Strategies for Effective Teaching

fourth edition

Allan C. Ornstein
St. John's University

Thomas J. Lasley, II
University of Dayton

Boston Burr Ridge, IL Dubuque, IA Madison, WI New York
San Francisco St. Louis Bangkok Bogotá Caracas Kuala Lumpur
Lisbon London Madrid Mexico City Milan Montreal New Delhi
Santiago Seoul Singapore Sydney Taipei Toronto

Higher Education

STRATEGIES FOR EFFECTIVE TEACHING, FOURTH EDITION

Published by McGraw-Hill, a business unit of The McGraw-Hill Companies, Inc., 1221 Avenue of the Americas, New York, NY 10020. Copyright © 2004 by The McGraw-Hill Companies, Inc. All rights reserved. Previous edition(s) 2000, 1995, 1990. All rights reserved. No part of this publication may be reproduced or distributed in any form or by any means, or stored in a database or retrieval system, without the prior written consent of The McGraw-Hill Companies, Inc., including, but not limited to, in any network or other electronic storage or transmission, or broadcast for distance learning.

Some ancillaries, including electronic and print components, may not be available to customers outside the United States.

This book is printed on acid-free paper.

Domestic   2 3 4 5 6 7 8 9 0 0 9 8 7 6 5 4

ISBN 0-07-256428-8

Vice president and editor-in-chief: *Thalia Dorwick*
Developmental editor: *Teresa Wise*
Senior marketing manager: *Pamela S. Cooper*
Project manager: *Mary Lee Harms*
Production supervisor: *Enboge Chong*
Media technology producer: *Lance Gerhart*
Senior designer: *Violeta Diaz*
Cover designer: *Laurie Anderson*
Interior designer: *Michael Remener*
Art editor: *Emma Ghiselli*
Associate photo research coordinator: *Natalia Peschiera*
Photo research: *Toni Michaels, PhotoFind*
Senior supplement producer: *David A. Welsh*
Compositor: *Thompson Type*
Typeface: *Times Roman*
Printer: *R. R. Donnelley/Crawfordsville, IN*

Library of Congress Cataloging-in-Publication Data

Ornstein, Allan C.
    Strategies for effective teaching / Allan C. Ornstein, Thomas J. Lasley, II; with technology
    viewpoints by Jackie Marshall Arnold.—4th ed.
      p. cm.
    Includes bibliographical references and indexes.
    ISBN 0-07-256428-8 (alk. paper)
    1.   Teaching. 2. Effective teaching. 3. Classroom management. 4. Lesson planning. 5.
         Teachers—Training of. I. Lasley, Thomas J. II Arnold, Jackie Marshall, 1971 – III.
         Title.

LB1025.3.O76 2004
371.102—dc21

                                                                                    2003046403

The Internet addresses listed in the text were accurate at the time of publication. The inclusion of a website does not indicate an endorsement by the authors or McGraw-Hill, and McGraw-Hill does not guarantee the accuracy of the information presented at these sites.

www.mhhe.com

Dedication

For Elizabeth Lasley who is studying to be a teacher; for Julianne Burt who is a beginning teacher; for Jennifer Hawkins who is now a veteran teacher; and, for Gina Henderson who lives to question teachers!

AND

For Stacey Ornstein who is thinking about teaching; Joel Ornstein who is now a professional student; Jason Ornstein who just graduated from F&M and is contemplating the future; and my two favorite teachers, Hans Kohn at C.C.N.Y. and Virgil Clift at N.Y.U.

Brief Contents

Contents

part one

Perspectives on Effective Teaching Performance 1

part two

The Technical Skills of Teaching   89

part three

Professional Growth　547

Tips for Teachers

Case Studies

Professional Viewpoints

Preface

Becoming a teacher is an extraordinarily complex venture. Some of what is needed for success is learned; some is attributable to who you are as an individual. This textbook argues for the *art* and *science* of teaching. The science of educational practice is growing; several chapters document what is now known. But you can know all that science and still be ineffective; and ironically, some individuals are relatively successful without knowing any of it. Such individuals may be good teachers, but they are not, at least in a technical sense, professionals. Professionals intentionally acquire a discrete body of specialized and theoretical knowledge (the type of knowledge that is now emerging about teaching), and they use that knowledge to help students learn.

This book is intended for any general methods or specialized methods class that seeks to show prospective teachers how to plan *what* to teach (objectives), how to determine *how* to teach (methods), how to reflect on what is taught (reflection), and how to assess whether students learned the requisite concepts (assessment).

As you begin your journey toward acquiring professional knowledge, you need to understand that successful teaching is predicated on several fundamental assumptions:

1. Teachers must possess thorough disciplinary knowledge.
2. Teachers must know the academic content standards for what they teach.
3. Teachers must know how learners learn in order to design meaningful instruction.
4. Teachers must know how to present content based on context and purpose.

Assumption 1 is fulfilled if you have a good general education. Assumption 2 is already addressed if you pursued disciplinary coursework in understanding and depth—that is, you earned a disciplinary major (or selected academic minors). Assumption 3 was fulfilled through educational psychology courses that emphasize work by people such as Jean Piaget, B. F. Skinner, Edward Thorndike, and L. S. Vygotsky. Assumption 4 is the focus of this book. Specifically, this book focuses on *how* to teach: the process of communicating what you know (and is known) in ways that help students construct their own knowledge.

Organization of This Text

The book is organized into three parts. Part I focuses on the art and science of teaching. Part II breaks down the teaching act into specific, discrete skills. And Part III addresses issues related to ongoing professional development and suggests ways in which the skills of teaching are part of both the art and science of what you do (or any teacher does) in the classroom.

Features of This Text

The book is based on six fundamental elements, making it highly useful to a prospective teacher in today's schools. It is research based, standards based, example based, reflection based, expert based, and technology based.

Research Basis

The book intentionally draws on the growing body of literature that shows that teachers really do make a difference in the achievement of students. In the 1960s, educators were told that family socioeconomic status was so important that teachers were "secondary." In the 1990s and 2000s, new "value-added" research suggests that teachers do dramatically influence student achievement. What students *bring* to school (the socioeconomic capital of their families) makes a difference. But what *happens* to them once they are at school is just as important. That means that you as a teacher are potentially just as important to a student's achievement as are the student's parents, and perhaps more important. What a responsibility *and* opportunity!

Standards Basis

Many states are embracing some type of standards (or criteria) for assessing teacher competence. Some of those standards are national in nature (PRAXIS series and INTASC), and others are developed at the state or regional level (such as California's CFASST). What is presented in the text is linked with the national standards. Chapters 3–12 begin with a specific description of the Pathwise/PRAXIS III and INTASC criteria and principles determined relevant to the content of each chapter (not everyone will agree with the alignment of these criteria to content; but you will be able to see how these standards may be connected to the skills or "inputs" of teaching). If you are in an INTASC or PRAXIS series state, the provided "markers" should be very helpful. Even if you are not, you should find them useful as a way to frame and think about the content.

Example Basis

One of the real problems with many methods texts is that they are heavy on theory and light on applications (examples). This text errs on the side of applications. Good teachers need theory, but that theory is meaningless if they do not know how to apply the knowledge. Many examples (tables, figures, charts, analogs) are provided to make certain that what is described theoretically can be applied practically. Case Studies and Tips for Teachers help connect the theory and practice. In some instances, we even illustrate specifically within the cases the connections to teaching standards criteria and principles. By doing this you should more directly see the theory-practice nexus.

Reflection Basis

During the 1990s the whole notion of reflecting-in-action and reflection-in-action became important professional dispositions that prospective teachers were expected to acquire. This text includes Questions for Reflection to help teachers think more deeply about some of the salient topics discussed. Once you start teaching you will need to learn how to reflect on what you are doing *as* you are doing it and to reflect on what you taught *after* you complete a lesson.

Expert Basis

Many individuals have shaped education in America. Many of their "voices" are part of this text—through Professional Viewpoints. Some of those viewpoints are written by current practicing teachers. All the writers are either those who have shaped teaching through their writing and thinking or those who are shaping it through their teaching. Both perspectives are extremely important and should help you see that many current educational issues are not new but are instead old problems that require your new thinking.

Technology Basis

The use of technology is increasingly prevalent for America's young people. Many of the preservice teachers who read this text are used to accessing Websites to gather information about topics of interest. Throughout the text, but especially in Chapter 7, you will find Website information that will be helpful in enhancing your effectiveness. Also added to this edition are Technology Viewpoints in each chapter to help you see how to use the technology that is now available.

Conclusion

We are privileged that you are reading this textbook as part of your journey to become a teacher. Our hope is that your teaching journey is a long and fruitful one and that our text stimulates you to learn even more about what it means to be a classroom teacher.

Reviewers Who Made This Text Possible

No textbook of this type is possible without the critical assistance of a number of very able reviewers. We are especially grateful to the following individuals for their thoughtful suggestions during the development of the fourth edition:

Caroline Diemer,
Liberty University

Barbara Divins,
Franklin College

Caroline Knight,
North Central University

Anne Mungai,
Adelphi University

Albert A. Stramiello,
Mercer University

To the Instructor

Strategies for Effective Teaching, fourth edition, is written for all who are interested in learning how to teach, improving their teaching, or teaching students how to learn. It will help prepare novice teachers for their new roles and provide seasoned teachers with new insights into *what* they are doing and *why* they are doing it.

The text focuses on the theory and practice of teaching. It attempts to blend theory with practice by reporting and analyzing important research and then presenting practical procedures and adaptive strategies for teachers to use. How do successful teachers start a lesson? How do they monitor classroom activities? How do they deal with disruptive students? How do they proceed with a student who doesn't know the answer? These are problems that teachers must deal with daily. The answers to these questions depend on how we apply the theory we have learned in our coursework to the classroom setting.

Strategies for Effective Teaching is also grounded in the INTASC standards and Pathwise PRAXIS criteria. Many states are using these as a means of ensuring quality teacher education and for creating a common language to discuss good teaching. Our hope is that you will be able to use this book to relate required teaching skills to defined and accepted teaching standards. And, that by using the ideas in this text, the learning of your students will be enhanced.

Prospective teachers and beginning teachers need to master theoretical concepts and principles and then *integrate* these concepts and principles into practice by developing specific methods and strategies that work on the job. The integration process, or the leap from theory to practice, is not easy. *Strategies for Effective Teaching* helps by interweaving practical strategies and methods with research. Many theories and practices are presented with the understanding that readers can pick and choose among them the ones that fit their personality and philosophy. In each chapter, look for *Tips for Teachers* and *Case Studies*. These instructional aids are designed to help the reader apply the theory to practice.

Strategies for Effective Teaching adopts a cognitive science approach, blending cognitive-developmental research with information-processing research. Consequently, a good deal of the subject matter is rooted in educational psychology, linguistics, and subject-related methods—and there is little that deals with the philosophy, history, or sociology of teaching.

Cognitive science focuses on how teachers teach and how learners learn, and it can be used to develop strategies that guide effective teaching and learning. This text presents research on how students process information, or what we call *learning strategies:* how to skim data, summarize information, take notes, do homework, read text material, take tests, and so forth. Existing research can also be used to teach students to think critically and creatively; to classify, infer, interpret, extrapolate, evaluate, and predict.

Research also exists to help identify effective teaching strategies. *Strategies for Effective Teaching* uses cognitive science research to discuss how to teach by explaining, questioning, monitoring, and reviewing; how to diagnose, assess, and place students into groups for instruction; how to teach basic skills, concepts, and problem solving; how to manage the surface behavior of students on an individual and group basis; how to plan for instruction and utilize instructional technology; and how to use textbooks and improve instructional materials.

The new emphasis in cognitive science is concerned not so much with students' answers (though clearly correct answers are important), but rather with how students derive answers and what strategies teachers use to help students learn requisite material. This book informs teachers about recent research on how students process information and how teachers can modify their instruction to help students learn more effectively.

The many distinctive features of this edition of *Strategies for Effective Teaching* include the following:

- Pathwise (PRAXIS Series) criteria and INTASC standards that ground teaching skills (see Chapters 3 to 12)
- Focusing questions at the beginning of each chapter to help orient the reader, set the stage for what is to follow, and highlight the main ideas of the chapter
- Easy-to-read headings and subheadings that facilitate understanding and illustrate relationships among ideas
- Short descriptors and categories that help classify and conceptualize information
- Tables and charts organized as overviews that make learning more meaningful
- Current research findings applied to classroom teaching
- *Professional Viewpoints,* the perspectives of experts in the field, written specifically for this text, that highlight a major concept or principle and/or give advice for both the beginning and the experienced teacher
- *Technology Viewpoints,* written by a media specialist who uses various forms of technology to enhance student learning and teacher professional development
- *Case Studies* that illustrate some of the salient educational problems and help readers see the real-world nature of the problems—some are anchored specifically to the Pathwise criteria
- *Questions for Reflection* in Chapters 1–11 to help readers critically reflect on the content
- Lists of practical tips that give insights into teaching
- Chapter summaries that present short lists of main ideas, in the same sequence as the chapter's narrative

To the Student

Strategies for Effective Teaching, fourth edition, has five major purposes. The first is to help beginning teachers develop an understanding of what goes on in the classroom and of what the job of teaching involves. Despite your familiarity with education from a student's point of view, you probably have limited experience with teaching from a teacher's point of view. And even if you are experienced, you can always integrate your own experiences about teaching with new information to achieve professional improvement and development.

A second purpose is to provide classroom teachers with concrete and realistic suggestions about ways of teaching—and how they can improve the teaching-learning process within their classrooms. Many teachers are unaware of their behaviors or the effects they have on students; others can sharpen their expertise in the methods and strategies that work with different students.

Another purpose is to apply theoretical and research-based data to teaching practices. Social scientists and educators have discovered many things about human behavior, and they have established many principles that can be translated into new practice in order to enhance student learning. Existing practices of the teacher can also be clarified and refined through an understanding of research. The idea is to convert "knowledge of teaching" into "knowledge of how to teach."

A fourth purpose is to show how teachers can make a difference and how they can have a positive influence on students. The data in this text suggest that teachers affect students, and that some teachers, because of their practices, have better results than others in terms of maximizing student success.

Finally, *Strategies for Effective Teaching* deals with how teachers can teach students how to learn—that is, with learning strategies that will increase students' chances for achievement and reduce the loss of human potential so pervasive in our society today. Knowing how to learn and ground personal decisions is the goal of the learner; helping students learn how to learn is the goal of the teacher. The extent to which students learn how to learn is influenced by how well the teacher can teach.

Allan C. Ornstein
Thomas J. Lasley II

Acknowledgments

Many people wrote the *Professional Viewpoints* features in *Strategies for Effective Teaching*. They were kind enough to take time from their busy schedules to jot down some valuable advice or personal views about teachers and teaching. Their thoughts add a timely and unusual dimension to the text while providing useful information in an appealing manner. We appreciate their contributions to this text. And finally, I'd like to acknowledge Esther who fulfills my life, and has provided me with much needed understanding, support, and encouragement while revising this book.

Allan C. Ornstein

Many people made it possible to revise this text. I give thanks to each for their particular contributions: Jane Perri, Debbie Byrd, Matt Sableski, and Josh Schrank for help with the photography; Tanya Marling for her assistance with keyboarding sections of the revised text; Carmen Giebelhaus and Susan Ferguson for their efforts to ensure that the INTASC and Pathwise Standards were aligned correctly (or at least logically!); Connie Bowman and Patricia Hart for their careful reading of selected sections of the text relative to PRAXIS and INTASC concepts; Melissa Bogan for her help with the copyrights and permissions; Brandy Flack for all of her proofreading and her work on the instructor's manual; Colleen Wildenhaus for assistance in reading the page proofs; Terri Wise for her editorial support; my colleague Mea Maio for doing most of the typing and for doing extra work so that I could be free to write; my wife, Janet, for allowing me to work on Saturday and not to do work around the house; and, of course, the University of Dayton for its wonderful support.

Thomas J. Lasley II

Perspectives on Effective Teaching Performance

This first part examines teacher behaviors and how those behaviors influence your ability to teach and a student's desire to learn. As you will readily notice, the teaching act is incredibly dynamic. It demands a great deal of teachers, physically and emotionally, but it also can pay real psychological rewards.

In these first two chapters we explore the art and science of teaching. We start in Chapter 1 with the art because it suggests the incredible power and complexity of teaching. In Chapter 2, we examine the growing body of scientific literature about teachers and teaching.

The Art of Effective Teaching

1. What reasons do people give for teaching? How do these reasons compare with your own reasons?

2. What does artful teaching look like and why do teachers need to know both the art and science of teaching?

3. What paradigms dominate teaching practice?

4. How do effective teachers encourage students to learn how to learn?

5. How do effective teachers foster student creativity?

6. How does constructivism foster the learning paradigm in the classroom?

7. Are teaching standards and constructivism incompatible?

This first chapter briefly asks why you wish to teach—with the hope that you will honestly explore your own reasons. Then the heart of the chapter examines the art of teaching: Why is it that some teachers have the same skills but experience different levels of success? That variation is due to the artful nature of the teaching act—some have that art; some do not. And, finally, the chapter examines how teaching influences student learning and creativity.

Reasons for Teaching

There are many ways to start a chapter on teaching. To paint a balanced picture of what teaching is, we begin with some general considerations about teachers. Then we move on to more precise discussions about teaching. The object of the chapter and text is to describe teachers, not only the teaching strategies that those teachers use. We begin with motives for choosing a career in teaching. Those who are entering the teaching profession and even those who are already teaching should ask themselves why they wish to teach.

One strong motivation for many teachers is their identification with adult models—parents and especially teachers—during their childhood. Research indicates that women are influenced by their parents slightly more than by their teachers in their decisions to become teachers. Men are influenced by their teachers more than twice as often as by their parents.[1]

The data suggest, further, that parents encourage their daughters more than their sons to become teachers. Perhaps this is due to the wider range of professional choices that have been available for men in the past and the traditional view that teaching is a respected occupation for women but not for men.[2] Although job opportunities for women have increased recently, in 2000 women still made up 74 percent of the public school teaching force, more than 80 percent of elementary teachers, and 45 percent of secondary teachers. These percentages have not changed much since the mid-1960s.[3] And the situation is just as lopsided by race. Government data suggest that the teaching force was less diverse (88 percent white in 1972 and 91 percent in 2000) and less gender balanced (31 percent male in 1961 and 26 percent in 2000).[4] The reason is that male teachers feel a greater need to make more money, and teachers' salaries are losing ground to inflation.

Many researchers have explored the idea that the choice of teaching as a career is based on early psychological factors. For example, Wright and Tuska contend that teaching is rooted in the expression of early yearnings and fantasies.[5] Dan Lortie holds that early teaching models are internalized during childhood and triggered in adulthood.[6] Although these two investigations have different theoretical bases, both hold that, to a considerable extent, the decision to teach is based on experiences that predate formal teacher training and go back to childhood. You might ask how accurate this is in your own case.

There are many motives, both idealistic and practical, for choosing a career in teaching. People who are thinking of entering the teaching profession—and even those who are already teaching—should ask themselves why they are making this choice. Their motives may include 1) a love of children, 2) a desire to impart specific content knowledge (i.e., mathematics or English), 3) an interest in and excitement about trying to change society, or 4) a desire to perform a valuable service to help society. Other reasons may include job security, pension benefits, or the perception of the relative ease of preparing for teaching compared with the training required by some other professions.[7]

It is especially essential for prospective teachers to understand the importance of this career decision. Your reasons for choosing teaching as a career will undoubtedly affect your attitude and behavior with your students when you eventually become a teacher. Whatever your reasons for wanting to teach, it might be helpful to consider your thoughts and feelings and those that have motivated others, such as your classmates, to become teachers. One way to do that is to examine the five categories in Table 1.1 and to determine which one best describes you.

QUESTION FOR REFLECTION

There is great debate currently about programs like Teach for America and whether they foster a long-term professional commitment to teaching. Do you think that

table 1.1   Categories of Reasons for Deciding to Teach

Type	Description
Crusader	One who seeks to change the system or society
Content Specialist	One who wants to teach a specific content area
Convert	One who starts another career but then "discovers" that teaching is really better for him or her
Free Floater	One who is in teaching until a "real" career choice emerges
Early Decider	One who knows from an early age that teaching is the right direction
	Which one best describes you?

Source: Based on Carolyn Bogad's five categories of student teachers as described in Nathalie J. Gehrke, *On Being a Teacher.* West Lafayette, Ind.: Kappa Delta Pi, 1987.

matters? Are teachers who plan to stay only a few years in teaching good for or detrimental to the profession of teaching? Why? Can you find research support for your position? Why do you think the teacher turnover patterns in Figure 1.1 are evidenced in American schools?

The Art of Effective Teaching

This chapter is intended to inspire you to see "the possible," regardless of the reason you selected for wanting to teach. Throughout the book, we'll explore why the possible becomes standard practice for some gifted teachers. In the actions of these people you will see the **art of teaching.** However, throughout the text you will also read about the **science of teaching.** Over twenty years ago, a researcher named Nate Gage argued for a better understanding of the scientific basis for the art of teaching. In essence, good teaching is neither exclusively art nor essentially science but rather a combination of both. Good teachers do things well and know conceptually why they do them well— they have an explanation for what grounds their practices. Good teachers also know what goals they plan to achieve and how they will "move" students toward realizing those goals. Good teachers are centered on learning, *student* learning. And having such a focus demands that teachers think about the art and science of teaching.

If you learn all the ideas in this book but focus on your behavior and not on what the students are learning, your effectiveness will be diminished. If you focus exclusively on the students and not on the content or the pedagogy (strategies) you should be using to enhance your teaching, you are nothing more than a high-priced, well-educated baby-sitter.

Carefully examine the following descriptions of "star" teachers depicted in the movies and you will see an emphasis on learning, not teaching. Some prominent researchers describe these teachers (Jaime Escalante and LouAnn Johnson) as oriented toward the learning paradigm. Roland Barth and Vito Perrone would describe the teachers as educators who care and teach with "heart."[8] We will begin our examination by

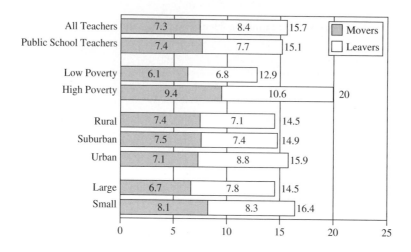

figure 1.1   Teacher Turnover in Public Schools.

Source: Adapted from Richard M. Ingersoll. "Teacher Turnover and Teacher Shortages: An Organizational Analysis." *American Educational Research Journal 38* (Fall 2001): 516: Reprinted with permission.

exploring the differences between the learning and instructional paradigms of teaching. Then we will use that understanding to begin to analyze teacher effectiveness.

Teaching Effectiveness in the Movies

A number of teacher movies draw attention to the power of effective teaching. *Stand and Deliver, Dangerous Minds,* and *Mr. Holland's Opus* are but a few of these films. Some of the movies capture the real lives of dynamic teachers (Jaime Escalante in *Stand and Deliver*); others are fictionalized depictions (Robin Williams as John Keating in *Dead Poet's Society*).

Well documented in the literature is the fact that classrooms are complex places. Movies capture that complexity in ways that stir an array of personal emotions. In *Stand and Deliver,* Jaime Escalante confronts difficult if not disrespectful students and makes them want to learn. As we watch him succeed, our personal passion to make a difference suggests that we, too, could make it at Garfield High School or at our own local high school. Even the most negative of teachers is inclined to think, "I know I can do as well," after exiting the cinema or turning off the video.

The movies, however, also offer a powerful lesson about the very nature of classroom teaching. In most of the popular teacher movies, we can see a shift in how the teachers view the students. Indeed, what makes these movies emotionally engaging is that a pedagogical "shift" occurs before our eyes, and once the shift occurs, neither the teacher nor the student (nor the viewer) is the same. Each is transformed.

Robert Barr and John Tagg focus on undergraduate education but their ideas have K–12 applications. They argue that within American classrooms two paradigms dominate: one instructional and one learning (see Table 1.2).[9] The ***instructional paradigm***

A focus on learning demands that teachers think about the art and science of teaching.

encompasses what the teacher does in the classroom (i.e., how the teacher presents content material). The teacher considers the teaching act as relatively remote from the learner: "I taught Hamlet, but the students didn't learn it." Instructional paradigm teachers (and administrators) talk in terms of technique and the quality of a technique: "He's a greater lecturer" or "She's fantastic with hands-on activities."

Learning paradigm teachers focus on whether and how students learn. What matters to them is a student's learning, not their own behavior. Ted Sizer's exhibition-based learning falls into the learning paradigm because in this approach the teacher places attention on the student's ability to construct and represent content understandings.[10] (For example, the student might be required to draw a freehand map of the world and situate on it a predetermined number of "key" countries.)

Most teachers and a majority of administrators work within the instructional paradigm. While they may not consciously espouse this theory, it emerges as their theory-in-use. They and the larger community they serve (parents and a variety of significant others) want to see students looking busy and getting their work done—indeed, for years many state legislatures worried more about the hours allocated for instruction rather than the learning outcomes expected of students. Instructional paradigm teachers focus on the tasks of teaching and often evidence a very high degree of

table 1.2   **The Two Paradigms in American Classrooms**

The Instructional Paradigm	*The Learning Paradigm*
Mission and Purposes	
• Provide/deliver instruction	• Produce learning
• Transfer knowledge from faculty to students	• Elicit student discovery and construction of knowledge
• Offer courses and programs	• Create powerful learning environments
• Improve the quality of instruction	• Improve the quality of learning
• Achieve access for diverse students	• Achieve success for diverse students
Teaching/Learning Structures	
• Atomistic; parts more important than whole	• Holistic; whole more important than parts
• Time held constant; learning varies	• Learning held constant; time varies
• One teacher, one classroom	• Whatever learning experience works
• Covering material	• Specified learning results
• Private assessment	• Public assessment

Adapted from: Robert Barr and John Tagg, "From Teaching to Learning." *Change* (June 1995): 16.

skill in keeping students focused on worksheets, workbook pages, or the "odd-numbered problems on p. 54."

Far fewer teachers embrace the learning paradigm. Teachers who are oriented in this way function very differently in their roles as facilitators of learning. They are constantly "reading" the students to determine how to create a better atmosphere for student growth. Learning paradigm teachers get outside themselves (personal performance) and get inside the minds of the *students:* How do *they* learn? How do *they* construct knowledge? How do *they* make sense of the world? How can I, as the teacher, participate in the learning process with my students?

Interestingly, research of the past decade may begin to nudge more teachers toward the learning paradigm. The value-added emphasis of researchers such as William Sanders suggests that one teacher makes a real difference in student learning and that exposure to strong teachers for three years in a row makes a *dramatic* difference (see Figure 1.2). The value-added focus is central to a larger debate on accountability that argues the merits and problems of the idea (how much academic growth can be measured?).[11]

What most of the excellent teacher movies depict is a pedagogical paradigm shift toward student learning. Mr. Holland (*Mr. Holland's Opus*) is a reluctant first-year teacher. He wants to be a composer, but reality forces him to find a teaching job. As the movie begins, Mr. Holland is "teaching," and his students are passively enduring his "performance." Mr. Holland feels defeated by the students' intellectual withdrawal. In one scene, he shares with his wife his sense of personal and pedagogical defeat:

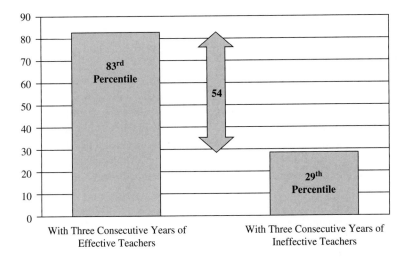

figure 1.2   Sanders' study concluded that fifth-grade math students who had three consecutive years of effective teachers scored in the eighty-third percentile. Students with three years of ineffective teachers scored in the twenty-ninth percentile.

Source: William L. Sanders and June C. Rivers. *Cumulative and Residual Effects of Teachers on Future Student Academic Achievement.* Knoxville, Tenn.: University of Tennessee Value-Added Research and Assessment Center, 1996.

Mr. Holland: "I hate teaching, Iris. I hate it! Nobody can teach these children! Nobody! I don't know what I'm going to do. They just sit there staring up at me. There's no one there. I've been trying to teach them."

Iris: "You've taught a lot of tough classes when they didn't listen. Did you quit and go home?"

Mr. Holland: "Wait a minute. Wait a minute. Aren't we supposed to be on the same side?"

Instead of accepting his assessment, Iris Holland challenges her husband to respect his audience. That respect necessitates a paradigm shift. It's subtle, but it's real. He starts with the music in the students' heads (*Lover's Concerto*) as a way of getting them to learn the music that is within his heart (by Johann Sebastian Bach). As the students make the connection, the teacher moves outside himself. The knowledge he seeks to teach is not "out there"; it is, instead, a part of the students' lived experiences. He just needs to tap that experience.

Similar shifts occur in other teacher movies. In *Dangerous Minds,* LouAnn Johnson wants students to learn about sentence structure. As an instructional paradigm teacher, she finds herself teaching but the students not learning. She searches frantically for assistance (e.g., she consults a colleague and even explores Lee Canter's *Assertive Discipline,* which we will examine in Chapter 9), but her application of simple solutions and more sophisticated discipline techniques does not help because they are part of the instructional paradigm as well. Finally, she is forced to start with the reality of the students; then, not only can she help them see the beauty of ideas within their reality, but she can also push them beyond their reality. She makes a change—she focuses on student learning.

In most of the Hollywood teacher movies the paradigm shift occurs soon after the teacher understands that the instructional paradigm simply will not work. In real classrooms, far too many teachers refuse to make the shift to a learning paradigm, and far too many administrators fail to encourage the shift. Many teachers stubbornly continue to use practices that they know are not working. In the language of Alcoholics Anonymous, "Insanity is doing the same thing over and over and expecting different results." Though a variety of reasons exist for this circumstance in teaching, we will suggest three.

The learning paradigm classroom is emotionally and intellectually demanding. The demands on a teacher who seeks to foster a learner-centered classroom are numerous. The teacher needs more time to plan lessons; must expend more effort to determine how to reach the students; and can use less teacher control to force students to conform to his or her personal will. Given the fact that the average American teacher is at school for 7.6 hours per day and that he or she is teaching (or on duty) for most of that 7.6 hours, it is little wonder that the instructional paradigm dominates American education.[12] Harold Stevenson and James Stigler documented this reality several years ago, and there is no reason to believe that the circumstance has changed since then. Indeed, Stevenson and Stigler argue that some of the success of the Japanese is attributable to enhanced teacher planning time: Japanese teachers are at school in excess of nine hours per day, but they teach for less than four.[13]

The learning paradigm teacher takes more personal risks and creates more administrative challenges. Dangerous Minds, Mr. Holland's Opus, or *Stand and Deliver* strike us with the number of directives issued (by the principal or school board) that require the teacher explicitly to "get in line" and implicitly to use the instructional paradigm. Most of the excellent teachers we know are not especially affable people. They are fighters. They fight for the students, and they are passionate about student learning. They do anything they have to do in order to make certain that students learn, even if it means confronting an administrator or tossing a disrespectful student out of the classroom.

The learning paradigm school is a "messy" place. Because learning is such a personal endeavor, schools that really embrace this paradigm struggle to find ways in which to connect students with their environment. Escalante offered special tutoring; Johnson used karate and a variety of very powerful pedagogical messages to connect students with ideas. Students, even those who are most unmotivated and defiant, are exploring, assessing, and examining their environment for ideas. In learning paradigm classrooms, the students become active learners rather than teacher-controlled intellectual pawns.

The curriculum for a learning paradigm teacher is a guide, not a dictate; as a consequence, the sequence of learning often conflicts with the prescribed learning sanctioned by the school. Learning is less linear and more nested in the students' experiences. Robert Fried explains why by describing the learning paradigm teacher:

> Some of the most passionate teachers are quiet, intense, thoughtful people. They patiently insist on high standards of quality in a language lab or drafting class. They talk with stu-

dents in conference about their work and where their talents and persistence might lead them. They stop to respond to a comment thrown out by a student that has more than a germ of truth in it. They bring in something from their current reading or their personal history that demonstrates the power of ideas.[14]

Teaching Effectiveness in Literature

The movie depictions of teachers make names such as Jaime Escalante almost household names. But anyone pursuing teaching as a career should also read about the lives and experiences of teachers with less glamorous realities. During the past couple of decades a number of authors have carefully studied good teachers and documented what they do to make the learning paradigm dominant in their classrooms.

Two examples of this literature base are Ken Macrorie's *Twenty Teachers* (1984) and Mike Rose's *Possible Lives: The Promise of Public Education in America* (1995). Both texts illustrate powerfully the ways in which learning paradigm teachers function. For example, from your own experience you know that instructional paradigm teachers often show films in class to keep students busy; the film becomes a celluloid baby-sitter. Notice, on the other hand, how Don Campbell uses films to help students learn. Campbell is one of the learning paradigm teachers that Marcrorie describes in *Twenty Teachers:*

> I have five sections of physics this year. I'll tell you what I did in class on the first day. I saw the students for just fifteen minutes, I told them what physics is—a way of understanding one's natural universe by codifying five aspects of it. We try to measure length, mass, time, electric fields, and magnetic fields.
>
> The next day I told them we were going to start this class out with a movie by Dr. Richard Little of the Massachusetts Institute of Technology, who put it together for the old Physical Science Study Committee Program sponsored by the National Science Foundation. In the film he does some rather simple experiments that would be difficult to perform in the classroom. The students go along with most of these and some of them begin to get caught up in the ideas. Then with the use of the camera he demonstrates refraction. The viewers of the film are placed in a swimming pool, down there underneath the water looking up at the feet of a swimmer hanging over the edge of the pool. When those feet separate from the swimmer, who seems to float in the air above the water, the film is demonstrating internal reflection and refraction. Dr. Little doesn't say what that is right away. Suddenly, my students want to see that part of the film again to check what they're seeing. Then they begin to think about the explanation, and I tell them that as we go along in this course, we're going to look at a lot of phenomena and then try to pull them together and explain them. Dr. Little makes that pitch, too.
>
> While the film is running, I stop it, run it back, and we talk about a point. Very quickly the kids realize they can ask questions, and some of them do. The film, which was meant to be part of the PSSC course, runs for 20 minutes, but we take the whole hour to go through it. The discussion becomes free flowing. Sometimes I initiate it, sometimes they do. When they start to ask, "Why did that happen?" or "What's going on there?" I tell them to remember the question and we'll take a look at it later. Maybe they will be able to answer it themselves. I start off giving students a chance to respond.[15]

What Don Campbell did was to take a movie that could have made students passive learners and forced them into more active learning. That's what effective teachers do—they take the ordinary and make it *extra-ordinary*. In *Possible Lives,* Mike Rose describes how one teacher, Michelle Taigue, makes *Oedipus the King* come to life for her students. *Oedipus* can be accessible or arcane, depending on how a teacher approaches it. Michele sought to make the Greek tragedy real for students by having them consider the parallels between what *was* to the Greeks and what *is* to Native American students. Michelle takes her class to the Center for Creative Photography (a gallery at a local university) and then she begins to teach.

> We [the students] spent an hour with the photographs, then Michelle walked to the center of the floor. We moved back farther toward the wall, giving her room. She slowly passed her hand over the photographs of the temples and started talking about the myth and the presence of the spiritual. She asked how the Greeks in *Oedipus the King* divined the meaning of events, and the students volunteered: "From the blind guy" and "that place, the o-oracle?" and "from birds—like my grandmother does." And she developed this into a discussion of the power of the spiritual and drew some specific comparisons between Greek mythology, her native Yaqui, and the students' Navajo and Hopi traditions. She paced back and forth, the hem of her maroon dress flipping around her ankles, and as she told these tales she assumed a range of storytellers' voices: old, cracking voices, children's voice, voices mixing Yaqui and Spanish, even animal clicks and trills.
>
> One of the stories she told was of Arachne, the proud Greek maiden who Athena turned into a spider. Both the Navajo and the Hopi have spider women in their lore—though each is a very different kind of figure from Arachne—and Michelle used this link to set out on the story. "Arachne was a maiden, beautiful, young, just about your age. . . ." And she stopped and turned, feigning mild puzzlement. She reached out to the girl closest to her. "Uh, Hana, how old are you?" "Sixteen," Hana said. "Ah, sixteen," repeated Michelle, not missing a beat. "That was ex*actly* her age. So, anyway, here's the lovely Arachne at her loom. . . ." And having drawn Hana—and, through Hana, all the girls—into the story, she continued telling us of Arachne's pride in her tapestries and her bold challenge to Athena, the best of the weavers among the goddesses. "So, of course, they had a contest," she exclaimed, her fingers picking up the air as though she were weaving the figures herself. "They spun and spun, and these beautiful gods and goddesses appeared in the fabric. Why, Hana, you could even see the expressions on the faces of the gods! And they spun and spun. And when they were done, whose tapestry do you think was better?" Murmurs here: "Athena's . . . no Arachne's . . . Whose?" "It was hard to tell," said Michelle, dropping her hands to her sides. "But Athena, indignant, shredded Arachne's tapestry (Michelle slashed the air) and turned her into a spider. She shriveled up and her arms got skinny and crooked, like this." The storyteller hooked her right arm and let it quiver. "And today this spider woman continues to weave her web. We see her all over . . . everywhere . . . all around us." The students were smiling; a few applauded. Michelle turned her head slightly, closing her eyes momentarily, dramatically, and raised a hand. She had more to say.
>
> She talked about the spider woman in Leslie Silko's *Ceremony* and about Navajo tales in which pride and retribution are the central themes. She shifted between the ancient Greek and the Native American, not looking for neat parallels, but suggesting correspondences. The myths and tales, she said, were "compelling and beautiful because they're so invested with power." But, though powerful, they were also present, kind of everyday. They were real for Michelle, not an artifact, not sealed away. I had read *Oedipus* a number of times in the past—had taught it, in fact—and had never understood, no, *felt,* the spiritual dimension of the play as I did sitting in that little room. I was suddenly curious to reread a classic that I figured I knew, that I had wrapped up in its historical gloss, nicely under control. But looking at Misrach's photographs and listening to Michelle made the world of the Greeks real and disturbing.[16]

Both of these teachers, Don Campbell and Michele Taigue, are able to move students toward a deeper understanding of ideas. Some might suggest that such teachers are exceptions. A few people have the gift and possess a capacity to make the classroom into something exceptional. We disagree. True, some teachers are naturally more creative, more reflective. But all teachers have the capacity to create the learning paradigm in their classrooms. However, in order for the *possible* to become a reality, teachers (YOU!) need to take pedagogical risks, try new approaches, explore different avenues for communicating content. Mike Rose observes that good teachers develop an understanding for variation, a phenomenon that we will explore empirically in Chapter 2, just as we have anecdotally in this chapter. In Rose's terms,

> [T]here is no one best way [to teach]: lecture-discussion, Socratic dialogue, laboratory demonstration, learning centers, small-group collaborative learning, a kind of artisans' workshop where students pursue independent projects. Not infrequently, these approaches existed in combination in the same classroom. In a number of cases, the current organization evolved. Teachers experimented with ways to create a common space where meaningful work could be done. This quality of reflective experimentation, of trying new things, of tinkering and adjusting, sometimes with uneven results, sometimes failing, was part of the history of many of the classrooms in *Possible Lives*.[17]

Books such as this one communicate to you the science of teaching. The following chapters describe in detail the multiplicity of detailed, empirically based information that we now have about what good teachers do. But the science of teaching is not enough. You also need to be artful in what you do in the classroom and to understand that art takes *time,* requires *reflection,* and demands *dedication.* To acquire the art you need to embrace three opportunities and deal with three threats.

Opportunity 1: Practice, practice, practice. Good teachers work hard at what they do, and just because an idea fails on one occasion does not mean the idea lacks merit. No golfer developed skill by playing once and no artist became proficient by creating one watercolor or oil painting. It takes time to become good at what you do. Take the time!

Opportunity 2: Watch, watch, watch. Observe good teachers in classrooms and read about good teachers in popular books. This chapter is about the artful dimension of teaching. You become aware that the art is possible as you watch *Mr. Holland's Opus, Stand and Deliver,* or *Dangerous Minds.* You can also see it in the lives of Ken Marcrorie's and Mike Rose's teachers. Good golfers watched other good golfers. Great artists studied other great artists. Similarly, we encourage you to find great teachers and watch them to see how they create vital classrooms.

Opportunity 3: Reflect, reflect, reflect. Think about how you teach. Consider what you are going to do and then reflect on what you did do. Teaching requires a lot of mental effort. Focus your effort on designing lessons that make sense, and then after the lesson reflect on what parts of the lesson did and did not accomplish what you intended.

These opportunities, however, will be difficult for you to see because of some very real threats. In *Dead Poet's Society,* John Keating is an English teacher who functions within the *learning* paradigm as a beginning teacher, a pedagogical neophyte. Such a circumstance is probably somewhat unique; it exists more frequently in fiction than in reality. Most new teachers start out with a certain passion, but because they are

so focused on surviving, they begin to unintentionally embrace the instructional paradigm; they then may, but most do not, shift to the learning paradigm. No empirical data
exist that document this assertion, but our guess is that the number who shift is relatively small and may be getting smaller. The reason may be the three threats that mili-
tate against teacher effectiveness.

Threat 1: Schools are busy, complex places. Most American teachers have little
time for planning and critical reflection. While at school they are either teaching or
monitoring students. Learning paradigm teachers need time: time to think and time to
plan. The nature of the learning paradigm is such that teachers need opportunities (and
that means time) to consider the learning needs of students if they are going to create
environments that meet those needs, and students will need to have time structures that
allow for the messiness of active learning. The difficult question is how to achieve that
goal. Schools and most educators treat learning as a linear process, and the school day
is structured to accommodate that assumption of linearity. Keep in mind, though, that
you, not the school structure, are the real key dynamic. Some schools are moving toward BLOCK scheduling as a means of enhancing teacher planning time. However,
some evidence is now emerging to suggest BLOCK scheduling may actually lower student performance even though it may enhance the overall school environment.[18] As we
suggested, schools are complex places but teachers are the key to effectiveness.

Threat 2: Canned programs and techniques abound. The proliferation of canned
or commercialized learning programs for dealing with students is clearly evident in the
multitude of teacher magazines. Too many teachers embrace these programs as possible solutions to the learning problem. One such technique, assertive discipline (see
Chapter 9), becomes a means of managing students, of keeping them on task, but behavioristic class structures subsequently influence student self-discipline in negative
ways. Direct instruction (see Chapter 5), another technique, teaches skills, but it falls
short in myriad ways of achieving higher learning outcomes (e.g., critical thinking or
problem solving). One prominent psychotherapist alluded to the way in which canned
approaches influence problem solving: "If the only tool you have is a hammer, you see
all problems as nails." This observation is equally apt for teachers. Many teachers enter
the classroom with too few tools. Give them assertive discipline or direct instruction or
whole language, and suddenly the classroom world is pounded into one shape—a shape
that may or may not fit each child's needs. Jaime Escalante's words are poignant in this
regard: "The most important thing is not knowing the subject [or the right discipline
technique]. The important thing is transmitting knowledge."[19] And, in order to transmit
knowledge, teachers need to become passionate about their own learning as well as the
learning of the students. That means, quite simply, moving beyond the surface of technique to the depth of ideas. In Robert Fried's words,

> Rightly understood, engaging students in content requires us to change our pedagogy by
> *limiting the amount of stuff we teach,* so that our students learn the important things well
> and dig deeply into the subject; by *posing interesting questions,* setting up a framework
> for inquiry; and then by *getting out of the way* to let the students do the work.[20]

Threat 3: Legislative mandates limit teachers' choices. Legislatures around the
country are seeking to solve the educational crisis by using their own strategies. For many,
the solution rests in one word: testing. By testing students more often and by making

schools more demanding, legislators theorize, America's goal of a world-class educational system can be attained. Many students are responding to testing mandates in the only way they know: withdrawal. That withdrawal is psychological at the younger age levels and physical once students are sixteen. Because testing implicitly promotes the instructional paradigm (a need to cover material), students who cannot achieve on the teacher's timeline or with the teacher's approach simply withdraw (drop out). Many city systems have high dropout rates and graduate fewer than 50 percent of their students. Students drop out once they realize they cannot compete. Raymond McDermott writes,

> Our schools divide people into halves; those who can and those who cannot. Dropouts are doing what the culture tells those in the losing half to do; they are getting out of the way. There are thousands of students every day who are insured success simply because the dropouts have disappeared from the competitive roles. Where would the successful be without the dropouts?[21]

The secret to lowering the number of dropouts and enhancing the graduation rate is not finding ways to make schools more demanding, though placing emphasis on academics can have positive effects on student learning. Rather, the secret is in finding ways to create a curriculum that is more responsive.[22] Escalante was not an easy teacher; he was a responsive one. Johnson did not cut the students a break; she simply broke the curriculum into pieces that the students could digest (after first seeking to understand their tastes).

In *Dead Poet's Society,* John Keating urges his students to "seize the day" (Carpe Diem!) and to write their own life "poems." If American education is to be competitive on a worldwide scale, American teachers will need to find ways to seize the day themselves. How? By disdaining an instructional paradigm that focuses on the teacher and embracing a learning paradigm that centers on the student. The shift is not easy, but it is just as possible in real classrooms as it is in the celluloid worlds of Michele Pfeiffer (LouAnn Johnson) and Richard Dreyfuss (Mr. Holland).

In Chapter 2, we will examine the rather substantial empirical data that document the science of teaching. As you read that information, reflect on the ways in which that science can be used to describe Jaime Escalante's or LouAnn Johnson's success. You will also notice that effective teachers enable students to learn how to learn. Effective teachers want students to learn what they are teaching. They also expect that students will go beyond what they are teaching. This is likely to occur when teachers are both *fair* and socially interactive with students. What does this mean specifically? In Stronge's words,

- Effective teachers consistently behave in a friendly and personal manner while maintaining appropriate teacher-student role structure.
- Effective teachers work *with* students as opposed to doing things *to* or *for* them.
- Productive interactions involve giving students responsibility and respect; also treating secondary students as adults when appropriate.
- Teachers who are considered effective allow students to participate in decision making.
- Effective teachers pay attention to what students have to say.
- Students indicate that effective teachers spend more time interacting and working directly with them than do ineffective teachers.

- When interacting with students, effective teachers demonstrate a sense of fun and a willingness to play or participate.
- Effective teachers have a good sense of humor and are willing to share jokes.[23]

The Concept of Learning How to Learn

The concept of learning in this text is not that the learner merely remains passive, reacts to stimuli, and waits for some reward. Here the learner is regarded as active and able to monitor and control cognitive activities. He or she acquires new information through assimilation and integrates it with previous information. Without this integration, new information would be lost to memory, and task performance dependent on the information would be unsuccessful.[24] Learning new information results in modification of long-term memory. The responsibility for engaging in learning—including control, direction, and focus—belongs to the individual.

Cognitive structures are searched When students want to identify, categorize, and process new information they search their cognitive structures. If the cognitive structures are disorganized, unclear, or not fully developed (for their age), then students cannot clearly identify, categorize, and assimilate new information. Of course, new learning based on previous learning should be meaningful to students—in context with prior knowledge and real-life experiences, regardless of whether the students are low or high achieving.

High-achieving students have a more expanded prior knowledge base, in terms of in-depth knowledge and multiple forms of knowledge, than do low-achieving students.[25] This mature knowledge base permits learners to integrate important and/or complex information into existing cognitive structures. Indeed, one of the premises grounding reform programs such as E. D. Hirsch's Core Knowledge (see *www.coreknowledge.org*) is that schools need to provide a content-rich curriculum so that students acquire the requisite background knowledge to handle increasingly complex cognitive tasks and then become better able to foster their own learning.

Those students who are capable of learning on their own are better able to 1) narrow, identify, or place information into preexisting categories; 2) sharpen prior information or distinguish from new information to avoid confusion or overlap; 3) tolerate or deal with ambiguous and unclear information without getting frustrated; and 4) assimilate existing schemata to interpret problematic situations.[26]

One of the central ideas of this text is that students do construct their own cognitive frameworks and structures (they make their own sense of the world), but teachers must necessarily guide that process using existing disciplinary frameworks. Teachers understand (or should understand) how disciplinary knowledge is organized. They provide a structure to ideas that students then make personal sense of when they study content material. The process of learning to learn assumes that students will use personal experiences to construct personal meanings and that the teacher has responsibility for shaping that process.

The world you are entering is a standards-based world. Clear standards for what students will learn place clear demands on how and what you assess. Good teachers know what and how to teach, but they also understand that students will also often assimilate that content in very different ways. The assessment process shows you what students have learned, and your role is to assess both whether it makes intellectual sense

A Technology Viewpoint from a Classroom Teacher

Jackie Marshall Arnold
K–12 Media Specialist

 Just as this chapter inspires you to see the artful possibilities in teaching, this section in each chapter of the book will focus on inspiring you to see the possibilities that technology enhancements can bring to your teaching. Artful instruction can be enhanced by teachers who choose to develop knowledge and skill with the ever-increasing range of new technology tools. With these tools in hand, a teacher can now diversify to students' needs, motivate the learners with creative presentations, foster inquiry as students learn material, allow students to demonstrate learning in meaningful ways, and much more. The following is a vignette demonstrating a teacher artfully incorporating technology into meaningful instruction.

Josie is a fourth-grade teacher. She has twenty-five students, six of whom are identified as learning disabled. Josie is struggling to help her students see authentic purposes of surveying, collecting data, and creating charts and graphs that will convey information in an interesting way. After collaborating with the school's media specialist, Josie decides to give her students the task of surveying and counting the biography section of the school's library. The students as a class determine the categories (male/female, African-American/Caucasian/Hispanic, etc.) Each student is assigned a group, and each group surveys a particular part of the biography section. Using a presentation system and spreadsheet software, the teacher facilitates the class bringing all the data together. The class is then given hands-on instruction on how to use the spreadsheet software, and class members create their own tables and charts. It is quickly noted that the library is inadequately representing women and minorities. The students then learn how to write letters and incorporate their tables and graphs into their letters to support their points. The students also work in groups to create presentations to share with the media specialist, principal, and district superintendent.

The media specialist challenges the students to help her improve the selection in the library. She creates a WebQuest in which the students are engaged in answering questions following Internet research on the important attributes of a high quality biography. The students conclude the effort by organizing fund-raisers and using a software program designed to support simulating basic accounting to keep track of their profits. Students, with the support of the media specialist, select and purchase the new biographies after extensive Internet and journal research. As a final project, students work on creating their own bookplates to put inside their purchases and create Web pages with digital photographs they took throughout the process to tell their story.

In this case study, Josie has taken an authentic learning situation, rooted in standards of her curriculum, and used technology enhancements to support student learning of those standards. Technologies such as the WebQuests were used to support inquiry, the creation of Web pages and multimedia presentations were used to support creativity, simulation software allowed for real life experiences, and more.

The artful teacher embraces technology as a tool. As you develop your teaching skills, consider ways in which technology can artfully contribute to the learning outcomes you pursue.

(i.e., it honors the cognitive structures of the students) and whether it conforms to the standards that are in place for a particular discipline. That is, students can create personal structures, but they must also know the recognized structures of an academic area.

We realize that this view is a contentious one. Some would want to allow the "life of the mind" of the student to dominate to permit personal freedom in what and how it is learned. They see in standards (and standardized testing) a fixation that all too often distracts students from genuine learning and from constructing their own meaning.[27] Others would argue for an educational world that is academically narrowly prescribed—the same standards for all and narrow assessment relative to those standards. In this book, however, we rely on Aristotle's "golden mean." Students need some freedom to explore, but to be successful they also all need to know certain things. The diversity of this country does not demand total academic openness. Rather, as one educator asserts, "in a society stratified along racial and economic lines 'the absence of [state] standards guarantees that educational opportunities for students will be stratified according to where one lives and what one's background is.'"[28] That circumstance cannot be permitted in a Democratic society. Diversity requires common academic standards to provide a common benchmark for assessment and provide students with equal opportunity.

Learning-to-learn skills are basic thinking skills that are used in all content areas. Learning paradigm teachers know how to foster learning-to-learn skills because they understand the dynamic nature of the learning process. Although some of these learning skills are generic and can be taught in isolation as general strategies, without reference to content, it is impossible to avoid teaching a certain number of subject matters, especially to upper (secondary) grades.[29] While a good mathematical learner may not be as good in English or history, for example, that does not mean there is no transfer of learning skills from one subject to another; rather, it may be less than we used to think. Jerome Bruner may have been right: Different disciplines have their own principles, concepts, and methods that are distinguished from those of other disciplines.[30] Or, as Lauren Resnick claimed, what is learned in one area is not easily transferable to another area of learning because it is context based.[31]

Yet another "school" believes generic learning skills can be taught to most students and transferred across subjects. Most of such learning skills can be incorporated into regular classroom activities or taught in a special course that incorporates cognitive processes that cut across subjects. Separate programs designed to teach thinking include Adler's Paideia Program, Feuerestein's Instrumental Enrichment, Lipham's Philosophy for Children (discussed later in greater detail), and Pogrow's Higher-Order Thinking Skills (HOTS).[32] These and other special thinking programs are designed to make all students independent learners in *all* subjects. The training begins early in the elementary grades, somewhere around the third or fourth grade. It continues thereafter with additional time devoted to these skills, perhaps twice the allotted time by sixth or seventh grade, when students must gather and organize increasing amounts of subject-related information. It cannot be postponed until high school, when the job of learning how to learn has become more difficult because of increasing academic deficiencies. (See Tips for Teachers 1.1.) A student who starts behind will stay behind unless educators create value-added instructional interventions that help close the gap. We'll discuss some of those strategies later in this text.

Critical Thinking

One of the most important things a teacher can do in the classroom, regardless of subject or grade level, is to make students aware of their own *metacognition* processes; that is, the processes involved in their own learning. Students should examine what

Strategies and Methods for Motivating Students

The teacher has the responsibility to help the learner feel and be successful. Students should not be bored but be interested in their schoolwork. What follows are some basic applications of theories of motivation for producing learner success in school.

1. *Be sure students can fulfill their basic school needs.* Provide time to discuss academic and social expectations, responsibilities, and behaviors.
2. *Make sure the classroom is comfortable, orderly, and pleasant.* A student's sense of physical and psychological comfort is affected by such factors as room temperature, light, furniture arrangement, pictures and bulletin boards, and cleanliness.
3. *Help students perceive classroom tasks as valuable.* Learners are motivated when they believe the tasks they perform are relevant to their personal needs, interests, and goals.
4. *Be sure tasks are suitable for students' capability.* If the tasks are too difficult, students will quickly become frustrated and lose self-confidence. If the tasks are too easy, they will eventually become bored and lose interest in the work.
5. *Recognize that students have different levels of anxieties and need for advancement.* Some students need extra time, support, or help because they seem to be unmotivated. Most of this behavior is a defense mechanism brought on by previous failure, lack of stimulation, or poor self-esteem. Other students are reared in environments that result in stress and the need to excel.
6. *Help students take appropriate responsibility for their successes and failures.* Students need to be taught that they cannot excel in all activities and that if they do not adequately perform in one area they can improve with effort and also excel in other areas. Build on the strengths of students; work around (don't ignore) their weaknesses through support and encouragement.
7. *Help students set reasonable goals.* Encourage students to set realistic, short-term goals. Discuss the need for planning, practice, and persistence.
8. *Provide variety in learning activities.* Changes in instructional activities help students pay attention and renew interest. Younger students and low-achieving students need more variety to avoid boredom.
9. *Use novel and interactive instructional methods.* The idea is to get students to ask, "Why?" "How come?" and "What will happen if I do *x, y,* or *z?*" The goal is to get students interested and then to think. Avoid too much "teacher talk;" it leads to a bored, passive audience.
10. *Use cooperative learning methods.* Get students to participate and work together. Have them work as a team so one student's success helps other students succeed. Cooperative learning also reduces stress and anxiety, especially among low-achieving students.
11. *Monitor students' work; provide feedback.* Knowledge of results, notes on homework or written assignments, and even nods or verbal praise reinforce effort and provide students with recognition for achievement.
12. *Provide ways for improving.* Comments about skill performance and on how to improve are important because they allow students to make corrections, avoid bad habits, and better understand content.

they are thinking about, make distinctions and comparisons, identify errors in their thinking, and make self-corrections. This is, in fact, what good (scientifically artful) teachers like those in *Twenty Teachers* or *Possible Lives* do: They make distinctions and comparisons in ways that illustrate the power of ideas.

Some argue that critical thinking is a form of intelligence that can be taught. The leading proponents of this school are Matthew Lipman, Robert Sternberg, and Robert

One of the most important things a teacher can do is to make students aware of their own metacognitive processes.

Ennis.[33] We'll consider a little about each of these individuals to suggest the power of their ideas.

Lipman's program was originally designed for elementary school grades but is applicable to all grades. He sought to develop the ability to use 1) concepts, 2) generalizations, 3) cause-effect relationships, 4) logical inferences, 5) consistencies and contradictions, 6) analogies, 7) part-whole and whole-part connections, 8) problem formulations, 9) reversibility of logical statements, and 10) applications of principles to real-life situations.[34]

In Lipman's program for teaching critical thinking, children spend a considerable portion of their time thinking about thinking and about ways in which effective thinking differs from ineffective thinking. After reading a series of stories, children engage in classroom discussions and exercises that encourage them to adopt the thinking processes depicted in the stories.[35] Lipman's assumptions are that children are by nature interested in such philosophical issues as truth, fairness, and personal identity and that children can and should learn to explore alternatives to their own viewpoints, to consider evidence, to make distinctions, and to draw conclusions.

Lipman distinguishes between ordinary thinking and critical thinking. Ordinary thinking is simple and lacks standards; ***critical thinking*** is more complex and is based on standards of objectivity, utility, or consistency. The goal is for teachers to help students move from ordinary to critical thinking, or 1) from guessing to estimating, 2) from preferring to evaluating, 3) from grouping to classifying, 4) from believing to assuming, 5) from inferring to inferring logically, 6) from associating concepts to grasping principles, 7) from noting relationships to noting relationships among relationships, 8) from supposing to hypothesizing, 9) from offering opinions without reasons to offering opinions with reasons, and 10) from making judgments without criteria to making judgments with criteria.[36]

Sternberg seeks to foster many of the same critical thinking skills but in a different way. He points to three categories of components of critical thinking: 1) metacomponents, which are higher-order mental processes used to plan, monitor, and evaluate what one is doing; 2) performance components, the actual steps one takes; and 3) knowledge-acquisition components, which are processes used to relate old material to new material and to apply new material.[37] Sternberg does not specify how to teach these skills; rather, he gives general guidelines for developing or selecting a program. He does suggest, however, when teachers do use all the skills that students can process information more effectively. That is, teachers do not emphasize critical thinking approaches in order to be pedagogically "cute" but to help students learn more and better.

Robert Ennis identifies thirteen attributes of critical thinkers. They tend to 1) be open-minded, 2) take a position (or change a position) when the evidence calls for it, 3) take into account the entire situation, 4) seek information, 5) seek precision in information, 6) deal in an orderly manner with parts of a complex whole, 7) look for options, 8) search for reasons, 9) seek a clear statement of the issue, 10) keep the original problem in mind, 11) use credible sources, 12) remain relevant to the point, and 13) be sensitive to the feelings and knowledge level of others.[38]

One might argue that all this fuss about thinking is nothing more than old-fashioned analysis and problem solving—what good teachers have been infusing into their classroom instruction for years. Moreover, it may be argued that teaching a person to think is like teaching someone to swing a golf club or cook a stew; it requires a holistic approach, not the structured efforts suggested by Lipman, Sternberg, and Ennis. "Trying to break thinking skills into discrete units may be helpful for diagnostic proposals," Sadler and Whimbey maintain, "but it does not seem . . . the right way in the teaching of such skills." Critical thinking is too complex to be divided into small steps or processes; teaching must involve "a student's total intellectual functioning, not . . . a set of narrowly defined skills."[39] Similarly, Fred Newmann argues that explicitly teaching thinking is too reductionist—it pays too much attention to parts rather than the whole. The best way to teach thought is to ask students to explain their thinking, to require them to support their answers with evidence, and to ask them thought-provoking (Socratic) questions.[40] Formulating thinking into discrete skills or a special unit or course is artificial, while dividing thinking skills by subject matter is unwieldy and mechanistic.

Perhaps the major criticism of thinking skills programs has been raised by Sternberg himself. He cautions that the kinds of critical thinking skills stressed in school and the way they are taught "inadequately [prepare] students for the kinds of problems they will face in everyday life."[41]

Unintentionally, thinking skills programs sometimes stress "right" answers instead of helping students decide and justify what to believe and do with regard to real world

Critical Thinking in the Everyday World

Robert J. Sternberg
IBM Professor of Psychology and Education
Yale University

 Every teacher believes she teaches children to think. If she didn't, she would probably have tried a different occupation. But the way we teach children to think in schools often has little to do with the everyday world, and, indeed, what works in school thinking may not work outside. For example, in the everyday world, we need to recognize problems when faced with them; in school, teachers hand problems to students. In the everyday world, we have to figure out the exact nature of the problem confronting us at a given time; in school, teachers define problems for us. In the everyday world, problems are highly contextualized: There is a great deal of background information that enters into our solutions to problems and the decisions we make.

For example, the information needed to decide whether to buy a car, and, if so, what kind to buy, can't be stated in a couple of sentences.

School problems, in contrast, are often decontextualized, with the result that children come to think that problems can be stated much more simply than is true outside academia. School problems, too, are well-structured: There is usually a clear path to a solution. In contrast, everyday problems tend to be ill-structured, with no clear path leading to an answer. Indeed, in everyday life, usually there is not one right answer, so unlike the multiple-choice and fill-in-the-blanks tests we give. Schools also ill-prepare us for working in groups, despite the fact that in the everyday world, there are few problems that are solved totally on one's own, without the need to talk to others about possible solutions. The bottom line is that to teach children to think, we need to teach them in a way that prepares them for life outside of school, not just life in the classroom, which may bear little resemblances to what goes on outside it.

problems.[42] Most problems and decisions in real life have social, economic, and psychological implications. They involve interpersonal relationships and judgments about people, personal stress and crisis, and dilemmas requiring responsibility and choice. How a person deals with illness, aging, or death or with less momentous events such as starting a new job or meeting new people has little to do with the way a person thinks in class or on critical thinking tests. But such life situations are important matters. In stressing cognitive skills, educators tend to ignore the realities of life. Being an A student in school guarantees little after school and in real life. There are many other factors associated with the outcomes of life—and many of them have little to do with critical thinking or even intelligence. Thus, we need to keep in mind social, psychological, and moral components of learning as well as "luck" or what some of us might call the unaccounted-for variables in the outcomes of life.[43]

Creative Thinking

In the past decade, the term *creativity* has been used to describe at least three different kinds of human abilities: the process by which a symbolic domain is altered; innovative problem-solving abilities; and personal expression through the arts.[44] When researching the lives of highly creative people, Howard Gardner and Mihaly Csikszentmihalyi found creativity to be an ability to shape or change a world view through one's ideas or works.[45] Csikszentmihalyi and Gardner discuss other applications of the terms *creative* and **creativity** from contemporary society, including to a range of abilities

Be a Great Teacher!

E. Paul Torrance
Distinguished Professor Emeritus of Psychology
University of Georgia

 There are far too few great teachers and society desperately needs them. Great teachers are great artists. Teaching is perhaps the greatest of the arts because the medium is the human mind and spirit.

My experience and research have made me aware of the importance of falling in love with what you are going to do—a dream, an image of the future. Positive images of the future are a powerful and magnetic force. These images of the future draw us on and energize us, giving us the courage and will to take important initiatives and move forward to new solutions and achievements. To dream and to plan, to be curious about the future, and to wonder how much of it can be influenced by our efforts are important aspects of our being human.

There is considerable evidence that our future image is a powerful motivating force and determines what we are motivated to learn and achieve. In fact, a person's image of the future may be a better predictor of future attainment than past performance.

I would encourage you to developing a future image of yourself as a great teacher—a new, positive, compelling, and exciting image. Then, fall in love with this image—your unique future image! You *can* become a great teacher—and that is a great thing!

from problem solving to personal artistic expressions. They did not however, find these abilities in their research into highly creative people. Csikszentmihalyi also points out that the terms *talent* and *genius* are often used as synonyms for creative abilities. However, he does not find that these designations apply to the creative individuals he interviewed.[46] What Gardner and Csikszentmihalyi point out is that creativity functions within a system in which the domain, the gatekeepers of the domain, and the new idea or pattern identified by an individual interact to shape or change the domain. Thus, highly creative individuals are a product of timing, culture, and personal creativity.

Tests do not always measure creativity accurately; in fact, researchers have difficulty agreeing on what creativity is and who is creative. All children are potentially creative, yet many parents and teachers impose so many restrictions on children's natural behaviors that the children learn that creativity gets them into trouble and earns them disapproval. Parents often react negatively to children's inquisitiveness and "messing around." Teachers and parents impose rules of order, conformity, and "normalcy" to suit themselves, not the children.

There are many types of creativity—artistic, dramatic, scientific, athletic, manual—yet we tend to use *creativity* as an all-encompassing term and usually limit its application to cognitive or intellectual endeavors. Educators tend to assess people as *smart* or *dumb* based on their performance in one or two areas of intelligence, say linguistic or mathematical ability. In fact, as a teacher, your goal is not really to assess how smart a student is, but rather to explore in what ways a student is smart and then to use those ways to help a student learn how to learn. Because of the narrow view of human abilities (a focus on narrowly defined intelligence) and this insensitivity to how individuals differ, schools often prevent the development of a positive self-concept in young children who have creative abilities other than in the cognitive domain. The potential talents of many creative children are lost because of our fixation on specific and limited kinds of knowledge.

Creative students are often puzzling to teachers. They are difficult to characterize, their novel answers are threatening, and their behavior often deviates from what is considered normal or proper. Curriculum specialists tend to ignore them in their plans, and teachers usually ignore them in their program and classroom assignments. Little money is earmarked to support special programs and personnel for them. Even if they recognize creativity, educators often lump "gifted" children together without distinguishing between intellectual and creative talents or between different types of creativity.

Robert Sternberg identified six attributes associated with creativity from a list of 131 mentioned by laypeople and professors in the arts, science, and business: 1) lack of conventionality, 2) intellectuality, 3) aesthetic taste and imagination, 4) decision-making skills and flexibility, 5) perspicacity (in questioning social norms), and 6) drive for accomplishment and recognition.[47] He also makes important distinctions among creativity, intelligence, and wisdom. Although they are mutually exclusive categories, they are interrelated constructs. Wisdom is more clearly associated with intelligence than is creativity, but it differs in its emphasis on mature judgment and use of experience in difficult situations. Creativity overlaps more with intelligence than it does with wisdom, but in creativity there is more emphasis on imagination and unconventional methods. Intelligence deals with logical and analytical constructs.

According to Carl Rogers, the essence of creativity is novelty, and hence, we have no standard by which to judge it. In fact, the more original the product, the more likely it is to be judged by contemporaries as foolish or evil.[48] The individual creates primarily because creating is self-satisfying and because the behavior or product is self-actualizing. (This is the humanistic side of creativity, even though the process and intellect involved in creating are cognitive in nature).

Little agreement exists on a definition of *creativity* except on that it represents a quality of mind and is associated with intelligence. For teachers, the definition of *creativity* comes down to how new ideas have their origin. We are dealing with processes that are both conscious and unconscious and both observable and unrecognizable. Because unconscious and unrecognizable processes are difficult to deal with in the classroom, there is often misunderstanding between teachers and creative students.

Teachers generally require ***reactive thinking*** from their students; that is, they expect them to react to questions, exercises, or test items and give a preferred answer. They tend to discourage *creative thinking;* that is, generating novel questions and answers. The reason is that teachers tend to overrely on teacher-centered strategies and underutilize inquiry-type models. This is the way most teachers were taught, and they feel uneasy about not having "right" answers. Some teachers do try to develop critical thinking in their students, but they need to go beyond reactive thinking and even beyond critical thinking to encourage learners to generate ideas on their own.

Society needs generative thinkers to plan, to make decisions, to deal with social and technological problems. Teachers need to let students know that having the absolutely right answer is not always possible, that depth of understanding is important, and that different activities require different abilities. Teachers need to understand that nearly all students have the potential for creative thinking and for asking questions, but they need practice in order to do so. In Case Study I.I, the teacher is using an ***inquiry approach*** to get

case study 1.1   Inquiry

Chad Raisch teaches sixth-grade social studies. He is interested in teaching his middle grade students how the growing of rice is determined by supply and demand.

He begins his lesson by briefly reviewing the concepts of supply and demand. He shows the students a Furby, which is an interactive computerized pet introduced in 1998 that sold for $30. At the time it was the hottest item on children's holiday gift lists, and auction bids for it online reached four figures. He shows the Furby to sudents in his class. The Furby responds to sound, music, talking, and light—it also says some simple words and phrases. The students observe the Furby. Mr. Raisch asks, "Why would customers spend so much for something so simple?"

He continues, "In fact some people paid almost 100 times what the Furby is worth! What I'd like for you to do is explore the answer to this question by asking me questions, but all must be answerable with a 'yes' or 'no.'" (Students in his class have been schooled in the yes/no format through exposure to weekly riddles.)

Jonathan asks, "Did a lot of children really want the Furby?"

Mr. Raisch responds, "Yes, it was really in tremendous demand."

"Was it easy to find places that had the Furby even though it was expensive?" Elizabeth queries.

"No, unfortunately, few stores were able to keep it in stock."

The students question Mr. Raisch for several minutes, asking questions such as "Was it originally expensive?" "Did children think the Furby was cool?" "Was the Furby originally scheduled to be sold during the holiday season?"

After students collect some data through the questioning, Mr. Raisch asks, "What ideas or generalization might explain the Furby phenomenon?"

Students proffer a wide variety of explanations. Mr. Raisch explores each one. Several students generate hypotheses that are finally shaped into "If demand is high and supply is low, the price for purchasing an item will dramatically increase."

Once students have a firm grasp on that idea, Mr. Raisch asks, "Class, what do you think that the producers did once they realized the Furby was a hit?" The students are very engaged now and offer lots of alternative theories.

As the lesson closes, Mr. Raisch asks the students to generate their own examples of the supply/demand phenomenon and to explain how prices are ultimately affected.

Reflections of Mr. Raisch about the Inquiry lesson

I vaguely remember my first few introductions to the relationship between supply, demand, and price. I think I know why. These concepts were not built on my prior knowledge or my past experiences. Instead, I "learned" these concepts by reading about them in a textbook accompanied by graphs detailing how price was affected by consumer demand and seller supply. Maybe I was dense, but I don't think so.

One of the great benefits of the inquiry method, as I have observed, is that it builds on the natural curiosity of learners and helps them become better thinkers. In the particular case of the Furby lesson, my students are asked to make sense out of something that at first might not make much sense. Through the course of gathering information through question asking, generating hypotheses, and analyzing hypotheses, students are able not only to build on and critique the ideas of others, but also to see that asking good questions is, in many respects, just as important as knowing the right answers. For in "solving" the discrepant event, you can't have one without the other.

The inquiry method can offer the teacher and learner a real opportunity for active and "personalized" learning. Because students can identify with the value of a Furby, or the latest Beanie Baby, or a mint Mickey Mantle baseball card, they can better understand how limited supply and consumer demand help determine the price of a good in a market economy.

Source: Thomas J. Lasley, Thomas J. Matczynski, and James B. Rowley, *Instructional Models: Strategies for Teaching in a Diverse Society,* 2nd ed. Belmont, Calif.: Wadsworth, 2002, pp. 168–9.

students to ask questions and think more deeply about content. Research is now beginning to emerge that documents that teachers who use higher order (inquiry oriented) thinking techniques and who provide their students with real hands-on examples tend to be more effective and to outperform teachers who simply transfer knowledge through lectures. This case study includes a brief description of the inquiry lesson and Chad Raisch's reflections on the teaching episode, which occurred during his first year of teaching. Pay particular attention to the way in which inquiry has the potential to foster both critical and creative thinking. Also, how could he have made the lesson even more hands-on?

In order to stimulate creative thinking, teachers should encourage students to make inferences, encourage them to think intuitively, and use inquiry-discovery teaching techniques. Three types of inferences have creative potential: 1) elaboration of characteristics, categories, or concepts (for example, a student is told some of the objects in a category are "right" and some are "wrong," and the challenge is to identify the category); 2) elaboration of causality (what were the causes of World War I? why did the compound turn into gas?); and 3) elaboration of background information (making inferences about possible effects of events or about facts from past events or about facts in order to make decisions and solve problems).[49]

Intuitive thinking is a cognitive process that has been discouraged by traditional teaching, which relies on facts and rote. A good thinker, according to Jerome Bruner, is creative and has an intuitive grasp of subject matter. Intuition is part of the process of discovery; investigating hunches and playing with ideas can lead to discoveries and additions to the storehouse of knowledge. The steps involved in intuitive thinking often cannot be differentiated or defined; intuition involves cognitive maneuvers "based on implicit perception of the total problem. The thinker arrives at an answer, which may be right or wrong, with little, if any, awareness of the process by which he reached it."[50] Teachers must encourage students to make educated guesses, to follow hunches, and to make leaps in thinking. To instill fear of being wrong, to discourage independent and/or innovative thinking, on the basis that the student does not have the right answer, means to stifle creativity.

The Role of the Teacher in Fostering Creativity

Teachers must encourage students to make educated guesses, to follow hunches, and to make leaps in thinking. Not having a clear account of how we obtain an answer is sometimes secondary; understanding the nuances and larger concepts is more important. And such understandings often require the use of creative imagery. Artful teachers have this ability. You see it in the efforts of Jaime Escalante when he pushes students to explore the concept of absolute zero. The concept is abstract but read this illustration carefully because it illustrates how good teachers use concrete examples to help students learn abstract, complex ideas. Also note the level of teacher creativity!

"You guys play basketball? You know the give and go?" He bounced an imaginary ball in front of him. He crouched with his back to an imaginary basket, passing the ball to an imaginary guard crossing on his right. He repeated the routine, this time passing to the left.

"The absolute value function is the give and go. I have two possibilities. If this fellow on this side is open, it is going to be from the left." He wrote $x < 0$ on the board. "If it is from the right, then $x > 0$."

"So my little ball is going to be the absolute value. I don't know which ball I'm going to use. This guy has two options, come from the left, he's gonna make it, or come from the right. Every time you see a number between two bars"—he wrote $[x]$ on the board—"you have to, you have to, you have to say, well all right, it's coming from the left or from the right. You have to break it down into two parts. I can do that."

He wrote

$|a| = a$ if $a > 0$
$|a| = -a$ if $a < 0$

"But you must take into consideration three positions, I call the three-second violation. Now. I don't really understand what is the three-second violation. Can somebody explain to me?

"I use the three-second violation my own way. The three-second violation is, this is one ball: $|x| < a;$ this is the second ball: $|x| = a;$ and the third ball: $|x| > a$. That right?"

"Yeah, right."

"How many you see?"

"Three."

"You know, you gonna be in bad shape if you don't know how to solve these three things." He thumped the board next to each expression. "When the *absolute value* is greater than a, when the *absolute value* is equal to it, when the *absolute value* is less than a. You have to *know* this three-second violation. Look."

He wrote, with sweeping gestures, the meaning of each expression in turn:

$-a < x < a$ $x = a$ $x < --$ or $x > a$
                     $x = -a$

"As soon as you see that absolute value of x is more than a, be able to say, immediately, minus a is more than x or x is more than a."

He assigned homework to underscore the point. Absolute value would be vital to understanding calculus. They had to get it down now. He glossed over some mathematical niceties, but it was important first to help his audience find the theater before he directed them to their seats.[51]

table 1.3   **Teaching Behaviors That Correlate with Student Inquiry-Discovery Behaviors**

The Teacher

1. Accepts student ideas
2. Develops student interests and creative potential
3. Recognizes personal limitations of students
4. Provides a stimulating and accepting environment
5. Has high expectations of students
6. Views learning beyond classroom boundaries
7. Develops effective communications skills
8. Wants students to apply knowledge
9. Puts more emphasis on process of learning than outcomes
10. Stimulates in-depth learning of subject
11. Allows students to pursue activities, thus allowing students to decide the point of closure
12. Creates in students a sense of ownership in learning
13. Permits student choices and decisions concerning classroom activities
14. Designs learning experiences around students' life experiences, needs, and interests
15. Encourages risk taking and a questioning attitude
16. Reduces classroom anxiety
17. Encourages divergent thinking and new ideas
18. Encourages frequent self-evaluation by students
19. Provides sufficient structure for students to understand goals, rules, and routines without stifling creative behavior
20. Provides students with an awareness of the interrelationships of science, technology, and social science.

Source: Adapted from Ronald J. Bonnstetter, "Teacher Behaviors That Facilitate New Goals." *Education and Urban Society* (November 1989): 31–32. John E. Penick and Ronald J. Bonnstetter, "Classroom Climate and Instruction." *Journal of Science Education and Technology* (June 1993): 394.

In inquiry-discovery techniques of teaching, students are not presented with subject matter in its final form; students devise and derive questions, answers, solutions, and information. The techniques can be adapted to students of all ages. Ronald Bonnstetter summarizes the most desirable teacher behaviors observed over a five-year period in more than 1,000 exemplary science programs across the country.[52] These behaviors were considered most effective in fostering inquiry-discovery skills among students in science courses. In general, the list of behaviors in Table 1.3 encourages students to "mess around," to explore, to experiment, to appreciate new techniques, to respect differing (as well as novel) ideas, and to make mistakes and learn from them. Students taught by teachers who exhibit these behaviors tend to be more creative, more innovative, and more at ease with themselves as well as their peers and teachers than are students taught by teachers who use more conventional methods of teaching.

Most people would agree that it is tremendously important to society that the creative abilities of our children and youth be identified and developed, that it is important for the welfare of our civilization. Teachers need to recognize that highly creative children learn in different ways and that children who have high IQs are not always highly creative and vice versa. The teacher needs the courage and maturity to accept students' first answers and to accept some degree of nonconforming behavior—not an easy thing to do. Teachers are better able to free and develop the creative capacities of their students when they embrace the learning paradigm.

In the final analysis, learning paradigm teachers learn to accept and encourage an inquiring and divergent mind—one that questions and challenges common thinking and is willing to avoid the ordinary and think of the unusual. The information age is upon us, and those who can digest, assimilate, and question data and see different perspectives and opportunities when they are confronted with problems will be better able to cope with the future. Managers and executives of business and industry and even of the government and military are going to have to learn to deal with creative people—who can creatively deal with complex information—in order to stay ahead. The more quickly teachers come to realize that a narrow classroom mold—one that breeds conformity, complacence, and rote learning—is old-fashioned and out of tune with the future, the better off will be our students, schools, and society.

The Learning Paradigm and Constructivism

We have discussed the different ways in which teachers attempt to foster more critical inquiry in students. The past decade has witnessed pedagogical battles about the efficacy of such dispositions. Some argue for imposing knowledge structures on students. These individuals, typically ideologically conservative, assert that we know certain things (a lot of things, in fact), and that teachers should impose what they know on students. Teachers possess knowledge and students need to absorb and be tested on that knowledge. Others suggest that, although structures are known within disciplines, that it makes more sense for students to discover them. Cognitive theorists argue that students construct (or make sense of) the information they receive in a way that makes personal sense to them.[53]

Many of the ideas in this book are constructivist. In Chapter 4, for example, we discuss the teaching strategy of concept formation, which is essentially constructivist in nature. That is, you will see how the teacher provides content but the students construct that information in a way that makes personal sense to them. We will also discuss the use of inquiry strategies at several points in the text. They are also essentially constructivist in nature because the student is using what he or she observes to construct a personal cognitive structure about some set of ideas or concepts.

Constructivists fall into different camps. Some are *empiricist oriented* and others are *radical.* The former "believe that knowledge is anchored in the external environment and exists independently of the learner's cognitive activities, so they tend to speak about helping learners construct accurate concepts." The latter assert that "knowledge resides in the construction of learners."[54] This book tends to be more empiricist oriented. The standards-based environment within which you will teach work demands that students acquire certain understandings and do so in a way that reflects accurately what is known in the various disciplines.

Some would suggest that there is also middle ground between the empiricist and radical constructionists—the dialectical constructivists or those who argue that knowledge emerges from an interaction between the internal (or cognitive) and the external (or environmental) factors. For the dialectical constructivist, there are multiple ways to construct knowledge, but some are better than others and not all defensible.[55]

It is not an unimportant issue in terms of a teacher's constructivist orientation. The empiricist and dialectical constructivists are concerned with students' accurate representations of the realities they confront. The radical constructivists believe that the world is not really knowable because context changes what one knows. As you can see the debate can be complex and, at times, it is acrimonius, especially so in the high-stakes, standards-based world of modern education. We will not ignore the debate but we will endeavor to take a more balanced view regarding constructivism.

We contend that the key to constructivism, whether empiricist oriented or radical, is that good teachers go well beyond the transfer of knowledge. At times that transfer is important as you will see when we discuss drill and practice approaches such as when you are teaching students how to multiply or wanting students to understand and use certain theorems, which, quite simply, they cannot or may not be able to rediscover. At other times, you will want students to have opportunities to reflect, inquire, and creatively think about ideas—to construct knowledge. We contend that good teachers—effective teachers—know how and when to do both: to know when to transfer knowledge (i.e., a skill or process) and to know when to engage students in the active construction of knowledge themselves. Such pedagogical knowledge entails use of both the science and the art of teaching. Who you are teaching, what you are teaching, and what your teaching objectives are will influence *how* you teach.

A Final Note

We conclude this chapter on the artful nature of teaching and the importance of teaching students how to learn with a caution. Some teachers become so preoccupied with teaching and learning that they fail to see how their daily actions contribute to the hidden messages of school. Those types of messages may be more powerful than any paradigm we adopt or critical thinking skills we encourage. Read carefully the words of one teacher and then consider how what you do (your daily actions) with kids may supersede anything you ever intentionally plan:

> One year I was working with this boy who had been a D student all the way through. I could hardly keep him in his seat. He was just a rascally boy. He never stepped over the line completely, but he was a thorn in my side all year long. In the lab he would always do something offbeat. By the end of the year he was coming along in his work o.k. I didn't see him after that for two or three years. Then one day here was this young man coming down the hallway dressed in a smart business suit, and lo and behold, it was that fellow. I said, "Well, what have you been doing?" and he said, "I've been in the Marines and I came back to thank you."
> I said, "What for?" because I thought I'd never taught that boy any science.
> And he said, "It's not for the science. It's because you taught me to be honest and to say what I observed. That was really important to me."
> I'll carry that with me forever.[56]

professional viewpoint

Providing the Space and the Time for the Construction of Meaning

Kathryn Kinnucan-Welsch
Associate Professor of Education
University of Dayton

 One of the aspects of teaching that I treasure most fondly is recalling those times that I was a participant in a powerful learning experience, one that offers a flash of insight, that "a-ha," leaving one changed forever. I recall such a time some years ago when I was working with a group of teachers who were trying to bring a more student-centered, constructivist way of being to their classrooms. We were talking about questioning and how often teachers ask those questions which merely require students to "guess what's in the teacher's head." Each of us took a turn role-playing by asking questions that would encourage students to think deeply about a concept, to grapple with alternative explanations. It suddenly hit me. I was still asking my students in preservice education classes to give me the right answer, to please the teacher.

After that flash of insight, I brought to my graduate and undergraduate classes a fresh perspective on what it means to encourage students to construct their own meaning and understanding of the immense knowledge base required of all teachers. My goal for developing teachers is that they engage in constructing their own knowledge, both in the disciplines and in pedagogy, so that they may bring a more constructivist orientation to their own classrooms. We learn best when we are actively engaged in making sense of what we are trying to learn. That is true for children as well as adults. In every classroom that will mean time for students to ponder, time to ask each other questions, time to explore possibilities. How teachers provide students the opportunity to construct meaning will evolve differently in every classroom. How might it evolve in yours?

Summary

1. The kind of teacher you choose to be is based in part on your reasons for teaching.
2. Teachers must provide motivating methods and materials for students, by recognizing that students are individuals with their own set of needs, abilities, and self-esteem.
3. Learning paradigm teachers focus on what students do to construct their own knowledge. Such teachers focus on the essence of the teaching act, not on the busyness of the students.
4. Students have different ways of thinking and learning, including but not limited to visual, auditory, and tactile processes.
5. Students can be taught learning-to-learn skills, critical thinking skills, and creative thinking skills. The idea is for the teacher to move from teaching the facts and right answers to problem solving and creative thinking.

Questions to Consider

1. Why is it important to understand your own reasons for teaching?
2. What factors keep teachers from becoming more like Jaime Escalante or LouAnn Johnson?
3. What teaching methods and approaches can be used to improve students' thinking skills?
4. What are the attributes of critical thinking and of creative thinking? Which type of thinking is more important for students to develop in school?
5. What are three ways for enhancing creative thinking? critical thinking?

Things to Do

1. Observe two or three teachers at work in the classroom and try to describe how they motivate their students. How successful are they in motivating their students?
2. Observe the same teachers and students again. Make a list of the dominant student behaviors that the teachers have to deal with.
3. Is the teacher you are observing a learning or instructional paradigm teacher? Explain.
4. Describe your own experiences with teachers. Which of your teachers have been learning paradigm teachers? Which instructional? Explain.
5. School success is partially based on students' abilities to think critically. Identify the things teachers can do to foster critical thinking among students.

Recommended Readings

Burkett, Elinor. *Another Planet: A Year in the Life of a Suburban High School.* New York: Harper Collins, 2001. This is a close examination of teacher and student lives in a suburban high school. Schools are busy, complex places and this text powerfully illustrates that reality.

Fried, Robert. *The Passionate Learner.* Boston: Beacon Press, 2001. This book offers a thoughtful description of how excellent teaching can be learned through practice and reflection.

Maran, Meredith. *Class Dismissed.* New York: St. Martin's Press, 2000. In this poignant examination of life in one urban American high school, Maran focuses on the lives of three high school seniors, illustrating implications both for how teachers teach and for how students learn.

Ornstein, Allan C. *Teaching and Schooling in America: Pre- and Post-September 11.* Boston: Allyn and Bacon, 2003. The author describes life and death, good and evil, peace and war, morality and immorality, equality and inequality.

Rose, Mike. *Possible Lives: The Promise of Public Education in America.* New York: Houghton Mifflin, 1995. This compilation of teacher stories is taken from different social and economic contexts.

Sternberg, Robert J. *Understanding and Teaching the Intuitive Mind.* Mahwah, N.J.: Erlbaum, 2001. Sternberg discusses the methods and findings of problem solving and intuitive thinking.

Key Terms

art of teaching 5	empiricist-oriented	learning paradigm 7
cognitive structures 16	constructivists 29	metacognition 18
creative thinking 22	inquiry approach 24	radical constructivists 29
creativity 22	instructional paradigm 6	reactive thinking 24
critical thinking 20	intuitive thinking 26	science of teaching 5

End Notes

1. Susan M. Johnson. *Teachers at Work.* New York: Basic Books, 1990. Ann Liberman and Lynne Miller, *Teachers—Their World and Their Work.* New York: Teachers College Press, Columbia University, 1992.
2. Larry Cuban. *How Teacher Taught,* 2nd ed. New York: Teachers College Press, Columbia University, 1993. John I. Goodlad, *Teachers for Our Nation's Schools.* San Francisco: Jossey-Bass, 1990.

3. *The Condition of Education,* 2001. Washington, D.C.: Government Printing Office, 2001, Tables 70, 80. *Digest of Education Statistics,* 2000. Washington, D.C.: Government Printing Office, 2001, Tables 70, 79.

4. "Measures to Woo Men to Teaching Jobs: Low Pay, Hard Work Cited for Declining Numbers." Retrieved July 5, 2002, from *http://fyi.cnn.com/2002/fyi/teachers.ednews/07/05/male.teachers.ap/index.html.* Digest of Education Statistics, 2000, Tables 70, 79.

5. Benjamin D. Wright and Shirley A. Tuska. "From a Dream to Life in the Psychology of Becoming a Teacher." *School Review* (September 1968): 259–393.

6. Dan Lortie. "Observations on Teaching as Work." In R. M. Travers (ed.), *Second Handbook of Research on Teaching.* Chicago: Rand McNally, 1973, 474–497.

7. Allan C. Ornstein and Daniel U. Levine. *Foundations of Education,* 8th ed. Boston: Houghton Mifflin, 2003. Nathalie J. Gehrke, *On Being a Teacher.* West Lafayette, Ind.: Kappa Delta Pi, 1987.

8. Roland S. Barth. *Learning by Heart.* San Francisco: Josey-Bass, 2001; Vito Perrone. *Teaching with Heart.* New York: Teachers College Press, 1998.

9. Robert Barr and John Tagg. "From Teaching to Learning." *Change* (June 1995): 16.

10. Theodore R. Sizer. *Horace's School.* Boston: Houghton Mifflin, 1992.

11. Dale Ballou. "Sizing Up Test Scores." *Education Next* (Summer 2002): 10–15.

12. Harold Stevenson and James Stigler. *The Learning Gap.* New York: Summit, 1992.

13. Ibid.

14. Robert Fried. *The Passionate Teacher.* Boston: Beacon Press, 1995, p. 12.

15. Ken Macrorie. *Twenty Teachers.* New York: Oxford University Press, 1984, pp. 138–139.

16. Mike Rose. *Possible Lives: The Promise of Public Education in America.* New York: Houghton-Mifflin, 1995, pp. 374–375. Note: Copyright © 1995 by Mike Rose. Reprinted by permission of Houghton Mifflin Company. All rights reserved.

17. Ibid., p. 421.

18. Clark Kauffman and Staci Hupp. "Scores Pip at 'Blocked' School." Retrieved July 3, 2002, from *http://www.dmregister.com/news/stories/c4780927/18611237.html.*

19. Jay Mathews. *Escalante: The Best Teacher in America.* New York: Henry Holt, 1988, p. 46.

20. Fried. *The Passionate Teacher,* p. 57.

21. Raymond McDermott. "Making Dropouts." In Henry Trueba, George Spindler, and Louise Spindler (eds.), *What Do Anthropologists Have to Say About Dropouts?* New York: Falmer Press, 1989, p. 20.

22. Allen C. Ornstein and Francis Hunkins. *Curriculum: Foundations, Principles, and Issues,* 4th ed. Boston: Allyn and Bacon, 2004.

23. James Stronge. *Qualities of Effective Teachers.* Washington, D.C.: Association for Supervisor and Curriculum Development, 2002, p. 17.

24. John Flavell. Cognitive Development, 2nd ed. Englewood Cliffs, N.J.: Prentice Hall, 1985. Robert Glaser, *Advances in Instructional Psychology,* vol. 4. Hillside, N.J.: Erlbaum, 1993.

25. Gaea Leinhardt. "What Research on Learning Tells Us About Teaching." *Educational Leadership* (April 1992): 20–25.

26. Charles Letteri. "Teaching Students How to Learn." *Theory Into Practice* (Spring 1985): 112–122. Richard E. Mayer. "Models for Understanding." *Review of Educational Research* (Spring 1988): 43–64. Richard S. Prawat. "The Value of Ideas." *Educational Researcher* (August–September 1993): 5–16.

27. Olaf Jorgenson and Rick Vanosdall. "The Death of Science?" *Phi Delta Kappan* (April 2002): 601–605.

28. Gary B. Nash, "Expert Opinion." In D. Meier, *Will Standards Save Public Education?* Boston: Beacon Press, 2000, p. 46.

29. Gerald G. Duffy. "Rethinking Strategy Instruction." *Elementary School Journal* (January 1993): 231–248. Alan H. Schoenfield. "Teaching Mathematical Thinking and Problem Solving." In L.B. Resnick and L. E. Klopfer (eds.), *Toward the Thinking Curriculum.* Alexandria, Va.: ASCD, 1989, pp. 83–103.

30. Jerome Bruner. *The Process of Education.* Cambridge, Mass.: Harvard University Press, 1960.

31. Lauren Resnick. *Education and Learning to Think.* Washington, D.C.: National Academy Press, 1987.

32. Justin Brown and Ellen Langer. "Mindfulness of Intelligence: A Comparison." *Educational Psychologist* (Summer 1990): 305–36. David Perkins, Eileen Jay, and Shari Tishman. "New Conceptions of Thinking." *Educational Psychologist* (Winter 1993): 67–75.

33. Cathy C. Block and Michael Pressby. *Comprehension Instruction.* New York: Gilford, 2001.
34. Matthew Lipman. "The Culturation of Reasoning Through Philosophy." *Educational Leadership* (September 1984): 51–56.
35. Matthew Lipman et al. *Philosophy for Children,* 2nd ed. Philadelphia: Temple University Press, 1980. Matthew Lipman. *Philosophy Goes to School.* Philadelphia: Temple University Press, 1988.
36. Matthew Lipman. "Critical Thinking—What Can It Be?" *Educational Leadership* (September 1988): 38–43.
37. Robert J. Sternberg. "How Can We Teach Intelligence?" *Educational Leadership* (September 1984): 38–48. Robert J. Sternberg, "Practical Intelligence for Success in School." *Educational Leadership* (September 1990): 35–39.
38. Robert H. Ennis. "A Logical Basis for Measuring Critical Thinking Skills." *Educational Leadership* (October 1985): 44–48. Robert H. Ennis. "Critical Thinking and Subject Specificity." *Educational Researcher* (April 1989): 4–10.
39. William A. Sadler, Jr. and Arthur Whimbey. "A Holistic Approach to Improving Thinking Skills." *Phi Delta Kappan* (November 1985): 200.
40. Fred Newmann. "Beyond Common Sense in Educational Restructuring: The Issues of Content and Linkage." *Educational Researcher* (March 1993): 4–13.
41. Robert J. Sternberg. "Teaching Critical Thinking: Possible Solutions." *Phi Delta Kappan* (December 1985): 277. Also see Robert J. Sternberg and Peter A. French, *Complex Problem Solving.* Hillsdale, N.J.: Erlbaum, 1991.
42. Ennis. "A Logical Basis for Measuring Critical Thinking Skills."
43. Allan C. Ornstein. *Teaching and Schooling in America: Pre- and Post-September 11.* Boston: Allyn and Bacon, 2003.
44. Mihaly Csikszentmihalyi. *Creativity: Flow and the Psychology of Discovery and Invention.* New York: Harper Collins, 1996. p. 8.
45. Howard Gardner. *Creating Minds: An Anatomy of Creativity Seen Through the Lives of Freud, Einstein, Picasso, Stravinsky, Eliot, Graham, and Gandhi.* New York: Basic Books, 1994. Mihaly Csikszentmihalyi. *Creativity: Flow and the Psychology of Discovery and Invention.* New York: Harper Collins, 1996.
46. Mihaly Csikszentmihalyi. *Creativity: Flow and the Psychology of Discovery and Invention.*
47. Robert J. Sternberg. "Intelligence, Wisdom, and Creativity: Three Is Better Than One." *Educational Psychologist* (Summer 1986): 175–190.
48. Carl Rogers. "Toward a Theory of Creativity." In M. Barkan and R.L. Mooney (eds.), *Conference on Creativity: A Report to the Rockefeller Foundation.* Columbus, Ohio: Ohio State University Press, 1953, pp. 73–82.
49. Paul Bloom. *How Children Learn the Meanings of Words.* Cambridge, MA: MIT Press, 2000. Robert Marzano. *Dimensions of Learning.* Alexandria, Va.: Association for Supervison and Curriculum Development, 1991.
50. Jerome S. Bruner. *The Process of Education.* Cambridge, Mass.: Harvard University Press, 1960, p 57.
51. Pp. 118–120 from *Escalante: The Best Teacher in America* by Jay Mathews. Copyright © 1988 by Jay Mathews. Reprinted by permission of Henry Holt and Company, LLC.
52. Ronald Bonnstetter Jr., J. E. Penick, & R. E. Yager. *Teachers in Exemplary Programs: How Do They Compare?* Washington, D.C.: National Science Teachers Association, 1983.
53. Jeanne Ellis Ormrod. *Human Learning.* Upper Saddle River, N.J.: Merrill, 1999. Virginia Richardson. *Handbook of Research on Teaching,* 4th ed. Washington, D.C.: American Educational Research Association, 2001.
54. Thomas L. Good and Jere Brophy. *Educational Psychology,* 5th ed. New York: Longman, 1995, p. 180.
55. Wayne K. Hoy and Cecil E. Miskel. *Educational Administration: Theory Research and Practice* 6th ed. Boston: McGraw Hill, 2001.
56. Macrorie. *Twenty Teachers.* London: Oxford University Press, 1990, p. 147.

The Effective Teacher

1. What is the difference between teacher *processes* and teacher *products?*

2. What is the relationship between how teachers teach and what students learn, and how does it influence accountability?

3. How does *what* you teach influence how you *should* teach?

4. What are the characteristics of a good teacher as defined in the research literature?

5. What is the difference between teacher *characteristics* and teacher *competencies?*

6. How can we determine teacher effectiveness?

7. How would you define an *expert* teacher and a *novice* teacher? How do experts and novices differ in the roles they assume in classroom instruction and classroom management?

8. What are some current alternative ways to understand how teachers teach and what they are thinking about when they are teaching?

9. How do effective teachers differentiate instruction to deal with student diversity?

As these focus questions suggest, understanding teacher competency and describing what makes some teachers effective and other teachers ineffective is not an easy endeavor. Although we have all spent lots of time in classrooms, the qualities defining teacher effectiveness are complex and at times almost contradictory.

In addition, everyone enters the discussion about teacher effectiveness with a variety of subjective views and dispositions. The reason for that is due, in part, to the fact that what works for one individual in terms of pedagogy may be less effective with a different learner. The goal in this chapter is to help you both understand and then utilize those general principles that educators know from research to shape how you might engage in actual classroom practice. To appreciate the research findings in this chapter, you might try this exercise. Make a list of teachers you have had about whom you have pleasant memories. Also list those teachers in whose classes you were not happy. What do you remember about the attitudes and behaviors of both types of teachers? As you read this chapter, a chapter that we have intentionally "packed" with a great deal of information on what we now know about teaching, think about how the attitudes and behaviors of the teachers on your two lists correspond to research findings and information about effective and ineffective teachers.

We will first review the research on effective teaching (the scientific basis for teaching) and then examine five basic aspects of teaching: teacher style, teacher interactions, teacher characteristics, teacher competencies, and teacher effects. It is in these aspects of teaching that the art of teaching becomes evident—knowledge alone does not make one effective; effectiveness comes in how that knowledge is used. In the early stages of research, up to the mid-1970s, theorists were concerned with *teacher processes;* that is, teacher behaviors, or the teaching that was going on in the classroom. The attempt to define and explain good teaching focused on teacher styles, teacher interactions, and teacher characteristics. From the 1970s to 1990s, researchers have become concerned with teacher products; that is, student outcomes. Specifically, are students achieving? Some of those same researchers have endeavored to assess the context of the teaching environment by focusing on qualitative and quantitative methods that more fully measure and describe the complexity of the classroom environment.

Review of the Research on Teaching: The Science

Over the years, thousands of studies have been conducted to identify the behaviors of successful and unsuccessful teachers. However, teaching is a complex act; what works in some situations with some students may not work in different school settings with different subjects, students, and goals. There will always be teachers who break many of the rules of procedures and methods and yet are profoundly successful. There also will always be teachers who follow the rules and are unsuccessful.

Until the late 1990s, some educational researchers maintained the impossibility of distinguishing significantly between "good" and "poor" or "effective" and "ineffective" teachers. They asserted that no one knows for sure or agrees about whom the competent teacher is, that few authorities can "define, prepare for, or measure teacher competence."[1] Many of these same researchers pointed out that disagreement over terms, problems in measurement, and the complexity of the teaching act are major reasons for the negligible results from studies of teacher behavior. The result is that "much of the data have been confusing, contradictory, or confirmations of common sense (i.e., a cheerful teacher is a good teacher), and that so-called acceptable findings have often been repudiated."[2] The more complex or unpredictable one views teaching as being, the more one is compelled toward concluding that it is difficult to agree upon generalizations about successful teaching, even if it is possible to agree on some propositions about what contributes to student success—for example, that successful teachers have a clear focus on student achievement and they allow students to show what they know in multiple ways.[3]

Other researchers and education theorists assert that appropriate teaching behaviors can be defined (and learned by teachers), that good or effective teachers can be distinguished from poor or ineffective teachers, and that the magnitude of the effect of these differences on students can be determined.[4] They conclude that the kinds of questions teachers ask, the ways they respond to students, their expectations of and attitudes toward students, their classroom management techniques, their teaching methods, and their general teaching behaviors (sometimes referred to as the *classroom climate*) all make a difference. However, even these researchers suggest that in some cases the positive effects of some teachers upon student performance may be masked or washed out by the relative negative effects of other teachers in the same school.[5] Negative teacher influences have greater impact than positive ones, in that students can be turned into nonlearners and experience loss of self-concept in a matter of just weeks as a result of a hostile or intimidating teacher.

Teachers may not be the only variables, or even the major ones, in the teaching-learning equation, but they can make a difference, either positive or negative. If teachers do not make a difference, then the profession has problems. If teachers do not make a difference, the notions of teacher evaluation, teacher accountability, and teacher performance are nonworkable; sound educational policy cannot be formulated; there is little hope for many students; and there is little value in trying to learn how to teach.

A landmark study by James Coleman in the 1960s questioned the significance of teacher impact. Coleman argued that most of the variability in student achievement was attributable to parental socioeconomic characteristics, not the teachers who taught them or the schools they attended.[6] Coleman's research was challenged directly by the work of William Sanders (from Tennessee) in the early 1990s. Sanders' *value-added* concept documented the power of the teacher. Parents, argued Sanders, are important. Teachers are potentially *more* important.

Each teacher adds value to a student's learning. The student enters school at point 1 (in terms of achievement) in September, and the teacher may move the student to point 2, point 3, or point 4 by May in terms of learning gains. Effective teachers foster at least one year of achievement growth in a school year. Furthermore, effective teachers are found in all types of districts and all types of schools. They are the ones whose students evidence the greatest achievement gains in the course of an academic school year. Whitehurst writes,

> Thus if a [female] math teacher has children who start the year at the 95th percentile and end the year at the 90th percentile, she would not be considered an exemplary teacher even if the performance of her students was the highest in the district. In contrast, a teacher who raised her students' performance from the 45th to the 60th percentile over the course

of a year would be deemed very effective even if her children performed below the average in the district. Value-added methods require that children be followed longitudinally; i.e., the same children must be tested each year and identified uniquely in the resulting database.[7]

There are many ways to look at teacher effectiveness. One focus can be teacher characteristics such as subject matter background or certification. Another can be specific teacher behaviors. We will analyze both.

As you read the material in this section, remember that teaching is not a total science. Good teachers do know, implicitly at least, what research has to say about student learning. But they also are bound implicitly by the following assumptions:

Assumption 1:   Research findings need to be critically examined and analyzed.

Assumption 2:   Research findings are not universally applicable.

Assumption 3:   Research-based "best" practices require critical reflection.

No research findings should be implemented without thoughtful consideration of their implications for the classroom. Teachers do not apply what they learn without critically examining what it potentially means for all students. They also understand that what they learn from research may not be applicable to all students in all situations. For example, research on direct instruction (see Chapter 5) suggests that it is a very powerful means of teaching skills and procedures. It is not, however, a particularly useful strategy for enhancing critical thinking or creativity. Teachers need to understand *who* they are teaching and *what* they are teaching in order to know *how* they should be teaching.

The process-product approach (focusing on teacher behaviors that influence student achievement) limited teachers' understanding of classrooms in a number of ways. It placed too much emphasis on specific types of teacher behaviors and on the frequency of those behaviors (i.e., how *often* does the teacher praise students or how *many* examples does the teacher provide) and insufficient attention to the ecology of the classroom —the multiple relationships that exist between teachers and students, in response to the natural setting of the classroom. Ecological understandings of the classroom do not obviate the process-product approach; they simply suggest the complexity of the classroom reality.

More empirical findings are needed if we are to establish stronger expectations concerning teacher effects. In the meantime, we must find strength and confidence in the belief that teachers can and do make a difference with students, with all students. Indeed, William Sanders found that value-added teachers succeeded, not simply with some students but with all students, at least to some extent.[8] Most of you will succeed—through experience, self-reflection, and focused observation in clinical or field settings. See Tips for Teachers 2.1.

Also required for your success is a clear understanding that the world into which you are entering is very different from the world of K–12 education in which you matriculated. In the past, *style* counted for teacher assessments. The content of what was taught was dictated by a locally developed curriculum guide or textbook. If students put in the seat time and received a good grade, they were perceived to have learned the material The emerging education world is less about style and more about *what* you teach and *how* effectively you teach it. Every discipline taught in schools now has academic content standards. Consequently, most activities that you engage your students in should relate to those standards. Your students will ultimately be assessed according to these standards, and you may be held accountable for their success or failure. How you teach still matters, at least to many administrators and policymakers, but only to the extent that it influences actual student achievement.

In the next sections we discuss teacher style and teacher characteristics. Such understandings help self-reflection because they assist you in thinking about your teaching and how that influences student learning. As you read these next sections use the information as a way of helping yourself reflect on the *how* (or process) of teaching but understand that you will be held accountable for *what* students learn.

One more note: Throughout the 1990s educators were concerned with diversity and teaching to diverse student populations. As the twenty-first century begins, researchers such as Ronald Ferguson at Harvard are focused on closing the achievement gaps among different groups of students and enhancing the academic status of all students. One of the best ways to do this is to define clear standards and then ensure that students have opportunities to learn and be assessed based on those standards.

Teacher Styles

Teaching style encompasses a teacher's stance, pattern of behavior, mode of performance, and attitude toward self and others. Penelope Peterson defines teacher style in terms of how teachers utilize space in the classroom, their choice of instructional activities and materials, and their method of student grouping.[9] Still others describe teacher style as an expressive aspect of teaching (characterizing the emotional relationship between students and teachers, such as *warm* or *businesslike*) and as an instrumental aspect (how teachers carry out the task of instruction, organize learning, and set classroom standards).[10]

Regardless of which definition of teacher style you prefer, the notion of a pattern is central to it. Certain behaviors and methods are evident over time, even with different students and in different classroom situations. There is a purpose or rationale—a predictable teacher pattern—even in different classroom contexts. Beginning teachers can modify aspects of teaching style dictated by personality through early experiences and perceptions and with appropriate training. As years pass, your own teacher style will become more ingrained and it will take a more powerful set of stimuli and more intense feedback to make changes. If you watch different teachers at work, including your college professors, you can sense that each one has a style of his or her own for teaching, for structuring the classroom, and for delivering the lesson.

Descriptive Models for Teaching: Historical Perspectives

Many educators have identified teaching styles in descriptive and colorful terms. Herbert Thelen compares teaching styles with characteristics of societal positions or with roles associated with other occupations. Frank Riessman's eight teaching styles describe personality types; they were originally based on observations of effective teachers of inner-city

tips for teachers 2.1

Observing Other Teachers to Improve Teaching Practices

 The saying "Teachers are born, not made" fails to take into account the wealth of knowledge we have about good teaching and how children learn. Teachers can supplement their pedagogical knowledge and practices by observing other good teachers. Assuming that your school has a policy of observation or your supervisor can make arrangements with experienced teachers, you will be able to see how other teachers organize their classrooms. Which of their practices are compatible with your approach to teaching and which might you be able to use? Here are some of the things to look for when you are observing:

Student-Teacher Interaction

1. What evidence was there that the teacher truly understood the needs of the students?
2. What techniques were used to encourage students' respect for others' turns to talk?
3. Which student behaviors in class were acceptable and which were unacceptable?
4. How did the teacher motivate students?
5. How did the teacher encourage student discussion?
6. What did the teacher do to encourage student thinking?
7. What evidence was there that the teacher responded to students' individual differences?
8. What evidence was there that the teacher fostered students' cognitive development?

Teaching-Learning Processes

1. Which instructional methods seemed to engage the students?
2. How did the teacher provide for transitions between instructional activities?
3. What practical life experiences (or activities) did the teacher use to integrate concepts being learned?
4. How did the teacher minimize student frustration with or confusion about the skills or concepts being taught?
5. How did the teacher encourage creative, imaginative work from students?
6. What instructional methods did the teacher use to make students think about ideas, opinions, or answers?
7. How did the teacher arrange the groups? What social factors were evident within the groups?
8. How did the teacher encourage independent (or individualized) student learning?
9. How did the teacher integrate the subject matter with other subjects?

Classroom Environment

1. How did the teacher utilize classroom space/equipment effectively?
2. What did you like and dislike about the physical environment of the classroom?

students, but they can be used for all teachers. More recently, Louis Rubin defined six kinds of teaching styles. These descriptions of teaching styles are summarized in Table 2.1. Though their work is dated in some respects, it continues to be a timeless and in many ways accurate description of teaching in many American classrooms.

There are also many other teacher styles. Teachers develop their own styles and teaching techniques based on their own physical and mental characteristics. Teachers must feel at ease in the classroom. If they are not genuinely themselves, students see through them and label them "phony." The social, psychological, and educational climates in the classroom and school also have something to do with determining teaching style. Nonetheless, no one should be locked into a "recommended style," regardless of conventional wisdom, contemporary history, or popular opinion. Teacher style is a matter of choice and comfort, and what works with one teacher may not work with another teacher. Similarly, operational definitions of *good teachers* and *good teaching*

table 2.1   Descriptions of Teaching Styles: Historical Perspectives

Thelen (1954)

1. *Socratic:* This teacher is a wise, somewhat crusty person who purposely gets into arguments with students over the subject matter through artful questioning.

2. *Town Meeting:* Teachers who adapt this style use a great deal of discussion and play a moderator role that enables students to work out answers to problems by themselves.

3. *Apprenticeship:* This person serves as a role model in the arenas of learning, occupational outlook, and perhaps even general life.

4. *Boss-Employee:* This teacher asserts his or her own authority and provides rewards and punishments to see that the work is done.

5. *Good-Old Team Person:* The students are like a group of players listening to the coach and working as a team.

Riessman (1967)

1. *Compulsive Type:* This teacher is fussy, teaches things over and over, and is concerned with functional order and structure.

2. *Boomer:* This teacher shouts out in a loud, strong voice, "You're going to learn." There is no nonsense in the classroom.

3. *Maverick:* Everybody loves this teacher, except perhaps the principal. He or she raises difficult questions and presents ideas that disturb.

4. *Coach:* This teacher is informal, earthy, and may be an athlete; he or she is physically expressive in conducting the class.

5. *Quiet One:* Sincere, calm, but definite, this teacher commands both respect and attention.

6. *Entertainer:* This teacher is free enough to joke and laugh with the students.

7. *Secular:* This person is relaxed and informal with children; he or she will have lunch with them or play ball with them.

8. *Academic:* This teacher is interested in knowledge and in the substance of ideas.

Rubin (1985)

1. *Explanatory:* The teacher is in command of the subject matter and explains particular aspects of the lesson.

2. *Inspiratory:* The teacher is stimulating and exhibits emotional involvement in teaching.

3. *Informative:* The teacher presents information through verbal statements. The student is expected to listen and follow the instructions of the teacher.

4. *Corrective:* The teacher provides feedback to the student—analyzing the work, diagnosing for errors, and presenting corrective advice.

5. *Interactive:* Through dialogue and questioning, the teacher facilitates the development of students' ideas.

6. *Programmatic:* The teacher guides the students' activities and facilitates self-instruction and independent learning.

Source: Adapted from Frank Riessman. *"Teachers of the Poor: A Five Point Plan." Journal of Teacher Education* (Fall 1967): 326–336. Louis Rubin. *Artistry in Teaching.* New York: Random House, 1985. Herbert A. Thelen. *Dynamics of Groups at Work.* Chicago: University of Chicago Press, 1954.

styles vary among and within school districts. There is no ideal teacher style—and no educational institution (school or college) should impose one for all teachers to use with all students.

Research on Teacher Styles

Lippitt and White laid the groundwork for a more formal classification of what a teacher does in the classroom. Initially, they developed an instrument for describing the "social atmosphere" of children's clubs and for quantifying the effects of group and individual behavior. The results have been generalized in numerous research studies and textbooks on teaching. The classic study used the classifications of authoritarian, democratic, and laissez-faire.[11]

The authoritarian teacher directs and controls all the activities of the classroom. This style shares some characteristics with what is now called *direct instruction*. The democratic teacher encourages group participation and is willing to let students share in the decision-making process. This behavior is typical of what is now called the *indirect teacher*, a teacher who fosters and encourages cooperative group work and student participation. The laissez-faire style provides no (or few) goals and directions for group or individual behavior. It is quite clear that, with the increased attention on academic standards and accountability, those laissez-faire teachers who may still be in classrooms will be confronting some profound challenges.

One of the most ambitious research studies on teacher styles was conducted by Ned Flanders and his associates between 1954 and 1970. Flanders focused on developing an instrument for quantifying verbal communication in the classroom. His work dominated the way in which teaching behaviors were analyzed throughout the late 1970s and 1980s.[12] Every three seconds, observers sorted teacher talk into one of four categories of indirect behavior or one of three categories of direct behavior. Student talk was categorized as response or initiation, and there was a final category representing silence or when the observer could not determine who was talking. The ten categories are shown in Table 2.2.

Flanders' indirect teacher tended to overlap with Lippitt's and White's democratic teacher, and Flanders' direct teacher tended to exhibit behaviors similar to Lippitt's and White's authoritarian teacher. Flanders found that students in the indirect classrooms learned more and exhibited more constructive and independent attitudes than did students in the direct classrooms. All types of students in all types of subject classes learned more working with the indirect (more flexible) teachers. In an interesting side note, Flanders found that as much as 80 percent of classroom time is generally consumed in teacher talk.

The following questions, developed by Amidon and Flanders in the 1970s, represented a possible direction for organizing and analyzing observations. Thirty years later, to what degree is this model still useful in describing what you have seen in classrooms? Does it help you understand student achievement?

1. What is the relationship of teacher talk to student talk? This can be answered by comparing the total number of observations in categories 1 to 7 with those in categories 8 and 9.

2. Is the teacher more direct or indirect? This can be answered by comparing categories 1 to 4 (indirect) with categories 5 to 7 (direct).

t a b l e 2 . 2   **Flanders' Classroom Interaction Analysis Scale**

Indirect Behavior

1. Accepts feeling: Accepts and clarifies the tone of feeling of the students in an unthreatening manner. Feelings may be positive or negative. Predicting or recalling feelings is included.

2. Praises or encourages: Praises or encourages student action or behavior. Jokes to release tension, but not at the expense of another individual; nodding head or saying "Um Hm?" or "Go on" are evidenced to encourage students.

3. Accepts and uses ideas of student: Clarifying, building ideas suggested by a student. As teacher brings more of his or her own ideas into play, shift to category 5.

4. Asks questions: Asking a question about content or procedure with the intent that a student will answer.

Direct Behavior

5. Lecturing: giving facts or opinions about content or procedure; expressing his or her own ideas, asking rhetorical questions.

6. Giving directions: Directions, commands, or orders with which students are expected to comply.

7. Criticizing or justifying authority: Statements intended to change student behavior from unacceptable to acceptable pattern; bawling someone out; stating why the teacher is doing what he or she is doing; extreme self-reference.

Student Talk

8. Response: Talk by students in response to teacher. Teacher initiates the contact or solicits student statement.

9. Initiation: Talk initiated by students. If "calling on" student is only to indicate who may talk next; observer must decide whether student wanted to talk.

Silence

10. Silence or confusion: Pauses, short periods of silence, and periods of confusion in which communication cannot be understood by the observer.

Source: Ned A Flanders. *Teacher Influence, Pupil Attitudes, and Achievement.* Washington, D.C.: Government Printing Office, 1965, p. 20. (Note: This version has been slightly adapted)

3. How much class time does the teacher spend lecturing? This can be answered by comparing category 5 with the total number of observations in categories 1 to 4 and 6 to 7.

4. Does the teacher ask divergent or convergent questions? This can be answered by comparing category 4 to categories 8 and 9.[13]

The data obtained from this system do not show when, why, or in what context teacher-student talk occurs, only how often particular types of interaction occur.

Nonetheless, the system is useful for making teachers aware of their interaction behaviors in the classroom.

The research literature that does exist offers mixed reviews on whether teacher directness or indirectness actually makes a difference in student achievement. The Flanders system may help reveal the style of teacher, but it does not suggest whether that style will produce a tangible achievement difference in students.

The Flanders system can be used to examine teacher-student verbal behaviors in any classroom, regardless of grade level or subject. Someone can observe the verbal behavior of a prospective, beginning, or even experienced teacher and categorize the teacher as direct or indirect.

Teaching Styles and Student Learning

The analysis of teaching styles eventually leads to two questions: Is student learning affected by a teacher's use of different styles? Are different teaching strategies effective for different students? Clear empirical evidence to support an answer to either of these questions does not exist. Let us assume that the answer is "yes" in both cases. If the assumption is true, the aim is to match the appropriate teacher style and strategies with the appropriate group of students in order to achieve the best teaching-learning situation. Depending on one's particular philosophy, matching teacher style and student need is accomplished in one of several ways.

Herbert Thelen argued that teachers recognize four kinds of students: good, bad, indifferent, and maladjusted. Each teacher places different students in these categories; students considered teachable by one teacher may not be by another. The proper fit between teacher and students results in the best kind of classroom or best group—what is defined as the *teachable* group. Thelen contends that homogeneous grouping is essential for a group to become more teachable. A teacher in such a group accomplishes more with students than do teachers in groups in which the range of ability and behavior is wide; moreover, it is easier to fit students and teachers in a homogeneous group. Any grouping that does not attempt to match students and teachers can have only "accidental success."[14]

Other researchers have addressed the problem of teachable groups and point out that effective teaching varies for students with different learning characteristics and socioeconomic backgrounds, as well as for different grade levels and subjects. For example, Donald Medley presents one of the most comprehensive reviews of 289 teacher process and product studies.[15] He concludes that effective teachers behave differently with different types of students. The most effective teachers of low socioeconomic status elementary school students who may be low achieving (1) spend less time discussing matters unrelated to lesson content, (2) present structured and sequential learning activities, (3) permit little time on independent and small group work, (4) initiate low-level and narrowly defined questions and are less likely to amplify or discuss student answers, (5) spend little time on and discourage student-initiated questions and comments, (6) provide less feedback on student-initiated questions, (7) engage in fewer teacher rebukes, and (8) spend less time on discipline matters. The optimum type of instruction, type of questions, and management techniques tend to be completely different for middle-class students. Table 2.3 provides a much more recent analysis of teacher behaviors appropriate for lower-achieving students. Compare those with Medley's.

table 2.3   **Teaching Lower-Achieving Students**

....

The teacher provides *active instruction* through lots of teacher-led instruction. Unstructured time is avoided and high levels of teacher-student interaction are encouraged.

The teacher *paces instruction* by breaking tasks into manageable segments and then carefully assesses student learning and creates instructional sequences based on that learning.

The teacher provides *remedial instruction* by understanding where students are as learners before proceeding further with instructional interventions.

The teacher builds *positive attitudes* by finding ways for students to experience success as learners. Teachers praise students for real accomplishments and good work.

Source: Adapted from Carolyn Evertson, Edmund T. Emmer, and Murray E. Worsham. *Classroom Management for Elementary Teachers,* 5th ed. Boston: Allyn & Bacon, 2000, pp. 216–219.

Three things are important to note from Medley's review. First, his notion of modifying teaching strategies for different students is similar to Thelen's "fit" between teachers and students. Teachable students for one teacher may be quite different from those for another, and not all students are easy to teach or even teachable under normal conditions. Some good teachers cannot successfully teach some types of problem students using approaches that they use with "nonproblem" students. Different students need different teaching techniques.

Second, Medley's description of effective teaching behaviors for low-socioeconomic status students does not resemble the current progressive model of instruction that many educators advocate (e.g., the use of inquiry approaches and self-discovery). The least effective teachers with low-socioeconomic status students are those who ask the most high-level and fewest low-level questions, whose students ask more questions and get more feedback, and who amplify or discuss student-initiated comments. Teachers who use more low-level questions and fewer high-level ones, whose students initiate fewer questions, and who tend not to discuss what students say are the most effective. Unquestionably, Medley's ideas are threatening and open to criticism, since they can lead to tracking students by ability and restricting low socioeconomic status students to limited cognitive experiences.[16]

Finally, Medley's ideas appear to be very much in line with teaching approaches that have been identified by current researchers as highly successful with low-achieving students, both at the elementary and secondary grade levels: basic skill, drill, time on task, feedback, competency, and mastery learning approaches. They coincide with instruction labeled *direct* and *explicit.*

Martin Haberman writes that "*Star teachers* conceive that their primary job is turning kids on to learning."[17] As a consequence, the star teacher begins to function in particular ways toward students. But just as important as those functions are the star teachers' attitudes toward students. For example, star teachers assume that problems are part of the teaching. Some teachers become discouraged because they expect the "perfect" class. It does not exist! And teachers who persist in trying to "find" it will be disappointed. Star teachers emerge as stars because they work to transform problems into possibilities for all students. It sounds trite, but it is also true.

The Science and Art of Teaching

Madeline Hunter*
University of California—Los Angeles

 Teaching is both a science and an art. The science is based on psychological research that identifies cause–effect relationships between teaching and learning. The art is how those relationships are implemented in successful and artistic teaching.

All excellent teaching does not look the same but it does contain the same basic psychological elements: In the same way, the Taj Mahal and the Lincoln Memorial are very different in appearance but they both commemorate a person, are made of marble, and follow the same principles of aesthetics and engineering.

Teaching in kindergarten or calculus, literature or auto shop manifests the same elements of instructional effectiveness. Teachers need to learn the science of pedagogy so they, in their own classrooms, with their own personalities, can implement it artistically.

Teaching excellence is not a genetically endowed power but a result of rigorous study and inspired performance.

*Madeline Hunter died in the early 1990s, but her presence is still felt throughout many American schools.

Interestingly, during the past few years more and more schools have been experimenting with systemic reform strategies that represent specific, almost scripted ways of teaching students. Such strategies will influence the instructional style a teacher uses. You may well be placed in a school that uses one of those approaches. They include but are not limited to Success for All (PreK–6), Direct Instruction (K–6), and Roots and Wings (Pre–K). Such systemic reform models do not take into consideration matching teacher style with learner characteristics. Rather, each has a defined structure, and teachers are expected to use that "scripted" approach in classroom instruction. Such models are drawing considerable attention in terms of their effectiveness (see Table 2.4).

As you begin your teaching career, you will be confronted by a wide variety of expectations for your behavior. You may be in a state that focuses on PRAXIS and INTASC standards, but you could conceivably be hired by a school that prescribes how you will teach, especially if you are in an urban or rural setting. Schools in those contexts are the ones most often using whole-school reform strategies.

Read the following description of a teacher who is using a form of scripted direct instruction (DI) to teach vocabulary, a method often found in lower elementary schools. As you read it, think about to what degree a teacher's style could influence the way in which instruction occurred. If you were hired into a school that used DI, could you adopt a teaching style that was more student-centered or laissez faire? Would it be appropriate? Should the principal allow it?

A teacher slowly circles her second-grade class, which is grouped in five rows of five children. Reading from a spiral notebook, she barks, "What word?" And the children, their eyes locked on a vocabulary list in their workbooks, cry out in unison, "Taste!" The teacher sharply snaps her fingers at the side of her head. "Next word! What word?"

"Ankle!"

Snap. "Next word! What word?"

"Tasted!"

table 2.4   **Unproven Designs**

Only three of twenty-four popular models of whole-school reform are supported by strong evidence that they improve student achievement.

Model of Whole-School Reform	Evidence of Positive Effect on Student Achievement	Year Introduced	Number of Schools Adopting the Model*
Accelerated Schools (K–8)	Marginal	1986	1,000
America's Choice (K–12)	No Research	1998	300
ATLAS Communities (PreK–12)	No Research	1992	63
Audrey Cohen College (K–12)	No Research	1970	16
Basic Schools Networks (K–12)	No Research	1992	150
Coalition of Essential Schools (K–12)	Mixed, Weak	1984	1,000
Community for Learning (K–12)	Promising	1990	92
Co-NECT (K–12)	No Research	1992	75
Core Knowledge (K–8)	Promising	1990	750
Different Ways of Knowing (K–7)	Promising	1989	412
Direct Instruction (K–6)	Strong	Late 1960s	150
Expeditionary Learning Outward Bound (K–12)	Promising	1992	65
The Foxfire Fund (K–12)	No Research	1966	N/A
High Schools That Work (K–12)	Strong	1987	860
High/Scope (K–3)	Marginal	1967	27
League of Professional Schools (K–12)	Marginal	1989	158
Modern Red Schoolhouse (K–12)	No Research	1993	50
Onward to Excellence (K–12)	Marginal	1981	1,000
Paideia (K–12)	Mixed, Weak	1982	80
Roots and Wings (PreK)	Marginal	1993	200
School Development Program (K–12)	Promising	1968	700
Success for All (PreK–6)	Strong	1987	1,130
Talent Development High School (9–12)	Marginal	1994	10
Urban Learning Centers (PreK–12)	No Research	1993	13

* As of October 30, 1998

Source: American Institute for Research (under contract to AASA, AFT, NAESP, NASSP, NEA). *An Educator's Guide to Schoolwide Reform.* 2003. See www.aasa.org/issues_and_insights/district_organization/Reform/ That site will provide current information on all of the reform initiatives.

Snap. And so on, down to the bottom of the column. "Great job! Touch on the first word of Column 4. Good touching! What word?"

You can hear the shouted call-and-response echoing up and down the hallways of Hamstead Hill, a school close to Baltimore's Inner Harbor that serves a predominantly working-class population. The shouting isn't absolutely necessary; Janet Mahoney, a third-grade teacher, says that she winces when she hears it. But since the DI script is mostly written in the imperative mode, students generally respond in unison, and communication on both sides is speedy and short, the classroom often descends into earsplitting [din]. At the same time, the transaction is anything but chaotic. One bit of information is separated from another by unmistakable punctuation—a fingersnap, a clicker, a clap.[18]

Another question to ask about this scenario is "Should direct instruction be used in teaching other types of content besides vocabulary?" Recently, some researchers have used extant research to show how different types of knowledge require different types of learning and, appropriately, different forms of teaching. These researchers illustrate how the ability of students (and their backgrounds) and levels of cognitive development influence capacity for learning. For example, let's assume that you are about to teach details (e.g., facts, time sequences, cause-effect relationships) to students. Marzano, Pickwing, and Pollock identify two generalizations to guide instruction:

1. Students should have systematic, multiple exposures to details.
2. Details are highly amenable to "dramatic" instruction.[19]

What we are suggesting is that *what* you teach may influence *how* you teach. And who you teach is important to the extent that you need to understand that different learners (whatever their gender, race, ethnicity, ability, age, or sexual orientation) may need different approaches to that same content, even though they are all capable of learning the content. (We will discuss instructional approaches more thoroughly in Chapter 5.)

The key is that teaching effectiveness is often shaped by where you teach as well as by the grade level at which you teach. Researchers are beginning to understand more fully the complexities of the cognitive process. A truly professional teacher is one who shapes his or her behavior to meet the unique needs of the students for whom he or she has responsibility. We want you to know more than one approach. The diversity of the students you teach demands that you know what they must learn and a variety of methods to help them learn it. Table 2.5 illustrates the effects of different instructional approaches. It also shows how instruction that is dramatic and involves the students actively in thinking about content creates the greatest achievement gains.

Teacher Expectations

In the previous section, we discussed teacher style and some of the complications that you might experience when embracing a personal style, especially if you are in a school that uses an approach such as direct instruction.

In this section we will discuss a matter that is somewhat less controversial: *teacher expectations.* One thing that almost all educators (and educational critics) agree on is that teacher expectations do influence student achievement.

Teachers communicate their expectations of students through myriad verbal and nonverbal cues. It is well established that these expectations affect the interaction between teachers and students and, eventually, the performance of students. In many cases *teacher expectations* become self-fulfilling prophecies; that is, if the teacher ex-

table 2.5   **Types of Instruction and Effect on Learning**

Instruction	Effect Size (ES) Immediately After Instruction	ES After 12 Months
Verbal Instruction	.74	.64
Visual Instruction	.90	.74
Dramatic Instruction	1.12	.80

Source: Robert J. Marzano, Debra J. Pickering, and Jane E. Pollack. *Classroom Instruction That Works.* Alexandria, Va.: Association for Supervision and Curriculum Development, 2001, p. 131.

Note to Reader: Effect size illustrates the amount of growth experienced by students receiving a "treatment" such as verbal instruction as compared to a control group. An ES of 1.0 would be a one standard deviation (or quite large) level of growth. Notice that *dramatic instruction* resulted in the largest short-term and long-term effect on learning.

pects students to be slow or exhibit deviant behavior, he or she treats them accordingly, and in response they adopt such behaviors.

The research on **teacher expectations** is rooted in the legal briefs and arguments of Kenneth and Mamie Clark prepared during the fight for desegregated schools in the late 1940s. They pointed out that prophesying low achievement for black students not only provides teachers with an excuse for their students' failure, but also communicates a sense of inevitable failure to the students.

The Clarks' thesis was given empirical support a few years later by Rosenthal's and Jacobsen's *Pygmalion in the Classroom*, a study of students in the San Francisco schools.[20] After controlling for the ability of students, teachers were told that there was reason to expect that certain students would perform better, and the expectancy was fulfilled. However, confidence in *Pygmalion* diminished when Robert Thorndike, one of the most respected measurement experts, pointed out that there were several flaws in the methodology and that the tests were unreliable.[21]

Interest in teacher expectations and the **self-fulfilling prophecy** reappeared in the 1970s and 1980s. Good and Brophy and then others outlined how teachers communicate expectations to students and in turn influence student behavior.

1. The teacher expects specific achievement and behavior from particular students.

2. Because of these different expectations, the teacher behaves differently toward various students.

3. This interaction suggests to students what achievement and behavior the teacher expects from them, which affects their self-concepts, motivation, and performance.

4. If the teacher's interaction is consistent over time, it will shape the students' achievement and behavior. High expectations for students will influence achievement at high levels, and low expectations will produce lower achievement.

5. With time, student achievement and behavior will conform more and more to the original expectations of the teacher.[22]

t a b l e 2 . 6   **Teacher Behavior with Low Achievers and High Achievers**

1. Waiting for less time for low achievers to answer questions: Teachers often give high-achieving students more time to respond than low-achieving students.

2. Interrupting low achievers more often: Teachers interrupt low achievers more often than high achievers when they make reading mistakes and/or are unable to sustain a discussion about the content or lesson.

3. Giving answers to low achievers: Teachers more frequently respond to incorrect responses of low achievers by giving them the answer or calling on another student to answer the question than they do with high achievers.

4. Rewarding inappropriate behavior: Teachers at times praise the inappropriate responses of low achievers, which serves to dramatize the weakness of such students.

5. Criticizing low achievers more often and praising them less often: Some teachers criticize low achievers more than high achievers, a practice that is likely to reduce initiative and risk-taking behavior. Moreover, low achievers seem less likely to be praised, even when they get the correct answer.

6. Not confirming responses of low achievers: Teachers sometimes respond to answers from low achievers with indifference. Even if the answers are correct, they call on other students to respond without confirming answers, a practice that is likely to sow seeds of doubt in low achievers concerning the adequacy of their response.

7. Paying less attention to low achievers: Teachers simply pay less attention to low achievers. For example, they smile more frequently at and maintain more eye contact with high achievers, give briefer and less informative feedback to low achievers' questions, and are less likely to follow through on time-consuming instructional methods with low achievers.

8. Calling on low achievers less often: Teachers seem inclined to call on high achievers more often than low achievers.

9. Using different interaction patterns: Contact patterns between teachers and students are different for high and low achievers. Public response patterns dominate in interaction with high achievers, but low achievers have more private contacts with teachers. For low achievers, private conferences may be a sign of inadequacy.

10. Seating low achievers farther from the teacher: Teachers often place low achievers in locations that are more distant from them.

11. Demanding less from low achievers: Teachers are more likely to demand little from and give up on low achievers and let them know it. Teachers demand more work from high achievers and ask more high-level questions.

12. Administering different tests and grades: Teachers often give low achievers less demanding tests and assignments. They are more likely to give high achievers the benefit of the doubt in borderline cases involving grades.

Source: Adapted from Thomas L. Good, "Two Decades of Research on Teacher Expectations: Findings and Future Directions." *Journal of Teacher Education* (July–August 1987): 32–47. Thomas L. Good and Jere E. Brophy, *Educational Psychology: A Realistic Approach,* 5th ed. New York: Longman, 1994, pp. 490–492.

Brophy and Good's model, in particular, shows that many teachers vary sharply in their interaction with high and low achievers (Table 2.6). The two researchers contend that it is not necessary for the teacher to engage in all the behaviors listed in the table to have an impact. For example, if a teacher assigns low achievers considerably less content than they can handle, that factor alone will inhibit their learning.

The most effective teacher is realistic about the differences between high and low achievers. The teacher who develops a rigid or stereotyped perception of students is likely to have a harmful effect on them. The teacher who understands that differences exist and adapts realistic methods and content accordingly (i.e., differentiates instruction) will have the most positive effect on students.

Labeling Students

Dona Kagan outlined a comprehensive model of how teachers (and students) alienate low achievers by making assumptions about their behavior and achievement, thus tracking them into a second-class status in classrooms and schools.[23] Once a label is attached to a student, according to Kagan, the teacher tends to adjust his or her teaching methods so they are consistent with the label ("underachiever," "slow learner," "disabled learner," etc.). The anticipation and expectations associated with the label constitute a "rational response" by the teacher in understanding and reacting to the students. This "typing" or labeling of students is often reinforced by school specialists, counselors, and psychologists, which in turn has a reinforcing effect on the teacher's perceptions and an overwhelming effect on the student.

Today, labeling is often unwittingly the outcome of state mandated tests in which low performing students are expected to perform low, despite their efforts or what they may have learned beyond what is assessed on standardized tests. Moreover, when minority students are "told" year after year that they perform lower than their white counterparts, they fulfill what Clarence Page and others call the "stereotype threat," which means that they perform lower on tests than their ability would suggest. The problem is traceable less to present-day racism than to the legacy of racism—an attitude that affects the perceptions and behaviors of far too many people in American society today.[24]

Little wonder, then, that some theorists attribute academic failure of some black students to an oppositional cultural frame of reference, an oppositional identity, and a continuous distrust of white educators. Dropping out of school for some low achievers and minority students might be regarded as a process of disengagement from school, a means of preserving one's own personal and cultural identity, and a way of alleviating the negative effects associated with low self-concept, low motivation, and low achievement—and only secondarily as fulfilling the expectations associated with school failure. In fact, dropouts are doing what dominant culture tells those in the losing half to do: They are getting out of the way.[25]

A dilemma evolves in helping teachers work with low achievers and with culturally diverse students. Generalizations are needed to inform teachers about various instructional methods and techniques that can be applied to students with differing backgrounds. On the other hand, a universal concept of multicultural education exposes teachers to the problems inherent in prejudging individuals on the basis of membership in a particular group.[26] Thus, we raise a number of questions to consider in context with your own teacher expectations and views of teaching low achievers or minority groups. How can you avoid the dangers inherent in generalizing about low achievers or diverse cultural groups? Given your own prior experiences, how can you be objective in examining your own views about low achievers or culturally different students?

Fortunately, there is evidence to indicate that when teachers connect learning to a student's background and culture, the student becomes engaged in his or her educational experiences. That is, the students of teachers who are able to show them the relevance of what they are learning are more inclined actually to learn the material.

Parents appreciate that some students need the relevance issue defined before they can learn. Others have no need for such relevance—they will learn to learn, regardless. Dodd and Konzal describe this phenomenon:

> . . . [D]ifferences among parents were apparent in the degree to which they talked about practices for students universally or for particular groups or individual students. Because some parents did not think the classics were relevant today, they thought they should be taught only to college-bound students; or, as [one parent] . . . put it, the student who was going to work in a gas station did not need algebra, chemistry, or Shakespeare.
>
> Other parents talked specifically about the relevance of particular practices for individual children. For example, [another parent] . . . said relevance was not an important issue for her daughter, a good student who would do whatever the teacher asked, but her son, who was a reluctant reader and writer, needed curriculum and methods with clear connections to the real world to motivate him. He "definitely needs writing to get him by in everyday life. . . . [H]e's going to need to know that if he ever had to write a business letter. . . . [H]e's going into business for himself."[27]

In a recent study of 140 high-poverty classrooms in fifteen schools and across three states, researchers examined the impact of teaching style on achievement and found that teachers who "taught for meaning" rather than focusing on basic skill development were more likely to respond to diversity by connecting students' backgrounds and culture to learning, achieving higher levels of student engagement and academic success.[28]

Teacher Traits

In the reams of research published on teacher behavior, the greatest amount concerns teacher traits. The problem is that researchers disagree on which teacher characteristics result in successful teaching, on how to categorize characteristics, and on how to define them. In this section we'll examine the research and debate that occurred on teacher traits during the middle part of the 1900s. Much of the material is still relevant in the early twenty-first century.

Teacher traits or characteristics have different meanings for different people. What one investigator considers warm behavior may differ from what another investigator considers it, just as they may disagree on the effects of such behavior. In addition, it can be assumed that a warm teacher would have a different effect on students according to age, sex, achievement level, socioeconomic class, ethnic group, subject, and classroom context.[29]

Such differences tend to operate for every teacher characteristic and to affect every study on teacher behavior. Although a list of teacher characteristics may be suitable for a particular study, the characteristics (as well as the results) cannot always be transferred to another study.

Yet, as Lee Shulman points out, teacher behavior researchers often disregard factors such as the time of day, school year, and content, and they will combine data from an early observation with data from another, later occasion. Data from the early part of the term may be combined with data from the later part of the term; data from one unit of content (which may require different teacher behaviors or techniques) may be combined with that from other units of content.[30] All these aggregations assume that instances of teaching over time have equal weights, which is rarely the case. The accuracy issue is further clouded when such studies are compared, integrated, and built upon each other to form theories or viewpoints about which teacher characteristics are most effective.

Despite such potential problems, many researchers feel that certain teacher characteristics can be defined and validated across the board and generalized from one study to another. In turn, many researchers feel that they can make recommendations from such generalizations for practices and behaviors in the classroom.

Research on Teacher Traits

Researchers have named literally thousands of *teacher characteristics* over the years. A. S. Barr organized these recommended behaviors into a manageable list in the 1950s.[31] Reviewing some fifty years of research, he identified twelve successful characteristics such as emotional stability. Other authorities have made summaries of teacher traits or characteristics, but Barr's work is considered more comprehensive even though it is somewhat dated. Many of the same characteristics that Barr identified are still clearly evident in the body of literature surfacing in the early part of the twenty-first century. What makes the newest research a bit different from the work of Barr is that researchers have now begun to document the value added by a single teacher or group of teachers. What William Sanders and other such researchers cannot document is what specific teacher characteristics or behaviors are related to student achievement. For this reason it is still relevant to review the contributions of early researchers such as A. S. Barr, who we describe as the "granddaddy of teacher behavior research," and David Ryans. Most—certainly *some*—of what they found will still be true for you and for the teachers who follow you.

While Barr presented an overview of hundreds of studies of teacher characteristics, which included characteristics such as reliability, cooperativeness, objectivity, emotional stability and intelligence, the single most comprehensive study was conducted by David Ryans.[32] More than 6,000 teachers in 1,700 schools were involved in the study over a six-year period. The objective was to identify through observations and self-ratings the most desirable teacher characteristics. Respondents were asked to identify and describe a teaching act that they felt made a difference between success or failure. These critical behaviors were reduced to a list of twenty-five effective behaviors and twenty-five ineffective behaviors (Table 2.7). The lists serve as good guidelines for beginning and even experienced teachers. The teacher should examine them in terms of his or her own personality and perceptions of good teaching or for what he or she defines as good teaching.

Ryans went on to develop a bipolar list of eighteen teacher characteristics (for example, original vs. conventional, patient vs. impatient, hostile vs. warm). Respondents were asked to identify the approximate position of teachers for each pair of characteristics. (Notice that most of this research is based on people's perceptions of good teaching, not actual measures of student achievement.)

t a b l e   2 . 7   **Ryans' Critical Teacher Behaviors**

Effective Behaviors	*Ineffective Behaviors*
1. Is alert, appears enthusiastic.	1. Is apathetic and dull and appears bored.
2. Appears interested in pupils and classroom activities.	2. Appears uninterested in pupils and classroom activities.
3. Is cheerful, optimistic.	3. Is depressed and pessimistic, appears unhappy.
4. Is self-controlled, not easily upset.	4. Loses temper, is easily upset.
5. Likes fun, has a sense of humor.	5. Is overly serious, too occupied for humor.
6. Recognizes and admits own mistakes.	6. Is unaware of, or fails to admit, own mistakes.
7. Is fair, impartial, and objective in treatment of pupils.	7. Is unfair or partial in dealing with pupils.
8. Is patient.	8. Is impatient.
9. Shows understanding and sympathy in working with pupils.	9. Is short with pupils, uses sarcastic remarks, or in ways shows lack of sympathy with pupils.
10. Is friendly and courteous in relations with pupils.	10. Is aloof and removed in relations with pupils.
11. Helps pupils with personal as well as educational problems.	11. Seems unaware of pupils' personal needs and problems.
12. Commends effort and gives praise for work well done.	12. Does not commend pupils, is disapproving and hypercritical.
13. Accepts pupils' efforts as sincere.	13. Is suspicious of pupils' motives.
14. Anticipates reactions of others in social situations.	14. Does not anticipate reactions of others in social situations.
15. Encourages pupils to try to do their best.	15. Makes no effort to encourage pupils to try to do their best.
16. Classroom procedure is planned and well organized.	16. Classroom procedure is without plan, disorganized.
17. Classroom procedure is flexible within overall plan.	17. Shows extreme rigidity of procedure, inability to depart from plan.
18. Anticipates individual needs.	18. Fails to provide for individual differences and needs of pupils.
19. Stimulates pupils through interesting and original materials and techniques.	19. Uses uninteresting materials and teaching techniques.
20. Conducts clear, practical demonstrations and explanations.	20. Demonstrations and explanations are not clear and are poorly conducted.
21. Is clear and thorough in giving directions.	21. Directions are incomplete, vague.
22. Encourages pupils to work through their own problems and evaluate their accomplishments.	22. Fails to give pupils opportunity to work out own problems or evaluate their own work.
23. Disciplines in a quiet, dignified, and positive manner.	23. Reprimands at length, ridicules, and resorts to cruel or meaningless form of correction.
24. Gives help willingly.	24. Fails to give help or gives it grudgingly.
25. Foresees and attempts to resolve potential difficulties.	25. Is unable to foresee and resolve potential difficulties.

Source: David G. Ryans. *Characteristics of Teachers*. Washington, D.C.: American Council on Education, 1960, p. 82. Reprinted with Permission.

The eighteen teacher characteristics were defined in detail and further grouped into three "patterns" of successful versus unsuccessful teachers:

1. *Pattern X:* understanding, friendly, and responsive versus aloof and egocentric
2. *Pattern Y:* responsible, businesslike, and systematic versus evading, unplanned, and slipshod
3. *Pattern Z:* stimulating, imaginative, and original versus dull and routine

Ryans singled out these three primary teacher patterns for further attention. Elementary teachers scored higher than secondary teachers on the scales of understanding and friendly classroom behavior (Pattern X). Differences between women and men were insignificant in the elementary schools, but in the secondary schools women consistently scored higher in Pattern X and in stimulating and imaginative classroom behavior (Pattern Z), and men tended to exhibit businesslike and systematic behaviors (Pattern Y). Younger teachers (under 45 years) scored higher than older teachers in patterns X and Z; older teachers scored higher in pattern Y.

A similar but more recent list of teacher characteristics was compiled by Bruce Tuckman, who has developed a feedback system for stimulating change in teacher behavior.[33] His instrument, which originally contained twenty-eight bipolar items, was expanded to thirty items (for example, creative versus routinized, cautious versus outspoken, assertive versus passive, quiet versus bubbly) on which teachers also were rated on a seven-point scale.

The thirty characteristics cluster into four teacher "dimensions," similar to Ryans' three patterns:

1. *Creative:* The creative teacher is imaginative, experimenting, and original; the noncreative teacher is routine, exacting, and cautious.
2. *Dynamic:* The dynamic teacher is outgoing, energetic, and extroverted; the nondynamic teacher is passive, withdrawn, and submissive.
3. *Organized:* The organized teacher is purposeful, resourceful, and in control; the disorganized teacher is capricious, erratic, and flighty.
4. *Warm:* The warm teacher is sociable, amiable, and patient; the cold teacher is unfriendly, hostile, and impatient.[34]

Because of the problem with lack of agreement in defining teacher characteristics, Wiggins and others recommended more precise terms—what they called ***teacher competencies.***[35] These competencies may or may not stem from broad teacher characteristics, but they are "specific items of behavior" that can be defined carefully for inclusion in a manual of instruction or in a teacher appraisal system. Examples of competencies include the following:

1. Uses a variety of instructional strategies.
2. Uses convergent and divergent inquiry strategies.
3. Establishes in instruction transitions and sequences that are varied.
4. Modifies instructional activities to accommodate learner needs.
5. Demonstrates ability to work with individuals, small groups, and large groups.

table 2.8   **Principals' Ranking of Effective Teacher Competencies**

Rank of importance	Competency	Definition
1	Task orientation	The extent to which the classroom is businesslike, the students spend their time on academic subjects, and the teacher presents clear goals to the students
2	Enthusiasm and interest	The amount of the teacher's vigor, power, and involvement
3	Direct instruction	The extent to which the teacher sets and articulates the learning goals, actively assesses student progress, and frequently makes class presentations illustrating how to do assigned work
4	Pacing	The extent to which the level of difficulty and the pace of the lesson is appropriate for the students' abilities and interests
5	Feedback	The extent to which the teacher provides the students with positive or negative feedback
6	Management	The extent to which the teacher is able to conduct the class without instruction being interrupted
7	Questioning	The extent to which the teacher asks questions at different levels and adjusts them appropriately in the classroom
8	Instructional time	The allocation of a period of time for a lesson adequate to cover the material yet flexible enough to allow for the unexpected
9	Variability	The amount of flexibility or adaptability of teaching methods; the amount of extra material in the classroom
10	Structuring	The extent to which the teacher directs instruction
11	Opportunity to learn criterion material	The extent to which criterion material is covered in class

Source: John W. Arnn and John N. Mangieri. "Effective Leadership for Effective Schools: A Survey of Principal Attitudes." *NASSP Bulletin* (February 1988): 4. Copyright (1988) National Association of Secondary School Principals. www.principals.org. Reprinted with permission.

6. Demonstrates knowledge in the subject areas.

7. Accurately assesses student achievement.

8. Articulates achievement targets for all students.[36]

It is especially important to determine which competencies school principals believe to be significant, since they invariably play a role in developing teacher evaluation plans, in observing and judging teachers (especially at the elementary and junior high level), and in assigning supervisors to evaluate teachers' performance (usually at the high school level). In a nationwide study of 202 secondary schools selected for special recognition for effectiveness in educating their students (conducted under the aegis of the U.S. Department of Education), principals were asked to identify and rank the competencies they emphasized with teachers.[37] Table 2.8 shows the top eleven competencies.

The five competencies most important for principals—task orientation, enthusiasm and interest, direct instruction, pacing, and feedback—emphasize the "active" dimension of teaching and businesslike behaviors. Principals of effective schools expect their teachers to teach in a way that can be observed and measured. Increasingly, principals expect teachers to exhibit teaching behaviors that make a value-added difference for students.

As you are reading this book, a new emphasis on standards is emerging—both the academic standards that students are to meet and the teaching standards that are to shape the way in which you teach. Sergiovanni and Starratt describe six characteristics of teachers who are successful in teaching to national discipline-based standards:

1. *The use of integrative units:* organizing the curriculum around larger themes

2. *The use of small group activities:* helping students work collaboratively

3. *The capacity to help students represent to ideas in order to learn:* using Venn diagrams and other representations to help students explore ideas

4. *The use of classroom workshops:* organizing time to ensure that students have some one-on-one time with the teacher to explore ideas

5. *The use of authentic ideas:* providing opportunities for students to think in "real-world" terms about classroom concepts

6. *The use of reflective assessment:* finding ways for students to show what they have learned and to reflect on its quality[38]

Their emphasis reflects a phenomenon that we discussed in Chapter 1, that effective teachers know content and know how to teach that content.

In the 1980s and 1990s, most measurements of teacher competence focused on minimal competencies. According to Arthur Wise, as school districts and administrators evaluate competencies of teachers, they spend "little time evaluating teachers who appear to be competent." Therefore, competent teachers often are not threatened by the process nor do they consider it useful. This does not mean that teacher competency instruments are invalid or unreliable measures, but only that their present utility is linked to identifying teacher incompetence. In some school districts that rely on a competencies approach, for example, "the absence of minimal teaching competence, especially the inability to manage the classroom, triggers remediation, probation, or intervention."[39]

Many school districts (even entire states such as Florida and North Carolina) developed in the 1980s and 1990s specific lists of teacher competencies as a basis for appraisal plans. Teachers who did not exhibit these explicit behaviors were often penalized, were labeled as "marginal" or "below standard," and in some cases may have risked losing their jobs. As you will see in Chapter 5, how you teach will be dictated by what (content) you plan to teach so evaluating teachers on these competencies holds them responsible for content over which they have no control. According to critics of the Florida and North Carolina systems, the competencies also tended to reflect a narrow and behaviorist view of a "good" teacher and to ignore humanistic or affective behaviors that also contribute to good teaching.[40]

These competencies are now evolving into specific ***teaching standards.*** This book relies on Pathwise Induction Programs-PRAXIS III and INTASC standards but some states have their own core teaching standards such as North Carolina. We will discuss the PRAXIS and INTASC in detail as an introduction to Chapters 3 through 11. The conceptual grounding for these standards came from research on teacher style, teacher characteristics, and teacher competencies. The researchers laid the foundation for the current teacher standards that many educators are now implementing and that will likely be used to assess your teaching.

The old teacher competencies focused heavily on actual teacher behaviors. The new teaching standards are much more oriented to pedagogy and content and the complexity of the classroom environment. The following two standards are from the National Council for the Accreditation of Teacher Education (NCATE) and the Interstate New Teacher and Support Consortium (INTASC) and illustrate this content and pedagogy nexus:

> *Example NCATE Standard:* Candidates preparing to work in schools as teachers or other professional school personnel know and demonstrate the content, pedagogical, and professional knowledge, skills, and dispositions necessary to help all students learn. Assessments indicate that candidates meet professional, state, and institutional standards.

> *Example INTASC Standard:* The teacher has a thorough understanding and knowledge of subject matter and uses such knowledge to create effective learning experiences for students.

QUESTIONS FOR REFLECTION

Many states are now implementing teaching standards similar to those outlined for NCATE and INTASC. North Carolina is one of those states that has been a real leader in this movement. On the surface the core standards appear clear, but what do you see if you look more closely? Select one of the standards from the following list and explain in detail what you would look for in the classroom of a teacher who demonstrated it effectively. Also, what behaviors do ethical teachers exhibit? How do they support the profession? After you have considered these questions visit the North Carolina website (www.ncptsc.org) and look at how they describe what each of these means for teachers.

Teachers Are Leaders

- Teachers lead in their classrooms.
- Teachers lead in the school.
- Teachers lead in advocating for schools and children.
- Teachers function effectively in a complex, dynamic environment.
- Teachers meet high ethical standards of practice.
- Teachers support the teaching profession.

Teachers Are Reflective About Their Practice

- Teachers analyze the results of teaching.
- Teachers collaborate with their colleagues.

- Teachers use research in their classrooms.
- Teachers continue to grow professionally.

Teachers Respect and Care About Students

- Teachers enjoy spending time in the company of children and young adults.
- Teachers learn all they can about each of their students.
- Teachers maintain the dignity of each student.
- Teachers express pride in their students' accomplishments.

Teacher Effects

This section examines the different research findings from the applied science literature, categorized by the researchers who popularized certain perspectives toward the research. The work of these individuals has shaped, directly or indirectly, much of what has emerged in the teaching standards now used by different states.

Rosenshine and Furst Model

Teacher behavior research has shown that teacher behaviors, as well as specific teaching principles and methods, make a difference in student achievement. Rosenshine and Furst analyzed some forty-two correlational studies in their often-quoted review of **process-product** research. They concluded that there were eleven **teacher processes** (behaviors or variables) strongly and consistently related to *student products* (outcomes or student achievement). The first five teacher processes showed the strongest correlation to positive outcomes:

1. Clarity of teacher's presentation and ability to organize classroom activities
2. Variability of media, materials, and activities used by the teacher
3. Enthusiasm, defined in terms of the teacher's movement, voice inflection, and the like
4. Task orientation or businesslike teacher behaviors, structured routines, and an academic focus
5. Student opportunity to learn; that is, the teacher's coverage of the material or content in class on which students are later tested[41]

The six remaining processes were classified as promising: use of student ideas, justified criticism, use of structuring comments, appropriate questions in terms of lower and higher cognitive level, probing or encouraging student elaboration, and challenging instructional materials.

Rosenshine himself later revised his conclusions; subsequent analysis showed that only two behaviors or processes consistently correlated with student achievement: (1) task orientation (later referred to as *direct instruction*) and (2) opportunity to learn (later referred to as *academic time, academic engaged time,* and *content covered*). On a third behavior, clarity, he wavered, pointing out that it seemed to be a correlate of student achievement for students above the fifth grade. The other eight processes appeared to be less important, and they varied in importance not only according to grade level, but also according to subject matter, instructional groups and activities, and students' social class and abilities.[42] Nevertheless, the original review remains a valuable study on how what the teacher does relates to how the students learn.

More recently, Rosenshine summarized the important instructional advances of the last thirty years and identified four key instructional procedures:

1. Providing procedural prompts
2. Teaching in small steps
3. Modeling the use of cognitive strategies
4. Directing and guiding student practice

Gage Model

Nate Gage analyzed forty-nine process-product studies. He identified four clusters of behaviors that show a strong relationship to student outcomes: (1) teacher indirectness, the willingness to accept student ideas and feelings, and the ability to provide a healthy emotional climate; (2) teacher praise, support and encouragement, use of humor to release tensions (but not at the expense of others), and attention to students' needs; (3) teacher acceptance, clarifying, building, and developing students' ideas; and (4) teacher criticism, reprimanding students, and justifying authority. The relationship between the last cluster and outcome was negative—when criticism occurred, student achievement was low.[43] In effect, the four clusters suggest the traditional notion of a democratic or warm teacher (a model emphasized for several decades).

From the evidence on teacher effects upon student achievement in reading and mathematics in the elementary grades, Gage presented successful teaching principles and methods that seem relevant for other grades as well. Bear in mind that they are commonsense strategies. They apply to many grade levels, and most experienced teachers are familiar with them. Nonetheless, they provide guidelines for education students or beginning teachers who say, "Just tell me how to teach." Here is a summary of the strategies:

1. Teachers should have a system of rules that allows students to attend to their personal and procedural needs without having to check with the teacher.
2. A teacher should move around the room, monitoring students' seat work and communicating an awareness of their behavior while also attending to their academic needs.
3. To ensure productive independent work by students, teachers should be sure that the assignments are interesting and worthwhile yet still easy enough to be completed by each student without teacher direction.
4. Teachers should keep to a minimum such activities as giving directions and organizing the class for instruction. Teachers can do this by writing the daily schedule on the board and establishing general procedures so students know where to go and what to do.

5. In selecting students to respond to questions, teachers should call on volunteers and nonvolunteers by name before asking questions to give all students a chance to answer and to alert the student to be called upon.

6. Teachers should always aim at getting less academically oriented students to give some kind of response to a question. Rephrasing, giving clues, or asking leading questions can be useful techniques for bringing forth some answer from a silent student, one who says, "I don't know," or one who answers incorrectly.

7. During reading group instruction, teachers should give a maximum amount of brief feedback and provide fast-paced activities of the "drill" type.[44]

Good and Brophy Model

Over the last twenty years, Good and Brophy have identified several factors related to effective teaching and student learning. They focus on basic principles of teaching but not teacher behaviors or characteristics, since both researchers contend that teachers today are looking more for principles of teaching than for prescriptions.

1. Clarity about instructional goals (objectives)

2. Knowledge about content and ways of teaching it

3. Variety in the use of teaching methods and media

4. "With-it-ness," awareness of what is going on, alertness in monitoring classroom activities

5. "Overlapping," sustaining an activity while doing something else at the same time

6. "Smoothness," sustaining proper lesson pacing and group momentum, not dwelling on minor points or wasting time dealing with individuals, and focusing on all the students

7. Seat-work instructions and management that initiate and focus on productive task engagement

8. Holding students accountable for learning, accepting responsibility for student learning

9. Setting realistic expectations in line with student abilities and behaviors

10. Giving realistic praise, not praise for its own sake

11. Flexibility in planning and adapting classroom activities

12. Task orientation and businesslike behavior in the teacher

13. Monitoring of students' understanding; providing appropriate feedback, giving praise, asking questions

14. Providing student opportunity to learn what is to be tested

15. Making comments that help structure learning of knowledge and concepts for students, helping students learn how to learn[45]

The fact that many of these behaviors are classroom management techniques and structured learning strategies suggests, quite logically, that good discipline is a prerequisite for good teaching.

Evertson and Emmer Model

The Evertson and Emmer model is similar to the Good and Brophy model (in fact, Evertson has written several texts and articles with Brophy). The models are similar in three ways: (1) teacher effectiveness is associated with specific teaching principles and methods; (2) organization and management of instructional activities are stressed; and (3) findings and conclusions are based heavily on process-product studies.

Nine basic teaching principles represent the core of Evertson's work with Emmer and, to a lesser extent, with Brophy. Effectiveness is identified as raising student achievement scores. Evertson and Emmer also focus a great deal on classroom management.

1. *Rules and procedures:* Rules and procedures are established and enforced and students are monitored for compliance.
2. *Consistency:* Similar expectations are maintained for activities and behavior at all times for all students. Inconsistency causes confusion in students about what is acceptable.
3. *Prompt management of inappropriate behavior:* Inappropriate behavior is attended to quickly to stop it and prevent its spread.
4. *Checking student work:* All student work, including seat-work, homework, and papers, is corrected, errors are discussed, and feedback is provided promptly.
5. *Interactive teaching:* This takes several forms and includes presenting and explaining new materials, question sessions, discussions, checking for student understanding, actively moving among students to correct work, providing feedback, and, if necessary, reteaching materials.
6. *Academic instruction, sometimes referred to as* academic learning time *or* academic engaged time: Attention is focused on the management of student work.
7. *Pacing:* Information is presented at a rate appropriate to the students' ability to comprehend it, not too rapidly or too slowly.
8. *Transitions:* Transitions from one activity to another are made rapidly, with minimum confusion about what to do next.
9. *Clarity:* Lessons are presented logically and sequentially. Clarity is enhanced by the use of instructional objectives and adequate illustrations and by keeping in touch with students.[46]

Teacher Qualities and Value-Added Teaching

We have now discussed teacher styles, teacher traits, and teacher effects. Most recently, researchers such as Whitehurst and Haycock (of the Education Trust) have explored those teacher qualities that might influence student achievement. If good teaching matters and if the research on teacher style, teacher traits, and even teacher effects is often mixed, is there any evidence about teacher qualities that are related to value-added teaching? The answer is yes. What follows are a set of questions about specific teacher qualities and the research-based answers. They add yet another dimension to what we know about the science of teaching.[47]

Question 1: Does strong content knowledge matter in a teacher?

Yes and No. It appears to make more of a difference at the secondary level than at the elementary level. A secondary teacher with an academic major in the subject he or she teaches will foster more enhanced student learning than will a teacher teaching similar students but without a major. At the elementary level, the degree to which advanced content work is needed is much less clear. Teachers need to know content, but how much they must know is dictated by who they teach.

Question 2: Does certification or licensure matter?

Yes and No. This issue is one that is hotly debated. Your answer will largely be dictated by your ideological disposition. Conservative critics of education say that licensure does not matter. Teacher education advocates suggest that it does. The answer is that we really don't know, though it does clearly appear that teachers with an understanding of student learning needs and how to address those needs have students who learn more.[48] The debate about whether licensure matters rages. What everyone does agree to, though, is that poor students are much more likely to have noncertified teachers and, as a consequence, they may have a teacher who lacks adequate content or pedagogical preparation.

Question 3: Does a teacher's general knowledge base matter?

Yes. This is where there is agreement. How well educated you are will influence how much your students learn. That is why general education courses and your personal intellectual development are important. Good teachers have better and more extensive knowledge, especially in terms of their verbal abilities.

Question 4: Does experience matter?

Yes. How much experience a teacher has does influence how much students learn. William Sanders argues that data collected in Tennessee and elsewhere suggest steady growth in student achievement for each year of a teacher's career up to about year seven. The achievement gains of students then plateau up to about twenty-two years of teaching experience, and then there is a slight diminution of student performance. So there appears to be a type of curvilinear relationship between teacher experience and student achievement.

Question 5: Does having a master's degree make a difference?

No. It does not appear that advanced degrees make a difference in terms of student achievement. Such a degree may help a teacher better understand teaching and what teaching entails, but it does not appear to influence student achievement.

In summary, based on the research of Whitehurst, Haycock, and others, it would seem that maximizing your effectiveness requires that you be well educated, that you

professional viewpoint

The Teacher with Wisdom

Neil Postman
Professor of Communication
New York University

 There is a sense in which the following aphorism is true: The dumber the teacher, the better the student. What is meant by this is that a teacher's knowledge can often be an obstacle to learning. If teachers know a great deal and spend most of the time telling what they know, students are often intimidated, rendered passive, and made entirely dependent on the source of knowledge. But this is not what most good teachers want to accomplish. What is required of teachers is to be restrained and to be sparing in how they employ their knowledge in a classroom. This is not to argue that teachers should, in fact, be ignorant. It is to say that they may use ignorance as a means of inviting students to participate actively in the quest for knowledge. For if students believe that everything is known and the teacher knows it, the students must remain outsiders to the "great conversation."

Of course, if the teacher is truly a learned person then there is no need for him or her to feign ignorance. A learned person knows how ignorant he is and, in teaching, simply gives more prominence and emphasis to what he does not know than to what he does. Moreover, truly learned teachers are never frightened or defensive about making what is not known the focus of their lessons.

know your content well, and that you find lots of different ways to get experience working with children. Further, if you evidence those qualities, you understand how to develop a personal professional teaching style that enables you to feel empowered, and you understand how to differentiate instruction and your behaviors based on who you teach, your students will learn more. You will create a value-added difference.

The Master Teacher

The national interest in education reform and excellence in teaching has focused considerable attention on teachers and the notion of the master teacher. The direct teaching behaviors suggested by the Rosenshine, Good, Brophy, and Evertson models correspond with Walter Doyle's task-oriented and businesslike master teacher. Such teachers "focus on academic goals, are careful and explicit in structuring activities, . . . promote high levels of student academic involvement and content coverage, furnish opportunities for controlled practice with feedback, hold students accountable for work, . . . have expectations that they will be successful in helping students learn, [and are] active in explaining concepts and procedures, promoting meaning and purpose for academic work, and monitoring comprehension."[49]

When 641 elementary and secondary teachers were asked to "rate criteria for recognition of a ***master teacher,***" they listed in rank order (1) has knowledge of subject matter, (2) encourages student achievement through positive reinforcement, (3) uses a variety of strategies and materials to meet the needs of all students, (4) maintains an organized and disciplined classroom, (5) stimulates students' active participation in class-

Excellence in teaching is recognized and rewarded by communities nationwide.

room activities, (6) maximizes student instruction time, (7) has high expectations of student performance, and (8) frequently monitors student progress and provides feedback regarding performance.[50]

Although the sample of teachers was predominately female (71 percent) and so it can be argued that the recommended behaviors reflect female norms, it must be noted as we shared earlier in this text that the teaching profession is predominately female. Most important, the teachers surveyed were experienced (77 percent had been teaching for at least eleven years), and their rank order list of criteria corresponds closely to the principals' rank order list (see Table 2.8) and to Doyle's notion of a master teacher.

Based on a study of several hundreds of teachers who teach in multiracial and multilinguistic schools, the *"star" teacher* research revealed a host of behaviors and attitudes that counter what many educators say make master or effective teachers.[51] Star teachers develop an ideology. These teachers do not use a prescribed theory to guide their practice; they do not refer directly to the research-based axioms or principles of

Piaget, Skinner, or the like. Star teachers do not consider the research on teacher effectiveness, school effectiveness or teacher style or teacher traits. They may be oblivious to and unconcerned with how researchers or experts in various subjects organize the content in their disciplines. Rather, they have internalized their own view of teaching, their own organization of subject matter, and their own practices through experience and self-discovery. Star teachers reflect on what they are doing in the classroom, why they are doing it, and the best way to do it in order to foster student success. These teachers are also guided by the expectations that inner-city and poor children can learn, think, and reflect.

Star teachers or master teachers are different from the average. They have an ideology about teaching and students that gives their performance a different meaning. They appear to be "mavericks" (see Table 2.1) and confident in the way they organize and operate their own classrooms. They are sensitive to their students, believe all students can learn, and teach in ways that make sense to their students, not necessarily according to what researchers or their administrators and colleagues have to say about teaching. These teachers seem to be driven by their own convictions of what is right, and not by how others interpret the teacher's role or teacher's pedagogy. They emerge as master teachers but they often do so based more on personal experiences than professional development.

Most significantly, master teachers are demanding but they are in a way that is affirming. No one expresses this more poignantly than Gloria Ladson-Billings. She identified specific conceptions that master teachers who understand how to make instruction culturally relevant have of themselves and others that shape what instruction looks like in their classrooms. Table 2.9 provides detail on her ideas. More importantly, it should provide a structure for you as you think about the characteristics of the effective or ineffective teachers you have had or have observed. How do teachers communicate so that all students can learn? How do teachers verbally or nonverbally communicate so that failure may be inevitable for some students? Watch, for example, as a teacher calls on students during a lesson. Are some students given more time to respond? Does the teacher elaborate on some student responses but not others? And, how does a teacher communicate a belief in students that they can succeed? Or, more disturbingly, that they are inclined to or will fail? (Review, again, Table 2.6)

Studies suggest that teachers understand how to deal differentially with learners, but the art requires that they do this without communicating a message regarding a student's potential as a learner. How is that possible? Read Case Study 2.1: Differentiation of Instruction and examine closely how one teacher accomplished this in teaching writing.

Cautions and Criticisms

Although the notions of teacher competencies and teacher effectiveness are often identified as something new in research efforts to describe good teaching, they are nothing more than a combination of teaching principles and methods that good teachers have been using for many years prior to this recent wave of research. What product-oriented researchers have accomplished is to summarize what we have known for a long time but often passed on in the form of "tips for teachers" or practical suggestions once crit-

Using Technology to Turn Kids on to Learning

Jackie Marshall Arnold
K–12 Media Specialist

 As Martin Haberman is quoted in this chapter, "Star teachers conceive that their primary job is turning kids on to learning." As many effective teachers know, a critical method for "turning kids on" involves the use of instructional technology. Students today are of the twenty-first century. Most have computer and Internet access. They come to today's classroom with technology experience and with expectations for using technology tools in their learning. An effective teacher in today's classroom will be prepared to use technology as a resource to motivate and enhance instruction.

The North Central Regional Educational Laboratory studies the use of effective technology in classrooms. From their research they have developed a framework that identifies "six categories of technology performance with indicators of high performance that supports engaged learning" (http://www.ncrel.org/sdrs/edtalk/body.pdf). They include the following:

- Forward-thinking, shared vision
- Effective teaching and learning practices
- Educator proficiency with effective teaching and learning practices
- Digital Age equity
- Robust access anywhere, anytime
- Systems and leadership

Research shows the necessity that technology be not just available, but also integrated in effective, engaging teaching. The effective teacher augments instruction with technology by providing access to meaningful, authentic tasks. Students are guided through the learning experience with active participation. Meaningful assessment and feedback are central to the process. The master teacher follows best teaching practices as documented by the authors of this book with technology as a critical tool.

What technologies could be used to support high performance learning and "turn kids on"? Recall the vignette from Chapter 1. The master, effective teacher used a realistic, engaging problem and allowed technology to support the learning. Students were using word processing programs to write letters, spreadsheet software to create tables and graphs, and presentation software to communicate their findings to interested parties.

Effective teachers will also find the use of video conferencing technology supportive in successful teaching. Distance learning (video conferencing) will allow students to interact directly with experts across the world. Students studying the Antarctica habitat can talk "live" with a scientist currently studying and living in the habitat. Virtual field trips will also allow students to travel to places never before thought possible. For example, viewing paintings throughout the Louvre is now easy with an Internet connection (http://www.louvre.fr/).

Finally, effective teachers will work to integrate technology tools in a manner that simulates real life experiences. Employers today are demanding employees who are team players and cooperative learners. A classroom designed to foster these characteristics will require not the stereotypical "one student to a computer" but rather small group instruction and collaboration.

In these settings, students will not only be "turned on to learning," but they also will be developing the knowledge, skills, and attitudes that will support them throughout life.

icized as mere recipes for teaching. These researchers confirm the basic principles and methods of experienced teachers. They give credibility to teaching practices by correlating teacher behaviors (processes) to student achievement (products). Product-oriented researchers also dispel the notion that teachers have little or no measurable effect on student achievement.

table 2.9   Conceptions of Self and Others

Culturally Relevant	Assimilationist
Teacher sees herself as an artist, teaching as an art.	Teacher sees herself as a technician, teaching as a technical task.
Teacher sees herself as part of the community and teaching as giving something back to the community; she encourages students to do the same.	Teacher sees herself as an individual who may or may not be a part of the community; she encourages achievement as a means to escape community.
Teacher believes all students can succeed.	Teacher believes failure is inevitable for some.
Teacher helps students make connections between their community, national, and global identities.	Teacher homogenizes students into one "American" identity.
Teacher sees teaching as "pulling knowledge out"—like "mining."	Teacher sees teaching as "putting knowledge into"—like "banking."

Source: Gloria Ladson-Billings. *Dreamkeepers.* San Francisco, Calif.: Jossey Bass, 1994, p. 34.

However, there is some danger in this product-oriented research. The conclusions overwhelmingly portray the effective teacher as task oriented, organized, and structured. But the teacher competency and teacher effectiveness models tend to overlook the friendly, warm, and democratic teacher; the creative teacher who is stimulating and imaginative; the dramatic teacher who bubbles with energy and enthusiasm; the philosophical teacher who encourages students to play with ideas and concepts; and the problem-solving teacher who requires that students think out the answers. In the product-oriented researchers' desire to identify and prescribe behaviors that are measurable and quantifiable, they overlook the emotional, qualitative, and interpretive descriptions of classrooms and the joys of teaching. Most of their research has been conducted at the elementary grade levels, where one would expect more social, psychological, and humanistic factors to be observed, recorded, and recommended as effective. A good portion of their work also deals with low achievers and at-risk students—perhaps the reason why many of their generalizations or principles coincide with classroom management and structured and controlling techniques.

The teacher effectiveness models also fail to consider that a good deal of effective teaching may not directly correlate with student achievement. For Maxine Greene, good teaching and learning involve values, experiences, insights, imagination, and appreciation—the "stuff" that cannot easily be observed or categorized. For her, teaching and learning are an existential encounter, a philosophical process involving ideas and creative inquiries that cannot easily be quantified.[52]

For Ornstein, good teaching in history, English, and the arts involves "remembering the dead" or moving students beyond the comfort of facts:

> . . . the lost souls who no longer exist because of human cruelty or hatred. Most of the voices and faces of the dead we never knew; therefore it is easy to become detached from their demise and treat them as an abstract statistic . . . Among the dead are some who were

case study 2.1   Differentiation of Instruction

Lori Turkey is a writing teacher. Notice how she uses differentiation to address all her students' needs.

I needed to come up with some strategies to help each student reach the goal of improved writing. I had to go back to the basics and remember to take small steps. Because my goal was to improve student writing through differentiation, I first needed to find out what my students felt they needed to work on in their own writing. So I developed some basic "sheets" for students to use in developing their portfolios. On the first sheet, the students stated how they were going to reach their goals; they decided what areas in writing they wanted to develop. One goal might be as simple as working on being a better speller. Then I sat down and talked with each student about the methods and strategies he or she could use to improve.

A conferencing sheet was used to document our discussions on how the students were doing with their writing or to record other things they might need to do to reach their goals. The students used a third sheet to keep track of their writing and record what they were working on. This sheet included the name of the story, the date the student began, and when it was completed.

I also decided that I needed the students' input on these sheets, so, when I introduced the idea of the sheets, we created our own forms to meet the needs of our classroom. I was impressed with their ideas. The students' suggestions were simple and user friendly. For example, they thought it was important for us to date and sign the conferencing sheet. We also felt we needed a rubric or some guidelines for correcting the writing. I told them I would look for examples and promised that they could give their input. At a workshop I gathered materials I could bring back to my students.

After organizing the considerable paperwork for the writing portfolios, I was still struggling with the lack of time to work with each student. So I decided to ask the class for suggestions. I was amazed with how creative and simple their ideas were. They suggested we create experts in the classroom to whom other students could go for help. We decided on the areas and the students who fit the roles. The areas we started with were spelling, punctuation, voice, introductions, and flow. We also decided to revisit the roles of the experts each month. This gave me enough time to conference with each student twice a month. While I still don't feel that this is enough time, it is a good start. And it's a "small step" to help students reach their goals.

If you could see the delight in my students' eyes when they achieve their goals, you would realize the importance of differentiation. When students can actually see their own growth through my drafts, they are motivated to do even more. Even the poor writers felt success and took pride in what they were able to produce. I found that one important element for success is making sure that the goals students choose match their ability. Sitting down and discussing students' chosen goals are essential. Having students give input with regard to goals as they begin to use portfolios helps them understand the expectations. Each individual knows what needs to be done in order to succeed.

Questions for Reflection:

1. Turkey describes the excitement of students when they achieve their goals. Why does that "experience" elude so many students? Are schools structured to mitigate that type of experience? If so, how?
2. What makes differentiation of instruction so difficult for so many teachers? Would it be better if schools and classrooms were more homogeneous? What problems might it create if school classrooms were truly homogeneous?
3. What teacher *style* or teacher *traits* do you see as most important for a teacher who wants to differentiate instruction for students?

Source: Lori Turkey. "Differentiation." *Phi Delta Kappan* (September 2002): 62. Reprinted with permission.

famous for something and are in our encyclopedias, but the vast majority have been forgotten and funneled into anonymity.[53]

What can be hoped for, argues Ornstein, is that the poet, painter, musician, and *teacher* "make use of the forgotten through their pen, canvas, lyrics," or classroom discussions in order for the living, including our children, to gain understanding, to learn from the past, to not repeat the mistakes of history, to correct the inequalities and injustices that influence the living, and to think more deeply about ideas.

Much of teaching involves caring, nurturing, and valuing behaviors—attributes that are not easily assessed by evaluation instruments. Elliot Eisner is concerned that what is not measurable goes unnoticed in a product-oriented teaching model. By breaking down the teaching act into dimensions, competencies, and criteria that can be defined operationally and quantified, educators overlook the hard-to-measure aspects, such as the personal, humanistic, and playful aspects of teaching. To say that excellence in teaching requires measurable behaviors and outcomes is to miss a substantial part of teaching—what some educators refer to as the artistry of teaching. And part of that artistry requires that adults create educational opportunities that are more personal and less bureaucratic.[54]

Teacher behaviors that correlate with measurable outcomes often lead to rote learning, "learning bits" and not wholes, memorization, automatic responses, and not high-order thinking. The new models also seem to miss moral and ethical outcomes, as well as social, personal, and self-actualizing factors related to learning and life—in effect, the affective domain of learning and the psychology of being human. In their attempt to observe and measure what teachers do and detail whether students improve their performance on reading or math tests, these models ignore the learners' imaginations, fantasies, intuitive thinking, dreams, hopes, and aspirations, and how teachers impact on these hard-to-define but very important aspects of students' lives. Learning experiences that deal with character, spiritual outlook, and philosophy are absent, too.[55]

The new and popular teacher competency and teacher effectiveness models create a rather narrow mold that misses many nuances of teaching. Many of these prescriptions (which the researchers call *principles*) themselves are old ideas bottled under new labels such as *with-it-ness, smoothness,* and *clarity.* They seem to confirm what effective teachers have been doing for many years, and although such confirmation is needed so that beginning teachers have a better yardstick or starting point, it is not enough. Tips for Teachers 2.2 offers ideas for considering the more affective side of teaching.

The Human Factor

Good teachers know, although they may not be able to prove it, that good teaching is really about caring and sharing; the capacity to accept, understand, and appreciate students on their terms and through their world; making students feel good about themselves; having positive attitudes and setting achievement goals; and getting all fired up with enthusiasm and a cheerful presence.[56] These are basically fuzzy qualities that the scientific theories and paradigms of teaching tend to overlook. Indeed, teachers who place high priority on humanistic and affective practices and on the personal and social development of their students are not really interested in devoting much time to the empirical or behavioral literature or in teaching small pieces of information that can be measured and correlated with their own teaching behaviors.

tips for teachers 2.2

Reaching and Teaching Students

 Most of the research on teacher competencies and teacher effectiveness stresses direct and explicit instructional techniques and overlooks attitudinal and motivational factors related to learning. What follows are some methods that deal with the human side of teaching children and youth. These methods, which have proven to be successful, complement and fill a void in the recent research on teaching, with special meaning for teaching at-risk students.

Achievement

1. Focus on teaching basic skills as well as higher cognitive functioning levels based on knowledge of the skills.
2. Develop individualization and differentiation approaches to learning.
3. Recognize absolute achievement and individual improvement by expanding achievement awards, sending letters to parents, and notifying school officials.
4. Involve parents in their children's learning, especially in high school grades.
5. Develop a peer-tutoring program using classmates or upper-grade students.

Attitude

1. Provide support, encouragement, and realistic praise.
2. Recognize good work, and provide confirmation of success.
3. Develop a class philosophy that each student is worthwhile and can learn.
4. Help students build self-esteem, a sense of responsibility, and self-respect.
5. Help students clarify values, deal with personal choices, and assume responsibility for themselves and for learning.
6. Involve students in school services and extracurricular activities to build self-confidence and group identification.
7. Invite successful people to act as mentors and to talk to students in class.
8. Enforce classroom rules; instill a sense of pride in the students and the classroom.
9. Involve students in real-life situations; encourage them to deal with personal issues.
10. Use community resources by bringing people into the schools and by taking students on field trips that help them connect school life with real life.

Source: Adapted from John V. Hamby. "How to Get an 'A' on Your Dropout Prevention Report Card." *Educational Leadership* (February 1989): 21–28. Bettie B. Youngs. "The Phoenix Curriculum." *Educational Leadership* (February 1989): 24.

Teachers who are confident about themselves tend not to be as concerned about their evaluation ratings or even about what the research has to say about their teacher behaviors. How does the profession reconcile the fact that so many competent teachers consider teacher research as "irrelevant and counterintuitive" to their own practice of teaching? Why do we often hear the complaint "That's all good theory, but it does not work in practice"?

Teaching is a people industry, and people (especially young people) perform best in places where they feel wanted and respected. To be sure, it is possible for a teacher to "disengage" or "disinvite" students by belittling them, ignoring them, undercutting them, comparing them to other siblings or students, or even "yessing" them (failing to hold them accountable for the right answer) and still perform well on other discrete competencies or behaviors associated with the teacher as a technician ("The teacher came to class on time," "The teacher checked homework on a regular basis," "The teacher was clear about objectives of the course," "The teacher graded quizzes on a timely basis," etc.). Such a competency-based model, checklist, or behaviorist approach is easy to find as we search for a research-based model of what is a "good" teacher. But it ignores being part of a helping or caring profession, being kind and generous, or working with students so they develop their own uniqueness.

Teacher research should focus on the learner, not only on content; on the feelings and attitudes of the student, not only on knowledge and skills (since feelings and attitudes will eventually determine what knowledge and skills are sought after and acquired); and on long-term development and growth of the students, not only on short-term objectives or specific tasks. But if teachers spend more time on the learner, on students' feelings and attitudes, and on the social or personal growth and development of students, they may be penalized when student outcomes (acquisition of little pieces of information) are correlated with their teaching effectiveness.

Students need to be encouraged and nurtured by their teachers, especially when they are young (certainly up to the end of middle school and junior high school). They are dependent on approval from significant adults—first their parents, then their teachers. Parents and teachers need to help young children and adolescents establish a source for self-esteem by focusing on their strengths, supporting them, discouraging negative self-talk, and helping them take control of their lives and live by their own values.[57]

People (including young people) with high esteem achieve at high levels; and the more one achieves, the better one feels about oneself. The opposite is also true. Students who fail to master the subject matter get down on themselves—and eventually give up. Students with low self-esteem give up quickly. In short, student esteem and achievement are related, as are student esteem and self-reliance.[58] If we can nurture the students' self-esteem, almost everything else will fall into place, including achievement scores and academic outcomes.

This builds a strong argument for creating success experiences for students to help them feel good about themselves. The long-term benefits are obvious. The more students learn to like themselves, the more they will achieve; and, the more they achieve, the more they will like themselves. But that's down the road; it takes time and nurturing for future benefits. It does not show up on a classroom or standardized test within a semester or school year. It doesn't help the teacher who is being evaluated by a content-driven or test-driven school administrator. It certainly does not benefit the teacher who is being evaluated for how many times he or she attended departmental meetings or on whether the classroom shades were even for aesthetic purposes.

Most research on teaching is concerned with the present—with processes and products that are measured in one term (or year) and by a standardized test of cognitive (not affective) outcomes. Thus, one might conclude that the teacher effectiveness research misses the main mark. Students need to engage in growth-enhancing experiences; we need to recognize that the most effective teachers endow their students with a "you can do it" attitude, with good feelings about themselves, which are indirectly but eventually directly related to cognitive achievement. While every teacher needs to demand high academic standards and teach the content, there needs to be understanding that the content interacts with the process. If the process can be cultivated in a humanistic way, then the outcomes of the content will be improved.[59] It is possible in real classrooms for this to occur. Jaime Escalante (*Stand and Deliver*) did it at Garfield High School with his calculus students and LouAnne Johnson (*Dangerous Minds*) did it with her high school English students. In this connection, the current research on teacher effectiveness needs to be revised to fit the context of varied teaching styles. Teachers need to incorporate specific teacher behaviors and methods that fit with their personality, philosophy, and goals. They need to pick and choose from a wide range of research and theory and to discard other teacher behaviors that conflict with their style, without being considered ineffective by evaluators.

Certain behaviors contribute to good teaching and enhanced student learning but there is little agreement on exactly what behaviors or methods are most important. Some teachers will learn most of the rules about "good" teaching, yet they will be unsuccessful. Other teachers will break many of the rules of "good" teaching, yet they will be profoundly successful. That's what Jaime Escalante did. He broke *certain* "rules," but he did so only to benefit the students. Some teachers will gain theoretical knowledge of "what works," but they will be unable to put the ideas into practice. Some teachers will move effortlessly through the school day, and others will consider teaching a chore. All this suggests that teaching cannot be reduced to a checklist or a precise model. Teaching is a holistic activity that deals with whole people (not tiny behaviors or competencies) and how people (teachers and students) develop and behave in a variety of classroom and school settings.

Beyond Effective Teaching: New Research, New Paradigms

For the last fifty years or more, research on teacher behavior has been linear and category based: It has focused on specific teacher styles, interactions, characteristics, competencies, or effects. It has either emphasized the process of teaching (how the teacher behaves in the classroom) or the products of teaching (student outcomes). As the twenty-first century begins, the research on teaching is beginning to examine the multifaceted nature and context of teaching: the relationship of teaching and learning, the subject matter knowledge of the teacher, how knowledge is taught, and how it relates to pedagogy.

This new emphasis goes beyond what the teacher is doing and explores teacher thinking from the perspectives of teachers themselves. The teacher is depicted as one who copes with a complex environment and simplifies it by attending to a small number of important tasks and synthesizing various kinds of information that continuously evolve. The impact of professional knowledge (that is, both subject matter and pedagogical knowledge, or knowing what you know and how well you know it) is now considered important for defining how teachers and students construct meaning for their respective roles and perform tasks related to those roles.

An alternative for understanding the nature of teaching has evolved—one that combines teaching and learning processes, incorporates holistic practices, goes beyond what teachers and students appear to be doing, and inquires into what they are thinking. This model relies on language and dialogue, not mathematical or statistical symbols, to

Research on teaching goes beyond what teachers and students are doing and inquires about what they are thinking.

provide the conceptual categories and organize the data. It uses the approaches that reformers, reconceptualists, and postliberal theoreticians have advocated: metaphors, stories, biographies and autobiographies, conversations (with experts), and voices (or narratives). Such research, which has surfaced within the last five to fifteen years, looks at teaching "from the inside." It focuses on the personal and practical knowledge of teachers, the culture of teaching, and the language and thoughts of teachers.

Metaphors

Teachers' knowledge, including the way they speak about teaching, does not exist only in propositional form, but also includes figurative language or ***metaphors.*** Because the thinking of teachers consists of personal experiences, images, and jargon, figurative language is central to the expression and understanding of the teachers' knowledge of pedagogy.[60]

Metaphors of space and time figure in teachers' descriptions of their work (i.e., "pacing a lesson," "covering the content," "moving on to the next part of the lesson").[61] The studies on teacher style, examined in the earlier part of the chapter, represent concepts and beliefs about teachers that can be considered metaphors: the teacher as a "boss," "coach," "comedian," or "maverick." The terms "master" teacher, "lead" teacher, "star" teacher, and "expert" teacher are also metaphors, or descriptors, used by current researchers to describe outstanding or effective teachers.

People use metaphors to explain or interpret reality. In traditional literature, this process of explanation and interpretation evolves through experience and study—without the influence of researchers' personal or cultural biases. But the use of metaphors also can be conceptualized in the literature of sociology to include ideas, values, and behaviors that derive in part from a person's position within the political and economic order. As an example, the notion of a Protestant work ethic is used by some to describe their business or economic success. Similarly, critical pedagogists and liberal theorists argue that personal and cultural factors such as gender, class, and caste influence the formation of knowledge, especially metaphors.[62] Indeed, during the 1980s and 1990s liberation theology became popular in Latin America in part because it "captured" how those who were disenfranchised could use religion to empower themselves to confront oppressors.

Stories

Increasingly, researchers are telling stories about teachers, their work, and how they teach, and teachers are telling stories about their own teaching experiences. Some researchers are describing these stories as portraits, especially when these portraits are intended to disclose something deeper about what it means to be a teacher.[63] Most stories are narrative and descriptive in nature, and they are rich and voluminous in language. This richness and high level of description can make points about teaching that would be difficult to convey through traditional research methods. Gathering such stories reflects the belief that there is much to learn from "authentic" teachers who tell their stories about experiences they might otherwise keep to themselves in an effort to engage students in higher levels of critical thought.[64]

Stories have important social and psychological meanings. Stories of teachers allow us to see connections between the practice of teaching and the human side of teaching. The stories of individual teachers allow us to see their knowledge and skills enacted in the real work of classrooms and lead us to appreciate their interactions at emotional and even moral levels with the people they teach.

Bel Kaufman, Herbert Kohl, and Jonathan Kozol's personalized stories have become best-sellers because of their "rich" descriptions. These stories create aesthetic and emotional landscapes of teaching and learning that would be missed by a clinically based process-product research study of teacher effectiveness. While some people criticize such personal teachers' stories for lacking scholarly reliability and accuracy—flaws they see as grounded in egoism or exaggeration—it is their personal nature that makes such stories so valuable to our understanding about teaching.

Stories of teachers written by researchers are less descriptive, less emotional, and less known. Nevertheless, they still provide us with insight into teachers' knowledge and experiences, and they provide unusual opportunities to get to know teachers on an emotional as well as intellectual level. Most important, these stories represent an important shift in the way researchers are willing to examine teachers' pedagogy and understanding of teaching.

Biographies and Autobiographies

Biography and autobiography give an even broader picture of a teacher's experience. Unity, wholeness, and a greater depth of understanding emerge when past experience is explored to make present action meaningful.[65] Whereas a biography comes through the filter of a second party, the autobiography fully permits the subject to present the information in his or her own way and on his or her own terms. An example of a teacher autobiography well worth reading is Sylvia Ashton-Warner's *Teacher*.[66]

As human beings, we all have stories to tell. Each person has a distinctive story shaped by a host of experiences from which emerge practices and a particular way of looking at the world. From *teacher* stories emerge a particular set of teaching experiences and practices, as well as a particular style of teaching and pedagogy.

Biographies and autobiographies of teachers are concerned with longitudinal aspects of personal and professional experiences, which can bring much detailed and insightful information to the reader. They help us reconstruct teachers' and students' experiences not available to us in typical professional literature on teaching.[67]

As opposed to autobiographies, biographies such as Jay Mathews's *Escalante: The Best Teacher in America* or Lynley Hood's *Sylvia*, which is a biography of Sylvia Ashton-Warner, suggest that the author is in a position of "authority" with respect to the life being described—hence, the thoughts and experiences of the author take on a sense of importance not always assumed in other stories.[68] While such biographies provide another perspective on a teacher's experience, we must question how accurate that perspective is.

Madeleine Grumet suggests a solution: Researchers should publish multiple accounts of teachers' knowledge and pedagogy, instead of single narratives. One problem with this solution is that it takes the stories out of the hands of the teachers themselves.[69]

The Expert Teacher

The **expert teacher** concept involves new research procedures—such as simulations, videotapes, and case studies—and a new language to describe the work and authority of teachers.[70] The research usually consists of small samples and in-depth studies (complete lessons and analysis of what transpired), in which expert (sometimes experienced) teachers are distinguished from novice (sometimes beginning) teachers. Experts usually are identified through administrator nominations, student achievement scores, or teacher awards (i.e., Teacher of the Year). Novices commonly are selected from groups of student teachers or first-year teachers.

Dreyfus and Dreyfus delineate five stages from novice to expert across fields of study. In stage one, the **novice teacher** is inflexible and follows principles and procedures the way he or she has learned them; the advanced beginner, in stage two, begins to combine theory with on-the-job experiences. By the third stage, the competent performer becomes more flexible and modifies principles and procedures to fit reality. At the next stage, the proficient performer recognizes patterns and relationships and has a holistic understanding of the processes involved. Experts, in stage five, have the same big picture in mind but respond effortlessly and fluidly in various situations.[71] Berliner and others illustrate this "stage five when they write that "expert teachers make classroom management and instruction look easy," although we know that teaching is a complex act, requiring the teacher "to do many many things at the same time."[72]

Data derived from recent studies suggest that expert and novice teachers teach, as well as perceive and analyze information about teaching, in different ways. Whereas experts are able to explain and interpret classroom events, novices provide detailed descriptions of what they did or saw and refrain from making interpretations. Experts recall or see multiple interactions and put interactions in the context of prior information and events, whereas novices recall specific facts about students or what happened in the classroom and provide literal and concrete descriptions of what occurred.

What experts (or experienced teachers) say or do about teaching is now considered important for building a science of teaching. Studies of expert and novice teachers show they differ in many specific areas of teaching and instruction.

1. *Information about students:* Experts are likely to refrain from making quick judgments about their students and tend to rely on their own experiences and gut feelings, whereas novices tend to lack confidence in their own judgments and are not sure where to start when they begin teaching. For example, experts look at student profiles left by previous teachers as reference material but don't place too much stock in them. Novices consider the previous teachers' comments on student information cards to be good starting points, even valid indicators of what to expect.[73]

2. *Student cues:* Experts tend to analyze student cues in terms of instruction, whereas novices analyze them in terms of classroom management. Expert teachers assess student responses in terms of monitoring student learning, providing feedback or assistance, and identifying ways instruction can be improved. Novices fear loss of control in the classroom. When given the opportunity to reassess their teaching on videotape, they focus on cues they missed that deal with students' inattentiveness or misbehavior. Although negative student cues appear to be of equal importance to experts and novices, positive cues figure more frequently in the discussion of expert teachers.[74]

3. *Starting points:* Experts make the classroom their own, often changing the instructional focus and methods of the previous teacher. Novices tend to follow the previous teachers' footsteps. Experts talk about starting over and breaking old routines; they tell us about how to get students going and how to determine where the students are in terms of understanding content. Novices, on the other hand, tend to begin where the previous teacher left off. They have trouble assessing where the students are, what their capabilities are, and how and where they are going.[75]

4. *Planning:* Experts engage in a good deal of intuitive and improvisational teaching. They begin with a simple plan or outline and fill in the details as the teaching-learning process unfolds and as they respond to students. Novices spend much more time planning, stay glued to the content, and are less inclined to deviate or respond to students' needs or interests while the lesson is in progress.[76]

5. *Students:* Experts seem to have a clear understanding of the types of students they are teaching and how to teach them. In a sense, they seem to "know" their students before they meet with them. Novices do not have a well-developed idea of the students they are teaching. Whereas novices have trouble beginning the new term, experts routinely find out just what it is the students already know and proceed accordingly.[77]

6. *Self-focus:* Expert teachers are less egocentric and more confident about their teaching. Novices pay more attention to themselves, worrying about their effectiveness as teachers and about potential discipline problems. Experts are willing to reflect on what they are doing, admit what they did wrong, and comment about changes they will make. Although novices recognize mistakes and contradictions in their teaching, they are defensive about their mistakes and seem to have many self-concerns and doubts about where and how to improve.[78]

Voice

The notion of voice sums up the new linguistic tools for describing what teachers do, how they do it, and what they think when they are teaching. *Voice* corresponds with such terms as the *teacher's perspective, teacher's frame of reference,* and *getting into the teacher's head.* The concern with voice permeates the teacher empowerment movement and the work of researchers who collaborate with teachers on teacher behavior projects. The idea should be considered against the backdrop of previous teacher silence and impotence in determining issues and practices that affect their lives as teachers. As Freeman Elbaz asserts, the fact that researchers are now willing to give credibility to teachers' knowledge, teachers' practices, and teachers' experiences helps redress an imbalance in the past of little recognition for teachers. The idea is that teachers have a right to speak and a role in speaking for teachers and about teaching.[79]

Although there are some serious attempts to include teachers' voices in the discussion, the key issue is to what extent these new methods permit the "authentic" expression of teachers to influence the field of teacher behavior research and teacher preparation programs. In the past, it has been difficult for teachers to establish a voice, especially one that commanded respect and authority, in the professional literature. The reason is simple: The researchers and theoreticians have dominated the field of inquiry and have decided what should be published.

With the exception of autobiographies and stories written by teachers, teachers' voices generally are filtered through and categorized by researchers' writings and publications. For decades, firsthand expressions of teacher experiences and wisdom (sometimes conveyed in the form of advice or recommendations) were considered as nothing more than "cookbook recipes" or lists of "dos and don'ts," irrelevant to the world of research on teaching. Recently, however, under umbrella terms such as *teacher thinking, teacher processes, teacher cognition, teacher practices,* and *practical knowledge,* taking what teachers have to say and adapting it and turning it into *professional knowledge, pedagogical knowledge,* or *teacher knowledge* have become acceptable and even fashionable. Yet although researchers are now collaborating with practitioners, taking teacher views seriously, and sometimes accepting teachers on equal terms as part of teacher training programs, teachers still do not always receive credit where it is due. Whereas in scholarly publications researchers and practitioners are named as co-authors, practitioners may be acknowledged only by pseudonyms such as "Nancy" or "Thomas." The cultures of schools and universities and of teachers and professors, should be compatible enough to bridge this gap in the near future.

We close this chapter with an example of one teacher's voice. As you read this passage, compare the ideas with many of those captured in this chapter. Also, notice what the author, Herbert Kohl, suggests is important that is *not* a part of the scientific base on effective teaching but is part of the affective approach.

> The idea of the teacher as a flawless moral exemplar is a devilish trap for the teacher as well as a burden for the child. I once had a pupil, Narciso, who was overburdened by the perfection of adults and especially of teachers. His father demanded he believe in this perfection as he demanded Narciso believe in and acquiesce to absolute authority. It was impossible to approach the boy for his fear and deference. I had terrified him. He wouldn't work or disobey. He existed frozen in silence. One day he happened to pass by a bar. Some other teachers and I were sitting having beers. He was crushed; *teachers don't do that.* He believed so much in what his father and some teachers wanted him to believe that his world collapsed. He stayed away from school for a while, then returned. He smiled and I returned the smile. After a while he was at ease in class and could be himself, delightful and defiant, sometimes brilliant, often lazy, an individual reacting in his unique way to what happened in the classroom.
>
> It is only in the world of Dick and Jane, Tom and Sally, that the *always* right and righteous people exist. In a way, most textbooks, and certainly the ones I had to use in the sixth grade, protect the pure image of the teacher by showing the child that somewhere in the ideal world that inspires books all people are as "good" as the teacher is supposed to be! . . . .
>
> Of course the teacher is a moral exemplar—an example of all the confusion, hypocrisy, and indecision, of all the mistakes, as well as the triumphs, of moral man. . . . Therefore, to be more than an example, to be an educator—someone capable of helping lead the child through the labyrinth of life—the teacher must be honest to the children about his mistakes and weaknesses; he must be able to say that he is wrong or sorry, that he hadn't anticipated the results of his remarks and regretted them, or hadn't understood what a child meant. It is the teacher's struggle to be moral that excites his pupils; it is honesty, not rightness, that moves children."[80]

Theory into Practice

Knowing the latest theories and research on teaching does not guarantee you will become a good teacher. The kind of teacher you become is to a large extent influenced by whether you are honest about your own strengths and weaknesses and willing to make changes in your teaching. The following questions should help you become more introspective about yourself and ideally more effective. The questions are divided into three areas: students, subject, and self. The no answers will suggest areas for you to strengthen.

Questions Related to Students

1. Am I genuinely interested in the education and welfare of my students?
2. Am I sensitive to the needs and abilities of my students?
3. Do I modify my instruction to meet these needs and abilities?
4. Do I respect the beliefs and feelings of my students? Do I respect and encourage diverse opinions among students?
5. Am I friendly and considerate to students? Do I encourage them to take responsibility for their own work?

Questions Related to Subject

1. Do I have sufficient knowledge of my subject matter?
2. Can I organize the content so that students get a clear understanding of the relationships between concepts and different real world problems?
3. Do I use a variety of methods, materials, and media to make the subject more relevant and interesting to students?
4. Do I provide class time, as well as my own professional time, assisting students who need additional time to learn the fundamentals of the subject?
5. Am I willing to spend time preparing my lessons and updating and improving my previous lessons? Do I base my lessons on established academic standards?

Questions Related to Self

1. Do I understand what are the nature and use of teacher assessment in my school?
2. Do I know what are the criteria to be used for teacher assessment?
3. Do I know what philosophical assumptions and learning theories undergird the teacher assessment program? Do the school philosophy and learning theories coincide with my personal views?
4. Am I willing to accept feedback from others?
5. Am I aware and accepting of my own behaviors that may need to be changed?

Summary

1. Research on teacher behavior has looked at teacher styles, teacher-student interactions, teacher characteristics, teacher competencies, and teacher effects. That research has now evolved to the point that teacher standards are being created.
2. Although much remains to be learned about successful teaching, research has identified some teacher behaviors that seem to be effective and influence student performance.
3. Recent research on effective teaching has shifted from the process of teaching to the products of teaching.

4. The classic, important research on teaching prior to the 1970s was the work of A. S. Barr, Ned Flanders, and David Ryans. These researchers focused on teacher styles, teacher-student interactions, and teacher characteristics—that is, the process, or what happens in the classroom or the behavior of the teacher.

5. In the 1970s and 1980s the research on teaching was based on the work of Jere Brophy, Carolyn Evertson, N. L. Gage, Thomas Good, Donald Medley, and Barak Rosenshine. Their research tends to focus on teacher effectiveness and on the products or results of teaching. In the 1990s and early 2000s, the research began to focus more on the value-added by a teacher in terms of student achievement.

6. As the 1990s unfolded, two basic trends influenced research on teaching. One was a focus on the nature of expertise in teaching and how expert and novice teachers differ in approach and in seeing and analyzing classroom events. The second trend prompted different forms of investigating teaching that were based on language and dialogue: metaphors, stories, biographies, autobiographies, expert opinions, and voice.

Questions to Consider

1. How would you describe your teaching style?
2. Do you think it matters whether a teacher is direct or indirect in how content is presented to students? Explain.
3. What teacher characteristics and competencies listed in the tables of this chapter seem most important to you? Why? Also, where can you see connections between those and the standards for teaching that we list in the preface for the next section of this book—see the INTASC standards.
4. What behaviors listed by Brophy and Good as well as Evertson and Emmer coincide with your own teacher style? What behaviors seem to conflict with your teacher style?
5. What makes an expert teacher an expert? How would you compare expert teachers with novice teachers?

Things to Do

1. Evaluate the behaviors Medley labels "effective" for low-income students. Discuss in class whether these behaviors make sense for low-income students of different gender, age, and with varied achievement levels.
2. Volunteer to teach a lesson in class for a topic you understand. Tape the lesson. Use a simplified version of the Flanders' interaction analysis scale (direct vs. indirect) to analyze your teaching and have peers analyze the tape. Note whether there is agreement among class members in categorizing your teacher behavior.
3. Recall three or four of your favorite teachers. Compare their teacher characteristics, as you remember them, with the list of effective characteristics compiled by Ryans (see Table 2.7). Which characteristics on Ryan's list do you think they possessed?
4. Interview several experienced teachers concerning the recommended teacher principles and methods of Rosenshine, Gage, Brophy, and Evertson. Do the teachers support or reject the recommendations? What reservations do teachers bring up? What do they like about the recommendations?

5. Observe two or three teachers (or professors) while they teach. Categorize them as novice, advanced beginning, competent, proficient, or expert. Defend your reasoning.

Recommended Readings

Gage, Nathaniel L. *The Scientific Basis of the Art of Teaching*. New York: Teachers College Press, Columbia University, 1978. This is a classic discussion of teacher effectiveness studies, successful teaching strategies, and the notion of teaching as a "practical" art with a scientific basis.

Good, Thomas L., and Jere E. Brophy. *Looking in Classrooms*, 9th ed. Boston, Mass.: Allyn and Bacon, 2003. An important book that helped move the field from the study of teacher processes to teacher products; it offers a convincing argument that teachers do make a difference.

Jackson, Philip W. *Life in Classrooms*, 2d ed. New York: Teachers College Press, Columbia University, 1990. Focusing on elementary classrooms, the author discusses various aspects of classroom life and teaching.

Joyce, Bruce, Marsha Weil, and Emily Calhoun. *Models of Teaching,* 6th ed. Needham Heights, Mass.: Allyn and Bacon, 2000. This book combines theory with practice and examines various cognitive and behavioral teaching models.

Ladson-Billings, Gloria. *Crossing over to Canaan*. San Francisco: Jossey-Bass, 2001. This book weaves together the art and science of teaching as it addresses the question "Can anybody teach these children?" Ladson-Billings asserts that all children can be taught if teachers hold high expectations for all students and see their potential, not just their problems.

Sarason, Seymour. *Teaching as a Performing Art*. New York: Teachers College Press, 1999. The author describes the teacher as a performer, a person with a grasp of content, ideas and skills who can then shape an audience.

Key Terms

expert teachers 78	self-fulfilling prophecies 51	teacher processes 61
master teacher 66	"star" teacher 67	teaching standards 59
metaphors 76	teacher characteristics 55	teaching style 41
novice teacher 78	teacher competencies 57	teacher traits 54
process-product 61	teacher expectations 50	value-added 39

End Notes

1. Bruce J. Biddle and William J. Ellena. "The Integration of Teacher Effectiveness." In B. J. Biddle and W. J. Ellena (eds.), *Contemporary Research on Teacher Effectiveness*. New York: Holt, Rinehart and Winston, 1964, p. 3.
2. Allan C. Ornstein. "Successful Teachers: Who They Are?" *American School Board Journal* (January 1993): 24–27. Also see Phillip W. Jackson. *Life in Classrooms,* 2d ed. New York: Teachers College Press, Columbia University, 1990.
3. Lee S. Shulman. "A Union of Insufficiencies: Strategies for Teacher Assessment." *Educational Leadership* (November 1988): 35–41. Gloria Ladson-Billings. *Crossing over to Canaan.* San Francisco: Jossey-Bass, 2001: 76.
4. Thomas L. Good and Jere E. Brophy. *Looking in Classrooms,* 9th ed. Boston, Mass.: Allyn and Bacon, 2003.
5. Thomas L. Good, Bruce J. Biddle, and Jere E. Brophy. *Teachers Make a Difference.* New York: Holt, Rinehart and Winston, 1975. Allan C. Ornstein. "Theoretical Issues Related to Teaching." *Education and Urban Society*

(November 1989): 96–105. Allan C. Ornstein. "A Look at Teacher Effectiveness Research: Theory and Practice." *NASSP Bulletin* (October 1990): 78–88.

6. James S. Coleman, Ernest Q. Campbell, Carol J. Hobson, James McPartland, Alexander M. Mood, Frederic D. Winfield, and Robert L. York. *Equality of Educational Opportunity.* Washington, DC: U.S. Government Printing Office, 1966.

7. Grover J. Whitehurst. "Research on Teacher Preparation and Professional Development." Washington, DC: United States Department of Education, 2002. See http://www.ed.gov/inits/preparingteachersconference/whitehurst.html

8. William Sanders and J. Rivers. *Cumulative and Residual Effects of Teachers on Future Student Academic Achievement.* Knoxville, Tenn.: University of Tennessee Value-Added Research Assessment Center, 1996. William Sanders. *Using Student Assessment Data to Guide Professional Development: Value Added Work in Ohio and Other States.* Presentation to the Governor's Commission on Teaching Success, Columbus, Ohio, July 2002.

9. Penelope L. Peterson. "Direct Instruction Reconsidered." In P. L. Peterson and H. J. Walberg (eds.), *Research on Teaching: Concepts, Findings, and Implications.* Berkeley, Calif.: McCutchan, 1979, pp. 57–69.

10. Susan L. Lytle and Marilyn Cochran-Smith. "Teacher Research as a Way of Knowing." *Harvard Educational Review* (Winter 1992): 447–474. Karen Zumwalt. "Alternate Routes to Teaching." *Journal of Teacher Education* (March–April 1992): 83–93.

11. Ronald Lippitt and Ralph K. White. "The Social Climate of Children's Groups." In R. G. Barker, J. S. Kounin, and H. F. Wright (eds.), *Child Behavior and Development.* New York: McGraw-Hill, 1943, pp. 485–508. Also see Kurt Lewin, Ronald Lippitt, and Ralph K. White. "Patterns of Aggressive Behavior in Experimentally Created Social Climates." *Journal of Social Psychology* (May 1939): 271–299.

12. Ned A. Flanders. *Teacher Influence, Pupil Attitudes, and Achievement.* Washington, D.C.: Government Printing Office, 1965. Ned A. Flanders. *Analyzing Teaching Behavior.* Reading, Mass.: Addison-Wesley, 1970.

13. Edmund J. Amidon and Ned A. Flanders. *The Role of the Teacher in the Classroom.* St. Paul, Minn.: Amidon & Associates, 1971. Also see Allan Ornstein. "Analyzing and Improving Teachers," In Hersholt S. Waxman and Herbert J. Walberg (eds.), *New Directions for Teaching.* Berkeley, CA: McCutchan, 1999: 17–62.

14. Herbert A. Thelen. *Classroom Grouping for Teachability.* New York: Wiley, 1967.

15. Donald M. Medley. *Teacher Competence and Teacher Effectiveness: A Review of Process-Product Research.* Washington, D.C.: American Association of Colleges for Teacher Education, 1977. Donald M. Medley. "The Effectiveness of Teachers." In P. L. Peterson and H. J. Walberg (eds.), *Research on Teaching: Concepts, Findings, and Implications.* Berkeley, Calif.: McCutchan, 1979, pp. 11–27.

16. Allan C. Ornstein. "How Good Are Teachers in Affecting Student Outcomes?" *NASSP Bulletin* (December 1992): 61–70. Michael S. Knapp and Patrick M. Shields. "Reconceiving Academic Instruction for the Children of Poverty." *Phi Delta Kappan* (June 1990): 753–758.

17. Martin Haberman. *Star Teachers of Children in Poverty.* West Lafayette, Ind.: Kappa Delta Pi, 1995.

18. James Traub. *Better by Design? A Consumer's Guide to Schoolwide Reform.* Washington, D.C.: Thomas B. Fordham Foundation, 1999, pp. 39–40.

19. Robert J. Marzano, Debra J. Pickering, and Jane E. Pollack. *Classroom Instruction That Works.* Alexandria, VA: Association for Supervision and Curriculum Development, 2001, pp. 129–131.

20. Robert Rosenthal and Lenore Jacobsen. *Pygmalion in the Classroom.* New York: Holt, Rinehart and Winston, 1968.

21. Robert Thorndike. "Review of Pygmalion in the Classroom." *American Educational Research Journal* (November 1968): 708–711.

22. Jere E. Brophy and Thomas L. Good. *Teacher-Student Relationships.* New York: Holt, Rinehart and Winston, 1974. Harris M. Cooper. "Pygmalion Grows Up: A Model for Teacher Expectation Communication and Performance Influence." *Review of Educational Research* (Summer 1979), 389–410. Harris M. Cooper and Thomas L. Good. *Pygmalion Grows Up.* New York: Longman, 1983.

23. Dona M. Kagan. "How Schools Alienate Students at Risk." *Education Psychologist* (Spring 1990): 105–125.

24. Jo Boaler. "When Learning no Longer Matters: Standardized Testing and the Creation of Inequality." *Phi Delta Kappan* (March 2003): 502–506.

25. John U. Ogbu. "Variability in Minority School Performance: A Problem in Search of an Explanation." *Anthropology and Education Quarterly* (December 1987): 312–334. John U. Ogbu. "Understanding Cultural Diversity and Learning." In A. C. Ornstein and L. Behar (eds.), *Curriculum Issues.* Needham Heights, Mass.: Allyn and Bacon, 1995, pp. 349–366. Henry Trueba, George Spindler, and Louise Spindler. *What Do Anthropologists Have to Say About Dropouts?* New York: Falmer Press, 1989. p. 20.

26. G. Williamson McDiarmid. "What to Do About Differences? A Study of Multicultural Education for Teacher Trainees." *Journal of Teacher Education* (March–April 1992): 83–93. Stephen J. Trachtenberg. "Multiculturalism Can Be Taught Only by Multicultural People." *Phi Delta Kappan* (April 1990): 610–611.

27. Anne Westcott Dodd and Jean L. Konzal. *Making Our High Schools Better.* New York: St. Martin's Griffin, 1999, p. 80.

28. Knapp and Shields. "Reconceiving Academic Instruction for the Children of Poverty," 753–758. Marilyn Cochran-Smith and Susan L. Lytle. "Interrogating Cultural Diversity: Inquiry and Action." *Journal of Teacher Education* (March–April 1992): 104–115,. Gary C. Wehlage and Robert A. Rutter. "Dropping Out: How Much Do Schools Contribute to the Problem?" *Teachers College Record* (May 1986): 374–392.

29. Allan C. Ornstein. "Research on Teaching: Issues and Trends." *Journal of Teacher Education* (November–December, 1985, pp. 27–31. Ornstein, "A Look at Teacher Effectiveness Research."

30. Lee S. Shulman. "Paradigms and Research Programs in the Study of Teaching." In M. C. Wittrock (ed.), *Handbook of Research on Teaching,* 3d ed. New York: Macmillan, 1986, pp. 3–36. Lee S. Shulman. "Ways of Seeing, Ways of Knowing: Ways of Teaching, Ways of Learning About Teaching." *Journal of Curriculum Studies* (September–October 1991): 393–396.

31. A. S. Barr. "Characteristics of Successful Teachers." *Phi Delta Kappan* (March 1958): 282–284.

32. David G. Ryans. *Characteristics of Teachers.* Washington, D.C.: American Council of Education, 1960.

33. Bruce W. Tuckman. "Feedback and the Change Process." *Phi Delta Kappan* (January 1986): 341–344. Bruce W. Tuckman. "An Interpersonal Construct Model of Teaching." Paper presented at the annual meeting of the American Educational Research Association, Chicago, April 1991.

34. Bruce W. Tuckman. "The Interpersonal Teacher Model." *Educational Forum* (Winter 1995): 177–185.

35. Grant Wiggins. *Educative Assessment.* San Francisco: Jossey-Bass, 1998.

36. Thomas Gibney and William Wiersma. "Using Profile Analysis for Student Teacher Evaluation." *Journal of Teacher Evaluation* (May–June 1986): 43; Richard J. Stiggins, "Assessment Crisis," *Phi Delta Kappan* (June 2002): 758–767.

37. John W. Arnn and John N. Mangieri. "Effective Leadership for Effective Schools: A Survey of Principal Attitudes." *NASSP Bulletin* (February 1988): 1–7.

38. Thomas J. Sergiovanni and Robert J. Starrett. *Supervision: A Redefinition,* 7th ed. Boston: McGraw-Hill, 2002.

39. Arthur E. Wise et al. "Teacher Evaluation: A Study of Effective Practices." *Elementary School Journal* (September 1985): 94.

40. Joseph O. Milner. "Working Together for Better Teacher Evaluation." *Phi Delta Kappan* (June 1991): 788–789. Allan C. Ornstein. "Teaching and Teacher Accountability." In A. C. Ornstein et al. (ed.),. *Contemporary Issues in Education* 3rd ed. Boston, Mass: Allyn and Bacon, 2003. 248–261.

41. Barak V. Rosenshine and Norma F. Furst. "Research in Teacher Performance Criteria." In B. O. Smith (ed.), *Research on Teacher Education.* Englewood Cliffs, N.J.: Prentice-Hall, 1971, pp. 37–72. Barak V. Rosenshine and Norma F. Furst. "The Use of Direct Observation to Study Teaching." In R. M. Travers (ed.), *Second Handbook of Research on Teaching.* Chicago: Rand McNally, 1973, pp. 122–183. Note that the first five processes also appear in Arnn and Mangieri's list of competencies (Table 2.8) but in different order of importance.

42. Barak V. Rosenshine. "Content, Time and Direct Instruction." In P. L. Peterson and H. J. Walberg (eds.), *Research on Teaching: Concepts, Findings, and Implications.* Berkeley, Calif.: McCutchan, 1979, pp. 28–56.

43. N. L. Gage. *The Scientific Basis of the Art of Teaching.* New York: Teachers College Press, Columbia University, 1978.

44. Ibid. The authors disagree with item 5; see Chapter 5, on questioning.

45. Thomas L. Good and Jere E. Brophy. "Teacher Behavior and Student Achievement." In M. C. Wittrock (ed.), *Handbook of Research on Teaching,* 3d ed. New York: Macmillan, 1986, pp. 328–375. Also see Andrew C.

Porter and Jere Brophy. "Synthesis of Research on Good Teaching." *Educational Leadership* (May 1988): 74–85. Thomas L. Good and Jere E. Brophy. *Looking in Classrooms,* 8th ed. New York: Addison Wesley, 2000.

46. Carolyn Evertson and Edmund T. Emmer. "Effective Management at the Beginning of the School Year in Junior High Classes." *Journal of Educational Psychology* (August 1982): 485–498. C. Evertson et al. *Classroom Management for Elementary Teachers,* 5th ed. Boston, Mass.: Allyn and Bacon, 2000.

47. Grover J. Whitehurst. "Research on Teacher Preparation and Professional Development." Washington, DC: United States Department of Education, 2002.

48. Ibid.

49. Walter Doyle. "Effective Teaching and the Concept of Master Teacher." *Elementary School Journal* (September 1985): 30. Also see Walter Doyle. "Curriculum and Pedagogy." In P. W. Jackson (ed.), *Handbook of Research on Curriculum.* New York: Macmillan, 1992, pp. 486–516.

50. Jann E. Azumi and James L. Lerman. "Selecting and Rewarding Master Teachers." *Elementary School Journal* (November 1987): 197.

51. Martin Haberman. "The Pedagogy of Poverty Versus Good Teaching." *Phi Delta Kappan* (December 1991): 290–294. Martin Haberman. "The Ideology of Star Teachers of Children of Poverty." *Educational Horizons* (Spring 1992): 125–129.

52. Maxine Greene. "Philosophy and Teaching." In M. C. Wittrock (ed.), *Handbook of Research on Teaching,* 3rd ed. New York: Macmillan, 1986, pp. 479–500. Maxine Greene. *The Dialectic of Teaching.* New York: Teachers College, Columbia University Press, 1988; Maxine Greene. *Variations on a Blue Guitar.* New York: Teachers College Press, 2001.

53. Allan C. Ornstein. *Teaching and Schooling in America: Pre and Post September 11.* Boston, Mass: Allyn and Bacon, 2003: 37.

54. Elliot W. Eisner. *The Educational Imagination,* 3d ed. New York: Macmillan, 1993. Deborah Meier. *Will Standards Save Public Education?* Boston: Beacon Press, 2000.

55. Allan C. Ornstein. "Teacher Effectiveness Research: Theoretical Considerations." In H. C. Waxman and H. J. Walberg (eds.), *Effective Teaching.* Berkeley, Calif.: McCutchan, 1991, pp. 63–80. See also John I. Goodlad. "Kudzu, Rabbits and School Reform." *Phi Delta Kappan* (September 2002): 16–23.

56. Parker Palmer. *The Courage to Teach.* San Francisco: Jossey-Bass, 1998.

57. Nel Noddings. *Educating Moral People.* New York: Teachers College Press, 2002.

58. Carol Ames. "Motivation: What Teachers Need to Know." *Teachers College Record* (Spring 1990): 409–421. Paul R. Burden and David M. Byrd. *Methods for Effective Teaching.* 2d ed. Boston: Allyn and Bacon, 2003.

59. Ornstein. "Teacher Effectiveness Research."

60. Christopher Clark. "Real Lessons from Imaginary Teachers." *Journal of Curriculum Studies* (September–October 1991): 429–434. Donna M. Kagan. "Ways of Evaluating Teacher Cognition." *Review of Educational Research* (Fall 1990): 419–469.

61. Hugh Munby. "A Qualitative Approach to the Study of Teachers' Beliefs." *Journal of Curriculum Studies* (April–May 1986): 197–209.

62. Peter McLaren. *Life in Schools.* Boston, Mass: Allyn and Bacon, 2003. Henry A. Giroux. "Curriculum, Multiculturalism, and the Politics of Identity." *NASSP Bulletin* (December 1992): 1–11. Peter C. Murrell, Jr. *African-Centered Pedagogy.* Albany, N.Y.: State University of New York, 2002.

63. Sara Lawrence Lightfoot and Jessica Huffman Davis. *The Art and Science of Portraiture.* San Francisco: Jossey-Bass, 1997.

64. Freeman Elbaz. "Research on Teachers' Knowledge: The Evolution of a Discourse." *Journal of Curriculum Studies* (January–February 1991): 1–19. Donna M. Marriott. "Ending the Silence." *Phi Delta Kappan* (March 2003): 496–501.

65. Raymond Butt and Daniele Raymond. "Arguments for Using Qualitative Approaches in Understanding Teacher Thinking: The Case for Biography." *Journal of Curriculum Theorizing* (Winter 1987): 62–93. Donna Kagan. "Research on Teacher Cognition." In A. C. Ornstein (ed.), *Teaching: Theory and Practice.* Needham Heights, Mass.: Allyn and Bacon, 1995, pp. 225–238.

66. Sylvia Asthon-Warner. *Teacher,* reissue ed. New York: Simon & Schuster Books, 1986.

67. Grace E. Grant. "Ways of Constructing Classroom Meaning: Two Stories About Knowing and Seeing." *Journal of Curriculum Studies* (September–October 1991): 397–408. Antoinette Errante. "But Sometimes You're Not Part of the Story." *Educational Researcher* (March 2000): 16–27.
68. Elbaz. "Research on Teachers' Knowledge." Diane R. Wood. "Teaching Narratives: A Source for Faculty Development and Evaluation." *Harvard Educational Review* (Winter 1992): 535–550.
69. Madeleine R. Grumet. "The Politics of Personal Knowledge." *Curriculum Inquiry* (Fall 1987): 319–329.
70. Donald C. Wesley. "Nurturing the Novices." *Phi Delta Kappan* (February 2003): 446–447.
71. Hubert L. Dreyfus and Stuart E. Dreyfus. *Mind over Machine.* New York: Free Press, 1986.
72. Katherine S. Cushing, Donna S. Sabers, and David C. Berliner. "Investigations of Expertise in Teaching." *Educational Horizons* (Spring 1992): 109.
73. Kathy Carter. "The Place of Story in Research on Teaching." *Educational Researcher* (January 1993): 5–12. Donna S. Sabers, Katherine S. Cushing, and David C. Berliner. "Differences Among Teachers in a Task Characterized by Simultaneity, Multidimensionality, and Immediacy." *American Educational Research Journal* (Spring 1991): 63–88.
74. Cecil M. Clark and Penelope L. Peterson. "Teachers' Thought Processes." In M. C. Wittrock (ed.) *Handbook of Research on Teaching.* 3rd ed. New York: Macmillan, 1986, pp. 255–296. Donna M. Kagan and Deborah J. Tippins. "Helping Student Teachers Attend to Student Cues." *Elementary School Journal* (March 1991): 343–356.
75. Cushing, Sabers, and Berliner, "Investigations of Expertise in Teaching." Carol Livingston and Hilda Borko. "Expert-Novice Differences in Teaching." *Journal of Teacher Education* (July–August 1989): 36–42.
76. Hilda Borko and Carol Livingston. "Cognition and Improvisation: Differences in Mathematics Instruction by Expert and Novice Teachers." *American Educational Research Journal* (Winter 1989): 473–498. Kathy Carter, Walter Doyle, and Mark Riney. "Expert-Novice Differences in Teaching." In Allan C. Ornstein (ed.), *Teaching: Theory and Practice.* Needham Heights, Mass.: Allyn and Bacon, 1995, pp. 257–272.
77. James Calderhead. "The Nature and Growth of Knowledge in Student Teaching." *Teaching and Teacher Education* (April 1992); 531–535. Kathy L. Carter. "Teachers' Knowledge and Learning to Teach." In W. R. Houston (ed.), *Handbook of Research on Teacher Education.* New York: Macmillan, 1990, pp. 291–310.
78. Kagan and Tippins. "Helping Student Teachers Attend to Student Cues." Terry M. Wildman et al. "Promoting Reflective Practice Among Beginning and Experienced Teachers." In R. T. Clift, W. R. Houston, and M. C. Pugach (eds.), *Encouraging Reflective Practice in Education.* New York: Teachers College Press, Columbia University, 1990, pp. 139–162.
79. Elbaz. "Research on Teachers' Knowledge."
80. Herbert Kohl. *36 Children.* New York: Plume, 1988, pp. 25–26.

Part II

The Technical Skills of Teaching

In the nine chapters that make up this section, we will explore the technical skills that are needed in order to use the science of teaching and move toward the artful practice of those skills. During the past several years, several organizations have structured those skills around certain domains or principles of practice. We selected two of those frameworks that have substantial popularity, Pathwise/PRAXIS III (ETS) and INTASC, and we will use those to introduce each of the skills of teaching. Provided in Tables II.1 and II.2 are the nineteen Pathwise assessment criteria (divided into four domains) and the ten INTASC principles.

As each technical skill of teaching is introduced, the Pathwise-PRAXIS criteria or INTASC standards that relate to each of the skills are identified. If you are in a state that uses either of these structures, this should help you connect the content of these chapters with those larger assessment schema.

Two important notes. First, we have attempted within each chapter to provide a set of activities for you to engage in or questions for you to reflect on. The purpose of these is to help you develop the dispositions and subsequently the performances that are needed for effective teaching. The criteria or standards sets a goal. To achieve those goals requires that you more completely develop and understand a body of knowledge. This text provides some of that requisite knowledge and should also provide a basis for learning the dispositions and performances essential for teaching effectiveness. Second, Pathwise is the mentoring framework for PRAXIS III, which is a more high-stakes assessment. Pathwise is for preservice teachers and beginning teacher mentors. PRAXIS III is for entry year teachers who are engaged in professional practice. Because this book is for preservice teachers, we will use the Pathwise designation.

Interestingly, Joseph Cadray has taken these same INTASC standards and graphically illustrated how they can be used in culturally responsive practices. Table II.3 was developed by Cadray. In essence, a culturally responsive teacher is one who understands the nexus between standards and classroom instruction and tries to shape instruction to maximize student involvement for *all* students. More importantly, there is not an incompatibility between well articulated teaching standards and the efforts by those preparing teachers to make novice educators more sensitive to the need for and appropriateness of culturally responsive pedagogy.

table II.1 Pathwise PRAXIS III Version

Domain A: Organizing Content Knowledge for Student Learning

A1: Becoming familiar with relevant aspects of students' background knowledge and experiences

A2: Articulating clear learning goals for the lesson that are appropriate for the students

A3: Demonstrating an understanding of the connections among the content that was learned previously, the current content, and the content that remains to be learned in the future

A4: Creating or selecting teaching methods, learning activities, and instructional materials or other resources that are appropriate for the students and that are aligned with the goals of the lesson

A5: Creating or selecting evaluation strategies that are appropriate for the students and that are aligned with the goals of the lesson

Domain B: Creating an Environment for Student Learning

B1: Creating a climate that promotes fairness

B2: Establishing and maintaining rapport with students

B3: Communicating challenging learning expectations to each student

B4: Establishing and maintaining consistent standards of classroom behavior

B5: Making the physical environment as safe and conducive to learning as possible

Domain C: Teaching for Student Learning

C1: Making learning goals and instructional procedures clear to students

C2: Making content comprehensible to students

C3: Encouraging students to extend their thinking

C4: Monitoring students' understanding of content through a variety of means, providing feedback to students to assist learning, and adjusting learning activities as the situation demands

C5: Using instructional time effectively

Domain D: Teacher Professionalism

D1: Reflecting on the extent to which the learning goals were met

D2: Building professional relationships with colleagues to share teaching insights and coordinate learning activities for students

D4: Communicating with parents or guardians about student learning

Credit: PRAXIS III: Classroom Performance Assessments materials selected from Development of the Knowledge Base for the PRAXIS III: Classroom Performance Assessments Assessment Criteria, 1994, by Carol Ann Dwyer. Reprinted by permission of Educational Testing Service, the copyright owner.

Disclaimer: Permission to reprint PRAXIS III: Classroom Performace Assessments materials does not constitute review or Endorsement by Educational Testing Service of this publication as a whole or of any other testing information it may contain.

table II.2 INTASC Standards

Principle 1: The teacher understands the central concepts, tools of inquiry, and structures of the discipline(s) he or she teaches and can create learning experiences that make these aspects of subject matter meaningful for students.

Principle 2: The teacher understands how children learn and develop and can provide learning opportunities that support their intellectual, social, and personal development.

Principle 3: The teacher understands how students differ in their approaches to learning and creates instructional opportunities that are adapted to diverse learners.

Principle 4: The teacher understands and uses a variety of instructional strategies to encourage students' development of critical thinking, problem solving, and performance skills.

Principle 5: The teacher uses an understanding of individual and group motivation and behavior to create a learning environment and encourages positive social interaction, active engagement in learning, and self-motivation.

Principle 6: The teacher uses knowledge of effective verbal, nonverbal, and media communication techniques to foster active inquiry, collaboration, and supportive interaction in the classroom.

Principle 7: The teacher plans instruction based upon knowledge of subject matter, students, the community, and curriculum goals.

Principle 8: The teacher understands and uses formal and informal assessment strategies to evaluate and ensure the continuous intellectual, social, and physical development of the learner.

Principle 9: The teacher is a reflective practitioner who continually evaluates the effects of his or her choices and actions on others (students, parents, and other professionals in the learning community) and who actively seeks opportunities to grow professionally.

Principle 10: The teacher fosters relationships with school colleagues, parents, and agencies in the larger community to support students' learning and well-being.

Source: See www.ccsso.org

Credit: PRAXIS III: Classroom Performance Assessments materials selected from Development of the Knowledge Base for the PRAXIS III: Classroom Performance Assessments Assessment Criteria, 1994, by Carol Ann Dwyer. Reprinted by permission of Educational Testing Service, the copyright owner.

table II.3 INTASC Standards and Practices

Standard 1

The teacher understands the central concepts, tools of inquiry, and structure of the fields of knowledge she or he teaches and can create learning experiences that make these aspects of subject matter meaningful for students.

The teacher integrates professional, content, and pedagogical knowledge to create learning experiences that make the content area meaningful for all students.
The teacher uses multiple representations and explanations and links them to students' prior understandings.

Standard 2

The teacher understands how children learn and develop and provides learning opportunities that support their intellectual, social, and personal development.

The teacher understands and appreciates cognitive processes involved in academic learning, including diverse learning styles.

Standard 3

The teacher understands how students differ in their approaches to learning and creates instructional opportunities that are adapted to diverse learners.

The teacher knows and is sensitive to diverse cultural groups globally and understands how ethnicity, class, gender, and other sociocultural factors influence students' learning and classroom climate.
The teacher understands students' families, cultures, and communities and uses this information as a basis for connecting to students' experiences.

Standard 4

The teacher understands and uses a variety of instructional strategies to encourage students' development of critical thinking, problem solving, and performance skills.

The teacher implements a variety of instructional and assessment strategies appropriate to diverse learners.

Standard 5

The teacher uses an understanding of individual and group motivation and behavior to create a learning environment that encourages positive social interaction, active engagement in learning, and self-motivation.

The teacher diagnoses and builds upon the personal, cultural, and historical experiences of learners from a variety of socioeconomic and ethnic backgrounds and develops meaningful instructional activities and positive, productive learning environments.

Credit: PRAXIS III: Classroom Performance Assessments materials selected from Development of the Knowledge Base for the PRAXIS III: Classroom Performance Assessments Assessment Criteria, 1994, by Carol Ann Dwyer. Reprinted by permission of Educational Testing Service, the copyright owner.

Disclaimer: Permission to reprint PRAXIS III: Classroom Performace Assessments materials does not constitute review or Endorsement by Educational Testing Service of this publication as a whole or of any other testing information it may contain.

table II.3   INTASC Standards and Practices (continued)

Standard 6

The teacher uses knowledge of effective verbal, nonverbal, and media communication techniques, including technology, to foster active inquiry, collaboration, and supportive interaction in the classroom.	The teacher communicates in ways that demonstrate sensitivity to cultural and gender differences. The teacher encourages students to express ideas in ways that help them acquire content.*

Standard 7

The teacher plans instruction based on knowledge of subject matter, students, the community, and curriculum goals.	The teacher plans learning opportunities that meet the developmental and individual needs of diverse learners.

Standard 8

The teacher understands and uses formal and informal assessment strategies to ensure the continuous intellectual, social, and physical development of the learner.	The teacher uses a variety of assessment techniques, including observation, portfolios, self-assessment, peer assessment, and projects, as well as teacher-made and standardized tests. This uses the experiences of the students to shape the learning activities of the classroom.*

Standard 9

The teacher is a reflective practitioner who continually evaluates the effects of his or her actions on others.	The teacher reflects on his or her personal background and life experiences in order to develop culturally responsive curricula and instructional practices.

Standard 10

The teacher fosters relationships with school colleagues, parents, and agencies in the larger community to support students' learning and well-being.	The teacher understands the influence of family participation on students' learning and involves families in students' learning. The teacher identifies and uses community resources in the classroom and understands teaching as situated in schools and communities.

Source: Adapted from and originally published in J. E. Cadray. *The Field Experiences Handbook.* Unpublished manuscript, Emory University, Atlanta, Georgia. 1999. * Note: A couple of new items have been added to the Cadray framework—see Standards 6 and 8.

Instructional Objectives

Pathwise criteria relevant to this chapter:

- *Becoming familiar with relevant aspects of students' background knowledge and experiences* (A1)
- *Articulating clear learning goals for the lesson that are appropriate for the students* (A2)
- *Making content comprehensible to students* (C1)

INTASC principles relevant to this chapter:

- *The teacher plans instruction based upon knowledge of subject matter, students, the community, and curriculum goals.* (Principle 7)

focusing questions

1. What should the schools teach?

2. How are aims, goals, and objectives formulated?

3. How are state and national standards influencing and shaping the formulation of instructional goals?

4. How do aims, goals, and objectives differ?

5. How would you characterize the approaches to writing objectives by the following: Tyler, Bloom, Gronlund, and Mager?

6. How does each approach differ? In what way do different learning objectives shape how a teacher teaches?

7. How specific should course objectives be? Classroom objectives?

T he world that you are entering as a new teacher looks a bit different from that of the teachers who taught you. Their world was one heavily oriented toward a form of teacher academic freedom, even in states with mandated curricula. Your world is one of clearly defined academic standards for students and of accountability for teachers and students relative to those standards. The 2002 No Child Left Behind legislation will leave no child untested and no teacher outside an accountability system. That means you must know what to teach (the content of this chapter), how to teach it (the content of chapters 4–7), and how to assess whether students have learned it (the content of Chapters 9 and 10).

Definitions of Terms

In figuring out what to teach, you will be guided by aims, goals, and objectives. Each of these tools will help you focus your teaching and plan units and lessons. You need to understand the purpose of each and how each can help you.

We use the term *aims,* or *purposes,* to refer to broad statements about the intent of education. They are descriptive, value-laden statements, written by panels, commissions, or policy-making groups at a societal (or national) level, that express a philosophy of education, concepts of the social role of schools, and the needs of children and youth. In short, they are broad guides for translating the needs of society into educational policy. Aims are usually somewhat vague in terms of how they will be achieved, but they are clear in terms of their focus. An aim is preparing students for democratic citizenship or citizenship preparation. But, what does the phrase "Preparing students for Democratic citizenship" mean? What do we have in mind when we stress "Citizenship preparation"?

Educators need to translate aims into statements that will describe what schools are expected to accomplish (which are more focused than statements about the purpose of education). These translations are called *goals.* Goals make it possible to organize learning experiences in terms of what the state, school district, or school decides to stress on a systemwide basis. In effect, *goals* are statements that cut across subjects and grade levels to represent the entire school program. Goals are more definite than aims, but they are still nonbehavioral and therefore nonobservable and nonmeasurable. Goals provide direction for educators, but they do not specify achievement levels or proficiency levels. Examples of goals are "Development of reading skills," "Appreciation of art," and "Understanding of mathematical/scientific concepts."

Goals are usually written by professional associations, state educational agencies, and local school districts to be published as school and curriculum guidelines for what all students should accomplish over their entire school careers. Although goals are usually developed at the local or regional level, a new movement proposes that one way of equalizing opportunity is to nationalize goals for education.[1] Because of the tremendous emphasis on assessment and accountability, more and more teachers are required (or elect through personal choice) to use state and national professional goals established by the learned societies or by state governments to prescribe content to be covered. Table 3.1 shows where national goals and standards for selected disciplinary areas can be accessed. You should review those goals and standards for the area you are responsible to teach. The daughter of one of the authors is in her first year of teaching as this book is

table 3.1   National Standards for Selected Disciplines

Art

From the Consortium of National Arts Education Associations:
artsedge.kennedy_center.org/professional_resources/standards/nat_standards/index.html

Social Studies

From the National Council for the Social Studies: www.ncss.org/standards/stitle.html

From the National Center for History In the Schools, UCLA: www.sscnet.ucla.edu/nchs/standards/

Science

From the National Science Teachers Association: www.nap.edu/books/0309053269/html/index.html

Mathematics

From the National Council of Teachers of Mathematics: www.nctm.org/standards/

English

From the National Council of Teachers of English: www.ncte.org/standards/

Music

From the National Association for Music Education: www.menc.org/publication/books/standards.htm

Foreign Language

From the American Council on the Teaching of Foreign Languages:
www.actfl.org/public/articles/details.cfm?id=33

being revised. She decided what to teach by using national and state (Indiana) standards in music education to determine her locally-defined instructional objectives.

QUESTIONS FOR REFLECTION

The emergence of national and state standards is a relatively recent phenomenon. Only one state (Iowa) still relies heavily on locally derived goals and objectives. What do you see as the advantages of state-prescribed goals and objectives? Will they make teaching more difficult or easier for novice practitioners? Consider the following real problem.

The new federal No Child Left Behind law requires that children in poorly performing (failing) schools be given the opportunity to attend better schools. However, each state can define *failure* in its own way. That means that a state with high academic standards may label as "failing" students who in another state would be "succeeding." Should standardized passing rates be adopted? Should each state be allowed to create its own definitions and then might some states lower standards to increase the number of succeeding students, saving themselves substantial costs? Read Professional Viewpoint 3.1 to gain more insight into state standards.

State Academic Standards

Chester E. Finn, Jr.
John M. Olin Fellow, Hudson Institute
President, Thomas B. Fordham Foundation

 State standards can be both a help and hindrance to teachers striving to develop an effective curriculum and pedagogy for their students.

They help by setting subject-matter parameters, delineating the knowledge and skills that the state deems essential, and thus providing a scaffolding on which district, school and teacher can construct their own version of what students will actually study.

They hinder by narrowing the curriculum to an unfortunate degree or—paradoxically—inflating it to absurd proportions, by establishing divisions that make it harder to bridge disciplines, by insisting on "coverage" of material that may be unrealistic or inappropriate in actual class settings, and occasionally by creating sequences that don't work for practitioners—yet must be honored because of the tests that accompany the standards. Still, state standards are a fact of life in most places, and the teachers ignore them at their (and their students') peril, particularly where assessments and ac-

countability mechanisms are keyed to them. It's best to view them as the skeleton of the curriculum and then work at supplying the flesh, the nerves, and the blood supply. This can actually be a blessing to teachers who need not fret over much about deciding what knowledge and skills to impart and who can instead concentrate on the sequence, materials and instructional methods most apt to succeed with their students.

This becomes far harder, of course, if the state did a mediocre job of developing its academic standards—and one is bound by them anyway. Unfortunately, this worrisome situation exists in many parts of the country, or did in 1997 when the Thomas B. Fordham Foundation undertook an appraisal of state standards in the five key subjects of English, math, science, history, and geography.

Our reviewers were generally dismayed by the vapidity and shoddiness of much that they found. The typical state's "grade" on the quality of its academic standards across the five subjects was D+. That's the bad news. The good news is that in every subject at least a few states developed exemplary standards—proof that this can be done well. I am also encouraged by the fact that many states took our criticism in a constructive vein and have indicated that improving their academic standards is a high priority. Let's hope they follow through.

Some educators question the rigor of the standards that all states (except Iowa) now have in place. The Thomas B. Fordham Foundation conducted an analysis of standards in selected teaching areas in the late 1990s. An example of the analyses for two states (one with a low and the other with a high assessment of science standards) is provided in Case Study 3.1: Standards. The Fordham Foundation study suggests that there may be unevenness in the quality of what states prescribe. That unevenness may have troublesome consequences for students or for school districts. It is important for you to remember that, regardless of what your state prescribes, what students learn depends on the choices that you, the teacher, make.

Objectives are descriptions of what eventually is to take place at the classroom level. They specify content and sometimes the proficiency level to be attained. Understanding why and how to use instructional *objectives* results in more effective teaching and testing. The use of instructional objectives helps the teacher focus on what students should know at the end of the lesson plan or unit plan (a series of lessons related to a specific topic) and, likewise, helps students know what is expected of them. Instructional objectives help the teacher plan for teaching and organize instruction; they identify what to teach and when to

case study 3.1   Examination of Science Standards for Arizona and Florida by the Thomas B. Fordham Foundation

Arizona State Science Standards (Highly Rated)

Arizona's standards, clear though relatively brief in 1997, earned an A in the previous review. Although the changes in the 1999 version are not extensive, they are very significant. The principal shortcoming of the 1997 version was the way in which evolution was masked. Though the content was treated in acceptable fashion, the word "evolution" was never mentioned, and the general effect was to distance evolution from its essential place at the center of the life sciences. This shortcoming has now been remedied by the addition of a number of explicit standards. These two are typical:

> Use scientific evidence to demonstrate that descent from common ancestors produced today's diversity for organisms over more than 3.5 billion years of evolution (Standard 4SC-P9).
>
> Explain prominent scientific theories of the origin of the universe (Big Bang Theory), the solar system (formation from a nebular cloud of dust and gas), and the life forms (evolution) (Standard 6SC-P1).

> *Unfortunately, human evolution is still not mentioned at all.*
> *There have been a few other minor changes in the interest of clarity. It is too bad, however, that Standard 5SC-E3 PO1 ("Define energy") has been removed from grades 4–5. "Define the law of conservation of energy" is retained at grades 6–8; one hopes that the student asked to do this knows by then what energy is! Addition of material concerning universal gravitation (5SC-P7) and the laws of thermodynamics (5SC-P8) at grades 9–12 is laudable but probably inadequate to be very useful. Modern astronomy is still shortchanged. All in all, however, a good set of standards has been improved.*

Florida State Science Standards (Poorly Rated)

The 1998 evaluation was based on the 1996 Florida Curriculum Framework—Science. This document contains a list of benchmarks together with Sample Performance Descriptions separated into four grade clusters. The benchmarks are unchanged but are now available in several formats. The one considered here, Grade Level Expectations for the Sunshine State Standards, lists the benchmarks by grade cluster (pre-K through grade 2, 3–5, and 6–8). Each benchmark is followed by a list of grade-specific grade-level expectations. These explicit grade-by-grade expectations appear to supplant the less grade-specific Sample Performance Descriptions. (A similar list for grades 9–12 is presumably in preparation.)

> *All of the shortcomings of the benchmarks are still present. And unfortunately, the grade-level expectations are no improvement over their predecessors in terms of clarity and scientific accuracy. As with the earlier document, there are occasional lapses in grade-level appropriateness. Often, an expectation is merely a verbatim copy or close paraphrase of the benchmark it is supposed to illustrate—sometimes*

over two or more successive grades. Worse, the expectations are sometimes irrelevant to the corresponding benchmarks.

Energy is discussed intelligently in a few places but no attention is given to defining the term, even though such technical terms as kinetic and potential are used. Modern astronomy, modern geology, and molecular biology are still shortchanged.

As in the earlier document, evolution is touched on very lightly—certainly not given its proper place as the central organizing principle of the life sciences—and the "E-word" is diligently avoided. The only relevant grade-level expectations that I have found are vague and inaccurate: "[The eighth grader] knows that the fossil record provides evidence that changes in the kinds of plants and animals in the environment have been occurring over time" (for Benchmark SC.F.2.3.4) and "[The seventh grader] knows that biological adaptations include changes in structures, behavior, or physiology that enhance reproductive success in a particular environment" (for Benchmark SC.G.1.3.2), of which the grade-level expectations are verbatim repetitions. There are a few references to competition and adaptation at earlier grade levels, but no direct reference is made to the evolutionary implications. Nor, unfortunately, is any information other than the fossil record discussed in an evolutionary context.

Graphs are introduced at first grade (!) but there is a paucity of development of this and other quantitative methods in the higher grades.

Questions for Reflection:

1. The Arizona analysis is interesting because of the controversy over the use of the term *evolution*. How would you deal with a topic such as evolution if the district you teach in uses a curriculum that "masks" its coverage?
2. What "e-word" topics are evident in your discipline? Should teachers have the freedom to teach content for all "e-word" topics?
3. Do you think teachers should have a voice in shaping state content standards? Why or why not? Who should decide what teachers teach?
4. Go to the Thomas B. Fordham Foundation website (see *www.edexcellence.net*) and examine the standards' analysis for your state. Talk to teachers who know your state standards to see if they concur with the Fordham Foundation analysis. Have your state standards changed since the Fordham Foundation analysis? If so, how?

Source: Retrieved on August 20, 2002, from http://edexcellence.net/library/soss2000/2000soss.html.

teach it and thus serve as a map or guide for both teachers and students. Instructional objectives are stated in observable and measurable terms, and they clarify whether what we intended was achieved or to what extent it was (or was not) achieved.

According to Hilda Taba, "The chief function of . . . objectives is to guide the making of . . . decisions on what to cover, what to emphasize, and what content to select, and what learning experiences to stress."[2] Because the possibilities of content,

Numerous large school districts now have their goals and standards outlined for parents on locally developed websites. They may even have suggestions for ways for parents to develop their own children's potential. Examples of websites that you might want to visit are the Academic Standards for Chicago Public Schools website (http://www.cps. k12.il.us/instruction/cas); and the California Standards for California Public Schools website (http://www.cde/ca/gov/standards). These are illustrative of what districts throughout the country are doing. If you want to see what the standards are for your state, visit www.achieve.org. Achieve was created to help states analyze, develop, and implement high academic standards. One additional note on goals is appropriate. For the purposes of simplicity we treat goals and standards as equivalent. They are really ways that educators are concisely attempting to define what students must know and be able to demonstrate.

Types of Objectives

Instructional objectives help the teacher focus on what students should know at the end of a lesson, unit, or course, and they also help students know what is expected of them. They help the teacher plan and organize instruction by identifying with more specificity than standards what is to be taught and when it is to be taught. Instructional objectives are stated in observable and measurable terms (outcomes, proficiencies, or competencies). Their specificity enables the teacher to determine whether what was intended was achieved and to what extent.

When we move from goals and standards to instructional objectives, the role and responsibility of the teacher become evident. Objectives are behavioral in nature and are more precise than goals. They are formulated on three levels, with increasing specificity: program, course, and classroom. Objectives at the classroom level can further be divided into unit plan and lesson plan objectives.

Program Objectives

Program objectives stem from the standards of the school and are written at the subject and grade level. Although they do not usually state specific content or competencies, they do focus on general content and behaviors. Like goals, they refer to the accomplishments of (and expectations for) all students, rather than to those of individual students.[10]

Nearly every state and school district have an overview or set of program objectives at the subject and grade levels to facilitate what teachers should be teaching. In most cases these instructional objectives are formulated by curriculum committees made up of administrative, teacher, and community (or parent) groups. Table 3.4 provides a detailed list of the instructional objectives for mathematics in Dayton, Ohio, and illustrates for the reader the program objectives on a vertical and horizontal basis. The Dayton curriculum shows how school district curricula are being structured to conform to both state mandates and national (in this case National Science Teacher Association) guidelines. It also shows the dynamic nature of the curriculum development process.

Good curriculum development is never complete. The standards and objectives in Table 3.4 were developed between 1992 and 1998. In 2004, the district likely will be forced to revise its curriculum again because of new academic content standards that

table 3.4 **Dayton Public Schools**
Mathematics Curriculum
Sample Strands, General Objectives, and Specific Objectives
Grade 5

Strand 1—Patterns, Relations and Functions	Specific Objective
The student will be able to . . .	
1. investigate patterns that occur when changing numerators and denominators in equivalent fractions and describe these patterns verbally.	1A. *(Knowledge/Skill)* Given five fraction or decimal patterns, the student will be able to complete each pattern to 70 percent accuracy.
Strand 2—Problem-Solving Strategies	**Specific Objective**
The student will be able to . . .	
2. read a problem carefully and identify subgoals that need to be attained in order to solve the problem.	2B. *(Concept)* The student will demonstrate understanding of the concept of problem solving by solving four word problems and explaining the steps taken to achieve his or her answer.
Strand 3—Numbers and Number Relations	**Specific Objective**
The student will be able to . . .	
3. multiply and divide decimals.	3A. *(Knowledge/Skills)* Given five multiplication and five division problems, the student will calculate accurately the solutions to 70 percent accuracy.

are now being promulgated for the state. As a new teacher you will find yourself in situations where the curriculum of the district will change over time and the burden is on you to know how to access and use the most recent standards in place for your field to design the learning experiences for your students.

Course Objectives

Course objectives are derived from program objectives and are formulated at the subject or departmental level. They categorize and organize content and sometimes concepts, problems, or behaviors, but they do not specify the exact content to be examined or the exact instructional methods and materials to be used. Course objectives are stated in the form of topics, concepts, or general behaviors.

table 3.4 **Dayton Public Schools**
Mathematics Curriculum
Sample Strands, General Objectives, and Specific Objectives
Grade 5 (continued)

Strand 3—Numbers and Number Relations	*Specific Objective (continued)*
4. find equivalent fractions.	4A. *(Knowledge/Skills)* Given ten fractional equivalency problems, the student will correctly identify and provide a missing numerator and write equivalent fractions to 70 percent accuracy.
6. order combinations of whole numbers, fractions, and decimals using the symbols <, ≤, >, ≥, and = and by placing them on the number line.	6A. *(Knowledge/Skills)* Given four graphing problems, the student will be able to order combinations of whole numbers, fractions, and decimals and place them on a number line to 70 percent accuracy.

Strand 4 – Geometry	*Specific Objective*
The student will be able to . . .	
1. compare and contrast angles in relation to right angles.	1A. *(Knowledge/Skills)* Given a set of six angles, the student will use a right angle to determine if the angles are obtuse or acute to 70 percent accuracy.
4. build models of previously encountered shapes and figures and describe the process in words.	4B. *(Concept)* The student will demonstrate understanding of the concept of geometric figures by using pattern blocks and geoboards and explaining in words how they were constructed.

Source: Adapted from the *Dayton Public Schools Mathematics Curriculum, Grade 5.* The Dayton Curriculum is based on the NCTM standard and reflects how goals and objectives for a local curriculum can be grounded on national standards. Developed in 1992 and revised in 1998.

Objectives stated as *topics* for an American history course might be "The Colonial Period," "The Revolutionary Period," "The Framing of the Constitution," "Manifest Destiny," "The Civil War Period," "The Reconstruction Period," "Industrialization and Colonialization," "Immigration and Nationalism," and "World War I." Objectives stated as *concepts* for a science course might be "Science and Knowledge," "Science and Method," "Science and Humanity," "Science and Environment," "Science, Products, and Technology," and "Science and Space." Examples of objectives stated as *general behaviors* (which are not easy to measure or observe) might be phrased "To develop critical thinking in . . . ," "To increase understanding of . . . ," and "To have experience for . . . ."

Course objectives (as well as program objectives) help the teacher organize the content in terms of scope (topics, concepts, behaviors to be covered), continuity (recurring and continuing opportunity to teach important content and practice certain skills and tasks), sequence (cumulative development or successive treatment of topics, concepts, or behaviors that build upon preceding ones), and integration (relationships of content in one course to content in another course).[11]

Classroom Objectives

Classroom objectives are usually formulated by the teacher. Classroom objectives divide course objectives into several units. Unit plan objectives usually encompass one to three weeks of instruction, organized in a sequence and corresponding to expectations for the entire class, not for particular individuals or groups. Unit plan objectives are then further divided to create *lesson plan objectives,* organized ideally around one day of instruction on a particular subject.

Unit Plan Objectives are usually categorized into topics or concepts. Recall the history course objective "The Framing of the Constitution." This topic might be divided into the following units: "To understand the system of American government," "To comprehend the rights of American citizens," "To identify characteristics of a democratic society," and "To apply the principles of American government to classroom and school activities."

The science objective written as the concept "Science and Method" might be broken down into the following unit plan objectives: "To organize inductive, deductive, and intuitive methods in answering questions about the (a) biological world, (b) chemical world, and (c) physical world"; "To organize scientific information according to (a) logic, (b) explanations, (c) causal relations, (d) hypotheses, and (e) projections"; "To acquire the methods of (a) inquiry, (b) experimentation, and (c) problem solving"; and "To show interest in scientific hobbies or projects."

Unit plan objectives are sometimes called *general instructional objectives.* They should be specific enough to provide direction for instruction but not so specific that they restrict the teacher's selection of instructional methods, materials, and activities. Several different instructional techniques—lectures, discussions, demonstrations, laboratory work, textbook assignments, inquiry, cooperative learning—might be used to achieve the unit plan objectives. If you are in a state that utilizes INTASC or PRAXIS, you will be required to perform certain planning tasks (e.g., create lesson plans with objectives appropriate to diverse learners) during, for example, your PRAXIS III performance assessment, which will occur during your first year of teaching.

Lesson Plan Objectives, sometimes called *specific instructional objectives,* further define the unit objectives by providing clear direction for teaching and testing. Instructional objectives at the lesson plan level state (1) expected behaviors in terms of specific skills, tasks, or attitudes and (2) content. They may also state (3) outcomes or goals, sometimes called *standards,* in terms of level of achievement, proficiency, or competency and (4) conditions of mastery. There is currently debate on how detailed these objectives should be and whether too much specificity narrows a teacher's options.

Lesson plan objectives are more specific than unit plan objectives. Whereas lesson plan objectives may include outcomes and conditions for a specific instructional sequence, unit plan objectives do not. Whereas lesson plan objectives usually include specific methods, materials, or activities, unit plan objectives may or may not, and if they do they make them more general. However, the two levels of objectives do have several characteristics in common. Such characteristics as described by Taba are listed in Table 3.5. Taba presents

table 3.5   **Characteristics of Instructional Objectives at the Classroom Level**

1. A statement of objectives should describe both the kind of behaviors expected and the content or the context to which that behavior applies.

2. Complex objectives need to be stated analytically and specifically enough so that there is no doubt as to the kind of behavior expected or what the behavior applies to.

3. Objectives should also be formulated so that clear distinctions are required among learners to attain different behaviors.

4. Objectives are developmental, representing roads to travel rather than terminal points.

5. Objectives should be realistic and should include only what can be translated into . . . classroom experience.

6. The scope of objectives should be broad enough to encompass all types of outcomes for which the school [or teacher] is responsible.

Source: Hilda Taba. *Curriculum Development: Theory and Practice.* New York: Harcourt Brace Jovanovich, 1962, pp. 200–205.

historical grounding for the lesson planning process. Her approach suggests the timelessness of good planning—set clear objectives that are understandable and relevant.

To understand the kind of specificity involved in the two levels of classroom objectives, consider this unit plan objective, stated as a concept: "To gain understanding of graphs." Lesson plan objectives for this unit might read as follows:

1. To identify different types of graphs when using different types of data

2. To identify important terms of a graph

3. To implement practical application of graphs

Some educators would feel that these lesson objectives are not specific enough, since they lack outcomes and mastery level.[12] They might rewrite them in the following way:

1. All students will be required to identify which sets of data are best represented by a bar graph, line graph, and circle graph. Seventy-five percent of the class are expected to earn 75 percent or higher.

2. High-achieving students will be required to demonstrate understanding of five terms associated with graphs by (a) defining them and (b) supplying appropriate illustrations of each term. No more than one error will be permitted for moving to the next sequence of material.

3. All students will be required to read an annual corporate report and translate the narrative into at least three graphs to state the financial condition of the company in terms of (a) income, (b) operating cost, and (c) assets and liabilities. A panel of three students must unanimously agree that the graphs are accurate.

There is also an emerging technological sophistication with which learning objectives can be developed and assessed. Teachers are pulling goals from websites and then developing objectives and posting those on school websites for administrators to review. You likely will begin teaching in such a situation and you may be attending an institution that requires you to use one of the Internet based resources to create and structure your lessons. Review Study 3.2: Technology for Assessment to see how assessment is connected to goal setting.

case study 3.2   Technology for Assessment

Consider the way Chad Raisch, an AP teacher in Centerville, Ohio, uses technology for assessing whether defined learning objectives are achieved.

One way I have been able to assess my students' mastery of classroom objectives is through the use of student-generated review activities. I teach two advanced placement social studies courses, both of which culminate in a different examination offered by the College Board each spring. I have found that consistent review of the material aids student understanding and will help them earn better scores on the AP test. To this end, I have my students create their own interactive review activities with the software program Hot Potatoes. Then we post them to our class website. In assessing student projects, I have utilized Rubistar (rubistar.4teachers.org), which helps teachers create rubrics for nearly any project-based activity, including multimedia design. This website offers an excellent tutorial; additionally, any rubric created on the site not only can be saved for up to a year, but also can be accessed and changed. What follows is a rubric I created for the student project mentioned, in only a few minutes.

Web Site Design: Interactive Review Activity—'Standard' Quiz

Teacher name: Mr. Raisch
Student name: _____

CATEGORY	Excellent (8)	Good (6)	Satisfactory (4)	Needs Improvement (2)
Background	Background is exceptionally attractive, is consistent across pages, adds to the theme or purpose of the site, and does not detract from readability.	Background is attractive, is consistent across pages, adds to the theme or purpose of the site, and does not detract from readability.	Background is consistent across pages and does not detract from readability.	Background detracts from the readability of the site.
Color Choices	Colors of background, fonts, unvisited and visited links form a pleasing palette, do not detract from the content, and are consistent across pages.	Colors of background, fonts, unvisited and visited links do not detract from the content and are consistent across pages.	Colors of background, fonts, unvisited and visited links do not detract from the content.	Colors of background, fonts, unvisited and visited links make the content hard to read or otherwise distract the reader.
Graphics	Graphics are related to the theme/purpose of the site, are	Graphics are related to the theme/purpose of the site,	Graphics are related to the theme/purpose of the site and are of good quality.	Graphics seem randomly chosen, are of low quality, or distract the reader.

CATEGORY	Excellent (8)	Good (6)	Satisfactory (4)	Needs Improvement (2)
Graphics (cont.)	thoughtfully cropped, are of high quality, and enhance reader interest or understanding.	are of good quality, and enhance reader interest or understanding.		
Links (content)	All links point to high quality, up-to-date, credible sites.	Almost all links point to high quality, up-to-date, credible sites.	Most links point to high quality, up-to-date, credible sites.	Fewer than $\frac{3}{4}$ of the links point to high quality, up-to-date, credible sites.
Copyright	Fair use guidelines are followed with clear, easy-to-locate, and accurate citations for all borrowed material. No material is included from websites that state that permission is required unless permission has been obtained.	Fair use guidelines are followed with clear, easy-to-locate and accurate citations for almost all borrowed material. No material is included from websites that state that permission is required unless permission has been obtained.	Fair use guidelines are followed with clear, easy-to-locate and accurate citations for most borrowed material. No material is included from websites that state that permission is required unless permission has been obtained.	Borrowed materials are not properly documented or material was borrowed without permission from a site that requires permission.
Spelling and Grammar	There are no errors in spelling, punctuation, or grammar in the final draft of the website.	There are 1–3 errors in spelling, punctuation, or grammar in the final draft of the website.	There are 4–5 errors in spelling, punctuation, or grammar in the final draft of the website.	There are more than 5 errors in spelling, punctuation, or grammar in the final draft of the website.
Content	The site has a well-stated clear purpose and theme that are carried out throughout the site.	The site has a clearly stated purpose and theme but may have one or two elements that do not seem to be related to it.	The purpose and theme of the site are somewhat muddy or vague.	The site lacks a purpose and theme.
Layout	The website has an exceptionally attractive and usable layout. It is easy to locate all	The website has an attractive and usable layout. It is easy to	The website has a usable layout but may appear busy or boring. It is easy to locate most of the	The website is cluttered looking or confusing. It is often difficult to locate important elements.

CATEGORY	Excellent (8)	Good (6)	Satisfactory (4)	Needs Improvement (2)
Layout (cont.)	important elements. White space, graphic elements, and/or alignment are used effectively to organize material.	locate all important elements.	important elements.	
Content Accuracy	All information provided by the student on the website is accurate, and all the requirements of the assignment have been met.	Almost all the information provided by the student on the website is accurate, and all require-ments of the assignment have been met.	Almost all of the information provided by the student on the website is accurate, and almost all of the requirements have been met.	There are several inaccuracies in the content provided by the students or many of the requirements were not met.
Learning of Material	The student has an exceptional understanding of the material included in the site and where to find additional information; can easily answer questions about the content and procedures used to make the website.	The student has a good understanding of the material included in the site; can easily answer questions about the content and procedures used to make the website.	The student has a fair understanding of the material included in the site; can easily answer most questions about the content and procedures used to make the website.	Student did not appear to learn much from this project; cannot answer most questions about the content and the procedures used to make the website.

QUESTIONS FOR REFLECTION

1. Visit the website that Chad Raisch refers to. In what ways might you be able to use it for content lessons you are teaching?
2. Chad Raisch discusses the use of rubrics with advanced placement students. What, if any, problems might you have with students who are not high performing?
3. Many states have the standards clearly posted on their department of educa-tion website. They also post sample lesson plans, along with detailed objec-tives. Do you think it is appropriate for teachers to access this information directly through a website similar to the way Chad Raisch has done it in his lesson? Or, should teachers develop their own?

Source: Based on rubric retrieved on August 20, 2002, from rubistar.4teachers.org/view_rubric.php3?id=321451.

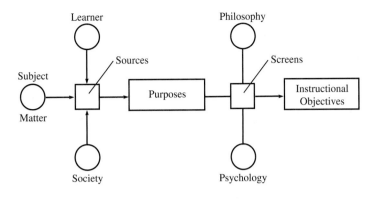

figure 3.2   Tyler's Method for Formulating Objectives.

Formulating Goals and Objectives

In our discussion so far, we have been using several words—*aims, goals, or standards, objectives*—that have subtle differences in meaning related to different levels of education (national to classroom) and different levels of abstractness. At one end of the continuum are the value-laden abstract aims of society; at the other end are concrete objectives describing specific behaviors. Most teachers tend to favor the middle of the continuum, where goals and objectives are observable but not necessarily stated as clearly measurable or, if measurable, stated without proficiency levels. They may use such terms as *list, describe,* and *identify* in writing their classroom objectives, but unless they are behaviorists or advocate outcome-based education, they may not always incorporate precise outcomes and conditions of mastery. There is no universal *right* way. What is right for you will likely be prescribed for you by your administrator.

Tyler Model

Ralph Tyler uses the term *purposes* when discussing what we call the goals of the school.[13] He indicates that educators need to identify purposes (goals) by gathering data from three sources: learners, society, and subject specialists. Educators then filter their identified purposes (or goals) through two screens: philosophy and psychology. What results from the screening are more specific and agreed-upon objectives, or what he calls *instructional objectives* (Figure 3.2).

Even though Tyler uses the term *instructional objectives,* he is not advocating narrow behavioral objectives. For Tyler, objectives cannot be deduced from tiny bits of data or only from objective data. The formulation of objectives involves the intelligence, insight, values, and attitudes of people involved in making decisions. Wise choices cannot be made without the most complete data available, but judgments must still prevail. We now turn to Tyler's three sources from which to select goals and two screens for refining goals into objectives.

Source 1, Studies of the Learners: The responsibility of the school is to help students meet their needs and develop to their fullest potential. Studies that focus on educational needs of students, that distinguish between what the schools do and what other social institutions do, that distinguish between what is done and what should be done, and that identify or differentiate gaps between students of the particular school (or school district) and students elsewhere, provide a basis for the selection of goals for the school program. It is possible to identify needs that are common to most students on a national, state, and local basis, as well as other needs that are common to all students in a school or to a certain group of students within a school or school district.

Source 2, Studies of Contemporary Life Outside of School: Educators must be aware of the tremendous impact of the increasingly rapid rate of change, the explosion of knowledge, and the increasing complexity of technology in our lives today and tomorrow. The trouble is that preparation for the future involves skills and knowledge that we may not fully understand today. As we analyze contemporary life, we need to study life at the community level in terms of needs, resources, and trends, as well as study larger societal issues that extend to state, national, and international levels. For example, in preparing students for the world of work, it is necessary to look at local work conditions and opportunities, but some students will move to other states or regions, requiring consideration of conditions and opportunities elsewhere as well. Further, we live in a "global village," one that is strongly interconnected: State, national, and international conditions eventually affect conditions at the community level.

Source 3, Suggestions from Subject Specialists: Every subject area has its professional associations that list goals and important knowledge in its field. Over the past several years, professional associations such as the National Council of Teachers of Mathematics and National Science Teachers Association have been more active in defining what students need to know (see again Table 3.1). A more detailed example is found in Table 3.6. Some agencies (such as BattelleforKids) are now creating materials that clearly illustrate for teachers the specific academic content standards for a state, the benchmarks and indicators by standards, and even the benchmarks and indicators by grade level (see, for example, www.battelleforkids.org).

Screen 1, The Use of Philosophy: Once purposes have been identified from studies of the learner, society, and subject areas, the educator must review and refine them in light of philosophy and psychology, or as Tyler says, filter them through two screens. As a school tries to outline its educational program, "the educational and social philosophy of the school can serve as the first screen."[14] We should be aware of the values and way of life we are trying to preserve and what aspect of society we wish to improve. Goals should be consistent with the democratic values and ideals of our society, in all aspects of living. In this country, education is for democracy, and this overriding philosophy must be reflected in our school goals.

Screen 2, The Use of Psychology: Goals must be in conformity with the psychology of learning; that is, the theories, concepts, and specific findings we accept. "A psychology of learning includes a unified formulation of the processes involved, such as how learning takes place, under what conditions, and what mechanisms and variables operate."[15] In formulating goals teachers need to consider how appropriate they are in terms of what is known about learning—whether they can be achieved, how they can be achieved, and what the cost and time will be. Teachers should reject goals that conflict with their viewpoints about the psychology of learning or that will compromise a student's potential for learning.

A great deal has occurred since Tyler first did his work in the early 1950s. Today, there is substantial controversy about how to use standards and specify goals and objectives. According to some critics of Tyler's work, there are simply so many goals and objectives, that teachers are forced to choose among them, which limits the freedom of a teacher. As a result, teachers are so focused on the prescribed curriculum that they fail to see the real needs of the learner. Wiggins and McTighe argue for establishing objectives, but they do so by carefully deciding what results they desire for students after reviewing national, state, and local standards. In essence, teachers must make choices. Some goals represent enduring understandings (i.e., the significant ideas that students need to explore and really "get inside of"), others are important to understand and do, and still others are worth being familiar with.[16] Four criteria or "filters" are used to answer the question "what is worthy and requiring of understanding?"

1. To what extent does the idea, topic, or process represent a "big idea" having enduring value in the classroom?
2. To what extent does the idea, topic, or process reside at the heart of the discipline?
3. To what extent does the idea, topic, or process require "uncoverage" (i.e., ideas that often have student misconceptions associated with them and require more in-depth explanation)?
4. To what extent does the idea, topic, or process offer potential for engaging students?[17]

Wiggins and McTighe then have teachers using standards to shape what is worthy and requiring of understanding. Table 3.7 depicts the process of using standards for determining what is worthy and then identifying learning experiences to teach that content. The important thing to note here is that teachers can start with standards/goals and move toward learning experiences or they can decide on the desired results and then plan back through what evidence (of learning) they want and then what learning experiences they need to provide. Notice that in Table 3.7 Wiggins and McTighe go from a focus on standards (clear objectives) to a process for how to teach students to achieve those learning goals—their stage 3.

The reason we highlight this process outlined by Wiggins and McTighe is because of the current debate concerning constructivism. In Chapter 1 we discussed briefly constructivism and its several variations. In general, constructivism is more student centered and focuses on helping students create and structure their own understandings and knowledge. Some critics of constructivism (e.g., Jeanne Chall) decry the use of student-centered approaches because they believe they compromise the quality of the learning environment; their argument is that the emphasis is on student centeredness at the expense of teacher-defined content.[18] Others argue that a form of constructivism and student-centered instruction is absolutely essential if students are truly going to learn how to learn.[19] In the next chapters we will more fully explore how you can act in a way that informs your practice and also moves beyond

table 3.6   **National Science Teachers Association Sample Learning Goals for Students: Science Content Standards**

Content Standard: K–12

Unifying Concepts and Processes

Content standard: As a result of activities in grades K–12, all students should develop understanding and abilities aligned with the following concepts and processes:

• Systems, order, and organization

• Evidence, models, and explanation

• Constancy, change, and measurement

• Evolution and equilibrium

• Form and function

Content Standards: K–4

Science as Inquiry

Content standard A: As a result of activities in grades K–4, all students should develop

• abilities necessary to do scientific inquiry.

• understanding about scientific inquiry.

Physical Science

Content standard B: As a result of the activities in grades K–4, all students should develop an understanding of

• properties of objects and materials.

• position and motion of objects.

• light, heat, electricity, and magnetism.

Life Science

Content standard C: As a result of the activities in grades K–4, all students should develop an understanding of

• the characteristics of organisms.

• the life cycles of organisms.

• organisms and environments.

---

the debate. Good teaching is not an either-or matter: teacher centeredness vs. student centeredness. It is, instead, what and how oriented—what goals and how to teach to them.

Taxonomy of Educational Objectives

Another way of formulating instructional objectives is to categorize the desired behaviors and outcomes into a system analogous to the classification of books in a library, the chemical elements in a periodic table, or the divisions of the animal kingdom. Through this system of categorization, known as a ***taxonomy of educational objectives,***

table 3.6   **National Science Teachers Association
Sample Learning Goals for Students:
Science Content Standards**

....

Earth and Space Science

Content standard D: As a result of the activities in grades K–4, all students should develop an understanding of

- properties of earth materials.
- objects in the sky.
- changes in earth and sky.

Science and Technology

Content standard E: As a result of the activities in grades K–4, all students should develop

- abilities of technological design.
- understanding about science and technology.
- abilities to distinguish between natural objects and objects made by humans.

Science in Personal and Social Perspectives

Content standard F: As a result of the activities in grades K–4, all students should develop an understanding of

- personal health.
- characteristics and changes in populations.
- types of resources.
- changes in environments.
- science and technology in local challenges.

History and Nature of Science

Content standard G: As a result of the activities in grades K–4, all students should develop an understanding of

- Science as a human endeavor.

Source: Lawrence F. Lowery (ed.) *NSTA Pathways to the Science Standards: Elementary School Edition.* Arlington, Va.: National Science Teachers Association, 1997, p. 134. See also the current (2003) website for an elaboration of these standards: www.nap.edu/readingroom/books/nses/html/index.html. Note: These are selected standards for K–12 and not inclusive of all that is required.

standards for classifying objectives have been established, and educators are able to be more precise in their language. The taxonomy is rooted in Tyler's ideas that all words in a scientific system should be defined in terms of observable events and that educational objectives should be defined operationally in terms of performances or outcomes. This method of formulating objectives can be used for writing objectives at the program and course level. By adding specific content, the objectives can be used at the classroom level, including the lesson plan level.

The educational taxonomy calls for the classification of learning into three domains: cognitive, affective, and psychomotor. The *Taxonomy of Educational Objectives, Handbook I: Cognitive Domain* was developed by a committee of thirty-six

table 3.7   The Big Picture of a Lesson Design Approach

Key Design Question	Design Considerations	Filters (Design Criteria)	What the Final Design Accomplishes
Stage 1: What is worthy and requiring of understanding?	National standards State standards District standards Regional topic opportunities Teacher expertise and interest	Enduring ideas Opportunities for authentic, discipline-based work Uncoverage* Engaging	Unit framed around enduring understandings and essential questions
Stage 2: What is evidence of understanding?	Six facets of understanding Continuum of assessment types	Valid Reliable Sufficient Authentic work Feasible Student friendly	Unit anchored in credible and educationally vital evidence of the desired understandings
Stage 3: What learning experiences and teaching promote understanding, interest, and excellence?	Research-based repertoire of learning and teaching strategies Essential and enabling knowledge and skill	Where is it going? Hook the students. Explore and equip. Rethink and revise. Exhibit and evaluate.	Coherent learning experiences and teaching that will evoke and develop the desired understandings, promote interest, and make excellent performance more likely

Source: Grant Wiggins and Jay McTighe. *Understanding by Design.* Alexandria, Virginia: Association for Supervision and Curriculum Development, 1998, p. 18. * Areas of student misunderstanding that require more explanation.

researchers from various universities headed by Benjamin Bloom.[20] The **cognitive domain** includes objectives that are related to recall or recognition of knowledge and the development of higher intellectual skills and abilities. David Krathwohl and associates created the *Taxonomy of Educational Objectives, Handbook II: Affective Domain.* The **affective domain** is concerned with aims and objectives related to interests, attitudes, and feelings.[21] The original group of researchers never completed the description of the **psychomotor domain,** which deals with manipulative and motor skills. However, Anita Harrow created such a classification of psychomotor objectives that comes close to satisfying the intent of the original group.[22] The fact that it was published by the same company that published the original two taxonomies adds to the validity of this version of the psychomotor domain.

In 2001, the Bloom Taxonomy was significantly revised. Because the vast majority of persons reading this book will be in programs that are implicitly or explicitly organized around the original structure, we have made a conscious decision to structure the domains in this textbook around the traditional framework, but we will rely on elements of the new as well. The new taxonomy has a knowledge dimension and a cognitive process dimension. The knowledge dimension focuses on factual, conceptual, procedural, and metacognitive knowledge. The metacognitive category is an especially significant addition because it focuses on the students' knowledge about cognition in general and personal cognition in particular. The categories in the cognitive dimension are outlined in Table 3.8. In the new taxonomy, the knowledge dimension is on one conceptual axis and the cognitive process is on another. Hence, for factual knowledge, teachers might identify learning objectives for cognitive processes involving remembering (Table 3.8, 1) or analyzing (Table 3.8, 4) or for procedural knowledge they might identify learning objectives for understanding (Table 3.8, 2) or creating (Table 3.8, 6). The old taxonomy included knowledge and cognitive process in one category. Here is the old model, and it is the taxonomy still used in most school districts.

Cognitive Domain

1. *Knowledge:* This level includes objectives related to (a) knowledge of specifics, such as terminology and facts; (b) knowledge of ways and means of dealing with specifics, such as conventions, trends and sequences, classifications and categories, criteria, and methodologies; and (c) knowledge of universals and abstractions, such as principles, generations, theories, and structures. Example: to identify the capital of France.

2. *Comprehension:* Objectives at this level relate to (a) translation, (b) interpretation, and (c) extrapolation of materials. Example: to interpret a table showing the population density of the world.

3. *Application:* Objectives at this level relate to the use of abstractions in particular situations. Example: to predict the probable effect of a change in temperature on a chemical.

4. *Analysis:* Objectives relate to breaking a whole into parts and distinguishing (a) elements, (b) relationships, and (c) organizational principles. Example: to deduce facts from a hypothesis.

5. *Synthesis:* Objectives relate to putting parts together in a new form such as (a) a unique communication, (b) a plan of operation, and (c) a set of abstract relations. Example: to produce an original piece of art.

6. *Evaluation:* This is the highest level of complexity and includes objectives related to judging in terms of (a) internal evidence or logical consistency and (b) external evidence or consistency with facts developed elsewhere. Example: to recognize fallacies in an argument.

Affective Domain

1. *Receiving:* These objectives are indicative of the learner's sensitivity to the existence of stimuli and include (a) awareness, (b) willingness to receive, and (c) selective attention. Example: to identify musical instruments by their sound.

2. *Responding:* These include active attention to stimuli such as (a) acquiescence, (b) willing responses, and (c) feelings of satisfaction. Example: to contribute to group discussions by asking questions.

t a b l e 3 . 8   **The Six Categories of the Cognitive Process Dimension and Related Cognitive Processes**

Process Categories	*Cognitive Processes and Examples*
1. REMEMBER—Retrieve relevant knowledge from long-term memory.	
1.1 RECOGNIZING	(e.g., recognize the dates of important events in U.S. history)
1.2 RECALLING	(e.g., recall the dates of important events in U.S. history)
2. UNDERSTAND—Construct meaning from instructional messages including oral, written, and graphic communications.	
2.1 INTERPRETING	(e.g., paraphrase important speeches and documents)
2.2 EXEMPLIFYING	(e.g., give examples of various artistic painting styles)
2.3 CLASSIFYING	(e.g., classify observed or described cases of mental disorders)
2.4 SUMMARIZING	(e.g., write a short summary of the events portrayed on videotapes)
2.5 INFERRING	(e.g., in learning a foreign language, infer grammatical principles from examples)
2.6 COMPARING	(e.g., compare historical events to contemporary situations)
2.7 EXPLAINING	(e.g., explain the causes of important eighteenth-century events in France)
3. APPLY—Carry out or use a procedure in a given situation.	
3.1 EXECUTING	(e.g., divide one whole number by another whole number, both with digits)
3.2 IMPLEMENTING	(e.g., determine in which situations Newton's second law is appropriate)
4. ANALYZE—Break material into constituent parts and determine how parts relate to one another and to an overall structure or purpose.	
4.1 DIFFERENTIATING	(e.g., distinguish between relevant and irrelevant numbers in a mathematical word problem)
4.2 ORGANIZING	(e.g., structure evidence in a historical description into evidence for or against a particular historical explanation)
4.3 ATTRIBUTING	(e.g., determine the point of view of the author of an essay in terms of his or her political perspective)
5. EVALUATE—Make judgments based on criteria and standards.	
5.1 CHECKING	(e.g., determine whether a scientist's conclusions follow from observed data)
5.2 CRITIQUING	(e.g., judge which of two methods is the best way to solve a given problem)
6. CREATE—Put elements together to form a coherent or functional whole, reorganize elements into a new pattern or structure.	
6.1 GENERATING	(e.g., generate hypotheses to account for an observed phenomenon)
6.2 PLANNING	(e.g., plan a research paper on a given historical topic)
6.3 PRODUCING	(e.g., build habitats for certain species for certain purposes)

Source: Lorin W. Anderson and David R. Krathwohl. *A Taxonomy for Learning, Teaching and Assessing.* © 2001, p. 31. Published by Allyn and Bacon, Boston, MA. Copyright © 2001 by Pearson Education. Reprinted by permission of the publisher.

3. *Valuing:* These include objectives regarding beliefs and evaluations in the form of (a) acceptance, (b) preference, and (c) commitment. Example: to argue over an issue involving health care.

4. *Organization:* This level involves (a) conceptualization of values and (b) organization of a value system. Example: to organize a meeting concerning a neighborhood's housing integration plan.

5. *Characterization:* This is the level of greatest complexity and includes behavior related to (a) a generalized set of values and (b) a characterization or philosophy of life. Example: to demonstrate in front of a government building on behalf of a cause or idea.

Psychomotor Domain

1. *Reflex movements:* Objectives relate to (a) segmental reflexes (involving one spinal segment) and (b) intersegmental reflexes (involving more than one spinal segment). Example: to contract a muscle.

2. *Fundamental movements:* Objectives relate to (a) walking, (b) running, (c) jumping, (d) pushing, (e) pulling, and (f) manipulating. Example: to run a 100-yard dash.

3. *Perceptual abilities:* Objectives relate to (a) kinesthetic, (b) visual, (c) auditory, (d) tactile, and (e) coordination abilities. Example: to distinguish distant and close sounds.

4. *Physical abilities:* Objectives relate to (a) endurance, (b) strength, (c) flexibility, (d) agility, (e) reaction-response time, and (f) dexterity. Example: to do five sit-ups.

5. *Skilled movements:* Objectives relate to (a) games, (b) sports, (c) dances, and (d) the arts. Example: to dance the basic steps of the waltz.

6. *Nondiscursive communication:* Objectives relate to expressive movement through (a) posture, (b) gestures, (c) facial expressions, and (d) creative movements. Example: to act a part in a play.

One point needs to be made about the cognitive domain. Bloom, in discussing the cognitive domain, asserts that "many teachers . . . prize knowledge . . . because of the simplicity with which it can be taught or learned."[23] Quite frequently we stop with the knowledge category, because it is easy to teach and test. All we have to do is ask our students: "What are three products of Brazil?" or "What is the chemical formula for water?" Another reason we can fail to move beyond the cognitive domain is that we may equate knowledge with intelligence. This is illustrated by the tendency to think that people who recall trivia information on a television quiz show are of superior intelligence. But it is not how much knowledge an individual possesses but what the individual can do with the knowledge that characterizes intelligence.

Once we study the taxonomy, it becomes apparent that most teaching and testing we have been exposed to as students have stressed knowledge—knowledge of facts, terms, conventions, classifications, categories, methods, and principles. As a teacher, you should not make the same mistake; rather, you should advance into other cognitive dimensions.

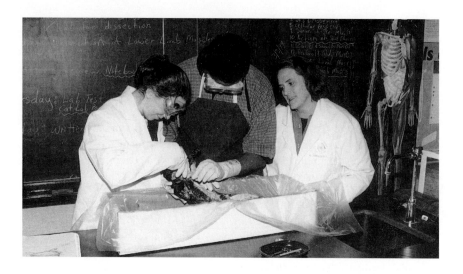

Achieving desired outcomes means that a teacher needs to know what knowledge students should acquire and what cognitive processes should be used to acquire it.

Establishing Specific Objectives

The three taxonomies describe levels of complexity from simple to more advanced. Each level is built upon and assumes acquisition of skills of the previous level. One must have knowledge of facts, for example, before one can comprehend material. The taxonomy as a whole is a useful source for developing educational objectives and for categorizing and grouping existing sets of objectives. Perhaps the greatest difficulty in using it is deciding between adjacent categories, particularly if the objectives have not been clearly stated. To avoid becoming frustrated while categorizing objectives into appropriate categories, classroom teachers are advised to work in groups and share opinions. By studying and using the taxonomy, they may eventually appreciate it as a valuable tool for identifying objectives and formulating test items.

After you have decided you want to use the taxonomy and after you have determined what you want your students to learn, you might systematically review the major classifications of the various domains to make sure you are familiar with each classification. You might then ask the following questions when formulating objectives in the cognitive domain:

1. *Knowledge:* What specific facts do you want the students to learn? What trends and sequences should they know? What classifications, categories, and methods are important for them to learn? What general principles and theories should they learn?

2. *Comprehension:* What types of translation will students need to perform? What types of interpretation? What types of extrapolation?

3. *Application:* What will students be required to perform or do to show they can use the information in practical situations?

4. *Analysis:* What kinds of elements should students be able to analyze? What relationships? What organizational principles?

5. *Synthesis:* What kinds of communication should students be able to synthesize? What kinds of operation? What kinds of abstraction?

6. *Evaluation:* What kinds of evaluation should students be able to perform? Can they use internal evidence? Can they use external evidence?

When asking these questions and when formulating instructional objectives according to the taxonomy, keep in mind that the classifications represent a hierarchy. Before students can deal with analysis, they must be able to function at the three previous levels; that is, knowledge, comprehension, and application. You should ask the same kinds of questions when writing objectives in the affective and psychomotor domains. Look at each level within the domain and ask what students are expected to achieve.

Tips for Teachers 3.1, 3.2, and 3.3 offer lists of key infinitives and direct objects for the cognitive, affective, and psychomotor domains. In all of these examples, no specific content is described so as to keep them applicable to all subjects.

General Objectives and Specific Learning Outcomes: The Gronlund Method

Norman Gronlund has developed a flexible way of formulating instructional objectives, whereby the teacher moves from a general objective to a series of specific learning outcomes, each related to the general objective. Gronlund's general objectives coincide with program (subject and grade) and course level objectives, and his specific learning outcomes coincide with unit plan and lesson plan objectives. He recommends that teachers start with general objectives because learning is too complex to be described in terms of specific behaviors or specific outcomes and because higher levels of thinking cannot be achieved by one specific behavior or outcome.

Gronlund has prepared a list of general objectives that can be used for almost any grade, subject, or course:

1. Knows basic terminology
2. Understands concepts and principles
3. Applies principles to new situations
4. Interprets charts and graphs
5. Demonstrates skill in critical thinking
6. Writes a well-organized theme
7. Appreciates poetry, art, literature, dance, etc.
8. Demonstrates scientific attitude
9. Evaluates the adequacy of an experiment[24]

Note that the behavior (verb) in each statement is general enough to permit a host of specific learning outcomes. There may be six or seven related specific outcomes for

tips for teachers 3.1

Key Words for the Taxonomy of Educational Objectives: Cognitive Domain

Taxonomy Classification	Examples of Infinitives	Examples of Direct Objects
1. Knowledge	To define, to distinguish, to acquire, to identify, to recall, to recognize	Vocabulary terms, terminology, meaning(s), definitions, referents, elements, facts, (sources), (names), (dates), (events), (persons), (places), (time periods), properties, examples, phenomena forms, conventions, uses, rules, ways, devices, symbols, representations, styles, formats, actions, processes, developments, trends, causes, relationships, influences, types, features, classes, sets, arrangements, classifications, categories, criteria, methods, techniques, uses, procedures, structures, formulations
2. Comprehension	To translate, to transform, to illustrate, to prepare, to read, to represent, to change, to rephrase, to restate, to interpret, to rearrange, to differentiate, to distinguish, to make, to explain, to demonstrate, to estimate, to infer, to conclude, to predict, to determine, to extend, to interpolate	Meanings, samples, definitions, abstractions, representations, words, phrases, relevancies, relationships, essentials, aspects, qualifications, conclusions, methods, theories, abstractions, consequences, implications, factors, ramifications, meanings, corollaries, effects, probabilities
3. Application	To apply, to generalize, to relate, to choose, to develop, to organize, to use, to employ, to transfer, to restructure, to classify Principles, laws, conclusions, effects, methods, theories, abstractions, situations, generalizations, processes, phenomena, procedures	Principles, laws, conclusions, effects, methods, theories, abstractions, situations, generalizations, processes, phenomena, procedures
4. Analysis	To distinguish, to detect, to identify, to classify, to discriminate, to recognize, to categorize, to analyze, to contrast, to compare, to distinguish, to deduce	Elements, hypotheses, conclusions, assumptions, arguments, particulars, relationships, interrelations, relevancies, themes, evidence, fallacies, cause-effects, consistencies, parts, ideas, assumptions, forms, patterns, purposes, points of view, techniques, biases, structures, themes, arrangements, organizations
5. Synthesis	To write, to tell, to relate, to produce, to transmit, to originate, to modify, to document, to propose, to plan, to design, to specify, to derive, to develop, to combine, to organize, to synthesize, to classify, to deduce, to develop, to formulate	Structures, patterns, products, performances, designs, works, communications, efforts, compositions, plans, objectives, specifications, operations, ways, solutions, means, phenomena, taxonomies, concepts, schemes, theories, relationships, abstractions, generalizations, hypotheses, discoveries
6. Evaluation	To judge, to argue, to validate, to assess, to decide, to consider, to compare, to contrast, to standardize, to appraise	Accuracies, consistencies, fallacies, reliability, flaws, errors, precision, exactness, ends, means, efficiency, economies, utility, alternatives, course of action, standards, theories, generalizations

Source: Newton S. Metfessel, William B. Michael, and Donald A. Kirsner, "Instrumentation of Bloom's and Krathwohl's Taxonomies for the Writing of Educational Objectives." *Psychology in the Schools* (July 1969): 227–231. Reprinted by permission of John Wiley & Sons, Inc.

Key Words for the Taxonomy of Educational Objectives: Affective Domain

Taxonomy Classification	Examples of Infinitives	Examples of Direct Objects
1. Receiving	To differentiate, to separate, to set apart, to share, to accumulate, to select, to combine, to accept, to select, to listen (for), to control	Sights, sounds, events, designs, arrangements, models, examples, shapes, sizes, meters, cadences, alternatives, answers, rhythms, nuances
2. Responding	To comply (with), to follow, to commend, to approve, to volunteer, to discuss, to practice, to play, to applaud, to acclaim, to augment	Directions, instructions, laws, policies, demonstrations, instruments, games, dramatic works, charades, speeches, plays, presentations, writings
3. Valuing	To increase measured proficiency in, to relinquish, to specify, to assist, to subsidize, to help, to support, to deny, to protest, to debate, to argue	Group memberships, artistic productions, musical productions, personal friendships, projects, viewpoints, arguments, deceptions, irrelevancies, abdications, irrationalities
4. Organization	To discuss, to theorize (on), to abstract, to compare, to balance, to organize, to define, to formulate	Parameters, codes, standards, goals, systems, approaches, criteria, limits
5. Characterization	To revise, to change, to complete, to require, to be rated high by peers in, to be rated high by superiors in, to avoid, to manage, to resolve, to resist	Plans, behaviors, methods, efforts, humanitarianism, ethics, integrity, maturity, extravagance(s), excesses, conflicts, exorbitancy/exorbitancies

Source: Newton S. Metfessel, William B. Michael, and Donald A. Kirsner. "Instrumentation of Bloom's and Krathwohl's Taxonomies for the Writing of Educational Objectives." *Psychology in the Schools* (July 1969): 227–231. Reprinted by permission of John Wiley & Sons, Inc.

each general objective that clarify what students will do to demonstrate achievement of the general objective.

Applying Gronlund's Objectives

The following two examples illustrate how to move students from general objectives to a series of related, intended learning outcomes.

I. Understands the meaning of concepts
    1. Explains the concept in own words
    2. Identifies the meaning of a concept in context
    3. Differentiates between proper and improper instances of a concept
    4. Distinguishes between two similar concepts on the basis of meaning
    5. Uses a concept to explain an everyday event

II. Demonstrates skill in critical thinking
    1. Distinguishes between fact and opinion
    2. Distinguishes between relevant and irrelevant information

Key Words for the Taxonomy of Educational Objectives: Psychomotor Domain

Taxonomy Classification	Examples of Infinitives	Examples of Direct Objects
1. Reflex movements	To flex, to stretch, to straighten, to extend, to inhibit, to lengthen, to shorten, to tense, to stiffen, to relax	Reflexes
2. Fundamental movements	To crawl, to creep, to slide, to walk, to run, to jump, to grasp, to reach, to tighten, to support, to handle	Changes location, moves in space while remaining in one place, moves extremities in coordinated fashion
3. Perceptual abilities	To catch, to bounce, to eat, to write, to balance, to bend, to draw from memory, to distinguish by touching, to explore	Discriminates visually, discriminates auditorially, discriminates kinesthetically, discriminates tactually, coordinates two or more perceptual abilities
4. Physical abilities	To endure, to improve, to increase, to stop, to start, to move precisely, to touch, to bend	Exerts tension, moves quickly, stops immediately, endures fatigue
5. Skilled movements	To waltz, to type, to play the piano, to plane, to file, to skate, to juggle, to paint, to dive, to fence, to golf, to change	Changes or modifies basic body movement patterns, uses a tool or implement in adaptive or skilled manner
6. Nondiscursive communication	To gesture, to stand, to sit, to express facially, to dance skillfully, to perform skillfully, to paint skillfully, to play skillfully	Moves expressively, moves interpretatively, communicates emotions, communicates aesthetically, expresses joy

Source: Adapted from Anita J. Harrow. *A Taxonomy of the Psychomotor Domain.* New York: McKay, 1972.

3. Identifies fallacious reasoning in written material
4. Identifies the limitations of given data
5. Formulates valid conclusions from given data
6. Identifies the assumptions underlying conclusions[27]

The learning outcomes listed are good examples of content-free objectives that can fit many different grade levels, subjects, and courses. Because Gronlund feels it is important to keep specific learning outcomes content free, they are not really applicable to the lesson plan level, which should be content oriented.

The teacher can add content to objectives. For example, an objective might be to identify three causes of World War I or to differentiate between a triangle and a rectangle. Gronlund maintains that once a teacher identifies content, there is a risk of writing too many objectives for each general objective or topic. But instead of making the objective to identify the causes of World War I, as most teachers would do, Gronlund would say the objective is to identify important historical causes and events. Instead of making the objective to differentiate between a triangle and a rectangle, the objective,

Using the Taxonomy

David R. Krathwohl
*Hannah Hammond Professor of Education, Emeritus
Syracuse University*

 I have always been surprised at how timid many individuals seem to be about modifying the taxonomy frameworks. I thought some words of encouragement from one of the taxonomy authors might make everyone freer to use them in their own way. Not only will we not take offense at your modifying them, we are delighted to have you make the structures your own and invest some of your talent in their further development.

Unlike the ten commandments, which are said to have come down from heaven, the taxonomies are not set in stone! They are just frameworks to make easier such tasks as curriculum and test development. Use them as jumping off places for modification; many people have. Look at how Christine McGuire changed the cognitive domain to better fit measuring the goals of medical education. She collapsed knowledge into two subcategories, expanded the application category (2.0, 3.0, and 4.0 below), and discarded the subcategories under evaluation and synthesis:

1.1 Items testing predominantly the recall of isolated information
1.2 Items testing recognition of meaning or implication
2.0 Generalization: Items requiring the student to select a relevant generalization to explain specific phenomena
3.0 Problem solving of a familiar type
3.1 Items requiring the student to make simple interpretations of data
3.2 Items requiring the student to apply a single principle or a standard combination of principles to a situation of a familiar type

4.0 Problem solving of an unfamiliar type
4.1 Items requiring the analysis of data
4.2 Items requiring the student to apply a unique combination of principles to solve a problem of a novel type
5.0 Evaluation: Items requiring the evaluation of a total situation
6.0 Synthesis: Items requiring synthesis of a variety of elements of knowledge into an original and meaningful whole[25]

The literature contains a variety of such adaptations of taxonomies. For example, all the chapter authors in Bloom, Hastings, and Madaus (specialists in art education, industrial arts, language arts, mathematics, pre-school, science, and social studies) struck off from ours to construct their own.[26] Consider these samples of their modifications of application:

- "functional application vs. expressive application"
- "solve routine problems, make comparisons, analyze data, and recognize patterns, isomorphisms, and symmetries"

These adaptations are a long way from the original framework aren't they? Many authors even blend affective and cognitive objectives in their structures.

Our experience suggests that the frameworks are most useful as you adapt them to fit your situation. Consider developing your own modifications or find one that fits your purposes.

Author's note: In 2001 David Krathwohl and Lorin Anderson revised Bloom's Taxonomy. This piece was written prior to the revision, but notice that Krathwohl suggests that teachers use the taxonomies "in their own way" and that he and others have now revised Bloom's work themselves. In essence, use the taxonomies to think about what students should learn and how you will have them learn it.

---

for Gronlund, is to differentiate between geometric shapes. Gronlund's content-free specific outcomes can be used up to the unit plan level; by including content they can be used at the lesson plan level.

Table 3.9 highlights Gronlund's steps for setting instructional objectives—both general and specific—and serves as a guide if you wish to adopt this method.

t a b l e   3 . 9   **Steps for Stating Instructional General Objectives and Specific Learning Outcomes**

Stating General Instructional Objectives

1. State each general objective as an intended learning outcome (i.e., pupils' terminal performance).
2. Begin each general objective with a verb (e.g., *knows, applies, interprets*).
3. State each general objective to include only one general learning outcome (e.g., not "Knows and understands").
4. State each general objective at the proper level of generality (i.e., it should encompass a readily definable domain of responses). Eight to twelve general objectives will usually suffice.
5. Keep each general objective sufficiently free of course content so that it can be used with various units of study.
6. State each general objective so that there is minimum overlap with other objectives.

Stating Specific Learning Outcomes

1. List beneath each general instructional objective a representative sample of specific learning outcomes that describes the terminal performance pupils are expected to demonstrate.
2. Begin each specific learning outcome with an action verb that specifies observable performance (e.g., *identifies, describes*). Check that each specific learning outcome is relevant to the general objective it describes.
3. Include a sufficient number of specific learning outcomes to describe adequately the performance of pupils who have attained the objective.
4. Keep the specific learning outcomes sufficiently free of course content so that the list can be used with various units of study.
5. Consult reference materials for the specific components of those complex outcomes that are difficult to define (e.g., critical thinking, scientific attitude, creativity).
6. Add a third level of specificity to the list of outcomes, if needed.

Source: Adapted from Norman E. Gronlund. *Measurement and Evaluation in Teaching,* 5th ed. New York: Macmillan, 1985, p. 46.

Specific Objectives: Mager Method

Robert Mager is more precise than Gronlund in his approach to formulating instructional objectives. His objectives have three components:

1. Behavior, or performance, which describes what the learner is expected to do. Example: to know, to use, to identify.
2. Condition, which describes under what circumstances or condition the performance is to occur. Example: given five sentences with adjectives . . . , based on the statement. . . .
3. Proficiency level, or criterion, which states an acceptable standard, competency, or achievement level. Example: 80 percent, 9 out of 10, judged correct by the teacher.[28]

Mager is controversial in his approach to writing instructional objectives, and therefore it might be worthwhile to state some of the arguments for and against his approach. Some educators (including Tyler and Gronlund) claim that Mager's method produces an unmanageable number of objectives, leads to trivia, and wastes time. They also contend that the approach leads to teaching that focuses on low levels of cognitive and psychomotor objectives, emphasizes learning of specific bits of information, and does not foster comprehension and whole learning.[29]

Mager and other educators argue that the approach clarifies what teachers intend, what students are expected to do, and what to test to show evidence of learning.[30] It provides a structured method for arranging sequences of skills, tasks, or content; provides a guide for determining instructional methods and materials; and adds precision for constructing tests. Most teachers prefer a less specific approach, corresponding more to the methods of Gronlund.

Applying Mager's Objectives

Using Mager's approach, a teacher could write hundreds of objectives for each unit, certainly for each course. If we selected his approach, we would first ask ourselves to identify or describe what the learner will be doing. Next we would identify or describe the conditions under which the behavior is to occur. Finally, we would state the performance criteria or achievement level we expect the learner to meet.

Here are some examples. The behavior, condition, and proficiency level are identified.

1. Given six primary colors, students will be able to identify five. The behavior is *to identify,* the condition is *given six primary colors,* and the proficiency level is *five out of six.*

2. Based on the reading passage in Chapter 7, students will compare the writing styles of Ernest Hemingway and John Steinbeck. Performance will be judged pass-fail by the teacher. The behavior is *to compare writing styles,* the condition is *after reading the passage in Chapter 7,* and the proficiency level is *to pass* (a subjective judgment by the teacher).

3. From the required list of 10 words, students will correctly spell 9. The behavior is *to spell,* the condition is *the required list of words,* and the proficiency level is *90 percent* (9 out of 10).

4. From the foul line, students will make 6 out of 10 baskets. The behavior is *to throw a basketball,* the condition is *from the foul line,* and the proficiency level is *60 percent* (6 out of 10).

5. The student will be able to complete a 100-item multiple-choice examination on the topic of pollution, with 80 items answered correctly within 60 minutes. The behavior is *to complete an exam,* the condition is *60 minutes,* and the proficiency level is *80 percent* (80 out of 100).

Mager lists eight phrases that he considers "fuzzy" and that should be avoided in formulating objectives: to know, to understand, to appreciate, to grasp the significance of, to enjoy, to believe, to have faith in, and to internalize. He lists nine phrases that are open to fewer interpretations and are more appropriate to use: to write, to recite, to identify, to sort, to solve, to construct, to build, to compare, and to contrast.

Writing Your Own Goals and Objectives

The task of writing goals and objectives for a school district, school, program, or course usually falls to a school committee. Individual classroom teachers are typically responsible for developing unit plans or lesson plans. For example, in the state of Ohio there are 600 school districts, and each one has its own course of study from which each teacher creates personal lesson plans. Ohio is a local control state, but state standards still exist that shape what teachers teach, and state assessment measures are being used now to determine whether students are learning requisite content. If you are a member of a district or school committee in any state, you should consult the following sources to make sure that your list corresponds to prescribed educational goals and objectives.

1. State standards (see www.achieve.org)
2. Learned society recommendations such as the National Council of Teachers of Mathematics (see again Table 3.1.)
3. Community concerns voiced by state and local business organizations and pressure groups
4. Parental concerns expressed in parental advisory committees, parent-teacher associations, and individual letters from parents
5. Professional literature on theories of learning and child development
6. Professional literature on student needs, assessments, and career choices[31]

Most published lists of objectives place primary emphasis on the cognitive domain; more limited attention is given to the affective and psychomotor domains. Lists of goals and objectives that have been published can be obtained from government agencies (state departments of education and regional educational agencies), professional agencies (Association of Supervision and Curriculum Development, Phi Delta Kappa), publishing companies and businesses, universities, and school districts. Objectives published by the government and schools can be obtained free of charge and, as noted, are often posted on websites by school districts or by state education agencies. Professional organizations may charge a nominal fee.

In formulating classroom-level objectives—for either unit or lesson plans—keep in mind the following concerns or general rules (see also Tips for Teachers 3.4).

1. They should be related to the developmental needs and tasks of the learners, which in turn are related to the age and experiences of the students.
2. They should be an outgrowth of diagnostic data (achievement, aptitude, personality, behavioral tests) and student records.
3. They should be consistent with professional and subject specialist opinions.
4. They should be consistent with teaching and learning theories and procedures.

Stating Classroom Objectives

 Theoretically sound and practical recommendations concerning the content and form of objectives are given here. These recommendations should help in the formulation of your own objectives at the unit plan and lesson plan level.

Content

1. Objectives should be appropriate in terms of the level of difficulty and prior learning experience of students.
2. Objectives should describe behaviors the teacher actually intends to act on in the classroom situation.
3. A useful objective will describe both the content and the cognitive process required for an appropriate student response.
4. The content of the objectives should be responsive to the needs of the individual and society.
5. A variety of types of knowledge should be expected, since most courses attempt to develop factual, conceptual, and procedural knowledge.

Form

1. Objectives should be stated in the form of expected student changes.
2. Objectives should be stated in behavioral or performance terms.
3. Objectives should be stated singly.
4. Objectives should be concise and trimmed of excessive verbiage.
5. Objectives should be grouped logically so they make sense in determining units of instruction and evaluation.
6. The conditions under which the expected student behavior will be observed should be specified.
7. If possible, the objective should contain criteria for acceptable performance. Criteria might involve time limits or a minimum number of correct responses.

Adapted from Allan C. Ornstein and Francis P. Hunkins. *Curriculum: Foundations, Principles and Issues,* 4th ed. Boston, Mass.: Allyn and Bacon, 2004. Grant Wiggins. *Educative Assessments.* San Francisco: Jossey-Bass, 1998.

5. They should build on student interests and strengths, not on adult interests and student weaknesses.

6. They should relate to the whole child and several domains of learning, not only to one aspect of learning or the cognitive domain.

7. They should foster lower- and higher-order thinking skills to cover the range of levels on Bloom's taxonomy.

8. They should be based on subject and grade level academic content standards.

9. They should be flexible enough to keep pace with changing educational and social situations.

Finally, no matter how carefully you plan your objectives, there are likely to be some unintended outcomes of instruction. These outcomes may be desirable or undesirable, and most are likely to fall into the affective domain of attitudes, feelings, and motivation about learning. For example, as a result of a language arts lesson on a Tolstoy novel, some students may become more interested in reading novels on their own or be motivated to read more books by Tolstoy. Other students may become bored with language arts or uninterested in reading novels. Even worse, teachers may fail to notice or may ignore such side effects, because they result more from the method than from the content of instruction and more from the teacher's behavior than from students' attitudes.

Additional Thoughts on Objectives

Both PRAXIS and INTASC require that teachers demonstrate an ability to create and define clearly articulated learning objectives. And even in those states that do not rely on PRAXIS or INTASC, teachers are expected to show that they can establish a meaningful lesson outline or guide. As a result, it is clear that as a teacher you are going to have to establish both general and specific objectives. At the present time and in almost all states the teacher uses the school district curriculum guide to establish specific learning objectives. This may change in the future. E. D. Hirsch, Jr. and others argue for nationalizing the curriculum. Hirsch contends that a nationalized curriculum better accommodates itself to a mobile student population—and American students are mobile.[32] Although it is doubtful that the nationalizing idea will immediately take hold, it is clear that the push for standards (and even national testing) will influence what you as a teacher might actually do when you enter the classroom.

Theory into Practice

Most teachers will be required to use objectives in the planning and implementation of their instruction. Depending on the philosophy and beliefs of your school (and supervisor), your formulation of objectives may be general or precise. What follows is a set of questions to cover both possibilities.

General Objectives

1. Have you determined the major objectives you wish to stress?
2. Are your objectives related to the goals of the school (grade level or department)?
3. Are your objectives related to sound principles of teaching and learning?
4. Are your objectives realistic in terms of students' abilities and the time and facilities available? Do students use different cognitive processes?
5. Are your objectives related to important learning outcomes?
6. Have you arranged the objectives according to some order of importance, domains of learning, or high-order/low-order cognitive, social, or psychological categories?
7. Have you arranged the content and activities of the subject so they correspond with the objectives?
8. Are you satisfied that your objectives coincide with the views (or values) of the parents and community? of established academic standards?

Precise Objectives

1. Have you clearly determined what you want the learner to accomplish? (Have you identified appropriate knowledge types and cognitive processes?)
2. Have you decided on who is to perform the desired behavior (e.g., the entire class, the more advanced group)?
3. Have you detailed through an action word the actual behavior to demonstrate mastery of the objective (e.g., to write, to describe)?

A Technology Viewpoint from a Classroom Teacher

Jackie Marshall Arnold
K–12 Media Specialist

 Creating and defining classroom objectives are critical to teaching. Creating instructional objectives should be done with great care and consideration to the many issues presented in this chapter. Technology can be a tool for teachers throughout this process.

Each national organization has defined standards that every teacher should be familiar with for his or her grade and subject. Each organization provides a website detailing those objectives (see table of organizations and their websites included in this chapter). Making a "bookmark" or a "favorite" of those sites would be a wise thing to keep those national guidelines close and at hand when you are writing objectives.

National standards also exist for technology skills in relation to students, teachers, and administrators. The International Society for Technology in Education (ISTE) has developed the National Educational Technology Standards (NETS) that define in six broad categories technological foundations that all students should have. In addition, ISTE has developed performance indicators that each student should have the opportunity to demonstrate at particular grade levels. These performance indicators and standards, as well as exemplary lessons and units integrating technology, can be found at ISTE's website (www.iste.org).

A critical component of instructional objectives is the assessment component. A well-created assessment will appropriately and creatively measure if the objective has been met. "Assessment of student achievement is changing, largely because today's students face a world that will demand new knowledge and abilities. In the global economy of the 21st century, students will need to understand the basics but also to think critically, to analyze, and to make inferences. Helping students develop these skills will require changes in assessment at the school and classroom level, as well as new approaches to large-scale, are high-stakes assessment" (NCREL, 1995). Classroom teachers can again rely on technology for assessment tools.

The Rubistar site that Chad Raisch (see Case Study 3.2) uses in his example is a fabulous free resource for teachers. By connecting to this site (http://rubistar.4teachers.org/) any teacher can create a rubric for any subject and save that rubric at the site for future use and revisions. A teacher can also use many previously created rubrics and adjust them for his or her own needs. The Rubistar site provides step-by-step directions that will allow a teacher to create his or her own personalized rubric in a short amount of time.

The Family Education Network also provides a site that can be of valuable use to any teacher. This site (www.teachervision.com) contains a lesson planning center. The center provides lesson plans with high quality objectives and online student activities. The site also houses a multitude of assessment resources including an online gradebook, quiz library, assessment forms, and alternative assessments.

Effective teachers who are creating high-quality objectives will look to the technology tools surrounding them to support their work. This Technology Viewpoint documents only a few of the multitude out there that can support the art and science of teaching.

4. Did you establish limiting and/or facilitating conditions under which the learner is to do what is asked (e.g., in one hour, with the textbook closed)?
5. Have you described the product or performance to be evaluated to determine whether the objective has been achieved (e.g., a report, a speech)?
6. Have you decided on a standard or achievement level that will be used to evaluate the success of the product or performance (e.g., 80 percent correct)?

Summary

1. Aims are broad statements about the intent of education as a whole. Goals or standards are statements about what students are expected to learn. Objectives specify content and behavior and sometimes a proficiency level to be achieved at some level of instruction.
2. Objectives are written at several levels, including program, grade, subject, course, classroom, unit plan, and lesson plan, and at several degrees of specificity, from broad to precise.
3. The most popular approaches to formulating objectives are based on the work of Tyler, Bloom, Gronlund, and Mager. Tyler identifies purposes and then to derive instructional objectives interprets them in the light of philosophical and psychological concerns.
4. Bloom's work (a taxonomy of educational objectives) entails three domains of learning: cognitive, affective, and psychomotor. The taxonomy was revised in 2001 to emphasize types of knowledge and cognitive processes.
5. Gronlund distinguishes between general objectives and specific learning outcomes.
6. Mager relies on three major characteristics for writing objectives: behavior, condition, and proficiency level.
7. A number of recommendations for writing objectives can facilitate teacher planning.

Questions to Consider

1. In terms of aims and goals, why is the question "What is the purpose of school?" so complex?
2. Why is it important for aims and goals to change as society changes?
3. What sources of information does Tyler recommend in formulating his objectives? Which source is most important? Why?
4. How does Gronlund distinguish between general objectives and specific learning outcomes?
5. What are the three components of Mager's objectives? Do teachers need to write objectives that include all three components?

Things to Do

1. Find a list of program or course goals in a curriculum guide and revise them to conform to the guidelines for writing objectives at a particular subject and grade level that you plan to teach.
2. Arrange the six categories of the cognitive domain into a hierarchy from simple to complex. Give an example of an instructional objective for each category for the content that you plan to teach.
3. Arrange the five categories of the affective domain into a hierarchy from simple to complex. Give an example of an instructional objective for each category.
4. Write six objectives for the subject you wish to teach at the lesson plan level. Use the methods of Bloom or Mager to write these objectives.

5. Identify the standards for your teaching area and examine them in relationship to a textbook that is being used by a local school district. Talk to a teacher in that district and inquire how he or she uses standards to shape classroom lessons.

Recommended Readings

Anderson, L. and Krathwohl, D. (eds). *Taxonomy for Learning, Teaching, and Assessing: A Revision of Bloom's Taxonomy of Educational Objectives.* New York: Longman, 2000. A revision of the taxonomical structure first put forth by Benjamin Bloom, this text illustrates the ways in which good instruction requires teachers to think broadly about the learning outcomes expected of students.

Bloom, Benjamin S., et al. *Taxonomy of Educational Objectives, Handbook I: Cognitive Domain.* New York: Longman, 1984. The *Taxonomy* describes six categories of the cognitive domain and identifies objectives and test items related to knowledge and problem-solving skills.

Krathwohl, David R., Benjamin S. Bloom, and Bertram Maisa. *Taxonomy of Educational Objectives, Handbook II: Affective Domain.* New York: Longman, 1984. This second part describes five categories of the affective domain and identifies objectives and test items related to feelings, attitudes, and values.

Marzano, Robert. *What Works in Schools.* Alexandria, Virginia: Association for Supervision and Curriculum Development, 2003. A wonderful synthesis of the curriculum and instruction implementation process that documents the various types of research supporting current practices.

Wiggins, G., and Jay McTighe. *Understanding by Design.* Alexandria, Virginia: Association for Supervision and Curriculum Development, 1998. This is an excellent text that helps teachers discern the difference between understanding and knowing. Many teachers think of covering content; the authors argue for striving to facilitate understanding.

Key Terms

affective domain 120	general instructional objectives 110	psychomotor domain 120
aims 96	goals 96	standards 110
classroom objectives 110	lesson plan objectives 110	taxonomy of educational objectives 118
cognitive domain 120	objectives 98	unit plan objectives 110
course objectives 108	program objectives 107	

End Notes

1. E. D. Hirsch Jr. *The Schools We Need.* New York: Doubleday, 1996.
2. Hilda Taba. *Curriculum Development: Theory and Practice.* New York: Harcourt Brace Jovanovich, 1962, p. 197.
3. Ibid.
4. Commission on the Reorganization of Secondary Education. *Cardinal Principles of Secondary Education.* Washington, D.C.: Government Printing Office, 1918.

5. National Commission on Excellence in Education. *A Nation at Risk: The Imperative for Reform.* Washington, D.C.: Government Printing Office, 1983.

6. Peter F. Oliva. *Developing the Curriculum,* 3d ed. New York: Harper Collins, 1992, p. 265.

7. Shirley M. Hufstedler. "The Once and Future K–12." *Phi Delta Kappan* (May 2002): 684–689. Allan C. Ornstein. "The National Reform of Education." *NASSP Bulletin* (September 1992): 89–105.

8. Myra P. Sadker and David M. Sadker. *Teachers, Schools, and Society.* New York: McGraw Hill, 1997, pp. 154–155.

9. James A. Banks. *Teaching Strategies for Ethnic Studies,* 7th ed. Boston, Mass.: Allyn and Bacon, 1993. Allan C. Ornstein and Francis P. Hunkins. *Curriculum: Foundations, Principles and Issues,* 4th ed. Boston, Mass.: Allyn and Bacon, 2004.

10. George J. Posner. *Analyzing the Curriculum.* New York: McGraw-Hill, 1992. George J. Posner and Alan N. Rudnitsky. *Course Design: A Guide to Curriculum Development for Teachers,* 4th ed. New York: Longman, 1994. Kevin B. Zook. *Instructional Design for Classroom Teaching and Learning.* Boston, Mass.: Allyn and Bacon, 2001.

11. Ronald C. Doll. *Curriculum Improvement: Decision Making and Process,* 10th ed. Needham Heights, Mass.: Allyn and Bacon, 1997. Allan C. Ornstein and Francis P. Hunkins. *Curriculum: Foundations, Principles, and Issues,* 2d ed. Needham Heights, Mass.: Allyn and Bacon, 1993.

12. W. James Popham. *Modern Educational Measurement,* 2d ed. Needham Heights, Mass.: Allyn and Bacon, 1990. Robert E. Slavin, *Educational Psychology: Theory into Practice,* 3d ed. Needham Heights, Mass.: Allyn and Bacon, 1992.

13. Ralph Tyler. *Basic Principles of Curriculum and Instruction.* Chicago: University of Chicago Press, 1949.

14. Ibid., p. 34.

15. Ibid., p. 41.

16. Grant Wiggins and Jay McTighe. *Understanding by Design.* Alexandra, VA: Association for Supervision and Curriculum Development, 1998, pp. 10–11.

17. Grant Wiggins. *Assessing Student Performance.* San Francisco: Jossey-Bass, 1999.

18. Jeanne Chall. *The Academic Achievement Challenge.* New York: Guilford Press, 2000.

19. John Bransford, Nancy Nye, and Helen Bateman. "Creating High Quality Learning Environments: Guidelines from Research on How People Learn." Presentation to the National Governor's Association, San Francisco, California, July 2002.

20. Benjamin S. Bloom, et al. *Taxonomy of Educational Objectives. Handbook I: Cognitive Domain.* New York: David McKay, 1956.

21. David R. Krathwohl, Benjamin S. Bloom, and Bertram Masia (eds.). *Taxonomy of Educational Objectives. Handbook II: Affective Domain.* New York: David McKay, 1964.

22. Anita J. Harrow. *Taxonomy of the Psychomotor Domain: A Guide for Developing Behavioral Objectives.* New York: McKay, 1972.

23. Benjamin S. Bloom, *Taxonomy of Educational Objectives, Handbook I, Cognitive Domain.* New York: David McKay, 1956, p. 34.

24. Norman E. Gronlund. *How to Write and Use Instructional Objectives,* 5th ed. New York: Macmillan, 1995, pp. 21 & 52–53. Norman E. Gronlund and Robert L. Linn. *Measurement and Evaluation in Teaching,* 7th ed. New York: Macmillan, 1995, pp. 41–42.

25. Christine McGuire. "A Process Approach to the Construction and Analysis of Medical Examinations." *The Journal of Medical Education,* vol. 38 (1963): 556–563.

26. Benjamin S. Bloom, J. Thomas Hastings, and George F. Madaus. *Handbook on Formative and Summative Evaluation of Student Learning.* New York: McGraw-Hill, 1971.

27. Norman E. Gronlund. *Assessment of Student Achievement.* Boston, Mass.: Allyn and Bacon, 2003

28. Robert F. Mager. *Preparing Instructional Objectives,* rev. ed. Belmont, Calif.: Fearon, 1984. The examples of each component are derived from the authors.

29. Ornstein and Hunkins, *Curriculum: Foundations, Principles, and Issues*; 4th ed. Boston, Mass.: Allyn and Bacon, 2004.

30. Lorin W. Anderson and David R. Krathwohl. *A Taxonomy for Learning, Teaching and Assessing.* Boston, Mass.: Allyn and Bacon , 2001. Popham, *Modern Educational Measurement.* Charles K. West, James A. Farmer, and Philip M. Wolff. *Instructional Design.* Needham Heights, Mass.: Allyn and Bacon, 1991.

31. Lynn L. Morris and Carol T. FitzGibbon, *How to Deal with Goals and Objectives.* Beverly Hills, Calif.: Sage, 1978. Michael Fullan. *The New Meaning of Change.* New York: Teachers College Press, 2001.

32. E. D. Hirsch, Jr. *The Schools We Need.* New York: Doubleday, 1996.

Instructional Planning

Pathwise criteria relevant to this chapter:

- Articulating clear learning goals for the lesson that are appropriate for the students (A2)
- Demonstrating an understanding of the connections between the content that was learned previously, the current content, and the content that remains to be learned in the future (A3)
- Creating or selecting teaching methods, learning activities, and instructional materials or other resources that are appropriate for the students and that are aligned with the goals of the lesson (A4)
- Making learning goals and instructional procedures clear to students (C1)
- Making content comprehensible to students (C2)

INTASC principles relevant to this chapter:

- The teacher understands the central concepts, tools of inquiry, and the structures of the discipline(s) he or she teaches and can create learning experiences that make these aspects of subject matter meaningful for students. (Principle 1)
- The teacher understands how children learn and develop and can provide learning opportunities that support their intellectual, social, and personal development. (Principle 2)
- The teacher understands and uses a variety of instructional strategies to encourage students' development of critical thinking, problem solving, and performance skills. (Principle 4)

focusing questions

1. How do teachers plan for instruction? At what levels do they plan?

2. How do teachers map a course of study?

3. What are the main components of a unit plan?

4. What are the main components of a lesson plan?

5. What components would be stressed in a mastery lesson plan? Creativity lesson plan?

6. How do unit and lesson plans facilitate teaching and instruction?

7. How does good planning relate to research available on how students learn and cognitive development?

8. How does a teacher decide whether to use methods of direct transmission or student construction of knowledge?

Effective planning is based on knowledge of 1) standards of the states; 2) the general goals of the school; 3) the objectives of the course or subject and the concomitant disciplinary standards; 4) students' abilities, aptitudes, needs, and interests; 5) content to be included and appropriate units into which the subject can be divided; and 6) techniques of short-range instruction or lesson planning.

Although planning is the shared responsibility of administrators, supervisors, and teachers, when you enter a school as a teacher, you must modify any existing plans and originate your own plans for instruction in the classroom. Those plans are represented in the curriculum (taught and hidden) that you emphasize in your classroom. As Table 4.1 illustrates, there are many different definitions of the curriculum as a plan. Each definition represents a different view of the learner and the learning process. A curriculum viewed as a plan represents a behaviorist interpretation, which includes a teacher-defined strategy for achieving desired goals or ends (and is rooted in the ideas of educators such as Ralph Tyler and Hilda Taba). Such an interpretation is quite different from viewing a curriculum as a set of experiences or activities (a progressive view where student interests drive instruction) or in terms of subject matter or academic content (a constructivist view, which we will discuss later).

How Teachers Plan

Teacher planning is a form of decision making. Planning a course, unit, or lesson involves making decisions in two areas: 1) subject matter (content) knowledge, concerning organization and presentation of content, knowledge of student understanding of content, and knowledge of how to teach the content; and 2) action system (pedagogical) knowledge, concerning teaching activities such as diagnosing, grouping, managing, and evaluating students and implementing instructional activities and learning experiences.[1] Both kinds of knowledge are needed for effective planning for instruction.

Some teachers have knowledge of subject matter but lack expertise in various aspects of action system knowledge. Research on out-of-field teachers (i.e., teachers who are teaching in areas in which they do not have an academic major) would suggest that they lack the content knowledge but may understand the process of grouping and managing students.[2]

John Zahorik, who sampled some 200 teachers, argues that most teachers do not engage in rational planning or make use of objectives. They tend to emphasize content,

table 4.1   Curriculum as a Plan: Some Definitions

The Curriculum is a planned program of learning opportunities to achieve broad educational goals and related objectives. (William Alexander)

The Curriculum is all of the learning of students that is planned by and directed by the school to attain its educational goals. (Ralph Tyler)

The Curriculum is a (set of) planned and guided learning experiences for the learners' continuous and willful growth. . . . (Daniel and Laura Tanner)

The Curriculum is a plan for learning. (Hilda Taba)

The Curriculum is a plan for what is to be taught and is composed of what is to be taught, to whom, when, and how. (John McNeil)

The Curriculum is planned actions for instruction. (James Macdonald)

The Curriculum of a school can be conceived of as a series of planned events that are intended to have educational consequences for one or more students. (Elliot Eisner)

Source: Jon W. Wiles. *Curriculum Essentials: A Resource for Educators.* Needham Heights, Mass.: Allyn & Bacon, 1999, p. 5. Copyright © by Pearson Education. Reprinted by permission of the publisher.

materials, resources, and learning activities.[3] Several years after Zahorik conducted his research, Clark and Peterson also found that teachers emphasize subject matter knowledge or content and instructional activities when planning a daily lesson. They spend the least time on planning objectives.[4]

Many teachers simply do not value the use of objectives or of detailed or elaborate lesson plans. Although researchers and professional educators tend to see logic in planned lessons, Elliot Eisner points out that most of what happens in the classroom cannot be observed, measured, or preplanned, and much of teaching is based on impulse and imagination and cannot be designed in advance.[5] There is, therefore, a tension between those who advocate detailed planning and those who suggest that teaching is too artful for such detailed planning. This textbook is oriented toward the former though we clearly acknowledge that good teachers do on occasion "teach to the moment" and rely on hunches and intuitive judgment.

The emergence of assessment measures that make public how much students are actually learning is impacting student learning. Assessments are based on standards that have been prescribed at the local, state, or national levels. Because teachers and schools are being held accountable for student performance on prescribed assessments, more teachers (and administrators) are ensuring a match between the taught curriculum and assessment. That makes sense! For teachers this means that they need to understand how to plan lessons around standards and the prescribed district curriculum and how to assess the growth of students using a variety of low-stakes testing measures (i.e., assessments that do not have retention or promotion consequences).

Standards are organized around the facts, concepts, principles, and skills that disciplinary experts believe every student at a grade level should know. Examples of such facts, concepts, principles, and skills categorized by various levels of learning are provided in Table 4.2. Standards do not prescribe the limits of what students learn, but rather establish a coherent structure for what is taught. Tomlinson observes,

t a b l e 4 . 2   **Examples of the Levels of Learning**

Levels of Learning	Science	Literature	History
Facts	Water boils at 212° C. Humans are mammals.	Katherine Paterson wrote *Bridge to Terebithia*. Definition of *plot* and definition of *character*	The Boston Tea Party helped to provoke the American Revolution. The first 10 amendments to the U.S. Constitution are called the *Bill of Rights*
Concepts	Interdependence Classification	Voice Heroes and antiheroes	Revolution Power, authority, and governance
Principles	All life forms are part of a food chain. Scientists classify animals according to patterns.	Authors use voices of characters as a way of sharing their own voices. Heroes are born of danger or uncertainty.	Revolutions are first evolutions. Liberty is constrained in all societies.
Attitudes	Conservation benefits our ecosystem. I am part of an important natural network.	Reading poetry is boring. Stories help me understand myself.	It's important to study history so we write the next chapters more wisely. Sometimes I am willing to give up some freedom to protect the welfare of others.
Skills	Creating a plan for an energy efficient school Interpreting data about costs and benefits of recycling	Using metaphorical language to establish personal voice. Linking heroes and antiheroes in literature with those of history and current life.	Constructing and supporting a position on an issue Drawing conclusions based on analyses of sound resources

Source: Carol Ann Tomlinson. *The Differentiated Classroom.* Alexandria, VA: Association for Supervision and Curriculum Development, 1999, p. 41.

Music	Math	Art	Reading
Strauss was The Waltz King. Definition of *clef*	Definition of *numerator* and *denominator* Definition of *prime numbers*	Monet was an Impressionist. Definition of *primary colors*	Definition of *vowel* and *consonant*
Tempo Jazz	Part and whole Number systems	Perspective Negative space	Main idea Context
The tempo of a piece of music helps to set the mood. Jazz is both structured and improvisational.	Wholes are made up of parts. The parts of a number system are interdependent.	Objects can be viewed and represented from a variety of perspectives. Negative space helps spotlight essential elements in a composition.	Effective paragraphs generally present and support a main idea. Pictures and sentences often help us figure out words we don't know.
Music helps me to express emotion. I don't care for jazz.	Math is too hard. Math is a way of talking about lots of things in my world.	I prefer Realism to Impressionism. Art helps me to see the world better.	I am a good reader. It's hard to "read between the lines."
Selecting a piece of music that conveys a particular emotion Writing an original jazz composition	Expressing parts and wholes in music and the stock market, with fractions and decimals Showing relationships among elements	Responding to a painting with both affective and cognitive awareness Presenting realistic and impressionistic views of an object	Locating main idea and supporting details in new articles Interpreting themes in stories

Standards should be a vehicle to ensure that students learn more coherently, more deeply, more broadly, and more durably. Sadly, when teachers feel pressure to cover standards in isolation, and when the standards are presented in the form of fragmented and sterile lists, genuine learning is hobbled, not enriched.[6]

Planning by Level of Instruction

Teachers should engage in four levels of planning: yearly (and in some cases semesters), unit, weekly, and daily. Planning at each level involves a set of goals, sources of information, forms or outlines, and criteria for judging the effectiveness of planning. Whereas yearly planning usually is framed around state and school district standards or curriculum guides, unit, weekly, and daily lesson planning permit wider latitude for teachers to develop their own plans, though teachers are still required to anchor what they teach to established goals and standards that exist in every disciplinary area. At the elementary school level, the principal is usually considered the instructional leader and is responsible for checking and evaluating the teachers' plans. At the secondary school level, the chair of the various subject or academic areas usually performs this professional role and works with teachers to improve instructional planning.

There are different sources of knowledge that influence teacher planning. Each of those will be discussed to some degree in this chapter, though the primary emphasis in Chapter 3 relates to how the goals of learning are identified and defined. Those goals emerge out of a context as illustrated by the following hierarchy:

National Standards

State Curricular Frameworks

District-Level Curriculum Guides

Teacher Unit Plans

Teacher Lesson Plans

Teacher Assessments

Notice that the top three are essentially controlled at the national, state, or district level, while the bottom three are under the direct decision-making of the teacher. The teacher makes general decisions with an awareness of national standards, state mandates and district requirements. So how do teachers make more specific decisions on what to include?

One researcher points out that middle-grade teachers rely most heavily on 1) previous successes and failures, 2) district curriculum guides, 3) textbook content, 4) student interest, 5) classroom management factors, 6) school calendar, and 7) prior experience when they plan at the yearly level. At the unit, weekly, and daily levels, they are mostly influenced by 1) availability of materials, 2) student interest, 3) schedule interruptions, 4) school calendar, 5) district curriculum guides, 6) textbook content, 7) classroom management, 8) classroom activity flow, and 9) prior experience.[7] According to Robert Yinger, planning is perceived as rational, logical, and structured and as being reinforced by a number of instructional and managerial routines. By the middle of the school year, about 85 percent of the instructional activities are routinized. In planning, teachers use instructional routines for questioning, monitoring, and managing students, as well as for coordinating classroom activities.[8]

But the teacher needs to include variety and flexibility in planning, as well as structure and routine, to take into account the students' differing developmental needs and interests. Some students, especially high achievers, divergent thinkers, and independent learners, learn more in nonstructured and independent situations, whereas many low achievers, convergent thinkers, and dependent learners prefer highly structured and directed environments.

The capacity of the teacher to differentiate instruction appears to be closely linked to student achievement across ability levels. Studies by William Sanders, who has established himself in education because of his value-added concept (how much value or learning is added by a teacher), suggest that the teachers most able to close the achievement gap between groups of students yet foster learning in all students are those who know how to differentiate instruction.[9] Chapter 2 provided one example of differentiation of instruction (Case Study 2.1). At other points throughout this text we'll examine how it is possible to match more closely teacher instruction with student learning needs. One way that that occurs is through good lesson planning.

Mental Versus Formal Planning

Gail McCutcheon maintains that the most valuable form of teacher planning at the classroom level is "the reflective thinking that many teachers engage in before writing a unit or lesson plan or while teaching a lesson [or even more important after teaching a lesson]."[10] Often the weekly or daily lesson plan is sketchily outlined. Much of what happens is a reflection of what happened in other years when the teacher taught a similar lesson. The structure develops as the teaching-learning process unfolds and as teachers and students interact in the classroom. Many actions related to planning cannot be predetermined in a classroom of thirty or more students who are rapidly interacting with their teacher.

Mental planning is the teacher's spontaneous response to events in the classroom; the teacher considers situations and responds intuitively. (Of course, that intuition must be well-grounded in subject matter and action system knowledge.) Mental planning is a part of teaching that is crucial for effectiveness, but it cannot easily be observed, recorded, or detailed. Therefore, it often goes unnoticed and unmentioned as part of the planning process.

Formal planning is what most educators and researchers recognize as a legitimate and necessary instructional activity. Perhaps it is examined so often simply because it can be prescribed, categorized, and classified. Formal planning is structured and task oriented; it suggests that teaching and instruction can be taught as part of teacher education and staff development. Further, if done correctly, it can be done to create a culturally responsive classroom and in a way that accommodates defined academic standards.

Specifically, the various academic standards created by organizations such as the National Council of Teachers of Mathematics (NCTM) and National Science Teachers Association (NSTA) can be used to create and organize lessons around certain culturally

table 4.3   Culturally Responsive Curriculum Principles

Instructional Examples (IE)

IE 1 =   Cultural examples used in the curriculum; inclusion

IE 2 =   Alternative perspectives

IE 3 =   Diversity and commonalities

IE 4 =   Culturally relevant and student-generated images/metaphors/examples

Student Engagement (SE)

SE 1 =   Purpose/curiosity/anticipation

SE 2 =   Multiple learning preferences

SE 3 =   Individual/unison/team communications

SE 4 =   Cooperative/competitive/individual goals

SE 5 =   Student choices/decision making

Assessment (A)

A 1 =   Ongoing assessment, using a range of materials

A 2 =   Assessment information to provide feedback and inform instruction

A 3 =   Special accommodations for special learners

Source: Jacqueline Jordan Irvine and Beverly Jeanne Armento. *Culturally Responsive Teaching.* Boston: McGraw Hill, 2001, p. 26. Reproduced with permission of the McGraw Hill Companies.

responsive principles. Beverly Armento takes three principles, one related to instruction, one to student engagement, and one to assessment and then examines how those principles can be embedded in lessons in ways that benefit diverse student groups.[11] A teacher identifies specific lesson objectives (related directly to established academic standards) and then identifies specific instructional strategies with an orientation to the principles outlined in Table 4.3. The teacher strives, for example, to allow different student voices to be heard (IE4) and to help students see the purpose for a lesson (SE1). These specific principles create an inclusiveness for the lesson but they do not compromise the rigor of what occurs. Lessons have clear objectives, are focused on standards and involve certain principles of culturally responsive instruction, and assess what students have learned through a range of materials and techniques and in ways that address the unique learning needs of special learners.

In essence, a ***culturally responsive classroom*** is one in which the teacher plans in a way that is inclusive, offers alternative perspectives, suggests commonalities as well as areas of diversity, and relies on some student-constructed (hence personally relevant) learning tasks. Further, students are engaged in learning as a result of understanding the purpose of learning, having a full range of learning modes available, using a full range of communication and interaction patterns, and appreciating the various choices that can and must be made while learning to learn. Finally, the teacher assesses what students learn in a way that is ongoing and formative in nature (i.e., provides feedback that shows students how they are progressing) and that accommodates special learners.[12] Notice that a culturally responsive curriculum does not mean you "take it easy" on the students. It means that you base instruction on defined academic standards and then try to make it relevant!

QUESTION FOR REFLECTION

The whole concept of culturally responsive teaching is controversial. Some conservative critics would argue that students learn best in highly teacher-centered classrooms, that content should be dictated by teachers, and that culturally responsive teaching (teaching that builds on student interests and backgrounds) is simply inappropriate. Many educators and especially many teacher trainers subscribe to the use of more student-centered strategies. They want to create classrooms where students' interests are considered part of the instructional sequence. The conflicting ideologies are increasingly evident in the debate about how to educate urban students. What approach do you subscribe to? Can you find research that supports your view? At the end of this chapter *The Academic Achievement Challenge* by Jeanne Chall is recommended. That book describes the problems with approaches similar to culturally responsive teaching. Chall argues for a highly teacher-centered approach. Find research that supports the culturally responsive, student-centered approach and compare what you discover with what Chall concludes. How do the types of students you teach potentially influence how you teach?

One way to begin to address this question is to examine the literature of two groups of educational writers. The first includes those who argue for culturally responsive teaching. For example, Gloria Ladson-Billings in her book *The Dreamkeepers* (see *Recommended Readings* at the end of the chapter) identifies specific characteristics of teachers who know how to deal with diverse student populations in classrooms. They see their role as one of "pulling knowledge out" of students rather than "pouring it in." In the second group, many conservative educational critics see culturally responsive teaching as a new form of student-centered instruction. Read articles from journals or newspapers such as *Education Next* to get a flavor of these critics' arguments. They assert that the limited skills of poor, urban students demand a more teacher-centered approach, and they claim that the evidence on student achievement backs them up.

Courses of Study

A long-range teacher guide is usually called a ***course of study*** or curriculum guide. In large school districts it is often prepared by a committee of experts. In small school districts the teachers, working as a group or as individuals, may develop their own, within limits defined by state guidelines or academic content standards. As a teacher plans, he or she must consider 1) needs assessment data, if available, for the

Good planning at the subject or grade level involves communication with colleagues.

school or district; 2) the goals of the school (or school district); 3) preassessment or placement evaluation data of the students, such as reading tests, aptitude tests, self-report inventories, and observational reports; and 4) instructional objectives of the course of study according to district or state guidelines and grade level or departmental publications.[13]

The course of study details the content, concepts, skills, and sometimes values to be taught for the entire course. Ideally, a prescriptive course of study places the teacher in a better position to do unit and lesson planning. The document helps guide and connect the goals and objectives of the course. It helps teachers view the course as a whole and to see existing relationships. The teacher must know, before the term or school year begins, what the important content areas, concepts, and skills of the course are. Some states require school districts to have courses of study, so you will need to see if one is available for the area you teach.

In general, the course of study provides a total view of the entire term's or year's work without specifying sequences or relationships of tasks. Read Case Study 4.1 to help you decide what you would do as a teacher trying to match the curriculum with the learner. The teacher, Bob Kimball, is trying to differentiate to accommodate different student levels of motivation and student ability.

Unit Plans

A *unit plan* is a blueprint to clarify what content will be taught by what learning experiences during a specific period of time. It incorporates goals and objectives from the course of study. One reason for developing unit plans is related to the theory that learning by wholes is more effective than piece-by-piece learning; units help learners

Bob Kimball had decided in his junior year of college to become a teacher. He wasn't quite sure what had convinced him to change his major from business administration, but it was clear that he wanted to work with young people. Fortunately, his first two years of college consisted mainly of general education courses, and after seeing an academic adviser, he was able to switch his major to mathematics education. . . .

Teaching, Bob concluded, would allow him to combine two things that were personally rewarding. First, he had always been a good mathematics student, and he found this subject to be personally challenging. He recognized that he did much better in mathematics than most other students. Second, holding a teaching post would make it possible for him to continue coaching—a job he had come to love. . . .

Just prior to graduation, Bob had interviews with six school districts. This culminated in three job offers. He decided to accept a position at Burtonville Middle School. There he would teach five classes of mathematics and coach the eighth-grade football team.

Burtonville is a suburban community that is continuing to grow. The middle school, which contains grades 6, 7 and 8, has an enrollment of just under 900 students. For the most part, the students come from middle-class families.

Bob was assigned to teach three sections of seventh-grade mathematics, an algebra class (taken by selected eighth-grade students), and a section of applied mathematics (a remedial-type class for eighth-grade students). This meant that Bob had to prepare for three different classes and coach football—a somewhat difficult assignment for a new teacher.

After just two or three weeks of school, it was clear to Bob that teaching the algebra class was the easiest assignment he had. The students were all bright; they were highly motivated. By contrast, his applied mathematics course was a real challenge. Increasingly, he found himself devoting more of his planning time to this course.

In observing students in the five classes assigned to him, Bob deduced that those in the applied class were far less motivated than the others. He had some students in his seventh-grade classes who were not highly motivated either, but they were a small portion of the class.

As the school year moved into October, Bob decided that his traditional approaches were not effective with the applied mathematics class. He was relying on the textbook to sequence instruction, and his teaching methodology consisted largely of lecturing on a concept and then having students do exercises or homework on the material he covered. Of the twenty-two students in this class, probably no more than five or six seemed to be paying attention at any given time. Often homework assignments were not completed, or they were done incorrectly. Weekly quizzes were serving to verify Bob's observations. Only a handful of students seemed to be mastering the material.

Pondering ways that he could improve his performance, Bob remembered two experiences from his college classes. One related to a teaching methods class in which the professor stressed the importance of developing daily lesson plans. He also recalled a video presentation in one of his educational psychology classes that showed how motivation was a key factor, especially with special-needs students. It featured an alternative school in California that was able to get students excited about learning. To do this, the teachers took risks; they strayed from traditional teaching methods and materials. For example, students were able to start their own company that specialized in removing graffiti from city property (a topic many of the students knew a great deal about). In doing this, they learned mathematics in a very practical way. And not only did they learn, they actually became excited about going to school.

Although Bob had been sketching out what he intended to do in each class, he really did not consider this to be detailed lesson planning. When he started the school year, he figured he would cover the content in the textbook over the course of the year (applied mathematics was a two-semester course). There were seventeen chapters in the book, and Bob thought that he would do one chapter approximately every two weeks.

Bob decided to change his teaching tactics to assure that (1) he would do more detailed planning, and (2) he would make the learning experiences more relevant for the students. He recognized that to do the latter, he might have to become far less reliant on his textbook. That might mean jumping around from fractions to multiplication to decimals. He decided that getting his students excited about learning mathematics was more important than following a prescribed path.

One of the first things that Bob did to pursue his new course of action was to develop a list of potential resource people and activities that he could integrate into his applied class. The list included the following:

- Invite a car salesman to talk to the class about how people finance cars. This will lead to a discussion of loans and interest rates.
- Invite a sportswriter from the local paper to discuss how baseball batting averages are calculated.
- Invite an owner of a boutique to discuss financial concepts related to operating a small business (e.g., calculating overhead expenses, estimating profits).
- Take a field trip to a manufacturing plant to see how workers are required to use mathematics in their jobs.
- Have the students create their own candy company so that they can manage funds.
- Study how much it costs to operate a car on an annual basis (e.g., cost of insurance, gasoline).

Each night before a scheduled activity, Bob detailed a plan of how he would spend each of the forty-seven minutes of class time. He wanted to make sure that the time would be used wisely. For the activity with the car salesman, for example, he decided that three class periods would be needed. His daily plans for [two of the] sessions are listed here:

Monday, November 2

10:00–10:05 Introduce Jack Davis of Burtonville Buick and outline for the students what he will be discussing.

10:05–10:35 Mr. Davis talks about the cost of new and used automobiles.

10:35–10:47 Time for student questions

Give students the following assignment: If a woman earns $35,000 per year and buys a used car for $6,300, what percent of her annual income does she spend on this one item?

Tuesday, November 3

10:00–10:05 Discuss assignment from previous day.

10:05–10:35 Mr. Davis discusses how car prices are determined (e.g., the value of options, the concept of depreciation).

10:35–10:47 Time for student questions

Give students the following assignment: A person buys a new car that has the following price breakdown: base price = $9,200; options = $3,100; dealer preparation costs = $410; sales tax = $460. What is the total price of the car? What percent of the total cost is due to options? What percent of the cost is due to dealer preparation and sales tax?

Although students reacted positively to special sessions such as those with Mr. Davis, subsequent quizzes and tests failed to show that students had progressed. By mid-November, Bob was truly concerned. Another cause for alarm was the fact that his principal had come to observe his teaching only once. He visited the algebra class in late September for twenty minutes and subsequently sent Bob a note saying, "Keep up the good work."

Mathematics at the school was in a combined department with science; and the chair of the department, a science teacher, had never even asked Bob how his classes were progressing. Feeling that he was pretty much on his own, he turned to a friend and colleague in the mathematics department, Sarah Allen. Although Sarah was only in her second year of teaching, she had already acquired a reputation as an outstanding instructor. The third full-time mathematics teacher in the department was Mr. Chambers, who kept to himself; Bob had barely gotten to know him.

After listening to Bob explain his difficulties with the applied mathematics class, Sarah asked if the same problems were evident in his four other classes. Bob said that they were not. It was his observation that the other students were responding well to his traditional approaches to teaching—especially the students in the algebra class.

"Although I think I have gotten the students more excited about mathematics, I'm not sure they are learning enough," Bob explained.

Sarah said, "What units are you covering during the first semester?"

"I started out following the chapters in the textbook; however, when I decided to try to liven things up for the students, we started jumping around a bit. I do plan my lessons daily. But I try to take advantage of whatever math skills are associated with the activity," Bob explained.

Having said that, Bob reached into his briefcase and pulled out a folder containing the three lesson plans that involved Mr. Davis, the car salesman. Sarah read each one and then asked, "What specifically were you trying to teach with these lessons?"

"Well, we were able to look at problems involving division and the students got exposure to interest and interest payments."

Sarah asked yet another question: "But how does that fit into your overall plans for instruction during this semester?"

"Right now my main objective is to find out what excites these students. I'm convinced that once they see that math is so necessary to their lives, they'll be more willing to learn." Bob paused and asked Sarah, "Do you think I am approaching this in the right way? Is there something I should be doing that I'm not? Now that football season is ending, I'll be able to devote a little more time to this class, and I want to make sure that I'm going in the right direction."

Put yourself in Sarah's position. What advice would you give Bob?

Questions for Reflection

1.   Do you agree with Bob's judgment that he has to use motivational techniques to get these students interested in studying mathematics? Why or why not?
2.   In your opinion, does Bob have a good perspective with regard to what he hopes to accomplish in this class? What evidence did you use to arrive at your answer?
3.   Do you classify Bob's activities as an attempt to use "discovery learning?" Why or why not?
4.   How do you assess Bob's decision to turn to Sarah for help? Should he have asked someone more experienced (e.g., the principal)? If you had teaching difficulties, to whom would you turn for help?
5.   Should low-achieving students be placed in one class? Would these students do better if they were dispersed among the other eighth-grade students?

Source: Adapted from T. J. Kowalski, R. A. Weaver, and K. T. Henson. *Case Studies of Beginning Teachers.* 5e. Published by Allyn and Bacon, Boston, Mass. Copyright © by Pearson Education. Reprinted by permission of the publisher.

see and make conceptual connections. Another is the need for teachers to plan experiences in advance to meet different kinds of objectives. Advance planning at the unit plan level enables teachers to be more effective in designing and structuring the instructional process. The overall view such planning provides helps teachers anticipate problems that may arise, especially in terms of prerequisite content, concepts, and skills.

Components of the Unit Plan

The unit plan may consist of six basic components. They are objectives, content, skills, activities, resources and materials, and assessment and evaluation (see Table 4.4). All should be considered when planning a unit, although in many cases all six components do not have to be specified.

table 4.4   Unit Plan Components

1. *Objectives*
    General objectives and specific objectives
    Behavioral objectives or nonbehavioral objectives (topics, problems, questions)

2. *Content*
    Knowledge (factual, conceptual, procedural)
    cognitive processes (remember, understand . . .)

3. *Skills*
    Work habits
    Discussion and specific communication skills
    Reading skills
    Writing skills
    Note-taking skills
    Dictionary skills
    Reference skills (table of contents, glossary, index, card catalog)
    Library skills
    Reporting and research skills
    Computer skills
    Interpreting skills (maps, charts, tables, graphs, legends)
    Inquiry skills (problem solving, experimenting, hypothesizing)
    Social skills (respecting rules, accepting criticism, poise and maturity, peer acceptance)
    Cooperative and competitive skills (leadership, self-concept, participation in group)

4. *Learning activities*
    Lectures and explanations
    Practice and drill
    Grouping activities (buzz sessions, panels, debates, forums)
    Role-playing, simulations, dramatizations
    Research, writing projects (stories, biographies, logs)
    Experiments, inquiry, and discovery
    Field trips
    Reviews

5. *Resources and materials*
    Written materials (books, pamphlets, magazines, newspapers)
    Audiovisual materials (films, records, slides, television, videotapes)
    Programmed or computer materials
    Models, replicas, charts, graphs, specimens

6. *Assessment and Evaluation*
    Demonstrations, exhibits, debates
    Reviews, summaries
    Quizzes, examinations
    Reteaching
    Remediation
    Exhibitions

Objectives

As was discussed in the previous chapter, objectives can be behavioral (e.g., given five fractions or decimal problems the student will be able to complete each pattern to 70 percent accuracy) or nonbehavioral (topics, problems, questions). Most teachers today rely on behavioral objectives partly because of recent emphasis on them in the professional literature. The method one uses as the core of a plan will depend on one's approach and the schools' approach to planning units.

Content

The scope of the content should be outlined. The content often includes two major categories: knowledge cognitive processes. The development of factual and procedural knowledge is usually more important at the elementary school level and with teachers who emphasize mastery learning, although types of knowledge are being emphasized by more educators at all levels because of high stakes testing. Abstract knowledge is more important at the secondary school level and with teachers who emphasize conceptual understandings. Teachers use the district's course of study and national or state standards to determine what knowledge and which cognitive processes to teach and even the sequence of the lessons.

Skills

Some teachers create what is often an optional list of cognitive and social skills. The skills should be based on the content to be taught but are sometimes listed separately from the content. Important skills to develop include critical thinking, critical reading, skimming and scanning, problem solving, reading graphic materials (maps, diagrams, charts, tables), library skills, composition and reporting skills, note-taking skills, homework skills, study skills, social and interpersonal skills, discussion and speaking skills, cooperative and competitive skills, and leadership skills.

Learning Activities

Learning activities, sometimes called *student activities,* should be based on students' needs and interests. Only special activities, such as guest speakers, field trips, debates and buzz sessions, research reports, projects, experiments, and summative examinations, need be listed. The recurring or common activities can be shown as part of the daily lesson plan.

Resources and Materials

The purpose of including resources and materials in the plan is to guide the teacher in assembling the reading material, library and research materials, and audiovisual equipment needed to carry out instruction. This list at the unit plan level should include only essential resources and materials. A list of resources is often included in a listing of learning activities and so is sometimes considered an optional element in a unit plan.

There is a wealth of lesson plans, units, websites and resources on-line that can be utilized as well. For example, the New York City Board of Education provides on its website (www.nycenet.edu/oit/netplans.htm) a variety of ways to use the internet as part of lesson planning. They include, for example, specific ideas on motivation and homework:

Movtivation: The teacher might use interesting facts from the internet to begin a discussion at the beginning of a period.

Homework: The teacher can create optional homework sites for students who have home internet access.

Organizing and Implementing Unit Plans

 As you prepare your unit and lesson plans, you should be aware of common mistakes. The idea is to minimize them by following guidelines that have proved to be practical, by discussing plans with your colleagues or supervisor, and by practicing. What follows is a list of suggestions that apply to all levels of unit planning and can be adapted to accommodate your school's requirements and your teaching style and instructional approach.

1. Ask your principal or supervisor for the standards and curriculum guides (or the course of study) pertaining to your subject and grade level.
2. Check the instructor's manual of the textbook or workbook, if you are using one; many have excellent examples of unit plans and many relate content to broader sets of disciplinary standards.
3. Consider vertical (different grades, same subject) and horizontal (same grade, different subjects) relationships of subject matter in formulating your unit plans. Be sure you understand the relationship between new information and prior knowledge.
4. Consider students' abilities, needs, and interests.
5. Decide on objectives and related content for the various units of the subject.
6. After objectives and content have been established, sequence the units.

7. Determine the order of the content by considering the cognitive processes (remembering, applying) and affective processes (attitudes, feelings, values) involved. You can use developmental theories, mastery learning, or task analysis to determine the order of the units.
8. Consider appropriate time allocation for each unit. Most units will take one to three weeks to complete.
9. Investigate resource materials and media available in your district and school; incorporate appropriate materials and media.
10. Provide opportunities for student practice and review.
11. Provide opportunities for evaluation (not necessarily testing or marks in early grades). Consider also what types of exhibitions might be appropriate.
12. Ask your colleagues or supervisor for feedback after you implement your unit plan; discuss questions, problems, and proposed modifications.
13. Rewrite or at least modify your unit plan whenever you teach the same subject and grade level; the world changes, classes change, and students differ.
14. Be patient. Do not expect immediate results. Practice will not make you perfect, but it will make you a better teacher.

Assessment and Evaluation Procedures

The major evaluation procedures and culminating activities, both formative and summative, should be included. Plans might list student exhibits and demonstrations, summary debates and discussions, quizzes and examinations, reteaching, remedial work, and special tutoring or training. Evaluation can be conducted by students or the teacher or both. The intent is to appraise whether the objectives have been achieved and to obtain information for improving the unit plan. We will discuss assessment and evaluation procedures in more depth in Chapters ten and eleven.

See Tips for Teachers 4.1 for some suggestions for organizing and implementing unit plans.

Approaches to Unit Planning

Teachers should check with supervisors before planning a unit. Some school districts have a preferred approach for developing units, and others permit more latitude for their teachers. For example, some supervisors require teachers to submit units for final approval, while other supervisors give more professional autonomy to teachers. What follows are basic approaches to unit planning that you may wish to consider. Regardless of the approach you use, it is imperative to consider depth over breadth when developing unit plans. Good teachers cover material but provide more opportunities for students to learn specific content material. Reform advocates in education such as E. D. Hirsch, Jr. reinforce this focus on specificity and depth:

> There is another inherent shortcoming in the overreliance on large-scale abstract objectives (as opposed to "mere" content) as a means of determining a curriculum. These general objectives do not compel either a definite or a coherent sequence of instruction. That is because the large conceptual scheme and its concrete expressions (through particular contents) have a very tenuous and uncertain relationship to each other. A big scheme is just too general to guide the teacher in the selection of particulars. For instance, one multigrade science objective in our superior local districts states, "Understand interactions of matter and energy." This is operationally equivalent to saying, "Understand physics, chemistry, and biology." The teachers who must decide what to include under such "objectives" are given little practical help.[14]

Taxonomic Approach

Table 4.5 illustrates a unit plan based on the taxonomy of educational objectives. The objectives are divided into three domains of learning: cognitive processes, attitudes and values, and psychomotor skills. The unit plan gives a daily problem that leads to the objectives and shows corresponding activities and materials and resources. Evaluation is not listed separately but is blended as part of the activities suggested for the ninth and tenth daily problem lessons. The approach requires that students use different cognitive processes to learn fully requisite content.

Topic Approach

Table 4.6 illustrates the topic or theme approach. The unit plan is organized by topics. Objectives introduce the lesson, but the topics serve as the major basis for outlining the unit and especially the lessons. The objectives coincide with the recommendation that content focus on concepts, skills, and values. Note that the objectives (related to knowledge, skills, and values) do not build upon one another (they are somewhat independent), nor are they divided into general and specific. The topics are arranged in the order in which they will be treated, suggesting that they correspond to the table of contents of a textbook. Indeed, it is appropriate to follow a text, as long as it is well-planned and the teacher knows when to modify or supplement the text with related activities and materials.

The topics also represent daily lesson plans. The activities listed are nonrecurring, special activities; repeated activities can be listed at the lesson plan level. The activities are listed in the order in which they will occur, but there is not one particular activity listed for each topic (as in Table 4.5). The evaluation component is separate and includes formative and summative tests, discussion, and feedback. Most secondary school teachers rely on the topic approach to unit planning, since they are subject or content oriented.

There is no right way to plan, though one method may better foster the types of learner outcomes that you desire. If you plan on using a taxonomic approach, you will likely be more oriented toward the explicit standards for your teaching area. What is prescribed? What is the sequence for the prescribed content? The topic approach identifies areas to be covered along with specific knowledge skills and attitudes for students to learn. If you use a topic approach, you might find it useful to review work by Howard Gardner on multiple intelligences and on an approach that he describes as "entry points" to learning. Gardner describes five such entry points:

Narrational: Presenting a strong or narrative about the topic or concept in question

Logical—Quantitative: Using numbers or deductive/scientific approaches to the topic or question

Foundational: Examining the philosophy and vocabulary that undergird the topic or concept

Aesthetic: Focusing on the sensory features of the topic or concept

Experiential: Using a hands-on approach where the student deals directly with materials that represent the topic or concept[15]

The one advantage of the Gardner "topic" or theme approach to unit planning is that it allows students to relate to content material in a more direct sense. The entry points foster a type of curriculum relevance and also may connect more with what we know about how the brain works and processes ideas. Brain researchers argue for using knowledge meaningfully, and that's precisely what Gardner's entry points approach accomplishes.

Guidelines for Developing Unit Plans

The number of units and the time allotted and emphasis for each unit are matters of judgment, although school practitioners tend to recommend about fifteen to thirty units for a year's course and about five to ten lessons per unit. Consideration is usually given to the organization of the textbook, the emphasis suggested by state and school district curriculum guides, and the special abilities, needs, and interests of the students. There is an increasing tendency for teachers to plan units around national, state, and school district testing programs.[16]

We've already examined the basic components of the unit plan. Now let us consider suggestions for dealing with some of the details. These suggestions are applicable for all subjects and grade levels:

1. Develop the unit plan with a particular class and group of students in mind.

2. Indicate the subject, grade level, and length of time to teach the unit.

3. Outline the unit around a general theme or idea (the unit title).

4. Identify the relevant standards on which your unit will be based.

5. Identify the general objectives, problems, or topics of the unit. Each objective, problem, or topic should correspond to a specific lesson plan

table 4.5   **Unit Plan: Taxonomic Approach for Environmental Science**

Problems	Cognitive Processes	Attitudes and Values
1. Identifying an environment	To identify environments based on physical and biological characteristics	To explore social and scientific issues; to ask questions
2. Comparing environments	To understand different environments	To discuss alternative viewpoints; to debate responsibility for health and welfare of others
3. Taking a field trip to compare environments	To analyze environments based on physical and biological characteristics	To formulate new ideas about natural resources
4. Experiencing other ways to compare environments	To evaluate environments based on physical and biological characteristics	To ask questions; to compare alternative viewpoints
5. Summarizing differences between environments	To evaluate different environments	To discuss balance and theorize ideas
6. Exploring the limits of environmental change	To deduce that environments change and still conserve their identity and that they lose identity when their capacity to change is exceeded	To ask questions; to define limits of biological and environmental systems
7. Understanding the consequences of changing environment	To appraise the results of changing environments	To seek alternative viewpoints; to revise ideas
8. Implementing a plan to improve the school environment	To recognize how to create environments that change and improve	To demonstrate responsibility for health and welfare of others
9. Surveying world environments that have changed	To detect how world environments have changed and assumed new identities	To demonstrate the need to use natural resources wisely; to organize a plan that contributes to the conservation of natural resources
10. Summarizing and evaluating	To remember facts, concepts, and principles	To argue, appraise, and judge in terms of scientific standards

Source: Adapted from Rita Peterson et al. *Science and Society: A Source Book for Elementary and Junior-High Science Teachers.* Columbus, Ohio: Merrill, 1984: pp. 166–167.

(discussed in the next section) and each should be tied directly (or indirectly) to an academic content standard.

6. Include one or more of the following: a) content and activities, b) cognitive processes and skills, c) psychomotor skills, and d) attitudes and values.

Psychomotor Skills	Learning Activities	Resources and Materials
	Class discussion	Video, internet
To use tools that call for fine adjustment and discrimination	Debates	Pictures, replicas, models
To visualize different environments; to listen to tour guides present relevant information	Field trip to museum	Tape recorder
To manipulate laboratory equipment	Experiment (see text)	Plants, rocks, soil
	Class discussion	Visiting expert
To handle plants, rocks, soil	Class discussion	Graphs and maps showing weather, volcanoes, mountains,
To use equipment that requires fine adjustments	Student interviews	"Old-timers" in community, old newspapers
To use and care for tools and equipment	Brainstorming sessions	Visiting administrator
	Oral reports judged by students	Technical journals, library materials
	Unit examination	

7. Identify methods for assessing and evaluating the outcomes of the unit. Possibly include a pretest and posttest to determine learning outcomes or improvement in learning.

8. Include resources (materials and media) needed to supplement the text.

t a b l e   4 . 6   **Unit Plan: Topic Approach for American History**

....

Objectives

   I.   Knowledge
   1.   To recognize that the U.S. Constitution is rooted in English law
   2.   To identify the causes and events leading to the forming of the U.S. Constitution
   3.   To argue the advantages and limitations of the U.S. Constitution
   4.   To illustrate how amendments are enacted

  II.   Skills
   1.   To expand vocabulary proficiency
   2.   To improve research skills
   3.   To improve oral reporting skills
   4.   To expand reading habits to include historical events and people
   5.   To develop debating techniques

 III.   Values
   1.   To develop an understanding that freedom is based on laws
   2.   To recognize the obligations of freedom (among free people)
   3.   To appreciate how rights are protected
   4.   To develop a more positive attitude toward minorities
   5.   To develop a more positive attitude toward classmates

Topics

   I.   Historical background of the Constitution
   1.   English common law
   2.   Magna Carta
   3.   Mayflower Compact
   4.   Colonial freedom
   5.   Taxation without representation
   6.   Boston Tea Party
   7.   First and second Constitutional Congress
   8.   Declaration of Independence
   9.   Age of Enlightenment and America

---

   9. Plan an effective way of introducing the unit, possibly through an overview exercise, problem, or recent event.

 10. Design parts of the unit for different types of learners (some hands-on activities, some inquiry strategies).

 11. Develop the unit to include the life experiences of the students or out-of-school activities such as field trips, or work in the library or community.

Lesson Plans

....

A *lesson plan* sets forth the instructional activities for each day; it is sometimes referred to as a *daily plan*. In general, the lesson plan should be planned around the fixed periods (usually thirty-five to fifty minutes) of the typical school schedule, allowing adequate time for teachers or students to arrive (if they are changing class-

II.   Bill of Rights and the Constitution
1.   Constitutional Convention
2.   Framing of the Constitution
3.   Bill of Rights
    a. Reasons
    b. Specific freedoms
4.   Powers reserved to the states
5.   Important amendments
    a. Thirteenth, Fourteenth, Fifteenth (slavery, due process, voting rights)
    b. Nineteenth (women's suffrage)
    c. Twentieth (progressive tax)
    d. Twenty-second (two-term limit to presidency)
    e. Others

Evaluation

1.   Short quiz for I. 1–9
2.   Graded reports with specific feedback for each student
3.   Discussion of students' roles as citizens in a free society; compare rights and responsibilities of American citizens with rights and responsibilities of students
4.   Unit test; review I. 1–9; II. 1–5

Activities

1.   (Selected video) introducing part I
2.   List of major points to be discussed in part I
3.   Homework—reading list for each topic or lesson (I. 1–9; II. 1–5)
4.   Television program on "American Freedom" and discussion after 1.9
5.   Field trip to historical museum as culminating activity for I and introduction to II
6.   Topics and reports for outside reading, with two-day discussion of reports after II.3
7.   Two-day debate (with four teams): "What's wrong with our Constitution?" "What's right with our Constitution?" after II.5
8.   Internet search of selected websites on teacher approved historical topic.

rooms) and to leave at the end of the period. Shorter blocks of time may be planned for younger students or for those whose attention span is limited. Longer time periods may be evidenced in high schools that have BLOCK scheduling (schools that schedule students into class, for example, every other day for longer time periods each day they do meet). Good timing or scheduling is an aid to good instruction and good classroom management.

Although special school activities may require shortened or lengthened periods, most lessons should be planned for full periods. Sometimes students need more or less time than planned to finish an activity or assignment, and teachers need to learn how to be flexible in adjusting timing. As teachers develop their planning and pacing skills, they learn to plan better schedules in advance and to plan supplementary activities and materials for use as the need arises. Supplementary activities might include performing a committee function, completing a research assignment, finishing a workbook assignment, illustrating a composition or report, working on a study activity, performing an honor or extra credit assignment, or tutoring another student. Supplementary materials

Lesson Plans and the Professional

Albert Shanker
Past President, American Federation of Teachers

 Should teachers be required to prepare lockstep lesson plans? Of course, teachers need to plan, and most of them do. But does each teacher have to do the same amount of planning and use the same format? Do all the plans have to be inspected on the same morning? Do some teachers plan better in their heads than on paper? More important, what are the plans for? They are supposed to help teachers focus and improve their instruction. But now, in many schools, teachers are not given a satisfactory rating, no matter how good they are as teachers, unless they have complied with the ritualistic planbook requirements. This is clear management incompetence. Would anybody rate Pavarotti a poor opera singer because he fails to fill out bureaucratic forms telling management how he intends to approach each aria?

This reminds me of the morning some thirty-five years ago when I appeared for the examination to become a New York City public school teacher. After we had assembled in the school cafeteria, someone appeared, blew a whistle, and ordered us to form a double line. We were then marched down a hall and told to form a single line to move to various classrooms in which we would take the test. Throughout this march, we continued to receive instructions. "Keep in single file." "Hurry up." "No talking." It was clear from the start that we were back in school. Even though we had gone to college and received our degrees, we were being treated very much like children again.

Rigid requirements for lesson plans are like that. They treat educated adults, veteran teachers among them, like children, requiring them to jump to a whistle and "keep in single file." Even after we have solved the problem of providing adequate financial rewards, we are not going to get good teachers or keep them so long as school management rewards blind obedience to authority above creativity and excellence.

Professionalism for teachers will come only through hard work. This will mean not only questioning outmoded practices but also offering better alternatives that serve the interest of student success, rather than bureaucratic convenience.

might include pictures, charts, and models to further demonstrate a major point in the lesson; review exercises for practice and drill; and a list of summary questions to review major points of the lesson.

To avoid omissions, or an over- or underemphasis on a particular topic, the teacher needs to consider his or her style of teaching and the students' abilities and interests. The teacher should review the progress of each day's lesson and periodically take notes on important student responses to different methods, media, and activities—to apply with another class or at another time. Inexperienced teachers need to plan the lessons in detail, follow the plan, and refer to it frequently. As they grow in experience and confidence, they become able to plan with less detail and rely more on their spontaneous responses to what happens in the classroom as the teaching-learning process unfolds (see Professional Viewpoint 4.1).

Lesson Plans by Authorities

Many current authorities who write about what a lesson plan should contain write from the point of view of direct instructional methods—that is, a view of the classroom in which teaching is teacher directed, methods and materials are sequenced, content is extensive and focused, students are provided with practice as the teacher checks or monitors the work, and the teacher provides evaluation of performance. The objectives are clearly stated in the beginning of the lesson, and a review either precedes or follows the statement of objectives. Learning takes place in an academic, teacher-centered environment. There is little mention of or concern about student needs or interests; emphasis is on student achievement.

The authors listed in Table 4.7 all exhibit this direct, step-by-step approach to learning. The categories or components are lined up within the table to show similarities among approaches. All lesson plan components and classroom events are controlled by the teacher, little provision is made for student choice or planning, and the classroom is highly structured and businesslike. Most important, the emphasis is on knowledge, skills, and tasks, as well as practice, review, and testing. Very few, if any, of the prescriptions seem directed to problem solving, critical thinking, or creativity, much less personal, social, or moral development.

Although the authorities listed in the table might not admit it or agree, their approaches apply mainly to the teaching of basic skills and discrete processes (i.e., how to do something in a step-by-step fashion) in basic subjects such as reading, mathematics, and foreign language, where practice and drill are often recommended. They are not as effective, if they can be used at all, in teaching inquiry or discovery learning or creative thinking. Nevertheless, since the explicit approaches do receive much attention in the professional literature and since they are applicable in more than one teaching area, they should be considered. Later, we will present a less direct, constructivist approach, that provides teachers with greater flexibility in teaching.

There are other types of lesson plan "authorities" as well—these authorities include other practicing teachers. Their efforts and ideas can be accessed through, for example, the Marco Polo website (marcopolo.worldcom.com). Such sites provide free lessons with many of the resources you will need to teach the lesson. Many of the practicing teachers we know rely heavily on the Marco Polo site as a resource for ideas. On the day that this chapter was written there were lesson plan ideas there on jazz history, music composition, economics, and Mount Everest. The Marco Polo type sites enable teachers to share with other teachers how to identify resources and materials that they can use to help build student understanding and to relate them to national and state standards.

Components of the Lesson Plan

There is no one ideal format to follow for a lesson plan. Teachers should modify the suggestions of methods experts and learning theorists to fit with their personal teaching style and the suggestions of their school or district. Both the PRAXIS and INTASC standards require careful attention to planning. And that planning is not done to show how you will keep students busy; it is done to document what they will learn. You may even be required to document how what you are teaching relates to specific academic standards and reference those in your plans.

One urban school district recommends that beginning teachers include the following components in a lesson plan:

1. Specific objectives of the lesson (and relate those to appropriate content standards)

t a b l e 4 . 7 **Lesson Plan Components by Authorities**

Mastery Learning *(Hunter)*	*Instructional Design* *(Gagné)*	*Instruction Behaviors* *(Good and Grouws, Good and Brophy)*
1. *Review:* Focus on previous lesson; ask students to review questions orally or in writing; ask students to summarize main points.	1. *Gain attention:* Alert students to what to expect; get students started on a routine or warm-up drill.	1. *Review:* Review concepts and skills related to homework; provide review exercises.
2. *Anticipatory set:* Focus students' attention on lesson to be presented; stimulate interest in new material.	2. *Inform learners of objective:* Activate the learners' motivation by informing them of the objective to be achieved.	2. *Development:* Promote student understanding of new material; provide examples, explanations, demonstrations.
3. *Objective:* State explicitly what will be learned; state rationale or how it will be useful.	3. *Recall prior knowledge:* Remind students of previously learned knowledge or concepts germane to new material; recall relevant prerequisites.	3. *Assess student comprehension:* Ask questions; provide controlled practice.
4. *Input:* Identify needed knowledge and skills for learning new lesson; present material in logical and sequenced steps.	4. *Present the stimulus material:* Present new knowledge or skills; indicate distinctive properties of the concepts to be learned.	4. *Seat work:* Provide uninterrupted seat work; get everyone involved; sustain momentum.
5. *Modeling:* Provide several demonstrations throughout the lesson.	5. *Provide learning guidance:* Elaborate on directions, provide assistance; integrate new information with previous (long-term memory) information.	5. *Accountability:* Check the students' work.
6. *Check for understanding:* Monitor students' work before they become involved in lesson activities; check to see they understand the directions or tasks.	6. *Elicit performance:* Suggest, do not specify, methods for performing tasks or problems; provide cues or directions, not answers (students are to provide answers).	6. *Homework:* Assign homework regularly; provide review problems.
7. *Guided practice:* Periodically ask students questions or pose problems and check answers. The same type of monitoring and response formats are involved in checking for understanding as in guided practice.	7. *Provide feedback:* Reinforce learning by checking students' work and providing frequent feedback, especially during the acquisition stage of the new material. Use feedback to adapt instruction to individual students.	7. *Special reviews:* Provide weekly reviews (exercises, quizzes) each Monday to enhance and maintain learning; provide monthly reviews every fourth Monday to further enhance and maintain learning.
8. *Independent practice:* Assign independent work or practice when it is reasonably certain that students can work on their own with minimal effort.	8. *Assess performance:* Inform students of their performance in terms of outcomes; establish an "expectancy" level.	
	9. *Ensure retention and transfer:* Utilize various instructional techniques to ensure retention (outline, classify information, use tables, charts, and diagrams). Enhance transfer of learning by providing a variety of cues, practice situations, and interlinking concepts.	

Source: Allan C. Ornstein. Secondary and Middle School Teaching Methods. Published by Allyn and Bacon, Boston, Mass. Copyright © 1992 by Pearson Education. Reprinted by permission of the publisher. (p. 141, 3/E)

2. Appropriate motivation to capture the students' interest and maintain it throughout the lesson

3. Development or outline of a lesson (sometimes referred to as *content* or *activities*)

4. Varied methods, including drill, questions, and demonstrations, designed to keep the lesson on track

5. Varied materials and media to supplement and clarify content

6. Provision for an assignment or homework [17]

The teacher can vary the components, how much time he or she spends on each component, and how much detail is included in each. With experience the teacher discovers the most useful components to include and the amount of detail needed in the plan as a whole.

There are also on-line lesson building sites now available to teachers such as TaskStream. Through these electronic sites, the components of the lesson plan can be customized based on user needs and can include rubric builders such as the one described by teacher Chad Raisch in Case Study 3.2. National and state standards are built into these sites and the user simply scrolls through the appropriate standards list in order to "pick and clip" selected objectives that are to be taught in lessons for a particular group of students and that meet the goals of a particular school.

Objectives

The first questions a teacher considers when sorting out the content he or she plans to teach are "What do I plan to teach?" and "What do I want the students to learn from the lesson that will be worthwhile?" The answers to these questions are the objectives; they form the backbone of the lesson. Motivation, methods, and materials are organized to achieve the objectives. Establishing objectives eliminates aimlessness and focuses teaching and learning.

Objectives may be phrased as statements or questions. (Most people think they can only be written as statements.) The question form encourages students to think. Regardless of how they are phrased, they should be written on the chalkboard or on a printed handout for students to see, or they should be stated at some point during the lesson. Here are some examples of general objectives for a lesson plan, written first as statements and then as questions:

Statement: To compare the prices of agricultural goods and industrial goods during the Depression

Question: Why did the prices of agricultural goods decline more than the prices of industrial goods during the Depression?

Statement: To explain how the production of oil in the Middle East affects economic conditions in the United States

Question: How does the production of oil in the Middle East affect economic conditions in the United States?

Statement: To identify how the skin protects people from diseases

Question: How does our skin protect us from diseases?

The major objective of a lesson may have ancillary (secondary) objectives. Ancillary objectives divide the lesson into segments and highlight or supplement important ideas. Here is an example of a lesson objective with two ancillary objectives (expressed as statements and then questions):

1a. *Lesson objective:* To explain the causes of World War I. *Ancillary objectives:* To compare nationalism, colonialism, and militarism; to distinguish between propaganda and facts.

1b. *Lesson objective:* What were the causes of World War I? *Ancillary objectives:* How are nationalism, colonialism, and militarism related? How can we distinguish between propaganda and facts?

Motivation

Motivational devices or activities arouse and maintain interest in the content to be taught. Fewer motivational devices are needed for students who are intrinsically motivated (that is, are motivated to learn to satisfy some inner need or interest) than for students who are extrinsically motivated (that is, require incentives or reinforcers for learning). Lesson planning and instruction typically relies on both forms of motivation, and motivation, as Case Study 4.1 illustrated, is often a major issue with some groups of students.

1. ***Intrinsic motivation:*** Intrinsic motivation involves sustaining or increasing the interest students already have in a topic or task. Intrinsic motivation is the best type of motivation because it starts with what the student wants to know. The teacher selects and organizes the lesson so that it will a) whet students' appetites at the beginning of the lesson; b) maintain student curiosity and involvement in the work by using surprise, doubt, or perplexity; novel as well as familiar materials; and interesting and varied methods; c) provide active and manipulative opportunities; d) permit student autonomy in organizing time and effort; and e) provide choices or alternatives to meet requirements of the lesson. Some activities and materials that can be used to enhance intrinsic motivation follow:

   a. *Challenging statements:* "Nuclear power plants are unnecessary and potentially dangerous."

   b. *Pictures and cartoons:* "How does this picture illustrate the American public's feelings about Japanese-made automobiles?"

   c. *Personal experiences* "What type of clothing is best to wear during freezing weather?" or "How does this content relate to you and your life?"

   d. *Problems:* "What metals conduct heat well? Why?"

   e. *Exploratory and creative activities:* "I need three volunteers to come to the chalkboard to fill in the blanks of the puzzle while the rest of you do it in your seats."

   f. *Charts, tables, graphs, maps:* "From a study of the chart, what characteristics do all these animals have in common?"

   g. *Anecdotes and stories:* "How does the paragraph I have just read convey the author's feelings about the South?"

Integrating Real-Life Experiences

Ralph W. Tyler
Former Director for Advanced Study in
The Behavioral Sciences
Stanford University

I have been teaching for more than sixty years. In every one of my classes I have found some students who have difficulty in learning what I had hoped the class would help them learn. At first, I thought these students were unable to learn and that they would never be successful in their schoolwork. But then, I noticed that many of them were learning to play games, to deliver newspapers, to plan for field trips, and to carry out many other activities.

I asked several students, "Why are you so good at learning things outside of school and seem to have difficulty with school work and with your homework?" Some said, "The things we learn outside of school are real, while schoolwork is dull and not real." Some others said, "The things we do outside of school are our jobs. In school we are doing your job."

From these experiences, I began to realize that I must give my students responsibility for jobs in school, on the playground, and in the neighborhood. Then, when they accepted these responsibilities, I helped them learn to meet these responsibilities successfully. Now, I try to find out from my students what they are trying to do, and then help them to learn how to use reading, mathematics, literature, science, art, and music by doing well in activities they believe to be important. As students understand that they need to learn what schools are expected to teach, I become their helper, not their slave driver. Then teaching becomes fun for me.

An illustration of one of those intrinsic motivators might help the reader see its power. Several years ago, one of the authors watched a high school teacher teach a lesson on the amendments to the Constitution and he made the content more powerful and relevant by using student personal experience. The teacher began the lesson by having the students stand, and then he made a series of statements and told students to sit depending on their response to his statements: "If you are not white, sit down. If you are not male, sit down. If you do not have two dollars in your pocket, sit down." At the end only two students were still standing. The teacher then explained that, without the amendments, only the standing students would be able to vote." See Professional Viewpoint above for more insight into intrinsic motivation.

2. **Extrinsic motivation.** Extrinsic motivation focuses more on behavioristic strategies. Activities that enhance success and reduce failure increase motivation. High-achieving students will persist longer than low-achieving students, even when experiencing failure, so incentives for learning are more important for average- and low-achieving students. They are important for all students when the subject matter or content is uninteresting or difficult.[18] But they must be used cautiously. The following principles can guide teachers in enhancing motivation through the use of both intrinsic and extrinsic approaches.

   a. *Provide clear directions:* Students must know exactly what they are expected to do and how they will be evaluated.

b. *Ensure a cognitive match:* Student motivation is highest when students work on tasks or problems appropriate to their achievement levels. When they are confused or when the work is above their abilities, they resist or give up. When it is below their abilities, they seek other interests or move through the lesson as fast as possible.

c. *Provide prompt feedback:* Feedback on student performance should be constructive and prompt. A long delay between behavior (or performance) and results diminishes the relationship between them.

d. *Relate past learning with present learning:* Use reinforcers to strengthen previously learned content.

e. *Provide frequent rewards:* No matter how powerful a reward, it may have little impact if it is provided infrequently. Small, frequent rewards are more effective than large, infrequent ones. Praise is a particularly powerful reward, especially if delivered in a natural voice to students for specific achievements.[19]

f. *Hold high expectations:* Students who are expected to learn will learn more and be motivated to learn more than students who are not expected to learn.

g. *Show instrumental value of what students learn:* Help students see how to use and apply what they are learning in the classroom.

One cautionary note: Limit the use of explicit extrinsic motivators such as rewards. They seem like an easy way to motivate, but they are not always the best way. Indeed, there are some critics who suggest that extrinsics should never be used. Paul Chance takes a more moderate stance:

> Rewards reduce motivation when they are given without regard to performance or when the performance standard is so high that students frequently fail. When students have a high rate of success and when those successes are rewarded, the rewards *do not have negative effects.* Indeed, success-contingent rewards tend to increase interest in the activity. . . .
>
> The evidence, then, shows that extrinsic rewards can either enhance or reduce interest in an activity, depending on how they are used. Still, it might be argued that, because extrinsic rewards *sometimes* cause problems, we might be wise to avoid their use altogether. The decision not to use extrinsic rewards amounts to a decision to rely on alternatives. What are those alternatives? And are they better than extrinsic rewards? [20]

Development

The development, sometimes called the *outline,* can be expressed as topics and subtopics, a series of broad or pivotal questions, or a list of activities (methods and materials). Most secondary teachers use topics or questions, and most elementary teachers use activities to try to foster student engagement with content.

 Emphasis on topics, concepts, or skills indicates a content orientation in teaching approach. Emphasis on activities has a more sociopsychological orientation; there is more stress on student needs and interests. For example, outlining the problems of the ozone layer on the chalkboard is content oriented. Interviewing someone about the ozone layer is an activity that encompasses a wide range of social stimuli.

Several criteria have been proposed for selecting and organizing appropriate content and experiences in the development section. The following are criteria for content developed by Ornstein and Hunkins [21]:

1. *Validity:* The content selected should be verifiable and standards based.

2. *Significance:* The content needs to be constantly reviewed so that worthwhile content—basic ideas, information, principles of the subject—is taught, and lessons do not become cluttered by masses of more trivial content now available through the "information explosion."

3. *Balance:* The content should promote macro and micro knowledge; students should experience the broad sweep of content, and they should have the opportunity to dig deep.

4. *Self-sufficiency:* The content should help students learn how to learn; it should help them gain maximum sufficiency in the most economic manner.

5. *Interest:* Content is best learned when it is interesting to the student. Some progressive educators urge that the student should be the focus of the teaching and learning process. What are the students' interests?

6. *Utility:* The content should be useful or practical in some situation outside the lesson, either to further other learning or in everyday experiences. How *usefulness* is defined depends on whether a teacher is subject centered or student centered, but most teachers would agree that useful content enhances the human potential of the learner.

7. *Learnability:* It should be within the capacity of the students to learn the content. There should be a cognitive match between the students' aptitudes and the subject (and between their abilities and academic tasks).

8. *Feasibility:* The teacher needs to consider the time needed, resources and materials available, curriculum guides, state and national tests, existing legislation, and the political climate of the community. There are limitations on what can be planned and taught.

The consideration of how to develop a lesson should include the use of activities and approaches that ensure congruence with what you teach. If you want students to learn problem-solving techniques, you need to, quite literally, give them problems. Indeed, one of the first premises of what Murrell calls "African-centered pedagogy" is "that human cognition and intellectual development are socially and culturally situated in human activity."[22] Murrell then goes on to observe, "You cannot teach children cooperative behavior without situating them in the activity of cooperative behavior; you cannot teach systematic inquiry without doing systematic inquiry."[23]

Methods—A Transmission View

Relying on the same methods day after day would be boring, even for adults. Different procedures sustain and enhance student motivation throughout the lesson. Many different procedures can be employed in a lesson. Four basic strategies for teaching specific concepts and discrete skills or processes are 1) explanations and lectures, 2) demonstrations and experiments, 3) questioning to check for understanding, and 4) practice and drill. (The next chapter also examines how questioning can also be included.) The extent to which each of these strategies is used depends on the type of lesson as well as the students, subject, and grade level. In Chapter 5, we'll explore these strategies and other methods at length but here we'll consider the order in which they are used. Notice that one begins with lecture (or teacher centered content delivery) which Madeline Hunter might describe as *input* (see Table 4.7), and one ends with practice/drill, which is both guided by the teacher and independent once students exhibit mastery.

1. *Lectures/explanations:* Teachers are often required to give short lectures and explanations to emphasize an important point, to fill in content gaps in the workbook or textbook, or to elaborate on a specific content area. Lecture can be used in combination with a number of other teaching methods—"buzz groups," controlled discussion, brainstorming, debates, audiotapes, etc.—to enhance lessons and student learning. According to Donald Bligh, "the task facing new lecturers is to decide [on] and invent combinations suitable for their purposes."[24] The classroom teacher must keep this in mind, as well. Short explanations may be embedded in the lesson without being noted in the plan. Keep in mind the 10–2 rule when lecturing. For every ten minutes of lecture, provide time for students to process the content through the use of some type of summary— see Summaries later in chapter.

   In planning an explanation or short lecture, the following characteristics are important to consider.

   a. *Sequence of discourse:* The lesson should follow a planned sequence, with few diversions or tangential discussions. Explanations should be included at proper places to maintain the sequence of the lesson.

   b. *Fluency:* The teacher should speak in clear, concise, complete, grammatical sentences.

   c. *Visual aids:* Pictures, tables, charts, models, and computer graphics or videos can be used to enhance verbal explanations.

   d. *Vocabulary:* The teacher should use the students' normal vocabulary for effective explanations. Technical or new terms pertaining to the content should be introduced and clearly defined during the explanation.

   e. *Inclusion of elements:* The major ideas of the lesson should be elaborated with specific descriptions or examples.

   f. *Explicit explanations:* Causal and logical relationships should be made explicit.[25]

2. *Demonstrations/experiments:* Demonstrations and experiments play an important role in inductive inquiry. They are ideal for creative and discovery methods of learning, whereby the teacher and students approach the subject matter by collecting data, observing, measuring, identifying, and examining causal relationships.

   Young students and low-achieving students will need more instruction and feedback from the teacher. Older and high-achieving students will work more

independently and participate more in demonstrations and experiments because they are better able to handle quantities of information, reorganize information into new forms, and transfer it to new learning situations.[26] The
following recommendations ensure the effectiveness of the demonstration and
experiment:

a. Plan and prepare for the demonstration (or experiment). Make certain that
    all materials needed are available when you begin. Practice the demonstra-
    tion (if you are conducting it for the first time) before the lesson to see
    what problems may arise.

b. Present the demonstration in context with what students have already
    learned or as a stimulus for searching for new knowledge.

c. Make provisions for full participation of the students.

d. Maintain control over the materials or equipment to the extent that the
    students are unable to work on their own.

e. Pose both close-ended and open-ended questions according to students'
    capacity for deductive and inductive responses. ("What is happening to the
    object?" is a close-ended question; "What can you generalize from . . . ?"
    is open ended.)

f. Encourage students to ask questions as they arise.

g. Encourage students to make observations first and then to make inferences
    and generalizations. Encourage them to look for and express new informa-
    tion and insights.

h. Allocate sufficient time so that a) the demonstration can be completed, b) stu-
    dents can discuss what they have observed, c) students can reach conclusions
    and apply principles they have learned, d) students can take notes or write
    about the demonstration, and e) materials can be collected and stored.

3. Questioning: Teachers should include questions to check for student under-
    standing of the content being presented. Such questions should

    a. be simple and direct.

    b. be asked in an order that corresponds to the content of the lesson.

    c. build on each other (that is, be sequential).

    d. challenge students, yet not be above the level of the class.

    e. be framed, when possible, to meet the needs and interests of the students.

    f. vary in difficulty and abstractness to encourage participation by different
        students.

    Good questioning, according to Jerome Bruner, leads to higher modes of
learning. We will discuss this more fully in the section on constructivism. In
asking questions that check for understanding of specific content, the teacher
limits what content students explore. In answering a thought-provoking
(higher-level) question, on the other hand, a high-achieving student explores
content, analyzes parts of it, reformulates it, and decides on the best method
to use for answering.[27] Thought-provoking questions usually ask how and

why, not when, where, who, or what, unless introduced by a provocative comment. Questions that call for a yes-or-no answer or for a specific right answer do not promote discussion or stimulate critical thinking or problem-solving strategies.

A lot of research now exists on questioning and on the efficacy of different approaches. Stronge provides the following synthesis of what we know about good questioning strategies used by teachers:

- Questions are most valuable when they receive responses—correct or incorrect—because responses encourage student engagement, demonstrate understanding or misconception, and further the discussion.

- The level of difficulty and cognitive level of questions should reflect the context for an optimal match; the level of the question should reflect the type of content, the goals of the lesson, and the students involved, with sufficient variance of question type within and across lessons to maintain interest and momentum.

- Questions should be considered carefully and prepared in advance of a lesson to ensure that they support the goals, emphasize the key points, and maintain appropriate levels of difficulty and complexity.

- In planning, implementing, and assessing, questions within a lesson should be considered as a sequence, not as isolated units.

- Wait time is an important aspect of questioning; longer wait times have been related to higher student achievement in several studies. However, amount of wait time should also be considered in terms of maintaining student engagement and lesson momentum.[28]

4. *Practice/drill:* There is general agreement that students need practice exercises to help them transfer new information into long-term memory and integrate new with old learning. Practice problems may come from workbooks, textbooks, and teacher-made materials. Practice, in the form of seat work, can be helpful for students if it is given for limited time periods (no more than ten minutes per class session), the instructions for it are clear, and it is integrated into the lesson (not assigned to fill time or to maintain order). Drill can be helpful for basic skills, such as reading, mathematics, and language, and in lower grades and with low-achieving students who need more practice to learn new skills or integrate information, but even with these types of students some balance of teaching approaches is needed.[29]

A short practice/drill session provides a quick and efficient way for teachers to check on the effectiveness of instruction before moving to the next stage or level in the lesson. It is well suited for mastery and direct methods of lesson planning and especially for low-achieving students.[30] Following are some drill techniques that can be used in lesson planning:

a. Ask pupils to repeat answers.

b. List facts or concepts to be remembered.

c. Identify characteristics or attributes of the content.

  d. Review answers to questions.

  e. State answers in different ways.

  f. Have volunteers answer a number of questions and discuss answers.

  g. Give a short quiz and have students grade papers.

  h. Assign exercises from the workbook or text.

  i. Monitor seat work and provide immediate feedback.

  j. Discuss or review common problems, as revealed by a short quiz or moni-
      toring of the seat work.

Methods—A Constructivist View

In the previous section, we discussed methods for teaching discrete skills and processes. Much of teaching involves such skills and processes (long division or how to solve a radical equation). The transmission view of teaching sees it as imparting to students what you know so they can use it just as you use it. But the constructivist view of teaching sees it as facilitating student co-construction of concepts. Table 4.8 clearly describes the differences between the two views. Methods for helping students explore content also need to be in your teaching skill set. What would this entail? Well, the constructivist approach is not as easily outlined as the transmission view. But here are some principles that should be evidenced:

- Students should be encouraged to express and develop their personal points of view.
- Students should be questioned by the teacher, but in a way that helps them critically reflect on ideas and engage in sustained discourse.
- Students should be exposed to ideas that might contradict their own beliefs.
- Students should be expected to communicate their ideas to others and to do so in a way that enables them to more clearly articulate and understand their personal views.[31]

As you can see, with the constructivism view, the control moves from the teacher to the student. We contend that good teachers (effective teachers) know when to teach from a transmission view and when to teach from a constructivist view. In the next chapter, we will examine some if-then statements to understand the conditions under which different approaches can be used.

Interestingly, though the transmission view advocates now tend to dominate education policymaking, the researchers involved in understanding how students learn (e.g., those involved in doing brain research) would more nearly conform to a constructivist view but their perspective also illustrates the merits of some transmission perspectives. The following principles of learning based on brain research reinforce the importance of finding ways to help students involve their interests in learning. The key is to do that so as to complement what is required by state or national academic standards. Doing so requires more thought on your part, but it results in more learning on the part of students. Notice that the first three relate more to a transmission view and the last three to a constructivist view—but a good learning environment does not make them mutually exclusive.

t a b l e   4 . 8   **Teaching and Learning as Transmission of Information versus as Social Construction of Knowledge**

Transmission View	*Social Construction View*
Knowledge is a fixed body of information transmitted from teacher or text to students.	Knowledge is developing interpretations co-constructed through discussion.
Texts and teacher are authoritative sources of expert knowledge to which students defer.	Authority for constructed knowledge resides in the arguments and evidence cited in its support by students as well as by texts or teacher; everyone has expertise to contribute.
Teacher is responsible for managing students' learning by providing information and leading students through activities and assignments.	Teacher and students share responsibility for initiating and guiding learning efforts.
Teacher explains, checks for understanding, and judges correctness of students' responses.	Teacher acts as discussion leader who poses questions, seeks clarifications, promotes dialogue, and helps group recognize areas of consensus and of continuing disagreement.
Students memorize or replicate what has been explained or modeled.	Students strive to make sense of new input by relating it to their prior knowledge and by collaborating in dialogue with others to co-construct shared understandings.
Discourse emphasizes drill and recitation in response to convergent questions; focus is on eliciting correct answers.	Discourse emphasizes reflective discussion of networks of connected knowledge; questions are more divergent but designed to develop understanding of the powerful ideas that anchor these networks; focus is on eliciting students' thinking.
Activities emphasize replication of models or applications that require following step-by-step algorithms.	Activities emphasize applications to authentic issues and problems that require higher-order thinking.
Students work mostly alone, practicing what has been transmitted to them in order to prepare themselves to compete for rewards by reproducing it on demand.	Students collaborate by acting as a learning community that constructs shared understandings through sustained dialogue.

Source: Thomas L. Good and Jere E. Brophy. *Looking in Classrooms.* 8th ed. 421. Published by Allyn and Bacon, Boston, Mass. Copyright © 2000 by Pearson Education. Reprinted by permission of the publisher.

1. Present new information within the context of prior knowledge and previously learned material.

2. Allow students to repeat learning tasks to cement them in memory.

3. Use mnemonics (or memory devices) that can significantly increase the memory of content.

4. Assign students active, hands-on tasks that require them to investigate, analyze, and solve problems using real world applications.

5. Allow students to use multiple ways to demonstrate learning.

6. Provide ways for students to engage in metacognitive learning, to think about how they think.[32]

Materials and Media

Media and materials, sometimes referred to as *resources* or *instructional aids,* facilitate understanding and foster learning by clarifying verbal abstractions and arousing interest in the lesson. Many materials and media are available. The teacher's selection should depend on the objectives and content of the lesson plan; the age, abilities, and interests of the students; the teacher's ability to use the resources; the availability of the materials and equipment; and the classroom time available. The materials and media can be in the form of 1) visuals such as posters, slides, graphs, films, computer simulations, and videos; 2) reading materials such as pamphlets, magazines, newspapers, reports, online information organized in a webquest, and books; 3) listening media such as radio, records, tapes, and television; 4) verbal activities such as speeches, debates, buzz sessions, forums, role-playing, and interviews; 5) motor activities such as games, simulations, experiments, exercises, and manipulative materials; and 6) construction activities such as collages, paintings, logs, maps, graphs, drawings, and models.

The materials and media should be

1. accurate and up-to-date.
2. large enough to be seen by all the students.
3. ready for use (check in advance of the lesson).
4. interesting and varied.
5. suited for developing the objective(s) of the lesson.
6. properly displayed and used throughout the lesson.

Many lessons fail because materials or media that were needed were inadequate, unavailable, or inappropriate for the level of the students. If students need to bring special materials for a task or project, they should be told far in advance so that they may obtain them. The teacher should be sure that necessary equipment is available, scheduled in advance, set up on the appropriate day, and in working order.

Summaries

Teachers cannot assume that learning is taking place in the class as a whole (or even with the majority) just because they have presented well-organized explanations and demonstrations or because some students give correct answers to questions. Some students might have been daydreaming or sitting there confused while other students answered questions and while the demonstrations took place. To ensure understanding of the lesson and to determine whether the objectives of the lesson have been achieved, teachers should include one or more of the following types of summaries:

1. ***Immediate summary:*** There should be a short review of each lesson in which the lesson as a whole and important or confusing parts are summarized. A short review can take the following forms:

technology viewpoint

A Technology Viewpoint from a Classroom Teacher

Jackie Marshall Arnold
K–12 Media Specialist

 Classroom teaching requires careful thought and planning. The North Central Regional Educational Laboratory (NCREL) recommends the following four steps when "transforming a lesson through the use of technology: 1) Define your goal, 2) Imagine teaching it, 3) Stop to consider whether technology could help, 4) Organize your new lesson" (NCREL's *Learning Point*, Fall 2002). A teacher interested in incorporating technology into a lesson will find it helpful to work through these four steps.

Technology can support teachers as they transition mental planning into formal planning. Concept mapping programs such as Inspiration will allow teachers formally and visually to plan units of study for any length of time. Publishing programs can be used to create personal templates for lesson plans so that information easily can be entered and changed in the flexible, dynamic world of teaching. Templates are also available at various websites such as http://www.lessonplanspage.com/ LessonTemplate.htm.

Technology can also support teachers as they choose lessons for their teaching. High quality lesson plans are available through a variety of websites. Teachers can develop their own lessons by critically reflecting on and reviewing existing lesson plans and units on the Internet. Kathy Schrock (supported by Discovery.com) has a rich supply of technology-enhanced lesson plans that teachers can access and adapt for their own teaching (http://school.discovery.com/schrockguide/). Educational sites, such as the Public Broadcasting System (www.pbs.org) also provide high quality lesson plans and resources for teachers. Finally, the North Central Regional Educational Laboratory provides a comprehensive lesson plan template that step-by-step allows teachers to plan for assessment, teaching strategies, and technology use (http://www.ncrtec.org/tl/lp/).

Materials and media greatly enhance a lesson plan. They also allow teachers to reach the diverse learning styles of students. Technology resources can support learners of all needs. Teachers need to know the learning styles of the students and design lesson plans with technology enhancements accordingly. Presentation software can support visual learners. Software that can scan and read any text to students will support auditory students. Kinesthetic students will benefit from the hands-on work involved in manipulating documents and programs. In addition, students with disabilities can use technologies to assist in their area of need. Programs such as Co-Writer and Write Out Loud now exist to support students who struggle putting their thoughts onto paper. Boardmaker and IntelliKeys allow physically handicapped students to interact and communicate in different ways.

Technology is a tool available to support teachers as they reflectively plan for students' learning and individual needs. It can support each step of the process: Software can support a teacher's planning process; Internet resources can provide enriching materials to augment existing content; experts can be found to conference with students from across the world. The possibilities are endless.

a. Posing several thought-provoking questions that summarize previous learning (or previous day's homework)

b. Asking for a comparison of what has already been learned with what is being learned

c. Asking a student to summarize the main ideas of the lesson; having other students make modifications and additions

     d. Assigning review questions (on the chalkboard or in the workbook or text-
       book)

     e. Administering a short quiz

2. ***Medial summary:*** During the lesson at some point when a major concept or
idea has been examined, it is advisable to present a medial summary—a series of pivotal questions or a problem that will bring together the information
that has been discussed. Medial summaries slow down the lesson; however,
they are important for low-achieving and young students who need more time
to comprehend new information and more links with prior knowledge.

3. ***Final summary:*** A final summary is needed to synthesize the basic ideas or
concepts of the lesson. If it is impossible to teach everything planned, then
you can end the lesson at some logical point and provide a summary of the
content covered. Each lesson should be concluded or brought to closure by a
summary activity, not by the bell. The summary activity enables students to
ensure that they understand what the teacher just taught.

As you move from education student to beginning teacher, you will have to acquire appropriate subject and pedagogical knowledge and develop your own beliefs about
teaching. Although teacher education programs can transmit some generalized principles of teaching and lesson planning, you need to learn to rely on your own experiences, capabilities, and reflections, incorporating them into your own classroom
practices. You can also improve your instruction by observing experienced teachers,
conversing with them, and getting feedback. Unfortunately, supervisors or principals
rarely visit classrooms to observe teachers and provide feedback, unless a teacher is
experiencing difficulties with the students or is new. Teachers need to interpret their
own instruction to grow professionally; they need mentors but they need to know how
to engage in self-reflection. The best barometers are the students. A teacher needs to
learn to understand his or her instruction from the perspective of students since they
are the ones being taught and the ones who observe the teacher on a daily basis. Which
students are engaged? Which are disengaged? Why?

    With experience, good teachers grow less egocentric (concerned about them-
selves) and more sensitive to student concerns. They learn to address the "Why?" question more thoughtfully. Such a shift in interest and focus helps them analyze what is
happening in the classroom on an ongoing basis. By learning to read your students'
verbal and nonverbal behavior, you will improve your instructional planning. As you
put yourself in the place of your students, you should become more attuned to them as
individuals—with particular needs and abilities—as opposed to viewing them as some
amorphous group with generic problems or concerns.[33]

Sample Lesson Plans

Three sample lesson plans are shown in Tables 4.9, 4.10, and 4.11 to illustrate how the
various components of the lesson can be used. The lesson plans are written for different
grade levels and subjects and are used to show the relationship of your overall instructional goals and the structure of a lesson. The following explanations give some sense of

what the teacher is trying to achieve. The words in italics coincide with the previously discussed components of a lesson plan; they serve as anchors or highlight the major ideas of the lessons. Notice, in particular, how the homework requires students to use other forms of intelligence in order to assimilate the meaning of the words.

Lesson Plan for Flexible Grouping (Table 4.9)

1. The *lesson topic* is derived from the unit plan on vocabulary development.

2. The *primary objective* is to teach the meaning of ten new words. The two secondary objectives accomplish the primary objective and enhance dictionary and writing skills.

3. The teacher immediately starts the lesson with a *review* of the previous homework. The class as a whole discusses the homework.

4. Only *materials* specific to the lesson are noted in the lesson plan.

5. The teacher uses the term *activities* to describe the development or outline, since the focus of attention is on classroom activities.

6. The class is divided into *two groups* for the activities. Group I is lower achieving than group II.

7. Both groups do similar *seat work*. Group I is given the extra step of alphabetizing for extra practice in the process. Group II understands the need for alphabetical order in searching through the dictionary, so this step is omitted. Group II is given another, more difficult task of dividing words into syllables to make up for the one task that was omitted. The teacher monitors the seat work of the students and helps anyone with individual problems.

8. After seat work, the two groups engage in different activities. The teacher works with one group while the other is involved in independent work. For group I the teacher provides a *medial summary* for feedback, review, and assessment. (Prompt and varied feedback and review are needed for the less-advanced group.) Group II engages in *independent* work, having selected their own books to read for enjoyment. The teacher then works with group II in a *summary* activity, connecting the original objective with the students' independent work, while group I does its independent assignment. Group I has fifteen fewer minutes for independent work and fifteen more minutes of teacher-directed summary work because these students need more teacher time, are less able to work independently of the teacher, and are likely to have more problems that need to be directly remediated.

9. The whole class receives the same *homework* assignment. Group I is permitted to start the homework in class so the assignment at home does not overwhelm them and so the teacher can check for understanding. The students use two forms of intelligence that they did not use during the formal lesson taught by the teacher, which fosters a type of intrinsic *motivation*.

Lesson Plan for Thinking Skills (Table 4.10)

1. The *lesson topic* can be part of a separate unit on critical thinking skills, or it can serve as an introductory lesson for a unit in almost any subject.

t a b l e   4 . 9   Flexible Grouping Lesson Plan

Lesson topic: Vocabulary

Objective: To define 10 new words.
1. To define the meaning of the words using a dictionary
2. To write the meaning of the new words in a sentence

Review: Both groups (10 minutes)
1. Correct homework, workbook, pp. 36–39.
2. Focus on questions, p. 39.

Materials: Dictionaries, logs, supplementary books

Development:

Group I Activities	Group II Activities
Seat work (15 minutes)	**Seat work (15 minutes)**
1. Alphabetize the following 10 words; explicit, implicit, appropriate, inappropriate, potential, encounter, diminish, enhance, master, alligator. 2. Find each new word in the dictionary. 3. Write a definition for each new word.	1. Find each of the following 10 words in the dictionary: explicit, implicit, appropriate, inappropriate, potential, encounter, diminish, enhance, master, alligator (same words for both groups). 2. Write a definition for each new word. 3. Divide each new word into syllables.
Medial summary (15 minutes)	**Independent work (15 minutes)**
1. Teach new words; students give examples and discuss meaning of new words.	1. Continue reading supplementary books. 2. Underline at least five new words in the pages you read. 3. Find their meaning in the dictionary.
Independent work (10 minutes)	**Final summary (10 minutes)**
1. Get up to date with logs. 2. Include the 10 new words in logs	1. Discuss the 10 assigned words plus the 5 words students have chosen in their independent reading.

Homework: Both groups
1. Develop a picture for the meaning of each word. (Artistic intelligence)
2. Create a song that has all 10 words. (Musical intelligence)

---

2. There is only one *objective.* It pertains to classifying—a critical thinking skill.

3. The *motivation* assumes a certain amount of abstract thinking on the part of the students. It is verbal as opposed to visual or auditory. The first question is divergent and open-ended. The second question is more convergent and focused. The short exercise provides students with a challenge, introduces them to the main part of the lesson, and shows how they handle certain information before the lesson. Some words (*elephant, donkey, Lincoln,* etc.) can be categorized into various groups, and *table* does not belong in any category. (It serves as irrelevant information to see how students handle it.)

4. The **development** is a set of *procedures* or operations to teach students how to classify information. The *pivotal questions* are to be introduced at different

t a b l e 4 . 1 0   **Thinking Skills Lesson Plan**

Lesson topic: Classifying information

Objective: To classify information on the basis of similar or common attributes

Motivation:
1. Into what groups would you classify the following information: Kennedy, table, elephant, Lincoln, Roosevelt, Chicago, Nixon, Boston, Bush, donkey, and San Francisco?
2. Why should we learn to classify information into categories or groups?

Procedures	Pivotal questions
1. **Development:** Discuss at least three reasons for classifying information.	1a. When do you classify information? Why? 1b. What happens to information that is not organized? Why?
2. Skim text (pp. 48–55) to get an idea of important items or ideas that might be classified.	
3. Agree on categories (groups or labels) to be used in classifying information in text.	3a. What advantages are there to the categories? 3b. What are their unifying attributes? 3c. What other categories could we have used? Explain.
4. Focus on three practice items in the text and agree on related categories for purpose of ensuring understanding.	
5. Read carefully the same pages and place selected items into appropriate categories.	6a. Why did you identify these items with those categories?
6. Discuss similar or common attributes.	6b. Why did you choose these common attributes as a category to classify the items? 6c. What other common attributes might you have chosen?
7. Modify (change, subtract, or add) categories, if necessary.	7a. Why did you change these categories? 7b. What can we do with the items that fit into more than one category? Which items fit into more than one category?
8. Repeat procedures using other important items; read pp. 56–63.	8. What categories did you select? Why?
9. Combine categories or subdivide into smaller categories?	9a. Why did you reclassify (add or subdivide) these categories. 9b. What should we do with the leftover items? Which ones are left over?

Summary:
1. What important things have you learned about classifying information?
2. What are different ways of classifying information?
3. When is it appropriate to subdivide categories?
4. Look at the chalkboard (text). Who wishes to categorize these five new items into one of the categories we have already established?

Homework:
1. Read Chapter 7. (Intrapersonal intelligence)
2. Classify important information into pro/con categories listed on p. 68. (Verbal intelligence)

stages of the lesson. They stimulate discussion, clarify points, and check understanding. They are divergent in nature and provide students with latitude in the way they can answer; the teacher must listen carefully to the responses, since the answers are not necessarily right or wrong but involve, in part, viewpoints and subjectivity.

5. The *summary* is a series of important or key questions that lead to a discussion and elaboration of what has been taught. The length of the summary discussion is based on the time permitted. Question 1 is vague, and students may not respond or may respond in a way that the teacher does not expect. Questions 2 and 3 are more focused. Question 4 leads to a good overview and reinforcement exercise. (The teacher may or may not have time to use it.)

6. The *homework* is based on the lesson and leads to a slightly more advanced type of thinking and relies on areas of verbal and intrapersonal intelligence.

Lesson Plan for Mastery (Table 4.11)

1. Subtraction as a *lesson topic* is introduced in the second grade in most school districts and continued in the third grade.

2. The *objective* is written in terms of a performance level.

3. Mastery learning lessons entail a good deal of practice and *review*.

4. The *motivation* is in the form of two separate problems that involve real-life experiences and interests.

5. Only unusual *materials* are listed. Popsicle sticks, baseball cards, or any other items easy to count can be used in lieu of checkers.

6. The *development* is in the form of problems and related activities. The problems, involving one- and two-digit numbers, coincide with the worksheet level the students have reached. The teacher explains each problem and then introduces the related activity. While students work on the activity, the teacher moves around the room and monitors their work. The problems get progressively more difficult. Each item that is missed by even a small percentage of students must be further explained, since the work builds on previous learning.

7. The teacher provides additional *practice* before asking students to complete the worksheet on their own. Only volunteers are called on because the work is new. Three items are explained. The teacher moves around the room monitoring the students' work and providing additional help when necessary.

8. As a *summary* all items are discussed. All items missed by students, especially those that are missed by 20 percent or more, are discussed in greater detail. Individuals' scores on the worksheet determine how much practice is needed the next day in the form of review.

9. The *homework* is related to the lesson; it is assigned and explained. The next day it will be reviewed. Peer teaching is quite simple. Just have students work in pairs and then have one of the students teach the process to his or her partner. The teacher should walk around the room to ensure that students are explaining the material correctly.

table 4.11   Mastery Learning Lesson Plan (Primary Grades)

Lesson topic: Subtraction

Objective: Students will compute the worksheet items on subtraction, with at least 80 percent accuracy after the lesson.

Review: Review yesterday's homework on subtraction.

Motivation (Sample items):

1. There are 25 students in the class, as you know. We are planning to go to a movie next Friday afternoon. Three of you—Joel, Jason, and Stacey—have soccer practice and will not attend the movie. How many tickets should we buy?
2. We are going to plan a Halloween party in class. Each of you may have one dessert choice with your milk. Most of us enjoy chocolate-chip cookies, but some might prefer vanilla-cream cookies. Let's see how many prefer vanilla-cream cookies. (Show of hands. Good.) Ten of you prefer the vanilla-cream cookies. Who can tell the class how many chocolate-chip cookies we will need for the party?

Materials: Overhead projector, checkers (pass out to students)

Development:

Problems	Activities
1. With overhead projector explain how to solve 11–5, 11–7.	1a. At their desks students use the checkers and perform 12–2, 12–5, 12–8.
	1b. Students record work (and answers) in their notebooks.
	1c. Discuss all items missed by more than 10 percent of the students.
2. With overhead projector explain 20–5, 20–10.	2a. At their desks students use the checkers and perform 21–3, 21–5, 21–7.
	2b. Repeat 1b.
	2c. Repeat 1c.
3. With overhead projector explain 22–6, 22–10, 22–15.	3a. At their desks students use the checkers and perform 23–5, 23–8, 23–12, 23–20.
	3b. Repeat 1b.
	3c. Repeat 1c.

Practice:

1. Hand out worksheet with subtraction problems.
2. Call on volunteer to do first sample item on worksheet.
3. Call on second and third volunteer to do next two sample items, then call on nonvolunteers.
4. Have students complete remaining worksheet on their own at their own pace.

Summary (evaluation):

1. With overhead projector show correct answers for all the items.
2. Ask students how many got each item right.
3. Discuss all the items, but reteach items that 20 percent or more missed.
4. Have students score their own papers and turn them in.

Homework:

1. Distribute homework or explain new worksheet that is to be answered.
2. Review assignment for next day.
3. Reteach problem items (items that 20 percent or more missed during previous lesson).

Teachers need to be aware of what is happening during the lesson and determine what is worthwhile and what needs to be modified.

Guidelines for Implementing Lesson Plans

You will need to consider several factors as you begin to move from planning to performance. Even after you have had some experience, it is wise to review the following factors to ensure your success in the execution of the lesson plan:

1. *Student differences:* You must consider individual and group differences as you plan your lesson and then teach it. Make provisions for student differences in ability, age, background, and reading level. The differences in how students learn are being accentuated because of the increased diversity of the student population. Teachers can capitalize on the unique learning dispositions of students from different backgrounds by understanding that different students learn in different ways. Be careful not to stereotype how students learn in classrooms. African-American students are not necessarily verbal learners any more than European-American students are analytical in their approach to learning. The key is to understand that you have different types of learners, and this fact requires that you organize the classroom in different ways and then examine critically how those different structures impact student learning and achievement. What students learn best in cooperative structures? Which ones benefit from independent structures? All students from all different types of ethnic and racial backgrounds can and do learn through some common strategies. But from the 1970s to the 1990s many researchers began to see that some approaches "played" more on certain students' cultural strengths. For example, Native Americans tend to stress interpersonal cooperation, and teachers who

understand that fact can better help Native American students achieve their full potential. Teachers should not interpret these cultural dispositions as keys to *how* a group learns, but rather should use them to understand *why* some students may adjust more quickly to one particular learning situation than to another.

2. *Length of period:* One of the major problems beginning teachers have is planning a lesson that will coincide with time allotted (the thirty, forty, or fifty minutes of each period; with BLOCK scheduling the time frame may be as much as 100 minutes). New teachers must learn to pace themselves and not plan too much (and have to end abruptly) or too little (and have nothing planned for the last five or ten minutes of the period). Remember to select fewer concepts but to find more ways to teach the concepts.

3. *Flexibility:* The teacher must be flexible—that is, prepared to develop a lesson along a path different from the one set down in the plan. Student reactions may make it necessary or desirable to elaborate on something included in the plan or to pursue something unexpected that arises as the lesson proceeds. Although effective teachers tend to encourage on-task behavior and discourage off-task behavior, they are willing to make corrections and take advantage of unforeseen developments. The basis for the change is more intuitive than objective, more unplanned than preplanned.

4. *Student participation:* Teachers must encourage the participation of the greatest number of students in each lesson. They should not permit a few students to dominate the lesson, and they should draw nonvolunteers into the lesson. They should not talk too much or dominate the lesson with teacher-directed activities. The need is to encourage student participation, student-to-student interaction, and increased performance among shy students, low-achieving students, and students on the sides and in the rear rows (as opposed to students in the middle or front of the room who tend to get the most attention).

5. *Student understanding:* There is often a gap between what students understand and what teachers think they understand. Part of the reason for this gap is the rapidity of the teaching process—so much happens at once that the teacher is unaware of everything that goes on in the classroom. Following are suggestions to increase student understanding as you teach the lesson:

   a. Insist that students respond to the questions put to them. Students who do not know answers or have trouble understanding the lesson tend to mumble or speak too quietly to be heard clearly, try to change the subject, or ask another question instead of responding to the original question. These are some of the strategies students adopt to outwit teachers.[34]

   b. If a student answer lacks detail, does not cover the major aspects of the problem, or is partially or totally incorrect, a) probe the student by rephrasing or simplifying the question, by using another question to lead the student toward the desired answer, or by providing additional information. As a last option, call on another student to help the first student.

   c. If, after calling on a few students, you are unable to obtain the desired response, you may have to reteach parts of the lesson. Although this is not

table 4.12   **Some Dos and Don'ts of Homework**

....

1. *Do not* ever give homework to teach complex skills.

2. *Do not* make up spur-of-the-moment homework assignments.

3. *Do not* assume that because there are no questions asked about a homework assignment, students have no questions about the assignment.

4. *Do not* expect students (even your best students) always to have their homework assignments completed successfully 100% of the time.

5. *Do* understand that not all types of homework assignments are equally valuable for all types of students.

6. *Do* explain the specific purpose of homework assignments and how to complete them.

7. *Do* listen to what students say about their experiences in completing your homework assignments.

8. *Do* acknowledge and be thankful for efforts students make to complete their homework.

Based on Harris Cooper, "Synthesis of Research on Homework." *Educational Leadership* (November, 1989): 90.

planned, you cannot ignore that several students are having problems understanding the lesson.

d. Prepare students for demonstrations and experiments, ask questions during these activities, and follow up with written exercises in which students analyze or synthesize what they observed or performed.

e. Include practice, review, or applications in every lesson. The amount of time you spend on these activities will depend on the students' abilities. Low-achieving and younger students need more practice, review, and concrete application.

f. Be sure to include medial and final summaries. Low-achieving and younger students need more medial summaries than high-achieving students.

Homework is a critical part of the process for fostering student understanding. Table 4.12 provides some dos and don'ts of homework.

6. *Assessment and evaluation:* At the end of a lesson, the teacher should have a clear idea about how the students reacted and whether they understood and were engaged in the lesson. To appraise your lesson plan, ask yourself the following questions:

a. Did my objectives align with state or local content standards?

b. Was the instruction congruent with the objectives?

c. Are certain questions targeted to the learning objectives?

d. Do I need to spend more time reviewing parts of the lesson?

e. Do I give feedback in a manner that is supportive and encouraging?

f. Were the questions appropriate? Which ones came up that were not planned and that can be used in the future? Did I incorporate higher-order questions?

g. What problems arose? How can I correct them?

h. Was there sufficient time to complete the lesson?

tips for teachers 4.2

Organizing and Implementing Lesson Plans

The teacher should always look for ways to improve the lesson plan. What follows are twenty-five research-based tips that correlate with student achievement. As many as possible (not necessarily all in one lesson) should be incorporated into portions of the lesson plan. Although most of the statements seem to be based on a mastery approach, the checklist can be used for most types of teaching.

1. Plan the lesson toward stated objectives or topics of the unit plan.
2. Make certain that lesson objectives are clear.
3. Develop objectives and activities that use a variety of higher-level and lower-level cognitive skills.
4. Provide a review of the previous lesson or integrate the previous lesson with the new lesson.
5. Indicate to students the objectives of the lesson; explain what is to be accomplished.
6. Present lesson with enthusiasm; motivate students.
7. Present the lesson at an appropriate pace, not too slow or too fast.

8. Explain things clearly. Be sure students understand what to do and how to do it.
9. Give students a chance to think about what is being taught.
10. Try to find out when students don't understand.
11. Provide sufficient time for practice.
12. Ask frequent questions; be sure they are challenging and relevant.
13. Provide explanations, demonstrations, or experiments.
14. Elaborate on difficult points of the lesson; give details, provide examples.
15. Choose activities that are interesting and promote success.
16. Incorporate supplementary materials and media.
17. Summarize the lesson.
18. Schedule seat work; monitor and assess student work.
19. Give homework, provide examples of how to do homework, and collect and check homework.
20. Evaluate (or reflect on) the lesson plan after teaching.

---

i. Did my students learn the skills, concepts, and generalizations I set out to teach in my learning objectives?

j. What did I fail to accomplish in the lesson?

k. What other forms of intelligence (musical, artistic, kinesthetic) might help students better understand the concepts?

A good teacher, no matter how experienced, is a critic of his or her lesson and seeks new ways to improve the teaching-learning situation. The teacher takes time for self-reflection and self-analysis. The teacher is aware of what is happening during the lesson and intuitively judges what is worthwhile and what needs to be modified for the next time the lesson plan is used. See Tips for Teachers 4.2 for more ideas for lesson improvement.

Theory into Practice

All school districts expect teachers to cover the appropriate goals/standards from the adopted course of study. Some on-line lesson/unit builders that are available are able to report on (and document) this kind of data if teachers create their lesson using one of these databases. LiveText and TaskStream are two such on-line approaches. School districts will have their own approaches that may be either electronic or paper and pencil oriented. In essence, unit planning and lesson planning will vary according to the school district and school in which you teach. Some school settings and supervisors will be quite prescriptive and expect you to follow a prescribed method. Your plans may be collected and checked on a regular basis. In other schools and with other supervisors, there will be no prescribed method and very little feedback or concern about your unit and lesson plans. Hence, you will be largely on your own when it comes to instructional planning. For this reason, you can use the following questions to avoid common mistakes and to guide you when you plan your own units and lessons.

Unit Planning

1. Did you consider state (or school district) requirements and standards as well as the course of study?
2. Did you read the instructor's manual for suggestions? Are there samples that you can modify to your students' abilities and needs?
3. Are you clear about your instructional objectives? Are they appropriate?
4. Does the content tie together with the objectives? Is the content interesting and relevant?
5. Do the skills tie together with the content? Do they allow for differences in student abilities and needs?
6. Did you include interesting and relevant learning activities? Do some of the activities extend beyond the classroom?
7. Did you include varied resources and materials? Did you supplement the text with other resources and materials?
8. Are your evaluation procedures appropriate? Do they help assess your objectives?
9. Is your plan flexible enough to accommodate various students—in terms of abilities, interests, and learning styles?
10. Is your plan detailed enough so that another person would understand it and know what you want to do?

Lesson Planning

1. Are your objectives clear in terms of the knowledge, skills, and values you wish to teach? Do they stem from the unit plan?
2. Is the content arranged in a logical order and in the way you wish to teach it?
3. Are your instructional methods clear? Do you vary the methods to prevent student boredom?
4. Are your materials and equipment ready to use? Did you order them far enough in advance?
5. Have you checked the previous work? Did you ask review questions or pose problems? Did you administer a short quiz on the previous lesson or homework? Did you reteach or provide additional practice when needed?

6. Have you checked the current work? Did you provide adequate summaries? Did you call on new volunteers? Did you reteach when necessary?
7. Are crucial or pivotal questions included?
8. Did you include an appropriate homework assignment? Were your directions clear? How did you check to see if the students understood yesterday's homework?
9. Have you budgeted sufficient time to complete the lesson? Did you finish too soon? Did you run out of time before finishing?
10. How do you intend to evaluate the lesson? Would you enjoy the lesson if you were a student? Would you learn from the lesson if you were a student?

Summary

1. Teachers plan at five different levels: yearly, term, unit, weekly, and daily.
2. Mapping takes place at different subject and grade levels; it helps clarify what content, skills, and values you wish to teach.
3. Teachers use national and state standards to shape the lesson goals and objectives.
4. The basic components of a unit plan are objectives, content, skills, activities, resources, and evaluation.
5. Two types of unit plans are the taxonomic and topic.
6. The basic components of a lesson plan are objectives, motivation, development, methods, materials and media, summaries, and homework.
7. Three lesson plans were discussed: flexible grouping, thinking skills, mastery learning.

Questions to Consider

1. Why do educators advise planning in cooperation with students? Why do many teachers ignore student input when planning?
2. What are the criteria for a good unit plan?
3. With what approach do you think a unit for your subject or grade could best be planned? Why?
4. Which are the most essential components to consider when planning a lesson? Why?
5. What are the problems of relying too heavily on either a transmission or social constructivist view of learning? Or is it preferable or possible to adopt just one view?

Things to Do

1. Prepare a unit for your subject or grade level grounded on existing content standards.
2. Speak to an experienced teacher. Ask the teacher to provide you with a series of unit plans for the subject or grade level you plan to teach. Examine the major components in class.
3. Select one of the units and list the activities and resources that could be incorporated into it.

4. Plan a lesson in your subject and grade level; then teach it using the lesson components listed in this chapter. What were the good parts of the lesson? What were the unsatisfactory parts?

5. List some common mistakes in lesson planning. Ask experienced teachers, "What are ways for preventing some of these mistakes?"

Recommended Readings

Beyer, Barry K. *Teaching Thinking Skills: A Handbook for Elementary School Teachers.* Needham Heights, Mass.: Allyn and Bacon, 1991. This book explores how teaching skills can be planned and taught in most elementary classrooms. It includes sample exercises and lesson plans.

Block, James H., Helene E. Efthim, and Robert B. Burns. *Building Effective Mastery Learning Schools.* New York: Longman, 1989. This mastery approach to teaching and learning includes how to plan unit plans and lesson plans for mastery.

Chall, Jeanne S. *The Academic Achievement Challenge.* New York: Guilford Press, 2002. This book examines the research on teacher-centered versus student-centered instructional approaches.

Good, Thomas L., and Jere E. Brophy. *Looking in Classrooms,* 9th ed. Boston, Mass.: Allyn and Bacon. 2003. This research-oriented book covers several aspects of teaching including lesson planning.

Irvine, Jacqueline Jordan, and Beverly Jeanne Armento. *Culturally Responsive Teaching.* Boston: McGraw Hill, 2001. This is a thoughtful exploration of how culturally responsive lessons can be planned around established disciplinary standards.

Ladson-Billings, Gloria. *Dreamkeepers.* San Francisco, Calif.: Jossey-Bass, 1994. This book describes the practices and characteristics of successful teachers working with students of color.

McNeil, John D. *Curriculum: The Teacher's Initiative,* 3rd ed. Columbus, OH: Merrill, 2003. The author describes a constructivist view on curriculum and teaching.

Key Terms

constructivist view 135	extrinsic motivation 169	medial summary 179
course of study 149	final summary 179	mental planning 147
culturally responsive	formal planning 147	transmission view 171
classroom 149	intrinsic motivation 168	unit plan 150
development 181	lesson plan 162	

End Notes

1. Paul V. Bredeson. *Designs for Learning.* Thousand Oaks, CA: Corwin Press, 2003. Pamela G. Grossman. "Why Models Matter." *Review of Educational Research* (Summer 1993): 171–80. John Solas. "Investigating Teacher and Student Thinking About the Process of Teaching and Learning." *Review of Educational Research* (Summer 1992): 205–225.

2. Craig D. Jerald and Richard M. Ingersoll. "All Talk, No Action: Putting an End to Out-of-Field Teaching." Washington, D.C.: Education Trust, 2002.

3. John A. Zahorik. "Teachers' Planning Models." *Educational Leadership* (November 1975): 134–139.

4. Christopher Clark. "Real Lessons from Imaginary Teachers." *Journal of Curriculum Studies* (September–October 1991): 429–434. Penelope L. Peterson, Christopher W. Marx, and Ronald M. Clark. "Teacher Planning,

Teacher Behavior, and Student Achievement." *American Educational Research Journal* (Summer 1978): 417–432.

5. Elliot W. Eisner. *The Educational Imagination,* 3d ed. New York: Macmillan, 1993.

6. Carol Ann Tomlinson. *The Differentiated Classroom.* Alexandria, VA: Association for Supervision and Curriculum Development, 1999, p. 40.

7. Deborah S. Brown. "Twelve Middle School Teachers' Planning." *Elementary School Journal* (September 1988): 69–87. Deborah S. Brown, "Descriptions of Two Novice Secondary Teachers' Planning." *Curriculum Inquiry* (Spring 1993): 34–45.

8. Robert J. Yinger, "A Study of Teacher Planning." *Elementary School Journal* (January 1980): 107–127.

9. William Sanders. "Value-Added Teaching." Presentation to the Governor's Commission on Teaching Success, Columbus, Ohio, 2002.

10. Gail McCutcheon. "How Do Elementary School Teachers Plan?" *Elementary School Journal* (September 1980): 4–23.

11. Jacqueline Jordon Irvine and Bevery Jeanne Armento. *Culturally Responsive Teaching.* Boston: McGraw Hill, 2001.

12. Beverly Jeanne Armento. "Principles of a Culturally Responsive Classroom." In J. Irvine and B. J. Armento (eds.). *Culturally Responsive Teaching.* Boston: McGraw Hill, 2001, p. 19–32.

13. Allan C. Ornstein. "Effective Course Planning by Mapping." *Kappa Delta Pi Record* (Fall 1990): 24–26. Allan C. Ornstein. *Educational Administration: Concepts and Practices,* 4th ed. Belmont, CA: Wadsworth, 2004.

14. E. D. Hirsch, Jr. *The Schools We Need and Why We Don't Have Them.* New York: Doubleday, 1996, p. 30.

15. Tomlinson. *The Differentiated Classroom,* pp. 81–82. See also Howard Gardner's video, *MI: Millenium.* Los Angeles, Calif: Into the Classroom Media, 2002.

16. W. James Popham. "Can High-Stakes Tests Be Developed at the Local Level*?" NASSP Bulletin* (February 1987): 77–84. Thomas R. Guskey. "Helping Standards Make the Grade." *Educational Leadership* (September 2001): 20–27.

17. *Getting Started in the Elementary School: A Manual for New Teachers,* rev. ed. New York: Board of Education of the City of New York, 1986.

18. Deborah J. Stipek. *Motivation to Learn,* 2d ed. Needham Heights, Mass.: Allyn and Bacon, 1993. Martin V. Covington. *Making the Grade: A Self-Worth Perspective on Motivation.* New York: Cambridge University Press, 1992.

19. Thomas L. Good and Jere E. Brophy, *Looking in Classrooms,* 8th ed. (New York: Longman, 2000): pp. 141-144.

20. Paul Chance. "The Rewards of Learning." *Phi Delta Kappan* (November 1992): 204.

21. Allan C. Ornstein and Francis P. Hunkins. *Curriculum: Foundations, Principles, and Issues,* 4th ed. Boston, Mass.: Allyn and Bacon, 2004.

22. Peter C. Murrell, Jr. *African-Centered Pedagogy.* (Albany, N.Y.: SUNY University Press of New York, 2002, p. 46.

23. Ibid.

24. Donald A. Bligh. *What's the Use of Lectures?* San Francisco, Calif.: Jossey-Bass Publishers, 2000, p. 282.

25. Kenneth A. Kiewra. "Aids to Lecture Learning." *Educational Psychologist* (Winter 1991): 37–53. Elizabeth Perrott. *Effective Teaching: A Practical Guide to Improving Your Teaching.* New York: Longman, 1982.

26 . Paul A. Schutz. "Goals in Self-Directed Behavior." *Educational Psychologist* (Winter 1991): 55–67. Kathryn R. Wentzel. "Social Competence at School: Relationship Between Social Responsibility and Academic Achievement." *Review of Educational Research* (Spring 1991): 1–24.

27. Jerome S. Bruner. *Toward a Theory of Instruction.* Cambridge, Mass.: Harvard University Press, 1966.

28. James H. Stronge. *Qualities of Effective Teachers.* Alexandria, VA: Association for Supervision and Curriculum Development, 2002, p. 48.

29. Kurt W. Fischer and L. Todd Rose. "Webs of Skill: How Students Learn." *Educational Leadership* (Novermber 2001): 6–13. Steven Zemelman, Harvey Daniels and Arthur Hyde. *Best Practice: New Standards for Teaching and Learning in America's Schools.* Portsmouth, NH: Heinemann, 1998.

30. Vito Perrone. "How to Engage Students in Learning." *Educational Leadership* (February 1994): 11–13. Frank Smith. "Learning to Read: The Never-Ending Debate." *Phi Delta Kappan* (February 1992): 432–441.

31. Thomas L. Good and Jere E. Brophy. *Looking in Classrooms,* 8th ed. New York: Longman, 2000.

32. Mariale M. Hardiman. "Connecting Brain Research with Dimensions of Learning." *Educational Leadership* (November 2001): 52–55.

33. Paul R. Burden and David M. Byrd. *Methods for Effective Teaching,* 3d ed. Boston: Allyn and Bacon, 2003.

34. Ruth Garner. "When Children Do Not Use Learning Strategies." *Review of Educational Research* (Winter 1990): 517–530. Donna M. Kagan and Deborah J. Tippins. "Helping Student Teachers Attend to Student Cues." *Elementary School Journal* (March 1991): 343–356. Marge Scherer. "Do Students Care about Learning?" *Educational Leadership* (September 2002): 12–17.

Instructional Strategies

Pathwise criteria relevant to this chapter:

- *Creating or selecting teaching methods, learning activities, and instructional materials or other resources that are appropriate for the students and that are aligned with the goals of the lesson. (A4)*
- *Making learning goals and instructional procedures clear to students. (C1)*
- *Making content comprehensible to students. (C2)*
- *Encouraging students to extend their thinking. (C3)*
- *Monitoring students' understanding of content through a variety of means, providing feedback to students to assist learning, and adjusting learning activities as the situation demands. (C4)*
- *Using instructional time effectively. (C5)*

INTASC principles relevant to this chapter:

- *The teacher understands and uses a variety of instructional strategies to encourage students' development of critical thinking, problem solving, and performance skills. (Principle 4)*
- *The teacher uses an understanding of individual and group motivation and behavior to create a learning environment and encourages positive social interaction, active engagement in learning, and self-motivation. (Principle 5)*

.... **focusing questions**

1. When is the method of practice and drill useful?

2. How can practice and drill be made most effective?

3. Why is the method of questioning crucial to good instruction?

4. What are the characteristics of well-formulated questions?

5. What are hierarchic and problem-solving lectures?

6.   Why should lecture times be limited?

7.   What are good strategies for student problem-solving and inquiry?

8.   How do varied methods (or what some term *adaptive pedagogy*) enhance the achievement of all students?

To appreciate instruction, we need to make a distinction between teaching and instruction. Teaching is the behavior of the teacher that evolves during the instructional process (the focus of Chapter 2). Instruction is the specific methods and activities by which the teacher influences learning (the focus of Chapters 3–9).

If teaching and instruction commingle correctly, the learning paradigm described in Chapter 1 results and the artful nature of teaching and learning emerges. In this chapter we will explore four instructional methods—the methods used most of the time by the great majority of teachers: 1) practice and drill, 2) questioning, 3) lecturing and explaining, 4) problem solving and experiential teaching. Each of these has been discussed to a limited degree in previous chapters, but in this chapter they will be organized around specific teaching-learning problems that you will confront in the classroom. These methods are supported by many years of research and practice and are foundational to a teaching repertoire. To help you better integrate the chapter, think of a concept or skill you will be teaching to your class. Which methods will you use? Why? What are the consequences of using these methods? When are these methods most effectively used? How do you make these methods work for your own teaching style? You will learn how to focus by using if-then statements. For example, if you want your students to memorize multiplication tables, then practice and drill are effective. If you want your students to think about how the multiplication tables work, then you might use questioning.

As new school structures and ideas about learning emerge, we find at their foundation new if-then statements. For example, in Alameda, California, Arthur Anderson and the Alameda Unified School District have created a project-based, open space school that organizes teachers and students as partners in learning in a very different way. Students do not function in classes the way most of us have experienced. They explore projects (or pursue their passions), and they engage in independent, self-directed learning. The if-then statement at work in this school might be "If you want your students to become independent, self-directed learners, then a project-based or inquiry approach." A similar passion-based learning approach occurs at The Met School headed by Dennis Littky in Providence, Rhode Island. In addition, an increasing number of students are now involved in virtual school experiences and they may not ever really be part of what we think of as a traditional classroom. Texas offers, in fact, a wide variety of virtual school courses that are aligned with its academic standards—to learn more visit http://www.texasvirtualschool.org. As the types of alternative and virtual programs begin to expand, more and more if-then statements will emerge.

No one illustrates this if-then relationship better than Bransford and his colleagues.[1] They argue that the appropriateness of a particular teaching technique depends on "1) the nature of the materials to be learned; 2) the nature of the skills, knowledge, and attitudes that learners bring to the situations; and 3) the goals of the learning situation and the assessments used to measure learning relative to these goals."[2]

They then go on to show how a teacher might select teaching techniques according to the desired if-then relationship. For example, if the teacher wants students to learn the characteristics of arteries, then students might use a mnemonic (or memory device) technique: "ART(ery) was *thick* around the middle so he wore pants with an *elastic* waistband."[3] This technique helps students learn that arteries are thick and elastic. However, if the teacher wants students to move to the question of *why* this is true (that is, why are arteries thick and elastic?), then the teacher may need to use a more inquiry-oriented strategy through which students experiment with different types of tubes (some hard and some elastic) to push liquids uphill.

The point is that the conditional (if-then) statement you make about your objectives determines your teaching strategy. You must also think about the goals for learning and the skill set that students bring with them to each learning task. "If students already know the properties of arteries, then they may be ready to consider the reasons for those properties."

The following instructional approaches suggest that teachers can (and must) use a range of teaching strategies and must know how to use both direct and indirect instructional models to foster student growth and development. The direct approaches such as practice and drill are transmission oriented (see Chapter 2) with the teacher explicitly teaching students the academic content they need to know. The indirect strategies are more constructivist oriented and require that students explore ideas to create more personally constructed understandings of salient concepts. Good teachers know when to use the different models and how to use them with students of different ability levels.

Instructional Approach I: Practice and Drill

If teaching a specific skill or process, then use practice and drill.

The mention of practice and drill summons up images of the old-fashioned schoolmaster, the drillmaster, who made learning a repetitive process whereby students either memorized their lessons or experienced the teacher's wrath. However, practice and drill is an instructional method that does serve certain purposes well and can be used to advantage in classrooms today. As we begin the twenty-first century, we now know both the strengths and limits of this approach. Practice and drill has a clear purpose: to help students learn discrete skills or processes *well*.

Applications of Practice and Drill

Practice and drill is a common method used by elementary teachers to teach the fundamentals, especially to young children. The method is also employed by secondary teachers working with students who still lack basic skills or knowledge of academic subject matter before they ask them to move on to other tasks or transfer their learning to a new situation. Some teachers believe lots of practice is essential in order to learn a

The Persistence of Practice and Drill

Herbert M. Klieband
Professor of Curriculum
University of Wisconsin—Madison

The decade of the 1890s was one in which a spirit of reform in education permeated the atmosphere. A young pediatrician, Joseph Mayer Rice, was caught up in this desire to remake American education and embarked on a tour of thirty-six American cities to observe what was going on in American schools. In one New York City school, Rice observed how children learned tiny bits of information by memorizing facts and reciting loudly and rapidly. Rice was properly outraged and dedicated himself to eradicating as far as possible such puerile forms of teaching.

Now, about a century later, such extreme forms of drill are virtually unknown, but all contemporary evidence indicates that the recitation remains the predominant form of classroom discourse. This is despite the fact that many astute and sensitive educational reformers have called for a much greater measure of teaching procedures that involve, say, critical thinking or discovery activities. But, even if teachers are not quite as rigid as in Rice's day, they continue to rely on ditto sheets and workbooks to an unconscionable extent.

Why, we may ask, have classroom practices changed so little from Rice's day to the present? To my way of thinking, the most plausible answer lies in a conflict between two seemingly compatible tasks that teachers are asked to perform: control and teaching. Hardly anyone will argue against the need for a measure of control in classroom situations in order to carry forward the task of teaching. In practice, however, the emphasis on control has so predominated that we can be counted as good teachers so long as our classrooms are orderly. It almost does not matter whether we really teach or not. Practice and drill of the sort that Rice observed persist not because they have specific pedagogical sanction but because they are proven instruments of control. It is only when teachers are able to see their primary role as teaching, not as enforcing a precarious order, that routine practice and drill will be relegated to their appropriately subordinate role in the classroom.

basic skill or task. As a result they repeatedly drill their students. Most teachers are less drill oriented and more open to other instructional approaches, but those different approaches rely heavily on Thorndike's **law of exercise,** which states that the more often a stimulus-response connection is made, the stronger it becomes. This law and Skinner's finding that reinforcement of a response increase the likelihood of its occurrence both provide some basis for the old maxim that practice makes perfect.[4]

Practice and drill can be provided by instructional techniques, such as computerized instruction, which relies on a schedule of reinforcement. In this approach instructional materials are arranged in logical order and broken down into units, called *frames,* that lead students through a program in small steps from the simplest to the most complex material. A program may have hundreds or thousands of frames. Repetition is used to maximize correct responses and to prevent misconceptions. Continuous reinforcement is supplied by getting answers right, and the program presents material in a way that enables students to have a high rate of success. From time to time, frames review previous material or present the same material in different contexts. After making a mistake, the student must practice more before he or she can advance to another level of difficulty.[5]

....

Workbooks are an excellent tool for practice and drill, yet overuse can lead to busy-work and student boredom.

Two methods of instruction are often associated with drill and practice or the transmission view of education: mastery learning and direct instruction.

Mastery Learning Methods

Instruction that is arranged in a logical, progressive order and that matches materials and activities to individual needs and abilities is most effective in fostering achievement. The basis of mastery learning is making certain that adequate learning and mastery of certain concepts and skills have taken place, usually through practice and drill, "before progressing to more complex concepts and skills."[6] Mastery instruction, especially when it is individualized, accommodates varying rates of learning among students.

A student who has difficulty attaining a specific level of performance or mastery can improve by working on the necessary prerequisites with practice and drill. The most important techniques for teaching simple tasks or reinforcing prior learning tasks involve practice and drill.

Direct Instruction Methods

One of the most popular forms of group-based drill and practice is direct instruction (DI). This model was first popularized by Siegfried Engelmann several decades ago as a means of teaching basic academic skills to students. It has grown in popularity recently

t a b l e   5 . 1   **Explicit (Direct) Instruction (Unscripted)**

....

1. *Daily reviews*
   Check previous day's work.
   Check homework.
   Reteach if necessary.

2. *Present new content/skills*
   Introduce with concrete examples.
   Proceed in small steps.
   Give detailed instructions and explanations if necessary.
   Gradually phase in material or task.

3. *Provide guided practice*
   Provide teacher-led practice.
   Provide varying contexts and exercises for student practice.
   Use prompts, cues, visuals, etc. when appropriate.
   Monitor students' work.
   Continue practice until student responses are firm.
   Aim for 80 percent or higher success rate.

4. *Provide feedback*
   Offer teacher-led feedback.
   Provide checklists.
   Correct by simplifying material or task, giving clues, explaining or reviewing steps.
   Reteach if necessary.

5. *Increase student responsibility*
   Diminish prompts, clues, explanations, etc.
   Increase complexity of material or task.
   Ensure student engagement during seat work.
   Monitor student work.
   Aim for 95 percent or higher success rate.

6. *Provide independent practice*
   Encourage students to work on their own.
   Provide extensive practice.
   Facilitate application of new examples.

7. *Weekly and monthly reviews*
   Check for understanding on irregular basis.
   Reteach if necessary.

Source: Adapted from Barak V. Rosenshine. "Teaching Functions in Instructional Programs." *Elementary School Journal* (March 1983): 338. Reprinted with permission.

as a result of the systemic reform efforts within many urban school contexts. Teachers ask questions in a rapid sequence by following a script and students respond with either a choral or individual response. Some teachers use the method for teaching vocabulary or specific skills. Other schools, such as the Cleveland, Ohio, public schools, adopt the approach for selected schools. See Case Study 5.1: Direct Instruction—One Approach for an example of the conflict one teacher experiences regarding using just one approach to teaching skills to students. The DI method can also be unscripted, consisting of a sequenced set of explicit teaching steps.[7] The teacher in such instances would follow the guidelines in Table 5.1 to conduct the lesson.

case study 5.1   Direct Instruction—One Approach

The use of direct instruction is being required in Ms. Simmons' school. Her principal has requested that all the teachers go through direct instruction (DI) training and begin during the next year to use DI in their teaching. He wants the school to be known as a DI school. As Ms. Simmons reviews the literature on DI she becomes aware that there are scripted approaches where the teacher is required to teach in a certain way and unscripted techniques that establish a sequence for presenting content but are not as prescriptive.

The principal provides Ms. Simmons with a videotape of a teacher who is using direct instruction to teach vocabulary to her sixth graders. He wants Ms. Simmons to see what DI looks like so that she can begin to prepare for planned DI professional development. An example of the scripted lesson, as it appears on the videotape, looks like the following:

> Teacher: "Class, spell the word mnemonic." The teacher says each letter as she writes the word on the board: "m-n-e-m-o-n-i-c. Say the word with me, class."
> Teacher and students: "m-n-e-m-o-n-i-c. Mnemonic."
> Teacher: "Right. Mnemonic is spelled m-n-e-m-o-n-i-c. Now, everyone, please write the word on your papers." Students write the words on their papers.
> Teacher: "Good. Now everyone say the word with me. Mnemonic. And it is spelled m-n-e-m-o-n-i-c. Now spell the word mnemonic, Susan."
> Susan: "M-N-E-M-O-N-I-C."
> Teacher: "Good. Leon, spell mnemonic."
> Leon: "M-n-e-m-o-n-i-c."
> Teacher: "Excellent. Class, spell mnemonic."
> Class: "M-n-e-m-o-n-i-c."
> Teacher: "That's great. The word mnemonic refers to a way of remembering things you do not want to forget. The next word is platonic."
> The teacher writes the word on the board and says each letter as she writes the word, "p-l-a-t-o-n-i-c. Say the word with me, class."
> Teacher and students: "P-l-a-t-o-n-i-c."

The lesson progresses through several words and their definitions. The teacher models spelling the words and has the students write and spell each one orally five times. By the time the students are done they have written each word, spelled it orally and have been provided feedback by the teacher.

After viewing the videotape of the scripted approach, Ms. Simmons then reviews articles on some of the more unscripted approaches that focus on the structure of a lesson (see Table 5.1) but do not prescribe the scripted presentation of content in a way that so clearly dictates teacher language and student responses similar to the approach described above.

Ms. Simmons begins to really understand the DI approach, scripted and unscripted. She also sees its utility for teaching some skills and processes. Her principal assures her that she will have lots of opportunity to both practice the technique and receive coaching on how to use it with students effectively. However, she has a reservation.

She recently read research from some international studies (the Third International Mathematics and Science Study or TIMSS) that suggests the reasons some students in foreign countries outperform American students is because teachers in other countries help students see the conceptual underpinnings of the ideas and skills being taught. In essence, the research suggests that good teachers don't teach just skills in isolation but they teach both skills and the conceptual grounding for those skills. It appears that her principal wants her to focus on one way to teach—through scripted DI.

Ms. Simmons is conflicted because she wants to be a good teacher and to be part of a successful school achievement enhancement effort, but she wonders whether it is possible to really teach effectively using only direct instruction methods. Her principal has not told her that DI is sufficient for accomplishing her major instructional goals but she is still concerned.

Questions for Reflection

1. Formal direction instruction (DI), in which teachers use scripted (and unscripted) approaches, is gaining in popularity. Would you be willing to teach in a school that focused singularly on it as an instructional approach? Could you use more inquiry oriented strategies to complement the DI approach? How?
2. Ms. Simmons is aware of some of the international comparative research that suggests effective teachers teach both skills/processes and the conceptual underpinnings for those skills and processes. Identify a skill you might teach for your content area or grade level. What conceptual understandings are part of ensuring that students really understand the skill fully?
3. What problems do you see that might occur for schools using the DI approach?
4. Identify what you would do if you were hired by a school district and then required to teach in ways that you felt did not provide sufficient and appropriate learning opportunities for students? How would you deal with the problem in a way that "protected" the learners?

The main goal of practice and drill is to make sure that students understand the prerequisite skills for the day's lesson. A high success rate on practice items is important for student learning. Similarly, short practice sessions at one sitting minimize the risk of student boredom or burnout. The amount of time for practice varies with age.

In elementary and secondary grades the technique of beginning a lesson by checking or reviewing the previous day's assignment is common in many direct instructional approaches. In a forty-five–minute period in mathematics, for example, educators recommend that daily practice and drill be used to start the lesson for approximately five to ten minutes, and that it be related to homework assignments and computation exercises. Educators also recommend practice as part of seat work activity, when students are engaged in learning new concepts and skills.[8] Practice and drill usage varies by subject and grade level. Teachers need to decide what concepts and skills require this type of focus to ensure that students learn content material sufficiently for mastery.

case study 5.2   Direct Instruction in a High School

Step 1—Present students with a brief explanation or description of the new term or phrase: A few days after the class had started reading the novel *Fahrenheit 451,* Mrs. Locke introduced a new word by telling one student that he should not read the book that was sitting on his desk. Naturally, the student looked surprised. She went on to say that he should read only those books approved by her. She walked over to another student and remarked that she noticed that he was keeping a journal and that it should be turned in at the end of the class to be "checked" in case the student had written anything incriminating. Finally, she told the students that they should always check with her before buying any new CDs so that she could approve their choices. The students looked at one another, wondering what was going on. After a long silence, Mrs. Locke asked the students to describe what she was doing. Ben said, "You were taking charge of our thinking." Joanne thought that she was being unfair. One student said that the teacher had no right to tell them what to read, write about, or listen to. Mrs. Locke explained to the students that they had just experienced a dramatization of the word *censorship.*

Step 2—Present students with a nonlinguistic representation of the new term or phrase: Mrs. Locke then drew a sketch on the board that depicted her dramatization of the word. The picture, she explained, showed a flame engulfing a book, a person speaking, a symbol of religion, and a newspaper.

Step 3—Ask students to generate their own explanations or descriptions of the term or phrase: Mrs. Locke asked the students to work in pairs to generate their own descriptions or explanations for the term *censorship.* Renatta wrote, "Censorship is wrong. It is taking away a person's right to think for himself."

Step 4—Ask students to create their own nonlinguistic representation of the term or phrase: The students also generated their own nonlinguistic representations. Most students used webbing techniques to represent the word, but some used sketches. One student drew a sketch of himself with bandanas around his eyes, his mouth, his ears, and his wrists to show that censorship was like a gag put on all of his senses.

Step 5—Periodically ask students to review the accuracy of their explanations and representations: For the next two weeks, as the students read the novel, they reviewed their definitions and sketches for the term *censorship,* adding new insights.

Questions for Reflection

1. Why does the teacher use nonlinguistic representations of the ideas to help the students understand the concept?
2. Why does the teacher ask students to create their own nonlinguistic representations? Is it really necessary for the students to do this kind of work given the way the teacher presents the concept?
3. Is it appropriate to use direct instruction to teach the concept of citizenship? That is, is the concept too abstract for use in a direct instruction lesson?

Source: Robert J. Marzano, Debra J. Pickering, and Jane E. Pollock. *Classroom Instruction That Works.* Alexandria, Va.: Association for Supervision and Curriculum Development, 2001, p. 129.

At the secondary level, unscripted direct instruction takes a slightly different form, but it still consists of a set of explicit steps. Marzano and colleagues provide an example of what it might look like when teaching new terms or phrases:

Step 1: Present students with a brief explanation or description of the new term or phrase.

Step 2: Present students with a nonlinguistic representation of the new term or phrase.

Step 3: Ask students to generate their own explanations or descriptions of the term or phrase.

Step 4: Ask students to create their own nonlinguistic representation of the term or phrase.

Step 5: Periodically ask students to review the accuracy of their explanations and representations.[9]

Notice the common elements of direct instruction, regardless of whether it is elementary or secondary focused: clear explanation of what is to be learned, teacher modeling, student practice, and repetition or drill.

Implementing Practice and Drill

In order to acquire many basic skills, especially in arithmetic, grammar, and foreign languages, you need to learn certain things to the point of automatic response, such as simple rules of grammar and speech, word recognition, and mathematical calculations (adding, subtracting, multiplying). These skills are needed for more advanced learning and are best learned through practice and drill.

Although practice and drill are accepted in theory, realistic guidelines need to be applied to the classroom setting. What follows is a list of guidelines based on practice and research:

1. *Practice must follow understanding and can enhance understanding:* Students will learn more easily and remember longer if they practice what they understand or have learned through prior and meaningful classroom experiences. At the same time, understanding can be further increased through practice and drill of what is to be learned.

2. *Practice is more effective if students have a desire to learn what is being practiced:* Students will practice what they believe has value or relevance and if they are motivated. For these reasons, it is important for the teacher to provide situational variety (repetition can become boring), interesting aspects of a particular skill as well as interesting drill items, situations in which students can use the skill or knowledge in other phases of learning, drill items related to students' experiences and interests, and explanations of the relationship between the skill or knowledge being learned and more advanced learning.

3. *Practice should be individualized:* Exercises should be organized so that each student can work independently at his or her own level of ability and rate of learning. In this way low-achieving students can devote more time to items that are difficult for them, and high-achieving students can advance without waiting for the others.

4. *Practice should be specific and systematic:* A drill exercise should be related to a specific objective or skill, and students should know in advance what is being practiced. Drill on specific skills in which students need practice will produce better results than will indiscriminate drill. Digressions should be avoided. A systematic, step-by-step procedure fits well with all learners, especially low-achieving students.

5. *Practice should be intermixed with different materials and parts of the lesson:* Drill items can constitute part of chalkboard exercises, mimeographed materials, workbook and textbook exercises, homework, and reviews for tests.[10] Drill may also be used in conjunction with independent seat work, small group learning, or student team learning.

6. *Practice should focus on a few skills rather than on many skills:* It is best to focus on one or two skills at one time and practice those few skills.

7. *Practice should be organized so that students experience high rates of achievement:* Effective drill is characterized by high rates of correct response. Correct responses serve as reinforcement. When students discover that their answers are correct, they are encouraged to go to the next question or item. This is especially important for students who learn slowly. Research suggests that most students need at least a 90 percent rate of correct response while doing practice and drill activities (also for completing homework) in material that has supposedly been learned.[11] Success rate can be lower for students who will not become overly confused or frustrated, as long as the teacher is available to correct their work immediately. These will be students who view themselves as competent.[12] They are often willing to persist even if they experience failure. Students who view themselves as incompetent will not persist in the same way.

8. *Practice should be organized so that students have immediate feedback:* Drills either should be student or teacher scored, with correct answers provided as soon as possible. The teacher needs to know scores or results in order to know if he or she can proceed to the next point or skill. The student, especially the low-achieving student, needs to know the correct responses immediately, not next week or when the teacher has had time to mark the papers.[13] Classroom practice also should be graded each day, with teacher suggestions given for what to do for wrong answers.

9. *Practice material should be used for diagnostic purposes:* Drill items should be constructed to reveal individual problem areas. Much of the practice material can be used for diagnostic purposes as long as the teacher knows what skills each student is working on and has mastered. Studying and keeping a record of students' performance can help the teacher recognize and treat problems before they become habits, seriously affect later work, or cause students to be branded as "remedial" or having a "learning disability."

10. *Practice material should provide progressive continuity between learning tasks:* Too often a skill is taught and left without testing. To foster continuous mastery and systematic recall, there should be a whole sequence of

tips for teachers 5.1

Improving Practice and Drill

 Research has identified several recommendations for improving practice and drill and other seat work activities to enhance academic learning:

1. *Have a clear system of rules and procedures for general behavior:* This allows students to deal with personal needs (for example, seeking permission to use the bathroom pass) and procedural routines (sharpening a pencil) without disturbing classmates.
2. *Move around the room to monitor students' seat work:* Students should feel that the teacher is aware of their behavior and alert to difficulties they may encounter. The extent of monitoring correlates with the students' academic abilities and need for teacher attention.
3. *Provide comments, explanations, and feedback:* The more recognition or attention students receive, the more they are willing to pursue seat work activities. Watch for signs of student confusion and deal with it quickly; this increases students' willingness to persist and helps you know how students are doing and helps you plan the next instructional task. Explain common problems immediately by interrupting the practice exercise if the problems are serious or after the practice if students can wait.
4. *Spend more time teaching and reteaching the basic skills:* Elementary and low-achieving students should be exposed to more skill focused learning, which require practice and drill. When students have difficulty, it is important to instruct in small steps to the point of overlearning.
5. *Use practice during and after learning:* Practice and drill should be used after teaching a specific skill or process. It is most effective mixed with other activities as learning progresses such as demonstrations, explanations, and questions, depending on the students' age and abilities. However, games and simulations for young children and field trips and buzz sessions for older students are not as effective (in terms of use of time) as practice and drill and other paper-and-pencil activities (for review or reteaching).
6. *Provide variety and challenge in practice and drill:* Practice can easily drift into busywork and frustrate or bore students if it is too easy, too difficult, or too monotonous.
7. *Keep students alert and focused on the task:* Teachers need to keep students on task—occasionally questioning them, calling on both volunteers and nonvolunteers, and elaborating on incorrect answers.
8. *Maintain a brisk pace:* There should be little confusion about what to do during practice and drill, and activities should not be interrupted by minor disturbances. A snap of the finger, eye contact, or other "signal" procedures should help deal with inattentive or disruptive students without stopping the lesson.

practice for a specific unit or course, with intermittent drill at desirable intervals. Practice should occur frequently; it should cover tasks in order of difficulty, and the range of items should be wide enough to connect prerequisite learning tasks with new learning tasks.[14] See Tips for Teachers 5.1 for more insight into how to use practice and drill effectively.

As you can see, drill and practice are not an uncomplicated strategy. They must be used purposefully to direct and then reinforce student learning. Read carefully Case Study 5.3: Drill and Practice and reflect on whether Ms. Garland is using the strategy correctly given the guidelines provided. Also, to help you think about instruction in a

case study 5.3   Drill and Practice

This case study illustrates how one teacher uses direct instruction. References to the relevant Pathwise (PRAXIS III) criteria are in parentheses.

Sarah Garland teaches kindergarten at an early childhood center. Several weeks before school begins, Ms. Garland meets individually with each one of her students in order to become familiar with their current knowledge base in emergent reading, writing, and math skills. (A1)

After reviewing the reading results Ms Garland determines that most students recognize the beginning uppercase letter and the lowercase letters in their own names. However, when assessing children on recognition of all twenty-six upper and twenty-six lower case letters, only five out of twenty-one students recognize all of them, six recognize close to half of the letters, and the other eleven students recognize fewer than one-third of the letters. Understanding the importance of recognizing letters as a precursor to reading, Ms. Garland designs a month-long drill and skill program based on "Building Blocks" by Patricia Cunningham to teach letter identification. The program offers the children an opportunity to learn the capital and lowercase letters in an authentic manner. (A2; A3)

At 9:00 A.M. on Monday, after completing one week of the program, Ms. Garland chooses Ben as the student of the day. The children are asked to choose a spot on the floor where they can see him well. (B5) Ben goes up to the front of the class. Ms. Garland explains that they will all learn some new things about Ben today. Also they will learn how to recognize the letters in Ben's name and learn to spell his name. (C1) She says that, by the time they are done today, they will be the authors of their sixth book! She teases by saying she is not sure if this is a kindergarten class or a second grade class because they are extremely smart. The children look up at her with grins on their faces. (B3)

Next Ms. Garland takes the time to interview Ben and ask questions such as "How old are you?" "How many brothers and sisters do you have?" and "What is your favorite thing to do after school?" (B2)

After the students learn some new things about Ben, Ms. Garland gives Ben three five-by-seven cards, each with a letter of his name on them. She purposely mixes them up and asks Ben to put them in the correct order. After he successfully completes the task, she asks Ben to point to the cards and say each letter of his name.

Because the children have completed a week of this program they are familiar with the next several steps. (C1) Ms. Garland asks Ben to lead the class in the Name Cheer. The entire class stands up. Ben begins by pointing to the "B" and says, "Give me a 'B'." The class yells, "B." "Give me an 'E,'" says Ben as he points to the letter card. "E," yells the class. "Give me an 'N'." "N." Ben continues, "What does that spell?" "Ben!" cheers the class. " Say it again," says Ben. "Ben!" "Louder!" "Ben!"

The class remains standing for the Name Chant. Again Ben points to each letter as the children look at the letter card. As they say the letter, they clap to its beat. They continue the verbal chant and clapping to finish spelling Ben's name. They re-

peat the chant several more times but add a different physical activity such as stomp-ing their feet, snapping their fingers, and slapping their thighs. (C2)

During the cheer and the chant Ms. Garland notes that each child is verbally and physically participating in this drill and practice activity. (B1) She also notes that each child is interested in the lesson. She thinks it is because learning the letters in Ben's name is relevant to them, since he is one of their classmates; and each child is given the opportunity both verbally and physically to participate in the lesson.

Ms. Garland asks the children to sit down on the floor. She points to a chart on which the five previous student-of-the-day names are located. She asks the class to compare Ben's name to the previously learned names: Ahmad, Alex, Allen, Amy, and Becky. She asks, "What do you notice about all of these names?" (C3) Some of the responses are "Both Ben's and Becky's name start with a B," "Ben has the same number of letters in his name as Amy," and "Allen ends in 'en' and so does Ben." Ms. Garland congratulates them on being such good letter detectives. (B2) She asks them some of her own questions in order to extend their thinking: "How many vow-els does Ben have in his name and how many does Ahmad have?" "Who has the most letters in their name?" "What are the names of these letters?" "Who has the shortest name?" "Besides Ben, who has an 'e' in their name?" "Who has a 'n'?" The children correctly respond.

Ms. Garland announces it is time to make Ben's very special book. She takes out a blank piece of paper and a sandwich bag filled with three papers with a letter of Ben's name on each. She asks the class, "With what letter does Ben's name begin?" "B," they respond. She pulls a capital B from the bag and glues it to the page. She points out that she starts on the left side of the paper. "OK, what letter is next?" "E," the students respond. Ms. Garland purposely puts the E upside down. Immediately some the of the children notice this isn't correct. She asked how they know. One child tells her it doesn't match the E on Ben's letter card. Ms. Garland praises the student for her bright idea of using the cards as a resource. She places the E in the correct position. She asks what the third and final letter in Ben's name is, and the students respond "N." She writes Ben's name with a crayon under the name and then draws a portrait of Ben. She proclaims that this is her page to put into Ben's very special book. Next each child gets to make a special page for Ben.

The students head back to their desks, and each child receives a piece of paper, a bag with the letters of Ben's name, and crayons. (B1) As the children work on their individual pages for Ben, Ms. Garland works her way around the room making sure children are gluing Ben's name in the correct letter order, starting at the left, are writing the letters properly, and are able to tell her the names of the let-ters in Ben's name. (C4) As she collects the papers, she checks each for accuracy and then congratulates each child on being such good beginning readers, writers, and artists. (B2) She puts all the pages together into a book and presents it to a grin-ning Ben.

Ms. Garland looks at the clock and sees that it is 9:26 A.M. This lesson took twenty-six minutes. She notes that the instructional time was used more effectively than the last five lessons. Last week the first two lessons took thirty-five minutes each and the other three about thirty minutes each. During this lesson, instructional *time was saved because she did not have to reteach the chant, because without much assistance the children were able to offer more information when comparing names, and because they remained on task. (C1) As an informal assessment she also notes that the majority of the children easily placed the letters of Ben's name in order and could name each letter in his name. A few children struggled but she guided them to use the room as a resource, to look at the large letter cards of Ben's name to help, and to repeat the chant. (D1) She plans on formally assessing the children on upper- and lowercase letter recognition at the end of the month once each child has had the opportunity to be student of the day. Because students also practice letter recognition daily in their learning centers and literacy stations, she hopes to see much improvement at the end of the month. (C4)*

Questions for Reflection

1. Can you see all the steps of the direct instruction process in Ms. Garland's approach? What are those steps?
2. If Ms. Garland wanted to foster a higher level thinking for her students, how might she do that given the skill she is trying to teach? Is it appropriate to try to extend student thinking when teaching a basic skill for students?
3. Ms. Garland is described as using informal and formal assessments. Identify what each of those might entail.
4. How might Ms. Garland record her observations or assessments?

Source: This case study was written by Melissa Mikesell, a teacher at West Carrolton Schools.

more focused way, the case study identifies ways in which the Pathwise criteria are part of the instructional process that Ms. Garland follows. The relevant criteria are provided in the parentheses.

Instructional Approach II: Questioning

If checking for student understanding, then use various forms of questioning.

Good teaching involves good questioning, especially when large groups of students are being taught. Skillful questioning can arouse the students' curiosity, stimulate their imaginations, and motivate them to search out new knowledge. It can challenge them, make them think, and help clarify concepts and problems related to the lesson. The type and sequence of the questions and how students respond to them influence the quality of classroom discussion and the effectiveness of instruction. Good teachers usually have skill in striking a balance between factual and thought-provoking questions and between questions that emphasize major points and that stimulate lively discussion. We discussed in Chapter 4 how questions could be used more narrowly to check for understanding. We now expand our discussion to consider how they can be used to help students both solidify concept understandings and develop or construct new ideas.

Types of Questions

Questions can be categorized in many ways: (1) according to thinking process involved, from low level to high level or (according to the cognitive taxonomy) from knowledge to evaluation; (2) according to the type of answer required, whether convergent or divergent; and (3) according to the degree of personal exploration, or valuing. Some authorities have also developed descriptive categories of questions that deal with academic tasks and activities.

Low-level questions emphasize memory and recall of information. When was the Declaration of Independence signed? Who won the Civil War? Where is the Statue of Liberty? These questions focus on facts and do not test understanding or problem-solving skills. They correspond to lower cognitive processes. Most typically, low-level questions begin with *what, when, where,* or *who* (especially when *who* refers to someone other than the person to whom a question is directed). Low-level questions have their place. They are used to assess readiness for complex and abstract thinking, and to see if students can deal with high-level questions that involve analysis, synthesis, and problem solving.

Low-level questions and highly explicit instruction can foster learning, especially with students who lack prerequisite knowledge and who are developing a knowledge base and need to experience basic understandings to build their confidence in learning. According to researchers, low-order questioning is effective for such students when it is used for instructional activities involving basic reading and math, or in any subject in which a basic foundation needs to be built and current learning is an extension of prior learning. The new low-order information must be related in a meaningful way to the knowledge and information the learner already possesses and done so in a way that enables learners to personally discuss and describe their thoughts and ideas.[18]

High-level questions go beyond memory and factual information and call for complex and abstract thinking. They usually begin with *how* or *why.* They typically are used after the teacher establishes that students possess certain fundamental understandings of the content. The ideal is to reach a balance between the two types of questions, with low-level questions typically preceding high-level questions. The trouble is that many teachers do not progress beyond the knowledge-oriented questions. In fact, according to researchers, it is not uncommon to find that 70 to 90 percent of the questions teachers ask are low level.[15]

Criticism of the use of low-level questions is complicated by recent research that indicates that low-level and narrowly defined questions (often evident in direct instructional approaches) characterize effective instructional programs for inner-city and low-achieving learners.[16] Some critics argue that teachers who ask high-level questions and encourage student-initiated comments and inquiry (or discovery of knowledge) are less effective with these types of students,[17] the reason being that these students lack a knowledge base and need more explicit instruction and low-level questions and feedback from teachers before they can move to problem-solving skills and high-level questions. The problem is that teachers often become set in their use of low-level questions (and concomitant low expectations) and thus keep these students permanently in a cognitively second-rate instructional program that fails to intellectually engage them and may be part of the reason for the achievement gap between diverse student groups that is evidenced in so many urban school environments.

A teacher might ask students in a history unit the low-level question "When was the Declaration of Independence signed?" But once students demonstrate command over some basic understandings, the teacher should move on to high-level questions: Why was it necessary for those involved in the American Revolution to sign the Declaration of Independence? What other alternative courses of action were available to the revolutionists? How would these other actions have affected history? Why did the North win the Civil War despite the fact that it lacked the superior military leadership of the South? How did the results of the war affect black-white relations for the remainder of the nineteenth century? Or this century? What does the Statue of Liberty mean to you? To an immigrant arriving in America by ship in 1920? To a Vietnamese or Haitian political refugee today? To a Hispanic worker today crossing the Rio Grande in search of a job?

These questions are obviously more advanced, more stimulating, and more challenging. They also all suggest the existence of *prior knowledge.* To some of them there are no absolutely right or wrong answers. The teacher wants to make the students think and to construct personal cognitive structures. As the questions become more advanced, they involve more abstractions and points of view. Asking high-level questions demands patience and clear thinking on the part of the teacher. Creating appropriate timing, sequencing, and phrasing is no easy task for even the experienced teacher, but such factors are critical in motivating pupils.[19]

The questions are ordered to make connections between what students already know and new information. Lower-order questions develop students' basic understanding of a concept or event so that teachers can then ask more complex questions.

Benjamin Bloom's cognitive taxonomy can be related to the categories of low-level and high-level questions just described. Low-level questioning and knowledge correspond to the knowledge category of the taxonomy—what Bloom calls the "simplest" form of learning and the "most common educational objective." [20] High-level questioning and problem-solving skills correspond to the next five categories of the taxonomy—comprehension, application, analysis, synthesis, and evaluation (see Table 5.2). As we saw in Chapter 3, the six categories of the cognitive taxonomy form a hierarchy of levels of complexity from simple to more advanced, with each level dependent upon the acquisition of skills at the lower levels. The sample questions in the table correspond to the cognitive categories of the taxonomy.

Convergent questions tend to have one correct or best answer. For this reason they are often mistakenly identified as low-level and knowledge questions, but they can also be formulated to demand the selecting of relevant concepts and the working out of problems dealing with steps and structure. Convergent questions can involve logic and complex data, abstract ideas, analogies, and multiple relationships. According to research, convergent questions can be used when students work on and attempt to solve difficult exercises in math and science, especially those involving analysis of equations and word problems.[21]

Divergent questions are often open-ended and usually have many appropriate, different answers. Stating a "right" answer is not always most important; rather, it is selecting a method for arriving at an answer. Students should be encouraged to state their reasoning and to provide supporting examples and evidence. Divergent questions are associated with high-level thinking processes and can encourage creative thinking and discovery learning. Often, convergent questions must be asked first to clarify what

t a b l e   5 . 2   **Questions Related to the Cognitive Taxonomy**

Category	Sample question
1.0 Knowledge	
1.1 Knowledge of specifics	Who discovered the Mississippi River?
1.2 Knowledge of ways and means of dealing with specifics	What word does an adjective modify?
1.3 Knowledge of universals and abstractions in a field	What is the best method for calculating the circumference of a circle?
2.0 Comprehension	
2.1 Translation	What do the words *hasta la vista* mean?
2.2 Interpretation	How do Democrats and Republicans differ in their view of spending?
2.3 Extrapolation	Given the present birth rate, what will be the world population by the year 2010?
3.0 Application	How has the *Miranda* decision affected civil liberties? Given a pie-shaped lot 120 ft. × 110 ft. × 100 ft. and village setback conditions of 15 ft. in all directions, what is the largest one-story home you can build on this lot?
4.0 Analysis	
4.1 Analysis of elements	How would you distinguish between fact and opinion in the article we read?
4.2 Analysis of relationships	How does Picasso organize colors, shapes, and sizes to produce images?
4.3 Analysis of organizational principles	How does John Steinbeck use his characters to discuss the notion of friendship in *Of Mice and Men?*
5.0 Synthesis	
5.1 Production of a unique communication	Who can write a simple melodic line?
5.2 Production of a plan or proposed set of operations	How would you go about determining the chemical weight of an unknown substance?
5.3 Derivation of a set of abstract relations	What are the common causes for cell breakdown in the cases of mutations, cancer, and aging?
6.0 Evaluation	
6.1 Judgment in terms of internal evidence	Who can show the fallacies of Hitler's *Mein Kampf?*
6.2 Judgment in terms of external evidence	Who can judge what is wrong with the architect's design for the plumbing and electricity?

Adapted from: Allan C. Ornstein. "Questioning: The Essence of Good Teaching." *NASSP Bulletin* (May 1987): 73–74.

students know before divergent questions are posed. But the ideal is to ask fewer convergent questions, especially low-level ones, and more divergent questions. The mix of convergent and divergent questions will reflect the students' abilities, the teacher's ability to phrase such questions, and the teacher's comfort with handling varied responses.

Convergent questions usually start with *what, who, when,* or *where;* divergent questions usually start with *how* or *why. What* or *who* questions, followed by *why,* are really divergent questions. For example, "*Who* won the Civil War?" leads to the ultimate question "*Why?*" The differences are highlighted by the sample questions in Table 5.3. Most teachers ask far more *what, who, when,* and *where* questions than *how* or *why* questions.[22] This is because the convergent questions are simple to phrase and to

table 5.3   Sample Convergent and Divergent Questions

Subject and Grade Level	Convergent Questions	Divergent Questions
Social studies, 5th–7th	Where did the Boston Tea Party take place? When did it take place?	Why did the Boston Tea Party take place? Why did it take place in Boston, not New York or Philadelphia?
Social studies, 7th–8th	What are the three products from Argentina?	How does wheat production in Argentina affect wheat export in our country?
English, 5th–7th	What is the verb in the sentence "The girl told the boy what to do"?	How do we write the present and future tense of the verb in the sentence "The girl told the boy what to do"?
English, 10th–11th	Who wrote *A Farewell to Arms*?	How might Hemingway's experience as a news reporter have affected his writing of the novel *A Farewell to Arms*?
Science, 2nd–5th	Which planet is closest to the sun? Who was the first American astronaut to travel in space?	How would you compare living conditions on Mercury with those on Earth? What planet, other than Earth, would you prefer to visit if you were an astronaut? Why?
Science, 9th–11th	What are two elements of water?	Why is water purified?
Math, 4th–5th	What is the definition of a triangle?	How have triangles influenced architecture?
Math, 6th–9th	What is the shortest distance between two points?	What is the best air route to take from New York City to Moscow? Why?

grade. They help keep students focused on specific data, and they give many students a chance to participate. Convergent questions thus make good questions for practice and review. Divergent questions require more flexibility on the part of the teacher. For the student they require the ability to cope with uncertainty about being right and with the possibility of not getting approval from the teacher. In general, the pace of questioning is slower. There is more opportunity for students to exchange ideas and differing opinions. There is also more chance for disagreement among students and between students and teacher—which is often discouraged or viewed as tangential by teachers.

Right Answers Count

In the majority of American classrooms, teachers ask convergent questions, which entail a "right" answer, and students are expected to give the answer—often resulting in teacher approval. These questions and answers, coupled with the students' need for approval (especially at the elementary grade level) permit teachers to dominate classroom interaction. According to Jules Henry, students "learn the signal response system called docility and thus obtain approval from the teacher."[23] Indeed, what usually counts in school are right answers, not necessarily how you arrived at the answer.

For low-achieving students and for students who need teacher approval, the magic word from the teacher is often *yes* or *right*. The teacher determines what is right in the classroom, and the easiest way to test students is to ask convergent questions. Divergent questions, on the other hand, lead to novel responses—responses that the teacher does not always expect, and responses that take up class time (or time out from the formal curriculum). This may be difficult to deal with for students who have come through the educational system being right-answer oriented or for teachers who have been trained to provide or look for correct answers.

John Holt points out that, as students become right-answer oriented, they become producers, producing what teachers want, not thinkers, constructing personal understandings of what the content suggests. It is only the rare student who is willing to play with ideas, not caring whether the teacher confirms an answer is right. The average child has a need to be right because that is what teachers in American schools expect: "She [the student] cannot bear to be wrong. When she is wrong . . . the only thing to do is to forget it as quickly as possible."[24] Few teachers understand that wrong answers are just as important as right answers. When students provide wrong answers they are showing the teacher how they are thinking about a particular question or idea and constructing the content, which suggests, then, what reteaching the teacher needs to do. Instead of dismissing wrong answers, ask students how they derived them and then make a decision on how to reteach. Interestingly, the Japanese, who consistently perform well in international comparisons, place more focus on *how* a student derived an answer than on whether a student has the right answer.

Asking questions to which there is only one right answer fosters a view of learning that is self-limiting—one that looks for simple solutions to complex problems, one that relies on authority rather than on rational judgment. It also breeds a rigid and narrow mind that fails to recognize or is unwilling to admit that facts and figures are screened through a filtering process of personal and social experience and interpretation.[25] The current academic standards emphasis in American education will likely enhance America's right-answer orientation. That need not be the case in your classroom. Remember, you want to teach content and to help students explore that content. To do that successfully requires variability.

Asking Questions Correctly

Good questioning is both a methodology and an art; there are certain rules to follow that have been found to apply in most cases, but good judgment is also needed. See Tips for Teachers 5.2 and 5.3 for some review of formulating questions and for some recommendations for procedures in asking questions.

In preparing for asking questions in class, a number of instructional strategies have been shown to be effective for a large number of different teachers and students. Most of these instructional strategies come from educational psychology and researchers who study teacher effectiveness, not from the curriculum, instruction, or teaching methods that one might think would contribute to this field of knowledge.

Wait-Time

The interval between asking a question and the student response is referred to as **wait-time.** One study by Mary Budd Rowe indicated that the average amount of time teachers wait is one second. Increasing the wait-time to three to four seconds has several

Don'ts in Asking Questions

 Good questioning techniques have to be developed slowly and over the years. They must become second nature, a habit. Just as you can form good or bad habits in driving a car or swinging a golf club, you can develop good and bad habits in questioning. Try to eliminate the don'ts from asking questions before they become ingrained as habits. What follows is a list of things a teacher should *not* do:

1. *Ask yes or no questions or questions that give a guesser a fifty-fifty chance of getting the right answer:* "Did Orwell write *Animal Farm?*" and "Who won the battle at Gettysburg?" are the kinds of questions that encourage guessing, impulsive thinking, and right-answer orientation, not conceptual thinking or problem solving. If the teacher accidentally asks this kind of question, he or she should follow up immediately with a why or how question.

2. *Ask indefinite or vague questions:* "What are the important cities of the United States?" and "How would you describe the following sentence?" are confusing questions and must be repeated or refined. Questions should be clearly worded and coincide with the intent of the teacher.

3. *Ask guessing questions:* Guessing questions can also be "yes" or "no" questions, indefinite or vague questions. Ask students to explain ideas and show relationships, rather than request detailed or trivial information.

4. *Ask double or multiple questions:* Asking, "What is the chemical formula for salt? What is its chemical weight?" confuses students. Which question does the teacher want answered?

5. *Ask suggestive or leading questions:* "Why was Andrew Jackson a great president?" appears to be asking for an opinion, but the opinion has already been given or implied.

6. *Ask fill-in questions:* In "The New Frontier occurred during whose presidency?" the question is embedded. It is better to express the question clearly: "Which president implemented the New Frontier?"

7. *Ask overload questions:* "In connection with pollution factors and the sun's rays, what conclusions can we make about the future water level?" and "How did Manifest Destiny lead to imperialism and colonialism, while enhancing the industrialization of the country?" are indefinite, multiple, and wordy. Trim excess verbiage, use simple rather than overly formal or obscure vocabulary, and ask clear, simple questions to avoid confusing the student.

8. *Ask tugging questions:* "What else?" and "Who else?" tug at the student and do not really encourage thought.

9. *Cross-examination questions:* You may be able to assist a student by asking a series of questions to draw out information. However, this should be distinguished from asking many or rapid questions of the same student, which not only can overwhelm the target student but can also make the rest of the class feel neglected.

10. *Call the name of a student before asking a question:* As soon as students know that someone else is responsible for the answer, their attention lessens. First ask a question, then pause to allow for comprehension, and then call on someone to answer it.

11. *Answer a question asked by a student if students should know the answer:* Turn the question back to the class and ask, "Who can answer that question?"

12. *Repeat questions or repeat answers given by students:* Reiteration fosters poor work habits and inattentiveness. A good practice is to say, "Who can repeat that question or that answer?"

13. *Exploit bright students or volunteers:* The rest of the class becomes inattentive and loses contact with the discussion.

14. *Allow choral responses or hand waving:* Both are conducive to undesirable behavior.

15. *Allow improper speech or incomplete answers to go unnoticed:* Young people are quick to cultivate wrong habits. Supply the correction without stopping the recitation.

Source: Adapted from Allan C. Ornstein. "Questioning The Essence of Good Teaching: Part II." *NASSP Bulletin* (February 1988): 77.

tips for teachers 5.3

Do's in Asking Questions

Now that you know what not to do after reading Tips for Teachers 5.2, here is a list of things to do in questioning. Practice them so they become second nature in your instructional process:

1. *Ask questions that are stimulating and not merely memory testing or dull:* A good teacher arouses students and makes them reflect with thought-provoking questions. Questions that ask for information recall will not sustain the attention of a class and that's when discipline and management problems begin.

2. *Ask questions that are commensurate with students' abilities:* Questions that are dramatically below or above the abilities of students will bore or confuse them. Target questions, even on difficult subjects, within the ability level of the majority of the class.

3. *Ask questions that are relevant to students:* Questions that draw on students' life experiences will be relevant.

4. *Ask questions that are sequential:* Questions and answers should be used as stepping stones to the next question. This contributes to continuous learning.

5. *Vary the length and difficulty of questions:* Questions should be diversified so that both high- and low-achieving students will be motivated to participate. Observe individual differences and phrase questions so that all students take part in the discussion.

6. *Ask questions that are clear and simple:* Questions should easily be understood and trimmed of excess verbiage.

7. *Encourage students to ask questions of each other and to make comments:* This results in students becoming active learners and cooperating on a cognitive and social level, essential for reflective thinking and social development. Good questions stimulate further questions, even questions by students. Encourage student comments and interaction and refer student questions and comments, even when they are directed at the teacher, to other students to promote discussion.

8. *Allow sufficient time for deliberation:* Pausing for a few seconds until several hands go up gives everyone, particularly the learners who need more time, a chance to consider the question. As a result, everyone profits from the discussion, and learning takes place for all.

9. *Follow up incorrect answers:* Take advantage of wrong or marginal answers. Probe the student's mind. Encourage the student to think about the question. Perhaps the student's thinking is partially correct, even novel.

10. *Follow up correct answers:* Use a correct answer as a lead to another question. A correct answer sometimes needs elaboration or can be used to stimulate student discussion.

11. *Call on nonvolunteers and volunteers:* Some students are shy and need coaxing from the teacher. Other students tend to daydream and need assistance from the teacher to keep attentive. Distribute questions among the entire class so that everyone can participate.

12. *Call on disruptive students:* This involves troublesome students without having to interrupt the lesson. It is important, however, not to call on them as a disciplinary technique. Call on "problem" students when they are already involved. Reinforce the behavior that you desire.

13. *Prepare five or six pivotal questions:* Such questions test students' understanding of the lesson as well as enhance the lesson unity and coherence.

14. *Write the objective and summary of the lesson as a question, preferably as a problem:* Questions encourage the class to think. The students are made to consider the new work when asked about it.

15. *Change your position and move around the room:* Teacher energy and vitality induce class activity, rapport, and socialization. They also foster an active audience and prevent daydreaming and disciplinary problems.

Source: Adapted from Allan C. Ornstein. "Questioning: The Essence of Good Teaching: Part II." *NASSP Bulletin* (February 1988): 77.

Teachers should call on a variety of volunteers and nonvolunteers to check for understanding.

beneficial effects on student responses: 1) length of response increases, 2) unsolicited but appropriate responses increase, 3) failure to respond decreases, 4) confidence (as reflected in an affirmative rather than a questioning tone of voice) increases, 5) speculative responses increase, 6) student-to-student responses increase, 7) evidence-inference statements increase, 8) student questions increase, and 9) responses from students rated by teachers as relatively slow increase.[26]

No negative side effects of increasing wait-time have been observed, and the positive effects are numerous. Yet many teachers do not employ this wait-time instructional strategy. Other data suggest that asking one to four questions per minute is reasonable and that beginning teachers ask too many questions, averaging only one second of wait-time.[27] Also, although all students need time to process information, low-achieving students need more time, but the data indicate that teachers tend to wait less time for an answer from the students they perceive as academically slow. Here the need is to be willing to slow down the lesson; cover fewer topics; focus on the most important ideas; ask more questions; and develop explanations.

Directing

The recommended strategy in directing questions to students is to ask the question and then call a student's name, because that way more students will think about it. Research on classroom management also confirms that it is better to be unpredictable in calling on students to answer questions but to do so in a way that maximizes participation. Indeed, Evertson and her colleagues suggest that "This can be done by using a checklist or shuffled stack of name cards. Some teachers [even] place a strip of construction paper on each student's desk as a marker. As a student contributes . . . the marker is removed."[28] On the other hand, when calling on students to read, using a predictable order seems to be more effective with the lower grades and with low-achieving students.[29] The reason is perhaps that predictability reduces anxiety, which is important for young children who are reading in front of the class.

The research also indicates that calling on nonvolunteers can be effective as long as students who are called on can answer the question most of the time. It is a good idea to call on nonvolunteers when it is believed that students can respond correctly, but it is not appropriate to embarrass them with their inability to answer the questions or to catch them off-task so that you can discipline them. This is probably true at all grade levels and subjects. If you call on a nonvolunteer and get an incorrect response, you can do two things: (1) match the correct statement to the wrong answer (e.g., if you ask, "What is the capital of New York?" and a student responds "Harrisburg" say, "Harrisburg is the capital of Pennsylvania; I want the capital of New York"); or (2) ask the student to explain a wrong answer. Quite frankly, some student explanations of wrong answers will make sense, which provides the teacher with more opportunities to probe and question. The key is that, to the extent possible, a teacher should stick with the student who was originally asked the question.

Although some research indicates that teachers should call on nonvolunteers no more than 15 percent of the time, practice indicates this figure may be too low.[30] By emphasizing volunteers, there is a tendency to call on high-achieving students more often than low-achieving students. Calling on more nonvolunteers increases the likelihood that low-achieving students will be included in the discussion. It is generally a good idea to call on low achievers who usually do not volunteer, and they should periodically be called on as nonvolunteers as long as they are likely to be able to answer the question correctly. If they do give a wrong answer, you have several choices. You can, as suggested earlier, (a) provide the right "lead" for the answer the student gave, (b) reword the question and probe, or (c) ask another student (through a question redirect) for a correction. We'll examine the redirect and probing options next.

Redirecting and Probing

If a student response to a question is incorrect or inadequate, an effective strategy is not to provide the answer, but to **redirect** the question to another student or to probe for a better answer from the same student. In general, teachers overuse redirecting. Redirecting the question is better for high-achieving students, but probing is better for low-achieving students. High-achieving students seem to be able to cope better with minor academic failure in front of their peers and thus are better able to accept redirection. This is especially true if a teacher knows how to "honor" a wrong answer. That is, treat the answer as logical but incorrect. Teacher persistence in seeking improved responses from low-achieving or at-risk students is a reflection of positive teacher expectations, which is important in trying to reach and teach such students.

In **probing** the teacher stays with the same student, asking for clarification, rephrasing the question or asking related questions, and restating the student's ideas. It is important not to overdo it, lest the probing become a cross-examination.[31] On the other hand, if the teacher feels that the student was not paying attention, it is best that he or she not probe and give the student a second chance; otherwise the teacher would unwittingly be condoning (even rewarding) the student's lack of attention. During the probing process the teacher may ask a series of easier questions that lead toward the answer to the original question. If the student answers correctly (either initially or in response to a rephrased question), the teacher may want to follow with a related question to pursue the implications of the answer and to ensure student understanding.

Probing is acceptable for all students. With high-achieving students it tends to foster high-level responses and discussion. With low-achieving students it tends to reduce the frequency of no responses or incorrect responses. In both cases probing is positively correlated with increased student achievement, especially if it fosters students' ability to engage in personal problem solving by pushing the students to solve intellectual problems themselves rather than to have them solved for them.[32]

Commenting and Praising

While research on the use of praise is mixed, it is generally agreed that honest, thoughtful praise increases achievement and motivation. Positive reactions can simply mean a smile, nod of approval, or brief comment ("Good," "Correct," "That's true") indicating approval or acceptance. Phoney praise or public praise can have detrimental effects.

Most teachers do not use sufficient or genuine praise while questioning or with other methods of instruction. Yet it is clear that praise and other positive reinforcement strategies can have positive effects on student behavior.[33] Experts have noted that praise of good answers to questions or good work in general needs to be spontaneous and genuine, not for the purpose of controlling student behavior or tacitly expressing teacher expectations.[34]

The research is also mixed about negative comments. It does suggest that teachers use criticism and disapproval sparingly, even less than praise, which is a good thing since criticism can have a detrimental effect on student achievement. Similarly, if used by a teacher in response to a student question or comment, criticism can curtail students' asking questions or responding to the teacher's questions.[35] Low achievers receive more criticism than high achievers—it is possible that low achievement causes teachers to use more criticism. Boys receive more criticism (and also more attention) from teachers than do girls—we know that boys often achieve less than girls because teachers tend to emphasize physical activities with boys and intellectual exercises with girls.[36] In other words, a correlation seems to exist between criticism (or negative attention) and lowered achievement, but a cause and effect relationship is uncertain.

We have explored a series of ideas and observations about questioning. Questions can be used for different reasons and to achieve different goals. Ideally, though, they are always used to assess what students know and how they are making sense of what the teacher is teaching.

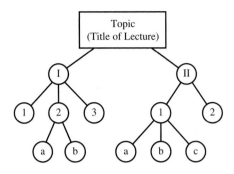

figure 5.1   Example of the Classification Hierarchy Form to Show "Links."

Source: Donald A. Bligh. *What's the Use of Lectures?* San Francisco: Jossey Bass, 2000: 70.

Instructional Approach III: Lecture

If seeking to present complex conceptual ideas efficiently, then use lecture.

Lecture or teacher-centered instruction is not inherently good or bad. The value of lecture is determined by whether the content must be taught for short-term memory or long-term retention. The longer you want students to remember something, the less oriented to lecture you should be for delivering content or the more you need to complement lecture with more interactive strategies such as discussion or cooperative learning. Students remember content longer when they actively engage the content. A lot of factual content simply does not need to be retained for long periods, but some conceptual material must be retained. Hence, a teacher may choose to lecture about some content (embrace a transmission view of knowledge) but then create opportunities for students to use that knowledge in ways that help them explore (or construct) their understandings of the content more fully (we will discuss the more student-centered constructivist orientation with Instructional Approach IV).

Lectures are divided into two types for our discussion:

1. Formal or *hierarchic* lectures last for most of or the entire class session with a modest number of student questions and comments. The teacher maintains primary control even during discussion times. Formal lectures should be used with more developmentally mature students who can sit for longer periods of time and take notes on their own. In a hierarchic lecture, different points of information are grouped under common headings (see Figures 5.1 and 5.2).

2. Informal, more *problem-centered* lectures last about five to ten minutes. The teacher starts with a problem, then gives students information, and subsequently explores arguments and solutions relative to the stated problem. Extensive student responses and questions focus on exploring the problem and its solution. Problem-solving lectures are more informal because the exchange between teachers and students is more fluid and less teacher-centered.[37]

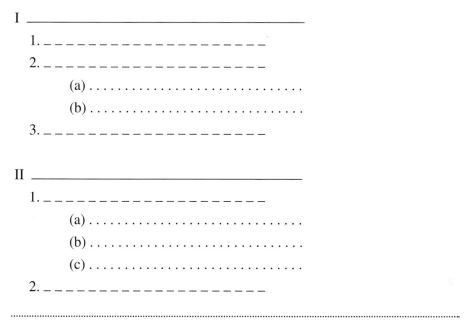

figure 5.2   Sequence and Probable Blackboard Organization of a Hierarchic Lecture.

Source: Donald A. Bligh. *What's the Use of Lectures?* San Francisco: Jossey Bass, 2000: 70.

Discussions are often an outgrowth of lectures. They are oral exchanges between the teacher and students or interactions among the students. Discussions permit students to respond to teacher statements, to ask questions, and to clarify ideas. The more involved students are in discussion, the more effective the exchange of ideas is likely to be, since students' thoughts tend to wander as teacher talk increases. Younger and low-achieving students become inattentive more readily than older and high-achieving students. The implication is clear: Teachers should make an effort to maintain student attention by limiting lecture and increasing discussion time. Discussions are opportunities for students to express their ideas; they are not structured for students to respond to a series of teacher questions—that is a recitation. One way to enhance discussions during lecture is to rely on informal cooperative learning strategies, which we will discuss more fully in Chapter 8.

One thing you will notice in discussions is that the social context in which you teach may influence the way in which students react to your lectures. Students from middle- and upper-class homes are often much more reticent to engage in heated verbal exchanges. Students from urban environments often relish heated verbal exchanges. Hence, as Brookfield and Preskill note, "What constitutes appropriate forms of classroom discourse is [often] much closer to middle-class than working-class speech norms."[38]

Problems of Lecturing

During lectures delivered by a teacher, there is little give-and-take between the teacher and students and among students. Lecturing is often described as "unnecessary," "dull," and a "waste of time." Formal, hierarchic lectures can be boring, especially when teachers do not allow for student response or when the lectures are not adequately prepared or are repetitive and lack stimulus variation. Attention span is correlated with age and ability, and with young and low-achieving students attention span is limited.[39] For such students it is essential that teacher talk in any form (especially lecturing and explaining) be limited to a few minutes' duration at any one time and be intermixed with other instructional activities (audio, visual, and physical). There should be more concrete activities than verbal and abstract presentations.

Lectures can quickly lead to boredom when the audience is passive for a lengthy period. One method for helping high school students learn from lectures and also for engaging them actively is for the teacher to prepare a series of questions about the content to be covered: "What is the main idea of . . . ?" "How does . . . affect . . . ?" "Why is . . . important?"[40] These types of questions help students identify main ideas, organize notes, and engage in critical thinking, as opposed to recording pieces of the lecture and memorizing the information—or even worse, drifting or losing concentration. The need is for students to integrate and anchor ideas of the lecture; that is, to become more involved in processing information as opposed to sitting passively. Another way to influence students' attention, comprehension, and engagement is by doing the following:

1. Varying the stimulation through voice tone (raise or lower your voice), visual stimuli (use gestures or move around while lecturing), or the introduction of novel stimuli (e.g., pictures of content being discussed)

2. Being enthusiastic about the ideas and putting energy into the actual presentation

3. Showing the relevance of the ideas to the students' lives[41]

Benefits of Lecturing and Explaining

Based on a review of several studies of the lecture method, Gage and Berliner feel that the lecture technique is appropriate when 1) the basic purpose is to disseminate information, 2) the information is not available elsewhere, 3) the information needs to be presented in a particular way or adapted to a particular group, 4) interest in a subject needs to be aroused, 5) the information needs to be remembered for a short time, and 6) the purpose is to introduce or explain other learning tasks. They further state that the lecture method is inappropriate when 1) objectives other than acquisition of information are sought; 2) long-term learning is desired; 3) the information is complex, abstract, or detailed; 4) learner participation is important for achieving the objectives; 5) higher cognitive learning, such as analysis and synthesis, is sought; and 6) students are below average in ability.[42]

There are administrative and practical reasons for using informal and brief lectures as well as explanations. These methods are well suited to large groups, and few materials and equipment are needed, giving the methods the additional benefit of being economical. The methods are flexible and can be used in regular classrooms, small groups, and large settings. Teachers who travel or change classrooms need only to carry with them their lesson plans or notes. Although good lectures need considerable preparation, their delivery does not require elaborate advance planning, advance ordering of

Enhancing Your Lectures

 There are numerous methods for improving your lectures and explanations in class. Evaluate your lesson with regard to the following guidelines:

1. Maintain eye contact with class.
2. Use handouts and overheads to help students follow the presentation and focus on important ideas.

3. Avoid high levels of detail unless supplemented by graphs, tables, or illustrations.
4. Write important information on the chalkboard.
5. Define new terms and concepts.
6. Provide an outline for note taking.
7. Present relevant examples to explain major ideas.
8. Relate new information to prior information.
9. Summarize important ideas.

materials, or advance scheduling of equipment. The fact that teachers are not dependent on others to carry out the lecture, explanation, or discussion makes it easy and comfortable for them. See Tips for Teachers 5.4 to find out how to enhance your lectures.

Presenting Lectures and Explanations

When preparing and presenting informal or brief lectures and providing explanations, you might consider the following steps and suggestions:

1. *Establish rapport with students:* At the beginning of a talk you should take measures to establish rapport with students. (Periodically telling a story or using humor helps maintain student interest in the subject and rapport with you.) Always keep in mind the need to maintain the interest of students and the fact that students will react to you first on a personal basis and then on a cognitive basis.

2. *Prepare lectures:* Outline the major concepts or ideas in advance, especially for hierarchic lectures. Indicate the corresponding activities and materials— say, in the lesson plan—to introduce at a certain point. Except for short passages or quotations to make a point, you should not read from notes. You must know the material well enough to speak clearly and with animation and to speak extemporaneously as you sense the need of the moment and the interests of the students.

3. *Control the length of lectures and explanations:* Brief lectures and explanations are suitable for elementary school students. Short lectures or explanations of five to ten minutes are acceptable at the middle grade and junior high school levels. High school students can tolerate longer periods of interesting teacher talk. Always try to limit your lecturing and explaining and use questions, discussions, various student activities, and media as supplementary tools of instruction. Overall, though, remember the 10-2 rule—approximately ten minutes of lecture require a couple of minutes of interaction to assess learning.

4. *Motivate students to pay attention:* Relevancy motivates students. To achieve relevance, you should consider the students' age, ability, educational

experiences, environment, interests, needs, perceived goals, and career aspirations. You can make the lesson more understandable and interesting by combining other methods, materials, and media with your talk. When students perceive the relevance of, understand, and are interested in the topic, they become success oriented and are more intrinsically motivated—that is, they pursue "the goal of achievement for the sake of achievement."[43]

5. *Establish structure and sequence:* A disorganized talk confuses and bores its audience. Present major concepts and difficult ideas in a linear and logical fashion, with examples and questions to test students' understanding. That is why it is important to use structures such as those in Figures 5.1 and 5.2. They "force" you to be clear and organized. Develop facts and concepts systematically and sequentially from statement to statement. Relate the overall topic to the topic of the previous lesson. Make your sentence structure and vocabulary appropriate for the students' level of development. Although this seems an obvious point, many beginning teachers speak over the vocabulary level and content understanding of students. Both hierarchic and problem-solving lectures require that you understand how you want to present content.

   The criteria for a structured lecture, according to researchers are 1) continuity, or a sequenced arrangement of ideas expressed in intelligible and grammatically correct sentences; 2) simplicity, or the absence of complex sentences and the use of language within the students' vocabulary range; and 3) explicitness, or the identification and explanation of major concepts and relationships.[44]

   Effective explanatory talk tends to correspond with what we often mean by coaching. More effective teachers engage in highly structured explanations and are 1) more responsive to student questions, 2) more adequate in presenting content, 3) more complete in providing specific information, and 4) better at giving students feedback to help them learn.[45]

6. *Provide appropriate graphic organizers:* Teachers can provide students with "graphic organizers" to help them assimilate content (see Figure 5.3). They can provide means for the students to organize the ideas to be presented in the lecture by telling them in advance what the lecture or explanation will focus on and how it will be structured. Research also suggests that teachers who use graphic organizers enhance student achievement.[46] (Figure 5.3 illustrates three different types of graphic organizers: expository, comparative, and sequential.) Another technique is to outline the major topics or parts of the lesson, either orally or in writing (on the chalkboard), as they unfold (not in advance) during the discussions. (See, again, Figures 5.1 and 5.2.) This is especially helpful when students are listening to the teacher and must select, process, and assimilate the information with which they are working.

7. *Avoid vagueness:* Lectures and explanations that are free of vague language are easier to follow and to understand. Researchers have labeled nine kinds of vague terms: 1) ambiguous designation—somewhere, somehow; 2) approximation—about, almost, nearly, sort of; 3) bluffing—anyway, as you know, so forth, to make a long story short; 4) error admission—I'm not sure, I guess, perhaps; 5) indeterminate amount—a couple, few, some,

Expository Organizer

Structure of Constitution

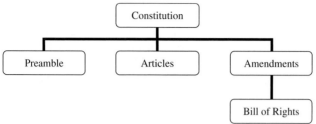

Comparative Organizer

How do 4th, 6th, and 8th Amendments relate relative to due process rights?

Amendments			
	4th	6th	8th
What does it say?			
What does it mean?			
When is it relevant to criminal process?			

Sequential Organizer

Dividing a decimal by a decimal

Step 1: Multiply the divisor and the dividend by the appropriate power of 10 that will make both divisor and dividend a whole number.

Step 2: Then divide as you would with any whole number.

figure 5.3   Types of Graphic Organizers.

many; 6) negated intensifiers—not many, not very much; 7) multiplicity—aspects, kind of, type; 8) possibility—chances are, perhaps, it seems, could be; and 9) probability—frequently, generally, usually, often.[47]

Another factor that leads to vagueness is discontinuous and irrelevant content. The content may be important at another time but, when introduced at an inappropriate time, it distracts from the main ideas. In a clear lecture, the sequence of ideas from sentence to sentence is clear, and the language is free of ill-defined and redundant words. Lecturers need to be clear and concise—using short and precise sentences; providing examples; using simple, jargon-free language; and including the minimum number of concepts to make a point. As a presenter or lecturer, you need to be decisive, avoid fillers and long pauses, and in general, display confidence in order to maintain your credibility.[48]

8. *Combine instructional materials and strategies:* The use of audiovisual aids and special materials and activities can liven a talk and reinforce its content. The use of informal cooperative learning strategies can also enhance lecture, which we will discuss in Chapter 8. Varied stimuli are important for all learners, but younger students especially benefit from less verbalization and more illustrations and activities. Display such aids only when you talk about them; explain visuals to your audience; use a marker or highlighter when using an overhead to focus students on key points; and use the k-i-s-s (keep it short and simple) principle—minimize detail. Make sure visuals (whether overhead or PowerPoints) are readable from the back of the room.

9. *Encourage students to take notes:* The activity of recording notes serves as an encoding (comprehension) function, helping to integrate content into long-term memory. Note takers outperform listeners (non–note takers) about four to one at the high school and college level. Effective note taking serves both a storage function and review function prior to tests.[49] You can also provide an outline for students to use in helping them take their notes.

10. *Summarize content:* Classroom discussions should always end with **final summaries** or conclusions, what some educators call *postorganizers.* The lesson may also have **internal summaries,** what some educators call *medial summaries, conceptual frameworks,* or *chunking strategies.*[50] *Medial summaries,* with accompanying summary activities and transitions, subdivide a lesson into clear parts. It is more important to incorporate medial summaries for low-achieving and young students than for high-achieving or older students.

    The best type of summary (medial or final) briefly reviews the presentation and gives students a chance to see whether they understand the material by asking them to explain ideas, provide examples, evaluate data, and do some exercises. It lets them know what they have learned and helps identify major ideas of the lesson.

    After the final summary, the teacher should explain related homework and prepare students for any problems they may encounter in it. Also, the teacher might establish a connection between the just-completed lesson and the next lesson.

ACTIVITY FOR REFLECTION

There is a wonderful scene in the movie *Ferris Bueller's Day Off* when the teacher (played by Ben Stein) is lecturing to students. He talks and then asks questions but he gives the students little time to respond. But, even if they did have time, they could not respond because they really are not listening. Watch that section of the movie and identify a way in which the same content could be delivered effectively. Stein is doing everything wrong for comedy effect, but it is funny because we have all experienced it. Identify specific things that he is doing wrong. How could he have done the lecture right? It would not, then, be funny, but it would be educational.

Instructional Approach IV: Student-Centered Learning

If fostering critical or creative thinking, then use strategies that emphasize student-centered learning.

A great deal of literature since the beginning of the twentieth century has focused on student problem solving and related thinking skills. Ever since Charles Judd (at the University of Chicago) and Edward Thorndike (at Columbia University) showed that learning could be explained in terms of general principles of thinking and methods of attacking problems transferred to different situations, educators and psychologists have worked to identify ways to teach students how to problem solve.

John Dewey's process of **reflective thinking** was considered the classic model for problem solving from 1910 until the 1950s, when Piaget and others introduced new models of various cognitive and information-processing strategies. Although Dewey's model is viewed as an oversimplification by cognition theorists, it is still considered practical, especially by science and math teachers.

Since one of the chief functions of school, for Dewey, was to improve the reasoning process, he recommended adopting the reflective thinking method for all subjects and grade levels. Reflective thinking involves five steps: 1) become aware of difficulty, 2) identify the problem, 3) assemble and classify data and formulate hypotheses, 4) accept or reject tentative hypotheses, and 5) formulate and evaluate conclusions.[51]

Dewey's reflective model is based on a mixture of theory and practice, and many problem-solving models today are also based on the same ingredients. For example, Bransford and Stein outline the IDEAL model for problem-solving: 1) identify the problem, 2) define it, 3) explore possible strategies, 4) act on the strategies, and 5) look at the effects of your efforts.[52]

A number of educators describe successful problem solving as **heuristic thinking**—that is, engaging in exploratory processes that have value only in that they may lead to the solution of a problem. Physicians often diagnose problems in this manner, for example, by doing tests to eliminate what is *not* the problem in order to narrow the possibilities down to a few probable diagnoses of what *is* the problem. Good physicians know how to diagnose and make appropriate prescriptions. Good teachers know their content, know how to assess students relative to that content, and know how to make appropriate interventions.[53] According to Newell's and Simon's method for dealing with a problem, the person first constructs a representation of the problem, called the *problem space,* and then works out a solution that involves a search through the problem space. The problem solver may break the problem into components, activate old information from memory, or seek new information. If an exploratory solution proves to be successful, the task ends.[54] If it fails, the person backtracks, sidetracks, or redefines the problem or method used to solve it.

In terms of actual teaching, the problem-solving process might look something like the three approaches presented in Table 5.4. In concept formation the teacher is teaching the students how to create their own concepts; in generalizing the teacher is teaching students to critically look at ideas; and in application of principles the teacher

table 5.4 Cognitive Operations and Levels of Questions

Overt Activity	Eliciting Questions
Cognitive task 1: concept formation	
1. Enumeration and listing	What did you see? Hear? Note?
2. Grouping together	What belongs together? On what criterion?
3. Labeling, categorizing	What would you call these groups? What belongs under what?
Cognitive task 2: generalizing and inferring	
1. Identifying points	What did you note? See? Find?
2. Explaining identified items of information	Why did such and such happen? Why is such and such true?
3. Making inferences or generalizations	What does this mean? What would you conclude? What generalizations can you make?
Cognitive task 3: application of principles	
1. Predicting consequences, explaining unfamiliar phenomena, hypotheses	What would happen if . . . ?
2. Explaining and supporting predictions and hypotheses	Why do you think this would happen?
3. Verifying predictions and hypotheses	What would it take for such and such to be true? Would it be true in all cases? At what times?

Source: Hilda Taba. *Teaching Strategies and Cognitive Functions in Elementary School Children, Cooperative Research Project No. 2404.* San Francisco: San Francisco State College, 1966, pp. 39–40, 42.

is teaching students how to predict. Look carefully at the questions in Table 5.4 to see the unique perspective of each approach.

Each of these approaches helps students explore ideas by constructing their own content understandings. In lecture, students learn the structure dictated by the teacher. In the more experiential, problem-solving models, students explore ideas on their own and derive more personally constructed understandings.

Does it make a difference whether the teacher hierarchically presents content (lectures) or the students construct it? The answer is yes. When students *induce* their own concepts, they tend to recall the information longer and better.[55] So the key to instructional variability is to understand that you want to make certain that students know the content and can recall it. That requires instructional variability, and that variability will lead to more successful student learning, especially if the teacher *knows* why he or she is varying the way content is presented. Teachers do not vary instructional approaches to be cute; they vary approaches to provide students with different entry points to learning. In Linda Darling Hammond's words, "In effective classrooms, teachers use diverse strategies ranging from whole class lecture and recitation to guided inquiry, small group work, discussions, independent work, projects, experiments . . . and teacher interaction with individuals and small groups."[56] And they use these different approaches to ensure that all students have multiple ways to assimilate content.

Students as Problem Solvers

Individuals are confronted with problems when they encounter situations to which they must respond but do not know immediately what the response should be. Regardless of the method, students need relevant information to assess a situation and arrive at a response—that is, to solve the problem. The strategies used relate to a student's age and the specific problem. Not all successful students will use the same strategy to solve the same problem, and often more than one strategy can be used.

Even in simple math, students use different strategies to solve problems and therefore have different frameworks about the relative difficulty of the problems. For example, if John has 6 marbles and Sally has 8, how many marbles do they have together? Most students simply add 6 and 8, in what we might term a *common strategy.* In a *joint strategy,* students add elements (6 + 6 = 12; 2 more is 14). With a *separate strategy;* students remove elements (8 + 8 = 16, 2 less is 14). A *part-part-whole strategy* involves undertaking two or more elements ("I tabulated both numbers by adding 1 and 6 and subtracting 1 from 8; that makes 7 + 7, which is 14"). All student approaches are potentially correct strategies.[57] As we discussed earlier, American teachers tend to emphasize a "right" strategy; the Japanese tend to stress that students be able to "defend" the strategy that they use to derive a correct answer.

As problems become more abstract, so do students' problem-solving strategies. The teacher who insists on one strategy and penalizes students who use another appropriate strategy is discouraging their problem-solving potential. American teachers need to become aware of how students process information and what strategies they use to solve problems in order to teach problem solving according to the way students think. They can do this by asking questions, listening to responses, and inspecting student work. They can also do it by using different types of deductive (lecture) and inductive (inquiry or problem solving) strategies that help different students understand the content.

Some basic problem-solving strategies do seem to emerge when the behavior of successful and unsuccessful problem solvers is explored. The more successful students do the following:

1. *Comprehend the problem:* Successful problem solvers react to selected cues and immediately begin to work out a solution. Unsuccessful students miss cues and often misinterpret the problem.

2. *Employ previous knowledge:* The successful students utilize previous knowledge to solve a new problem. The unsuccessful students possess the accessory information but do not utilize it. They often do not know where or how to start.

3. *Use active problem-solving behavior:* Successful students are more active and verbalize what they are doing. They simplify the problem, whenever possible, or break it down into parts. The unsuccessful students are unable to clarify or state concisely what they are doing. They often do not attempt to analyze the various parts.

4. *Display confidence toward problem solving:* The successful students have confidence and view the problem as a challenge. The unsuccessful students lack confidence, become frustrated, and give up.[58]

Metacognitive skills (or processes) are transferable competencies that play a significant role in student high-order thinking. Metacognitive skills represent knowledge of how to do something (usually involving a plan, a set of steps, or procedures) as well as the ability to evaluate and modify performance. Based on a review of the research, some metacognitive skills have been found to distinguish successful problem solvers from others and to translate into instructional methods:

1. *Comprehension monitoring:* knowing when one understands or does not understand something; evaluating one's performance
2. *Understanding decisions:* understanding what one is doing and the reasons why
3. *Planning:* taking time to develop a strategy; considering options; proceeding without impulse
4. *Estimating task difficulty:* estimating difficulty and allocating sufficient time for difficult problems
5. *Task presentation:* staying with the task; being able to ignore internal and external distractions; maintaining direction in one's thinking
6. *Coping strategies:* staying calm; being able to cope when things are not going easily; not giving up or becoming anxious or frustrated
7. *Internal cues:* searching for context clues when confronted with difficult or novel problems
8. *Retracking:* looking up definitions; rereading previous information; knowing when to backtrack
9. *Noting and correcting:* using logical approaches; double-checking; recognizing inconsistencies, contradictions, or gaps in performance
10. *Flexible approaches:* willingness to use alternative approaches; knowing when to search for another strategy; trying random approaches that are sensible and plausible when the original approach has been unsuccessful.[59]

It should be noted that low-achieving and younger students have fewer metacognitive skills than high-achieving and older students.[60] The implication for teaching is that an increase in knowledge of subject matter does not necessarily produce changes in metacognitive skills. These skills in general reflect high-order thinking processes that cannot be learned or developed overnight or in one subject. Developmental age is crucial in limiting potential metacognitive skills among students. An 8-year-old student is capable of just so much and cannot be pushed beyond his or her cognitive stage. According to Piaget, not until about age 11 is a child capable of employing many of these metacognitive skills (corresponding to formal mental operations), and not until approximately age 15 is the child capable of fully employing all metacognitive skills in an efficient manner.[61] One of the advantages of using multiple instructional approaches is that the teacher is explicitly helping students understand different ways to explore content.

Robert Sternberg points out that students do not have to rely on osmosis for learning how to problem solve. Teachers can encourage students to use their "practical intelligence" in schools where so much of their lives take place. Hence, there is a good deal of tacit knowledge that is not taught or verbalized per se but used explicitly by success-ful problem solvers. As a teacher, you need to help students manage and improve their problem-solving techniques by 1) taking notes; 2) getting organized; 3) understanding questions; 4) asking questions, especially when they don't know; 5) following direc-tions; 6) underlining main ideas in texts; 7) outlining text information and classroom discussions; 8) seeing likenesses and differences in subject matter; 9) keeping track of time; and 10) getting things done on time.[62]

Actually, most of these techniques are basic learning strategies that are based on common sense. They also correlate with school achievement. By providing knowledge of and practice in applying learning strategies the teacher invariably indirectly en-hances the self-concept and coping abilities of the students—which, in turn, provides the means for problem solving. Such confidence is essential for students to cope with minor frustration; to play with ideas; to take educated guesses; to delete, add, or mod-ify parts of problems; and to select a plan of action and carry it out. Various in-class support groups (e.g., peer tutors, sharing dyads, cooperative learning) can help relieve anxiety and stress associated with problem solving.

In Case Study 5.4: Concept Formation read how Ms. Wilson poses a conceptual problem about prejudice to students. The teacher wants the students to create their own concept and then explore the meaning of that concept in relationship to a broader con-cept: prejudice. This instructional technique is especially useful in helping students ex-plore and discuss ideas. We have observed videotapes of literally hundreds of concept formation lessons. The key is to find ways to help students explore old ideas in new ways and to make them think more deeply and thoughtfully. Read carefully how this teacher uses the strategy and then identify for your teaching area what you could teach using this strategy. When you use this teaching strategy, you will notice how many metacognitive skills such as reflecting, organizing, and structuring the students must use. Such skills enhance student learning and student retention of important content because they help students create their own connections with knowledge.

Students as Inquirers

While most teachers acknowledge that experiential approaches are important, many need help incorporating them into their lessons. Good and Grouws have identified five processes for mathematics, but they can be applied to the teaching-learning process in all subjects.

1. *Attending to prerequisites:* Solving new problems is based largely on under-standing previously learned skills and concepts of the subject. The teacher should use the skills and concepts mastered by the students as a basis for solving (new) problems.

2. *Attending to relationships:* Students need to understand how ideas are related; the teacher should emphasize meaning and interpretation of ideas to help them understand.

3. *Attending to representation:* The more the student is able to represent a prob-lem in context with concrete or real-world phenomena, the better able the stu-dent is to solve the problem.

case study 5.4   Concept Formation

Ms. Wilson is teaching a lesson on prejudice. The Iraq war is in its initial stages and many students have strong views about Iraq and about the American invasion. She wants students to appreciate how those views often breed prejudice, but she does not want to start with a formal definition of prejudice. Rather, she wants the students to derive their own understanding of the term and its meaning.

She begins by asking students to consider Gordon W. Allport's ladder of prejudice that outlines how people progress in their levels of enmity toward others.

I.   **Speech** or the process of talking negatively about a group.
II.   **Avoidance** or the disregard for a group that manifests the trait or characteristic perceived as "wrong."
III. **Discrimination** or the treatment of the "defined" group in a different, diminished way.
IV.   **Physical Attack** or the victimization of those who are within a threatened group.
V.   **Extermination** or the excessive use of physical attack to the point that it becomes deadly.

The students are asked to list the times when they have observed in their own lives or in their study of history when speech and avoidance relative to the treatment of a group of people have become commonplace and accepted as the "right" way to respond to others.

The students brainstorm a wide variety of personal examples where groups were treated differently and they also list historic instances that include:

•   Jim Crow laws
•   Segregation policies
•   Nuremberg laws
•   Ku Klux Klan

The personal examples include:

•   Name calling
•   Creating groups with special membership rules to exclude "undesirables."

The students and teacher spend a great deal of time talking through all the examples. She then asks the students to draw a large circle on some chart paper that she provides and to place terms within the circle that fit together and then to create a generic label for those terms. One group creates the following but can only think of three terms.

Ku Klux Klan
Street Gangs
Nazis

The students create a title for the grouping: Groups that See Themselves as Superior to Others

    The teacher asks the rest of the class two questions: (1) Can you think of other groups that you think fit into this category? and (2) Why might a feeling of superiority lead to "climbing" Allport's ladder of prejudice?

    The class identifies some other examples and spends the rest of the period discussing a definition of prejudice provided by the teacher. They also discuss the "concepts" that each group develops.

    The teacher collects all the concepts and she writes two questions under each grouping that the different groups will explore the next day. For the grouping provided above, the questions were:

1. Why did each group (Ku Klux Klan and Nazis) form? What events led to their creation?
2. Who have been the primary spokespersons for the views of the respective groups? How have they attempted to get their message out?

Questions for Reflection

1. What are the advantages of having students create their own concepts? What are the problems?
2. What other approaches could have been used to teach this same set of ideas about prejudice and its consequences? Would the teacher have been better off to just give them the concept, its definition, and then examples? Why or why not?

4. *Generalizability of concepts:* Teachers need to explain the general applicability of the idea; students should practice skills and processes that apply to many settings.

5. *Attending to language:* Teachers should use the precise terminology of their subject; students must learn basic terms and concepts of the subject.[63]

    The test for problem solving is the ability to apply or use the learned strategies in new or at least a variety of situations. Many times teachers erroneously think students have "mastered" relevant facts and procedures. In reality, according to Alan Schoenfeld, students often have learned a strategy blindly and can use it only in circumstances similar to those in which they were taught. When given a slightly different version of a problem, or when they must make inferences or leaps in thinking, they are stymied.[64] Similarly, most of the problems found in textbooks and those assigned for homework are not problems in the true sense. They are, instead, exercises or tasks that reinforce specific, usually rote, procedures for solving a problem. In math, for example, most word problems are solved by students who rely on a key word without fully understanding the procedures involved. A real problem presents a student with a difficulty; the answer cannot be obtained by relying on rote procedures. It calls for relating or rearranging learned concepts or procedures with new ideas generated by the problem. It is not straightforward. A student's understanding of the procedures and the transfer of that understanding to new situations are crucial. Most students cannot function in this arena because traditional instructional methods tend to emphasize rote procedures.

Teachers can help students become better problem solvers and inquirers by using a variety of student- and teacher-centered instructional approaches. Class time must incorporate experimental, discovery, and/or reflective processes and activities. An expectation or norm is created in the classroom that acquiring knowledge is only the first step to understanding and is not as important as actually using knowledge.

The Instructional Debate

We have examined four different instructional approaches in this chapter. Two of those strategies are largely teacher centered (practice and drill and lecturing) and two are primarily student centered (questioning and problem solving). You must achieve a balance among these strategies and match how you teach with what you want the students to learn.

Some conservative education reformers argue more forcefully for teacher-centered instruction.[65] After all, states now have clear academic standards in place (see www.achieve.org), and teachers are often expected to teach that content explicitly. Progressive reformers argue just the opposite. They assert that direct instruction (teacher-centered approaches) depresses learning and that teachers need to use approaches that help students discover the principles that are being taught. Alfie Kohn describes this clearly in an article about the difference between students learning through direct instruction and learning through discovery and principle-based instruction.

> A few years back, . . . a study published in the journal *Cognitive Development,* . . . looked at different ways of teaching children the concept of equivalence, as expressed in problems such as "4 + 6 + 9 = ___ + 9." Fourth and fifth graders, none of whom knew how to solve such problems, were divided into two groups. Some were taught the underlying principle ("The goal of a problem like this is to find . . ."), while others were given step-by-step instructions ("Add up all the numbers on the left side, and then subtract the number on the right side").
>
> Both approaches were effective at helping students solve problems just like the initial one. Consistent with other research, however, the principle-based approach was much better at helping [students] transfer their knowledge to a slightly different kind of problem—for example, multiplying and dividing numbers to reach equivalence. Direct instruction of a technique for helping students obtain the right answer produced shallow learning.[66]

Kohn reflects on the studies that he cites to argue his view:

> Regardless of the order in which these two kinds of instruction were presented, students who were taught both ways didn't do any better on the transfer problems than did those who were taught only the procedure—which means they did far worse than students who were taught only the principle. Teaching or understanding didn't offset the destructive effects of telling them how to get the answer. Any step-by-step instruction in how to solve such problems put learners at a disadvantage; the absence of such instruction was required for them to understand.[67]

Though on a conceptual level Kohn is right, on a practical level he misses the point. Good teachers (value-added teachers) possess a repertoire of strategies and they make de-

Methods for Teaching

Benjamin S. Bloom

Former Charles H. Swift Distinguished Service Professor,
Emeritus
University of Chicago

 There is much rote learning in schools throughout the world. However, in a small number of countries—for example, Japan, South Korea, Israel, and Thailand—I find great emphasis on such higher mental processes as problem solving, application of principles, analytical skills, and creativity. These countries have very active central curriculum centers charged with responsibility constantly to improve textbooks and other learning materials, and to provide inservice training for teachers, especially as it relates to the curriculum and teaching methods.

In these countries, subjects are taught as methods of inquiry into the nature of science, mathematics, the arts, and the social studies. Subjects are taught as much for the ways of thinking they represent as for their traditional content. Much of this learning makes use of observations, reflections on observations, experimentation with phenomena, and the use of firsthand data and daily experiences, as well as primary printed sources.

In sharp contrast to these teaching methods, teachers in the United States use textbooks that rarely pose real problems. The textbooks I observe emphasize specific content to be remembered and give students little opportunity to discover underlying concepts and principles—and even less opportunity to attack real problems in their environments. I estimate that over 90 percent of the test questions that American students are expected to answer deal with little more than remembered information. Our instructional materials, classroom teaching methods, and testing methods rarely rise above knowledge.

cisions on how to teach based on what they want students to learn and on what types of students they are teaching. Direct approaches can be efficacious; they can also diminish student discovery of knowledge and long-term retention of information. Student-centered instruction can foster inquiry; it can also lead to confusion and low achievement if students do not have sufficient academic guidance.

Experiential teaching forces tough choices. Open-ended questioning is essential in problem-solving classrooms, but such an approach takes time and hence limits content coverage. For example, it is very different to list the causes of the Vietnam War, the characteristics of a virus, or the social implications of Shakespeare's *Romeo and Juliet* for a group of tenth grade students than to ask those students to arrive at such understandings themselves.

It is one thing to demonstrate through direct instruction to fourth grade students how to fold a paper plane the right way so it flies, but it is totally different (and takes much longer) to encourage students to plan their own solutions, to discover on their own or in small groups how to fold and fly the planes. In the latter approach, the teacher might provide some clues to get them started, ask students to hypothesize functional models, and then at the end of the lesson ask students to reach a consensus on the common characteristics of planes that fly the farthest.[68] Such an approach is not time efficient, but it can extend substantially student understandings of academic content (see Professional Viewpoint 5.2).

The difference in approach between giving answers to students and having them search for answers may be summed up as *lecture* versus *experiential* teaching, direct instruction versus *inquiry-based* instruction, or *content-based* versus *process-based* learning. Does the teacher provide knowledge (lecture) or do the students construct knowledge? The more experimental types of learning generate more personal meaning for students and equip them to integrate learning into longer-term memory more easily; it is the learners who have generated, predicted, and evaluated the content. Teachers who use more inquiry and process-oriented approaches not only enhance student achievement but also foster long-term retention of the material that is learned.

New research on cognition shows that successful problem solving correlates with a particular mind-set. According to Robert Marzano, students' attitude toward school and learning and their own social concerns and self-concept are important dimensions for learning. Students develop "mental habits" that make them more or less efficient as problem solvers. For example, they learn to seek accuracy, test ideas, avoid impulsivity, and persist when answers are not apparent—which in part is based on how they perceive themselves in learning situations.[69]

Being able to translate these ideas into practice is another issue. It suggests that teachers take note of the broad social and psychological dimension of learning. On a cognitive level, it means slowing down the teaching-learning process and studying content in depth. It means using Socratic questions, asking students to clarify and redefine their thinking, as well as discussing, comparing, probing, and debating content—instructional methods that slow down teaching and learning. As a teacher, it means you must be willing to reveal or model your own thought processes—what you are thinking and how you are tackling a problem—and then ask your students to reveal their thinking during problem-solving tasks. It means sometimes discarding the lesson plan and just listening to your students as you pinpoint or focus on a concept, elaborate on one of their statements, or help them clarify an issue or problem.

It also means that you must familiarize yourself with several learning theories. Teachers must consider the students' developmental stages (Piaget) and how students use language (Vygotsky), process information (Ausubel, Sternberg), and construct meaning (Bruner, Vygotsky). These theories are appropriate for all learners of all ages and serve as the basis for problem solving in the classrooms. You cannot design your lesson plans in terms of experiential learning unless you have some appreciation and understanding of how students think.

It also means that you have to consider a constellation of factors as you structure a lesson. Bransford and his colleagues suggest that the appropriateness of a teaching strategy is dictated by three factors: the material to be learned, the "capital" (or skills, knowledge, and attitudes) that a learner brings to the learning task, and the goals of the learning situation, as well as the assessments to be used by the teacher.[70]

As you prepare to teach material, you must decide what students are to learn. Let's assume that you are teaching something complex like quantum theory. You could do drill and practice on different formulas to make certain the students knew what all the symbols meant. You could ask a series of questions about the differences between classical theory and quantum theory. You could deliver a hierarchic lecture on the history of quantum theory (Who shaped it? Challenged it?), or you could give students Schrodinger's Cat Measurement Problem: How can a cat be dead and alive at the same

Technology Viewpoint from a Classroom Teacher

Jackie Marshall Arnold
K–12 Media Specialist

"The first question children ask is why? Our job is to capture that natural curiosity and turn it into a lifelong passion for learning."—Dr. Robert Ballard

 Technology has for many years supported learning though drill and practice applications. These types of applications are plentiful for any grade level. Drill and practice can serve as a limited technology tool, allowing teachers to offer remediation or extension to students' learning. However, deeper technology uses can be found in problem-solving applications that allow children to ask and answer "why" questions and, as a consequence, own the learning in a deeper, richer way.

Simulation software applications are one technological tool that a teacher can use in a problem-solving environment. Using a simulation piece of software, students can experience a real-world phenomenon including physical, social, economic, and mathematical relationships. For example, programs exist that allow children to create a simulated city, adjusting the dynamics of the city to see the effects upon the citizens. Using LEGO™ sensors (such as touch, light, temperature, and rotation) and programming software, students can create and program their own adventure park, robot, greenhouse, and more. Software even exists now that allows students to "dissect" an imaginary frog without having to use the

"physical" frog. These examples are only a beginning to the many and varied simulation applications that exist. Simulation software will allow students to develop higher-order thinking skills while engaged in real world situations.

Another technical tool that facilitates the development of problem-solving abilities is called a WebQuest. WebQuests were developed by Bernie Dodge at San Diego State University. A WebQuest is an inquiry-based activity in which the students are guided through a structured problem using resources predominately found on the Web. WebQuests are designed to "use learners' time well, to focus on using information rather than looking for it, and to support learners' thinking at the levels of analysis, synthesis, and evaluation."[72] Teachers can create their own WebQuests or utilize previously created WebQuests. The WebQuest home page can be found at http://webquest.sdsu.edu/webquest.html. This site will give you an overview of WebQuests, examples, and a search engine that will allow you to access WebQuests matching your curriculum.

Research has documented the multiple advantages of teaching students problem-solving strategies. Teaching with a problem-solving approach allows for 1) emphasis on meaning, 2) increase in self direction, 3) a higher level of comprehension, 4) the development of collaborative interaction and interpersonal skills, and 5) an increase in motivation for learning content. An effective teacher will ensure students develop these lifelong skills. Tools such as the ones mentioned in this viewpoint will begin to provide the resources necessary for teachers to nurture those skills.

time? The last approach would require problem solving and inquiry and considerable teacher understanding of quantum theory.

Quantum theory is a good example because it is complex. Notice that even with complex ideas it is possible to make instructional decisions about what to teach and how to teach it. The learning goal you have dictates the teaching method you should use, but the teaching method is always used to engage students (all students) in the learning process.

Theory into Practice

Teachers and students across grade levels spend a majority of their classroom instructional time on practice and drill, questioning, explaining, and problem solving, inquiry and discovery. The remaining time is spent on other instructional methods and activities such as role-playing, simulations or games, small group discussions, independent projects, class reporting, and monitoring.[71]

Some basic recommendations in the form of questions can implement these various methods in classrooms:

1. Are your lessons planned in advance? Are they based on clear academic standards? Do students know what to expect and when to change activities? Is the pace of the lesson brisk? Do you slow down when further detail or explanation is warranted?
2. Are your materials and methods prepared in advance and incorporated without hindering the momentum of the lesson?
3. Do you combine explanations, illustrations, and demonstrations with your methods and with what is to be learned?
4. Does the lesson proceed in sequenced steps? Do academic tasks or skills build on the preceding ones? Are students helped to see relationships between previous and present learning?
5. Do you use practice and drill activities before and after other new learning to ensure that students have mastered required academic tasks? Have you incorporated practice exercises into several parts of the lesson, including preliminary reviews and end summaries?
6. Do you give younger students and low-achieving students more practice and drill activities than older and high-achieving students? Are practice exercises checked and corrected promptly?
7. In asking questions, do you make sure all students have the opportunity to respond by using a variety of types of questions (low-level, high-level, convergent, divergent, valuing, etc.)? Do you allow sufficient wait-time? Do you call on nonvolunteers as frequently as or more than volunteers? Do you call on low achievers as frequently as or more than high achievers?
8. Are you aiming at a high success rate in student responses to your questions? Do you ask easier or more concrete questions of low achievers to ensure high success rates?
9 Are your questions sequenced to ensure understanding and to build a knowledge base before proceeding to more difficult questions? Do you ask clear and concise questions? Or do you find you have to rephrase and repeat questions?
10. While lecturing or explaining, do you readily ask questions to maintain student attention and to gauge student understanding and progress? Do you test and assess students frequently?
11. Do you provide supportive groups in the classroom (i.e., sharing dyads, cooperative learning groups, tutors or homework helpers) to overcome anxiety in problem solving? Do you identify the strengths and resources of the students to enhance their confidence level?

12. Do you take time to model or show or let students discover *different* ways to solve problems, including how to compare, analyze, modify, guess, hypothesize, and predict? (Weak teachers explain problem concepts a second time, LOUDER. Strong teachers use different explanations, metaphors, or analogs.)
13. Do you modify your instructional approaches to ensure that classroom structures (such as tracking) do not limit instructional opportunities for some students?
14. Do you use different instructional approaches during the duration of a unit?

Summary

1. Most instructional activities can be categorized as one of four instructional methods: practice and drill, questioning, lecturing and problem solving or experiential. No one approach, whether teacher-centered or student-centered, is inherently good or bad. How you teach is dictated by who and what you teach.
2. The method of practice and drill has applications for teaching skills and processes.
3. Questioning is used as part of many different types of lessons: Types of questions include low level and high level, convergent and divergent, and valuing.
4. Lecturing is one of the oldest instructional methods. Different types of teacher talk can be effective with different students, but in general the length, complexity, and frequency of teacher talk should be reduced for younger and slower students.
5. Experiential and problem-solving approaches help students actively take responsibility for their own learning. Such approaches, which are inductive in nature, help students discover knowledge, not just assimilate teacher-identified content, and help them retain information better and longer.

Questions to Consider

1. Why is practice and drill used more often in elementary grades than secondary grades? Should it be?
2. What is the difference between convergent and divergent questions? Why do most teachers rely on convergent questions?
3. When should lecturing be used?
4. What are the advantages and disadvantages of student-centered approaches as an instructional method?
5. Does the national emphasis on academic standards suggest that teachers should favor one type of instruction over another?

Things to Do

1. List five recommendations for conducting practice and drill. Indicate any that you feel particularly comfortable or uncomfortable with as a teacher. Based on these preferences, what conclusions can you make about how you will use practice and drill?

2. Outline ten dos and don'ts in asking questions. Which of the don'ts have you most often experienced in your own education? Observe a classroom teacher during a field experience and identify dos and don'ts that you see in real practice.
3. Teach a short lesson to your class by asking questions. Have an observer use Tips for Teachers 5.2 and 5.3 as guides to assess how well you performed.
4. Develop a checklist for improving the lecture method. In doing so, review the procedures for preparing a lecture and the recommendations for lecturing. Then prepare a hierarchic lecture.
5. Select a concept or topic to teach. Identify how you might use each of the different strategies as you engage students in different learning tasks. How would you teach it through direct instruction? Through a problem-solving or experiential model?

Recommended Readings

Bligh, Donald A. *What's the Use of Lectures?* San Francisco: Jossey Bass, 2000. Bligh offers a thorough discussion of how and when to lecture.
Cathy Collins Block and Michael Pressley. *Comprehension Instruction.* New York: Guilford: 2001. Research-based cognitive practices and schema theory for teachers K–12.
Gage, N. L., and David C. Berliner. *Educational Psychology,* 6th ed. Boston: Houghton Mifflin, 1998. This is an examination of the research pertaining to practice and drill, lecturing, and problem solving—among other subjects.
Hargreaves, Andy, Lorna Earl, Shawn Moore, and Susan Manning. *Learning to Change.* San Francisco: Jossey-Bass, 2000. The authors focus on how reform proposals have brought new complexities to teaching practices.
Kohn, Alfie. *What To Look for in a Classroom* San Francisco: Jossey-Bass, 2000. The author raises several provocative issues that challenge traditional views on teaching and instruction.
Lasley, Thomas J., Thomas Matczynski, and James Rowley. *Instructional Models: Teaching Strategies for a Diverse Society.* Belmont Calif.: Wadsworth, 2002. The book that focuses on eight different specific teaching models can be used to teach students content and skills.
Tomlinson, Carole. *The Differentiated Classroom.* Alexandria, VA: Association for Supervision and Curriculum Development, 1999. This wonderful text describes how teachers can differentiate teaching to meet the diverse learning needs for students.

Key Terms

convergent questions 211	high-level questions 210	low-level questions 210
divergent questions 211	internal summaries 226	probing 219
final summaries 226	lectures 220	reflective thinking 227
heuristic thinking 229	law of exercise 198	wait-time 214

End Notes

1. John Bransford, Nancy Vye, and Helen Bateman. "Creating High Quality Learning Environments: Guidelines from Research on How People Learn." Paper presented at the National Governor's Association, San Francisco, California, July 2002.
2. Ibid, p.2.
3. Ibid.
4. Wilbert J. McKeachie. "Learning, Thinking, and Thorndike." *Educational Psychologist* (Spring 1990): 127–141. Richard M. Wolf. "In Memoriam—Robert Thorndike." *Educational Researcher* (April 1991): 22–23.

Developing your own instructional materials is an important part of good teaching.

Presenting Instructional Materials

The teacher must incorporate instructional materials into the unit plan and lesson plan and modify them in a way that considers the students' developmental stages or age, needs and interests, aptitudes, reading levels, prior knowledge, work habits, learning styles, and motivation. The following factors should be considered when presenting materials (published or teacher-made).

- *Understanding:* Understanding requires that the teacher match materials to the learner's abilities and prior knowledge. If students don't understand the material, frustration sets in, making learning even more difficult. The teacher must know whether the materials are appropriate for the students to begin with and whether the students are understanding the material as it is being presented. Teachers must check for student understanding—especially important when working with younger and slower-learning students and when teaching new information.

   Teachers can ask students questions to check for understanding or try to observe if students understand; if they know what they have learned; if they know what they need to know; and if they know how to detect errors and improve.[7]

- *Structuring:* Structuring involves organizing the material so it is clear to students. This means clearly stating directions, objectives, and main ideas. Internal and final summaries cover the content. Transitions between main ideas are smooth and well integrated. Writing is not vague. Sufficient examples are provided. New terms and concepts are defined. Adequate practice and review assignments reinforce new learning.[8] Clarity is especially important when new subject matter is introduced and when it is being integrated into previous learning.

- *Sequencing:* The teacher should arrange the material to provide continuous and cumulative learning and to give attention to prerequisite skills and concepts. There are four basic ways to sequence materials: 1) simple to complex—materials gradually increase in complexity and become broader and deeper in meaning; 2) parts to whole—parts of information are presented first to enable the student to grasp the whole; 3) whole to parts—whole concepts or generalizations are presented first to facilitate organizing and integrating new and isolated items, and 4) chronological (which is a favorite organizer for many teachers)—topics, ideas, or events are studied in the order in which they take place.[9]

- *Balancing:* The materials need to be vertically and horizontally related or balanced. Vertical relationships refer to a building of content and experiences at the lesson, unit, and course levels: Ninth-grade math concepts build on eighth-grade concepts, the second unit plan builds on the first, and so on. Horizontal relationships establish a multidisciplinary and unified view of different subjects: The content of a social studies course is related to English and science.

- *Explaining:* This refers to the way headings, terms, illustrations, and summary exercises are integrated and elucidate the content. Do the examples illustrate major concepts? Are the major ideas identified in chapter objectives and overviews? Do the headings outline a logical development of the content? Do the materials show relationships among topics, events, or facts to present an in-depth view of major concepts? The students should be able to discover important concepts and information and relate new knowledge to prior knowledge on their own through the materials. In short, the content of the materials should be explicit, related, and cumulative in nature.

- *Pacing.* This refers to how much and how quickly material is presented. The volume or length of material should not overwhelm students, but there must be enough to have an effect. As students get older, the amount of material can increase, the presentation can be longer and more complex, and the breadth and depth can be expanded.

- *Elaborating:* Students can learn better when they are learning in different ways. The idea is to teach students to transform information from one form to another and to apply new information to prior knowledge—by using various techniques such as comparing and contrasting, drawing analogies, drawing inferences, paraphrasing, summarizing, and predicting. Students can be taught a broad list of "generating" questions (e.g., previewing, self-questioning, visualizing) to use while reading materials. For "previewing," a good generating question for a narrative (storylike) text might be "Based on the title, what might be the focus of this story?" A student who is about to read expository material on the American Civil War might ask, "What do I already know about the events occurring during the war?" The teacher can also raise "generating" questions in class when discussing the materials: "What is the main idea of the story?" "If I lived during that period, how would I feel?" "What does this remind me of?" "How can I use the information in the project I am working on?" "How do I feel about the author's opinions?" "How can I put this material in my own words?"[10]

- *Motivating:* Instructional materials, according to Posner and Strike, may be classified as 1) concept related, drawing heavily on structure of knowledge or the concepts, principles, or theories of the subject; 2) inquiry related, derived from critical thinking skills and procedures employed by learning theorists or scholars in the field; 3) learner related, or related to the needs, interests, or experiences of the students; and 4) utilization related, showing how people can use or proceed with them in real-life situations.[11] The first two "organizers" seem to work best with intrinsically motivated (self-motivated) students, but all four draw on the intrinsic interests of students.

Embedded within all of these considerations is the teacher's awareness of the different types of learners in American classrooms. American classrooms evidence a great deal of diversity in students. Good teachers see the possibilities in all students regardless of the students' ethnic backgrounds or racial group affiliations. They also know how to use those backgrounds of the students to enhance the ways in which young people can learn content and experience success. There are many different ways to classify or think about students as learners, not as students of a particular racial or ethnic group. Teachers need to consider two primary ones: field dependent and field independent. Simply speaking, different students possess different cognitive styles and exhibit different levels of psychological differentiation. ***Field-dependent*** learners are those who tend to do best on verbal tasks that have a significant relational component. ***Field-independent*** learners are those who think more analytically and can process impersonal and often abstract ideas more effectively.[12]

There are several different cognitive styles that students possess. We use psychological differentiation (field-dependence and field independence) for illustrative purposes to show how important it is to recognize and teach with attention to student differences. If you treat all students the same and assume they are all field-independent learners, those who are field dependent will begin to experience frustration. Similarly, if you assume that the students are all field dependent, those who learn more analytically will become frustrated. Good and Brophy highlight research that illustrates the importance of teachers' accommodating different types of learners:

> . . . Field-independent and field-dependent students . . . [learned] content from taped lectures under four conditions: 1) no notes, 2) student's notes only; 3) outline framework plus student's notes, and 4) complete outline plus student's notes. [The researcher] . . . found that field-independent students performed well under the student's-notes-only condition, because they tended to take efficient notes and to organize them within an outline format. The field-dependent students, however, seemed to need the teacher-provided outline. [The researcher] . . . contended that the typical classroom procedure in which the teacher lectures and students take notes may favor the performance of field-independent students. To reduce this effect, he suggested that teachers provide students with external aids [or materials] (e.g., an outline on the board or a handout that organizes the presentation) that may help the field-dependent students without harming the field-independent students.[13]

As you can see, you do not use varied instructional materials to be "cute" or arbitrarily to satisfy a supervisor. You use them because there are a variety of different learners with different backgrounds in classrooms, and your goal is not content coverage but student learning. Teachers who practice adaptive pedagogy vary the way they teach and the materials that they use. They know that students who come to them from poor or rural or urban or highly ethnic communities need varied experiences that connect the standards to be achieved with the materials that are provided.

Textbooks

Traditionally, the textbook has been the most frequently used instructional material at all levels beyond the primary grades, and in some cases it is the only one used by the teacher. "The textbook and its partner, the workbook," asserts Eisner, "provide the curricular hub around which much of what is taught revolves."[14] In terms of purchasing decisions, textbooks receive the highest priority, with the exception of costly hardware such as computers and copying machines. Textbooks have a strong influence or even dominate the nature and sequence of a course and thus profoundly affect the learning experiences of most students.

Reliance on the textbook is consistent with the stress on written words as the main medium of education—as well as the way many teachers themselves were educated. Educators estimate that 70 to 95 percent of instructional time centers around some sort of textbook (or workbook for younger students) material.[15] This figure is supported by other research, especially in reading and math classrooms, where there is excessive dependence on textbooks.[16]

A number of teachers are now supplementing textbook material with information easily accessible through the Internet. The classroom world of the twentieth century was driven by textbooks. The learning world of the twenty-first century is driven by information access through the Internet. Case Study 6.1: Using the Web illustrates how one teacher is using the Internet to complement the students' textbook understandings and work.

Disadvantages

In order to have wide application and to increase potential sales, textbooks tend to be general, noncontroversial, and bland. They are usually written for a national audience, so they do not consider local issues or community problems. Because they are geared for the greatest number of "average" students, they may not meet the needs and interests of any particular group of students. Moreover, issues, topics, and data that might upset potential audiences or interest groups are omitted. A type of censorship is currently occurring that is creating heated ideological debate.[17] An example of this is provided in Case Study 6.2: Texas Textbooks. The case may seem extreme, but it is real and it represents part of the educational world you are about to enter.

Textbooks summarize large quantities of data and in so doing may become general and superficial and may discourage conceptual thinking, critical analysis, and evaluation. With the exception of mathematics textbooks, most quickly become outdated because of the rapid change of events. Because they are costly, however, they are often

case study 6.1   Using the Web

Chad Raisch is a second-year teacher. What follows is his account of how he uses the Internet with his students.

The range of learning opportunities for my students that supplements the textbooks I use in class has greatly increased because of the Internet. There is a host of activities my students can complete outside the confines of my classroom, provided they have access to an Internet connection. For instance, in my Advanced Placement American History course, I frequently assign review activities from the companion website for our book, *The American Nation,* 10th edition by Garraty and Carnes *[occawlonline.pearsoned.com/bookbind/pubbooks/garraty_awl/chapter1/deluxe.html].*

On that website, students can complete, among other things, interactive multiple choice and true/false review activities. The students can assess their own understanding of the course content by taking these quizzes. And, when they're done, they can submit their work for immediate feedback, which is often not the case in the regular classroom setting. Additionally, the teacher can set it up so that student quiz results are e-mailed directly to them. In addition to providing these standard types of assessment, the website provides a document based analysis writing activity for each chapter. Students read and analyze several primary sources online and then become historians themselves by crafting an argument based on their interpretation of the documents. Their assignments can be e-mailed to the teacher.

And that is not half of what this companion website or others like it offer to students and teachers. Other features include interactive maps and timelines, crossword puzzles, interactive matching and fill-in-the-blank activities, WebQuests, PowerPoint slide shows, glossaries, interactive flashcards, chapter outlines, chapter summaries, unit and chapter objectives, suggested resources, and a list of links to other sites on the Internet. If you have not tapped into the website that supplements your textbook, please give it a try. Such sites will open up technologically engrossing learning opportunities for your learners.

Questions for reflection

1. Chad Raisch asks you to tap into a website that supplements your textbook. Select a textbook for the content area you plan to teach and see whether you can do what he requests.
2. In what ways can the enhanced use of technology make your job easier? Harder? Does it ensure enhanced student learning?

used long after they should be replaced. There is also a concern that textbooks unnecessarily dumb down topics. Because some states require certain reading levels in the textbooks that they adopt, there is a tendency for publishers to modify sentences in ways that compromise the integrity of the ideas. Also problematic is the emphasis in the United States on breadth versus depth. Sadker and Sadker describe this as the "mentioning phenomenon," in which textbooks endeavor to mention everything so as not to forget anything. The by-product of this phenomenon is diminished student learning. Students who need richer descriptions of concepts with more examples are limited in their ability to acquire the content.[18]

case study 6.2   **Texas Textbooks**

The following article examines the case of Texas in the competitive textbook market and the states' disproportionate clout in the textbook industry.

Austin—What if a junior-high school textbook wrongly stated that John Marshall was the United States' first Supreme Court Chief Justice, instead of John Jay? Or that the Louisiana Purchase occurred in 1804, not 1803?

No one would fault textbook publishers for fixing factual errors like these found in recent textbooks. But when it comes to "fixing" harder to define social or political biases, what happens when publishers eager to make a sale are willing to edit content that special interest groups object to—or even submit their books to those groups for input *prior* to publication?

The practice of self-censorship is increasingly apparent here in Texas, where battles over textbook content are epic. For years, publishers have been held to the fire by conservatives who could make or break a textbook. But now, critics say, publishers are allowing conservative groups likely to raise the biggest fuss to discuss content before the books are made available for public review . . .

The annual textbook battle began [when] . . . the State Board of Education opened public hearings to consider 2003 social studies texts for all grades—a $345 million purchase. Special interest groups were here in force for the day-long event. The lobbying roster of 70 speakers included Hispanic college students and the NAACP wanting more minorities and women represented in textbooks, Christian groups seeking more conservative interpretations of issues, and social-studies teachers arguing against such tinkering.

Ever since well-known Texans Mel and Norma Gabler began poring over textbooks in the '60s in search of anti-Christian bias, critics have charged that the conservative right was trying to interject its agenda into the classroom. Conservatives over the years have battled such things as a photo of a woman carrying a briefcase, the theory of evolution, and "overkill of emphasis on cruelty to slaves."

In 1995, the legislature intervened and passed a law that said the State Board of Education could only reject books based on factual errors, not ideology.

But the board is also mandated by state law to approve books that are made of quality materials and that promote democracy, patriotism, and the free-enterprise system. And conservative members are finding ways to stretch the definitions to suit their beliefs.

Two recent examples: The state board rejected an environmental science book last year, in part, because it put the U.S. and the free enterprise system in a bad light as significant players in global warming. And, earlier this year, a history text was withdrawn by the publisher after board members objected to references of rampant prostitution in the American West in the 1800s.

Conservative groups contend ideas such as these are un-American or anti-free enterprise and should not be taught to children.

That would be fine, critics say, if decisions by the State Board of Education solely affected children in the Lone Star State. But because the textbook market in Texas is so large and financially attractive—with 4.1 million public school children it is second only to California in volume of books purchased—publishers often use books approved here nationwide.

"We're the 900-pound gorilla in the room," says board member David Bradley, referring to the clout Texas has in the publishing industry. "It's nice to be king."

Mr. Bradley revels in one tactic he tried to use to reject a math text in 1997. He objected to the book's discussions of poetry, the Vietnam War, and jalapeño recipes. Because his objections involved no factual errors and the new law prevented him from objecting on ideological grounds, he attacked the quality of the book by ripping its binding off.

While last year's focus on new science books produced some fireworks, Joe Bill Watkins, a lawyer with the Association of American Publishers in Washington, believes this year's battle over social studies books "offers a lot more potential for differences of opinion . . . [T]his is a delicate time. There's a lot at stake here."

The 29 publishers that submitted textbooks this year [want] to know how their books will fare and what will be asked of them.

At least some of the publishers provided their books prior to public review to the Texas Citizens for a Sound Economy, says Peggy Venable of that conservative group.

"Some folks here today disagree. They don't want American values reinforced in our schools," said Rep. Rick Green at the hearing. "But the vast majority of Texans think it is the right thing to do, that it is the primary purpose of our education system."

Some, however, believe the primary purpose of education is to embrace differences of opinion and encourage critical thinking.

The first book to be rejected by the state board since its new directive in 1995 was one such book: "Environmental Science: Creating a Sustainable Future." Used in colleges for the past 20 years, it was submitted for advanced-placement science classes. It received preliminary approval by the textbook committee of the Texas Education Agency. But school-board members rejected the text after the conservative Texas Public Policy Foundation (TPPF) report criticized it for statements about global warming and destruction of the environment—especially those that pointed to the U.S. role in these problems.

Dean DeChambeau, of the book's Massachusetts publisher, Jones and Bartlett, says the company agreed to fix the three factual errors found in the book. But of the other changes suggested by the TPPF report on the book, he says, "We steadfastly refused . . . because they wanted us to replace what they perceived as biased material with their own biased material."

. . . "There is absolutely no censorship here," says Chris Patterson, TPPF's director of educational research. The group recently released its findings on 28 of the proposed social studies books. None of them received failing grades.

Questions for reflection

1. What can you as a teacher do when you see that censorship has taken place relative to a topic that you deem essential for student understanding of a particular concept?

2. What contacts do you need to make before you teach a potentially controversial topic? Or, should you simply avoid controversial issues?

3. Are there some disciplinary areas where controversial topics are more evident? Is it possible that a particular discipline (e.g., mathematics) may not have controversy associated with it?

Source: This article first appeared in *The Christian Science Monitor* on July 22, 2002 and is reproduced with permission. Copyright © 2002 *The Christian Science Monitor,* (www.csmonitor.com). All rights reserved.

Advantages

Considering these criticisms, you might ask why teachers, when they have access to other instructional materials, rely so heavily on textbooks. The answer is, of course, that they offer many advantages. A textbook 1) provides an outline that the teacher can use in planning courses, units, and lessons; 2) summarizes a great deal of pertinent information; 3) enables the students to take home in convenient form most of the material they need to learn for the course; 4) provides a common resource for all students to follow; 5) provides the teacher with ideas regarding the organization of information and activities; 6) includes pictures, graphs, maps, and other illustrative material that facilitates understanding; 7) includes other teaching aids, such as summaries and review questions; and 8) relieves the teacher of preparing material for the course, thus allowing more time to prepare the lesson.[19]

Good textbooks have many desirable characteristics. They are well organized, coherent, unified, relatively up-to-date, accurate, and relatively unbiased. They have been scrutinized by scholars, educators, and minority groups. Their reading level and knowledge base match the developmental level of their intended audience. They are accompanied by teachers' manuals, test items, study guides, and activity guides. The textbook is an acceptable tool for instruction as long as it is selected with care and is kept in proper perspective so that it is not viewed as the only source of knowledge and it does not turn into the curriculum. In most cases you will have no choice about the textbook you use, but you can decide how to supplement the content covered in the textbook and what topics warrant extended coverage. Remember, most textbooks suffer from the mentioning phenomenon. To help you make a decision on where your *depth* decisions should be made, focus on the following:

1. *The school district's curriculum guide:* What does the district require that you teach?

2. *The academic standards for the state in which you teach:* What are the academic standards for your state and what topics *may not* be adequately covered in textbooks relative to defined standards?

Stereotyping

Basic readers and textbooks began to be criticized in the 1960s and 1970s as irrelevant to the social realities of the inner-city and minority child. Many years ago, Fantini and Weinstein suggested that school books depicted "happy, neat, wealthy, white people whose intact and loving families live only in clean, grassy suburbs. ...Ethnic [and racial] groups comprising so much of our population are often omitted" or included only "as children from other lands."[20] Such stereotypic representations are far less explicit than they used to be, but they are still evident.

According to one educator, for many years all American Indians in textbooks and readers were called "Big Horn" or "Shining Star"; people with Italian, Greek, or Polish names were likely to appear as peddlers or organ grinders, wearing red scarves and ragged clothes. Either there were no blacks, or one black boy might be inserted in the background. Yellow, brown, or black people were depicted in stories about China, India, and Africa, but they were always strangers and foreigners. Women were portrayed almost always as mothers, nurses, or teachers. Religion was rarely mentioned—except in relation to church attendance on Sunday morning. In short, the readers of these books were presented with a monocultural view of society. Nonwhite children were learning to read from books that either scarcely mentioned them, omitted them entirely, or represented them stereotypically.[21]

Today, many readers, workbooks, and textbooks exclude racial, ethnic, religious, and sexual stereotyping. (Obscenity, violence, and sexual topics are still generally avoided, as are such unpleasant issues as disease and death.) Major racial, ethnic, and minority groups, including the handicapped and elderly, tend to be better represented in story characters and pictures. Women are depicted as airplane pilots, police officers, construction workers, lawyers, and doctors. Blacks, Hispanics, and other minorities have professional and managerial jobs and are not all basketball players and musicians. Overt stereotyping is largely avoided in current textbooks.

Still, balanced textbook development remains an ongoing topic of debate. On one end of the political continuum are the charges that the content and pictures in textbooks still transmit racial and gender stereotypes—such as an overemphasis on science, capitalism, and formal rationality, values traditionally associated with the once-dominant (white, male) power group.[22] Critics maintain that subtle, tacit stereotyping still exists (e.g., women are portrayed as passive or mainly in service industries or family roles).[23] On the other end of the continuum is the criticism that too much pressure is being placed on publishers and now textbook authors to be "politically correct"—not just to reflect the cultures of all students but to disparage any hint of "common culture." Nearly everything that is European, white, or male is, according to critics, perceived as a vehicle for racism, sexism, and oppression.

Oakes and Lipton eloquently describe how a 1991 revision of a California text still compromises the real story of how pioneers expanded Westward and how American Indians responded. They first provide a quote from the text:

> Although some Indians were content on the missions, many others were unhappy with this new way of life. By living at the missions the Indians gave up their own culture, the way of life they had known in their tribal villages. They could only leave the mission grounds with permission from the padres. They were not free to hunt or to pick berries.
>
> Mission Indians were not allowed to return to their tribes once they agreed to take part in mission life. Some ran away. But soldiers usually brought them back and sometimes whipped them. Others wanted to revolt. They wanted to rise up against their leaders, the Spanish padres and the soldiers at the mission communities. . . .

Then Oakes and Lipton comment on the text:

> . . . [T]his version, waffles as it portrays the stunning violations of decency and human rights that California Indians endured. That "some Indians were content" must be seen as the moral equivalent of references to happy Negro slaves on the plantation. That the Indians "gave up" their culture seems close to a free and neutral choice. The text explains offenses against the Indians in the familiar language of what grownups do to naughty children—whippings, not being able to leave without permission, not free to hunt or pick berries. Indian deaths seem sanitized, kept a safe distance from the killers; disease, crop failure, and a change in diet reduce the Indian population by half, not theft of land and enslavement. On the other hand, Indians, with *their* offenses, are downright uncivilized; they violently revolt, attack and burn missions, and kill padres.[24]

We are forced to struggle with two opposing, highly emotional views about the politics of information and what textbook content is acceptable. Finding good literature or good texts that reconcile all these concerns is difficult. To accommodate some of the new criteria, many classic works of literature have been eliminated from the curriculum, and many bland texts and instructional materials have been included. Writes Connie Muther, "The idea is to please all and offend none [and thus] many textbooks [and related materials] have no clear point of view."[25] Although many new books portray the populace more accurately, they remain safe, boring, and watered down.

One of the authors (of this textbook) made it clear in a book about 9-11 that most texts are watered down for purposes of being neutral, entertaining, positive, and politically correct. He wrote the following opinionated introduction about textbooks:

> You may feel life is too difficult and there is no need to read a book that requires a literate mind. If you cannot be entertained by glossy pictures and smiling faces, or with sidebars of cartoons or case studies, then you might rationalize that you should not be bothered or expected to read or think about serious issues.

Later, the author puts the issue more directly in the reader's face, claiming his textbook is opinionated and deals with tough issues that most education textbooks avoid.

> . . . this is not intended to be light reading, or a "Dick and Jane" reader. For those with an urge to be politically correct on all topics, you will find plenty to be upset with—not willing to admit your own form of racial, ethnic, religious, or gender prejudice. Finally, there will be some who find fault that the content lacks restraint, sobriety and optimism, and that my expressions are somewhat disruptive and upsetting.

Finally, the author pokes fun at the publishing industry.

> Life has become pretty flat and dull when reading typical education texts. That the content has become so oblique and middle-of-the-road is a tribute to mainstream society that publishers wish to convey a neutral or positive picture of the human condition.[26]

Readability

Concern about student reading problems has prompted educators to identify textbooks and other reading materials that are suitable for specific student populations, especially below-average readers. One strategy used in this endeavor is *leveling.* It is a fairly subjective assessment method. *Reading formulas,* first devised in the 1920s to estimate the reading difficulty of a text, are another strategy. They have lately increased in popularity.

Some reading formulas count the number of syllables or the number of letters in a word; some count the number of words that are not on a specific word list; others measure sentence length; and still others remove words from a passage to test whether students can fill in the exact word that was removed.[27] Some formulas use graphs, regression statistics, and percentiles and range scores to calculate reading difficulty. Computer programs are now available for doing the counting and calculation chores involved in reading-level determinations. There are a variety of formulas in existence, and all attempt to provide educational professionals with a means of assessing text difficulty and suitability for potential readers.

The best known reading formula was developed by Edward Fry. It is an estimate of grade level based on average number of sentences and syllables in three passages taken at random.[28] The Raygor Reading Estimate, developed by Alton Raygor, is easier to use than the Fry method (counting letters instead of syllables) and is of equal accuracy.[29] Examples of other formulas are provided in Table 6.2.

Critics of the various reading formulas say that 1) they fail to consider students' prior knowledge, experience, and interests, all of which influence reading comprehension; 2) they assume that words with fewer syllables and shorter, simpler sentences are easier to comprehend than words with more syllables and longer sentences with subor-

table 6.2   **A Closer Look at Readability Formulas**

Because there are over 100 readability formulas, what follows is only a small sample.

Betts Levels

This formula is based on errors made in oral reading. The independent level is less than 5 percent errors; the instruction level is about 5 percent errors (one in twenty words); the frustration level is more than 5 percent errors.

Chinese

Because Chinese is written in characters, not words, you count the number of brush strokes per character.

Cloze

To use the cloze method to rank books, simply take a text passage and delete every fifth word, and then ask a group to fill in the blanks. This method is objective and accurate but time-consuming. To translate cloze scores to grade level see the Dale-Chall manuals.

The New Dale-Chall Readability Formula

You can obtain a grade level, and a cloze score if you wish, by taking a 100 word sample (every fiftieth page) and counting the number of sentences in the sample. Next, determine the number of unfamiliar words, which are those not on the Dale list of 3,000 words. Use the table to get grade level or cloze score. You need the manual for the tables and the 3,000 word list.

The Flesch Kincaid Reading Ease Formula

This formula is widely used in industry: Grade level = 4 (words/sentence) + 12 (syllables/word)–16.

The Fry Readability Graph

Randomly select a minimum of three 100-word samples and count the number of sentences in each sample. Then count the number of syllables in each sample. Average the sentence count and syllable count and use the graph to obtain grade level. The graph is not copyrighted.

Lix and Rix

These formulas are used in Europe for many languages. Lix is average sentence length plus average word length. Rix is the number of long words divided by sentence length.

Leveling

Each of several authors suggest a different mix of factors. [Leveling is a much more modern term and is used primarily at the beginning reading levels.]

Lexiles, DRP Units, ATOS Grade Level

These formulas are applied by large companies to a large number of books. It is perhaps best to buy their book lists.

Source: Edward Fry. "Readability Versus Leveling." *The Reading Teacher* (November 2002): 290. Reprinted with permission.

dinate clauses, which is not always true; 3) publishers have reacted to these formulas by adjusting sentence and word length to give the appearance of certain levels of readability without necessarily providing them;[30] and 4) strict adherence to formulas robs prose of the connective words, vocabulary, and sentence structure that make it interesting, comprehensible, and stylistically worth reading. In short, rigid following of reading formulas may result in the adoption of a boring and bland text. As a consequence, it is imperative for you as the teacher to determine the match between textbooks used by a school and the learning needs of students and then to supplement the textbook when additional resources are needed to ensure student learning.[31]

Another criticism of the readability formulas is that they are not useful with texts for young children in the very early grades. Because text passages frequently have fewer than 100 words, the formulas do not work with the texts appropriate for early grades. When formulas cannot be applied, teachers need to develop skill in making their own assessments by taking into account such factors as text length, the size and layout of the print, the vocabulary and concepts introduced, the pattern of language, and the illustrations that support the narrative (i.e., do they help clarify material?). In essence, teachers need to be attentive to the vocabulary of the books they use and develop skill in matching books to children.

Whatever their faults, reading formulas do help teachers assess reading difficulty and select printed material that is appropriate for the students' abilities. Since most teachers work with groups of students in which there is a range of abilities, it is advisable that the difficulty of the material not be more than one year below or above the average reading grade level of the group. If there is more than a one- to two-year spread in reading ability in a group, the teacher should use more than one set of instructional materials.

Some educators now urge that comprehendability, not readability, is the major quality to consider when adopting a text. Teachers and textbook committees are identifying various textbook aids such as structural overviews, introductory objectives, summaries, and review exercises as devices that contribute to comprehendability. One reading expert lists more than forty aids that might be considered when selecting a text.[32]

Cognitive Task Demands

Critics have found that textbooks in nearly every subject and grade level cover too many topics; the writing is superficial, choppy, and lacking in depth and breadth (as explained earlier, this phenomenon is called *mentioning*); and content wanders between the important and the trivial.[33] Many texts also fail to capture the imagination and interest of the students or make students think, and they spurn current knowledge about cognitive information and linguistic processing.[34] The so-called best textbooks are often designed to entertain and to be decorative, but they provide only "surface" information on topics, lack adequate integration of subject matter, and do not stretch the student's mind. They are unintentionally geared to oversimplify and to limit thinking.

Textbook adoption committees have contributed to the superficiality problem with their demands for topic coverage and easy-to-read prose. Special interest groups, with their political passions and legal challenges, have added to the problem, causing publishers to become politically sensitive to the content at the expense of linguistic and cognitive processes. Teachers have done their part, too, since far too many teachers emphasize "right" answers rather than a focus on exploring ideas critically.

Several years ago, Bennett and colleagues analyzed 417 language and math tasks assigned in texts by teachers and found that 60 percent were practice tasks, or content already known to the students. New tasks accounted for 25 percent, and tasks requiring students to discover, invent, or develop a new concept or problem made up 7 percent of the tasks. Another study found that approximately 84 percent of teachers rely on textually explicit instruction, a method of selecting verbatim information from the textbook or workbook to provide a correct answer to a question. Rarely do teachers employ textually implicit instruction, in which a correct answer requires students to make an inference from the textual information supplied. Even more rarely do they use scriptually implicit instruction, in which a correct answer requires students to go beyond the information given and call on prior knowledge and reasoning skills.[35]

Many teachers are unwilling or unable to change from textbooks that are characterized by low-level cognitive demands and divorced from how students think or reason. One might expect at least mathematics teachers to stress problem solving, but many teachers of mathematics, especially at the upper elementary and junior high school grades, are not much different from their colleagues in this regard. Indeed, some data strongly suggest that many of these "teachers don't know mathematics. [As a result] they assign the basic problems but skip word problems because word problems are harder to teach."[36]

Word problems can also require a level of content understanding that some teachers, even "reasonably well-trained" teachers, do not have. For example, in the early 1990s one researcher asked teacher candidates to create a story problem for $1\frac{3}{4}$ divided by $\frac{1}{2}$. According to Harriet Tyson,

> A whopping 69 percent of the elementary education students were unable to do so. But a surprising 55 percent of the mathematics majors and minors who were planning to teach in secondary schools were also unable to devise a life situation that would call for that division problem. All could "work" the problem, of course, through the mechanical approach they had learned. But in trying to imagine a real-life situation using $1\frac{3}{4}$ divided by $\frac{1}{2}$, many created a problem that involved dividing by 2 rather than by $\frac{1}{2}$. This study makes it clear that those math majors and minors didn't understand the *concept* of dividing by $\frac{1}{2}$. If they had, they would have known that dividing by 2 produces a smaller number, whereas dividing by $\frac{1}{2}$ produces a larger number. Engineers may not need to understand that concept, but teachers do.[37]

The point here is straightforward: Good teaching is intellectually demanding. It requires complex and sophisticated decision making, and textbooks cannot do that for a teacher. Textbooks are a resource, not a content mandate.

Textbook and Pedagogical Aids

Textbook aids, sometimes called *text-based aids, instructional aids, textbook elements,* or *reader aids,* are designed to enhance understanding of the content and to facilitate learning. Aids that appear at the beginning of a chapter include overviews, instructional objectives, and focusing questions (prequestions). Aids that occur throughout the chapter include headings, key terms in special type, marginal notes ("trigger items"), overview tables, outlines, discussions (point-counterpoint, pro-con), and illustrations such as graphs, charts, and pictures. Aids that come at the end of the chapter include summaries, discussion questions (postquestions), case studies, problems, review exercises, sample test questions, suggested activities, suggested readings, and glossaries.

Those aids used before students start to read the chapter acquaint them with the general approach and the information and concepts to be learned, and they can foster enhanced comprehension. The aids used while students are reading the chapter focus on organization of the content, provide examples, supply supplementary information, and repeat objectives. Those used after the chapter reinforce learning through summaries and exercises and encourage critical thinking through problems and activities. See Tips for Teachers 6.2 for insight into the use of textbook aids.

Pedagogical aids, sometimes called *instructional aids* or *teaching aids,* are materials designed for teacher use and provided as supplements to a textbook. They include 1) teachers' manuals; 2) test questions; 3) skills books or exercise books; 4) transparencies or cutouts to duplicate; 5) reinforcement activities; 6) enrichment activities; 7) behavioral objectives; 8) lesson plans; 9) bulletin board displays; 10) supplementary tables, graphs, charts, and maps; 11) parent involvement materials; 12) teacher resource binders; 13) computer software; and 14) audio- and videocassettes.[38]

The teacher may combine approaches and guide students with questions to facilitate comprehension: "Where is the information you need to know stated?" "Which words are unknown to you?" "Where in the text can you find a clue for understanding them?" "How do the tables and graphs help you understand?" "Why pay close attention to the bold print (or print in italics)?" "What do the marginal notes tell you?" "Does the order of discussion (homework) questions correspond with the order of the narrative?" Then teacher and class can practice finding the answer to selected questions in the discussion (homework) section.

Textbook aids in particular can facilitate the development of cognitive processes. Table 6.3 lists four developmental stages of cognitive processes and corresponding cognitive operations, reader activities, and their relationship to various textbook aids. In theory, the cognitive processes, operations, and reader activities each form an untested hierarchy in which one level is prerequisite to the next. The aids are not hierarchical but overlap—any one aid may facilitate learning at more than one level of the hierarchy.

Without good textbook aids, poor readers will learn little and capable readers will develop default strategies or partially ineffective strategies for processing text information. A default strategy is likely to involve focusing on topic sentences or unusual and/or isolated information, instead of main concepts and principles.[39] A default strategy also leads to copying and memorizing long lists of information, rather than organizing, inferring, and transferring ideas of the text. A textbook may have excellent aids; however, the teacher may not know how to make good use of them. (See Tips for Teachers 6.2.)

One other type of textbook aid (or supplement) has emerged recently as a consequence of the heavy emphasis on academic standards: supplements that align textbooks with state standards. For example, in Virginia, Harcourt Brace and Scott Foresman have brought K–3 textbooks in line with the Virginia Standards of Learning for history and social science. Publishers put out national textbooks but in states like Virginia (and Texas and California) special editions of texts are being published to align with state standards.[40] Prior to this development, teachers who focused heavily on state academic standards created their own supplements.

Reading Across the Content Areas

All teachers, whatever the subject or grade level, are reading teachers in the sense that they should help their students read and understand textbook material. Success on all types of tests and assessments requires reading ability, even success on math tests.

Student Use of Textbook Aids

 Textbook aids (textbook elements) have continued to grow, as publishers and authors respond to growing needs of teachers and textbook selection committee criteria for selecting texts. Following is a list of features now commonly found in textbooks, with questions to ask students to help them understand how to use these tools.

Features of Text:
Sample Questions for Students

Contents
1. How do you use the table of contents?
2. What is the difference between major and minor headings?
3. In what chapters would you find information about _____?

Index
1. What information do you find in an index?
2. On what pages would you find the following information _____?
3. Why is the subject on _____ cross-referenced?

Opening Material (overview, objective, focusing questions, outline)
1. What are the main points or topics of the chapter? How do we know?
2. Do the objectives correspond with the outline of the chapter?
3. In what section can we expect to find a discussion of _____?

Graphic Material (charts, graphs, diagrams) and tabular material
1. How does the legend at the bottom of the chart explain the meaning of data?
2. Based on the lines of graph, what will happen in the year 2010? What do the dotted lines represent?
3. Where in the narrative does the author explain the table?

Summaries
1. If you could read only one page to find out what the chapter is about, what page would you read? Why?

2. Where can we find a summary of the main ideas of the chapter?
3. Does the summary correspond to the major headings?

Pictures
1. Are the pictures relevant? Up-to-date?
2. What is the author trying to convey in this picture?
3. How do the pictures reveal the author's biases?

Headings
1. What main ideas can you derive from the headings? Subheadings?
2. How are the subheadings related to the headings?
3. On what pages would you find a discussion of _____?

Information sources (footnotes, references)
1. Where did the author get the information for the chapter?
2. Are the footnotes important? Up-to-date?
3. What references might you use to supplement those at the end of the chapter?

Key Terms in text
1. Which are the important terms on this page?
2. What are some terms in bold print? What are others in italics?
3. Where can you find the meaning of these terms in the text?

Marginal notes (or trigger items)
1. Do the marginal notes catch your eye?
2. Why are these terms or phrases noted in the margin?
3. Quickly find a discussion of the following topics: _____.

Supplementary discussion (point/counterpoint tables, list of suggestions, case studies)
1. Why are the point/counterpoint discussions interesting? Which side do you take?
2. What are the important issues on this topic?
3. Which tips make sense to you? Why?

End-of-chapter material (review exercises, questions, activities, sample test items)
1. Are the exercises meaningful? Do they tie into the text?
2. Which discussion questions seem controversial? Why?
3. Why should we do the activities?
4. Take a practice test. Answer the sample test questions to see what we need to study.

table 6.3   **Levels of Cognition and Reading, with Implications for Using Textbook Aids**

Cognitive Process	Cognitive Operations	Reader Activities	Textbook Aids
Identifying	Focusing on selective information Sequencing selective information	Copying Underlining Simple note taking or discussion	Overviews Instructional objectives Prequestions Key words or terms Marginal notes Summaries Review exercises
Conceptualizing	Classifying main ideas of text Comparing main ideas of text	Logical or structured note taking or discussion Distinguishing relevant information Relating points to each other	Headings, subheadings Marginal notes Point-counterpoint discussion Summaries Postquestions Problems Review exercises
Integrating	Analyzing main ideas of text Modifying ideas of text into variations or new ideas Deducing main ideas of text Expanding main ideas of text Applying main ideas of text to problems	Elaborate note taking or discussion Making generalizations Hierarchical ordering of items Making inferences from text information	Headings, subheadings Graphs, tables Models, paradigms Postquestions Case studies Problems Activities
Transferring	Evaluating text information Verifying text information Going beyond text information Predicting from text information	Elaborate note taking or discussion Evaluating, problem solving, and inferring based on text information Using text information to create new information	Graphs, tables Models, paradigms Simulations Case studies Problems Activities

Source: Allan C. Ornstein. "Textbook Instruction: Processes and Strategies." *NASSP Bulletin* (December 1989): 109. Copyright 1989 National Association of Secondary School Principals (www.principals.org). Reprinted with permission.

The problem is that there is an apparent lack of interest by many secondary teachers in combining reading instruction with disciplinary content instruction. Nationwide, for example, 44 percent of 466 teachers surveyed maintained reading instruction is not the responsibility of content area teachers. Moreover, 30 percent admit they lack the skills needed to participate in reading instruction or combine it with content instruction.[41] The great majority of secondary teachers (over 90 percent) report they assign pages to read without providing purpose for or comprehension guides for the reading.[42] The level of support a teacher needs to provide will vary with the information a teacher knows about each student. Table 6.4 outlines a set of considerations essential for using and selecting texts to enhance learning.[43]

Researchers suggest that students' comprehension of what they read in the content areas is enhanced by 1) previewing (by helping students with background knowl-

table 6.4   Text Information for Classrooms

Once you have gathered information about each student, you need to consider what texts you will use. The following steps facilitate this process:

1. *Identify the texts already available in the classroom:* these may include basals, anthologies, trade books, textbooks, magazines, poetry books, and picture books.

2. *Organize the texts to facilitate guided comprehension:* use the following questions to accomplish this:
   - Does this text add to existing content area study or knowledge?
   - Can this text be used in a genre study?
   - Does this text exemplify a particular style, structure, language pattern, or literary device? Can this text be used to teach a comprehension strategy?
   - Are there multiple copies of the text available?
   - Does this text match a particular student's interests?
   - Is this a good example of a text structure?
   - Is this text part of a series?
   - Is this text written by a favorite author?

   These questions can be used with both narrative and expository texts, which include individual stories in literature anthologies as well as individual articles within magazines.

3. *Acquire additional materials to assure ample accessible text for all readers:* it is important to have some small sets of books to use during teacher-guided comprehension groups, but it is also necessary to have in the classroom a wide array of texts, varying in type, genre, length, and content. These books must represent a wide range of readability and genre. It is important to include novels of varying length, nonfiction trade books, picture books, poetry books, and magazines.

   Keep in mind the following ideas when adding to classroom collections:
   - Content areas—nonfiction and narrative text to supplement studies in math, science, and social studies
   - Student interests—a variety of texts (fiction, nonfiction, poetry) to match students' interests
   - Read aloud—texts that offer examples of a variety of text structures and engaging story lines to be used to demonstrate comprehension processes and fluency
   - Anchor books—texts used in whole-group and small-group instruction to demonstrate a specific strategy or routine
   - Sets of books—small sets (four to six copies) of books to be used in guided comprehension groups; these should be based on students' levels as well as the strategies that can be taught and used
   - Text sets—series books, favorite author, genre, topic; several books that have a common characteristic

   Authors' note: The purpose of all these questions is to focus teacher decision making about texts.

Source: Maureen McLaughlin and MaryBeth Allen. *Guided Comprehension:* A Teaching Model for Grades 3–8. Newark, Del.: International Reading Association, 2002, pp. 68–69. Reprinted with permission.

edge); 2) relating their knowledge and experience (or making connections) to the information in the text, 3) relating one part of the text to another, 4) discussing and summarizing the meaning of important new words; and 5) self-questioning that entails having students create questions about the content as they are reading.[44] Students need practice in inferential reasoning and other comprehension processes but this cannot occur if they are occupied with word recognition and vocabulary demands or they simply do not comprehend the material.[45]

Relating the text to students' experience can be done through asking their opinions, having them imagine themselves part of the events described in the text, or having them think of examples from their own experience. Relating parts of the text to one another can be achieved by asking students to summarize and analyze main points, to explain relationships and elaborate with examples, and to note main and minor headings, marginal notes, key terms, and summary statements. Defining new terms can be accomplished by discussing in class selected terms that have conceptual meaning and encouraging students to use the dictionary and glossaries on their own. Providing repetitive sentence patterns and familiar words and concepts eases word recognition and comprehension tasks for students who have trouble reading. Paying close attention to instructional objectives or focusing questions and answering review questions can help students determine whether they understand the text material and what sections they need to reread or skim.

It is imperative that teachers become good observers of students as they read or engage in reading activities. Marie Carbo developed a wonderful observation guide that requires a focused observation of students while they are reading to diagnose reading style and then offers recommendations for what the teacher might do to enhance reader performance (see Table 6.5).

Advance organizers, developed by David Ausubel to enhance concept thinking, can be used in teaching students how to read.[46] The advance organizers characterize the general nature of the text, the major categories into which it can be divided, the similarities and differences among categories, and the examples within different categories. The organizers state the abstraction or generality under which data can be subsumed. To be useful, the organizers should be stated in terms that are already familiar to the students prior to their reading the text material.[47] They are especially useful when the text is poorly organized or students lack prerequisite knowledge of the subject. Although Ausubel and most other educators believe organizers should be presented before the text is read, others maintain that presenting them in the middle or after the text can also facilitate learning.[48]

Other types of textbook aids or cues—such as instructional objectives, overviews, prequestions, and specific instructions—presented prior to chapter reading can also facilitate learning of reading materials.[49] These aids are similar to advance organizers because they provide advance information about the nature of the material to be learned. In addition, postquestions and summary activities that apply textbook material to concepts, problems, or creative projects also enhance learning.

The idea is to get students to think out loud and to elaborate on the strategies they use to process information they read. Students use different strategies. If they become aware of what they are doing, they can improve their approaches to reading texts. Teachers should discuss these strategies with their students on a regular basis.

Metacognition and Text Structure

In general, ***narrative structure,*** which deals with a broad theme and conveys information in story form, is easier for readers to understand than is ***expository structure,*** which the reader encounters in textbooks. Children who learn to read in elementary school first learn through narratives. By the fourth or fifth grade, students begin to move into the more complex organizational patterns of the content areas that are conveyed through texts and expository writing. The emphasis on textbooks and thus expository structure increases with the grade level. Students who are unable to cope with this type of read-

Most children learn to read through narrative text and then move to expository text.

ing are bound to be low achievers since most learning in school depends on the ability to read and understand expository text.

Students, in general, have more difficulty with expository text than narrative text, because of insufficient prior knowledge, poor reading ability, lack of interest and motivation, and lack of sensitivity to how texts are organized.[50] In addition, a good many texts are poorly written, boring, and even confusing to students.[51] Narrative writing possesses a structure that likely will engage many readers who are unable to deal with the inherent abstractness of expository texts.

Researchers argue that the reason some students have more difficulty comprehending expository texts relates to their prior experiences. Specifically, the backgrounds of students will dictate the ease with which they can comprehend a text. Students from literary-rich home environments may be better able to comprehend expository texts that emphasize comparison-contrast, description, and cause and effect.[52] Students from poor socioeconomic areas or from homes that lack substantial reading materials may be limited by the background reading experiences they bring to expository text.

The teacher cannot take for granted that students understand text structure—that is, how information is organized, as well as the verbal and contextual cues (such as the headings and subheadings or the bold or italics print) that bring unity to the text. Good texts are written with certain expository structures that can be taught to students. Some of the common textbook structures are defined next.

t a b l e   6 . 5   **Reading Style Observation Guide (RSOG)**

Observation: The student . . .	Reading Style Diagnosis: The student . . .	Suggested Teaching Strategies: The teacher might . . .
1. is distracted by noise, looks up from reading at the slightest sound, places hands over ears, tries to quiet others.	prefers to read in a quiet environment.	provide quiet reading areas (study carrels and magic carpet sections); provide tape-recorded materials with headsets.
2. can read easily when other people are talking or music is playing.	prefers to read in an environment with talking and/or music.	permit student to listen to music through headsets while reading; establish small-group reading areas.
3. squirms, fidgets, or squints when reading near a window on a sunny day.	prefers to read in soft or dim light.	use plants, curtains, hanging beads, and dividers to block and diffuse light; add shaded lamps to reading sections; suggest student read in darker area of room.
4. seeks brightly lit areas for reading.	prefers to read in bright light.	allow student to read under bright lights and near windows.
5. wears many sweaters indoors.	prefers a warm environment.	encourage student to read in a warmer area and suggest sweaters.
6. perspires easily, wears light clothing.	prefers a cool environment.	encourage pupil to read in a cooler area and suggest light clothing.
7. is restless and moves in his seat while reading.	prefers an informal design.	allow the student to read while sitting on a pillow, carpeting, soft chair, or floor.
8. continually asks for teacher approval on reading work; enjoys sharing interests with teachers.	is teacher motivated.	encourage student to discuss reading interests with you and to share work with you after doing it; praise him or her; try small, teacher-directed reading group.
9. enjoys reading with the teacher.	prefers reading with adults.	schedule student to read with you often; try older tutors and adult volunteers.
10. cannot complete lengthy assignments.	is neither persistent nor responsible.	give short reading assignments and check them frequently; try programmed reading materials or multisensory instructional packages.
11. becomes confused by many choices of reading materials.	requires structure.	limit choices; give clear, simple directions; try a structured reading approach such as basal reader or programmed materials; provide a limited selection of reading resources based on child's interests.

Source: Copyright © Marie Carbo 1980. Reproduced from *What Every Principal Should Know About Teaching Reading.* National Reading Styles Institute, Syosset, NY 11791.

Observation: The student . . .	Reading Style Diagnosis: The student . . .	Suggested Teaching Strategies: The teacher might . . .
12. enjoys choices, demonstrates creativity when reading.	does not require structure.	provide many choices of reading materials; try an individualized reading program.
13. participates actively in group discussions; chooses to read with friends.	prefers to read with peers.	establish isolated small-group areas; provide reading games, activity cards; encourage writing and acting in plays or panels; try a language-experience approach.
14. shies away from others; reads best alone.	prefers to read alone.	provide programmed materials if structure is needed; use tape-recorded books, computers, multisensory activities for tactile/kinesmatic or unmotivated child.
15. remembers details in pictures; is a good speller; does not confuse visually similar words or letters; has a good sight vocabulary.	is a visual learner.	try a whole-word reading approach or structure; for variety, occasionally try a programmed learning sequence.
16. remembers directions and stories after hearing them; decodes words with ease; does not confuse similar-sounding words; enjoys listening activities.	is an auditory learner.	try a phonic or linguistic reading approach or structure; for variety, occasionally try a programmed learning sequence.
17. enjoys learning by touching; remembers words after tracing over and "feeling" them; likes to type, play reading games; is very active.	is a tactile/kinesmatic learner.	try a language-experience approach; use clay, sandpaper, and so on, to form words; try many reading games, model building, project work, and multisensory activities.
18. continually asks if it is lunch time or time for a snack when reading.	prefers intake while reading.	permit nutritious snacks during reading periods.
19. has difficulty reading in early morning; becomes more animated and attentive in the afternoon.	is better able to read in the late afternoon; may be even better at night!	schedule student to read in the late afternoon or send home "talking books" for evening work.
20. cannot sit still for long reading periods; becomes restless and sometimes misbehaves.	either requires mobility or different types of studies or methods.	allow snack breaks; provide manipulatives and reading games; have child read where movement is possible (floor, couch).

Response

Sometimes referred to as "question/answer," or "problem/solution," these structures are most common and crucial for meeting classroom or homework assignments. Often a problem is introduced, a plan discussed, an action presented, or an outcome described. The teacher needs to help students become aware of what is being asked and where the solution can be found or how the problem can be worked out. In the middle grades and with low achievers, students as a group should discuss the difficulties encountered and what they did about them.

Cause-Effect

Students need to be taught to search for main ideas: What is happening? To whom? Why? The teacher needs to clarify the task or problem, present guided practice to the group, and then introduce independent practice. Whereas most texts, especially in science, usually deal in cause-effect relationships, the process is often reversed in social studies texts to effect-cause—that is, an event is described and then the causes are explained.

Comparison-Contrast

This structure is common in most science and social studies texts. The author explains likenesses and differences—sometimes with tables, charts, or graphs. When tables or charts are used, categories and columns usually help cluster the information. Students must be taught to slow down, deduce, and extrapolate data from the tables, charts, or graphs.

Collection

Texts often classify, enumerate, or list information. Although this text structure is easy for students to understand, the information is more difficult to recall because of overload (the list is too long), and the information is rarely integrated into larger concepts. Students must be taught to summarize or synthesize from long lists. Most low achievers will attempt to memorize or write down long lists as opposed to conceptualizing the major points.

Generalizations

This structure is sometimes referred to as argument-persuasion in science texts and main ideas in social studies and English texts. The author presents concepts, summary data, or conclusions with supporting information. Students need to identify the generalizations and their supporting information for each chapter. One method is to view major topics in relation to subtopics.

Topics and Subtopics

Good textbooks sequence topics (sometimes called *headings*) in logical form and then integrate subtopics (or *subheadings*) within topics. Most middle school and junior high school texts contain between seven and fifteen pages per chapter; they should have three to four topics per chapter and two to four subtopics per topic. High school texts may have as many as twenty pages per chapter, although fifteen is the average. These texts should have four to five topics per chapter and the same number of subtopics per topic. More than four or five subtopics per topic will confuse or overload most readers.

Whole-to-Part Organization

Most texts are written with a whole-to-part strategy in mind—that is, the content is organized at several macro levels (whole book, parts, chapters, sections, subsections, and so on). Content does not just evolve; it is organized with a larger purpose and themes in mind. The material converges as opposed to branches—that is, it is organized in a way that brings material together. Decisions about content and how to focus on that content are made at each level of the text. Good text readers make use of similar macrostructures in their reading and thinking processes. However, all students must be encouraged to organize their expository reading around the overall organization of the text.[53]

Teachers in all content areas can foster awareness of text structure by having students make concrete graphic representations of the ideas within the text. Such strategies are referred to as mapping, networking, and graphing. They involve 1) representing—students develop a "graph" that represents basic concepts or ideas and relationships within and among the concepts and 2) outlining— students use and integrate headings, subheadings, and paragraphs in the text and complete (or fill in) the graphic representation.[54]

It is important that the teacher stress one strategy at a time and have students practice it and raise questions and comments to fill in gaps in understanding. The strategy a student adopts will provide more information about selected topics, as the student considers characteristics, specifics, explanations, and details. Ultimately, skilled readers will become sensitive to text structure, including pedagogical aids; they will use them if they are well structured; and they will process this structure along with prior knowledge of the topic in deciding what information is important to emphasize and how to integrate the new information.

It is also important for students to see how the teacher makes instructional decisions. Effective teachers make it possible for students to understand how the curriculum is organized and what parts of the content are intellectually perplexing. Knowledge evolves; it is not static. Students need to see the thinking of the teacher in order to become better thinkers themselves. This process represents a type of metacognitive teaching.[55]

Guidelines for Using Textbooks

The following general guidelines should help increase the value of the text for students:

1. *Do not become so hypnotized by the textbook that you follow it rigidly:* Supplement the textbook with other instructional aids and printed materials (such as paperback books, for all students, and journals, magazines, and reports for junior high and high school students). And be certain to determine if your state offers supplements that align state academic standards with textbook content.

2. *Adapt the textbook to the needs of the students and the objectives of the lesson:* Do not allow the textbook to determine exclusively either the teaching level or course content.

3. *Appraise the worth of the textbook by critically examining its content and structure:* See Tips for Teachers 6.3 for more information on this topic.

Beyond the Textbook

Diane Ravitch
Brown Chair in Education Studies, Brookings Institution

 Don't be afraid to be a critic of textbooks. Sometimes they contain inaccuracies or poor writing. Sometimes they don't provide enough background information for students to understand their meaning.

The biggest drawback of textbooks is that they may bore students. Today's students are accustomed to getting information about the world from television and movies; many of them know how to get information electronically. A textbook alone may not hold the students' interest.

When your students are turned off by the dull writing in their textbooks, blame the textbooks, not the kids.

Put yourself in the students' place and then ask yourself, would you read this if you didn't have to? Does it hold your attention? Would you be tempted to read more than the assigned number of pages? If the answer is "no" to all of these questions, then think about de-emphasizing the textbook in your classes.

The best way to use a textbook is to treat it like a reference work. Use it as background. The main source of learning should come from the other materials, experiences, and technology that you supply, either through hands-on activities (in or out of the classroom) or through the use of supplementary materials that are livelier, more vivid, and more motivating for students than the textbook.

QUESTIONS FOR REFLECTION

Research clearly demonstrates that a large gap exists between the reading achievement of disadvantaged students and their advantaged peer counterparts. A relationship also exists between socioeconomic status and reading achievement. That said, what does it suggest about the types of skills you may need to possess if you teach in an urban (low SES) middle school as opposed to a suburban (high SES) middle school? Consider the reading problems of students in both situations. If you want students to comprehend an expository text (a typical textbook) what must you do differently with students who come from a literary-poor environment as opposed to with those from a literary-rich one? Notice that these questions do not suggest an inherent difference in students' abilities. If student abilities are often a reflection of their experiences, how do you adjust for those differences?

As you consider possible solutions, consider what a wide variety of researchers have found relative to the most significant ways to close the academic achievement gap between diverse student groups.

- High quality teaching.
- Reduced class size.
- Clear standards of performance for students to achieve,
- Assessments that are clearly aligned to standards.
- Enhanced parental involvement in a child's education.

Which of these can you most directly impact? How?

Special note to reader: A wide variety of resources are now available on the achievement gap issue. See, for example, *Bridging the Great Divide: Broadening Perspectives on Closing the Achievement Gaps.* Naperville, IL: North Central Regional Educational Laboratory, 2002, – *www.ncrel.org*

Appraising the Worth of a Textbook

 Here are some questions to keep in mind when assessing the worth of a textbook for teacher and student. The first group of questions deals with text content, the second with mechanics, and the third with overall appraisal.

Content

1. Does the text coincide with the content and objectives of the course?
2. Is it up-to-date and accurate?
3. Is it comprehensive?
4. Is it adaptable to the students' needs, interests, and abilities?
5. Does it adequately and properly portray minorities and women?
6. Does it foster methodological approaches consistent with procedures used by teacher and school?
7. Does it reinforce the type of learning (such as critical thinking and problem solving) sought by the teacher and school?
8. Does it provide the student with a sense of accomplishment because it can be mastered and yet is still challenging?

Mechanics

1. Is the size appropriate?
2. Is the binding adequate?
3. Is the paper of adequate quality?
4. Are the objectives, headings, and summaries clear?
5. Are the contents and index well organized?
6. Is there a sufficient number of pictures, charts, maps, and so on appropriate for the students' level?
7. Does it come with instructional manuals and study guides?
8. Is it durable enough to last several years?
9. Is it reasonably priced relative to its quality? To its competitors?

Overall Appraisal

1. What are the outstanding features of the text?
2. What are the shortcomings of the text?
3. Do the outstanding features strongly override the shortcomings?

Source: Adapted from Allan C. Ornstein. "The Textbook Driven Curriculum." *Peabody Journal of Education* (Spring 1994): 71–72.

Workbook Materials

At the lower grade levels, workbooks are often used separately or independently to provide exercises for practice and drill in language arts, reading, and math. Along with the textbook, the workbook tends to dominate elementary school classrooms as the major instructional tool.

Teachers exhibit wide variations in the use of workbooks—those variations are based primarily on content area. Workbooks and other guide materials tend to be used chiefly in reading and language arts (as much as 19 percent of the instructional time), but they are used to a much more limited extent in social studies and in math.[56]

At the secondary grade levels, workbooks are often used in different content areas keyed to or as a supplement (rarely independently) to the textbook for the purpose of practice. For example, student manuals with drill exercises (sometimes problems) may be available that cover most of the course content. Students first engage in new learning derived from the textbook or another source; then the workbook is used to reinforce the new learning. Ideally, the exercises or problems are concrete examples of abstract learning. For this reason, many teachers view the workbook as a pedagogical aid and always check with publishers to see whether a workbook accompanies the textbook.

Disadvantages

The value of the workbook depends on how the teacher uses it. The workbook is sometimes used as a form of busywork, to keep students occupied, or even worse, as a substitute for teaching. Workbooks tend to overemphasize factual and low-level information. Students can spend hours, especially at the elementary grade level, filling in blanks, completing sentences, recognizing correct words, and working on simple mathematical computations. According to critics, workbook exercises have little to do with—and often discourage—critical thinking; creativity; developing a whole, abstract thought; or relevant hands-on activities and materials.[57] One way that some teachers deal with the fact orientation of workbooks is to supplement workbook assignments with questions or activities that require more higher-level thinking.[58]

The teacher may assign workbook exercises in order to keep students busy while he or she grades papers, performs clerical functions, or confers with an individual student or group of students. Such approaches are used, sometimes overused, in conjunction with seat work activities. When workbooks are assigned either as busywork or merely to facilitate seat work activities and fail to link the exercises in a meaningful way to new information or to content coverage, the routine produces what critics call *management mentality* in both students and teachers. Such dependence "de-skills" teachers (they become ineffective) and curtails creative instruction.[59]

Advantages

The merit of the workbook is that it performs the practice-and-drill function well. It is helpful for young students who need to learn a knowledge base and with low-achieving students who need extra concrete activities to understand abstract learning and repeated exercises to integrate new learning. To the extent that the workbook is used in one of these instructional contexts and that the exercises make learning more meaningful to students, it has value. In essence, workbooks can be very useful for skill reinforcement.

The criteria for judging a workbook's merit include the following: 1) exercises (or problems) are related to abstract or new learning; 2) exercises are interesting and maintain students' interest; 3) exercises exist in proper quantity—not too many or too few; 4) students understand the directions (young students and low-achieving students often don't understand written directions); 5) students can perform or answer the majority of the exercises (if they cannot, frustration will mount and most students will no longer persist); 6) teachers provide needed direction and guided practice to help students learn the necessary skills and strategies for workbook comprehension or performance (the sheer ability to do something does not guarantee performance); and 7) teachers use the exercises discriminately (they supplement with other instructional methods and materials).[60]

Workbooks are desirable for many students but especially important for students for whom learning to read is difficult. It is for these children that workbooks should be geared. For workbooks to be effective, Jean Osborn insists that they focus on a sequenced review of what has been taught, on the most important content, and on content that needs to be reinforced. Workbooks can provide 1) a means of practicing details of what has been taught; 2) extra practice for students who need it; 3) intermittent reviews of what has been taught; 4) ways for students to apply new learning with examples; 5) practice in following directions; 6) practice in a variety of formats that students will experience when they take tests; and 7) opportunity for students to work independently and at their own pace.[61]

Guidelines for Using Workbooks

In choosing, working with, or evaluating workbook materials, keep the following guidelines in mind. They should help you decide if the workbook materials are appropriate for your specific teaching and learning situation.

1. *Objectives:* Do the workbook materials meet the goals of the school? Which ones? Do the workbook materials meet the program objectives? Course objectives? Unit or lesson plan objectives?

2. *Readability:* What evidence is there that the workbook exercises coincide with the reading level of the students? Do the students understand the written directions? Wording of the exercises or problems?

3. *Utility:* What evidence is there that the workbook materials are helpful for the students? What evidence is there that students are interested in the exercises?

4. *Cognition:* Do the workbook exercises supplement or reinforce abstract thinking? Are the exercises intellectually stimulating? Are sample exercises or problems worked out step-by-step?

5. *Content coverage:* Do the exercises cover the content in depth? Do they have balance in terms of the scope and sequence of the content?

6. *Audiovisuals:* Is the workbook material user-friendly? Are there a variety of appropriate illustrations—charts, tables, pictures, drawings, etc.—to facilitate learning?

7. *Learning theory:* Do the workbook exercises coincide (or conflict) with current learning theory? Which theory? In what ways do the exercises stimulate learning? In what ways are individual differences provided for?

8. *Pedagogical aids:* Is the workbook used as a separate text or used in conjunction with another text? Does the workbook have a teacher edition or instructor's manual to provide assistance? Is the assistance valuable?

Journals, Magazines, and Newspapers

These are primary sources and are therefore excellent materials for enhancing thinking skills and research skills of students. Journals are the publications of professional and academic associations and as such are more technical than magazines and newspapers. Their uses with students are quite limited. The most popular magazines used by teachers are *Time, Newsweek,* and *U.S. News and World Report,* although there are many others that can supplement or be the focal point of learning. The magazines are topical and usually readily available to a large number of students either at home or through a school or local library. It is appropriate to start students with the local newspaper at the middle grade and junior high school level, but the teacher should also consider *The New York Times, Washington Post,* or *The Wall Street Journal* at the high school level. These papers are written at the tenth to twelfth grade reading level; carefully assess the reading abilities of your students before using these papers. Many local newspapers will even deliver copies (for a limited time) to the whole class if you need them for some type of systematic study.

To enrich content, teachers in most subjects can encourage students to read journals, magazines, and newspapers. Many of these publications are interesting and more informative and up-to-date than the textbook. Gathering suitable magazine and newspaper materials can be delegated to the class or it can be conducted primarily by the teacher.

Journal and magazine articles have not been sanitized or toned down to the same extent as textbooks. The content expresses a point of view, and it can be used to enhance thinking and research skills. Newspapers, in theory (not always in practice), deal in reporting, not analyzing or interpreting data. It is up to the student to draw conclusions about and evaluate what is being reported. Editorials, story columns, op-ed (opinion) columns, and letters to the editor are quite different, and students need to understand that such material is subjective. Although a student may understand that a particular point of view may be expressed in a journal, magazine, or newspaper article, he or she may be unable to identify distortions or biases and therefore accept the view as fact. In general, biases can be conveyed in eight ways: 1) through length, selection, and omission; 2) through placement; 3) by title, headline, or headings; 4) through pictures and captions; 5) through names and titles; 6) through statistics; 7) by reference source; and 8) by word selection and connotation.[62]

Although the teacher must use professional judgment in interpreting or assigning these instructional materials, students can learn to evaluate the information contained in them by being trained to answer the following questions: 1) Is the account slanted? 2) Is important information treated accurately? 3) Are controversial topics discussed rationally? 4) Is there a clear distinction between fact and opinion? 5) Do the headlines, captions, and opening statements present the news accurately? 6) Are editorials and commentaries clearly designated?[63]

The five most popular uses of journals and magazines in classrooms are for 1) extension activities, 2) recreational reading, 3) motivation to read, 4) change of pace, and 5) current information.[64] Use varies by grade and subject area. One study reports that in junior high school, 76 percent of the language arts teachers, 43 percent of the social studies teachers, and 23 percent of the science teachers used journals or magazines in their classrooms. In high school, 57 percent of the science teachers, 31 percent of the English teachers, and 24 percent of the social studies teachers use them. Actual frequency of use and type of student (student's ability or achievement) were not reported.[65]

Considering that textbooks are adopted for a period of five years or more in some states, it is not surprising that teachers across the curriculum look to current magazines for updated information in their respective subject areas. These magazines are excellent up-to-date instructional tools for promoting student research skills and for independent projects. They offer multiple viewpoints and thus encourage critical reading and controversial discussions, as well as in-depth understanding and learning of current and relevant content.

Guidelines for Using Journals, Magazines, and Newspapers

The following guidelines should assist teachers and students:

1. Be sure that journal, magazine, and newspaper articles are within the students' reading and comprehension range.

2. Select those materials that are readily available and affordable.

3. Make sure the journal, magazine, or newspaper articles are compatible with your teaching goals, given the fact that these materials often express a particular view.

4. Train students in reading and evaluating these materials. Children and adolescents tend to believe that whatever is printed is true. A useful project is a comparative analysis of articles that take different views on a controversial subject.

5. Train students in the use of card catalogs, periodical catalogs, and the classification and retrieval systems of journals and magazines so they can use these materials in independent study and research.

6. Many students, especially at the secondary school and college level, clip excerpts from journals and magazines (also books) or cut out entire articles found in the library. As a teacher you must make the work of the librarian easier by discouraging this habit before students go to the library.

7. Journal, magazine, and newspaper articles are excellent sources for student reports. Encourage students to take notes, summarize main ideas, and interpret ideas in these instructional materials.

8. These instructional materials are also excellent sources for thinking about ideas, selecting and using information for assignments, and identifying and solving problems independently or in a group. High-achieving students can work independently; low-achieving students will more likely need the security of the group and the assistance of the teacher.

9. Assist students in doing research reports by providing a list of journals and magazines that are relevant to the topic and can be understood by the student.

10. Keep a file of pertinent journal, magazine, and newspaper articles to supplement the text and incorporate into the unit or lesson plan. Update the file on a frequent basis.

Simulations and Games

Play is pleasurable and natural for children and adolescents, and simulations and games are formalized expressions of play. They provide a wide range of social and cognitive experiences. *Simulations* are abstractions of the real world, involving objects, processes, or situations. *Games* are activities that may include a variety of goals, rules, and rewards. Simulated games involve *situations* with associated goals, rules, and rewards.

Simulations have become increasingly popular among educators, after much success in military, business, medical, and public administrative arenas. Many simulations are now produced commercially for teachers, especially for use in conjunction with computers and VCRs. However, teacher-made simulations (not for computer and VCR use) are more often used in the classroom, since they can be geared to specific students, subjects, or grade levels. Several "how-to-do-it" publications have been produced by teacher associations for would-be developers of simulations and games.

One educator reports four advantages of simulations:

1. A simulation is [an excellent motivating device].
2. A successful simulation demands the use of many study skills and techniques . . . A practical relationship is forged between study and fun.
3. A full-dress simulation is a powerful way to make many . . . topics . . . come alive.
4. A successful simulation is very rewarding to the teacher. [He or she] takes a back seat to let things develop [and watches] students live, talk, and enter into [active learning].[66]

In short, simulations permit students to experience the nearest thing to reality. They come in a variety of forms. One excellent resource for identifying appropriate simulations for content material that you are teaching is the Marco Polo website (www.marcopolo-education.org/join_maillist.cfm). On the day that this chapter was being written, a teacher who wanted information on simulations that could be used to illustrate population and diversity statistics sent a request to that website. One response came from a teacher who suggested Population Pasta, which is located on the National Geographic (nationalgeographic.com/xpeditions) website. If you visit the site you will be given a mission ("translate dry population statistics into vivid graphics") and asked to accomplish it through a series of engaging hands-on activities. Two examples of missions are provided here. One is for younger children, and the other is for older students. The questions are oriented toward the K-12 students being taught.

> *Younger Xpeditioners:* Print the world map from the *Xpeditions Atlas.* Find and mark the ten countries with the most people. Would you like to live in one of the countries? Think about how your life would be different in a country with a larger population. What happens when more people live in the same amount of space?
>
> What would happen if more children joined a classroom in the middle of the school year? Would the classroom be a better place to learn? If the number of students double, what changes might your teacher have to make?
>
> *Older Xpeditioners:* Pick one of the ten most populous countries and print a map of it from the *Xpeditions Atlas.* On the map write the country's population, average income and life expectancy, based on statistics that can be found at the *Population Reference Bureau.* Create a theory about what life might be like in this country.
>
> Find the country's profile in the *Map Machine.* Does the information in the profile make you want to revise your theory?[67]

Games are more informal and cover a wide range of situations, whereas simulations reflect real-life situations and are more structured. Games have been an important instructional tool in kindergarten and elementary school dating back to the early nineteenth-century and educational pioneers such as Froebel, Pestolozzi, and, later, the play wing of the Progressive movement.

Almost any teacher guide, for almost all grade levels and subjects, will list several games for enriching learning. Educational games have social and cognitive purposes; they are not designed solely to amuse. Any game, however, may contribute to learning. For example, Monopoly is a game played for amusement, yet it has some value for young children in learning to count and deal with money. Checkers and chess, besides being amusing, challenge the mind; they involve math, logic, and sequencing of moves.

For younger students the value of the game may lie in the game itself, in the experience it gives them in learning to discriminate sounds or objects, to manipulate and gain facility in motor skills, or to play together and socialize.[68] For older students, the value may lie more in the postgame discussion, or what some educators call the *debriefing sessions*. (Simulations can also incorporate postactivity discussions or debriefing sessions.) Through proper questioning, the teacher brings out instances of questionable behavior, when the rules were ignored, and the reasons for such behavior. Life situations can be perceived as a series of games, in which there are winners and losers, in which there is cooperation and competition, and in which rules are broken and enforced. In this connection, games are an excellent means for teaching morality and ethics, value clarification, and affective education.

One potential negative of games is that by their very nature they tend to emphasize competition. Depending on the students and the situation, teachers need to assess whether the positives of the game outweigh whatever negatives emerge as students compete against one another.

Guidelines for Using Simulations and Games

Numerous simulations and games are commercially produced, but teachers must judge whether these are suitable for their students, whether they need modification or can be modified, or whether the teachers need to develop their own materials. Here are some guidelines to follow when incorporating simulations and games:

1. Every simulation and game must have an educational objective. Distinguish between amusement games and educational games, between game objectives and instructional objectives.

2. The purpose of using simulations is to enable students to understand the nature of a problem and how to solve the problem.

3. Games should be used for teaching thinking and socialization to children in the lower grades.

4. Simulations and games should be viewed as an experience for learning content. Students learn by organizing and familiarizing themselves with the content— by experiencing as much as possible the object, process, or situation.

5. Simulations and games must be related to the content (skills, concepts, values) you wish to teach; this content should correspond with reality, and the relationship between the real world and the simulation or game should be clarified to the participants.

6. The postgame (or postsimulation) discussion is crucial for older students to clarify skills, concepts, and values to be learned.

Technology ViewPoint from a Classroom Teacher

Jackie Marshall Arnold
K–12 media Specialist

 Simulations are powerful tools that provide realistic, problem-solving experiences that might otherwise be unimaginable. Simulations utilizing technology are powerful learning opportunities that teachers should explore to enhance their curriculum.

Quality simulation experiences can provide rich educational opportunities for students. Simulations promote higher-order thinking and problem-solving skills. They can allow students to work collaboratively. Simulations can model engaging, dynamic experiences and allow for learning opportunities in a cause and effect environment. Simulations allow students to understand complex issues through a virtual hands-on environment that will be beneficial for any style of learner.

Teachers will find many commercially created simulation software programs are available for purchase. Publishers like Tom Snyder (www.tomsnyder.com) provide a wealth of software options such as the software entitled *Decisions, Decisions.* This software package provides a variety of curricular topics and presents students with simulated problems and choices. Students engage in the issues, research the topic in-depth, and "decide" upon a solution to the problem.

Simulations also exist that allow students to have hands-on experiences that might otherwise not be possible. Lego Dacta™ products (http://www.lego.com/dacta/products/robotics.asp) provide the hardware and software necessary for students to create and simulate real-world objects. For example, stu-dents can build an *Intelligent House* equipped with garage doors, burglar alarms, lights, a greenhouse, and more. Students then can decide when the windows should be opened and closed, when the burglar alarm should be set, and what conditions the greenhouse needs to maximize plant growth. They then program their creation to do just these things. The learning possibilities are endless.

Simulations also allow students to have experiences in a "virtual" way. For example, students can use software to simulate the dissecting of a frog. Teachers will also find websites that simulate the process of frog dissection. An online tutorial experience entitled *Net-Frog* was designed by a team through the University of Virginia's Curry School of Education. This website (curry.edschool.virginia.edu/go/frog/) has won multiple awards. It simulates the entire frog dissection process using video clips and step-by-step feedback.

ThinkQuest has developed an interactive site entitled *Sim Rock Café* (library.thinkquest.org/50061/teachersmanual/index.html) that allows teachers to study the components of a high quality simulation and provides the resources needed for teachers to develop their own curricular based simulation. The site summarizes the advantages of simulations in two critical points: simulations, first, by definition, seek to replicate the real world and, second, demand the "utmost in critical thinking and accurate data." The site provides the resources, professional development, and links for any teacher to create his or her own simulation. Several examples of student and teacher created simulations can be viewed at the website and used in the classroom.

Source: Retrieved November 4, 2002, from the Sim Rock Café website at http://library.thinkquest.org/50061/teachersmanual/index.html

7. The postgame (or postsimulation) discussion should incorporate case studies, draw on student experiences, apply what was observed to real-life situations, and lead to suggestions for further study.

8. Employ a series of questions that require students to discuss their thoughts during the activity: What thoughts governed their behavior? What experiences resulted in certain behaviors? What strategies did they use to make

decisions to achieve their goals? Which strategies were most effective? Could they predict the behavior of others?

9. In most simulations and games, students will interact. Participants and observers should discuss the interaction, if they are old enough, in terms of cooperation and competition and rational and emotional behavior.

10. To determine whether your objectives have been achieved by the simulations or games, use some form of evaluation, feedback, or discussion.

Theory into Practice

For each subject and grade level, you need basic instructional materials to implement successful teaching and learning. Teachers, both beginning and experienced, should become familiar with the curriculum bulletins and guides for their subjects and grade levels. Such bulletins list necessary, recommended, and supplementary materials. Teachers should be familiar with the materials available in their school by discussing them with experienced colleagues or supervisors. Teachers must also find out how to construct supplementary materials in order to address areas of weakness in prescribed textbooks and materials used by a school district.

The following questions provide a guide for effective use of instructional materials.

1. What instructional materials do you plan to use?
2. What do you hope to achieve by using these materials? Do they correspond with your objectives? Do they help students meet defined academic standards?
3. How will you prepare students to use the instructional materials?
4. How will you incorporate the instructional materials into the lesson?
5. Is the content of the materials suitable for your students? Consider sequence, scope, vocabulary, and so on.
6. Are there a variety of materials to coincide with various topics of the lesson?
7. How will you follow up the presentation of the materials? Are your follow-up activities appropriate?
8. How do students react to the materials? Are they engaged by the materials? Are the students learning the required content?

Summary

1. Good teachers become better teachers when they use appropriate materials in their lessons. Good teachers relate the materials they use to the curriculum and academic standards for the subject they teach. Learning what materials to use and how to use them comes with experience.
2. Instructional materials may be printed (available from professional, governmental, and commercial sources) or duplicated (if teacher-made or copied from printed material).
3. Materials should be selected in terms of well-defined and agreed-upon criteria—e.g., do they coincide with the teacher's objectives, are they well organized and designed, and are they suited to the reading level of the students?

4. In presenting materials, teachers need to consider student understanding, structure, sequence, balance, explanation, pace, and elaboration strategies.
5. Types of instructional materials include textbooks and workbooks; journals, magazines, and newspapers; and simulations and games. Textbooks and workbooks tend to dominate as the major instructional materials in most classrooms.
6. Important aspects of selecting textbooks are stereotyping, readability, textbook and pedagogical aids, and aids to student comprehension.
7. Textbook aids are designed to facilitate student comprehension, and pedagogical aids are designed to facilitate the teacher's instruction.
8. Several strategies can be used for incorporating simulations and games into the daily lesson.

Questions to Consider

1. What is the main purpose of using instructional materials?
2. How would you determine if a textbook presents a stereotypical picture of an ethnic or religious group, gender, labor group, or any other minority?
3. Which textbook aids are most important? Why?
4. What are important factors to consider when supplementing the textbook with the workbook?
Is there a danger in using too many supplementary materials in a class? Explain.

Things to Do

1. Discuss with other prospective teachers ten questions to consider when evaluating instructional materials. Which questions or concepts are the most important? Why?
2. List five steps in developing your own instructional materials.
3. Prepare a checklist for evaluating textbooks. Select a textbook for your disciplinary area that is used in a proximate school district and evaluate it using *your* criteria and using the criteria we provide in this chapter.
4. Give specific guidelines for using the following materials: a) workbooks, b) journals and magazines, and c) simulations and games.
5. Carefully read the case study about Texas textbooks (6.2). Are there similar controversies in your state? What do they mean for what teachers might or might not be able to teach? And what do they mean for you as a prospective teacher?
6. Observe a classroom of students and select three or four students who are having difficulty focusing on the content material. Using the Reading Style Observational Guide (see Table 6.5), identify some specific instructional actions you might take to foster enhanced learning.
7. Visit the state department of education website for the state in which you teach. For example, if you live in Virginia, you would go to www.pen.k12.va.us. See if there is a link there to textbooks and instructional materials. What resources are listed for teachers to use in your disciplinary area? Does your state provide clear linkages to the mandated academic standards that you are expected to use?

Recommended Readings

Allington, Richard L. and Peter H. Johnston. *Reading to Learn.* New York: Guilford, 2002. Lessons from exemplary classrooms along with reading strategies and methods that work for teachers.

Ellington, Henry, Joannie Fowlie, and Monica Gordon. *Using Games and Simulations in the Classroom: A Practical Guide for Teachers.* New York: Kogan Page Ltd., 1998. This book explains how to develop and implement games and simulations at the primary and secondary levels—case studies are included.

Kellough, Richard D., and Noreen G. Kellough. *A Resource Guide for Teachers K–12.* Columbus, Ohio: Merrill, 1997. This book examines various methods, materials, and resources for teaching middle school students and how to incorporate these resources into lesson plans.

Morlan, John E., and Leonard J. Espinoza. *Preparation of Inexpensive Teaching Materials,* 6th ed. Belmont, Calif.: Fearon, 1998. Use this book to learn about several ways to plan, prepare, use and evaluate materials.

Pressley, Michael. *Reading Instruction that Works.* New York: Guilford, 2002. A focus on comprehension problems, decoding, vocabulary instruction, development of word knowledge and both skills and whole language instruction.

Strong, Richard, Harvey F. Silver, and Matthew J. Perini. *Teaching What Matters Most.* Alexandria, VA: Association for Supervision and Curriculum Development, 2001. This is a thoughtful analysis of how to use standards in ways that enhance instruction and foster student learning.

Vacca, Richard T., and JoAnne L. Vacca. *Content Area Reading.* New York: Longman, 1999. These reading practices across content areas help students improve their reading skills.

Key Terms

copyright law 249	games 253	pedagogical aids 264
expository structure 268	leveling 260	reading formulas 260
field-dependent learners 253	mentioning 262	simulations 279
field-independent learners 253	narrative structure 268	

End Notes

1. Elliot W. Eisner. "Why the Textbook Influences Curriculum." *Curriculum Review* (January-February 1987): 11–13. Elliot W. Eisner. "Who Decides What Schools Should Teach?" *Phi Delta Kappan* (March 1990): 523–526.

2. Linda G. Fielding and David P. Pearson. "Synthesis of Research: Reading Comprehension—What Works." *Educational Leadership* (February 1994): 62–68. Maureen McLaughlin and MaryBeth Allen, *Guided Comprehension: A Teaching Model for Grades 3–8.* Newark, Del.: International Reading Association, 2002.

3. James H. Block, Helen E. Efthim, and Robert B. Burns. *Building Effective Mastery Learning in Schools.* New York: Longman, 1989. Thomas L. Good and Jere E. Brophy. *Looking in Classrooms,* 8th ed. New York: Addison-Wesley, 2000.

4. Paul Burden and David M. Byrd. *Methods for Effective Teaching,* 3d ed. Needham Heights, MA: Allyn and Bacon, 2003.

5. American Library Association, *The New Copyright Law: Questions Teachers and Librarians Ask.* Washington, D.C.: ALA, 1977. Kenneth T. Murray. "Copyright and the Educator." *Phi Delta Kappan* (March 1994): 552–555.

6. American Library Association. *Copyright Primer for Librarians and Educators.* Washington, D.C.: ALA, 1986.

7. Rebecca Barr. *Teaching Reading in Elementary Classrooms.* New York: Longman, 1991. Elfrieda H. Hiebert and Barbara M. Taylor. *Getting Reading Right from the Start.* Needham Heights, Mass.: Allyn and Bacon, 1994.

8. Robert C. Calfee. "Organizing for Comprehension and Composition." In R. Dowler and W. Ellis eds., *Whole Language and the Creation of Literacy.* Baltimore: Dyslexia Society, 1991, pp. 111–129. Patricia G. Mathes and Joseph K. Torgensen. "A Call for Equity in Reading Instruction for All Students: A Response to Allington and Woodside-Jiron." *Educational Researcher* (August-September 2000): 4–15.

9. Allan C. Ornstein and Francis P. Hunkins. *Curriculum: Foundations, Principles, and Issues,* 4th ed. Boston, Mass.: Allyn and Bacon, 2003.

10. Gaea Leinhardt. "What Research on Learning Tells Us About Teaching." *Educational Leadership* (April 1992): 20–25. Claire E. Weinstein et al. "Helping Students Develop Strategies for Effective Learning." *Educational Leadership* (December–January 1989): 17–19. McLaughlin and Allen. *Guided Comprehension: A Teaching Model for Grades 3–8.*

11. George J. Posner and Alan N. Rudnitsky. *Course Design: A Guide to Curriculum Development for Teachers.* 6th ed. Boston: Allyn and Bacon, 2001. Jon Wiles. *Curriculum Essentials.* Boston, Mass.: Allyn and Bacon, 1999.

12. Thomas J. Lasley II, Thomas J. Matczynski, and James Rowley. *Instructional Models: Strategies for Teaching in a Diverse Society,* 2d ed. Belmont, Calif.: Wadsworth, 2002.

13. Thomas L. Good and Jere Brophy. *Educational Psychology,* 5th ed. New York: Longman, 1995: 531.

14. Eisner. "Why the Textbook Influences Curriculum," p. 111.

15. *Report on a National Study of the Nature and Quality of Instructional Materials Most Used by Teachers and Learners.* New York: Educational Products Information Exchange, 1987. And see Myra Pollock Sadker and David Miller Sadker. *Teachers, Schools and Society,* 5th ed. Boston: McGraw-Hill, 2000.

16. Arthur Woodward and David L. Elliott. "School Reform and Textbooks." *Educational Horizons* (Summer 1992): 176–180. Colleen Fairbanks. "Teaching and Learning Beyond the Text." *Journal of Curriculum Supervision* (Winter 1994): 155–173. Also see Randi Stone. *Best Practices for High School Classrooms:* Thousand Oaks, Calif.: Corwin Press, 2001.

17. Harriet Tyson Bernstein. *America's Textbook Fiasco: A Conspiracy of Good Intentions.* Washington, DC: Council for Basic Education, 1988; Joan DelFattore. *What Johnny Shouldn't Read: Textbook Censorship in America.* New Haven Conn.: Yale University Press, 1992; Kris Axtman. "Texas Wrangles Over Bias in School Textbooks," *Christian Science Monitor* (July 22, 2002). See www.csmonitor.com/2002/0722/p03501-ussc.html.

18. Sadker and Sadker. *Teachers, Schools, and Society.*

19. Cleo H. Cherryholmes. "Readers Research." *Journal of Curriculum Studies* (January–February 1993): 1–32. Allan C. Ornstein, "The Textbook Curriculum." *Educational Horizons* (Summer 1992): 167–169.

20. Mario D. Fantini and Gerald Weinstein. *The Disadvantaged: Challenge to Education.* New York: Harper & Row, 1968. p. 133. Also see Chris Stray. "Paradigms Regained: Towards a Historical Sociology of the Textbook." *Journal of Curriculum Studies* (January–February 1994): 1–30.

21. Allan C. Ornstein. "The Irrevelant Curriculum: A Review from Four Perspectives," *NASSP Bulletin* (September 1988): 26–32. Also see Elaine K. McEwan. *Teach Them All to Read.* Thousand Oaks, Calif.: Corwin Press, 2002.

22. Nathan Glazer, *We Are All Multiculturalists Now.* Cambridge, Mass.: Harvard University Press, 1997. Henry A. Giroux. "Curriculum, Multiculturalism, and the Politics of Identity." *NASSP Bulletin* (December 1992): 1–11.

23. Dennis Doyle. "The Unsacred Text." *American Education* (Summer 1984): 3–13. Connie Muther. "What Every Textbook Evaluator Should Know." *Educational Leadership* (April 1985): 4–8. Allan C. Ornstein. "The Textbook Driven Curriculum." *Peabody Journal of Education* (Spring 1994): 70–85.

24. Jeannie Oakes and Martin Lipton. *Teaching to Change the World.* Boston: McGraw Hill, 1999: 169–170.

25. Muther. "What Every Textbook Evaluator Should Know." p. 7. Also see Connie Muther. "Reflections on Textbooks and Teaching." *Educational Horizons* (Summer 1992): 194–200.

26. Allan C. Ornstein. *Teachers and Schooling in America: Pre and Post September 11.* Boston:Allyn and Bacon, 2003. xiv–xv.

27. Harold L. Herber and Joan N. Herber. *Teaching in Content Areas.* Needham Heights, Mass.: Allyn and Bacon, 1993. Michael C. McKenna and Richard D. Robinson. *Teaching Through Text.* New York: Longman, 1993.

28. Edward Fry. "Fry's Readability Graph: Clarification, Validity, and Extension to Level." *Journal of Reading* (December 1977): 242–252. Edward Fry. "Readability Versus Leveling." *The Reading Teacher* (November 2002): 286–291.

29. Alton L. Raygor and George B. Schick. *Reading at Efficient Rates.* 2d ed. New York: McGraw-Hill, 1980.

30. James P. Byrnes. *Cognitive Development and Learning in Instructional Contexts.* 2nd ed. Boston: Allyn and Bacon, 2001. Alice Davidson. "Readability—Appraising Text Difficulty." In R. C. Anderson, J. Osborn, and R. J. Tierney, eds., *Learning to Read in American Schools.* Hillsdale, N.J.: Erlbaum, 1984, pp. 121–139. Robert J. Tierney, John E. Readence, and Ernest K. Dishner. *Reading Strategies and Practices,* 3d ed. Needham Heights, Mass.: Allyn and Bacon, 1990.

31. Harriet T. Bernstein. "The New Politics of Textbook Adoption." *Education Digest* (December 1985): 12–15. Harriet T. Bernstein. "The Academy's Contribution to the Impoverishment of America's Textbooks." *Phi Delta Kappan* (November 1988): 193–198. Marie Carbo. "Eliminating the Need for Dumbed-Down Textbooks." *Educational Horizons* (Summer 1992): 189–193. Jess E. House and Rosemarye T. Taylor. "Leverage on Learning: Test Scores, Textbooks and Publishers." *Phi Delta Kappan* (March 2003): 537–541.

32. Robert A. Pavlik. "Tips on Texts." *Phi Delta Kappan* (September 1985): 86.

33. Bernstein. "The New Politics of Textbook Adoption." Peter W. Foltz and Walter Kintsch. "Readers' Strategies and Comprehension in Linear Text and Hyper Text." Paper presented at the annual meeting of the American Educational Research Association, Atlanta, Georgia, April 1993.

34. Rebecca Barr, Marilyn Sadow, and Camille Blachowicz. *Reading Diagnosis for Teachers.* 2d ed. New York: Longman, 1990; Robert Glaser, ed. *Advances in Instructional Psychology.* vol. 4. Hillsdale, N.J.: Erlbaum, 1993.

35. Neville Bennett and Clive Carré. *Learning to Teach.* New York: Routledge, 1991.

36. Ezra Bowen. "Flunking Grade in Math." *Time* (June 20, 1988): 79. Also see Anne L'Hafner. "Teaching-Methods Scales and Mathematics-Class Achievement." *American Educational Research Journal* (Spring 1993): 71–94. Jian jun Wang. "TIMSS Primary and Middle School Data." *Educational Researcher* (August-September 2001): 17–21.

37. Harriet Tyson. *Who Will Teach the Children?* San Francisco: Jossey-Bass, 1994, p. 10.

38. Sandra Conn. "Textbooks: Defining the New Criteria." *Media and Methods* (March–April 1988): 30–31, 64.

39. Richard L. Allington. "What I've Learned about Effective Reading Instruction." *Phi Delta Kappan* (June 2002): 740–747. Richard E. Mayer. "Aids to Text Comprehension." *Educational Psychologist* (Winter 1984): 30–42. Philip H. Winne, Lorraine Graham, and Leone Prock. "A Model of Poor Readers' Text-Based Inferencing." *Reading Research Quarterly* (January 1993): 52–69.

40. Jason Wermers. "Virginia Becoming Textbook Power." *Richmond Times Dispatch* (November 1, 2002). See www.timesdispatch.com.

41. Deborah Menke and Beth Davey. "Teachers' Views of Textbooks and Text Reading Instruction." *Journal of Reading* (March 1994): 464–470.

42. Sigmund A. Boloz and Donna H. Muri. "Supporting Literacy Is Everyone's Responsibility." *Reading Teacher* (February 1994): 388–391. Rebecca B. Sammons and Beth Davey. "Assessing Students' Skills in Using Textbooks." *Journal of Reading* (December–January 1994): 280–287.

43. McLaughlin and Allen. *Guided Comprehension.*

44. Ibid. See also Bonnie B. Armbruster. "Schema Theory and the Design of Content Area Textbooks." *Educational Psychologist* (Fall 1986): 253–268. Stephen Krashen. "Whole Language and the Great Plummet of 1987-92." *Phi Delta Kappan* (June 2002): 748–753. Richard F. West, Keith E. Stanovich, and Harold R. Mitchell. "Reading in the Real World and its Correlates." *Reading Research Quarterly* (January 1993): 34–51.

45. Amy Driscoll. *Psychology of Learning and Instruction* 2d ed. Boston: Allyn and Bacon, 2001. Dolores Durkin. *Teaching Them to Read,* 6th ed. Needham Heights, Mass.: Allyn and Bacon, 1993. Anne P. Sweet and Judith I. Anderson. *Reading Research into the Year 2000.* Hillsdale, N.J.: Erlbaum, 1993.

46. David P. Ausubel. "In Defense of Advance Organizers: A Reply to the Critics." *Review of Educational Research* (Spring 1978): 251–257.

47. Peter H. Johnson. *Constructive Evaluation of Literate Activity.* New York: Longman, 1992. McKenna and Robinson. *Teaching Through Text.*

48. Livingston Alexander, Ronald G. Frankiewicz, and Robert E. Williams. "Facilitation of Learning and Retention of Oral Instruction Using Advance and Post Organizers." *Journal of Educational Psychology* (October 1979): 701–707. Mayer. "Aids to Text Comprehension." Elizabeth U. Saul et al. "Students' Strategies for Making Text Make Sense." Paper presented at the annual meeting of the American Educational Research Association, Atlanta, Georgia, April 1993.

49. John A. Ellis et al. "Effect of Generic Advance Instructions on Learning a Classification Task" *Journal of Educational Psychology* (August 1986): 294–299. James Harley and Ivor K. Davies. "Preinstructional Strategies: The Role of Pretest, Behavioral Objectives, Overviews, and Advance Organizers." Review of Educational Research (Spring 1976): 239–265.

50. Bonnie B. Armbruster, Thomas H. Anderson, and Joyce Ostertag. "Teaching Text Structure to Improve Reading." *Reading Teacher* (November 1989): 130–137. Marilyn M. Ohlhausen and Cathy M. Roller. "The Operation of Text Structure and Content Schema in Isolation and in Interaction." *Reading Research Quarterly* (Winter 1988): 70–88. Raymond E. Wright and Sheldon Rosenberg. "Knowledge of Text Coherence and Expository Writing: A Developmental Study." *Journal of Educational Psychology* (March 1993): 152–158.

51. Bernstein. "The Academy's Contribution to the Impoverishment of America's Textbooks." Susan M. Hubbuch. "The Trouble with Textbooks." *High School Journal* (April–May 1989): 203–210. Allan C. Ornstein. "The Censored Curriculum: The Problems with Textbooks Today." *NASSP Bulletin* (November 1992): 1–9.

52.   McLaughlin and Allen. *Guided Comprehension.* Richard L. Allington and Peter H. Johnston. *Reading to Learn.* New York: Guilford, 2002.

53. Robert L. Hillerich. "The Value of Structure." *Teaching K–8* (March 1990): 78–81. Ornstein. "The Textbook Curriculum."

54. Beau F. Jones, Jean Pierce, and Barbara Hunter. "Teaching Students to Construct Graphic Representations." *Educational Leadership* (December1988–January 1989): 20–25. Patricia A. Herman et al. "Incidental Acquisition of Word Meaning from Expositions with Varied Text Features." *Reading Research Quarterly* (Summer 1987): 263–284. Ohlhausen and Roller. "The Operation of Text Structure and Content Schema in Isolation and in Interaction." Steffan Ohlsson. "Abstract Schema." *Educational Psychologist* (Winter 1993): 51–66.

55. Carol Ann Tomlinson. *The Differentiated Classroom.* (Alexandria, VA: Association for Supervision and Curriculum Development, 1999), p. 33.

56. Lauren A. Sosniak and Susan S. Stodolsky. "Teachers and Textbooks: Materials Use in Four Fourth-Grade Classrooms." *Elementary School Journal.* (January 1993): 249–276.

57. Richard L. Allington and Anne McGill-Franzen. "School Response to Reading Failure." *Elementary School Journal* (May 1989): 529–542. Ruth Gardner and Patricia A. Alexander. "Metacognition: Answered and Unanswered Questions." *Educational Psychologist* (Spring 1989): 143–158. Michael McKenna. *Help for Struggling Readers.* New York: Guilford, 2002.

58. Paul R. Burden and David Byrd. *Methods for Effective Teaching,* 3d ed. Boston: Allyn and Bacon, 2003.

59. Jack W. Humphrey. "There's No Simple Way to Build a Middle School Reading Program." *Phi Delta Kappan.* (June 2002): 754–757. David R. Olson and Janet W. Astington. "Thinking About Thinking." *Educational Psychologist* (Winter 1993): 7–24. Arthur Woodward. "Over-Programmed Materials: Taking the Teacher Out of Teaching." *American Educator* (Spring 1986): 26–31.

60. Patricia M. Cunningham. "What Would Make Workbooks Worthwhile?" In R. C. Anderson, J. Osborn, and R. J. Tierney, eds. *Learning to Read in American Schools.* Hillsdale, N.J.: Erlbaum, 1984, pp. 113–120. Bonnie J. Meyer. "Text Dimensions and Cognitive Processing." In H. Mandl, N. L. Stein, and T. Trabasso, eds. *Learn-*

ing and Comprehension of Text. Hillsdale, N.J.: Erlbaum, 1984, pp. 3–52. Edward P. St. John, Siri Ann Loescher, and Jeff S. Bardzell. *Improving Reading and Literacy in Grades 1–5.* Thousand Oaks, Calif.: Corwin Press, 2003.

61. Jean Osborn. "The Purpose, Uses, and Contents of Workbooks." In R. C. Anderson, J. Osborn and R. J. Tierney, eds. *Learning to Read in American Schools.* Hillsdale, NJ: Erlbaum, 1984, pp. 45–111.

62. Donald C. Olrich et al. *Teaching Strategies: A Guide to Better Instruction,* 3d ed. (Lexington, Mass.: Heath, 1990). Charles K. West, James A. Farmer, and Philip M. Wolff. *Instructional Design: Implications from Cognitive Science.* Needham Heights, Mass.: Allyn and Bacon, 1991.

63. Association of Teachers of Social Studies in the City of New York. *A Handbook for the Teaching of Social Studies,* 4th ed. Boston: Allyn and Bacon, 1977, p. 127.

64. Thomas C. Gee, Mary W. Olson, and Nora J. Forester. "Classroom Use of Specialized Magazines." *Clearing House* (October 1989): 53–55.

65. Ibid.

66. Edmund Sutro. "Full-Dress Simulations: A Total Learning Experience." *Social Education* (October 1985): p. 634.

67. See www.nationalgeographic.com/xpeditions.

68. Penelope Semrau and Barbara A. Boyer. *Using Interactive Video in Education.* Needham Heights, Mass.: Allyn and Bacon, 1994. Lillian Stephens. *Developing Thinking Skills Through Real-Life Activities.* Boston: Allyn and Bacon, 1988.

Technology in the Classroom

With the Special Assistance of
Jill Lindsey-North, Chad Raisch, and Jackie Marshall Arnold

Pathwise Criteria relevant to the content of this chapter:

- Creating or selecting teaching methods, learning activities, and instructional materials or other resources that are appropriate for the students and that are aligned with the goals of the lesson. (A4)
- Communicating challenging learning expectations to each student. (B3)
- Encouraging students to extend their thinking. (C3)
- Monitoring students' understanding of content through a variety of means, providing feedback to students to assist learning, and adjusting learning activities as the situation demands. (C4)
- Using instructional time effectively. (C5)

INTASC principles relevant to the content of this chapter:

- The teacher uses an understanding of individual and group motivation and behavior to create a learning environment that encourages positive social interaction, active engagement in learning, and self-motivation. (P5)
- The teacher uses knowledge of effective verbal, nonverbal, and media communication techniques to foster active inquiry, collaboration, and supportive interaction in the classroom. (P6)
- The teacher plans instruction based upon knowledge of subject matter, students, the community, and curriculum goals. (P7)
- The teacher fosters relationships with school colleagues, parents, and agencies in the larger community to support students' learning and well-being. (P10)

focusing questions

1. What technological aid do you consider most valuable in improving your instruction?

2. What problems are beginning teachers likely to have in using technology?

3. For what instructional purposes might films, videotapes, and audiotapes be used?

4. When is it best to use an overhead projector or PowerPoint within an instructional context?

5. How can teachers best use technology for improving instruction?

6. How do you expect to incorporate computers in the classroom?

This chapter deals with using technology to enhance student learning and to facilitate your own professional development. We have incorporated a technology viewpoint section in each chapter, but this chapter takes a broader, more comprehensive view.

Technology has changed the very nature of work, communications, and our understanding of the development of knowledge.[1] Gone are the days of teaching solely from a textbook or by using a blackboard. Teaching today requires the use of a variety of approaches, techniques, and information sources. The use of computers, scanners, CD-ROMs, music CDs, audiotapes, clip art, graphics, videos, cameras, overhead projectors and PowerPoints, cable television, and telecommunication systems can maximize curriculum content delivery and improve student learning.

The growing array of technological tools and multimedia options available offer teachers a vast repertoire of instructional options. Just what media and technologies you use will depend upon your teaching assignment, the technical capabilities available, and your own knowledge. Vast discrepancies in technological equipment and expertise exist between and among schools. One school may have one computer for every four or five students, another school may have one large computer lab where groups of students are allocated computer time, and another school may restrict computer usage to study halls. In addition, many students will not have access to computers or other technologies in their homes, and this may affect their skill level with technologies. These factors, along with others, will determine how you will incorporate technology into your instruction.

Appropriate student use of technologies can help them develop needed skills, maximize learning time, minimize paperwork, facilitate connections with their community and the world, offer numerous alternative points of view, and prepare them for a vocation. As a professional, your use of technology can enable you to maximize your time, provide professional development resources, engage in dialogue with fellow professionals and the public, and accomplish administrative tasks efficiently.

There are two opposing views about the influence of technology upon learning. First, there is the notion that technology is a vehicle for delivering instruction but has no substantial influence on student learning; that is, learning from any technical tool or media has little to do with the medium itself. What counts are such factors as the teacher's instructional strategies or lesson plan design. Although technology influences the manner in which instruction is delivered, it is unlikely to modify the cognitive process involved in learning.[2] The second view is that technological media present images or information to the learner whereby he or she constructs new knowledge. Learning is viewed as an active, constructive process in which new information is extracted from the environment

Technology can make learning come alive.

(media) and integrated with prior knowledge. In essence, the world is a rapidly changing environment that requires students to draw information and data from many different sources in order to build a real understanding of the complexity of ideas, which means that the students need sophisticated technology skills if they are to be successful.[3]

Three decades of research in the cognitive sciences support the notion that knowledge is transmitted to and actively constructed by each learner, who draws upon prior experiences, established attitudes, and beliefs in order to create and make meaning. The variety of information sources available through technologies offers continuous, self-directed learning opportunities for students, independent of direct instruction from a teacher. This is not to suggest that reading texts, direct instruction, and engaging in class discussions should be replaced by learning through technologies, but rather to highlight the benefits of employing a full range of learning opportunities. The role of the teacher can also be that of an advisor and assistant to the student, as a self-directed inquirer, who seeks to research and answer questions of import and interest.

A Rationale for Using Technology

Modern communication devices such as DVD players, VCRs, audiotapes, cable television, computers, CDs, and the Internet can provide multisensory learning and in-depth ways of gaining knowledge. Experiences with such media can make learning come alive. A multimedia dimension to learning is more appropriate for the diversity in learning styles and abilities of learners in most classrooms. The latest pedagogical tools that technology provides permit teachers to customize instruction to the needs and pace of a wide range of individual students—and all students do not have to be available or present at the same time in order for instruction to take place.[4]

Four key assumptions are at play in this argument for the merits of using technology in the classroom: 1) information in school can be independently learned from electronic media and data sources other than the teacher or text; 2) students are capable of assuming responsibility for their own learning, especially if the material presented is visually and auditorially stimulating; 3) students learn best when they control their rate of learning; and 4) teachers can be assisted to successfully integrate technological-based instruction.

Some educators are concerned about the developmental appropriateness of using technology with children in the preschool and elementary grades. These educators feel that the imagination is a critical element in creative problem solving and that the imagination is dulled by the onslaught of external images technology provides. They are also concerned that our emotions, when constantly elicited and manipulated by technology, begin to be blunted by the body's survival instincts. Finally, they feel that human conversation and interaction are gradually being replaced by the passive viewing technology generates.[5] Although these concerns have led some educators to avoid using any technologies, the majority of educators recognize these potential dangers and strive to balance their use of technology with other traditional teaching methodologies.

Teachers need to balance the advantages of technological instructional modes with their drawbacks. Although educational technology facilitates individualized and self-directed learning and provides an increasingly efficient and effective way to assess and use information, some research suggests that it can needlessly isolate young people from essential social interactions. It can reduce the social exchanges among students, which are often the avenue through which learning occurs. If the social setting is diminished, the class no longer struggles as a group to find answers or to critically assess information and reflect on issues or problems.[6]

Technology is evolving, and both its problems and possibilities are becoming evident. True, some students working only with drill and practice software have the potential of becoming isolated. Equally true, with the introduction of the Internet, the World Wide Web, e-mail, networks, and other technology, innovative teachers are finding interesting ways to use technology to create and support communities of learners within the classroom as well as learning communities that transcend the classroom.

Technology can support multiple learning styles and allow individual talents to flourish. Students working together in groups can develop high-quality multimedia presentations, search for Internet information that coordinates with the classroom curriculum, spend time learning with a partner using simulation software, develop a database of information that relates to current events, and much more. A teacher in a five- (or less) computer classroom needs to understand how the creative uses of technology and group work will nurture social interaction and learning simultaneously.

Students benefit from the variety and diversity of learning opportunities provided by the teacher. As you will see at the end of this chapter, research is beginning to emerge that shows how teachers who know how and when to use different instructional approaches can enhance student achievement.

We will discuss the various types of technologies that you will see in schools. Read Case Study 7.1: High Tech School for an example of what one school is doing to

case study 7.1   High-Tech School

San Pasqual Elementary School in Escondido, California, is reminiscent of an early 1900s farming community, complete with a big red barn, silo, town hall, and court-yard. But inside this old–fashioned-looking complex, sixth-grade students are combining digital photography and sound clips from websites on Egyptian deities and displaying their presentations on interactive white boards.

This state-of-the-art K–8 school is the brainchild of administrators, teachers, and parents, who in 1997 found themselves in desperate need of a larger facility for their one-school district. Today, the new "barn" houses a gymnasium and perform-ing arts center. Inside the "silo" is a library, complete with a cushion-filled reading tower. The "town hall" is, indeed, a meeting hall. And from Monday morning flag assemblies in the rustic courtyard, students head to classrooms that are one click away from the rest of the world via the Internet.

A farming community planted in orange and avocado groves and corn fields, San Pasqual is thirty miles northeast of San Diego, California. Although some fami-lies work in agriculture, most parents commute back and forth to San Diego. Roughly 30 percent of the school's 500 students are Hispanic; 65 percent are white. English language learners comprise 16 percent of the student population. Nineteen percent of the students qualify for free or reduced-priced lunches.

In recent years, San Pasqual has undergone tremendous growth. New housing developments have lured families away from the city and have more than doubled the school's student population. In 1997, with the school filled well beyond capacity, the district needed a new facility, and needed it fast.

Jeffrey Felix, San Pasqual Unified School District (SPUSD) superintendent and principal, led a committee of twenty parents and teachers through the process of plan-ning the new school. HMC Architects from San Diego helped identify and acquire a site, secure funding sources, design the school with plenty of input from the community, and oversee construction. Building plans incorporated the most robust technologies available, both to support teaching and learning and to maximize energy efficiency.

Easy Access to High-Tech Tools

Technology is everywhere. Every K–5 classroom has at least two computers. Most students in grades 6–8 have daily access to a notebook computer. Many students own a notebook and bring it to school. The school also provides financial assistance for students who would otherwise be unable to purchase one.

"When there is a need," says Ken Beeunas, the school's technology coordina-tor and sixth-grade teacher, "there is a computer available." All classrooms are ca-pable of handling many more computers than are currently in place.

San Pasqual sixth graders have used laptops for several years. Beeunas set up the program based on the "Anytime, Anywhere" model from Australia that aims to get technology into the hands of kids "24/7" and thus increase their familiarity and improve learning. High-speed wireless computers will be added in autumn 2002, enabling the sixth graders to work from anywhere within 150 feet of a base station.

Every teacher has his or her own classroom computer for research, presentations, communications, and record keeping. Professional development is ongoing and includes exploring new ways to integrate technology into all areas of study. "We want to make our use of technology as seamless as possible," says Beeunas, who helps teachers enhance their curriculum with technology.

Money-Saving Controls

Besides being wired for use by the students and staff, the school was built from the ground up for efficiency in operation. The temperature in each room is monitored and adjusted automatically by a central computer, and it can also be controlled locally from any computer in the school to accommodate personal preferences. When air conditioning is not needed, fans circulate to prevent stuffiness.

Lights are on automatic timers but can be switched on and off from within each room or via the computer network. Infrared heat-sensing motion detectors in each room also activate lights and are part of the building's security system. Building orientations make use of prevailing winds and mitigate effects of strong, direct sunlight. Deep roof overhangs provide shade. Such well-thought-out features combined with cost-efficient heating, air conditioning, and lighting systems earned the school a $25,000 rebate from the local power supplier and have saved money on monthly energy bills.

A Multiuse Library

A focal point of the new school is its library. The school's media specialist, Teri MacDonald, says the old 700-volume library "was shifted around from classroom to classroom as the school kept growing, ending up in a portable building with barely enough room to get between the stacks." Thanks to a state grant the collection is approaching 11,000 volumes and is easily housed in the new space.

The new library's accessible and comfortable facilities support the school's literacy goals and enable students to conduct research through various technologies. Every book in the collection is labeled by reading level to help students select books that match their abilities.

In addition, students needing extra practice in English can access software literacy programs on one of the fifteen computers there. Parents, too, can use the software during evening English classes launched just this year. "At first, it was very intimidating for them [the parents] to come into the library, let alone work on the computers," MacDonald says. "By the end of the school year, the library was buzzing with learning—small groups working with a teacher or all of the computer stations busy. The parents were very comfortable and happy with their success. We had parallel books [the same book in English and Spanish] for checkout to read at home with their children."

History Comes Alive

Over the past fifteen years, many SPUSD eighth graders have journeyed to historic United States monuments with teachers Bryce Bacher and Colby Strongberg after studying related topics in class. In the early years, Bacher says, "Research meant opening an encyclopedia, writing letters, requesting pamphlets." These days, however, students research the monuments on the Internet and create presentations to share with their classmates.

A greater sense of excitement and expectation is ignited through connecting with primary and secondary sources on relevant websites. Students interact directly with the people involved in the events they are studying and the places they are planning to visit. Whether they actually make the trip or not, students still bridge history through their virtual experiences from the comfortable and historic environment of the "Little School in the Valley."

Questions for reflection

1. What would need to occur for what is occurring at San Pasqual to be possible in the schools where you are doing field experiences?
2. What technology has not been evidenced in your field sites that you believe should be in evidence?
3. How are teachers using technology in the San Pasqual school to foster enhanced student achievement? Are there any "downsides" to their efforts that you can see?

Source: Paula Monsef, "A High Tech School with a Down Home Feel." *Edutopia* (Fall 2002): 6–7. Copyright © by the George Lucas Foundation, Edutopia Newsletter, also available at www.glef.org.

define the school as a place where students can work together to achieve their collective academic potential.

Chalkboards and Display Boards

Long before modern technologies were introduced in the classroom, teachers employed visual aids and innovative presentation strategies to help their students learn. Chalkboards, visual displays, records, filmstrips, slides, skits, and plays offered multisensory learning opportunities in the classroom. The ***chalkboard*** is perhaps the oldest and most traditional piece of equipment found in the classroom. Next to the textbook, it is the most widely used instructional aid. According to two educators, the chalkboard "is so omnipresent that many of us fail to think of it as a visual aid at all; yet most teachers would be hard put if they had no chalkboards available."[7]

There is usually one chalkboard at the front of the classroom and sometimes others at the sides or back. In older schools most of the chalkboards are black (hence the name), but because black tends to absorb light and make the room gloomy, the color is being changed. Light green and yellow reduce glare and eye strain, absorb less light, are cheerful, and provide a good contrast with white and colored chalk. Many schools now use ***dry-erase boards*** instead of chalkboards. The background of these boards is typically white, and teachers write on it with multicolored dry-erase markers. These dry-erase boards typically are more visually appealing than blackboards, can be cleaned easily, and have the advantage of leaving no chalk dust.

Chalkboards and dry-erase boards are popular because they allow for spontaneity, speed, and change. They can fit the tempo of any lesson in any subject and can be used for displaying pictures and important clippings; sketches and diagrams to help illustrate points of a lesson; lists of suggestions or items as they are offered; outlines, summaries, and assignments; and the working out of problems. The chalkboard and dry-erase board are particularly valuable for working out problems for the whole class to see. Because of their flexibility and familiarity, the chalkboard and dry-erase board are sometimes overused, but they should not be dismissed as outmoded.

A *display board* can be used for displaying student projects and progress; displaying current items of interest related to a lesson or unit; posting announcements, memos, and routine assignments; and decorating the room. There are several types: bulletin boards, pegboards, flannel boards, and magnetic boards. The boards stimulate student creativity and interest, promote student participation in the learning activity, and make the room more cheerful and student oriented. If there are no display boards in the room, a portion of the chalkboard can be reserved for this purpose, or a free-standing display board may be created.

Guidelines for Using Chalkboards and Dry-Erase Boards

1. Write legibly and large enough for all to see.
2. Don't talk toward the chalkboard or dry-erase board while writing on it. Write and then talk or talk and then write.
3. Organize your chalkboard or dry-erase board work ahead of time. When possible, outline items with a letter or numbering system. There are many possible systems, but use one system for consistency.
4. Don't clutter the boards. Limit your writing or drawing to major ideas of the lesson.
5. Don't use unusual or personal abbreviations.
6. Use colored dry-erase markers, chalk, rulers, string, stencils, and other materials to make your illustrations more effective.
7. Don't overuse the boards. Provide handouts of lengthy or complicated materials.

Overhead Projectors and Data/Video Projectors

The overhead projector and the data/video projector or video projection system offer technological options for presenting visual information. One of the greatest benefits of the overhead projector and computer projector is that the teacher or lecturer can face the audience while writing. The *data/video projector,* used in conjunction with Power-Point or HyperStudio, also offers the option of including music, video clips, and text that "fly-in" across the page upon command; in addition, documents can be scanned in

Educational Technology

Henry A. Giroux
Distinguished Waterbug
Professor of Education
Pennsylvania State University

As a working-class kid growing up in Providence, Rhode Island, I attended a high school that incorporated a rigid tracking system. Most white and black students who were economically disadvantaged like myself ended up in courses in which educational technology along with worksheets became the main vehicles for teaching. Films became both a reward for being quiet and carried the implicit suggestion that visual culture was simply about entertainment rather than a serious object of knowledge inquiry.

The technology of electronic mass media became a way of policing behavior while simultaneously allowing teachers to confirm the assumption that serious learning was largely about the culture of the book. When the lights went off in the class, I always felt relieved; at least, in the darkness I could imagine myself in the movie theater, a cultural space that offered a brief respite from the humiliations and boredom that constituted the daily experience of schooling for myself and others who did not grow up in middle-class households.

Maybe I am wrong, but I don't think schools have changed much. Though students largely inhabit a society of mass media, educational technology appropriates the new information systems in order to produce curricula that serve commercial interests. In the end, technological innovation is reduced to turning kids into good consumers rather than critical citizens.

The problem is that if students are to be critical citizens they will have to learn to be literate in a global world that is increasingly mediated by visual and electronic texts that are redefining the meaning of culture and knowledge. This is a technology that cannot be contained within the imperatives of profit or simply dismissed as entertainment. But, of course, the issue here is not about merely understanding the pedagogical importance of the new informational systems along with the popular and cultural forms that increasingly educate students outside of schools, but one of who is going to educate the educators? This is more than a technological issue; it is an ethical and political one.

to create a polished and entertaining presentation. Preparing this kind of presentation on the computer does require some expertise and can take time. (For online tutorials on Microsoft PowerPoint, go to www.microsoft.com/education; for HyperStudio go to www.education.umd.edu/blt/hyperstudio.) You will need to check with your building's technology support person to see if the equipment needed for computerized presentations is available for classroom teachers to use.

The **overhead projector** is relatively inexpensive and easy to use and has thus become standard equipment in many classrooms. Overhead transparencies can be made relatively quickly in most copy machines from any document that can be photocopied. Commercially prepared overhead transparencies are also available for many textbooks or can be purchased by general subject area. Overhead projectors also offer teachers the option of writing on transparencies during the class activity. This can be especially helpful when small groups work to produce information that is to be presented to the larger group. Each small group can create a handwritten transparency and project it for all to see.

Data/video projectors also provide instructional benefits for classroom use. Presentations can be made quickly and easily, once a teacher has some experience with the software program, and can then be stored for later use. Presentations can also easily be changed when needed. Students can share group work in a visually interesting way by quickly creating a slide or two. Using a data/video projector may also help students of diverse learning styles absorb information more easily.

Guidelines for Using Overhead and Data/Video Projectors

1. Keep the materials up-to-date.

2. Preview the materials or prepare them before class begins.

3. Be sure the materials are appropriate for the students' interests and maturity level and that they fulfill your instructional objective.

4. Be sure all students can see the surface on which the material is projected. Focus the materials properly.

5. Explain and discuss each of the projected materials.

Films

Other than television, *film* (or movies) is perhaps the most influential and seductive educational medium for transmitting ideas and persuading an audience. Because of the vivid images it presents, the motion picture has a dramatic impact on its audience. Films both interest and motivate students. Thousands of good films have been made expressly for educational purposes (an excellent Internet resource is teachwithmovies.org). A film is presented in a fixed, continuous sequence, and the speed is also fixed (unless the images are such that the projector or video equipment can be slowed down or the projection can be stopped). Because students are forced to think at the speed and in the sequence determined by the film, it tends to create a passive rather than an active mind-set. Giving students questions or patterns to be aware of while viewing the film may help engage a more active mind-set in the classroom.

Guidelines for Using Films

1. Preview the film to make sure it is appropriate to the students' interests and maturity level and to familiarize yourself with the content.

2. Arrange to have the video equipment (or the projector) set up in the classroom on the day scheduled for showing the video or film. Be sure to arrange for someone to run the projector if you do not know how.

3. Be sure all students can see the screen. The room should be dark enough to produce a quality picture.

4. Prepare the students for the presentation. A list of major points or questions to answer or a guide to the film is often helpful. Hand it out to the class before the showing.

5. Allow time for discussion after the film.

The Pencil Makes the Point

Harvey S. Long
Professor of Education
George Mason University

 Since the late 1950s, computer-literate educators have enthusiastically been promoting the use of computer technology in education. Until recently, that advocacy has involved solutions to either nonexistent or noncompelling problems. However, the advent of the microcomputer and the national focus on growing educational issues could foster the linking of technology-related solutions to compelling problems. Among these challenges are growing illiteracy; the need for education reform and restructure; and the challenge of teaching in the information age.

Having made the connection between a possible solution and a recognizable problem has, however, in turn generated still another difficulty—implementing a computer-based solution. There are on the average approximately thirty students sharing each computer in the country's elementary and secondary schools. If those computers were pencils, one would hardly consider the "bifunctional" pencil a viable student writing instrument. The multifunctional computer with a student-to-computer ratio of 30:1 could certainly be predicted to be equally ineffective in producing a national impact. . . .

Few would dispute that computers through networks provide access to information, to computing, and most certainly to people. But today, only one in five faculty actually uses computers in the teaching process. The remainder, either because of personal choice or the lack of access to computers, deny their students the benefits derived from information searches, interactive computing, and the elimination of teacher isolation through computer conferencing.

With pencils in the hands of virtually all students and teachers, the author of this text has chosen not to dedicate a segment to "pencil technology." I hope that practical thinking and logical implementation of computer technology will lead on similar terms to the demise of "pencil technology" as well.

Authors' note: Professor Long wrote this almost a decade ago. By 2003, computers were in virtually all schools. Yet many argue that a technology divide still exists in America. Is Professor Long's argument still relevent?

Television and Videos

Recent evidence suggests that television has become "a second school system" or cultural transmitter. Children under 10 years old watch television an average of thirty to thirty-five hours a week, or for about one-fifth of their waking hours. Research from the 1980s suggested that, by the time a child graduated from high school, he or she would spend 15,000 to 20,000 hours in front of the screen as compared to 12,000 to 13,000 hours in school. Before children reached age 6, they would spend more time in front of a television than they would talking to their fathers in their lifetimes.[8] There is absolutely little evidence to suggest that the situation has changed as we begin the twenty-first century. The danger in this situation relates to the inherent isolation of American youngsters from adults. Specifically, compared to young people in other industrialized cultures, American students spend almost twelve hours more per week in one another's company and away from adults.[9] We will discuss this fact in more detail later in this chapter. The key point here is that American young people are socialized by technology to a potentially greater extent than are young people of other cultures.

Rather than viewing television as a second school system, Neil Postman views it and other mass media (radio, comic books, movies) as the "first curriculum" because they appear to be affecting the way children develop learning skills and acquire knowledge and understanding.[10] According to Postman and others, television's curriculum is designed largely to maintain interest; the school's curriculum is supposed to have other purposes, such as mastery of thinking skills. In addition, watching television requires little effort and few skills; children do not have to think about or solve problems. Rather, they become accustomed to rapidly changing stimuli, quick answers, and "escapist" fantasies, not to mention overdoses of violent and sexual behaviors on the screen.

Television's Influence

The real effect of television watching and Internet use is still unknown. The American Psychological Association reports that television violence accounts for approximately 10 percent of the aggressive behavior evidenced by children.[11] The research on the possible pernicious effects of heavy television viewing for young people over the past several decades is now being coupled with new research on the potential negative influences of the Internet. The Web offers wonderful learning possibilities for young people. However, some emerging data suggest problems with diminished communication among family members, enhanced depression and isolation, and mitigated face-to-face interaction.[12]

The average child now witnesses more than 8,000 murders and about 100,000 other violent acts by the time he or she completes elementary school. Estimates are that by age 18, a young person will have seen 40,000 murders and another 200,000 acts of violence on television. Reviews of research have found that repeated exposure to violence on television promotes a tendency to engage in aggressive behavior, such as getting into fights and disrupting the play of others.[13] A lot depends, of course, on how much television students are actually watching. Though specific data are unavailable, it is clear that television viewing for young children, on average, is heavy—three to five hours per day (or as many as twenty-two hours per week). The negative effects come not just from watching television, but also from what is being watched. The Parent Teacher Association (PTA) and other parental and religious activist groups have lobbied for years (but with limited success) to curtail violent and sexual scenes on television, especially during prime time (7 to 10 p.m.).[14] Interestingly, despite all the best efforts of these groups, it is still quite clear that television represents a medium of very mixed messages in terms of its visual images.

Almost half the adolescents surveyed in one study admit to the negative influences of television—noting that television's value-system emphasizes antisocial behavior (e.g., drugs, violence, and sex are okay or even "cool"). The same percent maintains that television viewing often detracts from participation in more constructive and worthwhile activities. These students equate television viewing with wasting time and being lazy. A small number complain that "plopping down" in front of the television and watching suggestive commercials have an impact on snacking and eating of junk food.[15] And, Sadker and Sadker report that, for high school students, "each hour of daily television watching corresponds to a 9 percent greater risk of alcohol consumption and . . . if music videos are watched, the drinking risk rises to 31 percent."[16]

Despite the dominant view of children as passive victims of television, children (as young as age 7) often display considerable sophistication about the relationship between television and reality and a high degree of criticism about the influence of advertising. They also seem quite adept at criticizing television for its artificiality—bad acting, inept story lines, and conspicuous consumption. A conversation with any young person quickly reveals this fact. Some of this critical reaction may be due to the fact that they are aware that adults, particularly teachers and parents, often disapprove of their watching television and believe that it has harmful effects. Just as adults frequently displace their concerns on children, so older children and teenagers often assert that it is the younger viewers who are at risk and that they themselves are more "adult" and less at risk.

Furthermore, not all research supports negative conclusions about the impact of television on student conduct and attitudes. If utilized properly, television can have a positive influence on socialization and learning and can serve as a vehicle for information, education, news, and consumer literacy. Studies over the past twenty years indicate that selected educational programs for preschool and primary grade children such as *Sesame Street* and *The Electric Company* are associated with improved cooperative (prosocial) behavior and cognitive skills.[17] The key is to help young people become better consumers of television programming and to limit the amount of television that they watch to approximately two hours per day.

In the area of academics, most data suggest that, for upper elementary and secondary school students, watching television more than five hours a day is associated with lowered student achievement, especially when it takes students away from homework and fosters passivity in the learning process.[18] Research comparing U.S. students to students in ten other countries revealed that students from all other countries "watch less television and spend more time on homework than their American counterparts."[19] The real key appears to be associated with what American young people do with their free time. In other countries young people are involved in substantial school and school-related activities when they are "free." In America, young people may lag behind in international comparisons (although there is some debate about whether that assertion is completely true) because they have so little "free" time to study. Laurence Steinberg writes,

> The typical adolescent has about 120 waking hours each week (assuming an average of 7 hours of sleep per night). The average school day in the United States lasts 6.5 hours, accounting for between 30 and 35 hours each week. According to time-use studies, teenagers devote an additional 25 hours each week to eating, personal care, household chores, transportation, and the like.
>
> This leaves somewhere around 60 hours each week for students to apportion across a variety of other activities. If the American typical teenager is devoting between 20 and 25 hours weekly to socializing, between 15 and 20 hours weekly to a part-time job, between 10 and 15 hours weekly to an extracurricular activity, and between 10 and 15 hours weekly to television viewing, there isn't any time left over for studying outside of school—which explains why the national average for time spent on homework is less than 5 hours per week.
>
> When we consider that only 40 percent of the time spent in school is spent on academic activities, it becomes clear that little of the typical American student's time—something on the order of between 15 and 20 hours weekly, or only about 15 percent of his or her waking hours—is spent on endeavors likely to contribute to learning or achievement.[20]

There is still another possible ramification of television and other electronic media in shaping students' learning behaviors. The audio and visual stimuli may produce what Lev Vygotsky termed *spontaneous concepts*—ones that are not systematic, structured, or generalized into a larger mental framework. Spontaneous concepts differ from scientific concepts, which are characterized by a degree of distance from immediate experience and which arise from reading text or being exposed to the teaching-learning process (in which the learner engages in a dialogue with the teacher or other students).[21] Scientific concepts, if taught properly, involve "scaffolding"—that is, making connections and building upon previous knowledge. Good and Brophy explain the process with an exploration of how teachers teach problem solving effectively to children:

> . . . [One] feature is modeling and coaching through scaffolded tasks and dialogue. The teacher models by showing how scientific knowledge can be used to solve problems, then provides problem-solving opportunities. The students' initial attempts are scaffolded through simplification or clarification of tasks and through classroom dialogues in which teacher and students listen carefully and respond to one another, sometimes critically but in ways that reflect respectful attention to the speaker's ideas. In the photosynthesis unit, for example, students are asked at several points to answer sets of questions that require them to make predictions and explanations about plants. Scaffolding is provided via reminders of key ideas that need to be kept in mind or provision of chart outlines to help students make key comparisons (e.g., between food for plants and food for people).[22]

Spontaneous concepts indicate that television viewers process transient and low-level information and assume a passive role vis-à-vis any learning that takes place. On the other hand, reading and classroom discourse involve structured linguistic activities, active learning, and systematic thinking. We students typically will remember the main ideas of the last book they read, even a year later, especially if that experience was linguistically structured, required effort, and led to self-reflection. Television and videos can also offer structured, active learning opportunities when reflection and discussion accompany viewing, but that does not characterize the reality of the viewing experiences of most students. The potential power of television requires that teachers consider carefully how to use it as a scaffold for key concepts that are being taught, not a spontaneous experience.

Utilizing Television

Because of television's impact on acculturation and socialization of children and youth and its influence on almost all of society, educators cannot ignore this medium. They must 1) find ways to reverse the trend toward lower achievement resulting from too much time spent watching commercial television; 2) counteract the tendency to use television as a means of escape or as a social companion, which isolates some children (and adults) from contact with other people and participation in more worthwhile activities; and finally 3) find positive ways to incorporate the medium into the school curriculum. As Figure 7.1 shows, television viewing is a critical part of what happens in many American classrooms and accounts for almost 10 percent of the time that students are with teachers.

Two types of programming can be employed in schools. ***Educational television*** refers to programs produced for broadcast on commercial or public television stations that are intended to inform and develop understanding. Many commercial and public

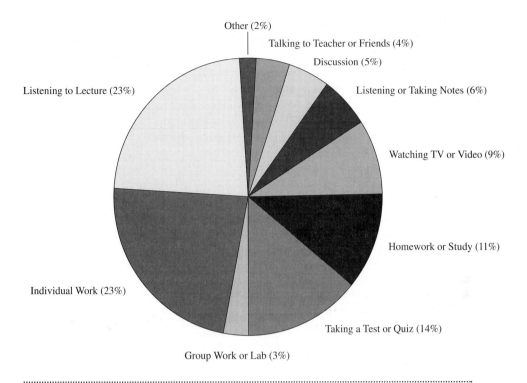

figure 7.1   Time Spent in Classroom Activities.

Source: M. Csikszentmihalyi and B. Schneider. *Becoming Adult.* New York: Basic Books, 2000, p. 144. Copyright by Mihaly Csikszentmihalyi and Barbara Schneider. Reprinted by permission of Basic Books, a member of Perseus Book, L.L.C.

television stations produce programs that fit educational goals and objectives. In particular, public television—broadcast in many large cities and delivered through cable across the nation—has real educational potential that has not been utilized fully by teachers.

Instructional television refers to programs produced by large school districts or colleges to teach specific subject matter in school. Some master teachers are used to teaching large numbers of classes simultaneously, with video providing greater flexibility in individual classroom scheduling. Although such programs are usually produced in advance, some schools have developed interactive and closed-circuit televised instruction so that students have the means of communicating with the instructor. In either case, we are talking about a cost-effective means of delivering education, especially in rural areas that might not have access to special or advanced academic courses.[23] Tips for Teachers 7.1 offers specific guidelines for teachers to use in making decisions about when and how to use television in the classroom.

Teachers can now select ***cable television*** programs specifically developed for educational purposes that are beamed into the classroom by satellite. Schools can subscribe (sometimes free of charge depending on the contract signed by the local government and cable company) to various commercial-free programs such as how to

tips for teachers 7.1

Key Questions for Active Viewing

 Productive uses of television in classrooms require connections—to the curriculum, to the learning styles of students, and to other resources that teachers can bring to bear on lessons. Here are key questions that teachers can ask themselves when using classroom resources involving technology:

- What is my purpose for using this video? Does it enrich the lesson?
- What are the best ways to focus the class on the video's content? What is the agenda for discussion and activity following the video?
- Is there more than one subject enriched by this video?
- Does the network airing the program have a website?
- Are there online resources that connect to this video?

- What online resources do I want my students to find?
- Are there opportunities to invite guests into the classroom who are experts on the topic shown in the video?
- What problem-solving techniques are useful in responding to this video?
- What specific curriculum connections can I cite for this video?

You don't have to answer all these questions or use only these questions. What counts is having an active purpose in a lesson before deciding to use resources from television.

Source: Donelle Blubaugh. "Bringing Cable into the Classroom." *Educational Leadership* (February 1999): 64.

improve writing, a daily or weekly series on ancient history or classical art, first-year Russian and other specialized languages, or world news. Some cable companies offer more than 100 channels, with a small number devoted specifically to educational programs. Such services are particularly useful for small, rural schools with limited resources, and in the case of subject matter that is highly expensive to teach or otherwise difficult to access in individual school districts.

Television has the potential for adding to students' knowledge. Students can learn about current events and scientific advances, be exposed to dramatic and musical performances, and become better acquainted with leading figures in the worlds of the arts, science, politics, and business. When used properly, television as an instructional aid can scaffold ideas; it can stimulate discussion and further study of the topic. It can bring the specialist and the expert teacher to class in front of hundreds of students at once or thousands of students over time. It can also enhance student achievement and motivation if properly used. Blubaugh cites research that connects educational programming with the school readiness of young children; the English, science, and math performance of high school students; and with lowered drop-out rates when schools use television, VCRs, and computers *properly.*[24]

Videotapes

The availability of *videotapes* makes using films and TV programs as instructional tools quite simple. Most schools have at least one TV/VCR for use in their media library as well as an array of cassette tapes. Local libraries loan DVDs and videocassettes, and tapes of national programs can generally be ordered from the producers. Written transcripts of broadcasts can also be purchased for study purposes.

Teachers and students can record classroom events and play back the recording in class through a VCR system attached to a television. Interviews, community meetings, special events, and students' projects can be recorded. Students can produce videos based on their own stories or research. Some large school districts now produce their own videos through recording departments and distribute them to surrounding school systems.

Guidelines for Using Television and Videos

1. Select programs to coincide with the learners' levels of interest and maturity and with instructional objectives. Consider the educational significance, quality, content, writing, and production.

2. Make sure the classroom or media center is suitable for viewing the program. Check the lights and shades, acoustic arrangements, seating facilities, and placement of the television.

3. Give students any necessary background data and tell them what to expect before viewing the program. You may want to hand out question sheets that focus on major points. These are especially helpful if students are assigned to watch a program at home.

4. Avoid using television as a lecturing device or a substitute for instruction. Integrate it into the lesson and discussion.

5. Hold a discussion after the program to analyze the main points

6. Discuss with your media specialist copyright issues before showing a tape that you have prerecorded.

Computers

Computer technology for school purposes has been available since the 1950s, but it is in the last few decades that computers have begun to have a major impact on classrooms and schools. In 1980 some 50,000 microcomputers were used in 15 percent of the nation's schools. In 1995 there were more than two million computers in use in nearly 99 percent of the schools. By 2001, student access was so prevalent that the ratio of students to computers (with internet access) was nearly 5 to 1.[25] As a result of the Goals 2000: Educating America Act passed by Congress in March 1994, schools across our nation are spending billions of federal dollars on computers, software, and related services in an attempt to meet the national priority of universal access to technology for teaching and learning.

Even with the current pervasiveness of computers, however, there still may be issues of equity access. In 2000, Holloway reported that Internet access was evident in only 39 percent of the classrooms with high concentrations of poverty but in 74 percent of the more affluent classrooms, but there is evidence of almost annual improvement. In 2001, the problem was still apparent but clearly more students in high poverty areas

Technology + Thinking = More Learning

Bob Lazzaro
Teacher
White Plains, New York

 Students walk into the classroom and immediately turn their attention to the ceiling-mounted 35-inch monitor. On display is an Internet website with today's e-mail from a sailboat racing across the ocean off the coast of Australia. Through satellite links the crew describes conditions on board the sixty-foot boat and their chances of placing well in the overall race.

After checking the exact location of the boat from the longitude and latitude coordinates listed on the website and logging it in their journals, the teacher directs one student to move to a weather website. Current conditions, as documented through a Doppler radar of precipitation and satellite photos of cloud covers, and predictions for the rest of the week are discussed and recorded as the student clicks through the site with the mouse.

Technology in the classroom is having a significant effect on the education of students across the country. Every day students are using more and more electronic resources and equipment such as computers, printers, scanners, VCRs, CD-ROMs, Internet websites, library card catalogs, and e-mail. Word processing programs, spreadsheets, and databases all make the manipulation of their work easier, but they do not eliminate the need for good thinking.

The well-known adage "garbage in, garbage out" still holds true. The garbage coming out may look better on a word processing program, but it will still stink the same. Students have been known to "ignore" all the suggestions given by a spell check program and turn in a piece of writing full of spelling errors. When the program checks the writing, it dutifully ignores the errors because it had previously been instructed to overlook them.

By the same token, once a rough draft is typed into the computer, editing and revising is so fast on a word processor that more time can be spent on learning advanced techniques of writing style rather than rewriting the piece by hand.

Technology will continue to be put into classrooms to help students learn. But student learning does not take place merely because their hands touch a keyboard. We must touch their minds, and technology can help us do that.

are gaining access.[26] In essence, Internet access is related to the income levels of families. Nothing surprising there. But that places special demands on teachers in contexts of low income to find ways to minimize the digital divide.

Current computer technology and related video and telecommunication technology have greater potential for enhancing the instructional and learning processes than did the computer technology of the past several decades. Unlike the old computers, the new technology can supplement complex interactions between learners and information bases. But, quite obviously, for that to occur students need access to the technology.

We are in the midst of an "information explosion," stemming from the computer generation of an ever-increasing and available quantity of information. People can participate in this explosion at three levels of computer knowledge: 1) *computer literacy,* or general knowledge of what computers are used for and some general experience in using them; 2) *computer competency,* or the ability to use the computer as a tool for particular purposes; and 3) *computer expertise,* or knowledge of how computers work. A new, fourth level of participation is computer entrepreneurship, which is more than expertise. An entrepreneur spends days and even nights working on games or prob-

There is an ever-increasing amount of information available because of computer technology.

lems, transmitting messages across the country or across oceans, devising ingenious games and software to sell, and swapping new software with fellow entrepreneurs. At best, entrepreneurs are freewheeling, creative types in a global technological revolution. At worst, they can become obsessed with technology in ways that may blind them to the ethics of responsible computer usage in society. Indeed, the World Wide Web exaggerates isolationist tendencies, and a generation of Internet addicts is now emerging.

As educators, we should aim at making our students computer-literate at an early age. Computer literacy might be "a fourth R," or fundamental skill. In this endeavour, several questions arise. How computer competent are teachers? Should every teacher be computer competent? Should every teacher be at least computer literate? What percentage of teachers in each school should have the skills to teach students how to use the computer? The International Society for Technology in Education (ISTE) is responsible for developing guidelines related to educational computing and technology integration. Teacher preparation programs to be accredited by The National Council for Accreditation of Teacher Education (NCATE), must incorporate these standards in their programs and provide opportunities for teacher education candidates to meet these standards. The ISTE standards cover three broad areas: basic computer/technology operations and concepts, personal and professional uses of technology, and the application

table 7.1   **Curriculum and Content Area Standards**

NETS for Teachers

Each of these six standards is followed by appropriate performance indicators. The standards document the types of technology skills teachers need for the classroom.

I. TECHNOLOGY OPERATIONS AND CONCEPTS.

   Teachers demonstrate a sound understanding of technology operations and concepts. Teachers:

   A. Demonstrate introductory knowledge, skills, and understanding of concepts related to technology (as described in the ISTE National Education *Technology Standards for Student*)

   B. Demonstrate continual growth in technology knowledge and skills to stay abreast of current and emerging technologies.

II. PLANNING AND DESIGNING LEARNING ENVIRONMENTS AND EXPERIENCES.

   Teachers plan and design effective learning environments and experiences supported by technology. Teachers:

   A. Design developmentally appropriate learning opportunities that apply technology-enhanced instructional strategies to support the diverse needs of learners.

   B. Apply current research on teaching and learning with technology when planning environments and experiences.

   C. Identify and locate technology resources and evaluate them for accuracy and suitability.

   D. Plan for the management of technology resources within the context of learning activities.

   E. Plan strategies to manage student learning in a technology-enhanced environment.

III. TECHING, LEARNING, AND THE CURRICULUM.

   Teachers implement curriculum plans that include methods and strategies for applying technology to maximize student learning. Teachers:

   A. Facilitate technology-enhanced experiences that address content standards and student technology standards.

   B. Use technology to support learner-centered strategies that address the diverse needs of students.

   C. Apply technology to develop students' higher order skills and creativity.

   D. Manage student learning activities in a technology-enhanced environment.

---

of technology in instruction (see Table 7.1). Within these three broad areas are six standards and appropriate performance indicators for those standards that are both a part of effective teacher education and essential to good teaching.

A teacher can become computer literate in workshops that meet for a few practice sessions. The time spent in training is fundamental to the teacher's ability to use the computer as an integral part of the teaching day, but a key factor is the attitude of the teacher. If the teacher is hesitant about using the computer, many children will pick

table 7.1   (continued)

NETS for Teachers

IV. ASSESSMENT AND EVALUATION.

Teachers apply technology to facilitate a variety of effective assessment evaluation strategies. Teachers:

A. Apply technology in assessing student learning of subject matter using a variety of assessment techniques.

B. Use technology resources to collect and analyze data, interpret results, and communicate findings to improve instructional practice and maximize student learning.

C. Apply multiple methods of evaluation to determine students' appropriate use of technology resources for learning, communication, and productivity.

V. PRODUCTIVITY AND PROFESSIONAL PRACTICE.

Teachers use technology to enhance their productivity and professional practice. Teachers:

A. Use technology resources to engage in ongoing professional development and lifelong learning.

B. Continually evaluate and reflect on professional practice to make informed decisions regarding the use of technology in support of student learning.

C. Apply technology to increase productivity.

D. Use technology to communicate and collaborate with peers, parents, and the larger community in order to nurture student learning.

VI. SOCIAL, ETHICAL, LEGAL, AND HUMAN ISSUES.

Teachers understand the social, ethical, legal, and human issues surrounding the use of technology in PK-12 schools and apply those principles in practice. Teachers:

A. Model and teach legal and ethical practice related to technology use.

B. Apply technology resources to enable and empower learners with diverse backgrounds, characteristics, and abilities.

C. Identify and use technology resources that affirm diversity.

D. Promote safe and healthy use of technology resources.

E. Facilitate equitable access to technology resources for all students.

Source: Reprinted with permission from *National Educational Technology Standards for Students*—Connecting Curriculum and Technology, copyright © 2000, ISTE (International Society for Technology in Education), 800.366.5191 (U.S. & Canada) or 541.302.3777 (Int'l), iste@iste.org, www.iste.org. All rights reserved.

up on this attitude. If the teacher is enthusiastic, children will learn more eagerly and more easily. A hesitant teacher could look to participate in a technology workshop or class being offered through professional development opportunities. These opportunities will allow a teacher's comfort level to increase and thus affect the attitude in the classroom.

Computers can be used in three fundamental learning phases: acquisition, transformation, and evaluation.

Acquisition.

Computers can be used by students to generate and retrieve three sources of information:

- *Information utilities:* Information, such as news, weather, sports, and stock market trends can be obtained through retrieval services.
- *Data banks and websites:* Students can access current information and opinions about reports, studies, and demographic trends using sources available on the Internet.
- *Computerized books:* Entire books are stored in electronic form or on computer discs. CD-ROMs—which combine graphics, pictures, and print—have the capability of creating dynamic and real-world representations missing from conventional printed books.

Transformation

Self-contained units or modules are available for use as instructional supplements or as self-contained programs. Interactive computer materials are also available through computerized video lessons that present the topic and guide the student through a series of exercises to test knowledge, understanding, and application of skills and concepts. For instance, many textbooks now have companion websites, which offer interactive review activities, chapter goals and summaries, interaction maps and timelines, primary-source writing activities, Internet activities, and a list of links for further review and research. Both approaches—self-contained units and modules—allow students to move at their own pace through the lessons.

Evaluation

Students can evaluate their learning meaningfully with rapid and accurate feedback from the computer. The computer can be programmed to respond to virtually any response the student makes. The computer can tell the student what information to review or when the answer is wrong. Not only do many companion websites for textbooks grade and offer immediate feedback for students, but such websites also allow students to e-mail their work to the instructor. With simulations, students can offer new kinds of responses and get immediate evaluation and feedback. In short, the computer allows students to evaluate learning by receiving essential information about the effects of their responses.[27]

Computer Software

Instructional software offerings, which have improved in quality and variety, are available for all subjects and grade levels. No longer do they cover only isolated topics or provide practice in only one or two skills. Current software can present whole units and courses of instruction.

Probably the most frequent criticism of educational software in general is the predominance in such software of drill and tutorial programs, which can also be viewed as a strength when specific skill acquisition is the goal of learning. Software has progressed to a highly interactive level. Whereas early software consisted of sequenced questions with specific answers, new software permits a variety of student responses with branching to appropriate levels of instruction. If the student fails to master a task or concept, the new drill and tutorial software breaks down the concept using analogies, examples, and suggestions rather than merely presenting a sequenced repetition of the subject matter. Still, teachers need to be very cautious in their use of drill-oriented software. The *Turning Points 2000* report documents the problem for eighth graders.

> . . . for eighth graders, "the use of computers to teach lower-order thinking skills was [found to be] negatively related to academic achievement and the social environment of the school . . . [L]ower-order activities included drill and practice primarily, though some learning games could be either higher or lower order and the use of computers to demonstrate new math topics could also be either higher or lower order, depending upon the topic. Higher-order activities included simulations and applications, along with some learning games and some topic demonstrations. We believe that this negative relationship between lower-order computer activities and academic achievement has implications for how computers are used in all subject areas. Apparently, "drill and kill" is still deadly even when it comes with bells, whistles, and a flashing cursor.[28]

Software beyond the standard "drill and practice" now exists in multitude. Teachers at any grade level will find an abundance of software that can support the learning process. Content-specific software supports a variety of topics including the rain forest, simple machines, and animals. In addition, software for student creativity and productivity will support the teaching of any subject. Multimedia software such as PowerPoint, HyperStudio, and Kid Pix allows for the creation of presentations on any topic. Other tool software (Excel, TimeLiner, Graph Club) will allow students to manage and manipulate data of any type. Consult with your media specialist or technology coordinator on the software that is available and any new software that will best support your curricular content.

In selecting or purchasing software, teachers need to consider how well the program sustains student interest and, most important, how well students receive and process information with it. More specifically, teachers need to focus on 1) how well the software appeals to both the eyes and the mind and how well visual and textual data are integrated; 2) how well the software helps students select and organize concepts and analyze and evaluate relationships; 3) how well the software promotes subjective, divergent, and creative thinking; and 4) to what extent the content fits with the teacher's instructional objectives and to the students' learning needs.[29] See Tips for Teachers 7.2 for a rubric on evaluating computer software. It is important that the software you use supports and enhances the instructional goals that you establish.

Amid the array of information systems available through computer software— CD-ROMs, Web pages, databases, and networks—the CD-ROM has particular educational potential. Its capacity is enormous. For example, an entire encyclopedia can be put on one CD through which the user experiences a world of data via a combination of audio, visual, and kinesthetic stimuli.

Whereas most school learning historically relies on audio stimuli (listening to the teacher) and is based on linear sequencing, the CD-ROM permits students to select from diverse topics and media, entering and exiting via a sequence of easy commands. The CD-ROM software brings life to learning through audio tracks such as music, speeches, and the voices of actual people; visual tracks such as printed text, graphs, pictures, news clippings, and films; and animation and motion. Rather than merely reading a conventional text on music, the student can use the CD-ROM to see a twenty-five-year-old film clip of a jazz artist (say, Dizzy Gillespie) in action; listen to a number of the music scores (the user can select which ones); go on to hear what other musicians or experts have to say about Gillespie (again, the user makes the selection); and finally read related text or supplementary magazine articles. Students can experience almost any topic with more depth and understanding than they could from just reading about it. There is some concern that these multimedia experiences entertain more than they educate—and don't really require the user to think other than superficially—but clearly they offer opportunities for learners to participate in their own learning in ways that were not previously possible.

QUESTION FOR REFLECTION

In this previous section we discussed how, for eighth graders, the drill and practice may have a detrimental effect on student academic achievement. In the previous chapter we talked about the need for using drill and practice and direct instruction approaches appropriately. Research is often inconclusive about what you should do with students. It gives direction but not specific answers. Identify ways in which you could use computer software for both lower-order skill practice and higher-order thinking skills. Be very specific. Identify a skill or concept that you would teach to students for your disciplinary area. What software (at different levels, lower and higher—see Bloom's taxonomy, for example, in Chapter 3) is available? Evaluate that software using Tips for Teachers 7.2.

Computer Simulations and Virtual Reality

It is not only the graphics and sound presentations that enhance the overall appeal of contemporary educational software, but also the computer simulations and virtual reality headsets by permitting students to vicariously experience real-life situations. Students can conduct experiments; experience past events, current trends, or future possibilities; and encounter "what-if" dilemmas—all through simulations. Through interactive learner participation software can promote logical thinking, hypothesizing, and the development of problem-solving strategies.

The idea of *computer simulations* as a method of teaching and learning is rooted in Newell's and Simon's classic text on problem solving. Newell and Simon theorized years ago that, if human cognition operates on internal representations and if computers can manipulate arbitrary symbol-structures, computer simulations have the potential to foster learning of knowledge, concepts, inferences, insights, and skills.[30] Their ideas still seem relevant in the first part of the twenty-first century. Computer simulations are not THE way to teach but rather one way to reinforce student acquisition of salient concepts and skills.

Because computer simulations contain explicit and implicit statements and tasks related to different capabilities as well as information-processing activities underlying performance, they are considered ideal starting points for observing student problem-solving skills. In addition, a simulation can be made increasingly more difficult to trace the

Software Evaluation

Name: _____   Date: _____

Gender: M/F (Circle one.)   Date of Birth:_____

Name of CD-ROM: _____

Rate the software on the following 20 criteria. Use a 1-5 scale with numbers meaning the following:

5 = Always   4 = Often   3 = To some extent   2 = Seldom   1 = Never

1. Skills needed to operate the program are in the range of a 7–10-year-old child. _____
2. It is easy to get in or out of any activity at any point. _____
3. The amount of reading required is appropriate for a 7-year-old child. _____
4. The amount of reading required is appropriate for a 10-year-old child. _____
5. The program survives the "pound the keyboard" test. _____
6. The child has control over the rate and order of display. _____
7. The program covers important content. _____
8. The program helps children develop understanding of concepts. _____
9. Graphics support the program's educational intentions. _____
10. The program has a good challenge range (i.e., it will grow with the child). _____
11. The program offers feedback that reinforces content. _____
12. The program fairly represents girls, minorities, and the disabled. _____
13. A child's ideas can be incorporated into the program. _____
14. The program teaches skills that children can transfer to other content. _____
15. The program covers material in depth. _____
16. The program is enjoyable for a 7–10-year-old to use. _____
17. Graphics are meaningful and enjoyable for children. _____
18. Speech and sounds are meaningful and enjoyable for children. _____
19. Challenge is fluid, or there is provision for the child to select his or her own level. _____
20. The program covers content that is meaningful to children. _____

On a scale of 1–6, with 6 meaning "Strongly Agree" and 1 meaning "Strong Disagree." please respond to the following statements:

a. I believe that this program can help children learn important lessons. _____
b. I believe that computers can help children learn important lessons. _____
c. I believe that teachers should make computers an essential component of their teaching. _____
d. I believe that computers will make schools better in the future. _____
e. I believe that computers will make the job of teaching easier in the future. _____

Source: Alex C. Pan and Stuart Z. Carroll. "Preservice Teachers Explore Instructional Software with Children." *The Educational Forum* (Summer 2002): 375. Reprinted with permission of Kappa Delta Pi, International Honor Society in Education.

performance of the learner. However, some researchers contend that computer simulations contribute little to an understanding of actual human problem solving because the simulations are based on oversimplified assumptions; the programs are written to work for a restricted set of examples; and performing the tasks does not necessarily coincide with the actual mental processes.[31]

Simulations can also encompass reaction-time tasks or real-life tasks to test the learner in a specified activity or subject matter. The complexity and challenge of the simulation can be changed to coincide with the skills of the learner. Many choices can be built into the program, so that, as learners advance, they are presented with different representative cases to address. An interesting modification permits different learners to participate jointly in the simulation at the same time, dividing up the tasks or problems so that each student has responsibility for a specific problem.

Interesting simulations can be accessed via the Internet. Through such simulations, participants can react over distance and take advantage of special training without traveling great distances. Indeed, computer-based simulations, games, and microworlds can be integrated into a system pulling together many different students from various parts of the local community, nation, or world. Students can interchange data via e-mail and modify the simulations to fit local conditions and present local problems.[32]

Finally, simulations can assist in learner self-evaluation by providing feedback on progress, recording and reviewing learning outcomes, and serving as a database for students to learn from each other. By showing other student attempts to solve a problem, the system helps learners avoid making the same mistakes. The same system can replay proper moves or behaviors for later review sessions. Through such retrieval systems, students can reflect on their own learning and that of others—not only learning a subject but also acquiring improved learning strategies in the process.

Virtual reality simulations are currently designed for entertainment purposes and are relatively expensive due to the special equipment required for the applications. Nevertheless, virtual reality equipment can transport the mind of the learner into an alternative experience, often one not otherwise possible within the confines of the traditional classroom. Learning that elicits emotional and physical sensations potentially adds to the memory enhancement of the content learned. However, some of the emotions elicited can also be harmful. The downside to virtual experiences will probably not be fully known for some time, but clearly any new technology holds both promise and challenges depending on how it is used.

For this reason, the moral and ethical implications of virtual reality applications must be weighed. Educators must put the well-being of students above all other considerations and use technologies wisely. The potential benefits of virtual reality learning will be explored in the twenty-first century. What must guide all applications, technological or others, is this question: Is this in the best interests of this particular student and this particular class?

Guidelines for Using Computers

Computers are beginning to impact the teaching-learning process. The following guidelines are for teachers as they implement and integrate computerized technology in classrooms and schools:

1. Use the computer in the classroom when its usage corresponds with curricular goals.

2. Preview software before it is purchased by the school or for the classroom.

3. Decide on what applications you want for the computer. Do you want to use it for practice and drill, problem solving, tutorial activities, simulations, games?

4. Establish criteria for use based on the objectives of your subject and the abilities and needs of your students.

5. Use software that is sound in terms of instructional and learning theory. It should be designed to foster students' critical thinking, development of problem-solving strategies, and creativity. It should be accurate, up-to-date, and clearly organized.

6. Integrate software and other traditional materials into a comprehensive curriculum and instructional package.

7. Encourage your students who have advanced knowledge of computing to network with other students—transmitting information from one computer to another. This can be arranged at the community, national, or international levels (as is the case of "e-mail pals").

8. Monitor Internet usage to ensure that students do not access inappropriate materials. Although filtering software like CyberPatrol is used by many districts to control access to inappropriate contents and sites, it is not 100 percent foolproof.

9. Build a relationship with your building's media specialist and/or technology support person to enhance your use of all educational technologies.

10. Check to see how software runs on the computer in your classroom before using it within a lesson.

11. Follow copyright and district guidelines when using software in your classroom.

Telecommunication Systems

Telecommunication systems refers to information exchanges between two or more locations connected by electronic media, including interactive computers, satellite and cable networks, television, and phone lines. Instruction is coming alive to new possibilities in all subject areas of telecommunication systems that are bringing people together in imaginative ways over vast distances. Given the computers already in classrooms, learning no longer revolves around seat work or the chalkboard. Indeed, substantial evidence already exists that within the first couple of years of the twenty-first century over half of all adolescents are using computers to access information on the Internet.[33] The textbook will take on different roles as this century evolves. It will no longer be the focus of learning but rather one among many sources of information. Acquiring and recalling new knowledge will not be the key in advanced educational courses because no one will be able to keep pace with it. Instead, being able to access data and network will be critical.

Teleconferences and Computer Conferences

Teleconferencing and video conferencing utilize similar technology. The difference is the audience. The word "conferencing" suggests a meeting or classroom with a specific purpose and an exchange of information. Participants come together at different locations for this exchange of information.

Teleconferences are now being used in many school districts. Groups of students can meet with teachers or other resource people through the computer monitor. The participants can watch, listen, ask questions, and make decisions, as if they were across the table from one another. It is a wonderful way for students to speak to a master teacher or expert or to communicate with their peers almost anywhere in the world. It is also an excellent way for small, rural schools to enable students to meet with other teachers, especially if the schools lack specialized personnel (for example, physics teachers).

Andrews and Marshall describe in detail one extended telelearning opportunity. As you read this example from J. Percy Page High School in Edmonton, Canada, note that the learning situation is not bound by a forty-five–minute class period or by a single teacher.

> Students in four locations have just gathered electronically. A student at the (Communications Research Centre) CRC welcomes the students from each location. Then Amy, one of our students, turns on her microphone and says, "We are pleased to present the topic of technology versus personal privacy and safety. Our group has created a video that demonstrates how your personal privacy and safety can be at risk owing to advances in technology." She waits, for what seems like an eternity, for the video to begin. When it does, it's going too fast: The screen is streaked and the sound is garbled.
>
> The group panics and turns to their teacher-facilitator. With a gentle reminder that they have done hours of research, she asks the students whether they can teach both sides of the issue without the video. After some quick brainstorming while the technician tries to get the video to stream in the correct speed, Amy and Gloria summarize both sides of the issue, with input from their classmates, and pose some questions: How have advances in technology affected our personal and national privacy and safety? What are the dangers created by this new age of technology and how can we protect ourselves?
>
> For the next hour, the student groups from across Canada debate a variety of issues concerning technology and privacy. Toronto students attempt to convince the other groups that the practice of capturing Internet protocol addresses when people visit Internet sites and then sending those people advertising equates to spying. Our students point out several additional ways that personal information can be obtained and discuss how we can protect our privacy. In the meantime, our technician fixes the video problem and our presentation closes with the student-created multimedia presentation.
>
> Next, an educational researcher from the University of Quebec appears on screen and asks the students to comment on what they have learned and what they think of this way of learning. The students offer insightful comments: "Other student groups offered many different points of view that my group never came up with," "We didn't know about IP tracing and some of the other safety issues regarding the Internet," and "This is a great way to learn—from one another."
>
> After a break, our panCanadian classroom resumes with a presentation by our tele-mentor, explorer, and renowned photographer Mike Beedel. His presentation on the plight of the spirit bear in British Columbia contains breathtaking images and thought-provoking narrations by author Pamela Coulston. Students from each region eagerly ask questions

about the elusive bear and its threatened habitat. The students decide to send letters and e-mails to government officials to express concern about the bear's survival. Mike provides the necessary addresses on a whiteboard that appears on everyone's screen. Once again, the session concludes with an evaluation led by the University of Quebec researcher.[34]

Networks allow users to contact others, conduct research, and share resources within a school or district or the global community. Via the network, information is transmitted from one computer to another in the form of text or graphic information, any time of the day for potentially much longer periods than class time, and without the receiving person(s) having to be present. Teachers can send assignments to students, for example, and students can send term papers back to teachers. Networking also provides a record of discussion; students can reread text, save it on a disk of their own, or print it at any time.

Electronic Mail

E-mail messages are stored in an electronic "mailbox" until the person receiving the messages accesses the system at his or her convenience. As almost every reader of this text now knows, the messages can be displayed on a computer screen, printed, and/or saved. Messages can be sent across continents and oceans. A class in New York City can communicate with a class in Chicago or Tokyo instantly. Many schools and colleges now have their own network for receiving and sending mail without worrying about long-distance charges. Of course, teachers and students can also communicate via fax machines, but this involves a telephone charge based on time consumption and local or long-distance rates.

Exchanges of e-mail correspondence are being used to teach written communication skills along with content learning in virtually every disciplinary field. The exchanges involve whole classrooms or individuals engaged in electronic pen-pal relationships with other students, professionals in disciplines related to a specific class activity, or people from other cultures and backgrounds. While pen-pal correspondence has been used for decades to promote such contacts, the advantage of e-mail is that it cuts down the time lag experienced with conventional mail; the technology also opens the possibility of sustained instantaneous written communication among participants.

The e-mail capacity of schools enhances the opportunity for children-teaching-children structures. Santrock describes the Fostering a Community of Learners (FCL) program of Anne Brown and Joe Campione, an effort that focuses on 6–12-year-old students and fosters student questioning and criticism through a variety of communication forms including e-mail.[35] The FCL-type programs that require students to explore topics through both fact-to-face and electronic communication illustrate the need for technological sophistication in twenty-first century teaching. The teacher of a class is no longer one adult, and the class of a teacher is no longer one set of same-aged students.

Students use e-mail to sustain personal relationships with peers. Educators are using it to help students explore their academic potential. For example, at the Ursuline Academy in Dallas, Texas, a telementoring program connects current students with experienced and successful women engineers at Texas Instruments. The program allows students and successful professionals to explore a wide range of personal and professional topics and to do so in a way that connects with real life.[36]

Courses OnLine

Colleges and universities have been offering independent study courses over the Internet for some time now. Students register and participate on-line at their convenience with a maximum time for completion. This is an excellent way for students to explore course content unavailable in their own institutions, and it is a preview of what may occur in the future.

Many universities in the western United States have joined together to form virtual universities. There is even one virtual law school in California (Concord University). Many other more mainstream institutions throughout the States offer on-line courses on topics of special interest.

The on-line learning experience once thought of as only an adult option is now a viable opportunity for young people who are in the elementary, middle, and high school grades. Students in K–12 classrooms are now availing themselves of a wide menu of on-line classes. That reality suggests real change for all of us who think of school as *a place*. In an earlier chapter we discussed that Texas offers virtual classes and Ohio now has virtual schools. Such opportunities suggest the wide range of skills that students need if they are going to be successful learners. Table 7.2 outlines the profiles for technology-literate students. What must students know to be successful in a global economy? Examine the list carefully and then consider how you need to use technology to help students develop the personal profile they will need for subsequent academic success.

Conclusions

What you accomplish in your classroom with the use of technology will depend upon the applications you utilize and how well those applications support your teaching goals. It will also depend on your school and its resources.

Many schools are caught in the middle ground with neither the financial resources to "move into the information age" nor the large number of disadvantaged students necessary to qualify for federal programs that fund technology.[37] Typically these schools have only two or three computers in a classroom or one large computer lab able to accommodate twenty-eight to thirty students. The computers they do have may be outdated—perhaps slow and unable to accommodate large software programs.

What you accomplish will also depend on your preparedness and computer ability (see Table 7.3) and the way you use the technology in your classroom (see Table 7.4). Research in the 1990s indicated that 30 to 60 percent of computer usage was spent acquiring technical mastery of computer software and typing/mouse skills and using the Internet.[38] As Figure 7.2 suggests, in many classrooms the emphasis on practice drills is still quite high. While computer skills are considered necessary for employability, some question the use of precious teaching time to teach younger students technical mastery over technology that is changing so rapidly. (See Professional Viewpoint 7.3 for another look at the concerns about instructional technology.)

table 7.2   **Profile for Technology Literate Students: Grades pre-K–12**

Prior to completion of grade 2, students will

1. use input devices (mouse, keyboard, remote control) and output devices (monitor, printer) to operate computers, VCRs, audiotapes, telephones, and other technologies.

2. use a variety of media and technology resources for directed and independent learning activities.

3. communicate about technology using developmentally appropriate and accurate terminology.

4. use multimedia resources (interactive books, educational software, elementary multimedia encyclopedias) to support learning.

5. work cooperatively and collaboratively with peers, family members, and others when using technology in the classroom.

6. demonstrate positive social and ethical behaviors when using technology.

7. practice responsible use of technology systems and software.

8. create multimedia products with support from teachers, family members, or student partners.

9. use technology resources (puzzles, logical thinking programs, writing tools, digital cameras, drawing tools) for problem solving, communication, and illustration of thoughts, ideas, and stories.

10. gather information and communicate with others using telecommunications, with support from teachers, family members, or student partners.

Prior to completion of grade 5, students will

1. use keyboards and other common input and output devices (including adaptive devices) efficiently and effectively.

2. discuss common uses of technology in daily life and advantages and disadvantages those uses provide.

3. discuss responsible uses of technology and information and describe personal consequences of inappropriate use.

4. use tools and peripherals to support personal productivity, to remediate skill deficits, and to facilitate learning throughout the curriculum.

5. use technology tools (multimedia authoring, presentation tools, Web tools, digital cameras, scanners) for individual and collaborative writing, communication, and publishing activities to create knowledge products for audiences inside and outside the classroom.

6. use telecommunications to access remote information, to communicate with others, and to pursue personal interests.

7. use telecommunications and online resources (e-mail, online discussions, Web environments) to participate in collaborative problem-solving activities.

8. use technology resources (calculators, probes, videos, educational software) for problem solving, self-directed learning, and extended learning activities.

9. determine when technology is useful and select the appropriate tools and technology resources to address tasks and problems.

10. evaluate the accuracy, relevance, appropriateness, comprehensiveness, and bias of electronic information sources.

Prior to completion of grade 8, students will

1. apply strategies for identifying and solving routine hardware and software problems.

2. demonstrate knowledge of current changes in information technologies and the effect those changes have on the workplace and on society.

(continued)

ta b l e 7 . 2 **continued**

....

3. exhibit legal and ethical behaviors when using information and technology and discuss consequences of misuse.

4. use content-specific tools, software, and simulations (environmental probes, graphing calculators, exploratory environments, Web tools) to support learning and research.

5. apply multimedia tools and peripherals to support personal productivity, group collaboration, and learning throughout the curriculum.

6. design, develop, publish, and present products (Web pages, videotapes) using technology resources that communicate curriculum concepts to audiences inside and outside the classroom.

7. collaborate with peers, experts, and others using telecommunications and collaborative tools to investigate curriculum-related problems, issues, and information and to develop solutions or products for audiences inside and outside the classroom.

8. select and use appropriate tools and technology resources to accomplish tasks and to solve problems.

9. demonstrate an understanding of concepts underlying hardware, software, and connectivity and of practical applications to learning and problem solving.

10. research and evaluate the accuracy, relevance, appropriateness, comprehensiveness, and bias of electronic information sources concerning real-world problems.

Prior to completion of grade 12, students will

1. identify capabilities and limitations of contemporary and emerging technology resources and assess the potential of these systems and services to address personal, lifelong learning, and workplace needs.

2. make informed choices among technology systems, resources, and services.

3. analyze advantages and disadvantages of widespread use and reliance on technology in the workplace and in society as a whole.

4. demonstrate and advocate legal and ethical behaviors regarding the use of technology and information.

5. use technology tools and resources for managing and communicating personal or professional information (finances, schedules, addresses, purchases, correspondence).

6. evaluate technology-based options, including distance and distributed education, for lifelong learning.

7. routinely and efficiently use online information resources for collaboration, research, publications, communications, and productivity.

8. select and apply technology tools for research, information analysis, problem solving, and decision making in content learning.

9. investigate and apply expert systems, intelligent agents, and simulations in real-world situations.

10. collaborate with peers, experts, and others to contribute to a content-related knowledge base by using technology to compile, synthesize, produce, and disseminate information, models, and other creative works.

Source: Reprinted with Permission from *National Educational Technology Standards for Students—Connecting Curriculum and Technology,* Copyright © 2000, ISTE (International Society for Technology in Education), 800.336.5191 (U.S. & Canada) or 541.302.3777 (Int'l), iste@iste.org, www.iste.org. All rights reserved.

table 7.3   **Access to Computers and Teacher Ability (1999)**

School and Teacher Characteristics	Not at all Prepared	Somewhat Prepared	Well Prepared	Very Well Prepared
All public school teachers with access to computers or the Internet at school	**13**	**53**	**23**	**10**
School Instructional Level				
Elementary School	12	55	23	10
Secondary School	15	50	23	12
Percent of students eligible for free or reduced price school lunch				
Less than 11 percent	10	53	25	12
11–30 percent	13	52	25	10
31–49 percent	14	51	24	10
50–70 percent	16	58	16	10
71 percent or more	13	55	22	10
Teaching experience				
3 or fewer years	10	46	31	13
4–9 years	10	49	28	13
10–19 years	14	55	21	10
40 or more years	16	58	19	8
Hours of professional development*				
0 hours	32	46	15	6
1–8 hours	19	55	20	6
9–32 hours	4	61	25	10
More than 32 hours	1	32	37	29
Type of work assigned to a moderate or large extent				
Use computer applications such as word processing, spreadsheets, etc.	4	45	33	19
Practice drills	4	54	27	14
Research using the Internet	4	43	34	19
Solve problems/analyze data	3	49	29	19
Research using CD-ROM	3	42	33	21
Produce multimedia reports/projects	5	38	33	24
Graphical presentation of materials	4	38	35	22
Demonstrations/simulations	2	34	37	28
Correspond with experts, authors, students from other schools, etc. via e-mail or Internet	4	32	34	30

*Professional development in the use of computers or the Internet within the last 3 years.

NOTE: Less than 1 percent of all public school teachers reported no computers or Internet were available to them anywhere in their school. These teachers were not included in the estimates presented in this table. percentages may not add to 100 because of rounding.

Source: U.S. Department of Education, National Center for Education Statistics, Fast Response Survey System. "Survey on Public School Teachers' Use of Computers and the Internet," FRSS 70, 1999.

table 7.4   Computer Use (1999)

School and Teacher Characteristics	Teacher Uses for Classroom Instruction	Computer applications[1]	Practice Drills	Research Using the Internet	Solve Problems and Analyze Data
Teacher Assigns to a Moderate or Large Extent					
All public school teachers with access to computers or the Internet at school	**66**	**41**	**31**	**30**	**27**
School instructional level					
Elementary school	68	41	39	25	31
Secondary school	60	42	12	41	20
Percent of students in school eligible for free or reduced price school lunch					
Less than 11 percent	71	55	26	39	25
11–30 percent	65	45	29	35	29
31–49 percent	65	39	33	29	26
50–70 percent	62	33	33	25	27
71 percent or more	64	61	35	18	27
Hours of professional development[3]					
0 hours	41	21	19	20	14
1–8 hours	56	36	26	28	24
9–32 hours	72	47	35	32	30
More than 32 hours	82	55	43	42	41

[1]Use computer applications such as word processing, spreadsheets, etc.

[2]Correspond with experts, authors, students, from other schools, etc., via e-mail or Internet.

[3]Professional development in the use of computers or the Internet within the last 3 years.

NOTE: Less than 1 percent of all public school teachers reported no computers or Internet were available to them anywhere in their school. These teachers were not included in the estimates presented in this table.

Source: U.S. Department of Education, National Center for Education Statistics, Fast Response Survey System. "Survey on Public School Teachers' Use of Computers and the Internet," FRSS 70, 1999.

The use of technology, especially computers and telecommunications, must be based on meeting the needs of students and the development of lifelong learning abilities. Technology represents a way to complement what is happening in the classroom and enhance student achievement. Some teachers see the work on computers or in using other forms of technology as "taking students away from" a focus on the teacher that some

table 7.4 (continued)

	Research Using CD-ROM	Produce Multimedia Reports/ Projects	Graphical Presentations of Materials	Demonstrations/ Simulations	Correspond with Others[2]
All public school teachers with access to computers or the Internet at school	**27**	**24**	**19**	**17**	**7**
School instructional level					
Elementary school	27	22	17	15	7
Secondary school	27	27	23	21	7
Percent of students in school eligible for free or reduced price school lunch					
Less than 11 percent	32	29	26	22	7
11–30 percent	27	23	18	16	9
31–49 percent	30	23	16	17	11
50–70 percent	24	25	19	13	5
71 percent or more	19	22	19	16	3
Hours of professional development					
0 hours	16	16	10	8	4
1–8 hours	24	20	16	13	7
9–32 hours	31	26	21	19	8
More than 32 hours	34	37	31	29	9

The header row is titled: *Teacher Assigns to a Moderate or Large Extent*

deem is essential for student learning. That is, in a high-stakes environment, should teachers encourage students to explore topics through a variety of methods, including both teacher-centered didactic and student-centered interactive methods? The results of work from the Consortium on Chicago School Research show why you should vary the way you help students access and use data:

> In a high-stakes testing environment, should teachers use so-called didactic methods—that is, lectures, drill and practice, and worksheets that encourage students to memorize facts and procedures—or an "interactive" approach that emphasizes inquiry-based, hands-on activities; knowledge-building discussions; and projects that connect students to their larger world?

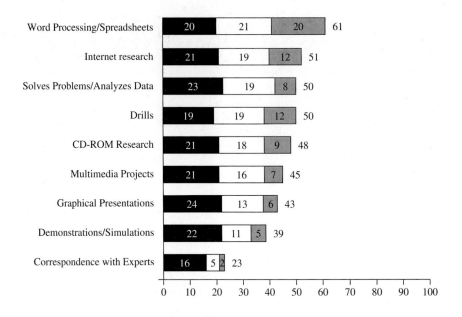

figure 7.2   Types of Computer Use (1999)

Note: Teachers who reported that computers were not available to them anywhere in the school were excluded from the analysis in this figure. Detail may not sum to totals due to rounding.

Source: U.S. Department of Education, National Center for Education Statistics, Fast Response Survey System, "Survey on Public School Teachers Use of Computers and the Internet," FRSS 70, 1999. (Originally published as figure 2.6 on p. 25 of the complete report from which this article is excerpted.)

Of course it's not an either/or question. Nearly all teachers use a mix of styles. But the Consortium report *Instruction and Achievement in Chicago Elementary Schools* shows that, in a single school year, Chicago elementary school students in classes with high levels of interactive instruction scored higher on year-end tests than the city average—5.1 percent higher in math, 5.2 percent in reading. Students in mostly didactic classrooms scored below the city average in both—3.9 percent lower in math, 3.4 percent in reading. The researchers suggest that students who learn in interactive classrooms through the eight-year course of elementary school may end up a year ahead academically of those who receive didactic instruction.

Whether teachers use didactic or interactive means, all of them face the issue of how—and how much—to review previous lessons before moving forward in the curriculum. The Consortium study found that students scored better on year-end tests when instructional review was limited—4.2 percent better than the city average in math, and 4.1 percent better in reading. "Although reviewing familiar content may help build a solid knowledge base for new learning, this could also diminish learning by taking away from teaching new material," the authors write.

Didactic instruction and review get used most after 5th grade; where behavioral problems and irregular attendance are usual; where students are low achievers; in large schools; and in schools with a predominantly African American and/or low income student body—

Some Quandaries in Instructional Technology

Harold G. Shane

Emeritus Professor and former Dean of Education
Indiana University–Bloomington

 Since the transistor (1947) and the single unit microchip (1959) made their debuts they have had an enormous and rapidly increasing impact on education. On the whole, electronic gear has created a milestone in the history of our schools— but the era of the "information society" could become something of a millstone around our necks unless we use instructional technology with a measure of wisdom.

Let us review a few of the major quandaries that are besetting us as we approach a new millennium. For one thing, young learners must be protected from the habit of letting a computer per se rather than their minds find answers!

Another problem resides in the way teachers use electronic tools in the learning milieu. We must also avoid acquiring a "frozen curriculum" dictated by the equipment used. A particular challenge resides in utilizing suitable learning tools for pupils' varied needs in diverse schools.

Space limitations preclude the review of many other problems, but at least two more should be mentioned. One of these is the composite use of electronic gear by young people for pranks, vandalism, and fraud. This must be discouraged.

Second, there is great, and generally unrecognized, danger in the electromagnetic pulse (EMP) phenomenon. The EMP, while harmless to humans, carries an energy surge which can cause electronic damage. We must not become too dependent on microelectronic support systems when an EMP blast, caused by a nuclear explosion or fire could render much of our equipment inoperative over most of the Continental United States. Patently our schools must not be so dependent on computers and robots that an EMP blast would render them virtually impotent.

all of which may suggest that those who might benefit most from interactive instruction aren't getting it. . . .

The Technology Viewpoint lists some resources for your use as you begin to incorporate technology into your classroom.

Theory into Practice

As educators, we must note that electronic media are increasingly supplementing, even replacing, traditional printed material in school and flooding our homes. Understanding and applying these new processes and systems are essential for students and teachers alike if they are to learn from and have control over technology.

The potential for learning is immense. Technology can promote individualized learning and react flexibly to student responses. It can promptly acknowledge correct answers; it can handle incorrect responses by giving students a second chance, easier questions or problems, or a review of the program or by

A Technology Viewpoint from a Classroom Teacher

Jackie Marshall Arnold
K–12 Media Specialist

 The World Wide Web can support you with a multitude of teacher-based resources. The following list is only the beginning of resources available for teachers:

Classroom Connect:
http://www.classroom.com/
This is a well-known provider of professional development and online teaching resources for K–12 teachers in all subject areas.

Kathy Schrock's Guide for Educators:
http://school.discovery.com/schrockguide/
This is a comprehensive list of sites for enhancing technology throughout the curriculum.

WWW for Teachers:
http://4teachers.org/
This site provides a multitude of resources for teachers, especially in the area of assessment.

Technology Software Tutorials:
http://www.internet4classrooms.com
This site provides links, web sites, and online modules that are easy to find and use.

Public Broadcasting System TeacherSource:
http://www.pbs.org/teachersource/
PBS provides lesson plans and activities tied to standards as well as a database to search for video and other links to quality education sites.

Education Planet—Educational Web Guide:
http://www.educationplanet.com/
An education-focused search engine, current standards-based lesson plans, parent resources, and much more are all part of this site.

Active Learning Practices for Schools:
http://learnweb.harvard.edu/alps/
Sponsored by Harvard University, this site provides resources, teaching techniques, and demonstrations to foster educational instruction.

Education World—Where Educators Go to Learn:
http://www.education-world.com/
This is a vast collection of high quality resources for planning lessons, integrating technology, finding standards, and more.

The WebQuest Page at San Diego State University:
http://webquest.sdsu.edu/

This site provides access to thousands of previously created projects as well as templates to create personalized projects. A WebQuest is a wonderful activity fostering student inquiry.

WebQuest was created in 1995 by Bernie Dodge as a means of helping teachers foster student learning through the internet. A WebQuest can be developed in almost any area and typically takes anywhere from one to three class sessions, or longer. The WebQuest structure consists of six elements:

Introduction or an overview of what WebQuest is.

Task or a description of what students will complete.

Information Sources or a listing of all the different resources students can use from the internet to content experts.

Process or the actual steps needed to complete the WebQuest.

Guidance or the input of teachers for how to complete the WebQuest.

Conclusion or closure of the activity.[40]

More information on WebQuest can be obtained by contacting Dodge's WebQuest page (edweb.sdsu/webquest/overview.htm)

showing them correct answers. A student's response to a question can determine what will be presented next. Technology gives teachers more knowledge and options to guide the process of learning, and it gives students more control over their learning.

In order to use technology effectively in the classroom, it is worthwhile to remember some general guidelines for operation. These guidelines are written in the form of questions regarding the equipment and media discussed in this chapter.

1. Are you familiar with the technological materials and equipment available in your classroom or media center? Have you found out what materials and equipment are available elsewhere in the school and what check-out procedures apply to their use?
3. Did you preview the materials and evaluate their availability for the lesson(s) you plan to teach?
4. Have you ordered the materials in advance? Did you allow enough time for delivery by the scheduled date?
5. Are you prepared to guide the students on what to look for while viewing, listening to, or reacting to the assigned media?
6. Did you allow time for a summary activity to highlight the main ideas of what the students saw or heard?

Summary

1. Basic guidelines related to using instructional technology include a) selecting equipment suitable to objectives, b) learning how to operate the equipment, and c) previewing the materials.
2. Visual images increase effectiveness of presentation of materials. Visual images can be incorporated into a presentation through the use of chalkboards, dry-erase boards, and display boards; films; and overhead projectors or PowerPoint software.
3. Two types of television programming for use in schools are educational television (informative programs produced by commercial and public television stations) and instructional television (programs produced by educators for specific teaching purposes).
4. Teachers and students can participate in these levels of computer use: computer literacy, computer competency, and computer expertise. All students should be at least computer literate. Examine the National Educational Technology Standards Project (NETS) profiles in Table 7.2.
5. All teachers should find ways to help students explore disciplinary concepts through Internet access. That access can be fostered in many different informal and formal ways.
6. The quality and variety of computer software have improved in recent years. The most challenging and interesting uses of computer-based instruction are in the growing number of simulations and interactive systems.
7. Telecommunication systems include teleconferences, electronic mail, and telecourses.

Questions to Consider

1. Do you agree that the chalkboard is still a valuable instructional aid? Explain. What are its limitations? Its advantages?
2. Some educators feel computers have revolutionized education. Do you agree? Explain.
3. What are important factors to consider in choosing appropriate video systems?
4. Should teachers encourage students to change their television and video habits? Can teachers really change student habits of television viewing?

Things to Do

1. Select one of the instructional technologies discussed in this chapter. Identify a specific way to teach a concept or skill using that form of technology.
2. Visit selected websites (see Technology Viewpoint) and determine how you might use those sites with K–12 students.
3. Review each of the NETS profile standards for K–12 students (Table 7.2). Which describe skills you do or do not possess?
4. Studies conducted by a host of independent researchers now document that the time students spend on learning activities (at home and at school) does influence their achievement gains. Identify specific things that you as a teacher can do to maximize the time students spend on learning goals that matter *outside* the classroom?
5. The ISTE website offers lots of different resources (see www.iste.org). Visit that website and identify some specific resources that would be helpful for you in constructing a lesson.

Recommended Readings

Bitter, Gary, and Melissa Pierson. *Using Technology in the Classroom,* 5th ed. Boston: Allyn & Bacon, 2002. This is a great place to start for educators wanting to incorporate technology in the classroom.

Cuban, Larry. *Oversold and Underused: Computers in Classrooms.* Cambridge, Mass.: Harvard University Press, 2001. This is a critical look at the actual use of computers by teachers and students in early childhood education, high school, and university classrooms.

Heinich, Robert, Michael Molenda, and James D. Russell. *Instructional Media and Technologies for Learning,* 7th ed. Upper Saddle River, N.J.: Prentice Hall, 2001. This book discusses how to select, develop, and use instructional media.

Kemp, Jerrold E., and Don C. Smellie. *Planning, Producing, and Using Instructional Technology,* 7th ed. New York: Harper Collins, 1998. This book shows how to integrate media with instruction.

McKenzie, Walter. *Multiple Intelligences and Instructional Technology: A Manual for Every Mind.* Eugene, Ore.: International Society for Technology in Education, 2002. This is a practical look at how to weave multiple intelligences theory with technology throughout your existing curriculum.

Papert, Seymour. *The Children's Machine: Rethinking School in the Age of the Computer.* New York: Basic Books, 1994. In a follow-up book to *Mindstorms,* the author discusses where the computer revolution went wrong—and where to go from there.

Sandholtz, Judith Haymore, Cathy Ringstaff, and David C. Dwyer. *Teaching with Technology: Creating Student-Centered Classrooms.* New York: Teacher's College Press, 1997. A report on the ten-year study trying to understand the role of teachers in a technology rich classroom using the Apple Classroom of the Future.

Key Terms

cable television 305	data/video projector 298	overhead projector 499
chalkboard 297	display board 298	telecommunication
computer competency 308	dry-erase board 297	systems 317
computer expertise 308	educational television 304	videotapes 306
computer literacy 308	film 300	virtual reality 316
computer simulations 314	instructional television 305	

End Notes

1. NCATE. *Technology and the New Professional Teacher: Preparing for the 21st Century in the Classroom.* Washington, D.C.: National Council for the Accreditation of Teacher Education, 1997. Mickey Revenaugh. "Toward a 24/7 Learning Community." *Educational Leadership* (October 2000): 25–28.
2. Curtis J. Bonk and Kira S. King. *Electronic Collaborators.* Mahurah, N.J.: Erlbaum, 1998. James Lockhard et al. *Microcomputers for the Twenty First Century.* New York: Longman, 1997.
3. Mary Elin Barnish. "International Learning in a High School Academy." *Educational Leadership* (November 2002): 79–82. Jacqueline Jordan Irvine and Beverly Jeanne Armento. *Culturally Responsive Teaching.* Boston: McGraw Hill, 2001.
4. Richard L. Allington. "You Can't Learn Much from Books You Can't Read." *Educational Leadership* (November 2002): 16–19. Simon Hooper and Lloyd P. Rieber. "Teaching with Technology." In A. C. Ornstein (ed.), *Teaching: Theory and Practice.* Needham Heights, Mass.: Allyn and Bacon, 1995, pp. 155–170. Joyce A. Burtch. "Technology Is for Everyone." *Educational Leadership* (February 1999): 33–34.
5. Christopher Belski-Sblendorio. "Push-Button Entertainment and the Health of the Soul." In Pamela Johnson Fenner and Karen L. Rivers (eds.), *Waldorf Education: A Family Guide.* Amesbury, Mass.: Michaelmas Press, 1995.
6. Judith O'Donnell Dooling. *"What Students Want to Learn About Computers."* Educational Leadership (October 2000): 20–24. Helen L. Harrington. "The Essence of Technology and the Education of Teachers." *Journal of Teacher Education* (January–February 1993): 5–15.
7. Leonard H. Clark and Irving S. Starr. *Secondary and Middle School Teaching Methods,* 6th ed. New York: Macmillan, 1991, p. 403. Joseph F. Callahan, Leonard H. Clark, and Richard D. Kellough. *Teaching in the Middle and Secondary Schools,* 7th ed. Columbus, OH: Merrill Prentice Hall, 2001.
8. Carla Kalin. *Television Violence and Children.* Retrieved on April 3, 2003 from http://interact.uoregon.edu/medialit/m1r/readings/articles/kalin.html. See also M. Lee Manning and Katherine T. Bucher. *Teaching in the Middle School.* Upper Saddle River, N.J.: Merrill Prentice Hall, 2001.
9. Mihaly Csikszentmihalyi and Barbara Schneider. *Becoming Adult.* New York: Basic Books, 2000.
10. Neil Postman. *Teaching as a Conserving Activity.* New York: Delacorte, 1979.
11. James Garbarino and Claire Bedand. *Parents Under Siege.* New York: A Touchstone Book, 2001.
12. Ibid.

13. See http://www.iptv.org/rtl/factoidz.cfm. Peter Plagens. *Big World, Small Screen.* Washington, D.C.: American Psychological Association, 1992, pp. 41–52. Mortimer B. Zuckerman. "The Victims of Violence." *U.S. News and World Report* (2 August 1993): 645.

14. Joan M. Bergstran. "Help Your Child Find Great Alternatives to Television." *PTA Journal* (April 1988): 15–17. Nancy L. Cecil. "Helping Children Become More Critical TV Watchers." *PTA Journal* (April 1988): 12–14.

15. Kathy A Krendal, Kathryn Lasky, and Robert Dawson. "How Television Affects Adolescents: Their Own Preceptions. *Educational Horizons* (Spring 1989): 89–91.

16. Myra Pollack Sadker and David Miller Sadker. *Teachers, Schools and Society.* Boston: McGraw Hill 2000, 462.

17. See http://www.iptv.org/rtl/factoid2.cfm. Mona Charen, "Kidvid Doing Battle with G.I. Joe" *The New York Times* (26 January 1992): H29. Fred D'Ignazio. "Why Should You Teach with TV? *Instructor* (March 1993): 24–28.

18. John W. Santrock. *Child Development,* (9th ed.) Boston: McGraw Hill, 2001.

19. Allan S. Vann. "Debunking Five Myths About Computers in Schools." *Principal* (January 1998): 53.

20. Laurence Steinberg. *Beyond the Classroom.* New York: Simon and Schuster, 1996, pp. 179–180.

21. Lev Vygotsky. *Thought and Language.* Cambridge, Mass.: MIT Press, 1962.

22. Thomas L. Good and Jere E. Brophy. *Looking in Classrooms,* 8th ed. Reading, Mass: Addison Wesley, 2000, p. 442.

23. Paula K. Montgomery. "Integrating Library, Media Research, and Information Skills." *Phi Delta Kappan* (March 1992): 529–532.

24. Donelle Blubaugh. "Bringing Cable into the Classroom." *Educational Leadership* (February 1999): 61–65.

25. Henry Becker. "Computer Use in United States Schools." Paper presented at the annual meeting of the American Educational Research Association, Boston, April 1990. *The Condition of Education.* Washington, D.C.: U.S. Government Printing Office, 1993, Tables 14, 36. Robert Heinich and James D. Russell. *Instructional Media and Technologies for Learning,* 6th ed. Columbus, Ohio: Merrill, 1999. Internet Access in U.S. Public Schools and Classrooms: 1994-2001. Washington, D.C.: National Center for Educational Statistics. Retrieved from: http://nces.ed.gov/pubs2002/internet/4.asp.

26. John H. Halloway. "The Digital Divide." *Educational Leadership* (October 2000): 90. Internet Access in U.S. Public Schools and Classrooms: 1994-2001. Washington, D.C.: National Center for Educational Statistics. Retrieved from: http://nces.ed.gov/pubs2002/internet/4.asp.

27. Joan Bissell, Anna Manring, and Veronica Rowland. *Cyber Education: The Internet and Worldwide Web for K-12 Educators.* Boston, Mass.: McGraw Hill 1998. Peter Smith and Samuel Dunn. "Human Quality Considerations in High Tech Education." *Educational Technology* (February 1987); 35–39. Ester R. Steinberg. *Computer Assisted Instruction.* Hillsdale, N.J.: Erlbaum, 1990.

28. Anthony W. Jackson and Gayle A. Davis. *Turning Points 2000.* New York: Teachers College Press, 2000, pp. 85–86.

29. Carol Tell. "The I-Generation—from Toddlers to Teenagers." *Educational Leadership* (October 2000): 8–13. Dennis Dewman. "Technology as Support for School Structure." *Phi Delta Kappan* (December 1992): 308–315.

30. Allen Newell and Herbert A. Simon. *Human Problem Solving.* Englewood Cliffs, N.J.: Prentice Hall, 1972.

31. Myron J. Atkins. "Evaluating Interactive Technologies for Learning." *Journal of Curriculum Studies* (July–August 1993): 333–423. Stephen T. Peverly. "Problems with the Knowledge-Based Explanation of Memory and Development." *Review of Educational Research* (Spring 1991): 71–93.

32. James A. Levine et al. "Education on the Electronic Frontier." *Contemporary Education Psychology* (March 1991: 46–51. Gwen Solomon. "The Computer as Electronic Doorway: Technology and the Promise of Empowerment." *Phi Delta Kappan* (December 1992): 327–329.

33. John W. Santrock. *Child Development*

34. Karen Andrews and Ken Marshall, "Making Learning Connections Through Telelearning," *Educational Leadership* (October 2000): 54.

35. John W. Santrock. *Child Development*

36. Carole Duff. "Online Mentoring." *Educational Leadership* (October 2000): 49–52.

37. Allan S. Vann. "Debunking Five Myths About Computers in Schools." *Principal* (January 1998): 53.

38. David Skinner. "Computers: Good for Education?" *Public Interest* (Summer 1997): 98–109.

39. Excerpted from David T. Gordon. "Moving Instruction to Center Stage." *Harvard Education Letter.* Volume 18:5 (September/October 2002), pp. 1–4. Copyright (c) 2002 by the President and Fellows of Harvard College. All rights reserved.

40. Susan Brooks-Young. "Set Out on a Web Quest." *Today's Catholic Teacher.* (November–December 2001): 13–15.

chapter 8

Instructional Grouping

Pathwise criteria relevant to the content of this chapter:

- Demonstrating an understanding of the connections between the content that was learned previously, the current content, and the content that remains to be learned in the future. (A3)
- Creating or selecting teaching methods, learning activities, and instructional materials or other resources that are appropriate for the students and that are aligned with the goals of the lesson. (A4)
- Making the physical environment as safe and conducive to learning as possible. (B5)
- Making content comprehensible to students. (C2)
- Monitoring students' understanding of content through a variety of means, providing feedback to students to assist learning, and adjusting learning activities as the situation demands. (C4)

INTASC principles relevant to the content of this chapter:

- The teacher understands how students differ in their approaches to learning and creates instructional opportunities that are adapted to diverse learners. (P3)
- The teacher understands and uses a variety of instructional strategies to encourage students' development of critical thinking, problem solving, and performance skills (P4)
- The teacher uses an understanding of individual and group motivation and behavior to create a learning environment that encourages positive social interaction, active engagement in learning, and self-motivation. (P5)

focusing questions

1. When is it appropriate to use whole-group, small-group, and individual instruction?

2. What are the advantages and disadvantages of the different types of instruction?

3.   How do teachers effectively organize students for different types of instruction?

4.   What methods can be used to individualize instruction? How does a teacher differentiate instruction to personalize it for students?

The most common means of organizing students for instruction is to group twenty-five to thirty students according to age and grade level and sometimes ability and assign them to a specific classroom and teacher. When instruction occurs in this type of setting, it is called a ***self-contained classroom.***

At the elementary school level a teacher is assigned to the class for the whole day. Students may travel as a class to another class one or two periods a day to receive special instruction (for example, in remedial reading, music, or physical education), or other teachers may visit the class to provide special instruction.

At the secondary level the self-contained classroom is modified by what is commonly called ***departmentalization.*** Students are assigned to a different teacher for each subject and may have six or seven different teachers each day. Departmentalization usually begins at the sixth, seventh, or eighth grade—depending on the school district and on the state. Ohio has licensure standards for teachers that make departmentalization prevalent in even the fourth and fifth grades.

There are three basic ways of grouping for instruction: 1) whole-group instruction, sometimes called *large-group instruction,* in which the entire class is taught as a group; 2) *small-group instruction,* in which the large group is broken up into subgroups according to ability, interest, project, or other criteria; and 3) *individualized instruction,* in which the individual student works alone or with another person on a specific task or assignment. Different groupings require different physical settings, so we will take a look at some designs for seating arrangement and then look at the characteristics of instruction for each grouping.

As you begin this chapter it is important that you clearly understand that, for students to learn, instruction must be vital. American teachers spend more time in front of students (actually teaching) than do teachers from many other countries such as those in Japan and China. And yet, U.S. students perform no better than their international counterparts.[1] Time makes a difference in student learning, but for it to make a value-added difference, what occurs must be vital, be linked to standards, and entail high expectations on your part for what the students will do. This chapter is about how you arrange the classroom environment for learning—but never forget that it is the substance of a lesson, not the arrangement of the desks, that really dictates whether the learning will be significant for students.

Classroom Seating Arrangements

Room arrangements are a reflection of your teaching philosophy. They also necessarily influence the types of interactions that occur in the classroom. In a classic study on teaching, Adams and Biddle found that, for the most part, what takes place in the classroom requires the attention of all the students. Teachers tend to stay in front of the classroom more than 85 percent of the time when teaching the whole class, but they change their location on the average once every thirty seconds. Elementary teachers tend to move around through the aisles more than do secondary teachers.[2]

Adams and Biddle further found that student participation is restricted by the environment or physical setting itself in ways in which neither the teacher nor students seem to be aware. It appeared to them that students who sit in the center of the room are the most active learners, or what they called "responders." The verbal interaction is so concentrated in this area of the classroom and in a line directly up the center of the room, where the teacher is in front most of the time, that they coined the term "action zone" to refer to this area (Figure 8.1).

Teachers who are student centered, indirect, and warm or friendly, as opposed to teacher centered, direct, and businesslike, tend to reject the traditional formal seating pattern of rows of students directly facing the teacher at the front of the classroom. Formal seating patterns tend to reduce student-to-student eye contact and student interaction and increase teacher control and student passivity. Student-centered teachers tend to favor informal seating patterns, such as rectangular (seminar), circular, and horseshoe (U-shaped) patterns, in which students face each other as well as the teacher (Figure 8.2).

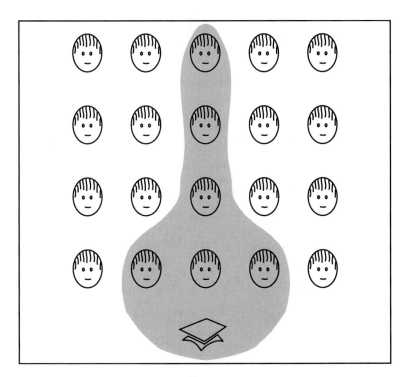

Front

figure 8.1   Classroom action zone.

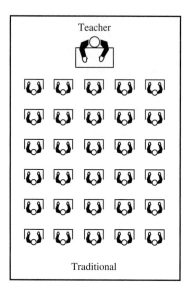

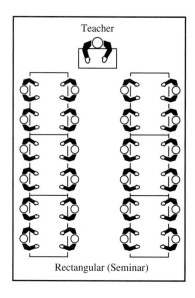

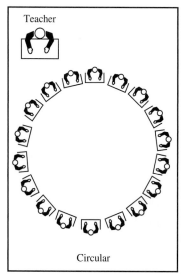

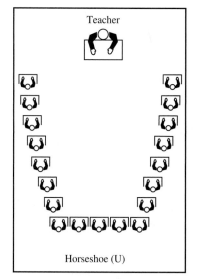

The teacher's desk is at the corner to avoid
neck strain among students in the front of
the classroom.

figure 8.2   Four seating patterns.

Some conservative reform critics would argue against using student-centered instruction and seating patterns. Others who are more progressivist in their approach
(and student centered in orientation) would argue for more open (and less traditional)
classroom arrangements. Neither argument is absolutely right. Your *goals* for instruction dictate how you arrange the classroom. A direct instruction lesson might require a

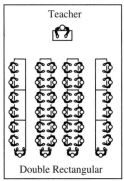

Teacher

Double Rectangular

Having rows of students separated by tables prevents students from sitting too close to each other and reduces potential discipline problems.

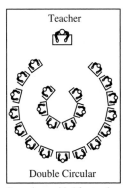

Teacher

Double Circular

Space is provided for teacher to move around and into smaller circle.

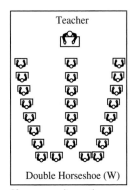

Teacher

Double Horseshoe (W)

If space permits, seating may be arranged to form a double U instead of a W.

figure 8.3   Three modified seating patterns.

traditional student-in-rows format. A jigsaw, cooperative learning lesson focused on the causes and consequences of the Civil War might require a very different classroom arrangement. Your learning goals, in essence, determine your classroom arrangement.

Special Classroom Designs

The rectangular, circular, and horseshoe arrangements in Figure 8.2 assume there are no more than twenty to twenty-five students. Double rectangular, double circular, and double horseshoe (W-shaped) arrangements are needed to accommodate more than twenty-five students (Figure 8.3).

An open classroom seating arrangement is appropriate for elementary, middle grade, and junior high school students (Figure 8.4). The many shelves, tables, and work areas allow for small-group and individualized instruction. The formal rows of fixed desks of the traditional classroom are gone. The desks are arranged in groups or clusters that can be moved. The open classroom increases student interaction and gives students the opportunity to move around and engage in different learning activities in different settings.

Figure 8.5 shows two additional seating designs—both of which correspond to special activities. The design on the left is well suited for whole-class debates and forums. The design on the right is conducive to cooperative learning or "buzz sessions." Whereas the seating patterns in Figures 8.2, 8.3, and 8.4 are home-based or permanent arrangements, the ones in Figure 8.5 are temporary designs.

Because of the resulting increased student interaction, discipline problems may arise with these special seating arrangements, unless the teacher has good managerial skills (see Chapter 9). However, all these designs allow the teacher flexibility in activities. They create feelings of group cohesion and cooperation, they allow students to work in small groups, and they also allow the teacher to present a demonstration, lead the class in a brainstorm or debate, or use audiovisual materials, among other methods.

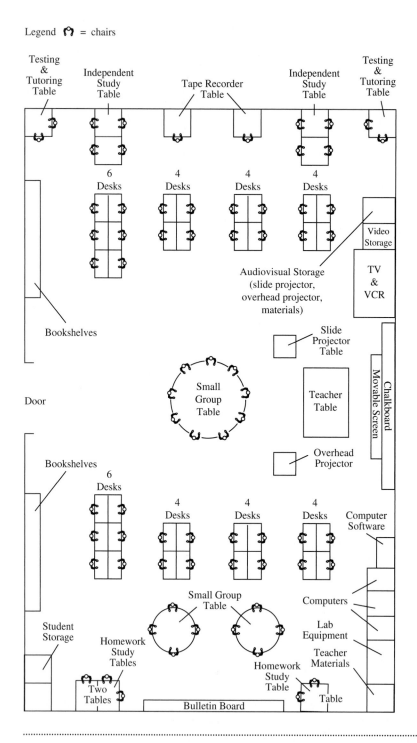

figure 8.4   An open-classroom seating pattern.

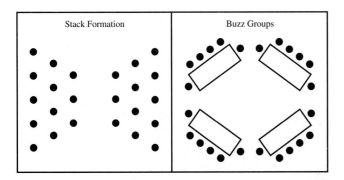

figure 8.5   Special Classroom Formation to Help Students in Groups.

Factors to Consider in Classroom Designs

Classroom design will be determined by the size of the room; the number of students in the class; the size and shape of tables and chairs; the amount of movable furniture; the location of fixed features such as doors, windows, closets, and chalkboard; the audiovisual equipment to be used; the school's philosophy; and the teacher's approach and experience. Several factors should be considered in arranging the classroom:

1. *Fixed features:* The teacher cannot change the "givens" of a room and must take into account the locations of doors, windows, closets, electric outlets, and so forth. For example, seats should not be too close to doors or closets. Electric equipment needs to be near an outlet, and wires should not run across the center of the room. (If they must, they should be taped to the floor.)

2. *Traffic areas:* High traffic areas, such as supply areas, the area around closets, and space near the pencil sharpener and wastebasket, need to be open and easily accessible. The teacher's desk should be located in a low traffic area.

3. *Work areas:* Work areas and study areas should be private and quiet, preferably in the corners or rear of the room, away from traffic lanes and noisy areas.

4. *Furniture and equipment:* The room, furniture, and equipment should be kept clean and in repair so that they can be used. Desks and chairs may be old, but they should be clean and smooth (make the appropriate requisition to the janitorial department or supervisor), and graphics and doodling on furniture should be discouraged immediately. The equipment should be stored in a designated space.

5. *Instructional materials:* All materials and equipment should be easily accessible so activities can begin and end promptly and clean up time can be minimized. Props and equipment that are not stored in closets should be kept in dead spaces away from traffic.

6. *Visibility:* The teacher should be able to see all students from any part of the room to reduce managerial problems and enhance instructional supervision. Students

Many factors determine classroom design.

should be able to see the teacher, chalkboard, projected images, and demonstrations without having to move their desks and without straining their necks.

7. *Flexibility:* The classroom design should be flexible enough so that it can be modified to meet the requirements of different activities and different groupings for instruction. As you look at your classroom flexibility, make certain that you are able to see all students and that all students can see you during whole class presentations.[3]

Elementary teachers often need to be more flexible, since they are teaching several subjects; they *can* be more flexible, since they rarely share the room with other teachers. The room is theirs in which to set up learning areas, interest areas, and work and study areas for reading, mathematics, science, and arts and crafts. At the secondary level, where teachers teach one subject and several teachers may share a room, the possibilities are reduced, but the room can still be divided into areas for small groups, audiovisual activities, projects, and independent study. Cooperation among the teachers who share the room is essential for a positive school climate.

Unfortunately, too few high school teachers are flexible in their classroom arrangements. Students usually sit in rows, facing the chalkboard and teacher, just as they did 100 years ago. One possible explanation is that most high school teachers stress content and ignore socialization and personal relations as classroom goals.

Only through experience and time will teachers learn if a given arrangement suits their teaching style and the needs of their students. It may take several tries and continual revision to come up with a classroom design that helps students work efficiently, in which materials and equipment can be used to their best advantage, from which unnecessary equipment is removed, and where the teacher finds it easy to instruct and to supervise the students.

Whole-Group Instruction

Whole-group instruction is the most traditional and common form of classroom organization. Teachers generally gear their teaching to the "mythical" average student on the assumption that this level of presentation will meet the needs of the greatest number of students. A common block of content (in any subject) is taught through whole-group instruction on the assumption that it is the most effective and convenient format for teaching it.[4]

In the large group, the teacher lectures, explains, and demonstrates material related to a topic, asks and answers questions in front of the entire class, provides the same practice and drill exercises to the entire class, works on the same problems with the entire class, and employs the same materials with all students. Instruction is directed toward the whole group, but the teacher may ask specific students to answer questions, monitor specific students as they carry out the assigned activities, and work with students on an individual basis.

Whole-group instruction can be an economical and efficient method. As we discussed in Chapter 5, this method is especially convenient for teaching the same skills or subject content to the entire class, administering tests, or setting group expectations. Bringing members of a class together for certain activities strengthens the feeling of belonging and can help establish a sense of community and class spirit. The whole group learns to cooperate by sharing available resources, setting up rules and regulations for the learning environment, and exchanging ideas. This method of grouping students is most effective for large numbers of students, especially when the focus is on learning distinct skills or processes (see Tips for Teachers 8.1). It is also one of the most common forms of instruction, despite the fact that a wide variety of educators have encouraged teachers to incorporate instructional alternatives that are more student centered.[3] Whole-group instruction is often used in conjunction with small group instruction: When working with whole groups, teachers usually present new information to the total group and then have students split off into smaller groups for review and practice or enrichment activities.

The critics of whole-group instruction contend that it fails to meet the needs and interests of individual students. Teachers who use this method tend to look upon students as a homogeneous group with common abilities, interests, styles of learning, and motivation. Instruction is geared to a hypothetical average student—a concept that only fits a few students in the class—and all students are expected to learn and perform within narrow limits. Students are evaluated, instructional methods and materials are selected, and learning is paced on the basis of the group average, with a tendency for high-achieving students eventually to become bored and low-achieving students eventually to become frustrated.[5] The uniqueness of each student is often lost in the large group context. Extroverted students tend to monopolize the teacher's time, and passive students usually are not heard from or do not receive necessary attention. Finally, students sometimes act out their behavioral problems in teacher-centered whole-group instructional formats.

tips for teachers 8.1

Components of Direct Instruction

 Evidence suggests that for teaching low-achieving and at-risk students in the whole-group setting, a high-structured approach is the most effective method. This approach today is often called *direct instruction* or *explicit instruction*. We discussed it in Chapter 5. The major aspects of direct instruction listed here are especially appropriate for teaching a specific skill, concept, or process:

1. Begin a lesson with a short statement of goals (and anchor those goals to defined academic standards).
2. Review previous, prerequisite learning.
3. Present new material in small steps, with student practice after each step.
4. Provide clear and detailed instructions and explanations.

5. Provide a high level of active practice for all students, and call on a variety of volunteers and nonvolunteers.
6. Guide students during initial practice and monitor and assess the ongoing practice of the students.
7. Check for student understanding by asking many questions of all students.
8. Provide systematic feedback and corrections.
9. Monitor and help students during seat work and independent practice.
10. Provide for review, testing, and assessment.

Source: Adapted from Barak Rosenshine. "Explicit Teaching and Teacher Training." *Journal of Teacher Education* (May–June 1987): 34. Since Rosenshine published his work on explicit instruction in the 1970s and 1980s, a variety of subtle variations have been introduced by all who have an interest in this form of instruction. The steps outlined are fundamental to the explicit approach and should be evidenced in any lesson that uses this approach.

Different group patterns are essential for variety, motivation, and flexibility in teaching and learning. They are also essential for meeting the needs of diverse learners who are now a part of American classrooms. Eugene Garcia describes teachers who are effective with language minority students:

> These [successful] teachers [of language minority students] organized a good portion of class time around a series of learning activities that children pursue either independently or with others. During science and math, children work in small groups doing a variety of hands-on activities designed to support their understanding of a particular concept . . . or subject. . . .[6]

To work effectively with the wide variety of students in whole-group learning classrooms, many educators are actively arguing for smaller classes, especially in the early grades. In the next section, we will discuss the research on class size. Clearly, the number of students you have makes a difference. The issue is how much of a difference in student achievement occurs if teachers have smaller classes?

Class Size and Achievement

Does class size affect whole-group learning? Some state legislatures think it does. In the late 1990s, California embraced smaller class size as a way of dealing with the learning needs of young children. Has it made a difference? Many researchers question whether slightly smaller class size makes a difference in achievement. (California looked at classes of twenty children, and Tennessee's Project STAR focused on classes of fifteen children). The key seems to be the interaction between class size and the effectiveness of the teacher's instructional practices. That is, a large class with an effective teacher may be better than a smaller class with an ineffective teacher. Indeed, many who are interested in class size effects are now calling for research that investigates the relationship between class size and the factors that help students learn.[7]

When it comes to improving student performance, common sense would indicate that there is a clear relationship between class size and student achievement. Conservative critics suggest that class size does not automatically lead to better student performance. For example, in one review of 152 studies that analyzed smaller classes and student achievement, 82 percent found no significant impact, 9 percent saw positive results, and about 9 percent found negative results.[8] That research has now been influenced by additional research that illustrates some of the complications (financial and practical) of smaller class size. For example, the California class size "experiment" resulted in many poorly qualified teachers being placed in classrooms. Nearly all schools needed more teachers, but schools in poor urban environments added the fewest number of highly qualified teachers.

In still another review of eight studies of low-achieving students, Robert Slavin found that differences in achievement levels of students in larger classes (twenty-two to thirty-seven students) compared to small classes (fifteen to twenty students) were insignificant. Across the eight studies the effect was only +.13—a low figure given that the average class size in the large groups was twenty-seven students compared to sixteen in the small groups (a 40 percent difference).[9] In another review, Slavin found that only when class size is reduced to a one-to-one teacher/student ratio, as in tutoring, does size make a truly dramatic difference.[10]

Although Glass and his colleagues received considerable attention when they concluded that class size under fifteen students had a positive effect on student achievement, the actual impact was only significant in a limited number of studies. Learning benefits did not really appear until class size was reduced to a very small number of students (three). The effects of class size and achievement were more positive in elementary grades than in middle grades and high school.[11]

In the largest single study ever performed (in Tennessee), kindergarten students were randomly assigned to classes of fifteen and twenty-five with an aide, and twenty-five without an aide; these configurations were retained through third grade. The study attributed almost zero impact to the presence of aides and only moderate positive effects to the smaller class size by the time students reached third grade; by the time the students were entering fourth grade, the difference was positive but insignificant.[12] Other statewide studies in Indiana and South Carolina at the primary level showed modest achievement effects when class sizes were reduced.[13]

At the secondary level, however, the impact of class size seems to have no significant influence on student achievement.[14] One possible reason is that class size may have different effects with different tracks (honors, academic, vocational, etc.); different subjects (English, social studies, etc.); different students (prior ability, motivation, study habits, high achieving versus low achieving); and/or different presentation of content (consistent review and practice, problem solving, questioning or discussion)—variables that may blur research results.

If reduced class size seems to have modest effects overall on school achievement and since reduction in class size is expensive (the cost in California is by some estimates close to one billion dollars), that cost should be weighed against the cost of other innovations to determine the best policy or programs for fostering academic achievement. For example, research suggests that increasing school attendance among students, increasing academic time in reading (or any other subject area), improving the quality of instruction (hiring better teachers for low-achieving students), and providing more review or practice for learning the material on tests have more positive effects than just reducing class size.[15]

Dividing the whole group (say twenty-five students) into smaller, homogeneous groups (four or five), with the teacher spending more time with the low-achieving groups is perhaps more beneficial than small whole-group instruction (say, fifteen students), as long as the teacher knows how to take advantage of the extra time for the low-achieving groups without shortchanging the other groups. Such different grouping patterns within whole groups also are essential for variety, motivation, and flexibility in teaching and learning.

What can we conclude? First, American schools have been trying to reduce the size of classes for years. In the 1970s, classes averaged 22.3 students, and in the 1990s, the average class size was 17, and some research from the *Digest of Education Statistics* suggests that in the early 2000s the class sizes are now getting even smaller.[16] Second, whether smaller class size makes a difference is difficult to ascertain. Through an analysis of National Assessment of Educational Progress (NAEP) data, Johnson examined variables related to race and ethnicity, parents' education, reading materials in a child's home, free and reduced lunch participation, gender and, of course, class size. Johnson concluded the following:

> After controlling for all these factors, researchers found that the difference in reading achievement on the 1998 NAEP reading assessment between students in small classes and students in large classes was statistically insignificant. That is, across the United States students in small classes did no better on average than those in large classes, assuming otherwise identified circumstances.[17]

Does that mean schools should not strive for smaller classes? Not if resources are available! What the class size research suggests, however, is that the key to a good learning environment is the teacher. That news is good for you. You are the key factor that will make a difference in a student's learning. Whether you have twenty-five or fifteen students, their learning depends primarily on what you do to structure the classroom into a meaningful environment. The tasks you assign and the learning experiences you arrange mean more than the number of students you have in the class.

QUESTIONS FOR REFLECTION

Although the relationship between class size and student achievement is unclear, class size can influence the quality of a teacher's life and students' educational experiences. For example, it is logical (and documented) that fewer students in a class result in fewer management and discipline problems for the teacher.[18] With smaller classes the teacher has a better set of options for dealing with the problems that do emerge. The teacher can use more one-on-one or personalized disciplinary techniques with fewer students. Consider factors other than discipline and management that may be influenced by class size: assessment of student learning, the use of effective teaching practices, the creation of a positive classroom learning community, and the time available to work with individual students.

Consider each of these "other factors" and compare results from having fifteen students as opposed to twenty-five. Also, are there times when larger classes are more advantageous? Why? Another issue to consider is why, even with smaller classes, the instructor tends not to change how instruction is delivered. Holloway documents that, even with smaller classes, teachers make "no substantial changes in their content coverage, grouping practices, or pedagogical strategies."[19] If that is true, what would be the argument for smaller classes?

Classroom Tasks

Instructional tasks are at the core of decisions about the classroom setting. Most teachers maintain control over instructional tasks by choosing what is to be taught, what materials and methods are to be used, and how much students are to be allowed to interact.

With the current emphasis on academic standards in most states, this circumstance is even more true than it was several years ago. Secondary school classrooms tend to be more controlled settings than elementary school classrooms. The key variable, of course, is the teacher and not the grade level. When the teacher has complete control over instruction, it is likely that most students, if not all, will be engaged in a single classroom task at one time and work toward the same goal with the same content. There are teachers, however, who do permit student input in planning content and activities. When students have input, it is likely that they will work on different classroom tasks.[20]

Teacher control over tasks affects the social setting and nature of evaluation. Under single-task conditions with high teacher control, students usually work alone, and evaluation of academic abilities and achievement is based on comparison to others in the class or to standardized achievement levels. Under multiple-task conditions with low teacher control, there is more social interaction and cooperative learning. Evaluation is conducted more on the basis of individual progress than on comparison to others.[21]

Classroom learning falls into one of three basic categories: 1) knowledge or facts (i.e., what is the capital of Chile?); 2) skills (i.e., reading, writing, spelling, computer literacy); or 3) high-order thinking processes (i.e., analysis, problem solving, concepts).[22] A majority of classroom tasks initiated by teachers in traditional classrooms are what might be called low level cognitive processes, involving facts or skills. Only a small portion are high-order cognitive tasks. The reason is that in a whole-group classroom setting, the range of ability is usually wide, and it is easier to keep things simple and focused so students can perform the tasks without frustration. Focusing on low-level tasks, facts or skills, and right answers, emphasizes short-term goals at the expense of critical thinking and integration of prior and past knowledge for long-term benefits. The idea is for the student to know the answer, not the process, and to complete the assignment on time and to get it out of the way (as if it were like taking medicine). Interestingly, one way that you can foster more process oriented (higher order) answers on the part of students is to engage yourself in more reflection about the lessons you teach. Your in-depth reflection will lead to more high level student thinking.

Most classroom tasks are initiated and structured by the teacher and focus on the acquisition and comprehension of knowledge. Students usually act in response to the teacher's expectations. Basically, classroom tasks that are initiated by the teacher fall into four categories: 1) incremental tasks, which focus on new skills or ideas and require recognition; 2) restructuring tasks, which involve the discovery of an idea or pattern and require some reorganization of data; 3) enrichment tasks, which involve application of familiar skills and ideas to new problems; and 4) practice tasks, which are aimed at making new skills and ideas automatic so they can be used in other task situations and for other cognitive processes.

In order to facilitate learning, the teacher must learn to match appropriate tasks with the students' abilities and background knowledge. Matching becomes more difficult as students get older and have the potential to learn more. It is also more difficult in heterogeneously grouped classrooms because of the range in students' abilities and interests. The teacher must consider which tasks contribute most to students' learning and when it is appropriate to introduce these tasks so students gain new insights and skills.

Success in matching can be judged by student performance. The more errors that students make in working on the tasks, the greater the mismatch. Fewer errors mean that students are capable of working on the tasks but not necessarily that a good match has been made, because the tasks may be too easy to contribute to learning. "Matched" tasks are at an appropriate level of difficulty and foster learning. "Mismatched" tasks are either too easy or too difficult. Matching tasks to student learning needs is one of the biggest challenges that new teachers and experienced teachers face. For example, the pattern of over- and underestimation of tasks was found in a study of twenty-one third- to sixth-grade classes in math, language arts, and social studies.[23] In this study 500 academic tasks were analyzed, and the extent of mismatching was significant for both high- and low-achieving students.

Teachers tend more often to overestimate than underestimate tasks. In fact, in the study cited, no teacher saw any task as too easy. Both types of mismatching lead to failure to meet the needs of the students. When tasks are underestimated, too many students are not learning up to potential, and they also may become bored. When tasks are overestimated, too many students fail to learn because they don't understand what they are being asked to do, and they are likely to become discouraged. If the assumption that matching becomes more difficult in the upper grades is correct, then mismatching may help explain why so many students drop out of school at adolescence. Far too many tasks are either too difficult or too easy for them to accomplish. As a result, they fail to understand the relevance of the tasks they are assigned.

Actually, understanding classroom tasks is not an "all-or-nothing" experience. Students seldom experience flashes of insight while in a classroom. Rather, they gain gradual understanding with further practice or explanation, as well as through exposure to a variety of tasks. High achievers more often than low achievers have a larger knowledge base (i.e., more prior learning that helps them acquire the new information faster) in the subject so they quickly integrate relevant information pertaining to the tasks; moreover, they have more confidence in their ability to learn so they remain on task and work on various tasks for longer periods without giving up. In fact, some are even challenged by difficult tasks. Not so for low achievers. Low achievers are often frustrated by difficult tasks—and easily give up. That is why varied instructional approaches are needed. Teachers who group students in one way (e.g., teacher-centered classrooms) give more advantage to one group of students (typically the high achievers—who need no advantage) and give more disadvantage to another group—the low achievers. Cooperative (student-centered) learning approaches, coupled with teacher-centered instruction, potentially maximize the learning for all students, especially if

1. students know why they are being asked to work together.

2. students are shown how to interact with one another.

3. student groups systematically analyze and reflect on their own effectiveness.[24]

A good deal of concept learning (high-order tasks) involves multidimensional understanding, not singular or specific representations.[25] That means that, in presenting new concepts such as symmetry, you need to help students learn the material in a number of different ways (e.g., drawing lines of symmetry on figures and having students look at different visual representations). A single task, or approach, repeated several times, may not represent effectively all features of a concept but rather captures only particular concept attributes. Thus, low-level tasks accompanied by concrete materials, often designed for low achievers, may have their limitations since this instructional approach fails to capture all the representations needed for full understanding. Thus the cycle of low achievement may be repeated by the way classroom tasks (involving facts and skills) are introduced by teachers. Think of this dilemma when you introduce tasks in your own classroom.

Instructional Variables

Researchers are focusing on elements of the classroom that teachers and schools can change, or what some call *alterable environments,* for purposes of measuring the effect they have on student achievement. According to Robert Slavin, there are four components of instruction: 1) quality of instruction, 2) appropriate level of instruction, 3) incentives to work on instructional tasks, and 4) time needed to learn tasks. He concludes that all four components must be adequate for instruction to be effective. For example, if the quality of instruction is low, it matters little how much students are motivated or how much time they have to learn.[26] Notice also that all four of these are matters that you as a teacher can control. Although there are limits to the total amount of time you have with students, you can dictate what you do with students when they are in your classroom.

Several years ago, Benjamin Bloom listed nineteen teaching and instructional variables based on a summary of several hundred studies conducted during the past half century. His research synthesized the impact these variables have on student achievement. The five most effective ones in rank order are 1) tutorial instruction (1:1 ratio), 2) instructional reinforcement, 3) feedback and correction, 4) cues and explanations, and 5) student class participation. The next most effective variables for student achievement are 6) improved reading and study skills, 7) cooperative learning, 8) graded homework, 9) classroom morale, and (10) initial cognitive prerequisites.[27]

Bloom concluded that the quality and quantity of instruction (teacher performance and time devoted to instruction) are the most important factors related to teaching and learning. Most of the instructional variables that are effective tend to be emphasized in individualized and small-group instruction. Bloom assumed that two or three variables "used together contribute to more learning than any one of them alone, especially those in the first five rankings."[28] In essence, it is not any one thing that you do but the array of practices that you have in place that begin to influence student achievement.

More recently, Good and Brophy have highlighted the notion that how the teacher behaves and arranges the learning environment and who he or she is teaching make a difference. Good teaching is not about doing one thing right but rather doing a combination of things correctly, purposefully, and in a timely manner. Good teachers alter how they arrange the class environment (whole class versus small group) and the focus of their teaching (thinking skill oriented versus learning time oriented). Good and Brophy write,

> Research findings sometimes reflect these complexities. . . . [For example] the effects of two contrasting interventions on fourth-grade students' mathematics achievement [have been compared by researchers]. In the thinking skills intervention, teachers learned how to teach the cognitive strategies of defining and describing, thinking of reasons, comparing, and summarizing. In the learning time intervention, teachers learned how to increase students' engagement and academic learning time. The researchers expected that the thinking skills intervention would produce better results than the learning time intervention, but the effects differed according to student achievement level. Higher-achieving classes did better with the thinking skills intervention, but lower-achieving classes did better with the learning time intervention. Within the classes that received the thinking skills intervention, however, lower achievers benefited more than the higher achievers. Thus, the same treatment can have different effects on different types of students.[29]

The general conclusion is that the classroom environment—that is, both the quality and quantity of instruction—can and must be modified for the students' benefit. The instructional variables (what you teach and how you teach it) provide excellent guidelines for improving instruction. The variables seem to be effective across school districts, ethnicity and gender, grade level, classroom size, and subject area. They deal mainly with the process, not with inputs or educational spending. They call attention to classroom variables that can be altered, rather than to such practices as IQ testing or to various cognitive deficits of students. You determine what can be altered. You decide how to adjust learning time for the whole group and when to develop thinking skills within small groups.

Guidelines for Teaching Whole Groups

When teaching whole groups or regular classes of twenty or more students, it is important to be organized and to start on time. You need to make good use of allocated time. Here are some practical suggestions to get the instructional ball rolling on the right path:

1. Be in the room before the class arrives. Your appearance helps the class start on time.
2. Ready your materials: attendance book, lesson plans, and other instructional materials (charts, pictures, maps) that you may need.

3. Obtain the full attention of the students. Start the students on a review exercise, warm-up drill, or set of problems. Explain instructions clearly and be sure students begin the assignment.

4. Attend to special student needs. While the students are completing the assignment, respond to special student requests or problems. Attend to one student at a time; otherwise, you may lose control.

5. Circulate among students. This bolsters classroom management and ensures that students are prepared with books, pens, assignments, and the like.

6. Check notebooks, homework, or other written work. If time permits, check to see that students have their notebooks, homework, or texts with them.

7. Review assignments. Take extra time to discuss or reteach specific aspects of the assignment.

8. Summarize the lesson. Learn to pace your lesson. Remind students that classwork continues until you give the word that the class has ended.

Small-Group Instruction

Dividing students into small groups seems to provide an opportunity for students to become more actively engaged in learning and for teachers to monitor student progress better. Between five and eight students seems to be an optimal number to ensure successful small-group activity. When there are fewer than five, especially in a group discussion, students tend to pair off rather than interact as a group.[30]

Small groupings can enhance student cooperation and social skills. Appropriate group experiences foster the development of democratic values, cultural pluralism, and appreciation for differences among people. Small-group instruction can provide interesting challenges, permits students to progress at their own pace, provides a psychologically safe situation in which to master the material, and encourages students to contribute to class activities.

Dividing the class into small groups helps the teacher monitor work and assess progress through questioning, discussions, and checking workbook exercises and quizzes geared for the particular group. Small groups also give the teacher a chance to introduce new skills at a level suited to particular students. Because the number of students assigned to each group is often determined by their progress, group size will vary. Students may move from group to group if their progress exceeds or falls below that of their assigned group. In effect, the teacher is using grouping to restructure a heterogeneously grouped class into several homogeneous subgroups.

Small groups are typically used in elementary school reading and mathematics. The teacher divides the class into two or three groups, depending on the number of students, their range of ability, and the number of groups the teacher is able to handle. The teacher usually works with one group at a time, while the other students do seat work or independent work.

The use of small groups can be extended beyond the typical grouping in elementary reading and mathematics to all grade levels and subjects. There are several other

Small group instruction plays an important role in the teaching-learning process.

reasons to form small groups: 1) special interests or skills in a particular topic or activity; 2) ability grouping or regrouping within a class for specific subjects (reading or mathematics) or specific content (different assignments or exercises), thus reducing the problems of heterogeneity in the classroom; and (3) integration, to enhance racial, ethnic, religious, or gender relations.

Regardless of the basis of the grouping, assignments given to small groups should be specific enough and within the range of the students' abilities and interests so that each group can work on its own without teacher support. This permits the teacher to single out one group for attention or to help individuals by explaining, questioning, redirecting, and encouraging.

Ability Grouping

The most common means of dealing with heterogeneity is to assign students to classes and programs according to ability. In high schools, students may be tracked into college preparatory, vocational or technical, and general programs. In many middle and junior high schools, students are sometimes assigned or ***ability grouped,*** to a class by ability and stay with that class as it moves from teacher to teacher. In a few cases, and more often in elementary schools, students are assigned to a class on the basis of a special characteristic, such as being gifted, handicapped, or bilingual. Elementary schools may use several types of ability grouping. In addition to the types used in the secondary schools, they may assign students to a heterogeneous class and then regroup them homogeneously by ability in selected areas, such as reading and mathematics.

Despite widespread criticism of **between-class ability grouping** (separate classes for students of different abilities), many teachers support the idea because of the ease of teaching a homogeneous group. In addition, many parents of high-achieving students perceive tracking to be in their children's best interests. Reality is also a consideration. By the time students are in middle school, the achievement and motivation gaps between the top third and lowest third achievers have grown extremely wide, and teachers cannot accommodate this range of student abilities. Hence, the norms of the school culture resist detracking.[31] In addition, a number of neoconservative education reform critics debunk detracking because they believe it results in "teaching to the average."

One primary criticism of separating students by ability is that it results in low expectations for low-ability students, lowered self-esteem, less instruction time, less homework, less learning, and worst of all, a compounding and stigmatizing effect on low achievers.[32] The negative consequences of these practices disproportionately affect minorities and female students in math classrooms. Given our democratic norms and the need to deal with diversity in schools (and society) and given the notion that abilities are multifaceted and developmental (not genetic), differences in abilities can become assets in classrooms rather than liabilities.[33]

Researchers have found that high-ability students benefit from separate ability groups because the curriculum and instruction are tailored to the students' abilities, and the classroom work and homework driving the group require extra effort. There are fewer competing values that curtail the academic ethos, and less time is devoted to management problems.[34]

But such arguments tend to run up against democratic thinking—that is, the drive to reduce inequality and differences (including outcomes) that may exist between high- and low-achieving students. Ability-grouping critics contend that the gains made by high achievers do not compensate for the loss of self-esteem and achievement among low achievers who often find themselves slotted into groups where the instruction is less engaging. It is not clear, however, whether performance of low-achieving groups suffers because the students themselves are less responsive, because of management problems, or because the instruction is really inferior, as critics suggest.

After reviewing sixty years of research on the issue, Slavin claimed that the achievement gains of all students (high and low achieving) in ability-grouped classes canceled each other out or "clustered closely around zero."[35] In other words, ability grouping rarely adds to overall achievement in a school (although it may for a particular class), but it often contributes to inequality (highs do better, lows do worse). In addition, studies show that instruction in mixed-ability, untracked classes more closely resembles instruction in high-achieving and middle-track classes than it does instruction in low-track classes—that is, the mixed-ability grouping tends to benefit low-ability students.[36] Similarly, average-ability students who are grouped in high-ability math classes achieve significantly higher math grades and higher scores on achievement tests than do their cohorts who are placed in average classes, perhaps since their teachers have higher expectations for them and the content is more advanced.[37]

No consensus from the research is evident to suggest exactly what teachers and administrators should do with regard to between-class ability grouping. However, some policy implications do emerge. Good and Brophy suggest, for example, that between-class ability grouping (or tracking) "should be minimized, should be delayed as long as possible, and when used, should be confined to grouping by curriculum rather than by ability or achievement."[38]

Within-class ability grouping, on the other hand, has been assessed as effective for almost all students. This is especially true if the groups are fluid and evolving. Students in heterogeneous classes who are regrouped homogeneously learn more than students in classes that do not use such grouping. This is especially true in reading and mathematics, for which within-class grouping is common, as well as for low-achieving students.[39]

The research data suggest that a small number of within-class groups (two or three) is better than a large number, permitting more monitoring by and feedback from the teacher and less seat work time and transition time.[40] For example, in a class of three ability groups, students spend approximately two-thirds of the time doing seat work without direct supervision; but with four groups they spend three-quarters of the class time doing seat work without the teacher monitoring their work.

When within-class ability groups are formed, students proceed at different paces on different materials. The tasks and assignments tend to be more flexible than those in between-class groups. Teachers also tend to try to increase the tempo of instruction and the amount of time for instruction in low-achieving within-class groups to bring students closer to the class mean.[41] There is less stigma for low-ability groups in within-class grouping than in between-class grouping, since grouping is only for part of the day and the class is integrated the rest of the time. Regrouping plans tend to be more flexible than with between-class groups, because moving students from group to group is less disruptive within a class than it is between classes. Finally, regrouping is most beneficial when it is based on achievement levels that can be assessed frequently (but not daily or weekly), so students can be regrouped during the school terms and when teachers adapt their instruction to the level and pace of the students' abilities and needs. Tips for Teachers 8.2 provides a synthesis of practices that teachers should consider in dealing with ability grouping practices.

Two researchers describe two approaches to within-class ability grouping. *Structural grouping* occurs when teachers form groups and then proceed to instruction. The groups may be formed in a variety of ways, but the grouping occurs before instruction and is appropriate when grouping by curriculum area. *Situational grouping,* which is the preferred approach, occurs when teachers form groups after instruction. The teacher sees who needs review or reinforcement and then moves students into groups based on their immediate needs.[42] Above all, researchers tend to agree that homogeneous grouping should be practiced partially and not completely—that is the segregation of students into permanent groups is not appropriate.

Peer Tutoring

Peer tutoring is the assignment of students to help one another on a one-to-one basis or in small groups in a variety of situations. There are three types of pairing: 1) students may tutor others within the same class; 2) older students may tutor students in lower grades outside of class; or 3) two students may work together and help each other as equals on learning activities. The purpose of the first two types is to pair a student who needs assistance with a tutor on a one-to-one basis, although small groups of two or

Grouping Practices in Classrooms

 Teachers and schools can provide alternatives to grouping without ignoring the needs of high-achieving and exceptional students. Here are some recommendations to consider:

1. *Postpone tracking:* Defer tracking as late as possible and implement it only in selected subjects at the middle school level. Organize elementary grades around within-class ability groups in reading and mathematics.
2. *Limit tracking.* At the high school level, limit ability grouping to a few academic subjects in which student differences in skill areas are critical for whole-group instruction or prerequisite requirements influence each step of learning.
3. *Modify placement procedures:* The use of a single criterion—such as the student's rank, report card average, or score on a standardized test—to determine track placement is misleading. Replace it with the use of recent grades and tests in each subject area.
4. *Make group assignments flexible:* Disband groups once they have achieved their goals, and regroup students for a new task.

5. *Provide tutoring assistance:* Encourage students having academic difficulties to participate in special tutoring or coaching sessions (before or after school) before assigning them to a lower track. Find ways to provide lower-achieving students with extra help.
6. *Limit the degree to which group membership determines other school experiences:* Group members of a group (reading or math) only for the learning time they have on one topic or activity.
7. *Use instructional alternatives:* Consider other useful methods such as mastery learning, continuous progress, independent study, and ungraded plans—all which permit students to complete subject units at different rates—for heterogeneous classes.

Source: Adapted from Jomills H. Braddock and James P. McPartland. "Alternatives to Tracking." *Educational Leadership* (April 1990): 76–79. Jeannie Oakes and Martin Lipton. "Detracking Schools: Early Lessons from the Field." *Phi Delta Kappan* (February 1992): 448–454. Thomas L. Good and Jere E. Brophy. *Looking in Classrooms,* 8th ed. New York: Addison Wesley Longman, 2000, pp. 281–282.

three tutees and one tutor can also be formed. The purpose of the third type, called *peer pairing* or *cooperative learning,* is more than tutoring.

Of the three pairing arrangements, peer tutoring within the same class is the most common in elementary and middle schools. A student who has mastered specific material or who has completed a lesson and has shown understanding of the material is paired with a student who needs help. The research suggests that, because students are less threatened by peers, they are more willing to ask fellow students questions that they fear the teacher might consider "silly." Jeanne Ormrod reports that in one study students in peer teaching situations asked 240 times more questions than they did during whole-class teaching.[43] In addition, students are less afraid in peer tutoring that fellow students might criticize them for being unable to understand an idea or problem after a second or third explanation.[44] It has also been found that a fellow student is sometimes better able to explain a concept in language that another student can grasp. Unfamiliar vocabulary is cut to a minimum, and sometimes a few choice slang terms can make a difficult concept comprehensible. Also, because the faster student has just learned the concept, he may be more aware than the teacher of what is giving the slower student difficulty. Peer tutors benefit from the relationship; their own understanding is reinforced by explaining the idea or problem, and their social skills are enhanced.[45] The teacher benefits by having additional time to work with students who have more severe learning problems.

David and Roger Johnson find these advantages of peer tutoring:

1. Peer tutors are often effective in teaching students who do not respond well to adults.

2. Peer tutoring can develop a bond of friendship between the tutor and tutee, which is important for integrating slow learners into the group.

3. Peer tutoring allows the teacher to teach a large group of students, but still gives slow learners the individual attention they need.

4. Tutors benefit by learning to teach a general skill that can be useful in an adult society.[46]

The help that one student gives another can be explanatory or terminal. Explanatory help consists of step-by-step accounts of how to do something. Terminal help consists of correcting an error or giving the correct answer without explaining how to obtain the answer or solve the problem. Most studies of explanatory and terminal help conclude that giving explanations aids the tutor in learning the material, whereas giving terminal help does not.[47] In giving explanations the tutor clarifies the material in her own mind, may see new relationships, and builds a better grasp of the material. Giving terminal help involves little restructuring of concepts.

Not surprisingly, receiving explanatory help is correlated with achievement. Students who receive terminal help or receive no help tend to learn less than do students who receive explanatory help.[48] The benefit of receiving explanations seems to be that it fills in incomplete understandings of the material and corrects misunderstandings; it also increases effort and motivation to learn. Receiving terminal help or receiving no help is frustrating and causes students to lose interest in learning.

In two separate studies (involving eight and fifteen classrooms respectively), the most effective tutoring situations occurred when the tutor 1) elaborated information, 2) directed attention to task features, 3) offered procedural assistance, and/or 4) showed how to use information. The problem is, however, that most student tutors do not provide adequate explanations unless explicitly trained.[49] With proper tutor training and experience, student questions during tutoring sessions—one indicator of learning activity—increase dramatically compared to the normal classroom setting.

Student questions in whole-classroom settings are infrequent and unsophisticated. The estimated frequency of student questions per hour ranges from 1.3 to 4.0, with an average of 3.0. Given an average class of 26.7 for the studies conducted on the frequency of questioning, the number of questions per student for one hour is 0.11 (3 questions ÷ 26.7). On the other hand, teachers ask 30 to 120 questions per hour or an average of 69—with math teachers tending to ask the most questions. Therefore, about 96 percent of the questions in a regular classroom are formulated by teachers.[50]

The low frequency and low sophistication of student questions may be attributed to student difficulty in identifying their own knowledge deficits (their inability to understand when they don't know or to discriminate superficial from necessary information) and their loss of self-esteem or the social barriers involved in asking questions in front of their peers. A one-to-one tutoring situation removes many of the barriers. Tutors, if experienced or trained properly, can tailor questions or explanations to a particular deficit. Peer embarrassment is minimized by the privacy of the sessions.

Benjamin Bloom argues that tutoring (with preferably a 1:1 student-student ratio and no more than 3:1) is the most effective method of grouping for instruction compared to conventional methods (30:1 student-teacher ratio) and even mastery learning methods (which he helped develop) when the mastery methods are used in a class of about thirty students. Bloom found that as many as 90 percent of the tutored students and 70 percent of the mastery learning students attained a level of increased achievement reached by only 20 percent of the students who received conventional instruction over a three-week period.[51] Figure 8.6 compares achievement with conventional, mastery, and tutor instruction.

The most effective tutoring programs, both for tutors and tutees, have the following characteristics: 1) procedural rules established by the teacher, 2) instruction focused on basic skills and content, 3) no more than three tutees per tutor and ideally one tutee per tutor, and 4) tutorial sessions of short duration, about four to eight weeks.[52] When a tutorial program with these features is combined with regular classroom instruction, "the students being tutored not only learned more than they did without tutoring, they also developed a more positive attitude about what they were studying." In addition, the "tutors learned more than students who did not tutor."[53]

There are, of course, some drawbacks as well. Peer tutoring is problematic if tutors do not believe they can really help other students because they fear losing face

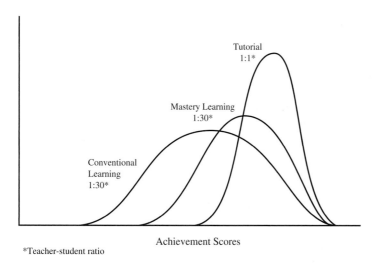

*Teacher-student ratio

....

figure 8.6   Achievement distribution for students with conventional, mastery learning, and tutor instruction.

Source: Benjamin S. Bloom, "The 2 Sigma Problem: The Search for Methods of Group Instruction as Effective as One-to-One Tutoring," in *Educational Researcher* (June–July 1984), 5. Reprinted by permission of the publisher.

(what happens if I can't help?) or if they perceive that they are too smart to help another student (why should I have to waste my time helping another student?). Teachers can limit these problems through the use of cross-age tutoring (fourth graders tutoring second graders) or through carefully constructed cooperative learning arrangements.

Guidelines for Peer Tutoring

Peer tutoring, like ability grouping, can be effective if implemented properly, but it takes substantial time and effort to get off to a good start. Following are some suggestions for effective peer tutoring:

1. Provide directions (or structure) for each tutor about time schedules and exactly what to do (for example, "Read the sentence to the group and get at least two students to identify the adjectives and nouns").
2. Prevent the tutor's assuming the role of substitute teacher. Where possible, use cross-age tutoring.
3. Be sure students understand their respective roles. The teacher should model appropriate tutor behavior and provide examples of what is to be achieved and how.
4. Plan tutoring arrangements so that tutors understand and use a mix of materials, media, and activities (for example, one week doing review and drill in the workbooks, the next week doing library research, the next week writing and discussing stories).
5. Inform parents of the organization, purpose, and procedures of the tutoring program.

Cooperative Learning

Cooperative learning is an instructional approach that received a lot of attention in the 1990s. It entails students working together in small groups instead of competing in a whole-group situation for recognition or grades. Rarely used in American classrooms before the 1970s, the idea is rooted in John Dewey's notion of group activities and group projects, as well as in his theories in *Democracy and Education* recommending that students work together to learn civic and social responsibility. Participating and sharing in mutual school experiences, Dewey maintained, prepares students for democratic living. Although reintroduced in the 1960s by Japanese educators to promote the ideal of teamwork and group effort, cooperative learning was popularized in the United States by Robert Slavin and the Johnsons (David and Roger) in the 1970s and 1980s.

In the traditional classroom structure, students compete for teacher recognition and grades, and the same students tend to be "winners" and "losers" over the years. High-achieving students continually receive rewards and are motivated to learn, and low-achieving students continually experience failure (or near-failure) and frustration, and subsequently many psychologically and then physically drop out of school. Reducing competition and increasing cooperation among students may diminish hostility, prejudice, and patterns of failure among many students.

This does not mean that competition has no place in the classroom or school. Even the advocates of cooperation feel that competition, under the right conditions and with

Meaningful Methods for Cooperative Learning

 Research on specific applications of cooperative learning, started in the 1970s, has now expanded in different parts of the world and includes various methods and techniques. Here are some practical questions for teachers to consider when organizing appropriate cooperative learning lessons:

1. Which cooperative learning model are you using? Why?
2. How did you form your groups? Did you consider ability, ethnicity, gender?
3. What objectives, directions, and timelines did the groups receive?
4. How did you motivate the students to perform as a group, to respect differences, and to interact with and accept peers from different ethnic, religious, or socioeconomic groups?
5. What have you observed about how the groups function? Do student groups use a variety of skills—reasoning, hypothesizing, predicting—or do they rely on rote procedures? Do students help one another understand concepts and skills?
6. What tasks will the groups be expected to perform during the cooperative lesson? Are the roles of students clear?
7. How will individual and group evaluation (academic and social) take place? Are students held accountable for individual learning through testing, individual work, or specific activities? Is the group accountable for its work and for the achievement of each member of the group?
8. Do you monitor group progress and intervene when necessary (when problems arise)? Do you merely provide answers, or do you assist groups in working out their problems?
9. Do you provide feedback about how progress is being made and about how problems can be resolved? Do you clarify, elaborate, and reteach when necessary?

evenly matched individuals or groups, can be a source of motivation, excitement, fun, and improved performance—for example, in simple drill activities, speed tasks, low-anxiety games, psychomotor activities, and athletics. Competition among groups is also accepted as a means for enhancing academic achievement for all grade levels and subjects, as long as two elements are present: group goals and individual accountability.[54] However, there are some data (a minority view) that suggest that group grading decreases individual motivation and lowers individual levels of performance, since the rewards are extrinsic. High-achieving students also feel the group activity is a waste of their time and express resentment in having to explain academic material to low achievers or uninterested students.[55]

According to a review of the research, cooperation among participants helps build 1) positive and coherent personal identity, 2) self-esteem, 3) knowledge and trust of others, 4) communication skills, 5) acceptance and support of others, 6) wholesome intergroup relationships, and 7) reduction of conflicts. The data also suggest that cooperation and group learning are considerably more effective in fostering these social and interpersonal skills than are competitive or individualistic efforts.[56] Most important, when cooperative learning methods are used, achievement effects are consistently positive compared to those of traditional methods. These conclusions applied in thirty-seven of forty-four controlled experiments at all grade levels (2–12); in all major subjects (although most of the research deals with grades 3–9 in reading and mathematics); and in a wide diversity of geographic settings[57] (see Tips for Teachers 8.3).

In cooperative learning, students divide the work among themselves, help one another (especially the slow members), praise and criticize one another's efforts and contributions, and receive a group performance score. It is not enough for a teacher simply to tell students to work together. They must have a reason and relate as a team. The idea is to create some form of interdependence "in such a way that each individual's actions benefit the group, and the group's actions benefit the individual."[58] The teacher needs to clarify learning goals, student roles, and expectations; divide resources within and among groups; provide tasks and rewards that promote team spirit; and, most important, provide some kind of incentive and recognition for individual achievement.

Formal cooperative learning strategies focus on some basic cooperative learning principles: positive interdependence between and among students, group processing of information, appropriate use of social skills, and individual and group accountability. For the formal groups, individual success and team success are easily tied together. Although some critics clearly articulate what they perceive as the damage done by formal types of structures (as a result of some intergroup competition), Robert Slavin and others have shown that formal structures can result in substantial increased student learning.

In formal cooperative learning, students share

- a goal to maximize the learning of all members.
- both individual and group responsibility for their learning goals.
- specific work goals that can be accomplished cooperatively.
- opportunities and obligations to learn and use interpersonal and small group skills.
- opportunities and obligations to reflect on both learning and peer interaction.[59]

The formal groups can take several different forms. Some are designed to work together for several days to complete a particular complex task. The following example by Marzano, Pickering, and Pollock illustrates this approach:

> Ms. Randall begins her high school economics lesson on trade and consumers by asking her 32 students to form eight groups of 4 by counting off from 1 to 8. The group members are each assigned a role: recorder, summarizer, technical advisor, and researcher. Each group is given the task of creating a product, using specific guidelines she has provided them. Over the course of four days, the students will work together to decide on a product, design it, and create a marketing display. They will try to sell their products to the other teams. Ms. Randall systemically monitors individuals and groups for social skills, problem-solving strategies, and group processing. She often asks students to self-assess on specific skills. In the final presentation of the product students must demonstrate their individual contributions, as well as the accomplishments of the group as a whole.[60]

Other formal cooperative learning approaches are structured around a particular team learning model. Student Teams-Achievement Divisions (STAD), Teams-Games-Tournaments (TGT), and Jigsaw are examples of team learning approaches:

> *Student Teams-Achievement Divisions (STAD):* Team membership consists of four students, based on heterogeneous abilities. The teacher presents the lesson to the whole group in one or two sessions, and then the class divides into teams for mastery. Students who have mastered the material help slower teammates. Drill and practice is stressed in groups, although students can engage in discus-

sion and questioning. Class quizzes are frequent, and student scores are averaged into a team score to ensure cooperation and assistance within groups. Quizzes are scored in terms of progress so that low-performing groups have the opportunity to gain recognition and improve. Team rewards are given based on the performance of the team as a "good," "great," or "super" team. Teams are changed every five or six weeks to give students an opportunity to work with other students and to give members of low-scoring teams a new chance.[61]

Teams-Games-Tournaments (TGT): Like STAD, TGT was developed by Robert Slavin. Instead of quizzes there are weekly "tournament tables" composed of three-member teams, with each member contributing points to the particular team score. Low achievers compete with other low achievers, and high achievers compete with other high achievers for equal points. Thus, the impact of low achievers is equal to that of high achievers. As with STAD, high-performing teams earn certificates or other team rewards. Student teams are changed weekly on the basis of individual performance to equalize them.[62]

Jigsaw: Originally designed for secondary schools (grades 7–12), Jigsaw has students work in small groups (four to five members) on specific academic tasks, assignments, or projects. They depend on each other for resources, information, and study assignments. Each team member becomes an "expert" in one area, meets with similar experts from other teams, and then returns to the original group to teach other team members.[63] After the time for team study, the students are tested and, once again based on each student's individual performance and the team performance, awards for "good," "great," and "super" team are given.

An example of a Jigsaw lesson is provided in Case Study 8.1: Cooperative Learning. Read the case study carefully to see whether you think it fits with the Jigsaw approach described here. How is it similar? Different? Also notice that for this case study the Pathwise criteria that relate to particular teacher behaviors or practices are identified in parentheses. The references to the criteria should help you think broadly about your teaching. Remember that Domain A (A) is planning and preparation, Domain B (B) is classroom environment, Domain C (C) is instruction and Domain D (D) is teacher professionalism.

Informal cooperative learning occurs when a teacher asks questions and then has students discuss among themselves or with the teacher a response, when teachers read stories or lecture and then ask questions, and when teachers ask questions in order to encourage students to summarize or synthesize ideas. Several forms of informal cooperative learning can be used. In general, informal approaches are clearly linked to other instructional strategies such as direct instruction. The following formats for informal groupings coupled with another teaching strategy such as direct instruction were developed by one educator:

1. Teacher asks a question that serves as an anticipatory set or advance organizer for the story, video, demonstration, or lecture that is to follow. Students discuss.

2. Teacher reads story, shows video, or delivers lecture—stopping every few minutes and asking students to discuss a teacher-prepared question or problem. Questions and problems might be factual or conceptual; they might

Heather McDonald teaches a fifth-grade class. The class has been studying the water cycle, the quantity of water on earth, and the limited amount of freshwater on earth. (A) She wants the class to understand what types of pollutants can seep into the freshwater supply and how these pollutants can damage wildlife. (A) She plans a lesson that spans two days.

On the first day, the goal for the class is to learn the definitions of the four major categories of pollution—chemical, thermal, organic, and ecological—and the types of pollutants that are classified under each category such as sediments, acid precipitation, and organic wastes. They will focus on a total of ten pollutants. (A) She uses the Jigsaw cooperative group arrangement to aid in the teaching of the lesson. (B) For the last two weeks the students have been in the same heterogeneous four-person groups known as Student Teams-Achievement Divisions (STAD). Ms. McDonald gives each STAD member a number from one to four. She divides them up into the new Jigsaw groups according to their numbers. She informs them that each member of the new group will become an expert on a particular pollution category and the types of pollutants that fall under each category. (B; C) Students work together for twenty minutes using resource materials to research the information, and then they return to their original STAD groups. Each expert member teaches the group about his or her category and the pollutants. Ms. McDonald moves around each group listening to the explanations. (C) After all members share their expertise, Ms. McDonald tells the class that this information will be used tomorrow in class. She briefly explains that tomorrow each group will receive a water sample of a different hypothetical river and analyze the pollutants in the sample based on the information they learned today. (A; C)

During her planning time later that day, Ms. McDonald makes and organizes the materials for the next day's lesson. She uses a resource book, Aquatic: Project WILD *by the Western Association of Fish and Wildlife Agencies and the Western Regional Environmental Education Council, to aid in lesson planning. She also cuts up different colored pieces of construction paper into one-inch square tokens. Each color represents a specific pollutant. She mixes them up and places them into four separate tubs, each representing a river. (A) Ms. McDonald checks to make sure there are enough materials for each group to complete the project successfully. (B)*

It is now 1:00 P.M. of the following day. The students come into the rooms, and Ms. McDonald greets them at the door. (B) They get settled into their groups. (B) Ms. McDonald restates that the information they learned yesterday will be put to use today. She explains that each group is a research team. Each team will take a freshwater sample from a different river. The goals of the group are to determine which rivers contain the most damaging pollutants to wildlife; to make inferences on how they may have appeared there; and to raise ideas as to how to diminish the amounts of these pollutants in the water source. (C; C)

She goes to the board and asks the class to give her the four categories of pollution and to briefly define them. The students successfully supply the answers. Then she asks for examples of the pollutants for each of the categories. As the class tells her the ten pollutants, she writes each one on the board in a different color of chalk. The class provides the answers in a swift manner, and she praises them on all being experts in the field. (B) She points out that the pollutants are written in chalk of specific colors and that these colors correspond to the color of pollutant in the water supply.

She explains the procedures of the activity. Each group will obtain a water sample, sort the contents by color, label each color group according to the pollutant's color, and make a bar graph that shows the level of each of the pollutants. She reminds them that each sample will be different because each water sample comes from a different river.

Ms. McDonald informs them that each team member of each research team will have a particular job. (B) She gives each group member a number from one to four. Before they begin the work in their groups, Ms. McDonald has them review the rules for group work, such as giving each person an opportunity to speak and correctly doing his or her assigned job. (B) She also mentions that they will be evaluated as a group on how well they work together, on how well they carry out each individual job, and on the graphing of the pollutants and the analysis of the pollutants. (A) She asks if there are any questions. There are none, probably due to the fact that the groups have been together for two weeks and are familiar with each other's work habits and with the cooperative group rules.

She asks for Researchers One from each group to come up to one of the rivers and take a water sample. Each person uses a $^1/4$-cup to scoop up the colorful tokens from the tub and spills the tokens into a sandwich bag.

Researchers Two from each group are asked to sort the tokens by color and label each pile by the pollutant's name according to the information on the board.

Ms. McDonald hands out a piece of graph paper and glue stick to each group. (B) She asks Researchers Three to count out the number of each kind of pollutant as Researchers Four graph the pollutants into a simple bar graph.

During each phase Ms. McDonald observes verbal conversations as well as the hands-on activity to see if the students are academically on task and working well together. (C) A student asks her a question about the task. She informs him to check with his group members first to see if they know the answer. They do and show him what to do. She notices one girl trying to pass the gluing onto a fellow member and overhears him say it is not his job, it is her job. The girl reluctantly begins gluing. Overall, she notes that the students are actively involved, and each is performing his or her job well and according to the instructions. (D)

When the bar graphs are complete, Ms. McDonald has the teams look at their graphs and discuss their findings. She reminds them that a pollutant with more than two tokens is considered a damaging pollutant to wildlife. She tells them to focus on these pollutants and to make inferences as to why that particular pollutant is found in this river and what can be done to lower the amount. (C) She also tells them to consider which pollutants are the most damaging to wildlife. She explains that each member is expected to participate fully and should be prepared to share this information with the class. She announces that Researchers Two should take notes. The groups discuss these questions for about fifteen minutes. Ms. McDonald asks Researchers One from each team to report the team's findings to the class. The class discusses these questions and possible solutions, what they learned from the activity, and what they can do in their lives to reduce the number of pollutants they are emitting into the environment. (C)

Ms. McDonald asks the class to take two or three minutes to focus on how well their group worked together, what did not go as well as expected, and what their group could do next time to improve its work. She walks around, listens to each group, and adds her opinion when necessary. (C)

At 1:50 P.M. the class is dismissed. (C) Ms. McDonald reflects on the lesson. Because she walked around, listened to discussions, and observed work from each group during the lesson she knows that the academic goals were met. As she focuses on the inferences made by the students and the evaluations made of the river samples, she feels they understand the importance of preserving our freshwater and how pollutants can damage wildlife. (D) Her next lesson will focus on water sources that contain a mixture of saltwater and freshwater, and types of species who live in these habitats. (A)

Questions for reflection:

1. Compare what Ms. McDonald did in this lesson to the steps articulated for the Jigsaw strategy. How is it consistent with the Jigsaw approach?
2. What should Ms. McDonald do if some group members are absent? How do teachers deal with student absenteeism during cooperative learning activities?
3. Positive interdependence is a critical part of cooperative learning. Where is that evident in this lesson?
4. What do you think Ms. McDonald should do differently to group the students for learning?
5. In what ways do you think Ms. McDonald's approach was effective? Ineffective?
6. Examine the domain designations highlighted in this case study. For one domain (e.g., A or B), what performance indicators would you look for to assess that the teacher is performing well? poorly?

Source: Case Study written by Melissa Mikesell, classroom teacher in West Carrollton, Ohio.

focus on the material that has just been presented or might help students bridge to a new segment of the presentation. Students discuss.

3. Teacher asks a question that helps students summarize and synthesize the material that has been presented and provides closure for the lesson. Students discuss.[64]

Following are two specific examples of informal cooperative learning strategies. Table 8.1 provides an example of other approaches. Notice that some, such as Round-Robin, help students get to know other students, and others, such as Numbered Heads Together help students master content material.

table 8.1   Overview of Selected Structure

Structure	Brief Description	Functions: Academic & Social
	Team Building	
Round-Robin	Each student in turn shares something with his or her teammates.	Expressing ideas and opinion, creation of stories, equal participation, getting acquainted with teammates.
	Class Building	
Corners	Each student moves to a corner of the room representing a teacher-determined alternative. Students discuss within corners and then listen to and paraphrase ideas from other corners.	Seeing alternative hypotheses, values, problem-solving approaches, knowing and respecting different points of view, meeting classmates
	Mastery	
Numbered Heads Together	The teacher asks a question, students consult to make sure everyone knows the answer, and then one student is called on to answer.	Review, checking for knowledge, comprehension, tutoring.
Color-Coded Co-op Cards	Students memorize facts using a flash card game. The game is structured so that there is a maximum probability of success at each step, moving from short-term to long-term memory. Scoring is based on improvement.	Memorizing facts, helping, praising
Pairs Check	Students work in pairs within groups of four. Within pairs students alternate—one solves a problem while the other coaches. After every two problems the pair checks to see if they have the same answers as the other pairs.	Practicing skills, helping, praising.

Source: Paul J. Vermette. *Making Cooperative Learning Work.* Upper Saddle River, N.J.: Prentice Hall, 1998, p. 23

Numbered Heads Together

1. The teacher has students number themselves off within their groups, so that each student has a number: 1, 2, 3, or 4. (Groups can consist of three to five students.)

2. The teacher asks a question.

3. The teacher tells the students to "put their heads together" to make sure that everyone on the team knows the answer. (All students need to discuss the material relevant to the question and be able to respond.)

4. The teacher calls a number (1, 2, 3, or 4) and the students with that number can raise their hands to respond.[65]

Think-Pair-Share

1. The teacher provides the students with a topic or idea.

2. The students then reflect independently on the meaning of the topic—the teacher should give students three to five seconds for independent thinking.

3. The students pair up with other students to discuss the topic and to share respective thoughts. (This can be a random pairing.)

4. The students then share their thoughts with the class—the teacher needs to wait after each student shares (three to five seconds) for all students to think about what has been shared.[66]

Marzano and his colleagues provide a description of what informal learning might look like in a classroom. As you read this illustration, compare it to the formal structures outlined earlier. Notice how the teacher is making no effort to create "arranged" teams or to assess how the pairs function together.

> Mr. Anderson likes to read aloud original source documents about slavery to his fifth graders. After reading for ten minutes, he gives the students a discussion task to complete in pairs for three to four minutes. The task requires students to answer a specific question that he provides. After each member of a pair formulates a response and discusses it with his or her partner, Mr. Anderson begins to read aloud again. After ten minutes, Mr. Anderson stops and asks students to complete a second paired discussion task. Occasionally, he asks two or three pairs to share a brief summary of their discussions. At the end of the class, Mr. Anderson asks the paired students to summarize in written form what they have learned from the readings and discussions and turn their summaries in to him.[67]

Guidelines for Cooperative Learning

David Johnson and Roger Johnson developed some strategies for cooperative approaches:

1. Determine goals and then decide on the appropriate formal or informal cooperative learning approach.

2. Arrange the classroom to promote cooperative goals.

3. Communicate intentions and expectations. Students need to understand what is being attempted.

4. Encourage a division of labor when appropriate. Students should understand their roles and responsibilities.

5. Encourage students to share ideas, materials, and resources. Students should look at each other and not the teacher.

6. Encourage supportive behavior and point out rejecting or hostile behavior. Behaviors such as silence, ridicule, personal criticism, one-upmanship, and superficial acceptance of an idea should be discussed.

7. Monitor the group. Check progress of individuals in a group and of the group as a whole. Explain and discuss problems, assist, and give praise as appropriate.

8. Evaluate the individual and group. In evaluation, focus on the group and its progress. Evaluate the individual in the context of the group's effort and achievement. Provide prompt feedback.

9. Reward the group for successful completion of its task.[68]

In a review of cooperative learning, the Johnsons point out that each lesson in cooperative learning should include five basic elements: 1) positive interdependence—students must feel they are responsible for their own learning and that of other members of the

Structured Teacher Observation
Form for Group Work Assessment

Assess the types of interactions using this matrix.

	John	Tom	Amanda	Lucette
Asks other group members questions	XX	X	X	
Takes notes on what others say		XX	X	
Helps others clarify their thoughts		XX	XXX	X
Rephrases the statements of others		XXXX		
Offers encouragement to other students	X	XX	X	XXX

figure 8.7

group; 2) face-to-face interaction—students must have the opportunity to explain what they are learning to each other; 3) individual accountability—each student must be held accountable for mastery of the assigned work; 4) social skills—each student must communicate effectively, maintain respect for group members, and work together to resolve conflicts; and 5) group processing—groups must be assessed to see how well they are working together and how they can improve.[69] Those assessments can take different forms. The teacher might keep some anecdotal notes on how groups function or make more structured observations using a matrix such as the one shown in Figure 8.7. The teacher might also ask students how they thought their groups functioned (see Figure 8.8).

Group Activities

Although there is no clear research showing that group activities, also known as *group projects,* correlate with student achievement, it is assumed that, under appropriate circumstances, instruction in small groups can be as effective as or more effective than relying on the teacher as the major source of learning. It is also assumed that many kinds of group activities 1) help teachers deal with differences among learners, 2) provide opportunity for students to plan and develop special projects on which groups can work together, and 3) increase student interaction and socialization. In short, they achieve social and emotional as well as cognitive purposes.

If planned and implemented properly, group activities tend to promote five group-oriented characteristics in the classroom: 1) task structures that lend themselves to cooperation among group members, 2) a chance for students to work at their own pace but think in terms of group goals, 3) the development of social and interpersonal skills among participants—students learn to communicate with and trust one another, 4) a reward structure based on the performance of the group (which encourages helping

Name:_____

Place checkmarks in the three boxes that best describe you in your work today.

Circle one behavior that you want to make sure you use tomorrow.

    ○ I stayed with my group.

    ○ I made sure my voice did not get TOO LOUD!

    ○ I reminded others to stay on task in an agreeable way.

    ○ I helped manage the materials and made sure they got put back in "good shape."

    ○ I participated.

    ○ I asked others to participate.

    ○ I helped my group make a plan.

    ○ I helped my group stick with the plan.

    ○ I helped summarize our work.

figure 8.8   Personal Assessment of Work in Groups.

Source: Lynda Baloche, *The Cooperative Classroom.* Upper Saddle River, NJ: Prentice Hall, 1998: 182. Reprinted by permission of Pearson Education Inc., Upper Saddle River, NJ.

behaviors), and 5) a variety of team-building strategies—students learn to work together, appreciate individual characteristics, and capitalize on individual strengths.

By participating in group activities, students engage in helping and sharing experiences. Ideally, they experience positive expectations of peers and learn to be considerate, cooperative, and responsible in mutual endeavors. If groups are organized properly, with clearly defined roles and/or rules, then positive discipline (actually self-discipline) should evolve as part of the classroom culture. Finally, students should come to appreciate and better understand people: their needs, intentions, and feelings. All of these new group learning experiences are important, since education and work environments increasingly involve people working together in programs, units, and departments.

According to researchers, when students (as well as adults) work on group projects, they need to focus on specific problems, not personalities; provide feedback that the receiver can understand; and provide feedback on actions that the receiver can change.[70] Honest communication demands that individuals learn to appreciate the strengths and uniqueness of others, to listen to others, and to give and receive supporting feedback—all of which require maturity, understanding, and respect. Effective student group activities can nurture and reinforce such qualities.

Group Techniques

During group activities, the teacher's role moves from engineer or director to facilitator or resource person, and many leadership functions transfer from the teacher to the students. Certain small-group techniques can assist students in their group projects and shift learning from originating with you to originating with them.

1. *Brainstorming* is a technique for eliciting large numbers of imaginative ideas or solutions to open-ended problems. Group members are encouraged to expand their thinking beyond the routine. All suggestions are accepted without judgment, and only after all the ideas are put before the group do the members begin to focus on a possible solution.

2. A *buzz session* provides an open environment in which group members can discuss their opinions without fear of being "wrong" or being ridiculed for holding an unpopular position. Buzz sessions can also serve to clarify a position or bring new information before the group to correct misconceptions.

3. The *debate* and *panel* are more structured in format than some of the other small-group techniques. In a debate, two positions on a controversial issue are presented formally; each debater is given a certain amount of time to state a position, to respond to questions from others in the group, and to pose questions to the other side. The panel is used to present information on an issue and, if possible, to arrive at group consensus. Several students (three to eight) may sit on a panel. Each panel member may make an opening statement, but there are no debates among panel members.

4. *Role-playing* and improvisation are techniques for stepping outside of one's own role and feelings and placing oneself in another's situation. Role-playing also serves as a technique for exploring intergroup attitudes and values.

5. *Fish bowl* is a technique in which group members give their full attention to what one individual wants to express. The whole group sits in a circle. Two chairs are placed in the center of the circle. A member who wants to express a point of view does so while sitting in one of the chairs. Any other member who wants to discuss the view takes the other chair, and the two converse while the others listen. To get into the discussion, students must wait for one chair to be vacated.

6. *Round table* is a quiet, informal group technique. Usually four or five students sit around a table conversing among themselves (similar to a buzz session) or before an audience (similar to a forum).

Using group techniques in flexible and imaginative ways can have important instructional advantages. They give students some control over their own behavior as well as over their own cognitive learning. Teachers can inject them into different lessons to meet the needs and interests of different groups. Teachers can use them to make activities more interesting and active. They can supplement lecture, questioning, and practice and drill methods.

Guidelines for Group Activities

Students can be assigned to group projects by interest, ability, friendship, or personality. The teacher must know the students and the objectives for using small groups before establishing the groups. If the objective is to get the job done expeditiously, the teacher should assign a strong leader to each group, rely on high-achieving students to lead the activities, avoid known personality conflicts, and limit the group size to five. If the objective is more interpersonal than cognitive, the students may be grouped according to their differences rather than similarities, and the groups might be larger.

In order to organize such group activities, consider the following recommendations. They are basically sequential, although each recommendation should be used only if it coincides with your circumstances and teaching style:

1. Decide on a group project that enhances specific objectives and outcomes.
2. Solicit volunteers for membership in group projects, reserving the right to decide final membership.
3. Go over directions for each phase of the group activity (in writing or orally) to the point of redundancy.
4. Explain the roles of participants, the way they are to interact, and potential problems. Give examples and model interactions.
5. Allot class time for groups to organize, plan, and develop some of their projects or assignments, with supervision as needed.
6. Allow group members to decide on the nature of the class presentation, within general rules that have been established.
7. Do not allow any individual to dominate the activities or responsibilities of the group.
8. Evaluate the completed group project with the students. Discuss problems and decisions participants had to face and the strategies chosen.

Individualizing Instruction for Enhanced Student Learning

Thus far we have examined different forms of whole-group and small-group instruction. These are by far the most common forms of instruction used in American classrooms. Another type of instruction is individualized. We will conclude this chapter with examples of such approaches. They are important to understand even though they are not evidenced in any "pure" form in many of today's schools. The individualized and mastery structures popular in the 1960s to 1980s represent important precursors for much of the instructional modeling that is evidenced today.

Individualized Instruction

Several systematic programs for individualized instruction were advanced in the 1970s and 1980s. Although the individualized instruction approaches varied somewhat, all the programs attempted to maximize individual learning by 1) diagnosing the student's entry achievement levels or learning deficiencies; 2) providing a one-to-one teacher-to-student or machine-to-student relationship; 3) introducing sequenced and structured instructional materials, frequently accompanied by practice and drill; and 4) permitting students to proceed at their own rate. Although the approaches combined behavioral and cognitive psychology, the behaviorist component seems more in evidence because of the stress on

Psychology of Instruction

Ernest R. Hilgard
Emeritus Professor of Psychology and Education
Stanford University

 The shift in emphasis in the last few years from a psychology of learning, which might hopefully be applied in the classroom, to a psychology of instruction has had promising consequences, encouraged both by the development of cognitive psychology and by a greater awareness of the contexts in which instruction is effective. A distinction between the mastery model, in which instruction is engineered to reach goals set by the teacher, is being contrasted with the acquiring of self-regulatory skills in which knowledge is structured for problem solving in various contexts.

If the teacher understands the difference between such strategies, steps can be taken to improve the interaction with the student as learner.

---

instructional objectives and drill exercises and small instructional units and sequenced materials that maximize student success. In essence, it was believed that learners would learn and be motivated if they experienced instruction "staged" to ensure success.

One of the early programs for individualized instruction was the Project on Individually Prescribed Instruction (IPI), developed at the University of Pittsburgh in the late 1950s and early 1960s. For every student an individual plan was prepared for each skill or subject based on a diagnosis of the student's proficiency levels. Learning tasks were individualized, and the student's progress was continually evaluated. Most important, the lessons for students were sequenced so that students could master skills within a single class period.[71]

Individually Guided Education (IGE) was a total educational system developed at the University of Wisconsin and introduced in several thousand schools. Planned variations were made in what and how each student would learn. The program included individual objectives, one-to-one relationships with teachers or tutors, diagnostic testing, independent study, small-group instruction, and large-group instruction.[72]

A more behaviorist and teacher-directed approach was the Personalized System of Instruction (PSI), sometimes called the *Keller plan* after its originator. It was developed initially for high school and college students. PSI made use of study guides, which would break a course down into small units with specific objectives. Individuals progressed through the units as quickly or slowly as they wished, mastered units (80 percent or better) before proceeding to the next unit, and acted as proctors (high-achieving students assisting others).[73]

Some reports on IPI, IGE, and PSI showed significant gains in student achievement, especially with low-achieving students who seemed to prefer a structured approach to learning.[74] Of the three programs, IPI and IGE were the most widely used and seemed to report the most consistent rise in student test scores. Because individualized plans were (and are) expensive to implement, most schools today continue to employ the "group" methods of instruction.[75]

The IPI, IGE, and PSI approaches, though once popular, are used today in only a very limited number of schools, and the research on them is even more limited. Indeed,

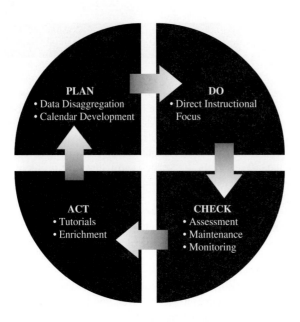

figure 8.9   PDCA Instructional Cycle.

Source: Patricia Davenport and Gerald Anderson, *Closing the Achievement Gap.* Houston, Texas: American Productivity and Quality Center, 2002: 60.

in the most recent issue of the *Handbook of Research on Teaching,* which was published in 2001 and is the most comprehensive synthesis of research on educational practices, only the IPI model is referenced.

Although these individualized approaches are out of vogue as "formal" strategies, they continue in instructionally mutated forms in many school districts today. Indeed, if you look at some school districts that are endeavoring to close the achievement gap between African-American and mainstream white students, you will see that they are using forms of individualized instruction to maximize the learning potential of typically disenfranchised and poorly performing students. That is, by identifying specific academic standards and diagnosing student prior knowledge of the requisite content, teachers are arranging learning experiences to ensure more student success (see Figure 8.9). After analyzing data on what students know or don't know, teachers provide appropriate instruction, check to see if students understand, and determine how students should continue their learning.

The PDCA (Plan-Do-Check-Act) instructional cycle in Figure 8.9 is predicated on securing and disaggregating data so that teachers can act (teach) in ways that make instructional sense for student learning. The first key is for a teacher to determine whether students are mastering the content prescribed by the school district. That occurs through careful assessment. The second key is to determine if all groups are mastering the content to the same degree, which can occur by disaggregating data by the different student groups. How are female students performing? Male students? African-American students? Are there apparent differences between and among the groups?

Once they have identified learning deficiencies, teachers make instructional decisions about how to cover the content, which can be done through whole-group, small-group, or even individualized models. As we will further discuss in Chapters 10 and 11, assessment is a critical key to good individualized instruction. You must know where your students are in their learning if you are going to teach them the particular academic skills they need for their future success.

Mastery Instruction

Mastery learning was associated originally with John Carroll and later with James Block and Benjamin Bloom and focused on specifically orienting instruction to ensure student acquisition of content. Their mastery learning ideas earned supporters particularly in urban school districts, where there was an obvious need to improve academic performance. It may seem unusual to those who really understand mastery learning to include it in the individualized instruction section since mastery learning is usually more focused on whole- (or large-) group instruction. It is included here because it constitutes a type of whole-group individualized model. The teacher teaches to a large group but seeks to identify those individual students who do not understand.

Carroll maintained that, if students are normally distributed by ability or aptitude for some academic subject and are provided appropriate instruction tailored to their individual characteristics, the majority should achieve mastery of the subject, and learning should be dramatically improved. He also held that, if a student does not spend sufficient time to learn a task, he or she will not master it. However, students vary in the amount of time they need to complete a task. Nearly all students (assuming no major learning disability) can achieve average outcomes if given sufficient time.[76] Mastery learning attempts to ensure that individual students have the time they need to learn the content taught in a whole group setting.

Carroll and, later, Robert Slavin distinguish between time needed to learn (based on student characteristics such as aptitude) and time available for learning (a factor that is under the teacher's control). High-achieving students need less time than low-achieving students to learn the same material. Group instruction, large or small, rarely accommodates varying learner characteristics or considers the time needed to learn. The teacher has the ability to vary instructional time for different individuals or groups of students with mastery instruction, especially for low-achieving students who usually need additional time.[77]

Block and Bloom argued that 90 percent of the public school students can learn much of the curriculum at the same level of mastery, with the slower 20 percent of students in this 90 percent needing 10 to 20 percent more time than the fastest 20 percent.[78] Although slower students require a longer period of time to learn the same materials, they can succeed if their initial level of knowledge is correctly diagnosed, and if they are taught with appropriate methods and materials in a sequential manner beginning at their initial competency level.

To accomplish this goal, criterion-reference tests (see Chapters 10 and 11) must be used to determine whether a student possesses skills required for success at each step of the learning sequence. Also, small units of instruction must be used. An entire course such as third-grade mathematics or seventh-grade social studies is too complex to be studied in large units. Instead it should be broken down into smaller pieces following some of the principles of programmed instruction.

In a review of more than twenty-five studies, Block and Burns found that 61 percent of the mastery-taught students scored significantly higher on achievement tests than nonmastery-taught students.[79] The results of studies of entire school districts show that mastery approaches are successful in teaching basic skills, such as reading and mathematics, that form the basis for later learning; moreover, inner-city students profit more from this approach than from traditional groupings for instruction.[80]

The favorable findings associated with the mastery approach do not mean that all the important questions have been answered. Mastery strategies have their critics. For example, some claim that, when basic skills—reading, writing, and mathematics—are broken down into discrete tasks that students can master, the students still do not acquire the more comprehensive skill (they cannot read, write, or compute any better). Students may show gains in small skill items, but this does not necessarily prove learning.[81] Critics ask a powerful, rhetorical question: What happened to the notions of wholeness and the importance of concepts and problem-solving skills? There are students who know the difference between a noun and a verb but who cannot write a whole sentence, much less a paragraph. Students may be capable of memorizing vocabulary words but still unable to read with comprehension (or understanding) at their grade level.

Traditionally, teachers have held time constant so that individual differences were reflected in achievement differences. A mastery learning situation, which varies time for learning among students, narrows achievement differences among students in favor of those who need extra time at the expense of other students.[82] In a situation in which high-achieving students must wait for slow students to catch up, and high achievers must wait for the teacher's attention (because the teacher spends an inordinate amount of time with low achievers so they can gain mastery), the high achievers may be discriminated against. As a result, they will become bored, and their learning outcomes will probably suffer.

These criticisms do not nullify the importance of mastery learning or other direct instructional approaches.[83] However, questions arise about whether any instructional approach that breaks learning into tiny, sequenced items has desirable end results for all students, especially high-achieving, talented, or creative students; whether all students need so much practice to master fundamental skills and tasks; and whether it is acceptable to vary instructional time to the disadvantage of higher achievers.

During the past two decades, mastery approaches have been adopted in more than 5,000 schools. The research suggests they require extensive diagnostic criterion-reference testing (see Chapter 10), and it is necessary to determine different standards of mastery for each class depending on the students' abilities. Teachers have to devise alternative assignments (remedial, corrective, or enrichment) for different students at different stages and at least two forms of tests to measure changes in learning. Teachers must cope with individual rates of learning and vary content coverage and time. It takes a master teacher who is willing to work hard to implement mastery instruction successfully. Actually, it takes a master teacher to implement any instructional method effectively. But if you look carefully at the mastery model, it consists of nothing more than solid instruction. In simplified form, mastery teaching consists of these steps:

1. Teach the lesson relying on large-group or whole-group instruction.

2. Give a "formative" quiz on a no-fault basis to assess student progress.

3. Based on the results, divide the class into a "mastery" group and "nonmastery" small group; 90 percent is considered mastery.

4. Give "enrichment" to the mastery group—group projects, independent study, etc.

5. Give "corrective" instruction to the nonmastery group—small study groups consisting of two or three students, individual tutoring, alternative instructional materials, rereading materials, practice and drill, etc.

6. Give a "summative" or final quiz on the unit or topic; students who achieved mastery on the "formative" quiz do not need to take this quiz.[84]

Personalized Instruction

A progressive (student-centered) variation of the individualized structure is the ***personalized instruction*** that is used in schools such as the Met School in Providence, Rhode Island and that focuses on a more personalized learning environment for all students. The Met School starts education by looking at the student, not at subject matter requirements and defined academic content standards. (Notice that a good bit of this text assumes that teachers begin by understanding the academic content standards for their state and then make decisions about how to teach that content.) As a result, Littky and Allen assert that, "Each Met student's education is one huge on-going conversation, maintained through daily interaction, regular contact among home and school and internship, learning-plan meetings, and more."[85] The Met School is not guided by Carnegie units but it is guided by a student's interests or intellectual passions. It is, in essence, an evolved example of an individualized (student-centered) construct at the secondary level.

Given the personalization, what assurances are there that students learn what they need to learn? Littky and Allen suggest that defined learning goals are in place but they are related to starting with the student, not the teacher's defined curriculum. They observe the following:

> Because a student's curriculum is individualized, not guided by mandatory courses or Carnegie Units, the Met has a list of required learning goals that provide crucial direction for each learning plan and ensure that students are adequately prepared for college, career, and citizenship. Though students have significant freedom to pursue their interests, each student is required to use those interests to master the schoolwide learning goals.
>
> The Met learning goals are skills and qualities that all students must demonstrate in order to graduate. Based on extensive research on how people learn and think, the goals are the qualities and abilities essential to success in any post–high school endeavor:
>
> - Empirical reasoning, or "How do I prove it?"
> - Symbolic/quantitative reasoning, or "How do I measure or represent it?"
> - Communication, or "How do I take in and express information?"
> - Social reasoning, or "What do other people have to say about this?"
> - Personal qualities, or "What do I bring to this process?"

professional viewpoint

On Being "Dumb"

Professor Anonymous
Heartland University

 I am writing as a parent and not in my usual role as professor.

It was two years ago when the standardized reading test, administered at the beginning of the term, sealed John's fate. The results revealed that his reading grade declined from 1 year above level in the previous school year to 1.2 years below level. He was shunted into the "slow" reading group by Mrs. Smith, his fourth-grade teacher, and was assigned three times a week to a special reading teacher, Mrs. Jones, who thrived on Prussian rules of order and drill activities.

The boy who only a few months ago during the summer had read for enjoyment the abridged versions (100–150 pages) of *Treasure Island, Robinson Crusoe, Swiss Family Robinson,* and *Dr. Jekyll and Mr. Hyde* was now unable to answer questions about "Tony's Visit to the Zoo" and unable to do his homework. The reading teacher's phone call at home confirmed his "lack of comprehension and inability to keep up with the class."

A new nailbiting habit, repeated outbursts at the dinner table, fights with his brother and sister, and frequent remarks about his new reading group and "dumbness"—all in six weeks—prompted me to make an appointment with the school principal, the popular Mr. Green, who knew every child in school by name and whose office magazine rack contained the latest issues of *Educational Leadership, Elementary Principal, Phi Delta Kappan,* and *Reading Teacher.*

When I mentioned John's behavior at home, the principal suggested further testing. "No," I responded. "If you test a child long enough, the school will find more things wrong with him and slap more labels on him." When I elaborated on my child's summer reading habits, Mr. Green pointed to recent research that concluded that poor readers don't understand what they read. Somewhat frustrated, I asserted, "Only a fool or nitwit would mis-read a book for one hour before bedtime each evening and then, after finishing the book, want to read another book."

The principal was flexible but did not give ground easily. He alluded to John's age—that he was the youngest person in his class—and then reviewed Piaget's development stages of growth. I responded with the principles of test reliability and boring methods of instruction. A compromise was eventually reached. My wife and I would make an appointment with the school social worker, so she could assess family conditions, and John would be retested.

After three additional weeks of school bureaucracy, the principal called with good news: John's retest score was .75 year above grade level. In order to preserve the reading teacher's ego, however, he suggested that the program transfer take place in January, when the semester ended.

John is in the sixth grade, today, still bored with his school reading assignments, but reading Dick Gregory, John Steinbeck, Jack London, and Pearl Buck for his own pleasure. It's sad to think what might have happened to my son had I not intervened. But what about all the children who don't have fathers sitting at the dinner table or checking homework, much less a parent with the knowledge to challenge the system? Armed with test data and reading labels, Mrs. Smith and Mrs. Jones had boxed a 9-year-old child into a no-win, no-escape situation—in which he could not fend or cope by himself. The school, with its professional jargon, had labeled and grouped a bright child so that he no longer wanted to learn and no longer felt he could learn. His means of expression was rebellion—stupidity in class and anger at home. In only a *few weeks,* the classroom's ability group coupled with the teacher's self-fulfilling prophecy had overshadowed the child's past performance and behavior.

My son had all the advantages: high SES, two educated parents, bright peer group, and a top-rated school—yet he could not cope with these new labels. Think of all the millions of students who don't have these advantages, in fact, who by chance are classified into the other side of the socioeconomic and school continuum. Then think of their test scores, their "stupidity" in school, and anger inside and outside of school. Ask yourself, as an educator, who is responsible; then ask yourself what you intend to do that is different from what Smith, Jones, and Green did.

The goals are general; they can be learned, practiced, and demonstrated in a variety of ways, allowing students to achieve them through almost any project or work experience of interest. In addition to guiding students' work, the learning goals demonstrate to the Met community and to the public our priorities for our students' academic learning and personal development.[86]

The power of the concept of personalized learning is that the focus is on the student, not on the teacher or on the defined standards a student needs to learn. We conclude this chapter on instructional grouping with a discussion of personalized learning because, whether you have thirty students or one student, your goal should be to determine how to make each student successful as a learner. There are no magic methods for making that happen, but the following suggestions provide a starting point:

1. Find ways to maximize student participation in what and how students will learn.

2. Know the academic content standards for your state and find ways to embed those in the lessons you teach.

3. Organize instruction so that the "whole" of what is taught is apparent to the students.

4. Know how to create working relationships and arrangements that maximize student success.

The Met school outlines the personalized approach at the secondary level, but schools in Maryland, Vermont, and Virginia have embraced personalized plans for students in regular classrooms. These personalized plans are used to help students pass proficiency tests and perform better on their academics. Obviously, such personalization takes time, and teachers are looking to parents and others to assist in building a learning approach for individual students.

The task of individualization requires that teachers find ways to differentiate instruction—which is yet another way to personalize learning. Good differentiated instruction uses whole-group, small-group, and individualized (even personalized) learning—it uses all the different strategies that we have discussed. Case Study 8.2 is from an article on differentiated instruction written by Carol Ann Tomlinson.[87] Read carefully how Ms. Cassell structures the multiple learning experiences for her students. Her goal is not to make learning fun, but rather to make it engaging so that all students can learn. As a result, they find that learning is fun.

Good teachers organize classrooms in many different ways to foster student learning. If they are teaching a basic skill or process, they may use a whole-class structure with direct-instruction practices. If they are teaching students to problem solve or engage in critical thinking, they may use small-group approaches, with some type of formal or informal cooperative learning. And, if they want to emphasize student personal interests, they may individualize (or personalize) instruction to allow students to follow their personal passions.

Good teachers do not have a single approach. And good teachers do not use varied approaches to be instructionally "cute." Rather, they use varied instructional models to achieve varied instructional goals. As the teacher uses those different models with students, student learning should be enhanced because students will learn to engage with

case study 8.2   **Differentiated Instruction**

Early in the unit, Ms. Cassell's students begin work, both at home and in class, on two sequential tasks that will extend throughout the unit as part of their larger study of ancient Rome. Both tasks are differentiated.

For the first task, students assume the role of someone from ancient Rome, such as a soldier, a teacher, a healer, a farmer, a slave, or a farmer's wife. Students base their choice solely on their own interests. They work both alone and with others who select the same topic and use a wide variety of print, video, computer, and human resources to understand what their life in ancient Rome would have been like.

Ultimately, students create a first-person data sheet that their classmates can use as a resource for their second task. The data sheet calls for the person in the role to provide accurate, interesting, and detailed information about what his or her daily schedule would be like, what he or she would eat and wear, where he or she would live, how he or she would be treated by the law, what sorts of problems or challenges he or she would face, the current events of the time, and so on.

Ms. Cassell works with both the whole class and small groups on evaluating the availability and appropriate use of data sources, writing effective paragraphs, and blending information from several sources into a coherent whole. Students use these skills as they develop the first-person data sheets. The teacher's goal is for each student to increase his or her skill level in each area.

The second task calls on students to compare and contrast their own lives with the lives of children of similar age in ancient Rome. Unlike the first task, which was based on student interest, this one is differentiated primarily on the basis of student readiness. The teacher assigns each student a scenario establishing his or her family context for the task: "You are the eldest son of a lawmaker living during the later years of the period known as Pax Romana," for example. Ms. Cassell bases the complexity of the scenario on the student's skill with researching and thinking about history. Most students work with families unlike those in their first task. Students who need continuity between the tasks, however, can continue in a role familiar from their first investigation.

All students use the previously developed first-person data sheets as well as a range of other resources to gather background information. They must address a common set of specified questions: How is what you eat shaped by the economics of your family and by your location? What is your level of education and how is that affected by your status in society? How is your life interdependent with the lives of others in ancient Rome? How will Rome change during your lifetime? How will those changes affect your life? All students must also meet certain research and writing criteria.

Despite the common elements, the task is differentiated in several ways. It is differentiated by interest because each student adds questions that are directed by personal interests: What games did children play? What was the practice of science like then? What were the purpose and style of art?

Readiness differentiation occurs because each student adds personal research and writing goals, often with the teacher's help, to his or her criteria for success. A wide range of research resources is available, including books with varied readability levels, video- and audiotapes, models, and access to informed people. The teacher also addresses readiness through small-group sessions in which she provides different sorts of teacher and peer support, different kinds of modeling, and different kinds of coaching for success, depending on the readiness levels of students.

Finally, the teacher adds to each student's investigation one specific question whose degree of difficulty is based on her most recent assessments of student knowledge, facility with research, and thinking about history. An example of a more complex question is "How will your life differ from that of the previous generation in your family, and how will your grandchildren's lives compare with yours?" A less complex, but still challenging question is "How will language change from the generation before you to two generations after you, and why will those changes take place?"

Learning-profile differentiation is reflected in the different media that students use to express their findings: journal entries, an oral monologue, or a videotape presentation. Guidelines for each type of product ensure quality and focus on essential understandings and skills established for the unit. Students may work alone or with a "parallel partner" who is working with the same role, although each student must ultimately produce his or her own product.

At other points in the study of ancient Rome, Ms. Cassell differentiates instruction. Sometimes she varies the sorts of graphic organizers that students use when they read, do research, or take notes in class. She may use review groups of mixed readiness and then conduct review games with students of like readiness working together. She works hard to ask a range of questions that move from concrete and familiar to abstract and unfamiliar in all class discussions. She sometimes provides homework options in which students select the tasks that they believe will help them understand important ideas or use important skills best. Of course, the class also plans, works, reviews, and debates as a whole group.

Ms. Cassell's class is highly likely to be effective for her varied learners, in part because she continually attempts to reach her students where they are and move them on—she differentiates instruction. The success of the differentiation, however, is not a stand-alone matter. It is successful because it is squarely rooted in student engagement plus student understanding.

This teacher knows where she wants her students to arrive at the end of their shared learning journey and where her students are along that journey at a given time. Because she is clear about the destination and the path of the travelers, she can effectively guide them, and she varies or differentiates her instruction to accomplish this goal. Further, her destination is not merely the amassing of data but rather the constructing of understanding. Her class provides a good example of the close and necessary relationship between effective curriculum and instruction and effective differentiation.

Questions for Reflection:

1. Ms. Cassell differentiated instruction in different ways. In what other ways might you differentiate instruction?
2. Do you think all teachers differentiate instruction as they should for the varied types of learners that they have in the classroom? Why or why not?
3. Why is it important for teachers to think about different ways to group for instruction when differentiating instruction?

Source: Excerpted from Carol Ann Tomlinson. "Mapping a Route Toward Differentiated Instruction." *Educational Leadership* (September 1999): 15–16.

the content in different ways. A teacher who organizes classes in different ways enables students to understand fully the structure of an academic discipline. A student will only half learn history if all he or she ever does is listen to a history teacher lecture on historical events.[88] Fuller understanding of those same events requires that the student work in small-group settings to discuss with peers the topic that is being explored and to work individually on topics to reinforce understandings or to follow more fully personal passions. In essence, good teachers are adaptive, and they evidence such a skill by using a variety of strategies dictated by the learning goals they hope to achieve.

Theory into Practice

Just as it is important to use different instructional methods and materials, it is important to mix instructional groupings to meet varied classroom conditions and student needs and to provide variety. No one grouping approach is appropriate for every circumstance. A mixture of whole-group, small-group, and individualized instruction should be used. Here are a few commonsense methods written as questions.

For Whole-Group Instruction

1. Is your classroom attractive and safe? Are the spacing and furnishings flexible?
2. Have you involved all students in the instructional activities? Do you avoid emphasizing teacher-student interaction on one side or in the middle of the room?
3. Have you arranged instructional materials and media equipment so that all students can readily see and participate in the activities?
4. Do you direct and monitor classroom activities?
5. Do you combine whole-group (direct-instruction) approaches with small-group (informal cooperative learning) approaches?
6. Are you able to make smooth transitions for large-group activities to either small-group or individualized instruction? Do you maintain a brisk pace when making transitions?

A Technology Viewpoint from a Classroom Teacher

Jackie Marshall Arnold
K–12 Media Specialist

 Instructional grouping can be a critical component when planning to use technology in today's classrooms. Effective teachers examine the objectives and activities of a lesson to determine the appropriate grouping arrangement for the technology being used. The NETS standards state that teachers need to "design, deliver, and assess student learning activities that integrate computers and other technology for *a variety of student grouping strategies* and for diverse student populations" (standard 1.3.3). Effective teachers study and apply a variety of instructional grouping strategies when utilizing technology.

Instructional technology applications can support individual instruction, small-group instruction, and whole-group instruction. For example, when all students need to master a new technology skill or application it is convenient to have the whole group in a computer lab mastering the skill or application together. In the same manner, if everyone has a report to type, having plenty of work stations for the entire group is a practical grouping arrangement.

Allowing the use of computers throughout the day via a rotating work station can be another efficient way to individualize computer assignments. Students can take turns going to the computer to complete a task that has previously been designed. Using this grouping strategy, every student can experience beneficial one-on-one time with a computer to engage in Internet searches, explore a curriculum connected simulation, work with a drill and practice piece of software, and much more.

With many classrooms now having one to five computers, many applications exist for small-group work at a computer. As some of the case studies presented in this text have described, grouping students at a computer can be a very successful and appropriate instructional strategy. For example, in cooperative learning groups students can work together to investigate websites, create graphs, develop websites, and much more. Teachers should carefully structure groups. For example, making sure there is one strong reader in each group is important to facilitate the great amount of reading that is necessary on many websites. Teachers may also choose to assign "roles" to students so that everyone knows his or her responsibilities. Example student roles include (but are not limited to) manager, timekeeper, mouse operator, and note taker. By giving an assignment and roles to each member of the group, everyone will know what the goal is and what they need to do to accomplish that goal.

A variety of instructional groupings can be used. Having one student per computer is highly appropriate at times, but teachers often stop here. Allowing students to work cooperatively in small groups at the computer will reap many benefits for your teaching and for student learning. Teachers using cooperative learning strategies have the opportunity to use technology to facilitate teamwork in an authentic work environment.

For Small-Group Instruction

1. Have you made sure students know what to do and how to proceed? Do they understand the objectives or tasks and when they have achieved them?
2. Have you made sure students are aware of their responsibilities while working in small groups?
3. Do you enhance communication and minimize conflicts by discussing appropriate behavior for individuals within groups?

4. When organizing groups, do you consider the abilities and interests of students? Do you mix groups by ethnicity, social class, and gender for purposes of integration and by ability so they are relatively equal on a cognitive basis?

5. Have you taken into account special learning and behavior problems? Do you separate students who do not work well together?

6. Do you permit students to work at their own pace within their respective groups? Do you permit each group to work at its own pace?

7. Do you monitor the work of each group? Do you make comments, ask questions, and assist the group as necessary?

8. Are you providing knowledge of group results by emphasizing the positive? Do you provide immediate feedback and group rewards for achievement?

Summary

1. Instruction may take place in whole-group, small-group, and individualized settings. The teacher is responsible for varying these three groupings according to the needs of the students and the objectives of the lesson.

2. Classroom seating arrangements include traditional, rectangular, circular, horseshoe, and various special formations designed for special activities.

3. Large-group or whole-group instruction is the most common form of classroom organization, suitable for the teacher when lecturing and explaining, questioning, and providing practice and drill.

4. Whole-group instruction tends to be geared to the average learner, and the students are expected to perform within a narrow range. Most classroom tasks performed by students are either too easy or too difficult.

5. Small groups give the teacher flexibility in instruction and an opportunity to introduce skills and tasks at the level suited to a particular group of students.

6. There are several methods for organizing students in small groups. Small-group activities are best conducted when group size is limited to five to eight students per group.

7. Individualized instruction permits the student to work alone at his or her own pace and level over short or long periods of time. Individualized instruction permits the teacher to adapt instruction to the abilities, needs, and interests of the learner.

8. Personalized learning is focused on the student and his or her learning needs.

Questions to Consider

1. What types of seating arrangements do you prefer during whole-group instruction? Does this suggest anything about your teaching approach?

2. Which small-group instructional methods do you prefer? Why?

3. How might class size influence how you teach in either a whole- or small-group situation?

5. In general, which methods do you expect to emphasize (or presently emphasize) in your own class—whole-group, small-group, or individualized? Why?

Things to Do

1. Discuss the advantages and disadvantages of three different seating arrangements for the subject level and grade level you wish to teach.
2. Observe two or three teachers at work in the classroom and describe in writing the classroom tasks taking place. Do the students appear to view the tasks as relevant to their lives?
3. Defend or criticize the nature of competitive and cooperative classrooms. Be sure to describe the advantages of each, whatever your overall preference. How would you change the reward structures in school?
4. Observe a tutoring program for students in a local school. How does the program operate in terms of student responsibilities?
5. In what content areas do students tutor other students?

Recommended Readings

Baloche, Lynda. *The Cooperative Classroom.* Upper Saddle River, N.J.: Prentice Hall, 1998. This book describes different types of formal and informal cooperative learning approaches.

Bloom, Benjamin S. *Human Characteristics and School Learning.* New York: McGraw-Hill, 1976. This classic text, which emphasizes individual instruction and school learning, offers mastery approaches to changing the level of learning and rate of learning.

Chubb, John E. and Tom Loveless, *Bridging the Achievement Gap.* Washington, DC: Brookings Institution Press, 2002. An exploration of the cause of the achievement gap between different student groups, with particular attention to ways of "bridging" the gap through different school and classroom practices.

Hacsi, Timothy. *Children as Pawns: The Politics of Educational Reform.* Cambridge, Mass: Harvard University Press, 2002. A thoughtful discussion of a wide range of issues with particular focus on class size research.

Marzano, Robert J., Debra J. Pickering, and Jane E. Pollock. *Classroom Instruction That Works.* Alexandria, VA: Association for Supervision and Curriculum Development, 2001. This text describes the different ways of teaching content and documents the research base to support each approach.

Slavin, Robert E. *Cooperative Learning: Theory, Research and Practice,* 2d ed. Upper Saddle River, N.J.: Prentice Hall, 1995. This book discusses how to set up and use cooperative learning in classrooms.

Vermette, Paul J. *Making Cooperative Learning Work.* Upper Saddle River, N.J.: Prentice Hall, 1998. This book describes how cooperative learning structures can be used to enhance student learning.

Key Terms

ability grouped 352	individualized instruction 370	personalized instruction 375
between-class ability grouping 353	informal cooperative learning 361	self-contained classroom 336
departmentalization 336	mastery learning 373	within-class ability grouping 354
formal cooperative learning 360	peer tutoring 354	

End Notes

1. Students Get More Face Time With Average Results." *USA Today* (October 30, 2002). Retrieved from http://www.usatoday.com/news/education/2002-10-30-students-average_xihtm.
2. Raymond S. Adams and Bruce J. Biddle. *Realities of Teaching* New York: Holt, Rinehart and Winston, 1970.

3. Edmund T. Emmer, Carolyn Evertson and Murray Worsham. *Classroom Management for Secondary Teachers,* 6th ed. Boston, Mass.: Allyn and Bacon, 2003. Carolyn Evertson, Edmund T. Emmer, and Murray E. Worsham. *Classroom Management for Elementary Teachers,* 6th ed. Boston: Allyn and Bacon, 2003.

4. Thomas L. Good and Jere E. Brophy. *Looking in Classrooms,* 8th ed. Reading, Mass: Addison Wesley, 2000.

5. Ibid. Larry Cuban. *Why Is It So Hard to Get Good Schools?* New York: Teachers College Press, 2003. Larry Cuban. *How Teachers Taught.* New York: Teachers College Press, Columbia University Press, 1993.

6. Eugene Garcia. "Effective Instruction for Language Minority Students: The Teacher." In Antonio Darder, Roldolfo D. Torres, and Henry Gutierrez (eds.), *Latinos and Education.* New York: Routledge, 1997, p. 368.

7. Timothy A. Hacsi. *Children as Pawns.* Cambridge, Mass.: Harvard University Press, 2002.

8. Eric A. Hanushek. "The Impact of Differential Expenditures on School Performance." *Educational Researcher* (May 1989): 45–51, 62.

9. Robert E. Slavin. "Class Size and Student Achievement: Small Effects of Small Classes." *Educational Psychologist* (Winter 1989): 99–110. Robert Slavin. "Putting the School Back in School Reform." *Educational Leadership* (January 2001): 22–27.

10. Robert E. Slavin. "Chapter 1: A Vision for the Next Quarter Century." *Phi Delta Kappan* (April 1991): 586–589.

11. Gene M. Glass and Mary L. Smith. *Meta-Analysis of Research on the Relationship of Class Size and Achievement.* San Francisco: Far West Laboratory for Educational Research and Development, 1978. Gene M. Glass et al. *School Class Size.* Beverly Hills, Calif.: Sage, 1982.

12. Barbara A. Nye. *The Lasting Benefit Study: A Continuing Analysis of the Effect of Small Class Size in Kindergarten Through Third Grade.* Nashville: Tennessee State University, 1991. Barbara A. Nye. "Smaller Classes Really Are Better." *American School Board Journal* (May 1992): 31–33.

13. Daniel J. Mueller, Clinton I. Chase, and James D. Walden, "Effects of Reduced Class Size in Primary Classes," *Educational Leadership* (February 1988): 48–50. Robert E. Slavin, Nancy L. Karweit, and Barbara A. Wasik. "Preventing Early School Failure: What Works?" *Educational Leadership* (December–January 1993): 10–17.

14. Gene Glass and Mary L. Smith. *Meta-Analysis of Research on the Relationship of Class Size and Achievement.* Glen E. Robinson, "Synthesis of Research on the Effects of Class Size." *Educational Leadership* (April 1990): 80–90. Also see, Stanley Pogrow. "The Unsubstantiated 'Success' of Success for All." *Phi Delta Kappan* (April 2000): 596–600.

15. Harris M. Cooper. "Does Reducing Student-to-Instructor Ratios Affect Achievement?" *Educational Psychologist* (Winter 1989): 79–88.

16. Kirk A. Johnson. "The Downside to Small Class Policies." *Educational Leadership* (February 2002): 27–29. *Digest of Education Statistics,* 2000. Washington, D.C.: United States Government Printing Office, 2001. Table 411.

17. Ibid., p. 29.

18. Patricia Handley. "Every Classroom Teachers' Dream." *Educational Leadership* (February 2002): 33–35.

19. John H. Holloway. "Do Smaller Classes Change Instruction?" *Educational Leadership* (February 2002): 91.

20. Ronald W. Marx and John Walsh. "Learning from Academic Tasks." *Elementary School Journal* (January 1988): 207–219. Stephen T. Peverly. "Problems with the Knowledge-Based Explanation of Memory and Development." *Review of Educational Research* (Spring 1991): 71–93.

21. Jacques S. Benninga et al. "Effects of Two Contrasting School Task and Incentive Structures on Children's Social Development." *Elementary School Journal* (November 1991): 149–168. Deborah Meier. "Standardization Versus Standards." *Phi Delta Kappan* (November 2002): 190–198.

22. Nancy S. Cole. "Conceptions of Educational Achievement." *Educational Researcher* (April 1990): 2–7.

23. Neville Bennett et al. "Task Processes in Mixed and Single Age Classes." *Education* (Fall 1987): 43–50. Neville Bennett and Clive Carré. *Learning to Teach.* New York: Routledge, 1993. Also see Weldon Zenger and Sharon Zenger. "Why Teach Certain Material at Specific Grade Levels?" *Phi Delta Kappan* (November 2002): 212–214.

24. Paul J. Vermette. *Making Cooperative Learning Work.* Upper Saddle River, N.J.: Merrill, Prentice Hall, 1998.

25. Thomas J. Lasley II, Thomas J. Matczynski, and James Rowley. *Instructional Models: Strategies for Teaching in a Diverse Society,* 2d ed. Belmont, Calif.: Wadsworth, 2002.

26. Robert E. Slavin. "A Theory of School and Classroom Organization." *Educational Psychologist* (Spring 1987): 89–128.

27. Benjamin S. Bloom. "The 2 Sigma Problem: The Search for Methods of Group Instruction as Effective as One-to-One Tutoring." *Educational Researcher* (June–July 1984): 4–16.

28. Ibid., p. 6. Also see Benjamin Bloom. "Helping All Children Learn." *Principal* (March 1988): 12–17.

29. Good and Brophy. *Looking in Classrooms,* p. 456.

30. David Johnson and Frank P. Johnson. *Joining Together: Group Theory and Group Skills,* 8th ed. Boston, Mass.: Allyn and Bacon, 2002. Robert E. Slavin. "Student Teams and Comparison Among Equals: Effects on Academic Performance and Student Attitudes." *Journal of Educational Psychology* (August 1978): 532–538. Noreen M. Webb. "Verbal Interaction and Learning in Peer-Directed Groups." *Theory into Teaching* (Winter 1985): 32–39.

31. Jomills H. Braddock and James M. McPartland. "Alternatives to Tracking," *Educational Leadership* (April 1990): 76–79. Jeannie Oakes and Martin Lipton. "Detracking Schools: Early Lessons from the Field." *Phi Delta Kappan* (February 1992): 448–454.

32. Thomas L. Good. "Two Decades of Research on Teacher Expectations." *Journal of Teacher Education* (July–August 1987): 32–47. Cloyd Hastings. "Ending Ability Grouping Is a Moral Imperative." *Educational Leadership* (October 1992): 14–18.

33. Jacqueline Jordon Irvine. *Educating Teachers for Diversity.* New York: Teachers College Press, 2003. Oakes and Lipton. "Detracking Schools." Anne Wheelock. "The Case for Untracking." *Educational Leadership* (October 1992): 14–18.

34. Adam Gamoran. *The Variable Effects of High School Tracking.* Madison, Wisc.: Center on Organization and Restructuring of Schools, University of Wisconsin–Madison, 1992. Ralph Scott. "Untracking Advocates Make Incredible Claims." *Educational Leadership* (October 1993): 79–81.

35. Robert E. Slavin. "Grouping for Instruction in the Elementary School." *Educational Psychologist* (Spring 1987): 12.

36. John Goodlad. *A Place Called School.* New York: McGraw Hill, 1984. Oakes. *Keeping Track: How Schools Structure Inequality.* New Haven, Conn.: Yale University Press, 1985.

37. Adam Gamoran. "Synthesis of Research: Is Ability Grouping Equitable*?" Educational Leadership* (October 1992): 11–14. De Wayne A. Mason et al. "Assigning Average-Achieving Eighth Graders to Advanced Mathematics Classes in an Urban Junior High." *Elementary School Journal* (May 1992): 587–599.

38. Good and Brophy. *Looking in Classrooms,* p. 278.

39. Adam Gamoran. "Synthesis of Research: Is Ability Grouping Equitable?" *Educational Leadership* (October 1992): 11–13. Jeanne Oakes. "Tracking in Secondary Schools." *Educational Psychologist* (Spring 1987): 129–153. De Wayne A. Mason and Thomas L. Good. "Effects of Two-Group and Whole-Class Teaching on Regrouped Elementary Students' Mathematics Achievement." *American Educational Research Journal* (September 1993): 328–360.

40. Elfrieda Heibert. "An Examination of Ability Grouping in Reading Instruction." *Reading Research Quarterly* (Winter 1983): 231–255.

41. Robert E. Slavin. "Ability Grouping and Student Achievement in Secondary Schools." *Review of Educational Research* (Fall 1990). Joseph S. Yarworth et al. "Organizing for Results in Elementary and Middle School Mathematics." *Educational Leadership* (October 1988): 61–67.

42. Good and Brophy. *Looking in Classrooms,* pp. 275–281.

43. Jeanne Ellis Ormrod. *Human Learning.* Upper Saddle River, N.J.: Prentice Hall, 1999.

44. Robert E. Slavin. "Mounting Evidence Supports the Achievement Effects of Success for All." *Phi Delta Kappan* (February 2002): 469–471. Theresa A. Thorkildsen. "Those Who Can, Tutor." *Journal of Educational Psychology* (March 1993): 82–190.

45. Marilyn J. Adam. *Beginning to Read.* Cambridge, Mass.: MIT Press, 1990. Penelope L. Peterson et al. "Ability X Treatment Interaction Effects on Children's Learning in Large-group and Small-group Approaches." *American Educational Research Journal* (Winter 1981): 453–473.

46. David Johnson and Roger Johnson. *Learning Together and Alone: Cooperative, Competitive and Individualistic Learning,* 5th ed. Boston, Mass.: Allyn and Bacon, 1998.

47. Susan R. Swing and Penelope L. Peterson. "The Relationship of Student Ability and Small-Group Interaction to Student Achievement." *American Educational Research Journal* (Summer 1982): 259–274. Noreen M. Webb. "Predicting Learning from Student Interaction: Defining the Interaction Variables." *Educational Psychologist* (Spring 1983): 33–41.

48. Nicola Findley. "In Their Own Ways." *Educational Leadership* (September 2002): 60–63. Panayota Mantzicopoulous et al. "Use of Search/Teach Tutoring Approach with Middle-Class Students at Risk for Reading Failure." *Elementary School Journal* (May 1992): 573–586.

49. Lynn S. Fuchs et al. "The Nature of Student Interactions During Peer Tutoring with and Without Peer Training and Experience." *American Educational Research Journal* (Spring 1994): 75–103. Noreen M. Webb. "Peer Interaction and Learning in Small Groups." *International Journal of Educational Research* (Spring 1989): 211–224.

50. William S. Carlsen. "Questioning in Classrooms: A Sociolinguistic Perspective." *Review of Educational Research* (Summer 1991): 157–178.

51. Benjamin Bloom. "Helping All Children Learn in Elementary School—and Beyond." *Principal* (March 1988): 12–17. Bloom. "The 2 Sigma Problem: The Search for Methods of Group Instruction as Effective as One-to-One Tutoring."

52. Peter A. Cohen, James A. Kulik, and Chen-Lin C. Kulik. "Educational Outcomes of Tutoring: A Meta-Analysis of Findings." *American Educational Research Journal* (Summer 1982): 237–248. Darrell Morris, Beverly Shaw, and Jan Perney. "Helping Low Readers in Grades 2 and 3: An After-School Volunteer Tutoring Program." *Elementary School Journal* (November 1990): 133–150. Linda Devin-Sheehan, Robert S. Feldman, and Vernon I. Allen. "Research on Children Tutoring Children: A Critical Review." *Review of Educational Research* (Summer 1976): 355–385.

53. *What Works: Research About Teaching and Learning.* Washington, D.C.: U.S. Government Printing Office, 1986, p. 36.

54. James W. Keefe and John W. Jenkins. "Personalized Instruction." *Phi Delta Kappan* (February 2002): 440–448. Robert E. Slavin. "Synthesis of Research on Cooperative Learning." *Educational Leadership* (February 1991): 71–82.

55. Alfie Kohn. "Group Grade Grubbing versus Cooperative Learning." *Educational Leadership* (February 1991): 83–87. Marian Matthews. "Gifted Students Talk About Cooperative Learning." *Educational Leadership* (October 1992): 48–50. Chip Wood. "Changing the Pace of School." *Phi Delta Kappan* (March 2002): 545–550.

56. David Johnson and Roger Johnson. *Joining Together: Group Therapy and Group Skills,* 5th ed. Needham Heights, Mass.: Allyn and Bacon, 1994). Robert E. Slavin. *Cooperative Learning: Theory, Research, and Practice.* Englewood Cliffs, N.J.: Prentice-Hall, 1990.

57. Slavin. "Synthesis of Research on Cooperative Learning." See also, Gayle H. Gregory and Carolyn Chapman. *Differentiated Instructional Strategies: One Size Doesn't Fit All.* Thousand Oaks, CA: Corwin Press, 2001.

58. Michael S. Meloth and Paul D. Deering. "Task Talk and Task Awareness Under Different Cooperative Learning Conditions." *American Educational Research Journal* (Spring 1994): 139.

59. Lynda A. Baloche. *The Cooperative Classroom.* Columbus, Ohio: Prentice Hall, 1998, p. 116.

60. Robert J. Marzano, Debra J. Pickering, and Jane E. Pollock. *Classroom Instruction That Works.* Alexandria, VA: Association for Supervision and Curriculum Development, 2001, p. 90.

61. Robert E. Slavin. *Using Student Team Learning,* 3d ed. Baltimore: Johns Hopkins University Press, 1986.

62. Robert E. Slavin. *School and Classroom Organization.* Hillsdale, N.J.: Erlbaum, 1988. Slavin. "Synthesis of Research on Cooperative Learning."

63. Elliot Aronson et al. *The Jigsaw Classroom.* Beverly Hills, Calif.: Sage Publications, 1978.

64. Baloche. *The Cooperative Classroom,* pp. 100–101.

65. Stanley Kagan. "The Structural Approach to Cooperative Learning." *Educational Researcher* (December–January 1989–1990): 13.

66. Thomas J. Lasley, Thomas J. Matczynski, and James Rowley. *Instructional Models: Strategies for Teaching in a Diverse Society.* Belmont, Calif.: Wadsworth, 2002: 315.

67. Marzano, Pickering, and Pollock. *Classroom Instruction That Works,* pp. 89–90.

68. David W. Johnson. *Reaching Out,* 5th ed. Needham Heights, Mass.: Allyn and Bacon, 1993.

69. Roger Johnson and David Johnson. "Toward a Cooperative Effort." *Educational Leadership* (April 1989): 80–81.

70. Roger Johnson and David Johnson. "Gifted Students Illustrate What Isn't Cooperative Learning." *Educational Leadership* (March 1993): 60–61. John A. Ross and Dennis Raphael. "Communication and Problem Solving Achievement in Cooperative Learning." *Journal of Curriculum Studies* (March–April 1990): 149–164.

71. Robert Glaser and Lauren B. Resnik. "Instructional Psychology." *Annual Review of Psychology* 23 (1972): 207–276. Also see Robert Glaser (ed.). *Advances in Instructional Psychology.* Hillsdale, N.J.: Erlbaum, 1978. Lorrie Shepard. "The Role of Classroom Assessment in Teaching and Learning." In Virginia Richardson (ed.), *Handbook of Research on Teaching,* 4th ed. Washington, D.C.: American Educational Research Association, 2001, pp. 1066–1011.

72. Herbert J. Klausmeier and Richard E. Ripple. *Learning and Human Abilities,* 3d ed. New York: Harper & Row, 1971. Also see Beverly A. Parsons. *Evaluative Inquiry: Using Evaluation to Promote Student Success.* Thousand Oaks, CA: Corwin Press, 2002.

73. Fred S. Keller. "Good-Bye Teacher." *Journal of Applied Behavioral Analysis* (April 1968): 79–84.

74. Margaret C. Wang and Herbert J. Walberg (eds.). *Adapting Instruction to Individual Differences.* Berkeley, Calif.: McCutchan, 1985. Also see Wang (ed.). *The Handbook of Adaptive Instruction.* Baltimore: Paul Brooks, 1992.

75. Mary A. Gunter, Thomas H. Estes, Jan Schwab, and Christine Hasbrouck Chaille. *Instruction: A Models Approach* 4th ed. Boston, Mass.: Allyn and Bacon, 2003. Deborah B. Strother. "Adapting Instruction to Individual Needs." *Phi Delta Kappan* (December 1985): 308–311. Also see Robert E. Slavin et al. *Preventing Early School Failure.* Needham Heights, Mass.: Allyn and Bacon, 1993.

76. John B. Carroll. "A Model of School Learning." *Teacher's College Record* (May 1963): 723–733.

77. John B. Carroll. "The Carroll Model: A 25-Year Retrospective and Prospective View." *Educational Researcher* (January–February 1989): 26–31. Robert E. Slavin. "Mastery Learning Reconsidered." *Review of Educational Research* (Summer 1987): 175–214.

78. James H. Block. *Mastery Learning: Theory and Practice.* New York: Holt, Rinehart and Winston, 1971. Benjamin Bloom. *Human Characteristics and School Learning.* New York: McGraw-Hill, 1976. Benjamin Bloom. *All Our Children Learning.* New York: McGraw-Hill, 1981.

79. James Block and Robert Burns. "Mastery Learning." In L. S. Shulman (ed.), *Review of Research in Education,* vol. 4. Itasca, Ill.: Peacock, 1976, pp. 118–145. Also see James Block, Helen Efthim, and Robert Burns. *Building Effective Mastery Learning Schools.* New York: Longman, 1989.

80. Thomas R. Guskey. "Helping Students Make the Grade." *Educational Leadership* (September 2001): 20–27. Daniel U. Levine. "Creating Effective Schools." *Phi Delta Kappan* (January 1991): 394–397. Daniel U. Levine and Allan C. Ornstein. "Reforms That Can Work." *American School Board Journal* (June 1993): 31–34.

81. Mary Ann Raywid. "Accountability: What's Worth Measuring?" *Phi Delta Kappan* (February 2002): 433–436. Allan C. Ornstein. "Comparing and Contrasting Norm-Reference Tests and Criterion-Reference Tests." *NASSP Bulletin* (October 1993): 28–39. Blaine R. Worthen and Vicki Spandel. "Putting the Standardized Test Debate in Perspective." *Educational Leadership* (February 1991): 65–70.

82. Marshal Arlin. "Time, Equality, and Mastery Learning." *Review of Educational* Research (Spring 1984): 65–86. Marshal Arlin. "Time Variability in Mastery Learning." *American Educational Research Journal* (Spring 1984): 103–120. Kevin Castner, Lorraine Costella, and Steven Hass. "Moving from Seat Time to Mastery." *Educational Leadership* (September 1993): 45–50.

83. Arthur K. Ellis and Jeffrey T. Fouts. *Research on Educational Innovations.* Larchmont, N.Y.: Eye on Education, 1997.

84. James Block. *Mastery Learning in Classroom Instruction.* New York: MacMillan, 1975.

85. Dennis Littky and Farrell Allen. "Whole-School Personalization, One Student at a Time." *Educational Leadership* (September 1999): 24–28.

86. Ibid, p. 28.

87. Carol Ann Tomlinson. "Mapping a Route Toward Differentiated Instruction." *Educational Leadership* (September 1999): 12–16.

88. Bruce Joyce and Beverly Showers. *Student Achievement Through Staff Development.* Alexandria, VA: Association for Supervision and Curriculum Development, 2002.

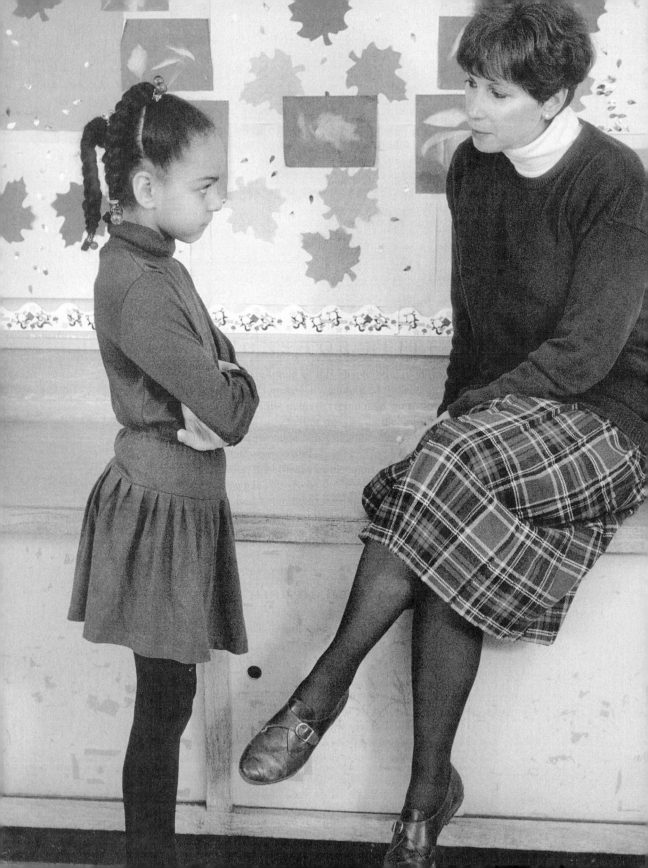

chapter 9

Classroom Management and Discipline

Pathwise criteria relevant to the content of this chapter:

- Creating a climate that promotes fairness (B1)
- Establishing and maintaining rapport with students (B2)
- Establishing and maintaining consistent standards of classroom behavior (B4)
- Making the physical environment as safe and conducive to learning as possible (B5)

INTASC principles relevant to the content of this chapter:

- The teacher uses an understanding of individual and group motivation and behavior to create a learning environment that encourages positive social interaction, active engagement in learning, and self-motivation. (P5)
- The teacher understands and uses formal and informal assessment strategies to evaluate and ensure the continuous intellectual, social, and physical development of the learner. (P8)
- The teacher fosters relationships with school colleagues, parents, and agencies in the larger community to support students' learning and well-being. (P10)

focusing questions

1. Why is classroom management an integral part of teaching?

2. What are some approaches to classroom management? Which ones best fit your personality and philosophy? How can similar management problems be handled in different ways?

3. What is the best way to choose the approach that best fits your classroom management goals?

4. What are some characteristics of successful classroom managers? How many of these characteristics coincide with your management behaviors?

5. How can preventive disciplinary measures improve classroom management? Which ones best fit your personality and philosophy?

6. How can you analyze your strengths and weaknesses as a classroom manager? What means or techniques would you use to evaluate your management abilities?

7. How does the use of technology potentially influence classroom management?

In order to teach, you must be able to manage your students. No matter how much potential you have as a teacher, if you are unable to control the climate in your classroom, little learning will take place. Classroom management is an integral part of teaching, and you can and must acquire techniques of managing students.

As you prepare to teach you need to understand two fundamentals. First, schools are largely governed by middle-class social rules. Second, student behavior is bound by the rules with which students are raised. Teachers have one set of expectations about how students should behave, but students come to school having learned a set of behaviors that may be incompatible with those teacher expectations. The vast majority of problems in classrooms are caused by conflicts between what the teacher expects and what the students have learned. To negotiate this conflict requires that teachers help students learn new sets of behaviors but also demands that teachers try to understand what it is that students bring with them to school. Because most teachers fail to understand the interplay between the school and home cultures, a large number of problems occur that limit teacher control and student learning.

The public widely considers inadequate classroom management and discipline to be the major educational problem, even though the media have centered on school busing, school financing, declining test scores, and student drug abuse. In annual Gallup polls in education taken among parents since the late 1960s, student discipline, or the lack of it, has been listed as the number one, two, or three school problem each year for almost three decades.[1]

According to a recent NEA teacher opinion poll, 90 percent of the teachers maintain that student misbehavior interferes with their teaching, and nearly 25 percent claim that it greatly interferes. The same poll revealed that approximately 100,000 teachers suffer personal verbal or physical attacks from students annually, most often in front of other students in the classroom.[2]

The problem of discipline is persistent, especially in inner-city schools, because 1) many students lack inner self-control and are unwilling to defer to teacher authority, 2) many teachers lack systematic methods for dealing with discipline problems, 3) many school administrators do not provide adequate support for teachers, and 4) many parents are not adequately involved in their children's education.

Approaches to Classroom Management

Your personality, philosophy, and teaching style will directly affect your managerial and disciplinary approach. There are many approaches, but the one you adopt must be comfortable for you and coincide with your personal characteristics.

We'll consider six approaches or models. Each is grounded in research and each is applicable to classrooms. Although they are presented as distinct approaches, they do share common features, and most teachers use them in some combination, depending on their personalities and the students' maturity. All are based on a mixture of psychology, classroom experience, and common sense. All blend elements of prevention with techniques for intervention. They differ in the degree of control and supervision exercised by the teacher and the relative emphasis on tasks and personalities. They form a continuum from firm, direct, and highly structured (high teacher control) to flexible, indirect, and democratic (moderate teacher control). Teachers, in general, should move from high teacher control to moderate control systems as the year progresses and as the maturity of students increases. That is, if the goal of the teacher is to foster student self-discipline (and that is what should occur), then the teacher needs to find ways to help students learn how to control their own behavior. That cannot occur if teachers are always directing and controlling students. Teachers may need to start their careers or the school year with high control, but as they create engaging lessons and as students come to understand the teachers' expectations, the students should begin to engage in more self-monitoring of their own behavior.

Assertive Approach: High Teacher Control

The **assertive approach** to classroom management requires that teachers specify rules of behavior and identify consequences for disobeying them; they also must communicate these rules and consequences clearly. The classroom is managed in such a way that students are not allowed to forget who is in charge of the classroom. According to Duke and Meckel, "Students come to realize that teachers expect them to behave in a certain way in class."[3] Teachers hold students accountable for their actions. For example, students who disobey rules might receive one warning and then be subject to a series of one or more sanctions.[4] The idea is for the teacher to respond to a student's misbehavior quickly and appropriately. Mild misbehavior is followed by mild sanctions, but if the misbehavior continues, the sanctions toughen. The approach assumes that misbehavior is contagious and will snowball (or ripple) unless checked early. If misbehavior is ignored or not stopped at an early stage, it will eventually become uncontrollable; more and more students will become disruptive.[5]

The assertive approach is based on Lee and Marlene Canter's model of discipline in which teachers insist on responsible behavior by their students. The teacher takes charge of the classroom immediately, sets the ground rules, and interacts with students in a calm yet forceful way.[6] The teacher is expected to combine clear expectations, an active response to misbehavior, and consistent follow-through with warmth and support for all students.

The technique assumes that good teachers can handle discipline problems on their own and that teaching failure is directly related to inability to maintain adequate classroom discipline. Success is, if not predicated on, at least correlated with good discipline. The approach probably is most effective with students who are emotionally immature and who are having difficulty controlling their own behavior.[7]

The Canters make the following suggestions for teachers applying assertive discipline:

1. Clearly identify positive expectations for students.
2. Take positions. (Say, "I like that" or "I don't like that.")
3. Use a firm tone of voice.
4. Use eye contact, gestures, and touches to supplement verbal messages.
5. Give and receive compliments genuinely.
6. Place demands on students and enforce them.
7. Set limits on students and enforce them.
8. Indicate consequences of behavior and why specific action is necessary.
9. Be calm and consistent; avoid emotion or threats.
10. Persist; enforce minimum rules; don't give up.[8]

The assertive model holds that teachers must establish firm management at the beginning of the year by 1) clarifying appropriate expectations of responsible behavior, 2) identifying existing or potential discipline problems, 3) deciding on negative and positive consequences of behavior that fit the students and situation, and 4) learning how to follow through and implement defined consequences. The plan is best achieved through mental rehearsal (having a good idea of what to do before something occurs) and practice (learning from mistakes).

Applied Science Approach: High Teacher Involvement

Well-run classrooms that are free from disruptions, in which students behave in an orderly manner and are highly involved in learning, are not accidental. They exist if teachers have a clear idea of the type of classroom conditions (arrangement, materials), student behaviors (rules, procedures), and instructional activities (assignments, tasks) they wish to produce. The ***applied science approach,*** developed by Evertson and Emmer, emphasizes the organization and management of students as they engage in academic work.[9] Much of their work is based on real-world observations of effective and ineffective classroom managers. Their work suggests that task orientation—that is, focusing on the businesslike and orderly accomplishment of academic work—leads to a clear set of procedures for students and teachers to follow.

Evertson and Emmer divide organizing and managing student work into three major categories: establishment and communication of work assignments, standards, and procedures; monitoring of student work; and provision of feedback to students.

1. *Clear communication of assignments and work requirements:* The teacher must establish and explain clearly to students work assignments, features of the work, standards to be met, and procedures.
   a. *Provide clear instruction for assignments:* Explanations should be made in both oral and written forms. In addition to telling the students about assignments, teachers should post assignments on the chalkboard or distribute duplicated copies. Students should be required to copy assignments posted on the chalkboard into their notebooks.

The classroom setting is a place where a structured and organized teacher is often successful.

     b. *Develop standards for the form, degree of neatness, and due dates of papers:* Before students start, they should be given general rules for all assignments: type of paper and writing material to use (pencil, pen, typewriter), page numbering system, form for headings, due dates, and so forth. Students will then know what is expected of them without having to be told each time.

     c. *Develop procedures for absent students:* Routines should be established for makeup work for students who missed class. Teachers must meet briefly with such students at a set time before or after school, assign class helpers who will be available at particular times of the day (usually during seat work activities) to help the students, and designate a place where students can pick up and turn in makeup work.

2. *Monitoring student work:* Monitoring student work helps the teacher detect students who are having difficulty and encourage students to keep working.

     a. *Monitor group work:* Before helping any individual student with work, the teacher must be sure that all students start work and are able to do the assignment; otherwise, some students will not even start the assignment and others may start incorrectly.

     b. *Monitor individual work:* You can monitor work in several ways, by circulating around the room and giving specific feedback where needed, having students bring their work to you one at a time at some designated point during an activity, and establishing due dates that correspond with stages in an assignment.

c. *Monitor completion of work:* Procedures for turning in work must be established and enforced. When all students are turning in work at the same time, the best procedure is to have the work passed in a given direction with no talking until all the work is collected.

d. *Maintain records of student work:* It is important for teachers to keep a record of the students' work and to incorporate it into the grade. The record should be divided into several headings, such as workbook assignments, major assignments or projects, daily homework, and quizzes and tests.

3. *Feedback to students:* Frequent, immediate, and specific feedback is important for enhancing academic monitoring and managerial procedures. Work in progress, homework, completed assignments, tests, and other work should be checked promptly.

a. *Focus attention on problems:* It is important for teachers to pay careful attention at the beginning of the year to completion of classroom and homework assignments. The first time a student fails to turn in an assignment without a good reason is the time to talk to the student. If the student needs help, provide it but insist at the same time that the student do the work. If the student has persistent problems completing work, then parental communication may be needed. Do not wait until the grading period is over to note the problems that exist.

b. *Focus attention on good work:* Part of giving feedback is acknowledging good work. This may be done by displaying the work, giving oral recognition, or providing written comments.[10]

According to Evertson and Emmer, an effective manager incorporates eleven managerial methods, all of which have been shown to correlate with improved student achievement and behavior. These methods are listed in Table 9.1.

The general approach and methods used by Evertson and Emmer are appropriate for both elementary and secondary teachers. The approach coincides with various instructional techniques, especially as a complement to teacher centered approaches such as direct instruction (see Chapter 5).

The applied science approach involves a high degree of "time on task" and "academic engaged time" for students. Time on task refers to the time allocated to learning and engaged time refers to the success students experience while completing a task. Successful students are typically engaged students. The idea is that when students are working on their tasks successfully and when those tasks have meaning and relevance, there is little opportunity for discipline problems to arise. The teacher organizes students' work, keeps students on task, monitors their work, gives them feedback, and holds them accountable by providing rewards and penalties.[11] It is a no-play, no-frills approach, corresponding to the old-fashioned "three Rs" and now packaged as part of the "academic productivity" movement in education.

table 9.1   **Methods of Effective Classroom Managers**

1. *Readying the classroom:* Classroom space, materials, and equipment are ready at the beginning of the year. Effective managers arrange their rooms better than others, and they cope more effectively with existing constraints.

2. *Planning rules and procedures:* Teachers make sure students understand and follow rules and procedures; they spend time at the beginning of the year explaining and reminding students of rules. They also provide feedback to students on rule compliance.

3. *Teaching rules and procedures:* Rules and procedures (lining up, turning in work) are systematically taught and reinforced. Most of these teachers teach their students to respond to certain cues or signals, such as a bell or the teacher's call for attention. They also discuss with students how their behavior conforms with expectations.

4. *Consequences:* Consequences for not following rules and procedures are clearly established by the teachers; there is consistent follow-through.

5. *Beginning of school activities:* The first few days are spent getting students ready to function as a coherent and cooperative group. Once the group is established, these teachers sustain a whole-group focus.

6. *Strategies for potential problems:* Strategies for dealing with potential problems are planned in advance. With these strategies teachers can deal with misbehavior more quickly than can less effective managers.

7. *Monitoring:* Student behavior is closely monitored; student academic work is also monitored.

8. *Stopping inappropriate behavior:* Inappropriate or disruptive behavior is handled promptly and consistently—before it worsens or spreads. The teacher has a variety of techniques to handle misbehavior.

9. *Organizing instruction:* Teachers organize instructional activities at suitable levels for all students in the class. There is a high degree of student success and content related to student interests.

10. *Student accountability:* Procedures have been developed for keeping students accountable for their work and behavior.

11. *Instructional clarity:* Teachers provide clear instructions; these help keep students on task and allow them to learn faster, and they reduce discipline problems. Directions are clear, and thus confusion is minimized.

Sources: Adapted from Edmund T. Emmer and Carolyn M. Evertson. "Synthesis of Research on Classroom Management." *Educational Leadership* (January 1981): 342–347. Carolyn M. Evertson and Catherine H. Randolph. "Classroom Management in the Learner-Centered Classroom." In A. C. Ornstein (ed.), *Teaching: Theory and Practice.* Needham Heights, Mass.: Allyn & Bacon, 1995, pp. 116–131. Catherine H. Randolph. "Perspectives on Classroom Management in Learner-Centered Schools." In Hersholt L. Waxman and Herbert J. Walberg (eds.), *New Direction for Teaching.* Berkeley, Calif.: McCutchan, 1999, pp. 249–268.

Behavior Modification Approach: High Teacher Intervention

Behavioral modification is rooted in the classic work of James Watson and the more recent work of B. F. Skinner. The ***behavior modification approach*** involves a variety of techniques and methods, ranging from simple rewards to elaborate reinforcement training. Behaviorists argue that behavior is shaped by environment, and so they pay limited attention to the causes of problems.

Teachers using the behavior modification approach strive to increase the occurrence of appropriate behavior through a system of rewards and reduce the likelihood of

Effective Classroom Management

Carolyn M. Evertson
Professor of Education and Educational Psychology
Vanderbilt University

 The foremost concern of new teachers is managing the classroom effectively, but, too often, managing effectively is seen as simply dealing with misbehavior. To view good classroom management as a set of strategies for disciplining students is to misunderstand the basis on which good management rests. Effective classroom managers are distinguished by their success in preventing problems from arising in the first place, rather than by special skills in dealing with problems once they occur. Good management practice begins on the first day of school with carefully organized, systematic plans for accomplishing classroom tasks and activities. Good managers also make clear their expectations for students' work and behavior, rules and procedures, routines for checking and monitoring student academic work, procedures for grading and giving feedback to students, incentives and deterrents, methods for grouping students, and a whole variety of seemingly minor but essential procedures. Proactive planning helps avert behavior problems by providing students with ways to be successful.

inappropriate behavior through punishments. According to Albert Bandura, such teachers would ask the following questions: 1) What is the specific behavior that requires modification and is the intention to (increase, reduce, or eliminate it)? 2) When does the behavior occur? 3) What are the consequences of the behavior? Or, what happens in the classroom when the behavior is exhibited? 4) How do these consequences reinforce inappropriate behavior? How can the consequences be altered? 5) How can appropriate behavior be reinforced?[12]

The basic principles of the behavioral modification approach are as follows:

1. Behavior is shaped by its consequences, not by the causes of problems in the history of the individual or by group conditions.

2. Behavior is strengthened by immediate reinforcers. ***Positive reinforcers*** are praise or rewards. ***Negative reinforcers*** take away or stop something that the student doesn't like or by removing a particular stimulus, an increase in behavior occurs.[13] For example, the student is reprimanded by the teacher; the student agrees to behave according to classroom rules, and the teacher stops reprimanding. In a negative reinforcing situation the student behaves in such a way as to remove aversive stimuli (such as nagging, scolding, and threats) from the environment.

3. Behavior is strengthened by systematic reinforcement (positive or negative). Behavior is weakened if not followed by reinforcement. Reinforcers can take several different forms: edible (candy), social (praise), material (tangible rewards), or token (stars, points).[14]

4. Students respond better to positive reinforcers than they do to punishment (aversive stimuli). Punishment can be used to reduce inappropriate behavior if used sparingly.

5. When a student is not rewarded for appropriate or adaptive behavior, inappropriate or maladaptive behavior may become increasingly dominant and will be utilized to obtain reinforcement.

6. Constant reinforcement—the reinforcement of a behavior every time it occurs—produces the best results, especially in new learning or conditioning situations.

7. Once the behavior has been learned, it is best maintained through intermittent reinforcement—the reinforcement of a behavior only occasionally.

8. Intermittent reinforcement schedules include a) variable ratio, supplying reinforcement at unpredictable intervals; b) fixed ratio, supplying reinforcement after a preselected number of responses; and c) fixed interval, supplying reinforcement at preselected intervals.[15]

9. There are several types of reinforcers, each of which may be positive or aversive. Examples of positive reinforcers are a) social reinforcers, such as verbal comments ("Right," "Correct," "That's good"), facial expressions, and gestures; b) graphic reinforcers, such as written words of encouragement, gold stars, and checks; c) tangible reinforcers, such as cookies and badges for young students and certificates and notes to parents for older students; and d) activity reinforcers, such as being a monitor or sitting near the teacher for young students and working with a friend or on a special project for older students.[16]

10. Rules are established and enforced. Students who follow rules are praised and rewarded in various ways. Students who break rules are either ignored, reminded about appropriate behavior, or punished immediately. The response to rule-breaking differs somewhat in different variations of the behavioral modification approach.

Each teacher has an undetermined value as a potential reinforcing agent for each student. This value is assigned initially by students on the basis of past experiences, and it changes as a result of the teacher's actions. The teacher must realize that this evaluation process is going on in the student, and that a positive relationship with the student will enhance the teacher's potential for influencing behavior in class. Moreover, the teacher is one of many adults who serve as reinforcing agents in the student's life. In order to facilitate the classroom management process, the teacher may have to enlist the support of others.

There are a number of systems or variations of behavioral modification that are applicable to classroom management. They basically build limits and consequences into behavior and employ various rules, rewards, and punishments. A well-known system utilized in various social learning situations is termed *modeling.*

Models are effective in modifying behavior to the degree that they capture attention, hold attention, and are imitated. Effective models may be parents, relatives, teachers, other adults (community residents), public figures (sports people, movie stars), and peers. The best models are those with whom individuals can identify on the basis of one or more of the following traits: 1) sex, 2) age, 3) ethnicity, 4) physical attractiveness, 5) personality attractiveness, 6) competence, 7) power, and 8) ability to reward imitators. Teachers who want to use modeling in classroom management should recognize that the first five are personal characteristics that are hard to change, but the last three are institutional and role characteristics that are easier to manipulate to increase the models' effectiveness.

Building good discipline through modeling includes the following.

1. *Demonstration:* Students know exactly what is expected. In addition to having expected behavior explained to them, they see and hear it.

2. *Attention:* Students focus their attention on what is being depicted or explained. The degree of attention correlates with the characteristics of the model (teacher) and the characteristics of the students.

3. *Practice:* Students are given opportunity to practice the appropriate behavior.

4. *Corrective feedback:* Students receive frequent, specific, and immediate feedback. Appropriate behavior is reinforced; inappropriate behavior is suppressed and corrected.

5. *Application:* Students are able to apply their learning in classroom activities (role-playing, modeling activities) and other real-life situations.[17]

Teachers who do not know much about how students learn from "modeling" produce less learning in their students and have more discipline problems than do teachers who are successful at using modeling.

Miltenberger describes several different ways in addition to modeling of using behavior modification in the classroom.

1. *"Catch them being good" approach:* The teacher observes students doing what he or she desires and then makes a positive statement: "I like how row one is sitting" or "I like how Bobby is working on his assignment."

2. *Rules-ignore-praise approach:* The teacher develops clear rules, ignores mild inappropriate behavior, and praises compliant actions.

3. *Rules-reward-punishment approach:* The teacher establishes clear rules and then rewards appropriate behavior and punishes infractions.

4. *Contingency management approach:* The teacher rewards appropriate behavior by creating tangible reinforcers that can be cashed in at some point for a variety of different rewards. One high school Algebra I teacher gave "lucky bucks" to students when they exhibited appropriate rule compliant (and positive mathematical) behavior in the classroom. The students then exchanged the lucky bucks for several different types of Girl Scout cookies.

5. *Contracting approach:* The teacher creates a contract that specifies the behaviors expected of a student and the rewards for appropriate behavior.[18]

Group Managerial Approach: Moderate Teacher Intervention

The group managerial approach to discipline is based on Jacob Kounin's research. Kounin was one of the first researchers to study systematically classroom management procedures, especially as they related teacher behaviors to student behaviors. The ***group managerial approach*** emphasizes the importance of responding immedi-

table 9.2 **Kounin's Behaviors and Categories for Observing Classroom Management**

Categories of Pupil Behavior

I. *Work Involvement*
   A. Involved
   B. Mildly involved
   C. Not involved

II. *Deviancy*
   A. No misbehavior
   B. Mild misbehavior
   C. Serious misbehavior

Categories of Teacher Management Behavior

I. *Desist Techniques*
   A. "With-it-ness"
      1. Dealing with students in a timely fashion
   B. Overlapping
      1. Dealing with multiple behaviors
   C. High Profile
      1. Publicly reprimanding a student
   D. Low Profile
      1. Moving closer to a misbehaving student

II. *Movement Management*
   A. Smootheness-Jerkiness
      1. Flip-flopping topics
      2. Abbreviating lessons
   B. Momentum
      1. Overdwelling
      2. Fragmenting lessons

III. *Group Focus*
   A. Alerting
      1. Encourage suspense
      2. Pick reciter randomly
      3. Call on nonvolunteers
      4. Present new materials
      5. Ignore group in favor of reciter
      6. Select reciter before asking question
      7. Ask question, then call reciter
   B. Accountability
      1. Ask students to hold up props
      2. Actively attend to mass unison response
      3. Call on others
      4. Ask for volunteers and nonvolunteers
      5. Require student to demonstrate performance
      6. Review frequently

Source: Adapted from Jacob Kounin. *Discipline and Group Management in Classrooms.* New York: Holt, Rinehart & Winston, 1970, Chaps. 3 and 7.

ately to group student behavior that might be inappropriate or undesirable in order to prevent problems rather than having to deal with problems after they emerge. He describes what he calls the "ripple effect."[19] If a student misbehaves but the teacher stops the misbehavior immediately, it remains an isolated incident and does not develop into a problem. If the misbehavior is not noticed, is inappropriately ignored, or is allowed to continue for too long, it often spreads throughout the group and becomes more serious and chronic.

Kounin analyzes classroom activities for purposes of management by dividing them into categories of pupil behavior and teacher management behavior (see Table 9.2). Major categories of pupil behavior are work involvement and deviancy. Major categories of teacher behavior are desist techniques, movement management, and group focus.

Work Involvement

Work involvement is the amount of time students spend engaged in assigned academic work. (It closely resembles what other researchers call "time on task" or "academic engaged time.") Students who are involved in work (writing in a workbook, reciting, reading, watching a demonstration) exhibit fewer disciplinary problems than do students who are not involved in any assigned task. If the teacher keeps students involved in work, there is less chance that boredom and discipline problems will arise.

Deviancy

Deviancy ranges from no misbehavior to serious misbehavior. *No misbehavior* means the student unwittingly is off task or is upsetting another student or teacher or is temporarily (nondisruptively) off task. *Mild misbehavior* includes such actions as whispering, making faces, teasing, reading a comic, and passing notes. *Serious misbehavior* is aggressive or harmful behavior that interferes with others or violates school or social codes. The point is to prevent mild misbehavior from degenerating into serious misbehavior. Mild misbehavior needs to be dealt with promptly.

Desist Techniques

Desist techniques are teacher actions taken to stop misbehavior. Kounin feels that they depend on two abilities. **With-it-ness** is the ability to react on target (react to the proper student) and in a timely fashion. It also involves communicating to students that the teacher knows what is happening or, as Kounin puts it, that the teacher "has eyes in the back of [his or her] head." **Overlapping** refers to the teacher's ability to handle more than one matter at a time. He or she can attend to more than one student at the same time—say, one student who is reciting and another student who is interrupting with a question or comment.

Movement Management

Movement management is the organization of behavior in transitions from task to task within and between lessons. Movement may be characterized as smooth or jerky. The terms are not especially sophisticated, but they are quite apt. *Smoothness* is an even and calm flow of activities. It involves uninterrupted work periods and short, fluid transitions that are made automatically and without disruption. In particular, the teacher 1) avoids unnecessary announcements and interruptions when students are busy doing work, 2) finishes one activity before starting on the next, and 3) doesn't abruptly end or start an activity. *Jerkiness* is a disorderly flow of activities. It may result if the teacher tries to do too many things at once or does not make clear to students the procedures for ending one task and changing to a new one. The teacher may have to shout during transitions, disorder may arise as students have to ask questions about what to do, and unengaged students may create disruptions. In order to prevent jerkiness, the teacher should avoid five subcategories of behavior:

1. The teacher is so immersed with a small group of students or activity that he or she ignores other students or misses an event that is potentially disruptive.

2. The teacher bursts into activities without assessing student readiness and gives orders, statements, or questions that only confuse the students.

3. The teacher ends an activity or drops a topic before it is completed.

4. The teacher ends an activity abruptly.

5. The teacher terminates one activity, goes to another, and then returns to the previously terminated activity. The teacher lacks clear direction and sequence of activities.

Movement management also involves *momentum*—that is, keeping activities at an appropriate pace. Momentum is slowed or impeded if the teacher engages in overdwelling or fragmentation. *Overdwelling* may take the form of giving explanations beyond what is necessary for most students' understanding or lecturing, preaching, nagging, overemphasizing, or giving too many directions. *Fragmentation* is giving too much detail, breaking things down into too many steps, or duplicating or repeating activities. For example, a teacher who calls students to the desk to read, one by one, when one student can read aloud while the others listen, is engaging in fragmentation.

Group Focus

Group focus refers to the students' concentration on the group activity or task. It can be achieved through what Kounin calls *alerting*. Alerting activities include creating suspense, presenting new material, choosing reciters randomly, and selecting reciters (see Table 9.2 for other methods Kounin lists). Group focus can also be achieved by using *accountability*. This involves such methods as asking students to hold up props, circulating to check the products of nonreciters, and requiring students to perform and then checking their performance (see Table 9.2).

In summary, Kounin believes that student engagement in lessons and activities is the key to successful classroom management. Students are expected to work and behave. The successful teacher monitors student work in a systematic fashion, clearly defines acceptable and unacceptable behavior, and exhibits with-it-ness and overlapping abilities. The successful teacher has a clear sense of direction and sequence for tasks. Smooth transitions are made from one activity to another, so that student attention is turned easily from one activity to another. Similarly, lessons are well paced.

Almost all the major applied science theorists of classroom management—Brophy, Doyle, Emmer, Evertson, and Good—have been influenced by Kounin. Much of what they have to say now was said by Kounin in some form thirty years ago.

In essence, Kounin argued that as a classroom manager, the teacher should do the following:

1. *Maintain a group focus:* The teacher needs to know what students need to do (to be organized) and then expect students to do what is outlined.

2. *Have a degree of group accountability:* The teacher makes all students feel a sense of responsibility for what happens in the classroom. All students feel included.

3. *Obtain the attention of the group:* The teacher finds ways to get students' attention easily and begins class on time.[20]

---

tips for teachers 9.1

Enhancing Your Classroom Management Approach

 How do you develop and maintain a positive approach to classroom management or whatever discipline approach you wish to adapt? Here are some practical suggestions that will work in most situations.

Affective Dimensions

1. *Be positive:* Stress what should be done, not what should not be done.
2. *Use encouragement:* Show that you appreciate hard work and good behavior.
3. *Trust:* Trust students, but don't be an easy mark. Make students feel you believe in them as long as they are honest with you and don't take advantage of you.
4. *Express interest:* Talk to individual students about what interests them, what they did over the weekend, and how schoolwork is progressing in other areas or subjects. Be sensitive and respectful of social trends, styles, and school events that affect the behavior of the group. Be aware that peer group pressure affects individual behavior.
5. *Be fair and consistent:* Don't have "pets" or "goats." Don't condemn an infraction one time and ignore it another time.
6. *Show respect; avoid sarcasm:* Be respectful and considerate toward students. Understand their needs and interests. Don't be arrogant or condescending or rely on one-upmanship to make a point.

Procedural Dimensions

7. *Establish classroom rules:* Make rules clear and concise and enforce them. *Your* rules should eventually be construed as *their* rules.
8. *Discuss consequences:* Students should understand the consequences of acceptable and unacceptable behavior. Invoke logical consequences—that is, use appropriate rewards and punishment. Don't punish too often; it loses its effect after a while.
9. *Establish routines:* Students should know what to do and under what conditions. Routine procedures provide an orderly and secure classroom environment.
10. *Confront misbehavior:* Don't ignore violations of rules or disruptions of routines. Deal with misbehavior in a way that does not interfere with your teaching. Don't accept or excuse serious or contagious misbehavior, even if you have to stop your teaching. If you ignore it, it will worsen.
11. *Reduce failure, promote success:* Academic failure should be kept to a minimum since it is a cause of frustration, withdrawal, and hostility. When students see themselves as winners and receive recognition for success, they become more civil, calm, and confident; they are easier to work with and teach.
12. *Set a good example:* Model what you preach and expect. For example, speak the way you want students to speak; keep an orderly room if you expect students to be orderly; check homework if you expect students to do the homework.

Kounin's greatest contribution may be his emphasis on prevention. Good teachers structure classroom environments so that misbehaviors are minimized if not prevented. Student misbehavior will never be eliminated totally, but a teacher who understands concepts such as "momentum" and "smoothness" will have far fewer misbehaviors than one who has too few activities or jumps from one lesson to another without proper transitions.

See Tips for Teachers 9.1 for an overview of some practical suggestions for effectively managing your classroom.

Acceptance Approach: Moderate Teacher Intervention

The *acceptance approach* to discipline is rooted in humanistic psychology. It maintains that every person has a prime need for acceptance. Students, like everyone else, strive for acceptance. They want to belong and to be liked by others who are important to them more than they want to learn. Similarly, they would rather behave than misbehave. The acceptance approach is also based on the democratic model of teaching in which the teacher provides leadership by establishing rules and consequences but at the same time allows students to participate in decisions and to make choices.

Rudolph Dreikurs is noted for a disciplinary approach based on the need for acceptance.[21] He maintains that acceptance by peers and teachers is the prerequisite for appropriate behavior and achievement in school. People try all kinds of behavior to get status and recognition. If they are not successful in receiving recognition through socially acceptable methods, then they will turn to mistaken goals that result in antisocial behavior. Dreikurs identifies four mistaken goals:

1. *Attention getting:* When students are not getting the recognition they desire, they often resort to attention-getting misbehavior. They want other students or the teacher to pay attention to them. They may act as "class clowns," ask special favors, continually seek help with assignments, or refuse to work unless the teacher hovers over them. They function as long as they obtain their peers' or teacher's attention. Teachers can determine if a misbehavior has this goal by asking, "Am I annoyed?"

2. *Power seeking:* Students may also express their desire for recognition by defying adults in what they perceive as a struggle for power. Their defiance is expressed in arguing, contradicting, teasing, temper tantrums, and low-level hostile behavior. If the students get the teacher to argue or fight with them, they win, because they succeed in feeling powerful. Teachers can determine if a misbehavior has this goal by asking, "Am I threatened?"

3. *Revenge seeking:* Students who fail to gain recognition through power may seek revenge. Their mistaken goal is to hurt others to make up for being hurt or feeling rejected and unloved. Students who seek revenge don't care about being punished. They are cruel, hostile, or violent toward others. Simple logic doesn't always work with them. Being punished gives them renewed cause for action. The more trouble they cause for themselves, the more justified they feel. Teachers can determine if a misbehavior has this goal by asking, "Am I hurt?"

4. *Withdrawal:* If students feel helpless and rejected, the goal of their behavior may become withdrawal from the social situation, rather than confrontation. They guard whatever little self-esteem they have by removing themselves from situations that test their abilities. Such withdrawal displays their feelings of inadequacy. If not helped, they eventually become isolated.[22]

The first thing teachers need to do is identify students' "mistaken goals." The type of misbehavior indicates the type of expectations students have or their goals.

1. If students stop the behavior and then repeat it, their goal tends to be getting attention.

Working together in small groups encourages cooperation and accountability.

2. If students refuse to stop or increase their misbehavior, their goal tends to be power seeking.

3. If students become hostile or violent, their goal tends to be revenge.

4. If students refuse to cooperate or participate, their goal tends to be withdrawal.

After teachers identify the student goals, they need to confront the students with an explanation of what they are doing. Dreikurs maintains that by doing this in a friendly, nonthreatening way, teachers can get students to examine—even change—their behavior. The teachers should then encourage students in their efforts to recognize their mistaken goals and to change their behavior. Dreikurs sees an important distinction between encouraging and praising. Encouragement consists of words or actions that convey respect and belief in students' abilities. It tells students they are accepted; it recognizes efforts, not necessarily achievements. Praise, on the other hand, is given when a task is achieved.

The teacher needs to be sure the students are aware of and understand the consequences of inappropriate behavior. The consequences must be as closely related to the misbehavior as possible, and the teacher must apply them consistently, immediately, and

table 9.3 **Strategies for Carrying out the Acceptance Approach (Some Examples)**

To Encourage Students	*To Enforce Consequences*
1. Be positive; avoid negative statements.	1. Give clear directions.
2. Encourage students to improve, not to be perfect.	2. Establish a relationship with each student based on mutual trust and respect.
3. Encourage effort; results are secondary if students try.	3. Use consequences that are logical; a direct relationship between misbehavior and consequences must be understood by students.
4. Teach students to learn from mistakes.	4. Perceive behavior in its proper perspective; avoid making issues out of trivial incidents.
5. Encourage student independence.	5. Permit students to assume responsibility for their own behavior.
6. Exhibit faith in students' abilities.	6. Combine friendliness with firmness; students must see the teacher as a friend, but limitations must be established.
7. Encourage cooperative or team effort among students.	7. Set limits at the beginning, but work toward a sense of responsibility on the part of the student.
8. Send positive notes home; note improvement.	8. Keep demands or rules simple.
9. Show pride in students' work; display it.	9. Mean what you say; carry out your rules.
10. Be optimistic, enthusiastic, supporting.	10. Close an incident quickly; mistakes are corrected, then forgotten.

Source: Adapted from Rudolph Dreikurs. *Maintaining Sanity in the Classroom,* 2d ed. New York: Harper & Row, 1982.

in a calm manner, displaying no anger or triumph. For example, failing to complete a homework assignment means staying after school and finishing it. Disturbing others in class results in isolation from the group for a short period. Students gradually learn that poor choices result in unpleasant consequences that are nobody's fault but their own. Eventually, students learn to control their actions and to make better decisions, and thus they reach a point at which they control their behavior through self-discipline.

Dreikurs suggests several strategies for working with students who exhibit mistaken goals to encourage them and to enforce consequences. Some examples of what he suggests are listed in Table 9.3.

Success Approach: Moderate Teacher Intervention

The *success approach* is rooted in humanistic psychology and the democratic model of teaching. Instead of dealing with inappropriate behavior and the consequences of such behavior, it deals with general psychological and social conditions. William Glasser, most noted for this approach, which he calls *reality therapy,* insists that, although teachers should not excuse bad behavior on the part of the student, they need to change whatever negative classroom conditions exist and improve conditions so they lead to student success.[23] One of those conditions is successful social relationships. Hence, a teacher may jointly establish rules with student assistance and then enforce those rules fairly.

Reality therapy consists of having a caring relationship with a student, keeping the focus on current behaviors (not past behavior), helping a student understand the personal responsibility for behavior, and then developing with the student a plan for behavior change and a commitment to that plan.

Control theory represents an expansion of Glasser's reality therapy. With control theory Glasser added the importance of the teacher attending to certain student needs such as belonging and love and control and freedom. Discipline problems are not isolated student actions. They occur because of a myriad of human needs, and teachers must be cognizant of those needs if behaviors are to be managed effectively.[24]

Glasser's noncoercive view of discipline is simple but powerful. Behavior is a matter of choice. Good behavior results from good choices; bad behavior results from bad choices. A teacher's job is to help students make good choices. Students make choices according to how they perceive the results of those choices. If bad behavior gets them what they want, they will make bad choices.

Students who have feelings of positive self-worth and who experience success will make good choices most of the time. The road to positive self-worth and to success begins with a good relationship with people who care. For some students school may be the only place where they meet people who genuinely care for them. Yet some students resist entering into positive relationships with adults, especially teachers. Teachers, therefore, must show that they care and are positive and be persistent about both. The emphasis is on helping—exactly what the teaching profession is about—and therefore the approach is attractive to many educators.

Glasser makes the following suggestions:

1. *Stress students' responsibility for their own behavior continually:* Since good behavior comes from good choices, on a regular basis clarify students' responsibility for their choices and behavior.

2. *Establish rules:* Rules are essential, and they should be established and agreed upon early in the term by the teacher and students. Rules should facilitate group achievement and group morale. Rules can be evaluated and changed, but as long as they are retained, they must be enforced.

3. *Accept no excuses:* The teacher should not accept excuses for inappropriate behavior as long as the student is able to distinguish right from wrong. This is especially true if the student has made a commitment to a rule.

4. *Utilize value judgments:* When students exhibit inappropriate behavior, the teacher should call on them to make value judgments about their behavior. This enhances the students' responsibility to make better choices.

5. *Suggest suitable alternatives to inappropriate behavior:* The students should make the choice, which reinforces their responsibility.

6. *Enforce reasonable consequences:* Reasonable consequences must follow whatever behavior the students choose. The consequences of inappropriate behavior should not be erratic, emotional, sarcastic, or physically punishing. The consequences of good behavior should be satisfying to students. The teacher should never manipulate events or make excuses so that reasonable consequences do not occur after a behavior is exhibited.

7. *Be persistent:* The teacher must make sure, repeatedly and constantly, that students are committed to desirable behavior. The teacher must always help students make choices and value judgments about bad choices.

8. *Continually review:* During a classroom meeting separate from academic activities discuss and develop these procedures. This is the time for students and teacher to seek plausible solutions to problems. Students should never be allowed to find fault with or place blame on others, to shout, or to threaten. If attention is directed to real matters of concern, a bonding or caring attitude between teacher and students may have a chance to take form.[25]

In a summary of his views, Glasser makes the point that teachers must be supportive of and meet with students who are beginning to exhibit difficulties, and they must get students involved in making rules, committing to the rules, and enforcing them. School must be a friendly, warm place, especially for students who have previously experienced failure in school. Student misbehavior is often intertwined with academic problems. The failing student, frustrated by an inability to function in the classroom, frequently expresses uneasiness by acting out. To correct an academic problem, the student, teacher, and school must make a specific commitment. But too often the student is unaware of how to deal with the problem, the teacher is too burdened with other problems, and the school lacks the resources for helping the student and teacher.[26]

For Glasser, school reform is not about stimulating teachers and students to work harder. People, including students, will not be more productive unless what is being asked of them is psychologically satisfying. We have to change school, not by changing the length of the school day or year or the amount of homework, but by making it more satisfying to students and more consistent with their interests, so that they gain a sense of power, fulfillment, and importance in the classroom. Solutions to the problems of discipline and achievement are related to and based primarily on making students feel that someone listens to them, thinks about them, cares for them, and feels they are important.

Many of Glasser's ideas involve time set aside for classroom meetings and group discussion. Glasser generally argues for three different types of meetings: social conduct meetings at which teachers and students discuss the students' behavior; open-ended meetings at which teachers and students discuss topics of intellectual significance; and curriculum meetings at which teachers and students discuss how well students are doing relative to curricular objectives.

On occasion, one-on-one conferences are also needed. The one-on-one sessions require that the teacher and student identify problem behaviors, indicate the specific reasons that behavior is problematic, and then seek specific ways to ameliorate the behavior. James Cangelosi provides an example of a teacher working with a student in one of these one-on-one sessions:

> For two consecutive days during the time Mr. Dean allocated for his high school industrial arts students to work on a project, Elmo either sat and stared into space or slept. Responding to this display of off-task behavior, Mr. Dean meets privately with Elmo. Mr. Dean takes a seat directly in front of Elmo so that he can readily achieve eye contact during the following conversation:

Mr. Dean: Thank you for coming. Tell me, Elmo, were you in shop class today?

Elmo: Yeah, you saw me there.

Mr. Dean: How long were you in shop class today?

Elmo: I was there the whole time; I didn't skip out or nothin'! Somebody else might of slipped out, but I didn't.

Mr. Dean: I don't want to talk about anybody else, just about what you did in shop class today.

Elmo: Maybe, Sandra was the one who—

Mr. Dean (interrupting): We're not going to talk about Sandra or anyone other than you and me. What did you do during the 55 minutes you spent in shop today?

Elmo: I don't know.

Mr. Dean: Tell me just one thing you remember doing in shop today.

Elmo: I watched you show us how to use that new machine.

Mr. Dean: And what did you do after I finished showing you how to use the drill press?

Elmo: I dunno, I guess I went to sleep.

Mr. Dean: Do you remember what I asked you to do right before you went to sleep?

Elmo: Work on my project, but I was tired.

Mr. Dean: I'm sorry you were tired, but would it be better for you to sleep in shop or get your project done?

Elmo: But the project is so boring!

Mr. Dean: I'm sorry you find the project boring. What happens if you don't finish your project by next Monday?

Elmo: I know, you told us. I don't pass shop.

Mr. Dean: Not passing shop, is that good or bad for you?

Elmo: That's bad, that's real bad!

Mr. Dean: Do you want to pass shop?

Elmo: Of course!

Mr. Dean: What will it take for you to pass shop?

Elmo: Do my project.

Mr. Dean: By when?

Elmo: Monday.

Mr. Dean: What must you do to have it done by Monday?

Elmo: I'll have to work on it this week.

Mr. Dean: When will you have time to work on it?

Elmo: In class, that's the only time you let us work on it.

Mr. Dean: And there are only two more class days for you to get it done. You don't have any time to waste. What are you going to do in class tomorrow when I direct the class to work on projects?

Elmo: I'm going to work on my project.

Mr. Dean: What if you're tired?

Elmo: I'll work on my project anyway.

Mr. Dean: You've made a smart choice. Would you be willing to write a note telling me that you will work on your project for the last 45 minutes of shop class tomorrow? I'll use the note to remind myself to leave you at least 45 minutes of class time for your project and I'll make a copy to keep to remind you of your commitment.[27]

Glasser's work continues to evolve. His concepts of reality therapy and control theory have further evolved with his publication of *The Quality School.* In this text he examines how the management of a school influences the behavior of the students. And in *Every Student Can Succeed* he offers specific strategies for teachers to use in creating quality schools.[28] In essence, Glasser argues that misbehavior does not occur in isolation.

The Glasser approach continues to be very popular with a wide variety of teachers and administrators. The straightforward approach requires that a teacher do the following:

1. Be involved with students on an ongoing basis. Be connected to the students in terms of knowing their interests and abilities.

2. Focus on behavior and deal with "what happened," not "who is to blame."

3. Help students learn to accept responsibility for behavior. As suggested previously, *accept no excuses.*

4. Help the student evaluate the behavior.

5. Develop a plan for preventing the behavior from recurring.

6. Help the student make a commitment to changing his or her behavior. This requires dialogue and a clear indication of the positive and negative consequences.

7. Monitor behavior on an ongoing basis.[29]

Implementing Alternative Approaches to Classroom Management

All six approaches have elements of prevention and intervention, and all, regardless of how firm or flexible they appear to be, require a set of rules, limitations, and consequences of behavior. In all the approaches students must complete academic work, and they are held accountable for their behavior and work. A brief overview of the six approaches is shown in Table 9.4.

All the approaches advocate having clear and well-communicated rules, but the firmer (teacher-centered) approaches expect the teacher to assert more power and authority with students. The moderate teacher intervention (MTI) approaches rely more on mutual trust and respect between teacher and students. The high teacher intervention (HTI) approaches look to the teacher to take control of the classroom and quickly establish rules. The moderate intervention approaches emphasize positive expectations of students; they have more faith in the students' ability to exhibit self-control and to work out the rules with their peers and the teacher.

Although all the approaches establish limitations, the MTI approaches permit greater latitude in enforcing rules and allow the students to share power with the teacher. Although all the approaches rely on consequences, the HTI approaches advocate stricter imposition of generally more severe sanctions as a consequence of disobedience. Punishment for inappropriate behavior is permissible as long as it is logical and related to the severity of the disturbance. The MTI approaches impose sanctions but emphasize making students aware that their behavior influences others, helping them to examine their behavior and helping them to identify the consequences of their misbehavior.

All the approaches hold students accountable for academic work. The HTI approaches limit students' socializing and group activities, determine academic tasks, and

table 9.4   Overview of Classroom Management Models

High Intervention Approaches

1. Assertive Approach
   a. Firm, assertive approach
   b. Insistence on appropriate behavior
   c. Clear limits and consequences
   d. Taking action promptly
   e. Follow-through, checking, and reinforcing rules

2. Applied Science Approach
   a. Identifying and enforcing school and classroom rules
   b. Procedures for seat work, teacher-led activities, transition between activities
   c. Purposeful academic instruction, student accountability
   d. Procedures for assignments and monitoring student work

3. Behavior Modification Approach
   a. Reinforcement through rewards
   b. Constant and then intermittent reinforcement to produce the best results
   c. Shaping desired behavior quickly and strongly
   d. Modeling appropriate behavior
   e. Use of verbal comments, observations, practice, prizes, etc.

Moderate Intervention Approaches

4. Group Management Approach
   a. Group focus and group management
   b. On task, work involvement
   c. With-it-ness, overlapping, smoothness, and momentum
   d. Variety and challenging instruction
   e. Teacher alertness, student accountability

5. Acceptance Approach
   a. Acceptance of and belonging to a group
   b. Student recognition and praise
   c. Routines and limitations
   d. Firmness and friendliness
   e. Teacher leadership, corrective action by teacher

6. Success Approach
   a. Student success and achievement
   b. Reasonable rules with reasonable consequences (some student input)
   c. Student responsibility and self-direction
   d. Good choices resulting in good behavior
   e. Teacher support, fairness, and warmth

case study 9.1   Solving a Classroom Problem with Different Management Styles

Ms. Bidwell, a first-year sixth-grade teacher, has done a terrific job of arranging her classroom to prevent problems. She has clear rules and she has even thought through the consequences for rule infractions. She has also articulated some very clear procedures for students to follow in turning in homework and for completing many of the routine tasks that students must do as part of their daily classroom activities. In essence, she has a classroom environment that is conducive to learning and that is arranged to prevent unnecessary problems.

Two students in her classroom simply refuse to do their homework and turn it in. They have done acceptable work on quizzes and they even participate reasonably well during classroom time, but they consistently fail to turn in their homework. She goes to two different teachers for advice. Because the boys are not turning in their homework, it is now starting to have a ripple effect in the classroom—others are now not turning in their work. Ms. Bidwell selects two teachers with very different disciplinary styles. One believes in high teacher control and uses a form of assertive discipline in her classroom. The other teacher uses a more moderate form of teacher control that is similar to Glasser's (success approach) strategy to deal with management problems.

Pretend that you are the high teacher control teacher. Reread that section of this text and make specific suggestions to Ms. Bidwell. Then pretend that you are the moderate teacher control teacher. What specific suggestions would you offer? Are there any similarities in what the two teachers would suggest? What are the big differences?

How would your suggestions change if Ms. Bidwell were a second-grade teacher? A high school English teacher? A high school advanced placement chemistry teacher?

demand that they complete assignments. Students are told what is expected of them and little time is spent on any activities other than academic work. The classroom is organized so that students' engagement in academic work is continuous. In the MTI approaches students are still accountable for academic work, but they participate in planning the curriculum, and socializing is tolerated. Engagement in academic tasks is less intense, and work is often performed on a cooperative or group basis.

In choosing an approach, teachers must be objective about their personality and philosophy and what they are trying to accomplish. It is important that they be honest about themselves—their strengths and weaknesses. To help determine the approach that is best, they must also consider their student populations—their developmental needs, abilities, and interests—and how they behave as a group. Adjustments in your approach may be required for certain classroom situations; reality, not theory, will dictate if adjustments are necessary. In general, HTI approaches are better for younger, more emotionally immature students. MTI approaches are better for older, more emotionally mature students. To explore the differences in the approaches, consider Case Study 9.1.

It challenges you to consider how the same behavior might be handled by teachers with different control philosophies.

Some teachers turn to package programs that are discussed in the professional literature or advertised as "reform" or quick fixes. It is wrong to assume that a process as complicated and multidimensional as managing students can be fully understood by reading a list of dos and don'ts or by attending a two-day workshop.

Certain rules are central to all the models, but they are conceptual and must be modified according to the classroom situation and personalities involved. The models should not be construed as set in stone, just as rules should not be viewed as inviolate. There are many gray areas involved in managing students that require common sense and maturity of the teacher. The models, if taken literally, limit teacher discretion and judgment.

The point is, teachers need to be flexible and examine the models in relationship to their own classroom situations and personalities. Each of the models is supported by some research, and all provide a way for teachers to respond to real discipline problems. You will likely use some combination of the strategies in your approach to disciplining. We seldom see teachers who are purists in terms of how to manage student behavior.

In considering what is best for you, you must consider your teaching style, your students' needs and abilities, and your school's policies. As you narrow your choices, remember that approaches overlap and are not mutually exclusive. Also remember that more than one approach may work for you. You may borrow ideas from various approaches and construct your own hybrid. The approach you finally arrive at should make sense to you on an intuitive basis. Don't let someone impose his or her teaching style or disciplinary approach on you. Remember, what works for one person (in the same school, even with the same students) may not work for another person because of the unique nature of personal chemistry.

As a new teacher, it is imperative that you begin by learning a relatively narrow set of skills and perhaps one HTI approach and one MTI approach. Expand the number of approaches as you develop your professional repertoire of skills and your understanding of classroom dynamics.

What follows are the *essential* survival management skills and the specific behaviors you *must* know how to exhibit. These are beginning points for the novice: a skill based strategy. As a veteran you will begin to shape and redefine them and you will find that you focus more on instruction to prevent problems than the disciplinary skills to deal with misbehaviors.

- *Skill 1:* Teachers should organize instruction to maximize student time on task.
  - *Behavior 1:* Start class on time.
  - *Behavior 2:* Move around the room to monitor student behavior.
  - *Behavior 3:* Establish clear procedures for turning in work.
  - *Behavior 4:* Establish clear routines for transition times.

- *Skill 2:* Teachers should identify and implement specific classroom rules.
  - *Behavior 1:* Rules should be reasonable, enforceable, and understandable.
  - *Behavior 2:* Rules must be taught to students. They must be rehearsed. The students must receive feedback on their rule comprehension.

- *Skill 3:* Teachers should know how to use both low- and high-profile desists in dealing with mild misbehavior. (Note: Low profile desists stop misbehavior without drawing attention to it. High profile desists stop misbehavior by drawing attention to it.)
  - *Behavior 1:* Use misbehaving students' names as part of the classroom lesson (low profile).
  - *Behavior 2:* Move close to the disruptive student (low profile).
  - *Behavior 3:* Use nonverbal cues such as eye contact (low profile).
- When behaviors 1–3 do not work, attempt the following:
  - *Behavior 4:* Say the student's name and direct the student toward appropriate and assigned tasks (high profile).
  - *Behavior 5:* Give punishment (detention) for misbehavior (high profile).
- *Skill 4:* Teachers should identify specific consequences for severe, chronic misbehavior.
  - *Behavior 1:* Know how and when to use different types of punishment.

Paul Burden identifies a large number of different low and moderate (Skill 3) behaviors. They include a process whereby the teacher first attempts to provide situational assistance and then moves to a low profile (mild) desist/response and then to a moderate response for behaviors that persist.[30] Table 9.5 provides an illustration of the behavior progression on the part of the teacher.

Burden's approach and the one suggested in this text are parallel in many respects. Always start with the lowest level response possible and then progress toward more serious interventions as student behaviors dictate. Both INTASC and PRAXIS have standards on managing a classroom. The approach suggested here parallels their requirements. The PRAXIS standards on classroom management and discipline focus on teacher intervention approaches. For example, if you are teaching in a state where PRAXIS III assessments are required, an assessor will enter your room during your first year of teaching and assess whether you "establish and maintain consistent standards of classroom behavior." That assessor is not necessarily looking to see *how* you keep order in your classroom as much as *whether* you keep order. The assessor will reflect on these types of questions when observing you: Are appropriate standards of behavior maintained in the classroom? What approaches does the teacher use to maintain those standards of behavior?

Then the PRAXIS assessor will use a certain scoring process to assess what you do. The assessor will want to know things like:

1. Do you respond to disruptive behavior when it occurs in the classroom? OR, do you allow student disruptive behavior to continue without a response?

2. Do you deal with misbehavior while still demonstrating a fundamental respect for a student? OR, do you deal with misbehavior in ways that mitigate student self-regard?

The PRAXIS assessment suggests implicitly that good classroom management results in standards of behavior that are co-constructed by teachers and students. What emerges may vary but if done properly, it should be a result to positively influence

t a b l e 9 . 5   **A Three-Step Response Plan to Misbehavior Using the Principle of Least Intervention**

Teacher Response	Step 1 Provide Situational Assistance	Step 2 Use Mild Responses	Step 3 Use Moderate Responses
Purpose	To help the student cope with the instructional situation and keep the student on task	To take nonpunitive actions to get the student back on task	To remove desired stimuli to decrease unwanted behavior
Sample Actions	• Remove distracting objects. • Provide support with routines. • Reinforce appropriate behaviors. • Boost student interest. • Provide cues. • Help student over hurdles. • Redirect the behavior. • Alter the lesson. • Provide nonpunitive time-out. • Modify the classroom environment.	*Nonverbal Responses* • Ignore the behavior. • Use nonverbal signals. • Stand near the student. • Touch the student. *Verbal Responses* • Call on the student during the lesson. • Use humor. • Send an I-message. • Use positive phrasing. • Remind students of the rules. • Give students choices. • Ask "What should you be doing?" • Give a verbal reprimand.	*Logical Consequences* • Withdraw privileges. • Change the seat assignment. • Write reflections on the problem. • Place student in time-out. • Hold student for detention. • Contact the parents. • Have student visit the principal.

Source: Paul R. Burden. *Classroom Management.* 2nd ed. New York: John Wiley, 2003, p. 204. This material is used by permission of John Wiley and Sons, Inc.

student learning and teacher comfort with the classroom atmosphere (see PRAXIS Standard B4).

The recommended approach (and that of Burden) parallels the disciplinary sequence that the Joneses recommend in their comprehensive classroom management approach. Specifically, they argue that the teacher should do the following:

• *When misbehavior occurs:* Nonverbally try to stop a misbehavior when it first occurs (e.g., make eye contact or move closer to a student). In essence, start by using a low profile desist.

• *If misbehavior does not stop:* Ask the misbehaving student to state the rule he or she has broken.

• *If misbehavior does not stop then:* Provide the misbehaving student with an option to stop the misbehavior or develop a plan for improving behavior.

• *If misbehavior does not stop then:* Ask the student to move to a designated area and develop a plan that addresses the following questions:

1. What rule did I violate?

2. What specific behaviors violated the rule?

3. What problems did my behavior cause for others in the classroom?

4. What can I do to be more responsible?

5. How can the teacher help me obey the rule?[31]

As you can see, there is a progression in the degree to which the student must clearly articulate the nature of the rule infraction. Remember, your goal is to enhance student responsibility and self-control. The way that becomes possible is by getting students to think about their misbehavior.

Discipline Issue 1: Dealing with Misbehaviors Through Punishment

Educators disagree about the extent to which misbehavior should be ignored. Some researchers have found that the best procedure is to ignore undesirable behavior while paying attention to and reinforcing desirable behavior. Some teachers take this finding to the extreme, hoping that if they ignore misbehavior, even persistent misbehavior, it will go away. If only that were true![32] Other researchers (especially the applied scientists) suggest that misbehavior should only be ignored if it is momentary, or if one student is involved, or if dealing with it may disrupt the entire class.[33] Ignoring sustained minor misbehavior leaves students with the impression that the teacher is unaware of what is going on or is unable to cope with it. In essence, minor misbehavior is likely to intensify unless it is addressed and dealt with.

Robert Slavin makes still another distinction. Many forms of misbehavior are motivated by the desire for peer attention and approval. Students who disobey the teacher are usually (consciously or unconsciously) weighing the effect of their defiance against their standing among classmates. This is especially true as students enter adolescence. Slavin concludes that ignoring misbehavior is ineffective if it is reinforced or encouraged by peers. Such behavior cannot be ignored, for it will worsen and attract more peer support.[34]

One of the authors of this book, Ornstein, makes still another distinction among misbehaving students. He asserted years ago that emotionally disturbed children and children who lack healthy ego development pose a special challenge. Their inability to get along with other children makes them isolated and rejected. Often, they are unaware of their responsibility for or contribution to events. They have almost no feelings of guilt and are not responsive to others' feelings. When they realize they are wrong, they tend to withdraw. He claims that "by threatening or punishing, the teacher makes the mistake of appearing hostile; in turn, these children feel they have a right to hate the teacher and be 'bad.'" It is advisable, Ornstein asserts, for the teacher "to be sympathetic," not overly assertive, and even to "make special allowances."[35] Is that advice appropriate for the Attention Deficit Disorder (ADD) or Attention Deficit Hyperactive Disorder (ADHD) child of the 2000s?

Cummings suggests that to a real degree it is. First, she outlines some specific behaviors that seem characteristic of ADD and ADHD students (see Table 9.6).[36] Second, she argues that teachers need to learn how to understand the students but that does NOT mean they need to tolerate the misbehavior. Rather, the teacher helps students learn goal-setting strategies like those articulated by Glasser or self-reflection techniques like the one

t a b l e 9 . 6   **Common Misbehaviors of ADD and ADHD Students**

· ·

- Playing with rulers, pencils, or other objects
- Tapping on desks or chairs
- Whistling or making inappropriate sounds
- Saying, "Shut-up" or verbally calling out inappropriate comments
- Invading the personal space of others
- Not sharing with others or taking material that belongs to others
- Sleeping in class or daydreaming extensively
- Talking during instruction or out of turn
- Blurting out answers, problems with impulse control
- Arguing with the teacher or talking back

Source: Adapted from Carol Cummings. *Winning Strategies for Classroom Management.* Alexandria, VA: Association for Supervision and Curriculum Development, 2000, p. 116.

provided in Table 9.7. In essence, it is important to work with such students to get them to think about their misbehavior. Incidently, whether students self-assess accurately is not nearly as important as just getting them to think about their behavior. Punishment is a last resort because it usually limits the degree to which a student looks at his or her own behavior, and it engenders more of a student response to the teacher's punishment behavior.

For situations in which it is decided that punishment is *appropriate,* the teacher must decide on its form and severity. The teacher should establish criteria for using it. Punishment is construed by behaviorists as an unpleasant stimulus that an individual will try to avoid. Common punishments, according to Gage and Berliner, range from soft reprimands (those experienced only by the student concerned), which we label low profile desists, to being publicly disciplined by the teacher to stop a misbehavior, to more serious consequences such as social isolation (detention, missed recess) and being reported to someone outside the classroom (disciplinarian, principal, parent).[37]

Corporal punishment should not be used. The negative side effects outweigh the temporary advantages of squashing inappropriate behavior. It tends to demoralize the class. Although it may keep young and physically immature students in check, it also creates anger and resentment. If it is to have any effect, the teacher will at some point have to use it with physically stronger students, and the teacher who backs down loses face and authority.

Although teachers need to know the negative consequences of corporal punishment, they also need to be aware of the fact that many U.S. parents use corporal punishment at home. Hence, many parents may encourage teachers to use a technique they like.[38] That does not justify its use. Many excellent teachers with difficult classes never paddle students. Learn how to discipline without paddling even if your state and school district permit it. You will be more effective and students will ultimately benefit.

It should be clear to the student why he or she is being punished. Moreover, the punishment should fit the misbehavior (overreacting will cause anger, suppressed hostility, or an emotional response from the student). The teacher should avoid punishing while angry or emotional.

table 9.7   **Self-Reflection**

Use this table and the following scale to measure your success in your
schoolwork and progress toward your goals:

Scale: 1 = seldom; 2 = sometimes; 3 = consistently

Where I Am Now			Topic	Where I Want to Be		
1	2	3	I turn my homework in on time.	1	2	3
1	2	3	I give good effort on class assignments.	1	2	3
1	2	3	I use my time wisely in class.	1	2	3
1	2	3	I try hard to produce quality work.	1	2	3
1	2	3	I work cooperatively with my classmates.	1	2	3

Source: Adapted from Carol Cummings. *Winning Strategies for Classroom Management.* Alexandria, VA: Association for
Supervision and Curriculum Development, 2000, p. 83.

One researcher, who refers to punishment as "management strategies," has assessed twenty-four common strategies employed by junior high school teachers.[39] The
sample consisted of 281 students and 80 teachers who were asked to rate the severity
of each strategy. The data reveal that teachers tend to employ as many relatively unsevere strategies as they do moderately severe and very severe strategies combined. Relatively unsevere strategies involve task assignments, removal of privileges, or a
classroom seating change. Moderately severe strategies impose constraints on students'
freedom or time, a trip to the principal's office, or detention after class. Very severe
strategies involve removal or transfer of the student; conferring with the parent; sham-
ing or insulting the student; or suspending the student. Although there were significant
differences between student and teacher mean ratings for about half the items, the rank
orderings of the strategies were similar (correlation of .84), implying comparable perceptions of the severity of punishment.

According to Good and Brophy, a number of general principles apply to meting
out punishment: 1) the threat of punishment is usually more effective than punishment
itself, especially when phrased in such a way that there are unknown consequences; 2)
punishment should be threatened or warned before implemented (but teachers should
threaten only once!); 3) the punishment should be accompanied with positive statements of expectations or rules, focusing on what the students should be doing; 4) punishment should be combined with negative reinforcement, so that the student must
improve to avoid the punishment; and (5) punishment should be systematic and delib-
erate.[40] Educators also point out that teachers should avoid punishing while angry or
emotional; punish when inappropriate behavior starts (don't wait until things build up);
and make their motivation clear (without preaching or overexplaining) while the student is being punished.[41] Two other suggestions are worth noting: 1) do not punish an
entire class or group because of the misbehavior of one student (this is a sign of weakness, and eventually the class or group will unite against you) and 2) avoid excessive

tips for teachers 9.2

Strategies for Managing Problem Students

 Following are general strategies for dealing with problem students, sometimes called "difficult" students, based on the experience of teachers. Although originally developed for junior high school inner-city students, the strategies apply to most school settings and grade levels.

1. Accept the students as they are, but build on and accentuate their positive qualities.
2. Be yourself, since these students can recognize phoniness and take offense at such deceit.
3. Be confident; take charge of the situation, and don't give up in front of the students.
4. Provide structure, since many of these students lack inner control and are restless and impulsive.
5. Explain your rules and routines so students understand them. Be sure your explanations are brief; otherwise you lose your effectiveness and you appear to be defensive or preaching. Also, explain why punished behavior is unacceptable.
6. Communicate the positive expectations that you expect the students to learn and that you require academic work.
7. Rely on motivation and not on your prowess to maintain order; an interesting lesson can keep the students on task.

8. Be a firm friend, but maintain a psychological and physical distance so your students know you are still the teacher.
9. Keep calm and keep your students calm, especially when conditions become tense or upsetting. It may be necessary to delay action until after class, when emotions have been calmed.
10. Administer punishment, whenever possible, privately.
11. Anticipate behavior; being able to judge what will happen if you or a student decide on a course of action may allow you to curtail many problems.
12. Expect, but don't accept, misbehavior. Learn to cope with misbehavior, but don't get upset or feel inadequate about it.
13. Follow through on consequences for misbehavior. It is acceptable to threaten once, but NOT repeatedly.
14. Inform students ahead of time that certain types of behavior will be punished.

Source: Adapted from Allan C. Ornstein. "Teaching the Disadvantaged." *Educational Forum* (January 1967): 215–223. Allan C. Ornstein. "The Education of the Disadvantaged." *Educational Research* (June 1982): 197–221. Jeanne Ellis Ormrod. *Educational Psychology: Developing Learners* 4th ed. Upper Saddle River, NJ: Merrill Prentice Hall, 2003.

punishment, since this may unite the students in self-defense against you. See Tips for Teachers 9.2 for more strategies.

It would be nice to say that teacher decisions are usually rational and reflective. Unfortunately, this is not so. Many managerial problems are caused by teachers themselves: by overreaction to minor incidents, by ignoring small problems and letting them build until they become out of control, or by meting out inappropriate punishment (mismatching the incident and response to the incident).

Educators would have you believe that the teachers' decisions in classrooms and reactions to student behavior are reflective in nature and can be understood within a psychological context of prior beliefs, personal perspectives, and embedded theories of behavior.[42] The fact is, the complexity and immediacy of many classroom situations require teachers to make intuitive rather than reflective or clinical decisions. Thus, disciplinary decisions, which are often complex and require immediate decisions, are likely to be more reactive than prescriptive and more influenced by prior social experiences and personality than well-thought-out techniques.

First-Day Procedures

Sara Eisenhardt
National Board Certified Teacher
Cincinnati, Ohio

 Classroom management is something that an accomplished teacher does almost intuitively. From my perspective, classroom management involves knowing my students and developing and consistently implementing comprehensive strategies for "doing the work." In twenty-five years of teaching I have developed a system for all the routines I needed to enable me to teach and my students to learn, which I modified according to each class's respective needs and dynamics. Developing these strategies is a very complex and challenging activity. It involves knowing your students and being able to predict how they might respond to particular situations. It involves identifying what you want them to know and be able to do by the end of the first day, week, month, etc., to enable them to shift their focus from the "routine" to the academic work you prepared. You must be clear about what you want them to know and be able to do, planning the most effective way to enable them to reach your goals.

The old saying "You don't know what you don't know until you learn it" certainly applied to one developing teacher I know and for whom I acted as an informal mentor. I drew a T-chart and asked him to identify what he wanted the students to know and be able to do by the end of the first day of school. He said he wanted the students to do a getting-acquainted activity. I reminded him that that was an activity and asked him to identify what he wanted them to know and be able to do. After exhausting his list of first day activities and still unable to identify what he wanted the students to "know and be able to do" and half-believing this was a trick question, he said he did not know the answer. One major difference between a highly effective teacher and

a less effective teacher is that the effective teacher clearly knows and understands why they do each and every activity.

I shared with him my strategy for communicating to the students how I want them to respond to my questions. I clarified the difference between when it is important for one student at a time to respond (communication of a conceptual understanding) and when I want the whole class to respond (recitation of facts). I showed him that when I want one student to respond, I raise my own hand as I ask the question and lower my hand when I call the student's name. This is what I want my students to do. I also explained that I want my students cognitively engaged the entire time they are in my class and so I teach them how to actively listen with their eyes, ears, and hearts as the student is responding. I explained that I always repeat this process as I encourage multiple perspectives and dialogue between students. I demonstrated how I preface a recitation or recall of information question with "Class, . . ." and a short pause to command their attention. Once I explained this to the teacher, he created a list of "know and do" that included things such as how to greet him and enter the classroom, how to store and collect materials, how to independently work on the Daily Calendar Math Problems, and how to participate in discussions and respond chorally. We worked collaboratively and developed connected and integrated lessons that taught the students the routines within the authentic context in which those routines would occur. He seemed to understand the importance of creating highly structured learning opportunities to teach the students classroom behaviors and routines and recognized that many of the challenges he faced were from the lack of effective management strategies.

If someone were to ask me what classroom management was, I would say, "knowledge of students–organization–clear communication–consistency–empathy."

Guidelines for Using Punishment

The guidelines listed here can be used for all disciplinary approaches. Underlying the guidelines is the idea that punishment should be flexible and tailored to the specific student and situation.

1. *Don't threaten the impossible:* Make sure the punishment can be carried out. Telling a student to stay after class at 3:00 P.M. when you have a 3:30 appointment with the dentist illustrates that you reacted hastily and cannot follow through.

2. *Don't assign extra homework as punishment:* This creates dislike for homework as well as the subject.

3. *Be sure the punishment follows the offense as soon as possible:* Don't impose punishment two days after the student misbehaves.

4. *When possible, be sure the punishment fits the misbehavior:* Don't overreact to mild misbehavior or underplay or ignore serious misbehavior.

5. *Be consistent with punishment:* If you punish one student for something, don't ignore it when another student does the same thing. However, students and circumstances differ, and there should be room for modification.

6. *Don't use double standards when punishing:* You should treat both genders the same way, and low-achieving and high-achieving students the same way. (Perhaps the only allowance or difference can be with emotionally disturbed children.) Avoid having teacher "pets."

7. *Don't personalize the situation:* React to misbehavior, not the student. Do not react to the student's anger or personal remarks. He or she usually doesn't mean them and is reacting out of emotion. Stay focused on the deed. Remind the student he doesn't mean what he is saying and that things will worsen unless he clamps down. When the student is out of control, the main thing is to get him to calm down. Punishment comes later, if it is required, after the student is calm.

8. *Document all serious incidents:* This is especially important if the misbehavior involves sending the student out of the room or possible suspension.[43]

QUESTIONS FOR REFLECTION

Some reform-minded educators argue that high academic standards and high expectations result in enhanced student achievement. Other educators who are more progressivist in orientation, feel that schools need to connect academic content with the real-world problems of students. In a recent *Miami Herald* (October 27, 2002) story, a reporter notes that teachers should change how they teach students to make classroom practices more culturally congruent in response to the diversity of American classrooms. Then the reporter quotes a University of South Florida professor discussing one strategy for working in a diverse classroom:

> Instead of classroom rules, the children . . . were presented with traditional African values associated with the Kwanzaa celebration, among them unity, self-determination, and faith. They also are encouraged to follow the "I got your back" concept of policing each other's behavior in the classroom.

Do you think this is an appropriate way to teach students who come from diverse environments? What might make it right for you? Wrong for you? Right for your students? Wrong for your students?

Discipline Issue 2: Preventing Misbehaviors Through Feedback, Trust, and Communication

David Johnson has written several books on interpersonal relations, cooperation, and self-actualization.[44] His methods of enhancing self-awareness, mutual trust, and communication among people serve as excellent preventive strategies. Johnson's methods correspond with flexible and democratic approaches to discipline such as the acceptance and success approaches. They might be used by anyone who wishes to build a humanistic classroom based on student rapport and understanding. The specific methods can be applied on a one-to-one basis or on a group basis in which teachers emphasize interpersonal relations and cooperative processes.

Building Self-Awareness Through Feedback

Feedback tells students what impact their actions are having on others. It is important for the teacher to provide feedback in a way that does not threaten the student. The more threatened and defensive the student becomes, the more likely it is that he or she will not understand the feedback correctly. Increasing a student's self-awareness through feedback gives the students a basis for making informed choices in future behavior. Follow these guidelines:

1. *Focus feedback on behavior, not on personality:* Refer to what the student does, not to what you believe her traits to be. The former is a response to what you see or hear, but the latter is an inference or interpretation about character.

2. *Focus feedback on objective descriptions, not on subjective judgments:* Refer to what occurs, not to your judgments of right or wrong, good or bad. Say, "You are not spelling the word correctly" or "We cannot hear you," rather than "You are a terrible speller" or "You don't know how to speak up in public."

3. *Focus feedback on a specific situation, not on abstract behavior:* Say, "Your homework has not been turned in for three days" instead of "You are so irresponsible." Feedback tied to a specific situation leads to self-awareness. Feedback that is abstract is open to interpretation and is often misunderstood.

4. *Focus feedback on the present, not on the past:* The more immediate the feedback, the more effective it is. Say, "You are becoming angry now as I talk to you," rather than "Sometimes you become angry."

5. *Focus feedback on actions that the person can change:* It does little good to tell a person that you don't like the color of his or her eyes. This is something that cannot be changed.

Developing and Maintaining Trust

To build a healthy relationship among students and between students and teacher, a climate of mutual trust must grow and develop. Fears of rejection or betrayal must be reduced, and acceptance, support, and respect must be promoted. Trust, like order, is not something that can be built once and forgotten about; it constantly changes and constantly needs nourishment. Consider these ideas about trust:

1. *Building trust:* Trust begins as people take the risk of disclosing more and more of their thoughts and feelings to each other. If they do not receive acceptance or support, they back off from the relationship. If they receive acceptance or support, they will continue to risk self-disclosure, and the relationship continues to grow.

2. *Being trusting:* The level of trust that develops between two people is related to both individuals' willingness and ability to be trusting. Each must be willing to risk the consequences of revealing oneself to and depending on the other person. Each must be openly accepting and supporting of the other to ensure that he or she experiences beneficial consequences from the risk taken.

3. *Trusting appropriately:* A person must be able to size up a situation and make a wise judgment about when, whom, and how much to trust. Trust is appropriate when a person is reasonably confident that the other person will not react in a way that will be harmful.

4. *Trusting as a self-fulfilling prophecy:* Assumptions affect an individual's behavior. That behavior often elicits the expected reactions from the other person, and the assumptions become a self-fulfilling prophecy. If you make other people feel they can trust you, they probably will.

Communicating Effectively

All behavior conveys messages. A person sends messages to evoke a response from the receiver. The messages and responses are verbal and nonverbal. Effective communication takes place when the receiver interprets the sender's messages in the way that was intended; effective communication enhances understanding and cooperation among individuals. Ineffective communication arises when there is a discrepancy between what the sender meant and what the receiver thought the sender meant. This reduces understanding and cooperation. Mutual trust enhances the possibility of effective communication; distrust is a primary cause of miscommunication. Skill in sending messages can increase communication between teachers and students. Follow these guidelines for effective communication:

1. *Use the first person singular:* Take responsibility for your own ideas or feelings. People doubt messages that use terms like "most people" and "some of your classmates." Say, "I think . . ." or "I feel . . .".

2. *Make messages complete and specific:* People often make incorrect assumptions about what their listeners know, leave out steps in describing their thinking, and do not mention specifics or ideas that will clarify their intent.

3. *Make verbal and nonverbal messages congruent:* Communication problems arise when a person's verbal and nonverbal messages are contradictory.

4. *Be varied in delivering key ideas:* Use more than one means of communication, such as verbal and nonverbal cues, to reinforce your message.

5. *Ask for feedback:* The only way to learn how a person is actually receiving and interpreting your message is to seek feedback from the receiver.

table 9.8   Politically Expedient Interventions

Problems	Quick-Fix Solutions
Not enough moral training in our educational institutions?	Allow prayer in schools or post the Ten Commandments in every classroom.
Too much violent imagery in the media?	Clamp down on violent movies, TV, and video games.
Too many guns, too easily available?	Institute more stringent gun control.
Youngsters are not respectful enough?	Make rules forcing them to call teachers "sir" and "ma'am."
Some students act differently from what is considered the norm?	Identify them and either keep them under surveillance, remove them from the school, or subject them to intensive therapy until they are able to be like everybody else.

Source: Elliot Aronson. *Nobody Left to Hate.* New York: W. H. Freeman/Owl Book, 2000, p. 9.

6. *Consider the listener's frame of reference:* The same information might be interpreted differently by a child than by an adult. It may be necessary to use different words or different nonverbal cues depending on the listener's age, maturity level, educational level, and cultural background.

7. *Make messages concrete:* It is important to be descriptive, to use verbs ("I like *working*"), adverbs ("Your homework is due *tomorrow*"), and adjectives ("Marco is an *excellent* student") to communicate your feelings clearly.

8. *Describe behavior without evaluating it:* Describe the student's behavior ("You are interrupting Alisha") rather than evaluating it ("You are self-centered and won't listen to anyone else's ideas").[45]

During the past several years there have been an alarming number of troubling incidents at schools involving violent actions by students. Great debate rages about who is at fault: teachers, parents, the students themselves, or society. Affixing blame seldom solves problems. One author has eloquently described actions or interventions that teachers and school personnel can take to prevent Columbine-like episodes. Many solutions are well intentioned but "off the mark." The key is to better match solutions with problems and that requires thought, dialogue, an understanding of young people, and research on what works.

Basically, there are two classes of intervention: root cause interventions and peripheral interventions. In my judgment, some of the so-called "cures" outlined in the box . . . [See Table 9.8] have merit; others are useless; still others are almost certain to cause more harm than good. But they are all peripheral interventions. None of them (not even the useful ones) succeed in getting to the root of the problem. If a peripheral intervention (like gun control or metal detectors, for example) proves to be useful, there is no reason why it cannot be utilized. But we must realize that the deeper underlying problem will remain. And before we implement any kind of intervention, we must make sure that there is evidence supporting its use. What is immediately apparent is that most of these "cures" are not based on solid evidence, but rest on emotion, wishful thinking, bias, and political expediency.[46]

tips for teachers 9.3

Suggestions for Analyzing Preventive Measures

 Some of the causes of misbehavior are beyond your control. Knowing what measures to take to avoid common discipline problems and to handle problem student behaviors will increase your time for teaching and your general effectiveness as a teacher. Here are suggestions for analyzing your measures for preventing student misbehavior:

1. Meet privately with other teachers to discuss problems and successful strategies for dealing with difficult students.
2. Identify and analyze the strengths of colleagues in dealing with discipline problems. Watch other teachers teach. What works for them with some students you find difficult to teach?
3. Determine which supervisors and administrators will provide support when necessary. What approach to dealing with misbehavior do they subscribe to?

4. Ask another teacher, supervisor, or administrator to visit your classroom on a regular basis to analyze your classroom management approach.
5. Communicate with parents on a regular basis to learn about their management philosophies for purposes of support and follow-up in the class.
6. Keep informed on current legal issues concerning discipline. Read education journals and state law digests; talk to union representatives.
7. Document carefully all serious student behavior problems.
8. Evaluate your expectations about your disciplinary measures and review what you ought to accomplish.

Source: Adapted from Daniel L. Duke and Adrienne M. Meckel. *Teacher's Guide to Classroom Management.* New York: Random House, 1984.

This chapter concludes with a discussion about prevention Many teachers think that the key to classroom management is knowing how to deal with students who are disruptive, but as we've said numerous times, the real key is to know how to prevent problems from occurring, or at least how to lessen the likelihood that they will occur. Prevention comes from creating an environment in which students are welcomed and learning is encouraged. (See Tips for Teachers 9.3 for suggestions for analyzing preventive measures.) To drive home the point about prevention, here is a vignette about a real (former) first-year teacher who has now drawn some national attention as a result of her work with urban students:

ABC News, on a *Prime Time Live* segment (April 4, 1998), captured the story of Susan Gruell, a first-year teacher in Long Beach, California. Ms. Gruell was struggling. Her students, at least some of them, wanted her to fail, and some even wanted to make her cry or break down in front of the class. One day, Ms. Gruell confiscated a student note that depicted in caricature a black boy with big lips. The caricature was derisive and degrading. Many teachers would have responded with high teacher control (and punishment) procedures. Ms. Gruell did not. She reacted, instead, out of a learning paradigm (recall Chapter 1). She wanted students to see what the note meant in personal and interpersonal terms. She introduced the concept of prejudice, drawing connections to the Holocaust and the Nazi dehumanizion of Jews. Her passion to help her students learn about why people act as they do rather than punish them for acting as they do started a journey for her class that was truly extraordinary. Over the next weeks and months they studied prejudice and injus-

First-Year Teacher

Julianne Burt
Teacher
Fort Wayne, Indiana

 To prepare for my first day of school as a first- through eighth-grade general music instructor I was forced to take it one thing at a time; if I'd thought of everything I need to do at once I would have gone crazy! Therefore I made a list of the most important things to accomplish before the start of school (i.e., the defined Indiana standards in music, grade level objectives and goals, classroom management strategies, classroom rules and consequences, decorations in the room). With so many things to do, I had to think about what the most important things to any students' education would be, and I started with my yearly objectives for each grade level, those being the things on which everything else is based.

I began by making my objectives for each grade and also used some of the objectives to enhance classroom management strategies, such as having daily music journals for grades three through eight. Students would walk into the class listening to music and immediately record journal reflections (appropriate to their grade level) in correct musical terminology.

Next I decided to focus on the rules and consequences for rule infractions in the classroom. I decided on these by researching what rules and consequences other teachers in the building were doing in their classrooms; I used this knowledge to make five short and straightforward rules that were appropriate for all grade levels as well as consequences that would fit each grade level individually.

Lastly, I began decorating the classroom. I made it a point to include things that would appeal to both younger and older students. I wanted the students to know that this was their classroom. For example, for older students I had a "Music Notes" bulletin board where students could find out about local news in the arts as well as any musical opportunities in the school and community. For the younger students there were brightly colored pictures and signs that encouraged creativity in the classroom and a friendly atmosphere.

By the first day of school, I felt mostly prepared, and my preparedness was due to my focus on what the important things were for student success in the classroom. My focus was not on impressing the other teachers, my mentor, or the principal or even on pleasing myself, but, with the best of my ability, I tried to keep my focus on what the students needed to learn and how they could reach the objectives set for them in the music classroom.

tice, in their lives and in the lives of others. The students were pulled outside of themselves to connect with lives of others such as Anne Frank and Zloto Vilapovich, people whose lives were changed or *ended* by prejudice. In the process, the students acquired an incentive to behave responsibly and maturely. They became so invested in their work that they no longer had any reason to misbehave.

This chapter introduced a great deal of information about how to manage students. Use that knowledge selectively. You need to have control of a classroom in order for students to learn. But you also really need to use good instructional strategies (and good planning), and you need to use prevention strategies and deal with problems when even the best plans fail.

The relationship between good classroom management and student learning is something that even the students understand. Almost all the students you teach want and expect you to have control of the class so that they can learn. A recent *Christian Science Monitor* article noted that 43 percent of teenagers believe that misbehavior of peers is hurting their learning. Equally important, 83 percent of all teachers and administrators assert that the major barrier to success of new teachers is classroom management.[47] Far too many new teachers are oversensitive to what misbehavior means (usually it is for attention; it is not directed at you!) and apprehensive about acting. If you watch good classroom managers, they do not take personally what students do (though they may reflect on what it means!), and they act to deal with misbehavior before it spreads. They also try to have a meaningful relationship with their students. Students who know you and know that you believe in them are much easier to manage. And, students who are engaged by what you plan as learning activities will be more on-task and successful.

Theory into Practice

To move from theory to the practice of good management and discipline, you need to consider some overview or wrap-up questions. Ideally you should be able to say "Yes" to all thirty of the following questions. This will probably not be the case if you have a problem managing students. More than five negative responses suggests you are probably contributing to your own problem and/or that you are heading for bigger problems unless you take corrective action.

	Yes	No
1. Background Information		
a. Do I know each student's personal needs as a learner?	☐	☐
b. Have I examined the student's records?	☐	☐
c. Have I spoken to colleagues (other teachers) about the student?	☐	☐
d. Is the student's home life psychologically safe and secure? (Does he or she eat a good breakfast, sleep enough, have a quiet place to work, etc.?)	☐	☐
e. Do I know which peers influence the student and what students he or she influences?	☐	☐
2. Attitude		
a. Do I interact positively with the student?	☐	☐
b. Do I listen to the student?	☐	☐
c. Do I show respect toward the student?	☐	☐
d. Do I provide helpful feedback?	☐	☐
e. Do I communicate high expectations to the student?	☐	☐
f. Do I compliment or praise the student when it is appropriate?	☐	☐
g. Do I recognize (call on the student) in class?	☐	☐
h. Do I emphasize the strengths of the student in front of the class?	☐	☐
3. Routines and Procedures		
a. Have the routines or rules been clearly stated to the student?	☐	☐
b. Are the classroom routines appropriate and succinct?	☐	☐
c. Is there consistent routine in the classroom that the student can understand and model?	☐	☐
d. Are the routines enforced equally with all students, including the student exhibiting inappropriate behavior?	☐	☐

A Technology Viewpoint from a Classroom Teacher

Jackie Marshall Arnold
K–12 Media Spcialist

 Teachers in classrooms of the twenty-first century will find themselves with several computers in their room and/or an available computer lab. Teachers of today will find expectations from administrators, parents, and students to use these machines, incorporating the technology into their teaching. However, using technology as an effective tool requires more knowledge than just how to turn them on and hoping students will use them appropriately. Teachers not only need technology skills, but they also need management skills to meet the challenges of using computers in the classroom.

It is important for teachers to understand that technology use does not always demand a computer for every student. Cooperative learning groups may be formed and given specific tasks to accomplish or problems to solve with technology tools. Depending on the age of the students, roles can be assigned to provide group structure, or groups can decide the roles of the members themselves. For example, in a group of four, one student can be the navigator, one the recorder, another the timekeeper, and another the manager. In this way, each student knows what is expected and the role that he or she is to provide.

Another management technique to support technology use in classrooms is a rotational schedule through which students move to different stations throughout the day. Once a schedule is in place and students become familiar with the schedule, you can use it to allow all students to utilize the technology. Scheduling can be challenging in the busy life of a classroom.

In developing your schedule make sure that it is consistent and fair to each student. Consider using the schedule during a limited time of the day, and gradually increase the schedule to include more time until you are satisfied with the time students have on the computer.

To increase student productivity while using technology consider the following suggestions:

1. Make sure that every student knows the goals of the project and provide them with a checklist of the tasks that they are to accomplish.
2. Discuss ahead of time the amount of time to be allowed for the project and provide benchmarks for the process.
3. Provide feedback and suggestions throughout the process (include incentives for effective use of time) rather than waiting until the end.
4. Define ineffective use of time and clearly explain the consequences of inappropriate behavior (loss of computer privileges, etc.).

Finally, to maximize students' use of technology, remember that you do not always have to be the only "expert" in the room. Train your students to support and help each other when they have a question or difficulty. Allow the "technology advanced" students in your room to provide leadership in helping students in need. Another suggestion is to survey parents and solicit help from those who have technology expertise and can share that knowledge with your students. A volunteer can provide a great deal of help with special projects or in the computer lab when everyone may need help at the same time.

Using technology in the classroom and in the computer lab will take time and practice for you to develop your own style and successful management and discipline techniques. Give yourself time—the rewards for you and your students will be great!

    e. Have I been clear about the consequences of inappropriate behavior? ☐ ☐

    f. Are the consequences fair and consistent with the misbehavior? ☐ ☐

    g. Do I remain calm when the student exhibits inappropriate behavior? ☐ ☐

4. Instruction
   a. Are the instructional demands appropriate to the ability and needs of the student? □ □
   b. Are the students interested in the classroom tasks? □ □
   c. Does each student understand how to do the homework? □ □
   d. Are special academic provisions (enrichment, tutorial) made for the students? □ □

5. Preventive Measures
   a. Have I followed through with my warnings to the students? □ □
   b. Have I changed a student's seat when problems warrant such a change? □ □
   c. Have I spoken to a student privately when misbehavior needs to be discussed? □ □
   d. Am I willing to spend extra time talking to and getting to know each student outside of class? □ □
   e. Have I communicated to each student's parent(s)? Is there consistent follow-up with the parent(s)? □ □
   f. Have I spoken to the guidance counselor or dean of discipline for advice about students who misbehave? □ □

Summary

1. Six approaches to establishing and maintaining good discipline are presented in this chapter. All establish clear rules and expectations, all include recommendations for preventive measures, and all are positive and practical. They differ in the degree of control exercised by the teacher and in the emphasis on tasks.
2. Which approach or combination of approaches a teacher adopts largely depends on the teacher's philosophy, personality, teaching style, and teaching situation. Teachers should begin their teaching by learning one high and one moderate intervention strategy extremely well. Do not try to use all of them until a couple of the approaches are fully mastered.
3. Punishment is sometimes necessary to enforce rules and regulations. Punishment should fit the situation and take into consideration the developmental stage of the student. It should also be in line with school policy.
4. Preventive measures for maintaining and enhancing discipline are based on the need to curtail classroom problems before they become disruptive and affect teaching.

Questions to Consider

1. What goals do you expect classroom management to achieve?
2. What approaches to classroom management do you prefer? Why?
3. How do a teacher's personality characteristics affect his or her disciplinary strategies?
4. Under what conditions, if any, might you touch a student? Under what conditions, if any, would you use corporal punishment?
5. Which preventive measures discussed in the chapter seem to coincide best with your personality and philosophy?

Things to Do

1. Arrange a conference with a teacher who is known as a "good" disciplinarian. Which of the approaches described in the chapter does the teacher's approach resemble? What are the constructive or positive factors in the teacher's methods and strategies?
2. Arrange to visit a nearby school to observe a teacher. Does that teacher have any special "tricks of the trade" for preventing disorder or confusion? What methods do you like? Dislike? Why? What low-profile desists are used? What moderate and high-profile approaches are used?
3. Prepare a list of preventive disciplinary techniques and common errors of discipline. Discuss the preventive techniques and common errors in class. Which common errors could have been prevented, with which preventive techniques?
4. Discuss in class how you would respond as a teacher to the following classroom situations: a) student constantly calls out; b) student refuses to do work; c) student uses improper language as an affront to a classmate; d) student begins to argue with another student.
5. Create a set of classroom rules for your first teaching assignment. Are they clear? Reasonable? Understandable? Have a peer critique them. Describe how you would teach them.

Recommended Readings

Burden, Paul. *Classroom Management: Creating a Successful Learning Community,* 2d ed. New York: John Wiley and Sons, 2003. A thoughtful research-based approach to classroom management that is appropriate for a wide range of teaching contexts.

Charles, C. M. *Building Classroom Discipline,* 7th ed. Boston: Allyn and Bacon, 2002. This book outlines various disciplinary models and practices.

Emmer, Edmond T., et al. *Classroom Management for Secondary Teachers,* 5th ed. Boston: Allyn and Bacon, 2000. A business-academic approach to organizing and controlling students, this book includes several practical techniques for secondary teachers.

Evertson, Carol M., et al. *Classroom Management for Elementary Teachers,* 4th ed. Boston: Allyn and Bacon, 2000. The companion book to the one above, this one is mainly for elementary teachers.

Carol Weinstein. *Secondary Classroom Management: Lessons from Research and Practice.* New York: McGraw Hill, 1996. This is an applied science approach to the research on classroom management and discipline.

Carol Weinstein. *Elementary Classroom Management: Lessons from Research and Practice.* New York: McGraw Hill, 1997. This is a companion book to the secondary text that focuses just on the elementary grades.

Charles Wolfgang. *Solving Discipline and Classroom Management Problems,* 5th ed. New York: John Wiley, 2002. This text surveys the different management strategies.

Key Terms

acceptance approach   403
applied science approach   392
assertive approach   341
behavior modification
   approach   395

control theory   406
desist techniques   400
group managerial approach   398
negative reinforcers   396
overlapping   400

positive reinforcers   396
reality therapy   405
success approach   405
with-it-ness   400

End Notes

1. The annual poll is published in the September or October issue of *Phi Delta Kappan.* See, for example, the September 1998 issue.
2. *Public and K–12 Teacher Members.* Washington, D.C.: National Education Association, 1993.
3. Daniel L. Duke and Adrienne M. Meckel. *Teacher's Guide to Classroom Management.* New York: Random House, 1984, p. 23.
4. Ronald C. Martella, J. Ron Nelson, Nancy E. Marchand-Martella, and Ronald Nelson. *Managing Disruptive Behavior in the Schools: A Schoolwide, Classroom and Individualized Social Learning Approach.* Boston, Mass.: Allyn and Bacon, 2002.
5. Allan C. Ornstein. "Techniques and Fundamentals for Teaching the Disadvantaged." *Journal of Negro Education* (Spring 1967): 136–145.
6. Lee Canter and Marlene Canter. *Assertive Discipline: Positive Behavior Management for Today's Classroom* 3d ed. Santa Monica, CA: Lee Canter et al, 2002. See also Lee Canter et al. *First Class Teacher: Success Strategies for New Teachers.* Santa Monica, Calif.: Canter and Associates, 1998.
7. Thomas J. Lasley. "A Teacher Development Model for Classroom Management." *Phi Delta Kappan* (September 1989): 36–38.
8. Canter and Canter. *Assertive Discipline.*
9. Carolyn M. Evertson et al. *Classroom Management for Elementary Teachers,* 5th ed. Boston: Allyn and Bacon, 2000. Edmund T. Emmer et al. *Classroom Management for Secondary Teachers,* 5th ed. Boston: Allyn and Bacon, 2000.
10. Ibid.
11. Allan C. Ornstein. "Emphasis on Student Outcomes Focuses Attention on Quality of Instruction." *NASSP Bulletin* (January 1987): 88–95. Allan C. Ornstein. "Teacher Effectiveness Research: Theoretical Considerations." In H. Waxman and H. J. Walberg (eds.), *Effective Teaching: Current Research.* Berkeley, Calif.: McCutchan, 1991, pp. 63–80.
12. Albert Bandura. *Principles of Behavioral Modification.* New York: Holt, Rinehart and Winston, 1969. Albert Bandura. *Social Foundations of Thought and Action: A Social-Cognitive Theory.* Englewood Cliffs, N.J.: Prentice-Hall, 1986.
13. B. F. Skinner. "The Evolution of Behavior." *Journal of Experimental Analysis of Behavior* (March 1984): 217–222. B. F. Skinner. "Cognitive Science and Behaviorism." *British Journal of Psychology* (August 1985): 291–301.
14. Paul A. Schutz. "Facilitating Self-Regulation in the Classroom." Paper presented at the annual meeting of the American Educational Research Association, New Orleans, April 1994. Paul R. Burden. *Classroom Management: Creating a Successful Learning Community.* New York: John Wiley, 2003.
15. Jack Snowman, Robert F. Biehler, and Curtis J. Bank. *Psychology Applied to Teaching,* 9th ed. Boston: Houghton Mifflin, 2000.
16. C. M. Charles. *Building Classroom Discipline,* 6th ed. New York: Longman, 1999.
17. Albert Bandura et al. "Representing Personal Determinants in Causal Structures." *Journal of Personality and Social Psychology* (June 1985): 406–414. Virginia W. Berninger and Robert D. Abbott. "The Unit of Analysis and the Constructive Process of the Learner." *Educational Psychologist* (Winter 1992): 223–242. B. F. Skinner. "The Evaluation of Verbal Behavior." *Journal of Experimental Analysis of Behavior* (January 1986): 115–122.
18. R. A. Miltenberger. *Behavior Modification.* Belmont, Calif.: Wadsworth, 2001.
19. Jacob S. Kounin. *Discipline and Group Management in Classroom.* New York: Holt, Rinehart and Winston, 1970. Jacob S. Kounin. *Discipline and Classroom Management.* New York: Holt, Rinehart and Winston, 1977.
20. Paul Burden. *Classroom Management.* 2d ed. New York: John Wiley, 2003, pp. 107–108.
21. Rudolph Dreikurs. *Psychology in the Classroom,* 2d ed. New York: Harper & Row, 1968. Rudolph Dreikurs and Pearl Cassel. *Discipline Without Tears,* rev. ed. New York: Dutton, 1988.
22. Rudolph Dreikurs, Bernice B. Grunwalk, and Floyd C. Pepper. *Maintaining Sanity in the Classroom,* 2d ed. New York: Harper & Row, 1982. Rudolph Dreikurs and Loren Grey. *Logical Consequences:*

A New Approach to Discipline. New York: Dutton, 1988. Rudolph Dreikurs. *Children: The Challenge.* New York: Dutton, 1990.

23. William W. Glasser. *Reality Therapy: A New Approach to Psychiatry.* New York: Harper & Row, 1965. William W. Glasser. *The Quality School: Managing Students Without Coercion.* New York: HarperCollins, 1990.

24. William W. Glasser, *School Without Failure.* New York: Harper & Row, 1969. Glasser. *The Quality School.*

25. William W. Glasser. *Control Theory in the Classroom.* New York: Harper & Row, 1986.

26. Ibid.

27. James S. Cangelosi. *Classroom Management Strategies,* 3d ed. New York: Longman, 1997, pp. 30–31.

28. William Glasser. *The Quality School: Managing Students Without Coercion,* 2d ed. New York: Harper Perennial, 1992. William Glasser. *Every Student Can Succeed.* Chatsworth, Calif.: Black Forest Press, 2000.

29. Evertson et al. *Classroom Management for Elementary Teachers.*

30. Burden. *Classroom Management,* pp. 198–215.

31. Vernon F. Jones and Louise S. Jones. *Comprehensive Classroom Management: Creating Positive Learning Environments for All Students,* 3d ed. Boston: Allyn and Bacon, 1995.

32. Carl Bereiter. "Implications of Connectionism for Thinking About Rules." *Educational Researcher* (April 1991): 10–16. Paul A. Schutz. "Goals in Self-Directed Behavior." *Educational Psychologist* (Winter 1991): 55–67.

33. Thomas L. Good and Jere E. Brophy. *Looking in Classrooms,* 8th ed. Reading, Mass: Addison Wesley, 2000.

34. Robert E. Slavin. *Cooperative Learning,* 2d ed. Needham Heights, Mass.: Allyn and Bacon, 1990. Robert E. Slavin. *Educational Psychology: Theory into Practice,* 6th ed. Needham Heights, Mass.: Allyn and Bacon, 2000.

35. Allan C. Ornstein. "Teaching the Disadvantaged." *Educational Forum* (January 1967): 221.

36. Carol Cummings. *Winning Strategies for Classroom Management.* Alexandria, VA: Association for Supervision and Curriculum Development, 2000.

37. N. L. Gage and David C. Berliner. *Educational Psychology,* 6th ed. Boston: Houghton Mifflin, 1998.

38. William Damon. *Greater Expectations.* New York: Free Press, 1992. Annette M. Iverson. *Building Competence in Classroom Management and Discipline,* 4th ed. Columbus, OH: Merrill Prentice Hall, 2003.

39. Moshe Zeidner. "The Relative Severity of Common Classroom Management Strategies: The Student's Perspective." *British Journal of Educational Psychology* (February 1988): 69–77.

40. Thomas L. Good and Jere E. Brophy. *Contemporary Educational Psychology,* 5th ed. New York; Longman, 1995. Good and Brophy. *Looking in Classrooms.*

41. Bob Algozzine and Pam Kay. *Preventing Problem Behavior.* Thousand Oaks, CA: Corwin Press, 2002. Tom V. Savage. *Teaching Self-Control Through Management and Discipline,* 2d ed. Needham Heights, Mass.: Allyn and Bacon, 1999.

42. Christopher M. Clark and Penelope L. Peterson. "Teachers' Thought Processes." In M. C. Wittrock (ed.), *Handbook of Research on Teaching,* 3d ed. New York: Macmillan, 1986, pp. 255–296. Bud Wellington. "The Promise of Reflective Practice." *Educational Leadership* (March 1991): 4–5.

43. Ornstein. "Techniques and Fundamentals for Teaching the Disadvantaged." Ornstein. "Teaching the Disadvantaged." Allan C. Ornstein. "A Difference Teachers Make: How Much?" *Educational Forum* (Fall 1984): 109–117. Also see Joseph E. Williams. "Principles of Discipline." *American School Board Journal* (February 1993): 27–209.

44. David W. Johnson. *Reaching Out: Interpersonal Effectiveness and Self-Actualization,* 6th ed. Needham Heights, Mass.: Allyn and Bacon, 1997.

45. Ibid.

46. Elliot Aronson. *Nobody Left to Hate.* New York: W. H. Freemanh? Owl Book, 2000.

47. J. Kehe. "It's 8 a.m., and Everything Is Not Under Control." *Christian Science Monitor* (October 8, 2002). Retrieved from http://ccmonitor.com/2002/1008/p14s01-lecl.html.

Academic Standards and Student Assessment

Pathwise criteria relevant to the content of this chapter:

- Creating or selecting evaluation strategies that are appropriate for the students and that are aligned with the goals of the lesson. (A5)
- Monitoring students' understanding of content through a variety of means, providing feedback to students to assist learning, and adjusting learning activities as the situation demands. (C4)
- Reflecting on the extent to which the learning goals were met. (D1)

INTASC principles relevant to the content of this chapter:

- The teacher understands and uses formal and informal assessment strategies to evaluate and ensure the continuous intellectual, social, and physical development of the learner. (P8)

focusing questions

1. How have academic standards influenced assessment?

2. What are the most common methods for testing reliability? Validity?

3. What are the differences between norm-reference measurements and criterion-reference measurements?

4. How can classroom tests be improved? What short-answer test questions generate the most controversy? Why? How can the teacher improve the writing and scoring of essay test questions?

5. What test-taking skills can be taught to students?

In these next two chapters we discuss the issues of standards, student assessment, and student and teacher accountability. During the past several years and especially with the passage of the No Child Left Behind legislation in 2002, educators have a "new" understanding of what it means to teach in an American classroom. Not all would concur that the emphasis on standards, assessment, and accountability has led (or will lead) to better education. But almost all would agree that it has and will impact schools and the teachers who teach in those schools.

Of the several different ways being used to improve the quality of schools (e.g., competition through the use of vouchers, legislated class size reductions), none offers the potential for such direct impact on teachers as does the standards movement. This chapter begins with a description of what the standards movement entails. We will then move to student assessment. In the next chapter we will deal with ways teachers evaluate the performance of students and how teachers, quite likely, will be evaluated and held accountable for what students learn.

Standards

All states except Iowa have some form of statewide standards in place. This book has stressed the need for you to know the standards for your discipline and for your state, and part of the reason for that is that your students will be assessed relative to those standards.

Standards evolve out of three basic propositions:

1. Students, teachers, and parents need a clear idea of what students will be expected to learn.
2. Teachers need to know whether students are learning what they need to learn.
3. Results should be connected with appropriate incentives and supports.[1]

These propositions are not ones that most people would contest, though clearly even the most innocuous of statements about standards will draw critics' comments. The point here is not to explore the complexity of the debate. Rather, the point is to understand that although standards are being contested, they are in place in most states and they will impact what and how you teach. Therefore, you should know about them and understand that most people who currently administer state and local education systems believe that standards are essential for improved education.

Standards and What They Mean

There are content standards for almost all disciplinary areas—they even exist now for the early childhood areas. Teachers need to know the content standards for the subjects that they teach even if they do not actively create lessons around those standards.

Good academic teaching standards have two essential qualities: clarity and parsimony.[2] *Clarity* means that sufficient detail is given to ensure that someone reading the standard will know what students are expected to learn. Clear standards tend to be free of jargon and ambiguity. *Parsimony* refers to the narrow focus of the standards. If they are written to ensure students learn *everything,* students will likely be unsuccessful.

As states set standards that are clear and focused, they also strive to ensure that the standards are reasonable yet rigorous. Some states also generate associated grade level indicators for defined standards. An example of associated grade level indicators for a standard is provided at www.battelleforkids.org.

Marzano argues that standards can improve student achievement, and many others who are concerned with educational reform would agree.[3] However, according to Marzano, for standards to make a difference, policymakers have to take some specific steps:

1. *Reduce the number of overall content standards and ensure clear focus:* Marzano claims that a review of the different content standards (see www.mcrel.org) turns up 130 documents across fourteen different disciplinary areas. Covering all that needs to be taught simply cannot be accomplished within a K–12 context.

2. *Create monitoring systems to track student progress:* Students are extremely mobile—they don't stick around at one school for their entire educational careers. How are teachers supposed to monitor students when the data for even the nonmobile students are often unavailable? Teachers need this data and they need to use it to clearly document the progress of students with a form of standards-based grading (i.e., plot the progress of students relative to specific standards).[4]

Marzano's recommendations are for the national, broad-level implementation of standards. What are the implications for a specific teacher? Teachers must decide what to teach, have a clear focus, find out what students have learned, and then remediate. The prescription is simple; the actual implementation process is a bit more complex.

Can Standards Make a Difference?

Those advocating for standards assert that they do make a difference in student achievement and that they can help close the achievement gap between white and black students. Schmoker and Marzano argue that the difference can be seen in many places such as the following:

- *Frederick County, Maryland,* where the number of students reaching well-defined and commonly assessed standards rose dramatically, lifting them from the middle to the highest tier in Maryland schools. Local assessments were deliberately aligned with standards as they were embedded in the state assessments.

- *Fort Logan Elementary School in Denver, Colorado,* where scores rose significantly when teams of teachers analyzed weaknesses in performance relative to grade-level standards. Each team reviewed test data and developed strategies for helping students learn in identified areas of difficulty. . . .

- *Amphitheater High School in Tucson, Arizona,* where teacher Bill Bendt routinely helps exceptional numbers of students pass advanced placement tests by carefully focusing instruction on the standards made explicit by the AP exam.[5]

Used appropriately and wisely by teachers, standards-based education can make a real value-added difference in the learning of students. Does that mean that you are locked into what you must teach? In most cases, the answer is *no.* Good teachers make decisions about what to teach and how to teach it. Schmoker and Marzano, though clear advocates for standards-based education, clearly argue that those at the school level (and at the classroom level) must "review the standards documents . . . [and] then exercise severe discipline in prioritizing on the basis of what students will most need if they are to become reflective thinkers, competent workers, and responsible citizens."[6]

Standards form the basis for the curriculum that you teach. Central to that process of identifying standards is a concomitant requirement that you as the teacher find ways to assess what you decide to teach. That assessment process is the focus of the remainder of this chapter. We will examine the different ways for you to know what the students know. If you have such knowledge and then understand how to use if effectively, the students will learn even more. The goal of assessment is not an objective grade for a report card, but a clear understanding by you and the student of what that student knows, does not know, and still needs to learn.

QUESTIONS FOR REFLECTION

As indicated at the beginning of this chapter, the focus on standards-based reform is not something that is universally embraced. Indeed, many argue that the narrow focus on standards results in an overemphasis on factual material and rote learning. Some also question whether the standards emphasis works against creating educational opportunities that help students achieve their full potential. In essence, although most states have embraced the standards reform focus, many educators continue to question the efficacy of the approach.

Articulate what you see as the arguments for and against standards-based education. You might begin by examining carefully the standards in your disciplinary area (or for the grade level that you want to teach). In what ways might standards make your job easier? More difficult?

Evaluating Student Learning

The process of evaluating student learning is now central to what it means to be a teacher. Good teachers know how to diagnose student learning, which means that they know how to use tests to assess what students know.

Evaluation is a two-step process. The first step is *measurement,* in which one or a series of tests generate data. That measurement process is the focus of this chapter. Once the measurement has occurred, judgments are made about the adequacy of the performance, usually in the context of instructional objectives. That judgment process will be the focus of Chapter 11. As you will see, just as you are making judgments, so, too, are others making judgments about your teaching.

Evaluation is also necessarily connected to testing and teaching. Some researchers assert that, when teachers teach material in a variety of ways, students are more likely to understand the content.[7] Indeed, teachers who require students to go beyond the rote memorization of content and to analyze and creatively and practi-

professional viewpoint

Testing What We Intend to Teach

Robert E. Yager
Professor of Science Education
University of Iowa

 Too often, testing never gets beyond seeing what a student can remember from reading, discussions, and/or class activities. And yet, the course goals and lesson objectives seldom begin with the verbs "remember" or "recall." It is reasonable, then, to expect skills and competencies in quizzes and examinations that coincide with the verb forms in the statement of goals and objectives.

Some who are intimately involved with competency-based and/or behavioral learning strategies are guilty of defining the competencies or behaviors for mastery as lists that can be transferred to test items that require recognition of definitions in multiple-choice items, matching terms with definitions, or a short answer item requiring a straightforward definition or elaboration. Such recall does not assure learning and often negates the value of identifying goals and objectives for the classroom.

Effective teachers use their goals to select a curriculum that is a vehicle for meeting those goals, instructional strategies to drive the vehicle, and skills in testing that match the actions used in the goal statements. Too many of us espouse general goals, proceed with telling students information that we know, and evaluate student retention of this information. Such is a common temptation for many beginning teachers. However, as we mature and have time to ponder what our testing actions do, we are humbled as we note the mismatch between what we purport to be our goals and the measures we select or create to assess student success.

cally engage with content remember the material better. You need to think about testing and evaluation as an extension of instruction, not as separate from the instructional process.

Criteria for Selecting Tests

Two major criteria for selecting tests, especially standardized tests, are reliability and validity. By *reliability* we mean that the test yields similar results when it is repeated over a short period of time or when a different form is used. A reliable test can be viewed as consistent, dependable, and stable. By *validity* we mean that the test measures what it is represented as measuring. An invalid test does not measure what it should. For example, a pen-and-pencil test is not suitable for measuring athletic abilities. A third criterion for selected tests is *usability,* which refers to its characteristics, such as cost and simplicity of administration, that make it a reasonable choice.

Reliability

Test reliability can be expressed numerically. A coefficient of .80 or higher indicates high reliability, .40 to .79 fair reliability, and less than .40 low reliability. Many standardized tests are comprised of several subtests or scales and thus have coefficients to correspond to each of the subtests, as well as the entire test. For example, reliability for a reading test might be reported as .86 for comprehension, .77 for vocabulary, .91 for analogies, and .85 for the test as a whole.

There are three basic methods for determining test reliability. In the method called *test-retest* a test is administered twice, usually with ten to thirty days between tests.[8] The rank ordering of individual test scores on the two tests is compared. If the rank ordering of scores is exactly the same, then the correlation coefficient is 1.00, or perfect reliability. A correlation of .86 indicates that the test is highly consistent over time.

A number of objections have been raised to the test-retest method. If the same items are used on both tests, the respondents' answers on the second test may be influenced by their memory of the first test and by discussions about the items with classmates or teachers between tests. If the interval between tests is too short, memorization is a factor. If the interval is too long, scores may change as a result of learning. The two test conditions might also differ. Lack of interest on the student's part during one of the test situations, a change in a student's health or diet, or a change in the mood of the student or the test administrator may affect the scores.

To overcome the problems introduced by repeated test items in the test-retest method, the *parallel forms* method may be used. In this method, two different but equivalent forms of the test are produced, and students are given both forms of the test. The correlation between scores on the two tests provides a good estimate of reliability. One drawback to this method is that parallel forms are not always available, especially with teacher-made tests but even with many standardized tests. And when two forms do exist they are not always equivalent and may differ in difficulty.[9] Also, the parallel forms method does not address the problem of differing test conditions.

The difficulties associated with the test-retest and parallel forms methods have led to the development of the *split-half reliability* method. In this method, a single test is split into reasonably equivalent halves, and these two subtests are used as if they were two separate tests to determine reliability coefficients. One common method of splitting a test is to score the even-numbered and odd-numbered items separately. Of course, splitting a test in half means that the reliability scores are determined by half the number of items. Too few items in calculations can lead to greater distortions and more chance effects. In short, test reliability is higher when the number of items is increased, because the test involves a larger sample of the material covered.[10]

Each of the measures (or different methods of estimating reliability) has different strengths and weaknesses. In general, there are more sources of error with the first two than with the split-half reliability method.[11] The key is to look not just at the numerical value of a reliability estimate, but also at the reported method.

Another type of reliability is *scorer* reliability. This refers to the consistency of the scorer (typically the teacher) in scoring test items. Quite obviously, a true/false test can be more reliably graded than an essay test. High scorer reliability is not always possible, but it is important than you as a grader understand the fact that you can increase or decrease scorer reliability by simply changing the type of test you give.

In conclusion, keep in mind that reliability can be enhanced generally by giving longer tests.

Validity

Depending on a person's knowledge of research and reason for administering the test, he or she can choose from many different types of validity. We will only examine those that a classroom teacher should know. You won't formally use these forms of validity in constructing teacher-made tests, but knowing them will help you shape your assessments. Professional testing services go to great expense to ensure that tests have validity. You should go to great effort to ensure that your tests have reasonable validity as well.

Content Validity

When constructing a test for a particular subject, teachers should ask whether the items adequately reflect the specific content of that subject. If test items can be answered on the basis of basic intelligence, general knowledge, or test wiseness, knowledge of the content of a course or knowledge of a subject is not being tested adequately. The test lacks content validity.

Of all the forms of validity, content validity is perhaps the most important one. An eighth-grade science test should measure scientific knowledge and skills taught in eighth grade, not reading comprehension, not mathematics, and not tenth-grade science.

Curricular Validity

A standardized test that covers a good sample of a subject, but not the subject or course as taught in a particular school, has content validity but not curricular validity. A test that reflects the knowledge and skills presented in a particular school's curriculum has curricular validity. In such a test the items adequately sample the content of the curriculum the students have been studying.[12]

The problem of curricular validity arises more often with standardized tests than with teacher-made tests. Many standardized tests have excellent content validity on a nationwide or statewide basis, but the items are not targeted for a local school basis.

Predictive Validity

Predictive validity is concerned with the relation of test scores to performance at some future time. For example, valid aptitude tests, administered in the twelfth grade or first year of college, should predict success in college. This is what the Scholastic Aptitude Tests (SATs) that students take in high school are supposed to do. Information on how a student is likely to perform in an area of study or work can be helpful in counseling students and in selecting students for different programs. (It is important to consider other factors as well, including previous grades and letters of recommendation.)

Usability

A test may be valid in content, but the questions may be so ambiguous or the directions so difficult to follow that a student who understands the material may give the wrong answer. Or the questions may be phrased in such a way that a student who does not understand the material may give the right answer. For example, students expect a true-false or multiple-choice item containing the word "always" or "never" to be false or an inappropriate choice. They sometimes answer such an item correctly when they are ignorant of the facts. By the same token, the vocabulary of the test should not be too difficult for students taking the test or the test will no longer be measuring only content but also reading comprehension. Placing too many difficult items in the front of the test will cause students to spend too much time on them at the expense of reaching items at the end that they could have answered easily.

Finally, if a test is too short, representative content will not be adequately tested—resulting in lower test validity.[14]

In general, for a test to be usable, it should be easy for students to understand, easy to administer and score, within budget limitations if it has to be purchased, suitable to the test conditions (for example, time available), and appropriate in its degree of difficulty.[13]

Standardized and Nonstandardized Tests

A *standardized test* is an instrument that contains a set of items that are administered and measured according to uniform scoring standards. The test has been pilot tested and administered to representative populations of similar individuals to obtain normative data. Most standardized tests are published and distributed by testing companies (such as Educational Testing Service and Psychological Corporation); publishing companies (such as Houghton Mifflin and Macmillan), which usually publish reading and math tests to accompany their textbooks; and universities (such as Iowa State University and Stanford University), which have developed and validated specific achievement and IQ tests.

The scores from standardized tests will typically appear in the student record, often called the *cumulative record*. Often these tests are scored externally.

Standardized tests are widely used in schools, and you most certainly have taken a number of them throughout your academic career. Standardized tests usually have high reliability coefficients and good validity, because they have been tested on representative sample populations. Most unreliable or invalid test items have been eliminated through pilot testing over the years. Normative data are useful in interpreting individual test scores and in ranking individual scores within a comparative population. However, normative data are less useful in special school or class situations in which the students have abilities, aptitudes, needs, or learning problems that are quite different from those of sample populations. A test manual should provide a comprehensive description of procedures used in establishing normative data. Although norms can be reported for almost any characteristic (gender, ethnicity, geographical setting, and so forth), such data are usually not shown or are incomplete for students who have special characteristics or backgrounds.

Sometimes an educator is concerned not with how well a student performs compared to other students, but with whether the student exhibits progress in learning. The educator establishes a set of objectives with corresponding proficiency or achievement levels and then determines whether the student can achieve at an acceptable level but does not compare the student to the normative population. The content of standardized tests does not always coincide with the content in a particular school or classroom—that is, the tests may lack curricular validity for that school or classroom.

Nonstandardized tests, usually referred to as *teacher-made tests* or classroom tests, have not been tested on several sample populations and therefore are not accompanied by normative data. These test scores cannot indicate an individual's position with reference to a larger sample. Standardized tests are usually administered only once or twice a year; teacher-made tests provide more frequent evaluations. Teacher-made tests are more closely related to the school's and/or teacher's objectives and content of the course. Who knows better than the teacher what content was covered and emphasized and hence should be tested? Who knows better than the teacher what the needs, interests, and strengths of the students are, when to test, and when, based on test outcomes, to proceed to the next instructional unit? We will discuss teacher made tests in more detail later in this chapter.

Norm-Reference Tests (NRTs)

In *norm-reference tests,* the performance of sample populations has been established and serves as a "basis for interpreting a [student's] relative test performance. A norm-reference measure allows comparisons between one individual and other individuals.[15] The purpose of norms, especially if the norms are based on a larger population, nationwide or statewide, is to compare the score of a student on a test with the scores of students from other schools. Suppose, for example, on a statewide achievement test that Jack's score places him in the 98th percentile in his school, and in the 58th percentile in the state. Although Jack's score is extremely high when compared with the scores of students in his school, it is barely above average compared to scores of a large pool of students. Students who attend inner-city schools may exhibit excellent performance when compared with classmates or peer groups but poor performance on a national or statewide basis. If their scores are compared only with those at other inner-city schools or even with the city norms rather than statewide or national norms, their percentile scores are likely to be higher since the norm group has lower scores than the larger population.

The standardized testing process has developed on a large scale recently.

Norm-reference tests tend to have high estimates of reliability and validity because the norms are based on large populations. Scores can demonstrate progress (or minimal progress) in learning over time.

Criterion-Reference Tests (CRTs)

Criterion-reference tests measure individuals' abilities in regard to a criterion—that is, a specific body of knowledge or skill. The tests are used to determine what students know or can do in a specific domain of learning rather than how their performance compares with other students.

Criterion-reference tests are usually locally or regionally developed. The criterion-reference tests allow the teacher to judge students' proficiency in specific content areas, and therefore they usually have better curricular validity than norm-reference tests. That is, the criterion-referenced tests are usually linked more directly to specific instructional objectives.

Criterion-reference measurements may be practical in areas of achievement that focus on the acquisition of specific knowledge (for example, the Civil War in history or gas laws in physics) and in special programs such as individually prescribed instruction, mastery learning, and adaptive instruction. What is important about this type of test is that it considers the context of the classroom, what has actually been taught, and learning that may not be reflected on textbook or other preplanned tests.[16] It is important to note, however, that it is difficult to develop reliable or valid criterion measurements that test for high-order or abstract thinking.

Your assessment should consider the kinds of learning (i.e., knowledge or problem solving) you expect from students, the content of the curriculum, and the context of the classroom. Your tests should be fair, provide incentives for students to learn, and give you information for purposes of instruction and curriculum decision making. See Tips for Teachers 10.1 for insight into how to improve your assessment procedures.

Differences Between Norm-Reference and Criterion-Reference Tests

The norm-reference test measures a student's level of achievement at a given period of time compared to other students elsewhere. Scores from a criterion-reference test, however, do not indicate a relative level of achievement or produce standards because no comparisons are made. The criterion-reference test indicates how proficient a student is in terms of a specific body of learning. It can measure changes in learning over time, but it cannot produce meaningful comparisons among students.

The norm-reference test is valuable for heterogeneous groups in which the range of abilities is wide and when the test is intended to measure a wide range of performance and then compare student performance. The criterion-reference test is more useful in homogeneous classroom situations in which the range of abilities is narrower and when the test is intended to measure a limited or predetermined range of objectives and outcomes. With norm-reference tests external standards can be used to make judgments about a student's performance relative to a geographically diverse student population; criterion-reference tests lack broad standards, and the interpretation of the scores is only as good as the process used to set the performance levels.[17]

Gronlund and Linn point out five differences between the two types:

1. Whereas the norm-reference test covers a large or general domain of learning tasks, with only a few items measuring each task, the criterion-reference test covers a limited or specific domain, with a relatively large number of items measuring each task.

2. The norm reference discriminates among students in terms of relative levels of learning or achievement, whereas the criterion reference focuses on description of what learning tasks students can or cannot perform.

3. The norm-reference test favors average difficulty and omits easy or difficult items; the criterion-reference test matches item difficulty to the difficulty of learning tasks and does not omit easy or difficult items.

4. The norm-reference test is used for survey or general testing, while the criterion-reference test is used for mastery or specific test situations.

Improving Your Assessment Procedures

The following tips reflect the assessment policy of the Washington-based National Forum on Assessment (an advocacy organization intent on protecting the rights of students) and the National Council on Measurement in Education. The suggestions can be used with norm-reference and criterion-reference tests.

1. Educational standards—specifying what students should know and be able to do—should be clearly defined before assessment procedures and exercises are developed. Assessment should be based on a consensus definition—based on input from teachers, administrators, parents, and policymakers—of what students are expected to learn and the expected level of performance.

2. The primary purpose of assessment systems should be to assist educators in improving instruction and advancing student learning. All purposes and procedures of assessment should benefit students; for example, the results should be used to improve instruction or remediate learning problems.

3. Assessment standards and procedures should be fair to all students. Assessment tasks and procedures must be sensitive to class, cultural, racial, and gender differences.

4. The assessment exercises should be valid and appropriate representations of the standards students are expected to achieve. A sound assessment system provides information about the full range of knowledge and skills students are to learn.

5. Assessment results should be reported in the context of other relevant information. Student performance should consist of a multiple system of indicators. Generally speaking, the more indicators there are, the more valid is the information about the student's performance.

6. Teachers should be involved in designing and using assessment systems. To correlate with instruction and to improve learning outcomes, teachers need to be involved in the assessment practices and be committed to and use the test outcomes for decisions involving curriculum and instruction.

7. It is inappropriate to limit instruction to the objectives of a test or assessment program. Tests should not drive the curriculum. Focusing on the specific content or skills of a test limits the students' ability to learn the larger content and skills of the subject or course.

8. Assessment practices and results should be understood by students, teachers, parents, and policymakers. Test results reported in technical terms, such as grade-equivalents and stanines, are often misunderstood or misleading to the public. Results should be reported in terms of educational standards or performance levels.

9. Assessment programs should provide appropriate information and interpretation when test scores are released to students, parents, employment agencies, or colleges and universities. The interpretation should describe in simple language (free of jargon) what the test covers, what the scores mean, the norms in which comparisons are being made, and how the scores will (or can) be used.

10. Assessment systems should be subject to continuous review and improvement. Even the so-called best testing (and grading) systems need to be modified to adapt to changing conditions (of community, class of students, etc.), resources (expenditures per student, staffing, etc.), and programs (class size, curriculum objectives, etc.).

See also Douglas B. Reeves. *Making Standards Work.* Denver, Co.: Center for Performance Assessment, 1998 for a more detailed discussion of these types of tips and especially the checklists on pp. 249–254.

5. Interpretation of a norm-reference score is based on a defined group, and the student is evaluated by his or her standing relative to that group. Interpretation of a criterion-reference score is based on a defined learning domain, and the student is evaluated by the items answered correctly.[18]

Criterion-reference tests are used by teachers to assess student performance relative to specific objectives, to develop more efficient and appropriate teaching strategies, and to fit the needs of the classroom population. Because norm-reference tests are prepared for many different school districts with different curricular and instructional emphases, they are unable to do these individualized things. Criterion-reference tests better coincide with the actual teaching-learning situation of a particular class or school and they tend to provide answers to questions that are quite specific: "What is the capital of Missouri? What river flows through eastern New York?" One problem with this type of test is that local school officials and teachers often lack the expertise in test construction needed to develop it. Norm-reference tests are usually more carefully constructed than are criterion-reference (teacher-made) tests, since the former are developed by test experts and test items are pilot tested and revised. Thus, it is recommended that teachers develop criterion-reference tests in a group, so they can exchange information with colleagues and perhaps with a test consultant.

Table 10.1 provides an overview of the difference between norm-reference and criterion-reference tests.

Types of Standardized Tests

There are basically four types of standardized tests: intelligence, achievement, aptitude, and personality.

Intelligence Tests

Intelligence tests have come under attack in recent years. Most school systems now use them only for special testing. The two most commonly used intelligence tests are the Stanford-Binet (SB) and the Wechsler Intelligence Scale for Children (WISC). The first is a group intelligence test; the second is administered on an individual basis. Intelligence tests sample a wide range of behaviors including, for example, general knowledge ("What is the square root of 25?"), vocabulary (with some intelligence tests scoring students pass-fail on definitions and giving points for different levels of definitions), comprehension, sequencing, analogical reasoning ("A is to B as D is to __?") and pattern completion.[19]

Achievement Tests

The use of *achievement tests* has increased in recent years, replacing intelligence testing as the prime source of information for educators about students and how they perform in comparison to each other. Every elementary student is exposed to a series of reading, language, and mathematics standardized tests to evaluate performance at various grade levels. There are several types of achievement tests:

1. The most common *survey* or *general achievement tests* are the Stanford Achievement Test—Ninth Edition (SAT9; grades 2 through 9) and the Iowa Test of Basic Skills (ITBS). These tests, used in a number of different states, give teachers a sense of what students have learned. The National Assessment of Educational Progress (NAEP) exams have been administered since 1969 and are designed to measure the knowledge and skills of American students in several different subject areas (mathematics, science, writing, U.S. history,

table 10.1   Comparison of Norm-Reference and Criterion-Reference Tests

Characteristic	Norm-Reference Test	Criterion-Reference Test
1. Major emphasis	Measures individual's achievement (or performance) in relation to a similar group at a specific time	Measures individual's change in achievement (or performance) over an extended period of time
	Survey test, achievement test	Mastery test, performance test
2. Reliability	High reliability; usually test items and scales are .90 or better	Usually unknown reliability; when test items are estimated, they are about .50 to .70
3. Validity	Content, construct, and predictive validity usually high	Content and curricular validity usually high if appropriate procedures are used
4. Usability	For diagnosing student difficulties; estimating student performance in a broad area; classifying students; and making decisions on how much a student has learned compared to others	For diagnosing student difficulties; estimating student performance in a specific area; certifying competency; and measuring what a student has learned over time
	Administration procedures standardized and consistent from class to class	Administration procedures usually vary among teachers or schools
	Large group testing	Small group, individual testing
5. Content covered	Usually covers a broad area of content or skills	Typically emphasizes a limited area of content or skills
	School (or teacher) has no control over content being tested	School (or teacher) has opportunity to select content
	Linked to expert opinion	Linked to local curriculum
6. Quality of test items	Generally high	Varies, based on ability of test writer
	Test items written by experts, pilot tested, and revised prior to distribution; poor items omitted before test is used	Test items written by teachers (or publishers); test items rarely pilot tested; poor items omitted after test has been used
7. Item selection	Test items discriminate among individuals to obtain variability of scores	Includes all items needed to assess performance; little or no attempt to deal with item difficulty
	Easy and confusing items usually omitted	Easy or confusing items rarely omitted
8. Student preparation	Studying rarely helps student obtain a better score, although familiarity with the test seems to improve scores	Studying will help student obtain a better score
	Students unable to obtain information from teachers about content covered	Students able to obtain information from teachers about content covered
9. Standards	Norms used to establish a standard or to classify students	Performance levels used to establish students' ability
	Intended outcomes are general, relative to performance of others	Intended outcomes are specific, relative to a specified level
	Score determined by a ranking, average, or stanine	Score determined by an absolute number (e.g., 83 percent right)

Source: Adapted from Allan C. Ornstein. "Norm-Referenced and Criterion-Referenced Tests." *NASSP Bulletin* (October 1993): 28–40.

civics, geography, and the arts). The No Child Left Behind (NCLB) legislation of 2002 changed the stakes with regard to the use of NAEP tests. Whereas NAEP testing was at one time optional, the NCLB now requires that states receiving Title I funds participate in the state NAEP testing in reading and mathematics at grades 4 and 8 every two years. Participation in the areas of science and writing remains optional.[20]

2. Many elementary and junior high school students are required to take *diagnostic tests,* usually in the basic skills and in study skills, to reveal strengths and weaknesses for purposes of placement and formulation of an appropriate instructional program. One of the several different diagnostic tests commonly used by schools is the Stanford Diagnostic Reading Test 4 (SDRT4). This test intended for lower-achieving students includes items that focus on phonetic analysis, vocabulary, comprehension, and scanning. The SDRT4 mixes difficult and easy items. On most diagnostic tests the items are ordered by level of difficulty.[21]

3. An increasing number of students in many school systems must pass *proficiency tests* to prove they are competent in reading, language, and math. Students who fail are provided some type of mediation. In some cases the tests are used as "break points" or "gate guards" between elementary, junior high, and high school and as a requirement for graduation from high school. Students in some states are denied promotion or a diploma until they pass the examinations.[22]

   One of the real problems with the proficiency tests in many states is the fact that they are still not linked to clear standards. For example, in 2002 only sixteen states had grade-by-grade tests in reading and math, and only nine of those states had tests aligned with their standards.[23] This circumstance is changing rapidly, but the reality in many states is poor alignment between standards and proficiency tests. Further, even where alignment is required by a state, the phase-in process may limit for several years the alignment that is possible.

4. *Subject exit tests* are used in a few school systems at the high school level. Students must pass tests to graduate, to receive a particular diploma, or to enroll in certain programs. For example, New York uses the Regent's examination in basic academic subject areas (English, history, science, mathematics, foreign language) as a screen for eligibility to matriculate full-time in a state college or university; the student must also pass these examinations to receive an academic diploma. These exams also may be considered competency tests.

   A variation on the subject exit tests is the Oregon Certificate of Initial Master (CIM). The CIM must be completed by the end of the tenth grade. Students must exhibit both content and applicational knowledge. Evidence of student acquisition of the knowledge will come, in part, from on-demand performance assessments that are both state and local in character, with teacher usage of discipline-based scoring guides—see Table 10.2.[24]

Aptitude Tests

The difference between aptitude and achievement tests is mainly one of purpose. Achievement tests provide information about present achievement or past learning on a cumulative basis. **Aptitude tests** predict achievement or what students have the capacity to learn. Whereas achievement tests deal with content that the schools teach (or should be teaching), aptitude tests may stress what is *not* taught in schools. There are two common types of aptitude tests:

table 10.2   **Example of Oregon Discipline-Based Scoring Guide (One Section of the Science Inquiry Scoring Guide)**

Use of Contents and Concepts *(always scored)*

Science concepts and principles used accurately.

HIGH
(5/6)
- Scientific facts and concepts are accurately and appropriately used.
- Scientific vocabulary is accurately used when describing and explaining processes and concepts.
- Illustrations and models help explain processes and concepts.
- Previous learning or experience is directly related to the concepts.

MID-RANGE
(3/4)
- Scientific facts and concepts are used, but some may be inaccurately applied or are incomplete.
- Some scientific vocabulary is accurately used.
- Illustrations and models offer some help in explaining processes and concepts.
- Connections of previous learning or experiences are indirectly related to scientific concepts.

LOW
(1/2)
- Scientific facts and concepts are not used accurately or are omitted.
- Scientific vocabulary is used incorrectly or not used.
- Illustrations and models do not help explain scientific processes and concepts or they are omitted.
- Connections of previous learning or experiences are inappropriately related to scientific concepts or are omitted.

Source: Ron Smith and Steve Sherrell. "Milestones on the Road to a Certificate of Initial Mastery." *Educational Leadership* (December 1996–January 1997): 46–51

1. Most students who wish to go on to college have to take a number of *general aptitude tests* to provide information to college admissions officers. You probably took the Scholastic Aptitude Test (SAT) or the American College Testing program (ACT) exam. Students applying to graduate school may take the Miller Analogies Test (MAT) or the Graduate Record Examination (GRE). The MAT is a general aptitude test in logic and language skills. The GRE is a general aptitude test, but the advanced parts are considered a professional aptitude test.

2. *Special* or *talent aptitude tests* are frequently administered as screening devices for students who wish to enroll in a special school (such as for music, art, or science) or for students who wish to enroll in a special course (such as an honors course or a college course with credit) or a special program (such as a creative writing or computer program). Specialized batteries of tests are available for assessing clerical ability (Hay Aptitude Battery Test), mechanical ability (SRA Mechanical Aptitude Test), psychomotor ability (Minnesota Manual Dexterity Test), artistic ability (the Meier Art Test), and musical ability (The Musical Aptitude Profile).[25]

Personality Tests

Personality tests are generally used for special placement of students with learning problems or adjustment problems. Most students in school are not tested for personality. The most commonly used personality tests are the California Test of Personality and the

Thematic Apperception Test, both are intended for use in primary grades through college and designed to measure various social and personal adjustment areas. Other types of tests that measure a person's qualities include:

1. A number of general *attitudinal scales,* which estimate attitudes in diverse economic, political, social, and religious areas, are available; among the more common ones are the Allport Submission Reaction Study and the Allport-Vernon-Lindsey Study of Values.

2. The *occupational attitudinal tests . . .* the Occupational Interest Inventory is suitable for students with at least a sixth-grade reading level, and the Kuder Preference Record is designed for high school and college students.

Questions to Consider in Selecting Tests

Hundreds of standardized tests exist, and selecting an appropriate one is difficult. Individual classroom teachers usually do not have to make this choice, but you may be called upon to make selections if you serve as a member of a test or evaluation committee for your school district. What follows are twelve questions to assist you in selecting an appropriate standardized test. They are based on criteria formulated by W. James Popham.

1. *Is the achievement test in harmony with course instructional objectives?* An achievement test should correspond with the objectives of the course, and it should assess the important knowledge, concepts, and skills of the course.

2. *Do the test items measure a representative sample of the learning tasks?* The test items cannot measure the entire course or subject matter, but they should cover the major objectives and content.

3. *Are the test items appropriate for measuring the desired outcomes of learning?* The test items should correspond to behaviors or performance levels consistent with the course level.

4. *Does the test fit the particular uses that will be made of the results?* For example, a diagnostic achievement test should be used for analyzing student difficulties, but an aptitude test should be used for predicting future performance in a given subject or program.

5. *Is the achievement test reliable?* The test should report reliability coefficients for different types of students, and they should be high for the student group you are testing.

6. *Does the test have retest potential?* Equivalent forms of the test should be available so that students can be retested if necessary. There should also be evidence that the alternative forms are equivalent.

7. *Is the test valid?* Standardized tests usually have poor curricular validity, but . . . should have good construct validity [e.g., show relationship to intelligence].

8. *Is the test free of obvious bias?* It is difficult to find a test that is totally free of bias toward all student groups, but teachers should look for tests that are considered culturally fair (or at least sensitive toward minority groups) and that provide normative data (reliability and validity data) for minority groups.

9. *Is the test appropriate for students?* The test must be suitable for the persons being tested in terms of reading level, clarity of instructions, visual layout, and so forth. It must be at the appropriate level of difficulty for students of a given age, grade level, and cultural background.

10. *Does the test improve learning?* Achievement tests should be seen as part of the teaching and learning process. This means a test should provide feedback to teachers and students and be used to guide and improve the teacher's instruction and the student's learning.

11. *Is the test easy to administer?* Tests that can be administered to large groups are more usable than tests that can only be given to small groups or individuals. Tests that require less time and are still reliable are more usable than lengthy tests.

12. *Is the cost of the test acceptable?* The total cost of the test, including the time involved in administering and scoring it, should be commensurate with the benefits to be derived. If similar information can be obtained by some other method that is just as reliable and valid and less costly, then that method should be considered.[26]

Test Strengths and Limitations

We have examined the different forms of tests that are typically developed by external vendors and that might be administered within a school district. Before we examine how some of these large-scale tests are being used for high-stakes purposes, let's consider some of the strengths and weaknesses of standardized tests. *Test Talk* distributed by the Center for Education Policy, is intended to help educators understand some of the practical problems associated with testing.[27] It outlines several strengths and weaknesses that warrant your attention relative to large-scale tests that are administered to a wide range of students.

- *Strength 1:* Large-scale tests can provide greater consistency in data gathered on students than could be found in an individual teacher's classroom assessments. The types of classroom assessments (portfolios, quizzes) teachers use provide rich information on students within particular classrooms, but such data cannot be used for comparative purposes across schools or school districts.
- *Strength 2:* Large-scale tests can provide excellent summaries of what students understand about a particular content area. They can also indicate whether students have met defined standards for a particular grade level.
- *Strength 3:* Large scale tests are typically efficient and cost effective for schools to administer. They produce a lot of information and do so at a cost that is reasonable as compared to what would be incurred if teachers were to develop similar types of measures. In essence, large-scale tests can produce substantial comparative data at a reasonably low cost.
- *Weakness 1:* Large-scale tests have a "standard error of measurement" that indicates the degree to which a student's test performance might vary: "If a student

earns a score of 410 on [a test such as the California High School Exit Exam] . . .
developers are 95% confident that the student's true score lies between 434 and
386—a standard error of plus or minus 24 points."[28] Test scores are not precise
measures. Rather, they are close approximations. Students who repeat taking a test
may score slightly higher or lower, but the "new" score should be in the error of
measurement of the "old" score.

- *Weakness 2:* Large-scale tests contain only a sample of all the possible questions
  on a topic. Regardless of how comprehensive a large-scale test is, there is no way
  such a test can measure comprehensively all the information a teacher has covered. Large-scale tests have a sample of items and that sample provides a "snap-
  shot" of what students know. A further problem relates to how difficult test items
  should be. Test items that do the best job of differentiating students are those answerable by half the students.[29] That means that, for some types of tests (those
  that are norm referenced), the test makers must create items of medium difficulty.
- *Weakness 3:* Large-scale tests are inclined to volatility. External factors influence
  student performance and that may create substantial year-to-year variations in
  how students perform in a particular classroom or school. The volatility influences
  how you should look at high or low student performance. Be very slow to render
  judgments. To clearly understand how students are performing make certain that
  you do the following:

  - Educate yourself on tests and testing problems.
  - Assess whether the tests that your state uses for accountability purposes are
    aligned with the state (and local) curriculum standards. That is one reason
    this chapter starts with a discussion of standards. Know the standards for your
    state and know whether tests (large-scale and classroom level) are aligned
    with them.
  - Use multiple measures to assess what students know and do not make a major
    decision about a student's promotion or graduation based on any one measure.[30]

That final item is extremely important. It sets the stage for a brief discussion of high-
stakes testing.

High-Stakes Tests

High-stakes tests—whose results impact important decisions—evolved from the minimum competency and basic skill tests of the 1980s. In some cases, under pressure from
the public, states began to impose "gatekeeping" tests for student promotion at selected
grades, "exit" tests for high school graduation or a diploma, and "certifying" tests for
beginning teachers.

In the 1990s the stakes were increased and, with the passage of the No Child Left
Behind legislation in 2002, the stakes for many students became truly "high." School
districts began to use the California Achievement Test (CAT) in the lower grades and
the Scholastic Aptitude Test (SAT) in the upper grades, as well as other statewide
achievement tests, to compare schools and hold teachers and school administrators accountable for the outcomes. State assessments also increased in number and complexity, and an incentive system was tied into the process. Most school districts today either

are rewarded for improvement with increased allocation of funds and bonuses for teacher salaries or penalized for continuous failure by reductions in funding and even loss of accreditation. Indeed, by 2002 half of the 27 states that use high-stakes tests rated schools primarily or solely based on student test scores.[31]

Local, state, and national testing programs have taken on such importance that standardized tests now drive the curriculum and affect the school culture in many school districts. The pressure is so great on schools (and teachers!) to produce achievement gains that it is not uncommon for many to find ways to exclude low-achieving students, who might lower the average test scores, from taking these tests, justifying the practice by classifying the students as handicapped or limited–English-speaking. Some teachers (and schools) fearful of negative ratings may avoid taking at-risk students or students with special needs, thus compromising the educational chances of disadvantaged students who already are served by a high percentage of inexperienced teachers. Still other teachers (and administrators) have been criticized for teaching to the tests and even for cheating in order to raise test scores.

Read the paper on almost any day and you can find a story related to high-stakes testing. On the day this chapter was written, the *Hartford Courant* (Connecticut) carried a story about the Connecticut Academic Performance Test (CAPT). The results from the most recent CAPT administration showed that half of the state's tenth graders fell short of the required passing score. The results produced considerable debate, with critics contending that the test was too difficult and advocates suggesting that any "able" student should know what is required by the test.[32]

When people are not arguing about whether tests are too rigorous or too easy, they are debating what material is actually covered on the test. Tomlinson, for example, argues that all of the No Child Left Behind's emphasis on testing and proficiency provides far too little attention to the academic growth of students *beyond proficiency.* That is, schools are (or may be) attending so much to making students proficient that they fail to really address many of the important academic growth questions that must be answered if schools are to be effective learning environments.[33]

Teacher-Made Tests

Teachers are expected to write their own classroom tests. Most of these tests will be subject related, will focus on a specific domain of learning, and will assess whether a subject has been mastered and when it is time to move on to a new content area. It is estimated by one researcher that a student may take as many as 400 to 1,000 teacher-constructed tests prior to high school graduation.[34] Teachers must create assessment mechanisms that match (or align with) the curriculum and do so with some sensitivity to the particular group of students that is being taught. Given the number of tests students take, such alignment is imperative.

It may be said that teachers and schools are in the business of testing and that they are highly influenced (sometimes hypnotized) by test scores. However, according to researchers, the bulk of the testing is done with teacher-made tests that have unknown reliability, and most teachers do not know how to check for reliability or how to ensure appropriate weighing of content (which impacts on validity) even though most

A teacher must keep many things in mind when preparing and evaluating tests.

teachers have increased the time devoted to testing.[35] Analysis of teacher-made tests reveals that about 80 percent of test questions emphasize knowledge or specific content, that tests frequently do not give adequate directions or explain scoring, and that about 15 to 20 percent contain grammatical, spelling, and punctuation errors.[36]

In spite of their limitations, classroom tests still serve important and useful purposes. Teacher-made tests should have high content validity largely because in most cases the material being tested by the teacher is the material that was just taught. In addition, they provide timely information related to 1) helping teachers understand what students do and do not know, 2) helping teachers know how to group students for appropriate remediation, 3) monitoring student academic progress, and 4) evaluating pupils on their performance.

Accommodating Special-Needs Students

As teachers assess students, it is often necessary to accommodate students who present special learning needs. Such students develop best when they are placed in the least restrictive educational setting, which in many instances will be your classroom. They may need special consideration for testing. Just as you must find ways to teach them essential content, you must also assess whether they have learned what you taught. Some students require adaptations in order to be successful learners. The adaptations that are needed depend on the uniqueness of each learner. Tips for Teachers 10.2 describes various adaptation and intervention possibilities. Case Study 10.1 addresses

For Students Needing Adaptations in Testing/Assessment

- Provide students with handout/test copies that are easy to read (typed, clear language, at least double-spaced, clean copies, ample margins).
- Avoid handwritten tests.
- On vocabulary tests give the definition and have students supply the word, rather than providing the word, and having the student write out the definition.
- Provide word banks to select from for fill-in-the-blank tests.
- Allow extended time for completing the test.
- Give the exam in the classroom and then in a small group or with the special education teacher, and then average the two grades.
- Provide students an example when possible of different types of test questions they will be responsible for on the exam.
- Provide more work space on the tests (particularly for math).
- Allow students to use graph paper or other paper to solve math problems that they then attach to the test, rather than requiring that computation be done on the limited work space directly on the test.
- Enlarge the print on the test.
- Divide a test in parts, administering it on different days rather than rushing students to complete lengthy tests in one class period.
- Allow students to take the test orally after taking it in written form to add points to their scores if they are able to demonstrate greater knowledge/mastery than shown on written tests (especially for essay questions).
- Administer frequent short quizzes throughout the teaching unit and review them the next day; this provides feedback to students on their understanding of the material. These short quizzes do not need to be graded for a score but should help students in their learning and confidence prior to the exam.
- Substitute an oral for a written test as appropriate.
- Assign take-home tests on occasion.
- Allow taped tests if needed, and permit students to tape record answers to essay questions rather than write them.
- Read test items orally to students.
- Don't penalize for spelling., grammar, etc., on tests that are measuring mastery of content in other areas.

- Read aloud the directions for the different parts of the test before students begin the exam.
- Give reduced spelling lists to students who struggle with spelling: for example, 15 words rather than 20 to 25. When dictating the words on the test, dictate those 15 words in any order first; then continue with the other words for the rest of the class. Those students using modified lists have the option of trying the additional words for bonus points . . .
- Score tests for the number correct/total number assigned per student (which can be shortened assignments or tests for individual students).
- Eliminate the need for students with writing difficulties to copy test questions from the board or book before answering.
- Teach students the strategies and skills needed for taking a variety of tests (true-false, multiple choice, fill in the blank, essay, fill in the bubble, etc.).
- Practice all types of testing formats.
- Collaborate with special educators to rewrite the tests for special needs students (shorter sentences, simplified vocabulary, easier to read format).
- Avoid questions that are worded in a way to deliberately trick the student.
- Write multiple-choice questions with choices listed vertically rather than horizontally (as they are easier to read).
- Utilize portfolio assessment (progress evaluated on individual performance and improvement as opposed to comparing to other students).
- Reduce weight of test grade.
- Color the processing signs on math tests for students who don't focus well on details and make careless errors due to inattention. For example, highlight yellow = addition problem, green = subtraction, blue = multiplication.
- Utilize privacy boards at desks during testing time and/or find other means of reducing distractions when students are testing.
- Allow the use of a calculator on math tests that are assessing problem solving skills.

Source: Adapted from Sandra F. Rief and Julie A Heinmburge. *How to Reach and Teach All Students in the Inclusive Classroom.* West Nyack, N.Y.: Center for Applied Research in Education, 1996, pp. 200–202. This material is used by permission of John Wiley and Sons, Inc.

case study 10.1   Assessing Student Progress: Making Accommodations

As your read this case, notice that the Pathwise criteria that are relevant are placed in parenthesis.

The school year at Roosevelt Middle School begins next week. Mr. Titus stops by to pick up his seventh-grade class rosters and organize his classroom for the first week of school. He's been teaching seventh-grade language arts at this middle school for three years and is finally beginning to feel comfortable in his position. Last spring, he took an extended period of time to reflect on what content, teaching strategies, and assessments were most effective in enabling his students to achieve the language arts performance indicators specified in the academic content standards for the State of Ohio—see www.battelleforkids.org (D). To reach his conclusions, he used the results of his students' performance on the seventh grade off-year standardized achievement tests as well as their language arts portfolios and end-of-the year small group interviews.

In the process, Mr. Titus also identified a number of areas that needed improvement (D). Analysis of student data showed a discrepancy between the quality of work on his students' language arts portfolios and their achievement on the standardized reading and writing achievement tests. Actually, he was quite disappointed when he received the standardized tests results. He had anticipated that his students would perform at a higher level on the standardized measures. During his end-of-year interviews with his students, he found that at least a third of them mentioned "freezing" when they saw the standardized achievement tests and "going blank" on questions for which they thought they had learned the answers! (A) As a result, they were underachieving.

He thought that perhaps his students' underachievement on the standardized achievement tests was at least in part due to mismatches among the learning objectives, seventh-grade reading and writing state performance indicators, in-class assessments, and standardized tests (D). As a result, he took a summer graduate class that provided him with numerous opportunities to explore a wide variety of reading and writing assessments and to develop lesson and unit plans on which the learning objectives and assessment were aligned with the performance indicators. He did his class project on test anxiety and developed a unit on test-taking strategies that he plans to incorporate into his first six weeks' plans.

He is excited to have the opportunity to use what he learned this past summer in his classes this fall until he looks at his rosters. Yes, there are still the same three double-blocked seventh-grade language arts classes, but there is a note attached to the roster. Quickly reading the note, he finds out that each of his two smaller language arts classes has students who are, for the first time, being mainstreamed into a general education classroom. Language Arts section 7-1 has twenty-four students, five of whom have identified mild to moderate special needs. Section 7-2 has twenty-two students, three of whom have identified mild to moderate special needs and one, Josh, who has always been in a self-contained class for students with multiple disabilities. All three of the sections have at least two students who have been identified as gifted. He always has had "gifted" students in his classes but seldom any students with disabilities. Their previous language arts instruction has been in their special education classes. Unfortunately, neither the guidance counselor nor the principal is available to talk with Mr. Titus the day he stops to pick up his rosters (D), so Mr. Titus tries to locate one of the fifth- and sixth-grade intervention specialist teachers to find out more about these students (A1).

Mr. Titus locates the sixth-grade intervention specialist teacher and requests to see the Individual Education Programs (IEPs) for the identified students. He finds out that their reading and writing skills range from kindergarten through fourth-grade skill levels and that the student with multiple disabilities (Josh) basically is nonverbal and communicates using a Vanguard computer/assistive communication device (A). All students with identified disabilities have language arts goals that can be considered to be at least in a few components of the seventh-grade reading and writing performance indicators and he is expected to help these students reach their IEP goals.

He also finds out that all but Josh will be expected to take the off-year standardized seventh-grade reading and language arts tests. Josh will be required to complete a district-approved alternative assessment. However, all the students he has who are on IEPs do have specific testing accommodations listed on their IEPs. The sixth-grade intervention specialist assures Mr. Titus that the seventh-grade intervention specialist, Mrs. Lacey, will be available to help him plan but probably will have only limited time to spend with the identified students while they are in his classroom.

Mr. Titus is discouraged. As he planned his lessons and units for the first six weeks, he did not take into account such a wide range of skill levels. His unit on enhancing test-taking skills assumes that his students will be taking the standardized tests using traditional formats. And he has never had to adapt classroom assessments to be consistent with IEP-approved accommodations. He also is worried that in an effort to meet the needs of the students who are performing significantly below grade level, he will not challenge his students who have been identified as gifted.

Mr. Titus also makes plans to meet with Mrs. Lacey during the first week of school to discuss testing accommodations. He is not sure what is considered an "allowable accommodation" and what is not and how to explain to his students that some students get twice as much time to take a test, others have a reader, and some may even have a totally different test. He also anticipates many calls from parents, so he plans to include a section in his monthly newsletter home about learning differences and multiple forms of assessment (D). Perhaps all the work he did over the summer on alternative assessments and alignment of curriculum and instruction with content standards actually will help him work with these students with special needs. And he thought he had it all under control. You are asked to help Mr. Titus. Write a draft of the newsletter that Mr. Titus can consider sending to the parents. What information on learning differences would you provide? What information on accommodations would it be appropriate to include? (See Tips 10.2.)

Questions for Reflection:

1. A major issue associated with enhancing student achievement is knowing how to use student assessment data to identify what students' future learning should entail. Talk to a teacher in a K–12 situation about how he or she uses data about student performance to structure student learning activities.

2. Mr. Titus focused on test anxiety and test-taking strategies. Identify specific ways you can help students be less anxious and more prepared to take tests.

3. This case again uses the Pathwise-PRAXIS criteria. There are references to domains A and D, but not to B and C. Why? Do you think there are areas in which domains B and C should be referenced? Explain.

Case written by Dr. Linda Morrow, Muskingum College.

some of the complexities associated with assessing the needs of students with exceptionalities and determining the types of accommodations that you have to make to address their special learning problems. As you read the case study and the newsletter, you might find it useful to consult *Assessing One and All* by Stephen Elliott and colleagues. See the Recommended Readings at the end of this chapter.

In general, the testing accommodations that you might have to make for a student fall into four categories: time accommodations (e.g., administer a test in shorter periods with more breaks), setting accommodations (e.g., permit a student to work in a private study carrel), format accommodations (e.g., use a Braille transcription of a test), and recording accommodations (e.g., use an adult to record a student's responses).[37] Teachers must be aware of new changes in federal legislation. One way to monitor the legislative changes is to access the Council for Exceptional Children website at http://www.cec.sped.org and then click the Public Policy and Legislative Information link.

Differences Between Short-Answer and Essay Tests

Most classroom tests fall into two categories: short-answer tests (multiple choice, matching, completion, and true-false), sometimes called selected response *objective tests,* and essay (or discussion) tests, sometimes called constructed response *free-response tests.* **Short-answer tests** require the student to supply a specific and brief answer, usually one or two words; essay tests require the student to organize and express an answer in his or her own words, not restricted to a list of responses.

An **essay test** usually consists of a few questions, each requiring a lengthy answer. A short-answer test consists of many questions, each taking little time to answer. Content sampling and reliability are likely to be superior in short-answer tests. Essay tests provide an opportunity for high-level thinking, including analysis, synthesis, and evaluation. Most short-answer items emphasize low-level thinking or memorization, not advanced cognitive operations.

The quality (reliability, validity, usability) of an objective test depends primarily on the skill of the test constructor, whereas the quality of the essay test depends mainly on the skill of the person grading the test. Short-answer tests take longer to prepare but are easier to grade. Essay tests may be easier to prepare but are more difficult to grade.

table 10.3   **Reasons for Selecting Short-Answer or Essay Tests**

Short Answer (multiple choice, matching, completion, true-false)	Essay
1. Provides good item pool	1. Calls for higher levels of cognitive thinking
2. Samples objectives and broad content	2. Measures students' ability to select and organize ideas
3. Is independent of writing ability (quality of handwriting, spelling) and verbal fluency	3. Tests writing ability
4. Discourages bluffing by writing or talking "around the topic"	4. Eliminates guessing or answering by process of elimination
5. Is easy and quick to score	5. Measures problem-thinking skills
6. Scoring and grading are reliable procedures	6. Encourages originality and unconventional answers
7. Scoring is more objective	7. Scoring is more subjective, though good rubrics limit subjectivity

Short-answer items tend to be explicit, with only one correct answer. Essays permit the student to express an individual style and opinion; the answer is open to interpretation, and there may be more than one answer. Short-answer tests are susceptible to guessing and cheating; essay tests are susceptible to bluffing (writing "around" the answer) unless the teacher has a clear rubric for grading them.[38] Table 10.3 provides an overview of some relative advantages of short-answer and essay tests.

According to Mehrens and Lehmann, there are several factors to consider in choosing between short-answer and essay tests:

1. *Purpose of the test:* If you want to measure written expression or critical thinking, then use an essay. If you want to measure broad knowledge of the subject or results of learning, then use short-answer items.

2. *Time:* The time saved in preparing an essay test is often used up in grading the responses. If you are rushed before the test and have sufficient time after it, you might choose an essay examination. If you must process the results in one or two days, you should use short-answer items—provided you have sufficient time to write good questions.

3. *Numbers tested:* If there are only a few students, the essay test is practical. If the class is large or if you have several different classes, short-answer tests are recommended.

4. *Facilities:* If typing and reproduction facilities are limited, you may be forced to rely on essay tests. You can administer completion and true-false questions by reading the questions aloud, but it is best that all short-answer tests be typed, reproduced, and put in front of students to respond to at their own pace.

5. *Age of students:* Not until about the fifth or sixth grade should students be required to answer essay questions. Older students (sixth grade and above) can deal with a variety of types of short-answer items, but younger students are confused by changing item formats and accompanying directions.

tips for teachers 10.3

Preparing Classroom Tests

 Teacher-made tests are frequently the major basis for evaluating students' progress in school. Good tests do not just happen! They require appropriate planning so that instructional objectives, curriculum content, and instructional materials are related in some meaningful fashion. Here is a checklist to consider when preparing your classroom tests:

1. Have the expectations for what students are expected to know been clearly communicated?
2. What is the purpose of the test? Why am I giving it?
3. What skills, knowledge, attitudes, and so on, do I want to measure?
4. Have I clearly defined my instructional objectives in terms of student behavior?
5. Do the test items match the objectives?
6. Are the objectives tied to standards and are they both communicated to students in language they understand?
7. What kind of test (item format) do I want to use? Why?
8. How long should the test be?
9. How difficult should the test be?
10. What should be the discrimination level of my test items?
11. How will I arrange the various item formats?
12. How will I arrange the items within each item format?
13. What do I need to do to prepare students for taking the test?
14. How are the pupils to record their answers to objective items? On separate answer sheets? On the test booklet?
15. How is the objective portion to be scored? By hand or machine?
16. How is the essay portion to be graded? Will a rubric be used?
17. For objective items, should guessing instructions be given? Should a correction for guessing be applied?
18. How are the test scores to be tabulated?
19. How are scores (grades, or level of competency) to be assigned?
20. How are the test results to be reported?

Source: Adapted from *Measurement and Evaluation in Education and Psychology,* 3rd edition by Mehrens/Lehmann © 1991. Reprinted with permission of Wadsworth, a division of Thomson Learning: www.thomsonrights.com. Fax 800-730-2215

6. *Teacher's skill:* Some types of items (true-false) are easier to write than others, and teachers tend to prefer one type over another. However, different types should be included. Test writing is a skill that can be improved with practice.[39] See Tips for Teachers 10.3 for insight into how.

Before we discuss the different types of assessments, let's focus on a critical question about which type of assessment is preferred: selected-response or constructed response? The answer, quite simply, is that the goal is balanced assessment, so both are needed. Good teachers collect achievement data about students in different ways. Your goals dictate your approach. What is clear is that you need to know how to develop and use a myriad of different assessments ranging from short-answer (selected response) to essay (constructed response).

Short-Answer Tests

Short-answer or selected response tests include multiple choice, matching, completion, and true-false. Regardless of the type of objective test, writing the test questions or items generally involves finding the most appropriate manner in which to pose problems to students. The test questions or items often involve the recall of information, exemplified by knowledge of facts, terms, names, or rules, but they can also involve higher-order cognitive abilities. (Multiple-choice items are easier to devise for testing advanced cognitive abilities; the other short-answer types are more difficult.) Consider these suggestions when preparing and writing short-answer tests:

1. The test items should measure all the important objectives and outcomes of instruction.

2. The test items should not focus on esoteric or unimportant content.

3. The test items should be phrased clearly so that a knowledgeable person will not be confused or respond to a wrong choice. The test items should not contain clues that might enable an uninformed person to answer correctly.

4. Trick or trivia test items should be avoided since they penalize students who know the material and benefit students who rely on guessing or chance.

5. Test items should not be interrelated. Knowing the answer to one item should not furnish the answer to another.

6. Test items should be grammatically correct.

7. Test items should be appropriate to the students' age level, reading level, and cognitive and developmental levels.

8. Test items should not be racially, ethnically, or gender biased.

9. Test items should have a definite correct answer, that is, an answer that all experts (other teachers) can agree on.

10. Tests should not be the only basis for evaluating the students' classroom performance or for deriving a grade for a subject.

In order to write an appropriate test the teacher must obviously know the course content (specific knowledge, skills, concepts, common misconceptions, difficult areas, etc.). But knowledge of content is not enough. The teacher must be able to translate the objectives of the course into test items that will differentiate between students who know the material and those who do not and that will measure qualitative differences (preferably in higher-order thinking) related to the course as well as knowledge.

Multiple-Choice Questions

These are the most popular objective test items, especially at the secondary level. Some students think they are fun to answer because they see the task almost as a puzzle, putting pieces together: doing easy pieces first and saving the hard pieces for last. The basic form of the ***multiple-choice test*** item is a stem or lead, which defines the problem and is to be completed by one of a number of alternatives or choices. There should be only one correct response, and the other alternatives should be plausible but incorrect. For this reason the incorrect alternatives are sometimes referred to as "distractors." In most cases three or four alternatives are given along with the correct item.

The idea in writing the question is to have the knowledgeable student choose the correct answer and not be distracted by the other alternatives; the other alternatives serve to distract the less knowledgeable student. The effect of guessing is reduced but not totally eliminated by increasing the number of alternatives. In a twenty-five–item

professional viewpoint

Rules of Thumb for Taking a Short-Answer Test

Bruce W. Tuckman
Professor of Educational Research
Florida State University

Once upon a time, when I was a student, I was a good test taker. While all my friends were busy being overcome by test anxiety and forgetting everything they had crammed into their heads the night before, I was being focused and super "cool" and looking for any advantage I could get. I figured that all was fair in love, war, and taking a test. I had studied hard, outlined all my notes and all the chapters that would be covered, and tried to figure out what the teacher thought was important enough to ask about on the test. But I also had some ideas about what kinds of clues to look for on the test itself. Back then I was working on intuition, but today, as a person who teaches teachers how to build tests, I have tried to specify what all those clues I used to use were so that the teachers I taught wouldn't inadvertently provide them for their students.

Since we don't want to reward test-taking skills as a substitute for acquiring knowledge through hard work such as coming to class and studying, these are the clues that students should not be given in the tests that you build:

1. Do not include any obviously wrong answer choices. If you do, students can just cross them out and thereby reduce their odds of guessing the incorrect answer.

2. Do not write one item that actually contains the answer to another item on the same test. If you do, clever students will skim over the whole test, find the items that overlap, and then use one to answer the other.

3. Do not make the right answer choice longer, more complex, or in any way visibly different from the wrong answer choices or else the wise test taker, when in doubt, will always choose the "meatier" choice and invariably be right.

4. Do not follow a pattern in choosing what choice, a, b, c, d, or e, will be the correct choice. Pick letters out of a hat or use some other truly random procedure. Otherwise, when in doubt, the "wily fox" will choose the letter choice that has not been right for the longest time.

5. Make all the answer choices grammatically consistent with the question. Any choices that are not will be automatically disregarded by the sharp-eyed student.

Beyond these five rules of thumb, in scoring the test include a penalty for guessing (for example, test score equals number right minus number wrong) if you do not want students to benefit unduly from guessing. In addition, while giving the test be wary of students who ask a lot of questions about the items that require you to give them explanations. You may be giving away the right answer without knowing it.

If you want to try to help your students, tell them to skip items they cannot answer and come back to them, to guess at answers they do not know (if there is no penalty for guessing), and to try to answer each question before they look at the answer choices. And wish them EFFORT rather than luck.

four-alternative multiple-choice test, the probability of obtaining a score of at least 70 percent by chance alone is 1 in 1,000. To achieve a similar freedom from the effect of guessing in a true-false test requires 200 items.[40]

The use of plausible distractors helps the teacher control the difficulty of the test. They should not be tricky or trivial. The major limitation of the multiple-choice format is that the distractors are often difficult to construct, particularly as the number of choices increases to five. Unless the teacher knows the content of the course well, he or she is usually limited in the number of good multiple-choice test items that can be constructed.

Following are three examples of multiple-choice questions. The first tests simple knowledge, the second the application of a formula, and the third the application of a concept.

1. Henry Kissinger is a well-known (a) corporate lawyer, (b) avant-garde playwright, (c) surrealist artist, (d) international statesman, (e) pop musician.
2. What temperature, in degrees Fahrenheit, is equivalent to 10° Centigrade? (a) 0°F (b) 32°F (c) 50°F (d) 72°F (e) 100°F
3. Based on the map provided, which product is most likely to be exported from Bango (a fictitious country for which longitude, latitude, and topography are shown)? (a) fish (b) oranges (c) pine lumber (d) corn.

Like the other forms of tests, good multiple-choice test items are difficult to construct. Although some teachers disdain multiple-choice (recognition) items because of their perceived simplicity, they are, in fact, if well constructed, very intellectually demanding. Multiple-choice items take time to develop and can come in several different forms: direct question, incomplete statement, and best answer. An example of each is provided here:

- *Direct question:*
  In what war was Thadeus Lowe's invention The Intrepid (an observational balloon) first used for making observations of troop movements?

  A. War of 1812
  B. Mexican-American War
  C. Civil War
  D. Spanish American War

- *Incomplete statement form:*
  The higher education institution that trained the most military officers for the Civil War was ____.

  A. Harvard College.
  B. West Point.
  C. Annapolis.
  D. Oberlin College.

- *Best answer:*
  Which of the following best explains why Black regiments were not more prominent in fighting for the North?

  A. Most Blacks refused to fight for the North.
  B. Northern Whites, like Southerners, held stereotypes that the Blacks were not brave enough to fight.
  C. Too few Blacks were in the North and those limited numbers made it difficult to form Black regiments.
  D. Training the Blacks was difficult because they were relatively unskilled.

Guidelines for Writing Multiple-Choice Questions

Here are some suggestions for writing multiple-choice questions:

1. Use, where possible, a direct question rather than an incomplete statement in the stem. (A direct question will result in less vagueness and ambiguity, especially among inexperienced test writers.)

2. Avoid negative statements in the stem, since they lead to confusion.

3. Use numbers to label stems and letters to label alternatives.

4. Avoid absolute terms ("always," "never," "none"), especially in the alternatives; a testwise person usually avoids answers that include them.

5. Each distractor should be reasonable and plausible.

6. Arrange alternatives so that they are parallel in content, form, length, and grammar. Avoid making the correct alternative different from wrong alternatives: longer or shorter, more precisely stated, having a part of speech others lack.

7. Make certain correct responses are in random order. Do not use one particular letter more often than others or create a pattern for the placement of correct responses.

8. Use alternatives such as "All of the above" and "None of the above" sparingly.

Matching Questions

In a ***matching test*** there are usually two columns of items. For each item in one column, the student is required to select a correct (or matching) item in the other. The items may be names, terms, places, phrases, quotations, statements, or events. The basis for choosing must be carefully explained in the directions.

Matching questions have the advantages of covering a large amount and variety of content, being interesting to students (almost like a game), and being easy to score. Matching questions may be considered a modification of multiple-choice questions in which alternatives are listed in another column instead of in a series following a stem. The questions are easier to construct than multiple-choice questions, however, since only one response item has to be constructed for each stem.

One problem with matching tests, according to test experts, is finding homogeneous test and response items that are significant in terms of objectives and learning outcomes. A test writer may start with a few good items in both columns but may find it necessary to add insignificant or secondary information to maintain homogeneity.[41] Another problem is that matching questions often require recall rather than comprehension and more sophisticated levels of thinking. Higher levels of cognition may be called for in matching questions that involve analogies, cause and effect, complex relationships, and theories, but such items are harder to construct.[42]

Here is an example of a matching exercise.

Famous American presidents are listed in column A, and descriptive phrases relating to their administration are listed in column B. Place the letter of the phrase that describes each president in the space provided. Each match is worth 1 point.

Column A: Presidents

___ 1. George Washington
___ 2. Thomas Jefferson
___ 3. Abraham Lincoln
___ 4. Woodrow Wilson
___ 5. Franklin Roosevelt

Column B: Descriptions or Events

a. Civil War president
b. "New Deal"
c. First American president
d. Purchased Louisiana Territory
e. "New Frontier"
f. World War I president

Guidelines for Writing Matching Questions

The following suggestions may improve the construction of matching questions:

1. Provide directions that briefly and clearly indicate the basis for matching items in column A with items in column B.

2. Ensure that column A contains no more than ten test items; five or six items is probably ideal.

3. Provide more responses in column B than there are premises in column A in order to prevent answering the last one or two items by simple elimination. Column B should contain six or seven items if column A contains five. A list of ten items in column A should be accompanied by about eleven or twelve items in column B.

4. Number the column A items, as they will be graded as individual questions, and letter column B items.

5. Present column A or B items in a logical order (and preferably B), such as alphabetically or chronologically (but not one that gives away the answer), so the students can scan them quickly in search for correct answers.

6. Ensure that items in both columns are similar in terms of content, form, grammar, and length. Dissimilar alternatives in column B give clues to the testwise student.

7. Avoid negative statements (in either column), since they confuse students.

Completion Questions

The **completion tests** present sentences from which certain words are omitted. The student is to fill in the blank to complete the meaning. This type of short-answer question, sometimes called a *fill-in* or *fill-in-the-blank* question, is suitable for measuring a wide variety of content. Although it usually tests recall of information, it can also demand thought and ability to understand relationships and make inferences. Little opportunity for guessing and for obtaining clues is provided, as it is with other short-answer questions.

The major problem of this type of test question is that the answers are not always entirely objective, so the scoring for the teacher is time-consuming, and the grading outcomes may vary with the grader. Combining multiple-choice and completion is an effective method for reducing ambiguity in test items and making scoring more objective. However, this combination does restore the opportunity for guessing.

The following examples illustrate how guessing is reduced. To answer the completion item (question 1), the student must know the capital of Illinois. To arrive at an answer to the multiple-choice question (question 2), the student may eliminate alternatives through knowledge about them or simply choose one of them as a guess.

1. The capital of Illinois is _____.

2. The capital of Illinois is (a) Utica, (b) Columbus, (c) Springfield, (d) Cedar Rapids.

Guidelines for Writing Completion Questions

Here are general suggestions for writing completion items:

1. Ensure that completion items have only one possible correct answer.
2. Ensure that the fill-in is plausible to the knowledgeable student; it should not be based on trivia or trick data.
3. Use one blank, or certainly no more than two, in any item, since more than two blanks leads to confusion and ambiguity.
4. Use completion items that are specific terms (person, place, object, concept), since an item requiring a more general phrase may elicit more subjective responses and be harder to score.

True-False Questions

Of all types of short-answer questions used in education, the ***true-false test*** question is the most controversial. Advocates contend that the basis of "logical reasoning is to test the truth or falsity of propositions" and that "a student's command of a particular area of knowledge is indicated by his [or her] success in judging the truth or falsity of propositions related to it."[43] The main advantages of true-false items are their ease of construction and ease of scoring. A true-false test can cover a large content area and can present a large number of items in a prescribed time period. This allows the teacher to obtain a good estimate of the students' knowledge. If the items are carefully constructed, they can also be used to test understanding of principles.

Critics assert that true-false items have almost no value, since they encourage, and even reward, guessing, and measure memorization rather than understanding. Others note that true-false questions tend to elicit the response set of acquiescence—that is, the response of people who say, "yes" (or "True") when in doubt.[44] The disadvantages of true-false questions outweigh their advantages unless the items are well-written. Precise language that is appropriate for the students taking the test is essential so that ambiguity and reading ability do not distort test results.

Here are two examples of ambiguous true-false questions.

1. Australia, the island continent, was discovered by Captain Cook.
2. Early in his career, Will Rogers said, "I never met a man I didn't like."
3. A body immersed in a fluid is buoyed up by a force equal to half the weight of the fluid displaced.

In question 1 two statements are made, and it is unclear whether the student is to respond to both or only one; moreover, the meanings of *island* and *continent* are also being tested. In question 2, is the student being asked whether Rogers made the statement early or late in his career or whether this is the exact statement? A testwise person might say "False," because there are two ways of being wrong in this question, but the answer is "True."

Guessing is the biggest disadvantage to true-false tests. When students guess, they have a fifty-fifty chance of being right. Clues in the items and being testwise improve these odds. The purpose of the test is to measure what students know, not how lucky or clever they are. This disadvantage can be compensated for to some extent by increasing the number of test items and by penalizing (deducting a quarter point or one-third point) for an incorrect answer. True-false items should be used sparingly for older students, who are more testwise and able to sense clues in questions. They are more appropriate for younger students, who respond more to the content than to the format of questions.

Guidelines for Writing True-False Questions

Here are some suggestions for writing true-false items:

1. Ensure that each true-false item tests an important concept or piece of information.

2. Ensure that true-false statements are completely true or false, without exception.

3. Avoid specific determiners and absolute statements ("never," "only," "none," "always"), since they are unintentional clues. Most important, do not use them in statements you want to be considered true.

4. Avoid qualifying statements and words that involve judgment and interpretation ("few," "most," "usually"). Most important, do not use them in statements you want to be considered false.

5. Avoid negative statements and double negatives, since they confuse students and may cause knowledgeable students to give the wrong answer.

6. Avoid verbatim textbook and workbook statements, since use of such statements promotes memorization.

7. Use the same form and length for true and false statements. For example, do not make true statements consistently longer than false statements; testwise students will recognize a pattern.

8. Present a similar number of true and false items.

9. Use simple grammatical structures. Avoid dependent clauses and compound sentences, since they may distract the student from the central idea. There is also a tendency for the knowledgeable student to see a more complex item as a trick question or to read more into the meaning than is intended.

Overview of Short-Answer Questions

Table 10.4 summarizes many of the points we have discussed. The different types of short-answer tests all have advantages and disadvantages. Different teachers will have different preferences. Although each type has features that make it useful for specific testing situations, the different types can be used together to add variety and to test different types and levels of knowledge.

Multiple-choice questions are the most difficult and time-consuming items to construct. However, they can be used more readily to test higher levels of learning than can the other short-test items. Matching questions are also difficult and time-consuming to write, but they are interesting for students and can be used for variety. Completion questions are open to subjective interpretation and scoring, but they can be used also to test higher levels of learning. True-false questions force students to choose between alternatives, and they are a good way of assessing in a general sense what students know or do not know.

table 10.4   Advantages and Limitations of Short-Answer Test Questions.

Question Type	Advantages	Disadvantages
Multiple choice	1. Flexibility in measuring objectives or content 2. Well-constructed items have potential to measure high-level thinking 3. Easy to score; little interpretation to count correct responses	1. A correct answer can sometimes be determined without knowledge of content 2. Susceptible to guessing and eliminating incorrect choices 3. Time-consuming to write
Matching	1. Relatively easy to write, easy to score 2. Well suited to measure associations 3. May be used to test a large body of content; many options available	1. Often necessary to use single words or short phrases 2. Cannot be used to assess all types of thinking; lists or individual pieces of information assess limited knowledge 3. Harder to write than other short-answer items because all items must fit together and be distinguishable from each other
Completion	1. Easy to write test items 2. Minimal guessing; clues are not given in choices or alternatives 3. Can test knowledge of what, who, where, and how many 4. No distractors, options, or choices to worry about	1. Difficult to score 2. Some answers are subjective or open to interpretation 3. Usually measures simple recall or factual information 4. Test items are sometimes confusing or ambiguous; constrained by grammar
True-False	1. Easiest test items to write; easy to score 2. Comprehensive sampling of objectives or content 3. Guessing can be minimized by a built-in penalty 4. No distractors to worry about; highly reliable and valid items	1. Sometimes ambiguous or too broad 2. Simplicity in cognitive demands; measures low-level thinking 3. Susceptible to guessing 4. Dependence on absolute judgments, right or wrong

Source: Adapted from Norman E. Gronlund and Robert L. Linn, *Measurement and Evaluation in Teaching,* 6th ed. New York: Macmillan, 1990.

Essay Questions

Short-answer questions are not intended, especially for most teacher-developed tests, to measure divergent thinking or subjective or imaginative thought. To learn how a student thinks, attacks a problem, writes, and utilizes cognitive resources, something beyond the short-answer test is needed. Essay questions, especially where there is no specific right answer, produce evaluation data of considerable value. One test expert, in fact, considers the essay to be "the most authentic type of testing" for middle school students on up through college and perhaps the best one for "measuring higher mental processes."[45]

Authorities disagree on how structured and specific essay questions should be. For example, some authorities advocate using words such as "why," "how," and "what consequences." They claim questions worded in this way (which we call *type 1 essay questions*) call for a command of essential knowledge and concepts and require students to integrate the subject matter, analyze data, make inferences, and show cause-effect relations.[46] Other educators urge words such as "discuss," "examine," and "explain," claiming that this wording (*type 2 essay questions*) gives the student less latitude in responding but provides the teacher with an opportunity to learn how the student thinks.[47] Although more restricted than the first type, this type of question may still lead to tangential responses by some students. It is useful when the object is to see how well the student can select, reject, and organize data from several sources. Others advocate more precision by providing more structure and focus in a question by using words such as "compare" and "contrast"[48] (*type 3 questions*). In addition to giving more direction to the student, such wording demands that the student select and organize specific data. Table 10.5 lists thought processes elicited by different essay questions.

In effect, the descriptions of the different types stress different degrees of freedom permitted the student in organizing a response to a question. The first two types of essay questions allow an "extended response"; they can lead to disjointed, irrelevant, superficial, or unexpected discussions by students who have difficulty organizing their thoughts on paper. The third type of essay question suggests a "focused response"; it can lead to simple recall of information and a mass of details.

Essay questions can be used effectively for determining how well a student can analyze, synthesize, evaluate, think logically, solve problems, and hypothesize. They can also show how well he or she can organize thoughts, support a point of view, and create ideas, methods, and solutions. The complexity of the questions and the complexity of thinking expected of the student can be adjusted to correspond to students' ages, abilities, and experience. Another advantage is the ease and short time involved in constructing an essay question. The major disadvantages of essay questions are the considerable time needed to read and evaluate answers and the subjectivity of scoring. The length and complexity of the answer as well as the standards for responding can lead to reliability problems in scoring.

Some studies report that independent grading of the same essay by several teachers results in appraisals ranging from excellent to failing. This variation illustrates a wide range in criteria for evaluation among teachers. Even worse, one study showed that the same teacher grading the same essay at different times gave the essay significantly different grades.[49] It has also been demonstrated that teachers are influenced by such factors as penmanship, quality of composition, and spelling, even when they are supposed to grade on content alone.[50]

One way to increase the reliability of an essay test is to increase the number of questions and restrict the length of the answers. The more specific and restricted the question, the less ambiguous it is to the teacher and the less affected it will be by interpretation or subjectivity in scoring.[51] Another way is for teachers to develop an outline of what information a desirable answer might contain. The more clearly the teacher defines the expected outcomes, the more reliably the various student responses can be graded. Note that "more reliably" is not reliability. The reason for this is clear: Essay tests are somewhat subjective and because of that fact there will always be a level of unreliability in assessing student responses.

An entire test composed of essay questions can cover only limited content because only a few questions can be answered in a given time period. However, this limitation is balanced by the fact that in studying for an essay test high-achieving students are likely to look at the subject or course as a whole and at the relationships of ideas, concepts, and principles.

t a b l e 1 0 . 5   Sample Thought Questions and Cognitive Levels of Thinking

1. Comparing
   a. Compare the following two people for . . .
   b. Describe the similarities and differences between . . .

2. Classifying
   a. Group the following items according to . . .
   b. What common characteristics do the items below have?

3. Outlining
   a. Outline the procedures you would use to calculate . . .
   b. Discuss the advantages of . . .

4. Summarizing
   a. State the major points of . . .
   b. Describe the principles of . . .

5. Organizing
   a. Trace the history of . . .
   b. Examine the development of . . .

6. Analyzing
   a. Describe the errors in the following argument . . .
   b. What data are needed to . . . ?

7. Applying
   a. Clarify the methods of . . . for purposes of . . .
   b. Diagnose the causes of . . .

8. Inferring
   a. Why did the author say . . . ?
   b. How would (person X) more likely react to . . . ?

9. Deducing
   a. Formulate criteria for . . .
   b. Based on the premise of . . . , propose a valid conclusion.

10. Synthesizing
    a. How would you end the story of . . . ?
    b. Describe a plan for . . .

11. Justifying
    a. Provide a rationale for . . .
    b. Which alternatives below do you agree with? Why?

12. Identifying
    a. Identify three characteristics of . . .
    b. Based on the following . . . identify two qualities of . . .

13. Predicting
    a. Describe the likely outcomes of . . .
    b. What will most likely happen if . . . ? Why?

Source: Allan C. Ornstein. "Essay Tests: Use, Development and Grading." *Clearing House* (January–February 1992): 176. Heldref Publications. See also Norman E. Gronlund, Robert L. Linn. *Measurements and Evaluation in Teaching,* 6th ed. New York: Macmillan, 1990.

The essay answer is affected by the student's ability to organize written responses. Many students can comprehend and deal with abstract data but have problems writing or showing that they understand the material in an essay examination. Students may freeze and write only short responses, write in a disjointed fashion, or express only low-level knowledge. One way to alleviate this problem is to discuss in detail how to write an essay answer. Sadly, few teachers take the time to teach students how to write essay answers. They often expect English teachers to perform this task, and English teachers are often so busy teaching grammar, spelling, and punctuation that they cannot approach the mechanics of essay writing.

On the other hand, there are students who write well but haven't learned the course content. Their writing ability may conceal their lack of specific knowledge. It is important for the teacher to be able to differentiate irrelevant facts and ideas from relevant information. Even though essay questions appear to be easy to write, careful construction is necessary to test students' cognitive abilities—that is, to write valid questions. Many essay questions can be turned around by the student so that he or she merely lists facts without applying information to specific situations, without integrating it with other information, and without showing an understanding of concepts. "What were the causes of World War II?" can be answered by listing specific causes without integrating them. A better question would be "Assume that Winston Churchill, Franklin Roosevelt, and Adolph Hitler were invited to speak to an audience on the causes of World War II. What might each of them say? What might each select as the most important causal factors? On what points would they agree? Disagree?"

Factors to be considered in deciding whether to use essay questions are the difficulty and time involved in grading essays, the low reliability of grading, the limited sampling of content, the validity of the essay itself, the ease in formulating questions, the testing of advanced levels of cognition, and the fostering of the integration of the subject as a whole. Many teachers take advantage of what both short-answer questions and essay questions have to offer by writing tests consisting of both, perhaps 40 to 60 percent short-answer and the remainder essay. This balance to some extent is determined by grade level. In the upper grades there is a tendency to require students to answer more essay questions since it is believed they should have the ability to formulate acceptable answers. According to Piagetian developmental stages, students should begin to be able to handle essays (actually short essays) at the formal operation stage, beginning at age 11.

Guidelines for Writing Essay Questions

Here are suggestions for preparing and scoring essay tests:

1. Make directions specific, indicating just what the student is to write about. Write up to three or four sentences of directions if necessary.

2. Word each question as simply and clearly as possible.

3. Allow sufficient time for students to answer the questions. A good rule of thumb is for the teacher to estimate how long he or she would take to answer the questions and then multiply this time by two or three depending on the students' age and abilities. Suggest a time allotment for each question so students can pace themselves.

4. Ask questions that require considerable thought. Use essay questions to focus assessment on organizing data, analysis, interpretation, and formulating theories rather than on reporting facts.

5. Give students a choice of questions, such as, two out of three, so as not to penalize students who may know the subject as a whole but be limited in the particular area asked about.[52]

6. Determine in advance how much weight will be given to each question or part of a question. Give this information on the test and then score accordingly.

7. Explain your scoring technique to students before the test. It should be clear to them what weight will be given to knowledge, development and organization of ideas, grammar, punctuation, spelling, penmanship, and any other factor to be considered in evaluation.

8. Be consistent in your scoring technique for all students. Try to conceal the name of the student whose answer you are grading to reduce biases that have little to do with the quality of the student's response and more to do with the "halo effect" (the tendency to grade students according to impressions of their capabilities, attitudes, or behavior).

9. Grade one question at a time, rather than one test paper at a time, to increase reliability in scoring. This technique makes it easier to compare and evaluate responses to each specific question.

10. Write comments on the test paper for the student, noting good points and explaining how answers could be improved. Do not compare a student to others when making comments.

Authentic Assessments

Authentic assessments such as research projects, group projects, scientific experiments, oral presentations, exhibits, and portfolios for various subject areas allow teachers to monitor and assess what students know. Authentic assessment techniques encourage learners to stretch their capacities, undertake independent assignments, and generate new ideas and projects. Teachers are expected to act as facilitators and coaches during the instructional process, engage learners in a dialogue, and ask them to defend their ideas during the assessment process.

According to critics, standardized tests do not tap the high-order skills and abilities that students need in later life. They encourage students to do little more than recall information instead of preparing them to solve problems, evaluate alternatives, and create ideas or products.[53] Authentic tests, however, assess essential skills or tasks. They are not needlessly intrusive or esoteric; they are contextualized and involve complex thought processes, not atomized tasks or isolated bits of information.

The students are graded in reference to a performance standard or expectation, not on a curve or absolute standard. The scoring system (or rubric) is multifaceted instead of issuing one aggregate grade, and self-assessment is part of the assessment process. Authentic tests often involve a panel, such as classmates or other teachers in the role of examiner. They do not rely on time constraints. The performance provides room for various student learning styles, aptitudes, and interests—and comparisons among students are minimized.[54]

| | PRIMARY | | | |

SIMULATION GAME RUBRIC

Criteria	1	2	3	4
Clearly stated Goal of Game	No goal	Vague goal	Goal stated, but difficult to reach	Clearly stated and attainable goal
Directions for Game	No directions	Directions are provided, but they are unclear	Clear directions provided	Clear and concise directions
Visuals for the Game	No visuals	Simple graphics provided	Clear diagram of game provided	Diagrams are clear and creative
Originality	Copied from another game	Ordinary idea	Ordinary idea with a different twist	Novel idea
Group Effort	Group members did not work well together	Members worked well some of the time	Members worked well most of the time	All members worked well together all the time

☐ Self Assessment

☐ Group Assessment

☐ Teacher Assessment

Grading Scale
18–20 points = A
15–17 points = B
10–14 points = C
9 or below = Not Yet

Total Points
_____
(20)

figure 10.1

Source: Kay Burke, *How to Assesss Authentic Learning* (Arlington Heights, Illinois: Merrill Prentice Hall, 1999): p. 51.

Teachers can create rubrics for a wide variety of authentic assessments that they might conduct to assess the communication skills of students, portfolios, oral presentations, oral readings performed by students, performance tasks, problem solving, or even simulations. Examples of rubrics for the primary, middle, and high school levels are provided in Figures 10.1, 10.2, and 10.3. Each of the examples offers a different way of thinking about a rubric (for a simulation, for a cooperative learning situation and for a situation in which students are endeavoring to solve a problem).

You need to observe some specific things about these rubrics, because they will suggest something about how you create your own.

OBSERVE whether these are holistic or analytical rubrics. They are analytical if they assess certain criteria (e.g., identifies certain problems) to different levels of performance, and holistic if they give a single rating or score for a student's performance.

OBSERVE whether a rubric could be used on lots of different tasks or would be useful for only a specific task. Figure 10.1, 10.2, and 10.3 are generic. One that you might devise for classroom lesson assignment for a unit on something like Egyptian art would be specific for a task.

MIDDLE SCHOOL

GROUP WORK CHECKLIST

Self-assessment of my cooperative group skills for our team project.

1. I have participated in all tasks.   1   2   3   4   ☐
   - I performed my assigned role
   - I helped team members
   - I contributed to the group

2. I have used time appropriately   1   2   3   4   ☐
   - I stayed on task
   - I monitored my team's activities
   - I did not wait until the "last
     minute" to finish our project

3. I behaved appropriately   1   2   3   4   ☐
   - I was courteous to everyone
   - I did not use put-downs
   - I used appropriate language

Scale
11–12 points = A
9–10 points = B
7–8 points = C
6 or below = Not Yet

Comments:
_____
_____
_____

Final Score ☐
Final Grade ☐

Signed: _____ Date: _____

figure 10.2

Source: Kay Burke, *How to Assesss Authentic Learning* (Arlington Heights, Illinois: Merrill Prentice Hall, 1999): p. 51.

There is a tendency to be reductionistic in creating rubrics, resulting in an over-simplified view of the learner and what he or she knows. Wiggins and McTighe ask teachers to think about rubrics in more complex ways. Good rubrics, they argue, enable teachers to view student explanations in a range from the naïve to the complex and sophisticated. In Wiggins's words, "understanding is a matter of degree."[55] What you are trying to do with a rubric is see the degree of understanding. If you are assessing an application, for example, the novice (naïve) level will reflect a lot of scripted effort (following the steps), but at the masterful level, the performance is fluid and flexible. With rubrics you are attempting to assess *where* the learner is and what type of growth is still required.

There is no right way to develop a rubric but there are some preferred steps, which are nicely articulated by Arter and McTighe:

1. Study what experts say relative to what you plan to assess and see if some rubrics already exist that you can use.

2. Make a list of those performance indicators that you want to see evidenced in the students' work.

HIGH SCHOOL

PROBLEM-SOLVING RUBRIC

Criteria	Novice	In Progress	Meets Expectations	Exceeds Expectations
Identifies Real Problem	Problem? What problem?	Someone else points out there is a problem	Recognizes there is a problem	Identifies "real" problem
Gathers Facts	Does not recognize the need to gather facts	Is able to gather one fact on own	Knows where to look to obtain additional facts	Accesses information to obtain all necessary facts
Brainstorms Possible Solutions	Does not generate any solutions	Generates one idea with someone's assistance	Generates two or three solutions independently	Generates four creative solutions independently
Evaluates Effectiveness of Possible Solutions	Does not evaluate the effectiveness of proposal solutions	Recognizes pluses and minuses of some of the solutions	Takes time to analyze effectiveness of each possible solution	Uses reflection to decide what to do differently next time

figure 10.3

Source: Kay Burke, *How to Assesss Authentic Learning* (Arlington Heights, Illinois: Merrill Prentice Hall, 1999): p. 51.

3. Collect some of the students' work and test the rubric. Does the rubric capture the qualitative differences in the students' work?

4. Sort the students' work into defined quality groupings. Do the groupings illustrate the real qualitative differences?[56]

In authentic performance assessments, the students and teachers become part of a learning community. Standards are clear, agreed upon, and in line with the goals of the school, so students are not surprised by them. Students have a chance to modify or revise their performance. Their work is important enough to be a source of public learning and public display—providing classmates an opportunity to learn from one another. Authentic assessments are designed to be representative of performance in the subject or field. Greater attention is paid in this type of assessment to aligning teaching, learning, and assessment. Students take an active role in their own assessment—to the extent of defending their ideas publicly.

The enthusiasm among many educators for authentic assessments reflects disappointment with formal tests (e.g., multiple-choice tests), which are viewed as too restrictive in providing evidence of students' real learning. In authentic assessments the responses of the learner are considered important.

Authentic assessment is a generic term that embraces a variety of assessment strategies. There are several different types of authentic assessments that teachers can use: portfolios, performance-based assessment, and project work. Perhaps the most prominent of the strategies is portfolios.

Portfolios

Portfolios (which we will also discuss in Chapter 11 as a means of summatively sharing information about what a student has accomplished) are a compilation of a student's best work—a record of completed work. Long popular with artists and photographers, portfolios have emerged as a new means of documenting what students accomplish. Paulson, Paulson, and Meyer, offer guidelines for working with portfolios:

1. Developing a portfolio offers the student an opportunity to learn about learning. Therefore, the end product must contain information that shows that a student has engaged in self-reflection.

2. The portfolio is something that is done *by* the student, not *to* the student. Portfolio assessment offers a concrete way for students to learn to value their own work and, by extension, to value themselves as learners. Therefore, the student must be involved in selecting the pieces to be included.

3. The portfolio is separate and different from the student's cumulative folder. Scores and other cumulative folder information that are held in central depositories should be included in a portfolio only if they take on new meaning within the context of the other exhibits found there.

4. The portfolio must convey explicitly or implicitly the student's activities; for example, the rationale (purpose for forming the portfolio), intents (its goals), contents (the actual displays), standards (what is good and not-so-good performance), and judgments (what the contents tell us).

5. The portfolio may serve a different purpose during the year from the purpose it serves at the end. Some material may be kept in a portfolio because it is instructional, such as partially finished work on problem areas. At the end of the year, however, the portfolio may contain only material that the student is willing to make public.

6. A portfolio may have multiple purposes, but these must not conflict. A student's personal goals and interests are reflected in his or her selection of materials, but information included may also reflect the interests of teachers, parents, or the district. One purpose that is almost universal in student portfolios is showing progress on the goals represented in the instructional program.

7. The portfolio should contain information that illustrates growth. There are many ways to demonstrate growth. The most obvious is by including a series of examples of actual records of school performance that show how the student's skills have improved. Changes observed on interest inventories, in records of outside activities such as reading, or on attitude measures are other ways to illustrate a student's growth.[57]

There are a number of different types of portfolios. Elementary teachers might consider having students develop a portfolio that deals with (a) writing (with a wide variety of writing samples), (b) literacy and includes the material students have read or have written about, (c) a unit to include all the different materials generated as part of a unit assigned by the teachers, or even (d) standards, which would illustrate the ways in which students are meeting or are fulfilling standards dictated by the state or school district.[58]

Each of these portfolios represents a different way of showing what students are learning within the classroom. The type of portfolio will also be dictated by the purpose you have in mind:

- Are you trying to document student performance relative to local or state standards?
- Are you trying to document a student's developmental growth?

Performance-Based Assessment

Another form of authentic assessment is what is described as ***performance-based assessment.*** This type of assessment requires that students demonstrate in some tangible way their knowledge or skill relative to a specific task that is contrived, rather than real. Some of the emerging state standardized tests have performance components to them. For example, the CAPT test in Connecticut requires students to perform a chemical experiment, to use Algebra to solve a practical problem, and to write a persuasive letter that demonstrates a personal capacity to fashion a clear, lucid argument in writing. Advocates for the CAPT believe that the performance assessments are forcing school districts to create curricula that involve students with *real* problems that will foster enhanced analytical skills.

Perhaps one of the most popular representations of performance assessment is Sizer's concept of "exhibitions." Sizer, who is founder of the Coalition of Essential Schools, argues that a "student must exhibit the products of his learning. If he does that well, he can convince himself that he can use knowledge and he can so convince others. It is the academic equivalent of being able to sink free throws in basketball."[59] Table 10.6 provides several examples of exhibitions that students must perform to demonstrate their memory skills. Exhibitions can emerge in a variety of forms—some require memory, others require writing, and others entail some form of skill demonstration. Each exhibition, though, holds the common element of making students *do* what the teacher wants them to *know.* Exhibitions enable students to represent knowledge in more personal and ideally, meaningful ways. Personal representations foster greater ownership of ideas and help students be more motivated in their learning.

Project Work

A third form of authentic assessment is ***project work.*** Whereas performances tend to require short-term demonstration of a skill (reciting a poem), a project is a more long-term and often collaborative endeavor. Greeno and Hall note that

> Teachers who engage their students in these project-based activities usually have groups of students present their work to the rest of the class. In some projects, presentations by students are videotaped and submitted to a panel of reviewers, as well as being seen by

table 10.6   An Exhibition: Performance from Memory

As part of your final Exhibitions, you must show yourself and us that you can do the following, from memory:

1.   Recite a poem or song or story that is special to your family or community.

2.   Draw a map of the world, freehand (conventional Mercator projection), and be prepared to place properly on your map at least twelve of fifteen members of the United Nations that we shall randomly select for you.

3.   Draw a map of the United States, freehand, and accurately position on your map at least twelve of fifteen states that we will select for you at random.

4.   Identify and answer questions about the current United States president and vice president, this state's two United States senators, the representative from your district, your state representative and senator, and the mayor of this city.

5.   Recite for us from memory a speech from history or literature that you find compelling and that we agree is appropriate for this exercise.

6.   Present a time line since 1750 that you have assembled over the last several years and be prepared to answer questions about any event that appears on it.

7.   Be prepared to identify five birds, insects, trees, mammals, flowers, and plants from our immediate local environment.

8.   At a time mutually agreed on, we shall give you a text or an analogous "problem" (such as a machine to disassemble and reassemble) and three days in which to memorize or master it. We will ask you then to show us how well you have done this exercise.

9.   Be prepared to reflect with us on how you completed this memory task; that is, how you best "learned" to memorize.

Source: "An Exhibition from Memory," from *Horace's School* by Theodore R. Sizer, Copyright (c) 1992 by Theodore R. Sizer. Reprinted by permission of Houghton Mifflin Co. All rights reserved.

students in other classes who are working on projects involving the same problems. These presentations are a major source of information for assessment and a valuable learning activity. Teachers in the Middle-School Mathematics Through Applications Project have found it essential to have presentations midway through students' work. The presentations are reviewed by teachers and by other groups of students. The students preparing presentations learn to evaluate alternative ways of representing their ideas and findings. Those reviewing other students' presentations learn ways of judging the effectiveness of representations for communicating understanding.[60]

Students work over an extended time period to show what they know and to earn some recognition, reward, or grade. Projects foster a certain measure of student self-discipline and motivation. Indeed, the daughter of one of the authors had a project-oriented German teacher who substantially enhanced her self-discipline and motivation. The projects were unique opportunities for the daughter to demonstrate what she knew in representational forms that "played to" her personal strengths.

These forms of alternative assessment, asserts Rothman, cause "students to demonstrate complex thinking, not just isolated skills. . . . These assessments . . . challenge the view, implicit in multiple-choice tests, that there is only one right answer to every question and that the goal is to find it and to find it quickly."[61] These forms of assessment, are also tied to helping students become more active in constructing their own knowledge before demonstrating what they know. Elliot Eisner poignantly writes,

> Performance assessment is aimed at moving away from testing practices that require students to select the single correct answer from an array of four or five distractors to a practice that requires students to create evidence through performance that will enable assessors to make valid judgments about "what they know and can do" in situations that matter. Performance assessment is the most important development in evaluation since the invention of the short-answer test and its extensive use during World War I.[62]

Performance-based assessment has its drawbacks. Such assessments require teacher thought and significant student time. (However, when evaluating the time taken for performance-based assessment it is important to remember that the time students take to generate products or performances for assessment is also learning time.) Another drawback is the difficulty of assessing student performance and projects unless teachers create and use clear scoring rubrics.

Administering and Returning Tests

You need to decide when and how to give tests. Teachers who consider testing important often give several tests at short intervals of time. Those for whom testing is not so vital may give fewer tests. Teachers who prefer a mastery or competence approach to instruction generally give many criterion-reference tests for the purposes of diagnosing, checking on learning progress, and individualizing instruction, as well as for grading student performance. Those who prefer a broad, cognitive approach may rely on fewer classroom tests that assess student knowledge of the subject matter. Whatever their approach to testing, it is recommended that teachers announce tests (or any assessment) well in advance. Discuss what will be covered, how it will be evaluated, and how much it will count toward a final grade. In Chapter 11, we will discuss more fully the grading process and the options you might consider.

Test-Taking Skills

Conditions other than students' knowledge can affect student performance on tests. One such factor is their general test-taking ability, which is completely apart from the subject matter of particular tests. Test-taking skills are important for all students. Almost any student who has taken a few tests and who has common sense can learn certain skills that will improve his or her scores. Developing good test-taking strategies should not be construed as amoral or dishonest. Rather it is a way of reducing anxiety in test situations. A number of test authorities contend that all students should be given training in test-wiseness.[63]

Important test-taking skills can be taught to students. When students are given practice in diagnosing test questions and in strategies involved in taking tests, their test scores usually improve (although researchers differ as to the size of the effect).[64]

Tips for Teachers 10.4 will help you prepare students for test taking. You will note that some of the ideas are related to general test-taking skills and others to test-specific skills that might be useful if tests are not constructed properly by developers.

tips for teachers 10.4

Testwise Strategies

 Testing is an integral part of the education process, and it affects the lives of all students. As students become more testwise, the better they should perform on classroom and standardized tests. The following suggestions are aimed at high school and college students:

1. Get a good night's sleep prior to major tests and don't sit near a friend.
2. Read the test directions and each test item carefully.
3. Be aware that both human scorers and machine scorers place a premium on neatness and legibility.
4. Establish a pace that will permit you sufficient time to finish; check the time periodically to see if you are maintaining the pace.
5. Do easy items first; bypass difficult test questions or problems and return to them as time permits.
6. If credit is given only for the number of right answers or if correction for guessing is less severe than a wrong response (e.g., -1 for a wrong response and +1 for a correct response), it is appropriate to guess.
7. Eliminate items you know are incorrect on matching or multiple-choice questions before guessing.
8. Make use of relevant content information on other test items and options.
9. Don't get stuck on one item or question.
10. Recognize idiosyncrasies of the test constructor that differentiate correct and incorrect options; for example, notice whether correct (or incorrect) options a) are longer or shorter, b) are more general or specific, c) are placed in certain logi-

cal positions within each set of options, d) include or exclude one pair of diametrically opposed statements, and e) are grammatically inconsistent or consistent with the stem.

11. Use of *an* instead of *a* may imply that the correct response begins with a consonant. Eliminate alternatives.
12. True items may be longer than false items because they require qualifying phrases.
13. Words such as "always," "never," and "none" are associated with false items.
14. Words such as "usually," "often," and "many" are associated with true items.
15. On multiple choice tests, if you cannot finish then fill in all the remaining answers with the same letter if there is no penalty for guessing.
16. Periodically check to be sure the item number and answer number match, especially when using an answer sheet.
17. Reflect on and outline an essay before starting to write; decide how much time you can afford for that question given the available time. In all cases, attempt an answer, no matter how poor, to gain some points.
18. Write short paragraphs for an essay; develop one idea or concept in each paragraph to make your points easier for the reader (teacher) to discern. Include several short paragraphs as opposed to a few long paragraphs that tend to blend or fuse distinct ideas.
19. If time permits, return to omitted items (if any); then check answers and correct careless mistakes.

See Anita Woolfolk. *Educational Psychology* 7th ed. Boston, Allyn and Bacon, 1998, pp. 546-547.

For example, here are some general test-taking strategies:

1. Attend carefully to the test directions and then periodically check your work to make sure you are following them exactly.
2. Ask questions if you are unclear about what to do.[65]
3. Consistent studying or review over the duration of the course is more effective than cramming.

Here are examples of some test-specific strategies:

1. The answer option that is longest or most precisely stated is likely correct.
2. The use of vague words ("some," "often") in one of the answers usually signals the correct option.[66]

Provided here are some specific examples of test-taking strategies in reading. Reading is critical to students' academic growth in all academic areas and is a part of the standardized assessment process found in states as a result of the No Child Left Behind legislation.

1. Whisper read the title/subtitles. Predict what the passage is about.
2. Carefully study any charts, graphs, or diagrams.
3. Number the paragraphs.
4. Whisper read the questions carefully, circling the key words. Make sure you understand what the question is asking.
5. Beginning with the title, whisper read the passage thoroughly at least two times. Make a mental picture of what you are reading.
6. Whisper read the first question and answer choices, getting an idea of what the answer may be. Do not bubble in your answer choice.
7. Return to the passage and underline the clues that support the possible answer.
8. Return to the question and eliminate the wrong answers.
9. Bubble in the correct answer and record the paragraph's number where the answer/clues were located. Remember, you have to prove your answer is correct.
10. Repeat steps 6 through 9 for the remainder of the questions.
11. Check to make sure you answered all questions reasonably.[67]

Test Routines

Both short-answer and essay tests must be administered carefully to avoid confusion. You should establish a routine for handing out the test questions and answer sheets, papers, or booklets. The answer sheets, papers, or booklets should be passed out first, for example, with the exact number for each row given to the first student in each row who then passes them back along the row. Students should be instructed to fill out information required on the answer papers, such as their names and class. To avoid confusion the test itself should not be handed out until the answer papers or booklets have been distributed. To save time, insert the answer paper into the test and then hand out both.

Before the test begins, be sure that students understand the directions and questions; that the test papers are clear, complete, and in proper order; and that students have any necessary supplies, such as pencil or pen, ruler, calculator, or dictionary. You need to have on hand extra copies of the test and extra supplies.

Establish a procedure for clarifying directions and test items during test time. Once the test begins, a student with a question should raise his or her hand without talking out loud or disturbing classmates. With young students, go to the student's desk and whisper. Older students may be permitted to come to you. If several students have the same question or a problem with the same item, interrupt the students briefly to clarify it for all. This should be done sparingly to limit distractions.

To further reduce distractions or interruptions, close the door to the hallway and post a sign, "Testing—Do Not Disturb," on the door. Late students will disturb the others no matter how quiet they are in picking up the test papers and getting seated. Unless they have a proper pass or excuse for being late, do not give them extra time to complete the examination. If students enter the room late for a standardized examination, they should not be permitted to take the exam since the norms are based partially on time allotments.

Pressure on students for good grades (or for successful performance on high-stakes tests) causes some to cheat. Short-answer teacher-made tests are particularly susceptible to student cheating, because a student can easily see someone else's answer by glancing at his or her paper.[68] To reduce cheating, have students sit in alternate seats if sufficient seating is available or have students sit at a distance from each other if seats can be moved. Using two versions of the same test or dividing the test into two parts and having students in alternate rows start on different parts also helps reduce cheating. One of the best deterrents to cheating is your presence. To what extent you need to police students during the test depends on how common cheating is. Even if there is no cheating problem, stay alert and don't bury your head in a book while the test is being administered.

Defined routines should be established for collecting tests at the end of the period. Remind students who finish early to review their answers. When the test period ends, the papers should be collected in an orderly fashion. For example, you might ask that papers be passed forward to the first student in each row where you collect them.

Table 10.7 lists some things a teacher can do to improve test conditions and help students perform to their full potential. Most of these strategies are geared to limiting confusion and interruptions before and during the test, ensuring that students know what to do, curtailing their anxieties and nervousness, and motivating them to do their best.

Test Anxiety

Test anxiety (that is, potentially debilitating emotions and worry) among students is common and should not be ignored. Most of us studying to become teachers can recall our own anxieties about certain subjects (usually our weaker ones), about certain tests (midterms, finals, and standardized) when the stakes were high, and with certain teachers who used test scores and grades as a weapon and who rarely gave students the benefit of the doubt.

Elementary teachers particularly report a host of anxiety-related symptoms experienced by their students. The six most common are 1) excessive concern over time limitations, 44 percent; 2) perceptions of freezing temperatures in the testing classroom, 41 percent; 3) headaches, 40 percent; 4) irritability, 38 percent; 5) increased aggression, 33 percent; and 6) stomachaches, 29 percent. Secondary teachers report fewer signs of stress, probably because of greater student experience in taking tests. Nonetheless, older student symptoms are 1) truancy, 29 percent; 2) increased aggression, 25 percent; 3) irritability, 21 percent; 4) excessive concern over time limitations, 17 percent; 5) complaints about freezing classroom temperatures, 14 percent; and 6) headaches, 12 percent.[69]

Anxiety is the highest during standardized tests. More than 80 percent of high-school student respondents in one state felt that scores on standardized tests are not a true reflection of what they have learned, and more than 65 percent felt too much is at stake with the exam.[70] Though this research is now a decade old, there is little new research to suggest that such findings are now invalid. Teachers express similar anxiety over state-mandated and annual achievement tests. Nearly 40 percent report feeling pressure from administrators to raise test scores, and over two-thirds feel threatened by the results of the tests.[71]

The anxiety of tests is not likely to be mitigated anytime soon. Consider that in Texas starting in 2005 a student has to successfully pass TAAS (the Texas proficiency exam) to graduate from high school, and in Louisiana a student is retained in either the fourth or eighth grade if he or she fails the mandated proficiency exam. Given such tests, student anxiety will be high and manifest itself in everything from physical symptoms (headaches and irritability) to social dysfunctions (cheating and aggressivity).

A review of 562 studies, involving more than 20,000 students, shows that test anxiety correlates with feelings of academic inadequacy, helplessness, and anticipation of failure. A child's original view of self, before entering school, is likely to be positive. However, after grade 4, students who exhibit high test anxiety wish to leave the test situation and consistently score low on tests, a pattern that reinforces a negative self-image. Performance on tests also strongly varies with students' perceptions of the test's difficulty; average-achieving students are impacted more than other groups.[72]

The high test anxiety/low test performance cycle is difficult to reverse. Incentives, praise, rewards, and prompt feedback all have minimal benefits, as do frequent tests, detailed test instructions, and test reviews. What works best, according to the research, is to teach students study skills (how to take good notes or how to use memory devices to remember information) and test-taking skills.[73]

Teachers can also help to reduce anxiety on teacher-made tests by a) eliminating time requirements *when* what they are trying to measure is not how quickly students perform, b) explaining to the students very carefully the assessment procedures that are to be used, and c) simply affirming with students that the purpose of testing is to *assess* what students know and need to learn—tests are not "gotcha" situations.[74]

Little things, in essence, can make a difference in reducing student anxiety around tests. Imagine yourself as a student with a teacher who is preparing to administer a standardized test telling you, "You really need to do well on this because poor performance will have serious consequences for you." Now consider yourself with another teacher prior to taking the same test. This one says, "Class, you have worked hard. Now try to do your best work on this test."

Returning Tests and Feedback

One major problem you might confront is the speed with which the results of standardized tests are provided for you. Unlike teacher-made tests, which can be graded quickly, standardized tests are returned by outside sources often after a significant time lag.

t a b l e 1 0 . 7   **Test Giver's List of Things to Do**

1.   Before giving a standardized test
     a. Order and check test materials (in advance of the testing date).
     b. Be sure there are sufficient tests and answer sheets.
     c. Securely store all test materials until the testing date.
     d. Read the testing instructions, including how to administer the test.

2.   Before giving a teacher-made test
     a. Check the questions for errors and clarity.
     b. Be sure there are sufficient tests and answer sheets.
     c. Be sure the test pages are sequenced properly.
     d. Securely store all test materials until the testing date.
     e. Announce the testing date; avoid days that are before holidays or coincide with major events.

3.   Be sure classroom conditions are adequate:
     a. Is there adequate work space, desks, chairs?
     b. Is there sufficient light, heat, and ventilation?
     c. Is it a quiet location?

4.   Study the test materials before the test:
     a. Are the directions clear?
     b. Are the time limits clear?

5.   Minimize distractions and interruptions during the testing period:
     a. Decide the order in which materials are to be distributed and collected.
     b. Be sure that students have pencils or pens and other needed supplies. Have extra pencils or pens handy for students who are unprepared.
     c. Close the hallway door.
     d. Post a sign: "Testing in Progress: Do Not Disturb."
     e. Decide what students who finish early are to do.

6.   Motivate students to do their best:
     a. Explain the purpose of the test.
     b. Ask students to do their best: "I will be pleased if you try your best."
     c. Reduce test anxiety: "Take it easy." "Take a deep breath." "Shake your fingers and wrists." "Relax, it's only a test."

7.   Reassure students; provide positive expectations and strategies:
     a. "Some test questions are difficult. Don't worry if you can't answer all of them."
     b. "If you don't finish, don't worry about it. Just try your best."

Teacher-made tests should be returned to students as quickly as possible. As you return the papers, make some general comments to the class about your awareness of the group effort, the level of achievement, and general problems or specific areas of the test that gave students trouble.

Discuss in class each question on the test, giving particular emphasis to questions that many students missed. If the missed test items are fundamental for mastery, take extra time to explain the material and provide similar but different exercises for students to review. Some teachers call on volunteers to redo and explain parts of the test that were missed, although this method may not always be the most profitable use of time.

To students who have achieved a good grade, especially an unexpectedly good grade, provide approval. Give students who have performed poorly special help in the form of extra reading, selective homework, or tutoring. In some cases, you may retest them after they have restudied the material. Meet with students who have ques-

table 10.7   (continued)

....

      c.   "Don't work too fast—you might start making careless mistakes."

      d.   "Don't work too slowly—you could start falling behind. Work at a moderate pace."

      e.   "Don't dwell on a difficult question; return to it when you finish and if there is time to do so."

      f.   "Pay close attention to your work and to the time."

      g.   "Good luck" (or better, "I know you'll do well").

8.   Follow directions and monitor time:

      a.   Distribute materials according to the predetermined time allotment.

      b.   Read test directions, if permitted.

      c.   Give the signal to start.

      d.   Do not help students during the test, except for mechanics (e.g., providing an extra pencil or answer sheet).

      e.   Stick to the time schedule, especially if you are administering a standardized test.

      f.   Periodically post or announce time; provide five- to ten-minute time announcements during the last fifteen to twenty minutes of test.

9.   Observe significant events:

      a.   Pay attention to students; monitor the test situation.

      b.   Make sure students are following directions and answering in the correct place.

      c.   Note if any student is displaying behavior that might affect his or her test results; curtail cheating.

      d.   Note any major distractions or interruptions that could affect the test results. If administering a standardized test, report these problems to the administration.

10.   Collect test materials:

      a.   Attend to students who finish early; remind them to check their answers before handing in the test.

      b.   Collect materials promptly and without confusion.

      c.   If administering a teacher-made test, perhaps provide a few minutes extra for slow students or students who walked in late. Use good judgment.

      d.   Count and check to see that all materials have been turned in.

11.   Help students know when to guess

      a.   yes . . . when only right answers are scored.

      b.   yes . . . when some alternatives can be eliminated.

      c.   no . . . if a penalty is assessed for guessing.

Source: Adapted from Norman E. Gronlund. *Measurement and Evaluation of Teaching,* 5th ed. New York: Macmillan, 1985. Anita E. Woolfolk. *Educational Psychology* 7th ed. Boston, Mass.: Allyn and Bacon, 1998.

tions about their grades after class privately or possibly in a small group if several students have the same question. Regardless of the type of test, make some comments about the individual student's answers and progress, directing more personal comments toward the younger children. Personal comments, as long as they are objective and positive, help motivate students and make them aware that they need to improve in specific areas.

The Purpose of Assessment

....

As we conclude this chapter, it is important to review the purpose of all the testing you might be responsible for as a teacher. You test (assess) in order to help students learn requisite content and to achieve learning goals effectively. A teacher who has clear standards of learning and who knows what the local district requires and the state mandates is in a good position to make certain that each child learns to his or her full potential. Good assessment starts with knowing what you need to teach and why and how you will teach it. The assessment process itself is most effective when you use a variety of strategies to measure what students have learned and to figure out whether you need to reteach any material they failed to learn.

If you are a teacher in a standards based classroom, you will find yourself using all the tools we articulated in this chapter. More specifically, you will be able to address or consider the following:

1. The specific content standards in place for the areas of instructional responsibility that you have.
2. The benchmark standards in place for students in your school and state. What must the students know at grades 4 or 8 or 10? What does that require that you assess at the grade level you teach?
3. The relative strengths and weaknesses of students you teach. You need to know what students know or do not know relative to the standards. That will dictate what you teach and how you teach them.
4. The students need to be held accountable for achieving the standards and the learning goals you establish. Help students see that their success is important and that will lead to your success.[75]

In the next chapter we will discuss what happens after the assessments are made: The teacher holds students accountable for their learning by making an evaluation (or judgment) of their progress. It seems fitting that, especially in the case of standardized tests, the teacher is then held accountable for what the students learned as a result of his or her instruction.

Theory into Practice

Although the specific purposes of tests and intended use of outcomes vary among teachers and schools, tests play an important part in the life of students and teachers. One of your goals as a teacher should be to improve your tests. Here is a checklist to use when constructing your classroom and/or criterion-reference tests:

1. Is my test appropriate?
   a. Does it match defined standards?
   b. Does it fit my objectives?
   c. Do the test items reflect a wide representation of subject content and skills?
   d. Does the test have credible and worthwhile items to anchor the scoring system?
   e. Does it consider reality: the conditions of the classroom, school, and community?

Technology Viewpoint from a Classroom Teacher

Jackie Marshall Arnold
K–12 Media Specialist

 Assessments are a critical component of any lesson. An effective teacher understands what it is that the students should learn and makes plans for how to assess that learning. The work of Wiggins and McTighe in *Understanding by Design* (1998) details three stages of planning. Effective planning begins first with identifying desired results, then determining acceptable evidence, and, last, planning the learning experiences and instruction (Wiggins and McTighe, p. 9). Many teachers will plan the instruction first without fully understanding what the goal is and how to tell if the goal has been achieved.

Consider the assessment of the use of technology as an example. The assessment may be formal or informal. For example, if the assignment involves students using the Internet to gather information on a topic, a teacher can quickly and informally assess individual or group work as it happens. Assessment of this type might include determining how the groups are working with each other, whether they are staying on topic and finding the necessary information, and whether they are recording the information in a way that can be used and shared later.

Technology use can be assessed more formally. An effective teacher can identify the technology skills that students should gain through the learning process and then plan how that knowledge will be demonstrated. For example, if the desired result is that students be proficient with a presentation software program, then the acceptable evidence could be a presentation based upon a particular content being studied. The effective teacher would then plan the experiences and instruction that would support students in learning the particular instructional content as well as the software.

Technology assessments can also be an ongoing process. Many teachers are now supporting students in creating individual electronic portfolios. These portfolios can authentically illustrate and assess a student's technology skills and understandings (or lack thereof) and provide the student a showcase piece of his or her work. The following sites are rich in information for those who would like to learn more about electronic portfolios and their applications: http://electronicportfolios.com/, http://www.ash.udel.edu/ash/teacher/portfolio.html, and http://www.hyperstudio.com/showcase/portfolio.html

Finally, it is important for students to understand what will be assessed and how it will be assessed. They need to have a clear description of the assessment tool. Using rubrics to assess technology projects is an excellent way to accomplish these goals. Rubistar (http://rubistar.4teachers.org) is a high-quality site that provides teachers an easy step-by-step process to create their own personalized rubrics or use ones already designed. Categories of created rubrics are easily accessible for website design, multimedia projects, HyperStudio projects, and more.

Assessment plans should always be done at the beginning of the planning stage, not at the end. Teachers need carefully to consider what it is they want their students to know, whether it is a technology skill or content-based knowledge. Effective teachers know where they want their students to go and how to know when they arrive.

2. Is my test valid?
   a. Does it discriminate between performance levels?
   b. Does it fit external and agreed-upon standards?
   c. Will my colleagues in the subject or at the grade level agree that all necessary items are included?
   d. Does the test measure actual performance, not the students' reading levels or simple recall of information?

3. Is my test reliable?
   a. Are all test items clear and understandable?
   b. Are the items consistent with test performance?
   c. Are there at least two items per objective, and do students who get one item of a pair correct get the other item correct?
   d. Are there sufficient test items to measure important content and skills?
4. Is my test usable?
   a. Is my test short enough to avoid being tedious?
   b. Does it have sufficient breadth and depth to allow for generalizations about student performance?
   c. Are there clear and standard procedures for administration of the test?
   d. Is it authentic: Does it measure worthwhile behaviors and tasks, not what is easy to score?

Summary

1. Good teachers know the standards for their local district and for their state.
2. A good test is reliable and valid. Methods for establishing reliability are test-retest, parallel test forms, and split-half reliability. Forms of validity are content, curricular, construct, criterion, and predictive, with content validity being most important.
3. There are two major types of tests: norm reference and criterion reference. Norm-reference tests measure how a student performs relative to other students. Criterion-reference tests measure a student's progress and appraise his or her ability relative to a specific criterion.
4. For general appraisal of an individual's performance or behavior, the standardized (norm-reference) test is an excellent instrument. There are four basic types of standardized tests: intelligence, achievement, aptitude, and personality.
5. Teacher-made tests may be short-answer tests or essay tests. Short-answer questions include multiple choice, matching, completion, and true-false. Essay, or free-response, questions also include discussion questions.
6. Proper test administration reduces confusion, curtails students' anxieties, and motivates and helps them do as well as possible.
7. Important test-taking skills can be taught to students.

Questions to Consider

1. What are the academic standards for the subject you teach?
2. How does the curriculum for a school district match established state academic standards?
3. What are the advantages and disadvantages of a norm-reference test?
4. What are the advantages and disadvantages of a criterion-reference test?
5. What are the advantages of teacher-made tests over standardized tests? What are the advantages of standardized tests over teacher-made tests?

Things to Do

1. Explain the differences between reliability and validity.
2. Visit a school and talk to a few teachers, the school counselor, or one of the administrators about the standardized tests the school uses. Try to find out which ones are used and why. What are the advantages and disadvantages of the tests? Report back to the class.
3. Discuss in class five guidelines for constructing multiple-choice questions and five guidelines for constructing matching questions.
4. Develop five essay questions (in the subject you plan to teach or are teaching) that test critical thinking.
5. Invite a test specialist to class to discuss strategies that students can learn to increase their test-wiseness.

Recommended Readings

Airasian, Peter W. *Classroom Assessment: Concepts and Applications,* 4th ed. Boston, Mass.: McGraw-Hill, 2001. This book focuses on assessment needs of preservice teachers, including special emphasis on standardized testing, performance tests, and authentic testing.

Burke, Kay. *How to Assess Authentic Learning,* 3rd ed. Arlington Heights, Ill.: Merrill Prentice Hall, 1999. This resource documents the different ways teachers can assess student learning by using alternative assessment protocols.

Elliot, Stephen N., Jeffrey P. Braden, and Jennifer L. White. *Assessing One and All.* Arlington, Va.: Council for Exceptional Children, 2001. This excellent resource helps readers understand how to assess the wide variety of learners evidenced in most classrooms.

Norman E. Gronlund. *Assessment of Student Achievement,* 7th ed. Boston, Mass.: Allyn and Bacon, 2003. A thoughtful description of the development and use of practical assessment tools for teachers.

Popham, W. James. *Classroom Assessment: What Teachers Need to Know,* 3rd ed. Boston, Mass.: Allyn and Bacon, 2001. This book describes the differences between norm-reference and criterion-reference tests and their applications.

Salvia, John, and James Ysseldyke. *Assessment,* 8th ed. Boston: Houghton Mifflin, 2001. This is a wonderful comprehensive resource for understanding all the different formal and informal assessment approaches that teachers might use.

Wiggins, G., and Jay McTighe. *Understanding by Design.* Alexandria, Va.: Association for Supervision and Curriculum Development, 1998. This wonderful book describes the subtle differences between *understanding* and *knowing* and how teachers explore and assess those differences.

Key Terms

End Notes

1. Matthew Gandal and Jennifer Vranek. "Standards: Here Today, Here Tomorrow." *Educational Leadership* (September 2001): 7–13.
2. Ibid.
3. Marge Scherer. "How and Why Standards Can Improve Student Achievement." *Educational Leadership* (September 2001): 14–18.
4. Ibid.
5. Mike Schmoker and Robert J. Marzano. "Realizing the Promise of Standards-Based Education." *Educational Leadership* (March 1999): 17–18.
6. Ibid., p. 20.
7. Robert Sternberg, Bruce Torff, and Elena Grigorenko. "Teaching for Successful Intelligence Raises Achievement." *Phi Delta Kappan* (May, 1998): 667–669.
8. William A. Mehrens and Irvin J. Lehmann. *Measurement and Evaluation in Education and Psychology,* 3d ed. Ft. Worth, Tex.: Holt, Rinehart, 1991.
9. Jum C. Nunnally. "Reliability of Measurement." In M. C. Wittrock (ed.), *Encyclopedia of Educational Research,* 5th ed. New York: Macmillan, 1982. pp. 1589–1601. Ross E. Traub and Glenn L. Rowley. "Understanding Reliability." *Educational Measurement* (Spring 1991): 37–45.
10. John Sylvia and James Ysseldyke. *Assessment,* 8th ed. Boston: Houghton Mifflin, 2001.
11. William A. Mehrens and Irvin J. Lehmann. *Using Standardized Tests in Education.* New York: Longman, 1987, pp. 64–65.
12. Samuel Messick. "Validity." *Educational Measurement,* 3d ed. New York: Macmillan, 1989, pp. 13–103. Pamela A. Moss. "Shifting Conceptions of Validity in Educational Measurement." *Review of Educational Research* (Fall 1992): 229–258.
13. Norman E. Gronlund and Robert L. Linn. *Measurement and Evaluation in Teaching,* 6th ed. New York: Macmillan, 1990. Tom Kubiszyn, Gary Borich and J. N. Reddy. *Educational Testing and Measurement: Classroom Application and Practice,* 7th ed. New York: John Wiley and Sons, 2002.
14. Gronlund and Linn. *Measurement and Evaluation in Teaching.* Robert M. Thorndike, George K. Cunningham, Robert L. Thorndike, and Elizabeth P. Hagen. *Measurement and Evaluation in Psychology and Evaluation,* 5th ed. New York: Macmillan, 1992.
15. N. L. Gage and David C. Berliner. *Educational Psychology,* 5th ed. Boston: Houghton Mifflin, 1992, p. 572.
16. Peter W. Airasian. "Perspectives on Measurement Instruction." *Educational Measurement* (Spring 1991): 13–16. Herbert C. Rudman. "Classroom Instruction and Tests." *NASSP Bulletin* (February 1987): 3–22. Robert E. Stake. "The Teacher, Standardized Testing and Prospects of Revolution." *Phi Delta Kappan* (November 1991): 241–247.
17. Ronald K. Hambleton et al. "Criterion-Referenced Testing and Measurement: A Review of Technical Issues and Developments." *Review of Educational Research* (Winter 1988): 1–47. Robert L. Linn. "Educational Testing and Assessment." *American Psychologist* (October 1985\6): 1153–1160. Grant Wiggins. "Creating Tests Worth Taking." *Educational Leadership* (May 1992): 26–34.
18. Gronlund and Linn. *Measurement and Evaluation in Teaching.*
19. John Sylvia and James Ysseldyke. *Assessment.*
20. See http://nces.ed.gov./nationsreportcard/about/state.asp.12/4/2002.
21. Ibid.
22. Peter W. Airasian. "Teacher Assessments." *NASSP Bulletin* (October 1993): 55–65. Allan C. Ornstein. "Accountability Report from the USA." *Journal of Curriculum Studies* (December 1985): 437–439. Allan C. Ornstein. "Teaching and Teacher Accountability." In Allan C. Ornstein et al., *Contemporary Issues in Curriculum* Boston, Mass.: Allyn and Bacon, 2003: pp. 248–261.

23. Retrieved from http://w.../standardform3?openform&parentunid.9/14/2002:p.1.

24. Ron Smith and Steve Sherrell. "Milestones on the Road to a Certificate of Initial Mastery." *Educational Leadership* (December 1996–January 1997): 46–51.

25. Robert J. Drummond. *Appraisal Procedures for Counselors and Helping Professionals.* Upper Saddle River, N.J.: Merrill Prentice Hall, 2000.

26. W. James Popham. *Modern Educational Measurement,* 3d ed. Needham Heights, Mass.: Allyn and Bacon, 1999.

27. Nancy Kober. *Test Talk for Leaders.* Washington, D.C.: Center for Education Policy, 2002.

28. Ibid., p. 9.

29. Ibid.

30. Ibid.

31. Heather Voke. "What Do We Know About Sanctions and Rewards?" *Infobrief.* Alexandria, VA: Association for Supervision and Curriculum Development, 2002: Retrieved from http://www.ascd.org/readingroom/infobrief/issue31.html.

32. Robert A. Frahm. "Is the Test too Hard, or Are the Schools too Soft?" *The Hartford Courant* (November 12, 2002). Retrieved from http://www.nl.newsbank.com/nlsearch.asp

33. Carol Ann Tomlinson. "Proficiency Is Not Enough." *Education Week* (November 6, 2002): 36 and 38.

34. William A. Mehrens. "Educational Tests: Blessing or Curse?" Unpublished paper. 1987. William A. Mehrens. "Facts About Samples, Fantasies, and Domains." *Educational Measurement* (Summer 1991): 23–25.

35. Claudia Meek. "Classroom Crisis: It's About Time." *Phi Delta Kappan* April 2003: 592–595. William A. Mehrens and Irvin J. Lehmann. "Using Teacher-Made Measurement Devices." *NASSP Bulletin* (February 1987): 36–44. W. James Popham. "Can High-Stakes Tests Be Developed at the Local Level?" *NASSP Bulletin* (February 1987): 77–84.

36. Margaret Fleming and Barbara Chambers. "Teacher-Made Tests: Windows in the Classroom." In W. E. Hathaway (ed.), *Testing in Schools.* San Francisco: Jossey-Bass, 1983. pp. 29–38. Richard J. Stiggins. "Relevant Classroom Assessment Training for Teachers." *Educational Measurement* (Spring 1991): 7–12.

37. Stephen N. Elliot, Jeffrey P. Bradon, and Jennifer L. White. *Assessing One and All.* Arlington, Va.: Council for Exceptional Children, 2001, p. 115.

38. Robert L. Ebel and David A. Frisbie. *Essentials of Educational Measurement,* 5th ed. Needham Heights, Mass.: Allyn and Bacon, 1991. Thorndike et al. *Measurement and Evaluation in Psychology and Evaluation.*

39. Mehrens and Lehmann. *Measurement and Evaluation in Education and Psychology.* The fifth point is mainly based on the author's ideas about testing students at various ages.

40. David A. Payne. *Measuring and Evaluating Educational Outcomes.* New York: Macmillan, 1992.

41. Kenneth D. Hopkins, Julian C. Stanley, and B. R. Hopkins. *Educational and Psychological Measurement and Evaluation,* 7th ed. Needham Heights, Mass.: Allyn and Bacon, 1990.

42. Benjamin S. Bloom, J. Thomas Hastings, and George F. Madaus. *Evaluation to Improve Learning* New York: McGraw-Hill, 1981. George K. Cunningham. *Educational and Psychological Measurement,* 2d ed. New York: Macmillan, 1992.

43. Ebel and Frisbie. *Essentials of Educational Measurement,* pp. 164–165.

44. Gage and Berliner. *Educational Psychology.* W. James Popham. *Educational Evaluation,* 3d. ed. Needham Heights, Mass.: Allyn and Bacon, 1993.

45. Bruce W. Tuckman. "Evaluating the Alternative to Multiple-Choice Testing for Teachers." *Contemporary Education* (Summer 1991): 299–300.

46. Allan C. Ornstein. "Questioning: The Essence of Good Teaching." *NASSP Bulletin* (February 1988): 72–80. Barak V. Rosenshine and Carla Meister. "The Use of Scaffolds for Teaching Higher-Level Cognitive Strategies." *Educational Leadership* (April 1992): 26–33.

47. Penelope L. Peterson. "Toward an Understanding of What We Know About School Learning." *Review of Educational Research* (Fall 1993): 319–326. Francis P. Hunkins. *Teaching Thinking Through Effective Questioning,* 2d ed. Needham Heights, Mass.: Gordon, 1995.

48. Gronlund and Linn. *Measurement and Evaluation in Teaching.*

49. Peter W. Airasian. *Classroom Assessment: Concepts and Applications,* 4th ed. Boston, Mass.: McGraw-Hill, 2001.

50. Ray Bull and Julia Stevens. "The Effects of Attractiveness of Writer and Penmanship on Essay Grades." *Journal of Occupational Psychology* (April 1979): 53–59. Jon C. Marshall and Jerry M. Powers. "Writing Neatness, Composition Errors, and Essay Grades." *Journal of Educational Measurement* (Summer 1969): 97–101.

51. Bruce W. Tuckman. "The Essay Test: A Look at the Advantages and Disadvantages." *NASSP Bulletin* (October 1993): 20–27.

52. Most authorities (for example, Ebel, Gronlund, and Payne) recommend that students answer all questions and that no choice be provided because a common set of questions tends to increase reliability in scoring while options tend to distort results. However, weighed against this advantage is the fact that being able to select an area they know well increases students' morale, reduces test anxiety, and gives them a greater chance to show they can organize and interpret the subject matter.

53. Linda Darling-Hammond. "The Case for Authentic Assessment." *NASSP Bulletin* (November 1993): 18–26. Lorrie A. Shepard. "Psychometrician's Beliefs About Learning." *Educational Researcher* (October 1991): 2–15.

54. Grant Wiggins. "Teaching to the (Authentic) Test." *Educational Leadership* (April 1989): 41–47. Wiggins. "Creating Tests Worth Taking." Grant Wiggins. *Assessing Student Performance* San Francisco, Calif.: Jossey-Bass, 1993.

55. Grant Wiggins and Jay McTighe. *Understanding by Design* Alexandria, Va.: Association for Supervision and Curriculum Development, 1998, p. 74.

56. Judith Arter and Jay McTighe. *Scoring Rubrics in the Classroom.* Thousand Oaks, CA: Corwin Press, 2001.

57. F. Leon Paulson, Pearl R. Paulson, and Carol A. Meyer. "What Makes a Portfolio a Portfolio." *Educational Leadership* (February 1991): 60–63.

58. Kay Burke. *How to Assess Authentic Learning.* Arlington Heights, Ill.: Merrill Prentice Hall, 1999.

59. Ted Sizer. *Horace's School.* Boston: Houghton Mifflin, 1992, p. 25.

60. James Greeno and James G. Hall. "Practicing Representation: Learning with and About Representational Forms." *Phi Delta Kappan* (January 1997): 363.

61. Robert Rothman. *Measuring Up.* San Francisco: Jossey-Bass, 1995, p. 72.

62. Elliot Eisner. "The Uses and Limits of Performance Assessment." *Phi Delta Kappan* (May 1999): 659.

63. Darling-Hammond. "The Implications of Testing Policy for Quality and Equality." Madaus. "The Effects of Important Tests on Students."

64. Henry S. Dyer. "The Effects of Coaching for Scholastic Aptitude." *NASSP Bulletin* (February 1987): 46–53. Samuel Messick. "Issue and Equity in the Coaching Controversy: Implications for Educational Testing and Practice." *Educational Psychologist* (Summer 1982): 67–91.

65. Stephen N. Elliot, Jeffrey P. Braden, Jennifer L. White. *Assessing One and All.* Arlington, Va.: Council for Exceptional Children, 2001, 115.

66. Ibid., p. 115.

67. Patricia Davenport and Gerald Anderson. *Closing the Achievement Gap: No Excuses.* Houston, Tex.: American Productivity and Quality Center, 2002, p. 88.

68. Jane Canner. "Regaining the Public Trust: A Review of School Testing Programs, Practices." *NASSP Bulletin* (September 1992): 6–15. Dale D. Johnson and Bonnie Johnson. *High Stakes: Children, Testing, and Failure in American Schools.* Lanham, Maryland: Rowman and Littlefield, 2002.

69. Susan B. Nolan, Thomas M. Haladyna, and Nancy S. Hass. "Uses and Abuses of Achievement Tests." *Educational Measurement* (Summer 1992): 9–15.

70. Nancy S. Hass. "Standardized Testing in Arizona." Technical Report 89–3. Phoenix: Arizona State University West, 1989.

71. Marshall L. Smith et al. "Put to the Test: The Effects of External Testing on Teachers." *Educational Researcher* (November 1991): 8–11. Nolan. "Uses and Abuses of Achievement Tests."

72. Ray Hembree. "Correlates, Causes, Effects and Treatments of Test Anxiety." *Review of Educational Research* (Spring 1988): 47–77.

73. Ibid.

74. Jeanne Ellis Ormrod. *Educational Psychology,* 4th ed. Upper Saddle River, N.J.: Merrill Prentice Hall 2003.

75. Marc Tucker and Judy B. Codding. *Standards for Our Schools.* San Francisco, CA: Jossey-Bass, 1998.

Student Evaluation and Teacher Accountability

Pathwise criteria relevant to the content of this chapter:

- Creating or selecting evaluation strategies that are appropriate for the students and that are aligned with the goals for the lesson. (A5)
- Monitoring students' understanding of content through a variety of means, providing feedback to students to assist learning, and adjusting learning activities as the situation demands. (C4)

INTASC principles relevant to the content of this chapter:

- The teacher understands and uses formal and informal assessment strategies to evaluate and ensure the continuous intellectual, social, and physical development of the learner. (P 8)

focusing questions

1. What is meant by the term *evaluation?*

2. What informal and formal methods are available for assessing students?

3. What are the advantages and disadvantages of absolute grade standards and relative grade standards?

4. How is traditional grading similar to or different from standards-based grading?

5. Why is it important to communicate with parents about their children's work and progress? How might communication with parents be improved?

6. What is the relationship between student performance and teacher accountability?

7. When is accountability a potential threat to teachers? How can it be used as an opportunity?

Testing students is more objective than evaluation, since it is based on quantifiable data. Evaluation is more subjective, since it involves human judgment. We make evaluations of people and their performance not only in school, but also on the job and at home. Similarly, we make evaluations of consumer goods (food, clothing, cameras, televisions) and services (auto repair, insurance, medical treatment, legal advice). We use various kinds of information, including test data and other objective measurements to do these evaluations. As teachers, we strive to reduce the chance for misjudgment in the evaluation of students by carefully designing evaluation procedures.

Students must feel that their academic efforts will lead to success. The evaluation process should motivate them; it should encourage them to set progressively higher goals for personal achievement. Students must feel that the evaluation of their performance is objective and the criteria are the same for all students. If students feel the evaluation process will lead to failure, or if they feel the process is unfair, then they will be discouraged by it.

The evaluation process should also be realistic. Students should be able to assess their own performance in relation to that of classmates and normative standards. In a class in which most students cannot read well, a student who is an average reader may get an inflated impression of his or her real abilities. Evaluations are more effective when students are provided with valid norms of what constitutes success. Evaluation is also more effective when teachers think beyond the use of just criterion or normative tests. Good teachers provide students with a wide variety of ways to *show* what they know.[1]

Every student, during his or her school career, will experience the pain of failure and the joy of success as a result of the evaluation process. The student must learn, according to Philip Jackson, "to adapt to the continued and pervasive spirit of evaluation that will dominate . . . [the] school year." Although school is not the only place "where the student is made aware of his strengths and weaknesses," school evaluation is the most common type and has the most lasting impact on how students view themselves.[2]

The impact of school evaluation is profound because students are forming their identities during their school years, because they are going through their most critical stages of development at that time, and because they lack defensive mechanisms to ward off extreme or continuous negative evaluations. Whether evaluation focuses on academic work, social behavior, or personal qualities, it affects the student's reputation among his or her peers, confidence in his or her abilities, and motivation to work. The student's popularity, confidence, personal adjustment, career goals, and even physical and mental health are related to the judgments that others communicate to him or her throughout school. We are what we see ourselves to be, and like it or not, we see ourselves as others perceive and evaluate us. The self is a social product that emerges as we grow and interact with others. Many students psychologically or physically drop out of school because they simply do not believe they can learn *and* they have learned that from teachers.

Types of Evaluation

There are four basic evaluation techniques that are appropriate for and commonly used in the classroom: 1) placement evaluation, which helps to determine student placement or categorization before instruction begins; 2) diagnostic evaluation, which is a means

Daniel L. Stufflebeam

Professor and Director, The Evaluation Center
Western Michigan University

professional viewpoint

Reasons for Evaluation

The most important reasons to evaluate are:

1. To assure that one is doing all one can to help each student to learn
2. To find ways to conduct group instruction as efficiently and effectively as possible
3. To provide students and their parents with progress reports they can use to guide the learning process
4. To certify levels of achievement
5. To provide records and reports that will help other professionals work with individual students

It is noteworthy that four of the five purposes denote the need for individualized evaluation and continuous assessment and feedback. While evaluation is also needed to assist the search for efficient teaching methods that work well with groups, it is crucial that the teacher become skilled in those kinds of evaluation that can lead to individual diagnoses, reinforcement, and direction for growth. Unfortunately, many of the evaluation devices for sale, especially standardized tests, and many of the evaluation designs in the literature, especially pre-test/post-test designs, have little utility to teachers for doing the types of evaluation that are most important to them and to the individual students and families they serve. Hence, teachers should not fall into a pattern of using whatever standardized measures are available but instead should become proficient in designing evaluations that produce useful information about their students, and in devising homespun instruments that will respond well to the pertinent data requirements.

of discovering and monitoring learning difficulties; 3) formative evaluation, which monitors student progress; and 4) summative evaluation, which measures the products of instruction at the end of instruction.

Placement Evaluation

Placement evaluation, sometimes called *preassessment,* takes place before instruction. The teacher wants to find out what knowledge and skills the students have mastered in order to establish a starting point of instruction. Sufficient mastery might suggest that some instructional units may be skipped or treated briefly. Insufficient mastery suggests that certain basic knowledge or skills should be emphasized. Students who are required to begin at a level that is too difficult or beyond their understanding will encounter frustration and will most likely be unable to gain new knowledge and skills. Students who are required to review old material they already know are wasting instructional time and may eventually become bored.

It is also important to find out how much a student knows and what his or her interests and work habits are in order to decide on the best *type* of instruction (group or independent, inductive or deductive) and instructional *materials* for that student. We finished the last chapter with a reference to standards-based reform. That reform has implications for how you teach. Specifically, you must be able to assess student strengths and weaknesses in order to identify strategies for moving students forward in their own learning.

A third reason for placement evaluation is to assign students to specific learning groups. Although this procedure may lead to tracking, which is criticized by many researchers, teachers find that appropriately grouping students facilitates teaching and learning. Placement evaluation is based on readiness tests, aptitude tests, pretests on course objectives, and teacher observational techniques, and teacher assessment of student progress toward achieving certain content standards.

Diagnostic Evaluation

Diagnostic evaluation attempts to discover the causes of students' learning or behavioral problems. If a student continues to fail a particular subject or is unable to learn basic skills in elementary school or basic content in secondary school, diagnosis of the cause of the failure may point to ways to remedy it. According to Bruce Tuckman, "where proficiency has not been demonstrated, remedial instruction aimed directly at those [deficiencies] can be instituted." Evaluation can "provide the kind of information that will make it possible to overcome failure."[3]

In many cases diagnostic and formative evaluation (discussed next) overlap. Formative evaluation is mainly concerned with student progress, but the lack of progress may indicate a problem, which should then be investigated with more specific diagnostic evaluation. According to Gronlund and Linn, formative evaluation serves as a guide to general, everyday treatment, but diagnostic evaluation is necessary for detailed, remedial treatment.[4]

Some diagnostic information is developed as a result of the administration of a standardized test (see Chapter 10). Such tests are intended to examine specific social, academic, or emotional dispositions that the child evidences.[5] Other diagnostics are prepared by teachers in order to assess what students are doing wrong and why they are behaving the way they are. One problem with standardized tests is that they tend to be broad and they may not yield the type of detailed information that you need. Teacher-made diagnostics can be much more focused.

Formative Evaluation

Formative evaluation and *summative evaluation* are terms coined by Michael Scriven in his analysis of program and curriculum evaluation.[6] Formative evaluation monitors student progress during the learning process, while summative evaluation measures the final results at the end of an instructional unit or term. Benjamin Bloom and his associates describe formative evaluation as a major tool of instruction: "Too often in the past evaluation has been entirely summative in nature, taking place only at the end of the unit, chapter, course, or semester, when it is too late, at least for that particular group of students, to modify either . . . the teaching [or] learning . . . process."[7]

If evaluation is to help the teacher and student, it should take place not only at the end point of instruction, but also at various points during the teaching-learning process when modifications can be made. Instruction can be modified, based on the feedback that formative evaluation yields, to correct learning problems or to move ahead more rapidly.

Formative evaluation focuses on small, comparatively independent units of instruction and a narrow range of objectives. It is based on teacher-made and published tests administered throughout the term, on homework, on classroom performance of

Evaluating Students in Schools

Martin Haberman
Professor of Curriculum and Instruction
University of Wisconsin—Milwaukee

 I learned two lessons while teaching second grade in the stone age. The first was from Arthur, who should have been in a special class but we liked each other and I never sent him to the school psychologist to be tested. Arthur had trouble learning anything and if he did, he had trouble remembering it the next hour. In order to "encourage" him (but also to be fair to the others) I gave him C's on his first report card. The next day he came in with a black eye and some facial cuts. His sister explained that their parents had beaten him because he hadn't come home with all A's. After meeting the parents I learned that they were religious zealots who believed that God told them to beat Arthur to shape him up; indeed, it was their duty. I saw to it that

Arthur got all A's on his subsequent report cards and included some specific information on the permanent record of just what Arthur's achievements were in the various subjects.

My second lesson also came from parents. Martha was a "sweet" little second grader who played with a doll all day, every day. When I met with her father, I was surprised to see a Danish sailor who was at least 6 foot 6 inches. He picked Martha up and perched her on his shoulder while I gave him one-half hour of jargon about how he might interpret norm-reference test scores related to Martha's achievement. I used every bit of jargon that I knew. But I noticed he was holding her just like she held her doll and the only thing I thought to say was that it was a real pleasure to have Martha in class.

I never did learn how to communicate honestly with abusive parents but with doting ones I learned to enjoy how much they loved their kids. I'll bet some people might not think this has anything to do with "evaluation."

students, on informal teacher observations of students, on student-teacher conferences, and on parent-teacher conferences.

Formative assessment and evaluation are critical to student success. A systematic review of assessment studies by a group of researchers revealed that enhanced formative assessments resulted in "significant and substantial learning gains" for students.[8] And those learning gains appear to be even more dramatic for the lower achievers. If teachers use assessments in ways that show students can improve their performance, enhanced student learning appears to be a real and substantive result. Teachers can do this by determining specific ways in which students can use more practice on skills or by revising what and how to teach based on what students need to learn.

Summative Evaluation

Summative evaluation takes place at the end of an instructional unit or course. It is designed to determine the extent to which the instructional objectives have been achieved by the students, and it is used primarily to certify or grade students.[9] Summative evaluation also can be used to judge the effectiveness of a teacher or a particular curriculum or program. Whereas formative evaluation provides a tentative judgment of teaching and learning, summative evaluation, coming when teaching and learning are over, is a final judgment.

Summative evaluation focuses on a wide range of objectives and relies on an accumulation of student work and performance. Although teacher-made tests can be used

table 11.1   Types of Evaluation

Type	Function	Illustrative Instruments Used
Placement	Determines skills, degree of mastery before instruction to determine appropriate level and mode of teaching	Readiness tests, aptitude tests, pretests, observations, interviews, personality profiles, self-reports, videotapes, anecdotal reports from previous teachers
Diagnostic	Determines causes (cognitive, physical, emotional, social) of serious learning problems to indicate remedial techniques	Published diagnostic tests, teacher-made diagnostic tests, observations, interviews anecdotal reports from current teachers.
Formative	Determines learning progress; provides feedback to facilitate learning and to correct teaching errors	Teacher-made tests, tests from test publishers, observations, checklists
Summative	Determines end-of-course achievement or student performance on state-wide proficiency tests	Teacher-made tests, rating scales, standardized tests administered locally or on a state-wide basis.

Source: Adapted from Peter Airasian. *Classroom Assessment.* New York: McGraw-Hill, 1991. Norman E. Gronlund and Robert L. Linn. *Measurement and Evaluation in Teaching,* 6th ed. New York: McGraw-Hill, 1990.

for this purpose, summative evaluation is often based on formal observation scales or ratings and standardized tests.

Table 11.1 provides a summary of the four types of evaluation a teacher can use during the instructional process. Understand that the problem with this construct of evaluation is that it focuses almost exclusively on the child. It does not take into consideration context; that is, how do environmental factors influence the problems young people face? Our approach addresses the child, it does not take into account context. That is yet another factor you must consider (see Martin Haberman Professional Viewpoint).

Evaluation Methods and Approaches

Everyone to some degree is evaluated and makes evaluations on a daily and informal basis. Students and teachers continuously evaluate each other informally in class. When teachers observe students at work or answer students' questions, they are engaging in **informal evaluation.** When evaluation is impressionistic or based on thoughtful hunches, it is informal. **Formal evaluation** is more precise and defined and usually entails a lot more planning on the part of the teacher. As you will see as we examine different ways to collect data, some forms of assessment have both formal and informal elements.

Evaluation without tests (or informal evaluation) occurs on a daily basis and is considered by Philip Jackson to be more powerful and influential than tests. He asserts that students quickly come to realize "when things are right or wrong, good or bad, largely as a result of what the teacher tells them." In such *teacher judgment,* the teacher "continuously makes judgments of students' work and behavior [and communicates] that judgment to the students in question and to others."[10]

A second source of daily informal evaluation is the *judgment of peers.* Jackson observes that "Sometimes the class as a whole is invited to participate in the evaluation of a student's work, as when the teacher asks, 'Who can correct Billy?' or 'How many believe that Shirley read the poem with a lot of expression?' At times an obvious error evokes 'laughter' or destructive criticism, while outstanding performance wins 'spontaneous applause.'"[11] Little urging on the part of the teacher is needed, although the teacher may consciously or unconsciously egg the students on.

A third source of daily informal evaluation is student *self-judgment.* Students appraise their own performance without the "intervention of an outside judge." This type of evaluation is more difficult to discern and describe, but it occurs throughout instruction, such as when the student works on the chalkboard and knows that the work is correct or incorrect even if the teacher does not bother to indicate one way or another.[12]

There are many other types of evaluation that are both *private,* such as IQ and personality test scores (which may lead to labeling) or certain communications to parents or other teachers about students, and *public,* such as the display of work for others to see or a teacher review for the class of someone's mistake. Evaluations in class and school never cease.

Although some educators criticize the evaluation process, evaluation is necessary. Although it can be argued that tests are not always necessary for grading, classifying, or judging students, evaluation is. Teachers need to evaluate students' performance and progress toward defined school and state standards; otherwise, they are relinquishing an important role. On the other hand, the evaluation process should consider the student's feelings and self-concept; it should avoid labels that lead to traps, embarrassment, and despair in students whose performance is less than average. Various informal methods and approaches that can be used to supplement formal test data are summarized in Tips for Teachers 11.1.

Specific Evaluation Techniques and Tools

Teachers use a wide variety of assessment strategies to evaluate student academic growth. Some require the collection of explicit data about student learning and others gather more informal types of information. Each type of data, however, should give you a sense of *what* and *how much* students are learning so that you can evaluate performance. In most instances you will have considerable discretion in selecting how to assess student learning. But remember that a good assessment is based on clearly defined objectives. Alignment is critical to good teaching: objectives ➔ instruction ➔ assessment.

Quizzes

Quizzes are brief informal assessments of student knowledge. They provide a basis for checking understanding and for evaluating student daily progress. Some teachers give unannounced quizzes (or "pop" quizzes) at irregular intervals, especially quizzes related to specific assignments. Others give regular, scheduled quizzes to assess learning over a short period of time, say a week or two. Quizzes encourage students to keep up with the assignments, and they show them their strengths and weaknesses in learning.

Frequent and systematic monitoring of students' work and progress through short quizzes helps teachers improve instruction and student learning. Errors that students make serve as early warning signals of learning problems that then can be corrected before they worsen. According to researchers, student effort and achievement improve

Alternative Assessment Criteria

 The Aurora (Colorado) School District has implemented a nontraditional method of grading students based on judging the abilities of students to perform complex tasks that are not just cognitive but also psychological, social, and civic in nature. The five categories, which the district calls the "big outcomes," and their nineteen components or examples can be used for all grade levels and subjects. This new method suggests a radical change in student assessment. Here are the criteria:

1. Self-directed learner
   a. Sets priorities and achieves goals.
   b. Monitors and evaluates progress.
   c. Creates options for self.
   d. Assumes responsibility for actions.
   e. Creates a positive vision for self and future.
2. Collaborative worker
   a. Monitors own behavior.
   b. Assesses and manages group functioning.
   c. Demonstrates interactive communication.
   d. Demonstrates consideration for individual differences.

3. Complex thinker
   a. Uses a wide variety of strategies for managing complex issues.
   b. Selects strategies appropriate to the resolution of complex issues and applies the strategies with accuracy and thoroughness.
   c. Accesses and uses topic-relevant knowledge.
4. Quality producer
   a. Creates products that achieve their purpose.
   b. Creates products appropriate to the intended audience.
   c. Creates products that reflect craftsmanship.
   d. Uses appropriate resources/technology.
5. Community contributor
   a. Demonstrates knowledge about his or her diverse communities.
   b. Takes action.
   c. Reflects on role as a community contributor.

Source: Nora Redding. "Assessing the Big Outcomes." *Educational Leadership* (May 1992): 50.

when teachers provide frequent evaluation and prompt feedback on quizzes.[13] Quizzes are relatively easy to develop, administer, and grade, thus providing an avenue for multiple and prompt evaluation.

In essence, student performance and progress can be measured through a variety of methods other than the pencil-and-paper tests described in the previous chapter, although testing is the most common source of data and should be included as part of the total evaluation.

Observation of Student Work

The teacher has the opportunity to watch students perform various tasks on a daily basis, under various conditions, and either alone or with different students. The teacher observes students more or less continually simply by virtue of being in the classroom, but he or she needs to know what to look for and to have some relatively objective system for collecting and assessing data.

Although the teacher should observe all students, individuals who exhibit atypical behavior or learning outcomes are often singled out for special study. The keys to

The teacher has the opportunity to watch students perform various tasks, under various conditions, on a daily basis.

good observation are objectivity and documentation. Teachers cannot depend on memory or vague statements, such as "Trent misbehaves in class." They must keep accurate, specific written records that contain objective statements of what students are doing: "Cheli is unable to use apostrophes correctly with possessive nouns" or "Han was out of his seat five times today without permission."

If observations are free from bias and tempered with common sense, this informal, nonstandardized evaluation method can provide more insightful information about a student than would test scores alone. The key for a teacher is to make observations of students and then make specific learning prescriptions based on those observations.

There are many different types of observation instruments you can use to evaluate students. Some teachers create learning prescriptions that highlight strengths and weaknesses but also outline specific ideas for improving weaknesses (see Tips for Teachers 11.2). One of the simplest instruments is a *sign instrument* on which you simply indicate the presence or absence of a behavior (see Table 11.2). Another form of simple observation instrument is a rating instrument, on which you evaluate the degree to which some behavior is occurring in the classroom. Table 11.3 is an example of a rating instrument. There are many other types of instruments that you can use, but these are two of the simplest and easiest. The first one would be appropriate for collecting information simultaneously on a large number of students. The second one is oriented toward individual assessments.

tips for teachers 11.2

Learning Prescription

Name   Lionel   Age   5   Date   1/20

Areas of Strength and Confidence
1. *Does manipulative activities well by self*
2. *Performs or participates in music and rhythm activities*
3. *Has good small motor coordination*

Areas Needing Strengthening
1. *Needs to develop large motor skills*
2. *Needs to learn to play with others*
3. *Needs to develop small motor skills of writing, drawing, cutting*

Activities to Help
1. *Bring in pair of left-handed scissors and have Lionel cut out pictures of cars from magazine to make a car scrapbook with one of the other boys.*
2. *Bring a hammer, nails, and tree stump; ask Lionel to help another child with pounding nails to make rhythm instrument shaker.*
3. *Have Lionel and other children paint the rhythm instruments they make.*

Source: Observing Development of Young Children. p. 208. 3/e by Beaty, Janice, © Reprinted by permission of Pearson Education, Inc., Upper Saddle River, NJ.

Observation data are valuable for understanding the daily performance of students in a more detailed way. Don't trust your memory to recall how a student is behaving. Purposefully collect observation data to better determine how students are behaving and what skills they do or do not possess.

Group and Peer Evaluation and Feedback

Teachers can set aside a time to allow students to participate in establishing instructional objectives and to evaluate their strengths and limitations and their own progress in learning. Students can evaluate themselves or their classmates on study habits and homework, class participation, quizzes, workbook or textbook activities, and other activities. They can keep anecdotal reports or logs about their own work in which they record successes and difficulties. They can check off assignments they complete and evaluate their work in group discussions. Evaluation techniques such as these make it possible for teachers to diagnose and measure student progress quickly and efficiently. These group evaluation strategies can be especially useful when teachers use cooperative learning strategies.

Group and peer evaluation enhances student interaction and enables students to learn from one another. It can also enhance group spirit and contribute to student empowerment. Research suggests, too, that when students provide and receive feedback to and from peers about their academic work, social responsibility and student achievement are enhanced.[14] Students can serve as peer evaluators for quizzes or peer editors

table 11.2   Student Behavior Observation Checklist

Identify behaviors that you would like to observe during a cooperative learning lesson. List those behaviors and then evaluate the degree to which students evidence the behavior during cooperative learning lessons. (We have identified some common misbehaviors for illustrative purposes.)

Teacher:_____ Class:_____ Date: _____

Target Skills: _____

Mark observed behaviors with a + and behaviors not observed with a –.

Name of students	Leaves seat without permission	Is late to class	Is disruptive to classroom activities	Keeps other students from doing work	Comments
1					
2					
3					
4					
5					
6					
7					
8					
9					
10					
11					
12					
13					
14					
15					
16					
17					
18					
19					
20					

for written projects. Ideally, the answers or a preset of criteria should be provided to enable students to evaluate others.

Students can also provide valuable ideas and information to each other regarding various cooperative activities and projects. Here the teacher's role in initiating and fostering trust and cooperation among students is important. Teachers can promote these aims by 1) encouraging students to contribute openly, 2) sharing materials and resources, 3) expressing acceptance and support during their interactions, and 4) pointing out rejecting and nonsupportive behaviors that hinder peer evaluation and cooperation.[15]

table 11.3   **Student Skill Checklist**

Directions: Identify specific skills that you expect students to demonstrate in a particular learning context and assess the degree to which you believe students possess that skill.

Student: _____

Date Observed:_____

Time Observed:_____

	Not Evident	*Somewhat Evident*	*Very Evident*
1. Students demonstrate an ability to think critically about an issue.	———	———	———
2. Skill 2:_____ _____ _____ _____ _____	———	———	———
3. Skill 3:_____ _____ _____ _____ _____	———	———	———
4. Skill 4:_____ _____ _____ _____ _____	———	———	———

Recitations

Many teachers consider a student's participation in class to be an essential source of data for evaluation. Teachers are impressed by students who volunteer, develop their thoughts logically, and discuss relevant facts and relationships. Answering the teacher's questions frequently and carrying out assignments in class are considered evidence of progress. The inability to answer questions and the inability to perform assignments in class are indications of learning problems or lack of motivation. The key during recitation is to make certain that full student participation is evidenced. Some teachers call on a small group of volunteers who know the content well and ignore a larger group of nonvolunteer students who may either fail to understand the content or be unwilling to participate. All students need to learn, and it is the responsibility of the teacher to find ways to help all students engage in the learning process.

In fact, there may be a number of reasons students do not respond to teachers correctly. Observers outline some possibilities:

A particular feature of the talk between teacher and pupils is the asking of questions by the teacher. . . . One common problem is that, following a question, teachers do not wait long enough to allow pupils to think out their answers. When a teacher answers his or her own question after only two or three seconds and when a minute of silence is not tolerable, there is no possibility that a pupil can think out what to say.

There are then two consequences. One is that, because the only questions that can produce answers in such a short time are questions of fact, these predominate. The other is that pupils don't even try to think out a response. Because they know that the answer, followed by another question, will come along in a few seconds, there is no point in trying. . . .

There are several ways to break this particular cycle. They involve giving pupils time to respond; asking them to discuss their thinking in pairs or in small groups, so that a respondent is speaking on behalf of others; giving pupils a choice between different possible answers and asking them to vote on the options; asking all of them to write down an answer and then reading out a selected few; and so on. What is essential is that any dialogue should evoke thoughtful reflection in which all pupils can be encouraged to take part, for only then can the formative process start to work.[16]

Homework

The teacher can learn much about students' achievements and attitudes by checking homework carefully. A good rule is not to assign homework unless it is going to be checked in some way, preferably by you, in some cases by another student, or by the student him- or herself. The idea is to provide prompt feedback to the student, preferably emphasizing the positive aspects of work while making one or two major recommendations for improvement. As Walberg points out, student achievement increases significantly when teachers assign homework on a regular basis, students conscientiously do it, and teacher comments and feedback are provided when the work is completed.[17] But, for homework to be effective in accomplishing its purposes, it must be assigned properly. Table 11.4 outlines general teacher guidelines for assigning homework.

Good and Brophy suggest that homework can be effective in fostering student learning and is advantageous for accomplishing teacher-defined goals if the teacher is seeking to achieve any of the following purposes: providing practice in a skill or procedures, preparing students for exams or summative learning experiences, enhancing personal student development in a particular area, or fostering parent-child relations (e.g., finding ways for parents and children to talk about ideas together).[18]

Notebooks and Note-Taking

Notebooks should be used as an assessment tool for evaluating students' writing and understanding of subject matter in elementary school and, to a lesser extent, in the middle grades and junior high school.

Note taking is more important for secondary school students, especially at the high school level. At this level students should begin to be able to take notes on some of the unwritten ideas that emerge from the classroom discussions. Good note taking consists of arranging information in a systematic form, focusing on major points of discussion, condensing material, and integrating new with old information.[19] Verbatim note taking or simple paraphrasing or listing of information is not as effective.[20]

table 11.4   **Homework Dos and Don'ts**

The following homework dos and don'ts are part of a selective list of the most important considerations.

For Principals

1. *Don't* believe everything you hear about a teacher's homework practices.
2. *Don't* expect all teachers to be equally enthusiastic about a schoolwide homework policy.
3. *Don't* expect a schoolwide homework policy to please all parents.
4. *Don't* expect teachers with the heaviest instructional loads to assign as much homework as those with the lightest loads.
5. *Do* check out all rumors that come your way about teachers' homework practices.
6. *Do* put the teachers you least expect to be pleased by a schoolwide homework policy on the committee that formulates it.
7. *Do* involve parents in the development of schoolwide homework policies.
8. *Do* everything possible to assist teachers with managing homework paper loads, including use of school aides and parent volunteers.

For Teachers

1. *Don't* ever give homework as punishment.
2. *Don't* make up spur-of-the-moment homework assignments.
3. *Don't* assume that because there are no questions asked about a homework assignment students have no questions about the assignment.
4. *Don't* expect students (even your best students) always to have their homework assignments completed.
5. *Do* understand that not all types of homework assignments are equally valuable for all types of students.
6. *Do* explain the specific purpose of every homework assignment.
7. *Do* listen to what students say about their experiences in completing your homework assignments.
8. *Do* acknowledge and be thankful for efforts students make to complete their homework.

Note taking can take different forms. One especially useful form is summarizing. Students synthesize the material that they have been learning by analyzing the notes they have taken and by writing a brief summary. Such strategies are well established in areas such as reading for their effectiveness in enhancing student achievement.[21] Once the summaries are written, you can collect and read them to see what understandings and misunderstandings the students have, or you can pair students and have them share and evaluate the material.

Reports, Themes, and Research Papers

Written work serves as an excellent way to assess students' ability to organize thoughts, to research topics, and to develop new ideas. In evaluating projects, the teacher should look to see how well students have developed their thoughts in terms of explanations, logic, and relationship of ideas; whether ideas are expressed clearly; whether facts are documented or distinguished from opinion; and what conclusions or recommendations are evidenced. Spelling and grammar should not be the focus of evaluating students' work but neither should they be dismissed; rather, the *emphasis* should be on the thinking process of the students, their use of reference materials, and their ability to keep to the topic and develop it logically.

For Parents

1. *Don't* try to help with homework if you are confused and really cannot figure out what is expected.

2. *Don't* hesitate to have your child explain legitimate reasons that homework simply cannot be completed.

3. *Don't* place yourself in an adversarial role between your child and the teachers over homework issues until all other alternatives are exhausted.

4. *Don't* feel your child always has to be doing "something productive." (There are few things sadder than a burned-out 14 year-olds.)

5. *Do* make sure your child really needs help before offering to help with homework.

6. *Do* help your child see a purpose or some value in homework assignments.

7. *Do* encourage your children to complete assignments after absences from school.

8. *Do* suggest an alternative to watching TV on nights when no homework is assigned, such as sharing a magazine article, enjoying a game together, or going to an exhibit or concert.

For Students

1. *Don't* expect that your parents will be able to help with all your homework. (Parents forget things they have learned, and some of what is taught in school today is foreign to adults.)

2. *Don't* ask teachers to help with any homework assignment you really can complete independently.

3. *Don't* confuse excuses for incomplete homework assignments with legitimate reasons.

4. *Don't* think doing your homework "most of the time" will be satisfactory for those classes in which homework counts the most. (In such classes, even a 75 percent completion rate may not be enough.)

5. *Do* ask your parents for help with your homework only when you really need help.

6. *Do* ask the teacher to help before or after class if you are confused about a homework assignment.

7. *Do* explain to teachers legitimate reasons that sometimes make it impossible to complete some homework assignments.

8. *Do* make every effort to complete homework assignments when they are very important for a particular class.

Source: D. A. England and J. K. Flatley's "Homework Do's and Don'ts." *Homework—and Why.* Bloomington, Ind.: Phi Delta Kappa, 1985, pp. 36–38.

Quite obviously, how you grade and assess student work is largely dictated by your purpose in making the assignment. Your instructional goals and the rubrics you will use in assessing student work should be transparent to students. Some teachers hand out performance standards with assignments, communicating to the student what he or she is expected to do and how it will be graded.[22] Zmuda and Tomaino observe that, with such evaluation explicitness, "the grading process . . . [becomes] concrete, up front, and honest."[23]

Chapter 10 highlighted how rubrics can be used to assess student performance. In evaluating student work it is imperative that you use formal or informal rubrics. Table 11.5 is another example of a rubric for use in evaluating persuasive writing. The key to any rubric is that it have clear criteria and that it define gradations of quality for the criteria. The rubric in Table 11.5 is analytic and generic. That is, it evaluates levels of performance on several criteria and it could be used for any persuasive essay.

Discussions and Debates

Evaluating oral work is more difficult than evaluating written samples, but oral work may reveal creative and critical thinking that cannot be measured with other methods. David and Roger Johnson and others point out that, when students freely discuss topics

table 11.5   Instructional Rubric for a Persuasive Essay

Criteria	Gradations of Quality			
	4	3	2	1
The claim	I make a claim and explain why it is controversial.	I make a claim but don't explain why it is controversial.	My claim is buried, confused, and/or unclear.	I don't say what my argument or claim is.
Reasons in support of the claim	I give clear and accurate reasons in support of my claim.	I give reasons in support of my claim, but I overlook important reasons.	I give one or two weak reasons that don't support my claim and/or irrelevant or confusing reasons.	I don't give reasons in support of my claim.
Reasons against the claim	I discuss the reasons against my claim and explain why it is valid anyway.	I discuss the reasons against my claim but neglect some or don't explain why the claim still stands.	I say that there are reasons against the claim, but I don't discuss them.	I don't acknowledge or discuss reasons against the claim.
Organization	My writing has a compelling opening, an informative middle and a satisfying conclusion.	My writing has a beginning, middle, and an end.	My organization is rough but workable. I may sometimes get off topic.	My writing is aimless and disorganized.
Voice and tone	It sounds like I care about my argument. I tell how I think and feel about it.	My tone is OK, but my paper could have been written by anyone. I need to tell how I think and feel.	My writing is bland or pretentious. There is either no hint of a real person in it, or it sounds like I'm faking it.	My writing is too formal or informal. It sounds like I don't like the topic of the essay.
Word choice	The words that I use are striking but natural, varied, and vivid.	I make some fine and some routine word choices.	The words that I use are often dull or uninspired or sound like I'm trying too hard to impress.	I use the same words over and over. Some words may be confusing.
Sentence fluency	My sentences are clear, complete, and of varying lengths.	I have well-constructed sentences. My essay marches along but doesn't dance.	My sentences are often awkward run-ons or fragments.	Many run-on sentences and sentence fragments make my essay hard to read.
Conventions	I use correct grammar, punctuation, and spelling.	I have a few errors to fix, but I generally use correct conventions.	I have enough errors in my essay to distract the reader	Numerous errors make my paper hard to read.

Source: Heidi Goodrich Andrade. "Using Rubrics to Promote Thinking and Learning." *Educational Leadership* (February 2000): 17.

that are of interest to them, their thinking is based on many skills, insights, and experiences not evidenced in a one-hour written test.[24] In discussion and debate students discover, in front of their peers, that they can succeed. Because they are in front of their peers, it is essential that no humiliation, no sarcasm, and no negativism be introduced into the discussion or evaluation process.

During discussions students can be rated not only on their mastery of and ability to analyze material, but also on several social and cognitive characteristics. Such characteristics include the way in which the student 1) accepts ideas of others, 2) initiates ideas, 3) gives opinions, 4) helps others, 5) seeks information, 6) tries to make the best decision as opposed to trying to "win," 7) encourages others to contribute, 8) works well with all group members, 9) raises provocative questions, 10) listens to others, 11) disagrees in a constructive fashion, 12) shows willingness to reverse an opinion, and 13) makes an overall positive contribution to the group.[25]

Before discussing the assignment of grades, we need to summarize. First, there are multiple layers of assessment. School districts will administer large-scale assessments (common assessments required in all teachers' classrooms), and teachers have the option to decide on a variety of classroom assessments. The former have efficacy in determining the overall performance of a school or school district or group of teachers, while the latter are most useful in helping students (and parents) understand specific strengths and weaknesses associated with the particular content that has been taught. Your classroom assessments are important because they provide detailed information and feedback regarding a particular student's academic growth. With such information you are now ready to consider the assignment of a grade.

Traditional Grading

The purpose of grading is somewhat different for teachers at different grade levels. Some studies indicate that elementary school teachers tend to say they give grades because the school district requires it, not because grades as a yardstick for achievement are important to them. In contrast, secondary school teachers feel grades are necessary for informing students, other teachers, and colleges about performance.[26] The same studies show that elementary school teachers rely heavily on their observations of student participation in class, motivation, and attitudes. Secondary school teachers assign grades mainly on the basis of test results and specific assignments.

Teachers need to recognize that young students (grade 2 or lower) have a limited understanding of the meaning of grades and that understanding of grading concepts increases with age. Grades at the elementary level are usually for the benefit of parents. Parents expect to see how a student stands, and, regrettably, that usually means in relationship to other students in class. It is not until the upper grades that most students understand complex schemes such as a grading curve, grade point average, and weighted grading. Older students are more likely to be critical of grading practices and less accepting of low grades received than are younger students.[27] Such findings indicate that teachers might consider postponing formal grading until grades 5 or 6, if school policy permits, and that teachers should expect concern and even criticism among older students regarding "issued" grades, especially since they increasingly see grades as important for their future.

There are a number of general purposes for testing and grading: 1) *certification,* or assurance that a student has mastered specific content or achieved a certain level of accomplishment; 2) *selection,* or identifying or grouping students for certain educational paths or programs; and 3) *motivation,* or emphasizing specific material or skills to be learned and helping students to understand and improve their performance.[28]

Interestingly, traditional grading is often taking a back seat in terms of importance to the standardized testing occurring in many schools and school districts. The high stakes testing is all too often supplanting in significance the tradtitional grades that emerge from a series of low stakes assessment teacher measures. As a new teacher, pressures will be on you to address and deal with the demands and requirements of standardized testing. That reality, however, should not mitigate your daily instructional decision making regarding the learning needs of each student. You will know the students best and no standardized test can assess better in a single day what you assess over a period of weeks.

Grades often result in a group of students being "winners" or "losers" from grade to grade. Indeed, one way in which teachers determine grades is by comparing students' performances, which might be referred to as norm-referenced grading. To paraphrase Robert Slavin: In the usual, competitive reward structure, the probability of one student's receiving a reward (or good grade) is negatively related to the probability of another student's receiving a reward.[29] Also, a demonstrable relationship exists between formal instruction and student performance at all grade levels, but constructing tests and grading accurately to reflect classroom tasks and intended learning are difficult for most teachers. Although teachers report that they feel they are able to interpret test results and transfer test scores into grades or grade equivalents, when teachers are tested on these abilities, the majority make some type of misinterpretation.[30]

Assigning grades to students' schoolwork is subjective. Teachers are required to make judgments, and few, if any, teachers are purely objective in making assessments. What test items should be included and how the items should be weighted are matters of judgment. Should points be deducted for partially wrong answers? How many As or Bs or Fs should be awarded? Will grading be on a curve or absolute? And what about all those special cases ("I lost my notebook") and problems ("I was sick last week")? Are students to be allowed to retake an exam because the results deviate from past performance? Should extra credit assignments be used to modify grades and to what extent? If test modification, additional tests, or extra credit assignments are permitted, then teachers are forced into a more subjective role. But, if a teacher fails to consider extraneous circumstances, possibly modifying the scoring results, then it can be argued that grades are being used as a weapon, certainly as a cold symbol of learning. It can also be argued that students are entitled to extra coaching and practice, but retaking exams or extra credit is unfair because it may improve the grades of some but not all students.

Homework is another consideration. Who should grade the homework, students or teacher? Prompt scoring by students enables the teacher to decide promptly what material needs further analysis. When the teacher grades the homework, his or her paper load is increased and feedback to students is delayed. Yet in the very act of grading homework, teachers add to their information about the specific thinking skills and problems of the students. Moreover, researchers point out that, when the teacher takes time to write encouraging and constructive comments on the homework (or other student papers), it has positive measurable effects on achievement.[31]

Homework may be important in the learning process, but there is a question about whether it should be counted in the grading system. Some educators say no. There are similar questions about lowering grades for minor discipline problems (for example, chewing gum), not typing a paper, not doing an assignment on time, and coming to class late. A student whose behavior is unacceptable must be held accountable, but some educators are against reducing grades as a deterrent.[32] Many teachers, however, take another view, especially when classroom discipline is at stake.

There is also considerable disagreement about the value of using routine class activities, class participation, recitations, oral reading, chalkboard work, oral presentations, and even reports as part of the grade system. Although such practices broaden the base of information on student performance and also give students a chance to be evaluated on grounds other than tests, there are serious questions about the quality of information they provide. For example, some students "talk a good game" and know little, while others are introverted or shy but know the material. Other educators maintain that grades should be divided into primary measures of performance (unit tests, term papers) and secondary measures (homework, quizzes). The secondary measures are considered less important and are given less weight, since their purpose is to prepare students to achieve the primary learning outcomes.[33]

Regardless of what you think about grading, considerable evidence supports its efficacy for improving student learning, especially when the grading process is conducted in a fair and objective manner. E. D. Hirsch writes,

> It has been shown convincingly that tests and grades strongly contribute to effective teaching. This commonsense conjecture was confirmed by research conducted after the anti-grade, pass/fail mode of grading had become popular at colleges and universities in the 1960s and 70s. Quite unambiguous analysis showed that students who took courses for a grade studied harder and learned more than students who took the course for intrinsic interest alone.[34]

Traditional grading, as you can see, has subjectivity built into it. Much of that subjectiveness occurs as you compare one student's performance to that of others, as you assess a student's individual ability (How is the student working in comparison to personal potential?) and as you measure the student's individual progress over time. Based on all the data you collect, a judgment about a grade is made.

Clearly, traditional grading is what most preservice teachers will have experienced. There are other ways to assess students, however. One of those is more criterion-referenced, where student performance is measured against a defined standard.

Standards-Based Grading

In Chapter 10 and at a number of points in this chapter we have examined the increased importance that educators are now placing on standards and on using those to assess student performance. Some teachers are now even creating criterion-referenced grading systems that are based on established standards. Colby writes about the complex but necessary relationship that teachers now deal with as they use standards and predefined performance levels to guide instruction and then find ways of aligning assessment procedures.[35] Colby highlights a four-step grading process:

Step 1: Create a workable format for documenting information—provide one page for each student and list on each page the curriculum standards that every student should know.

table 11.6   **Extract from a Standards-Based Grade Book—Grade Two**

Name_____

+ Has demonstrated proficiency of Learner Outcomes	P = performance assessment
* In progress on Learner Outcomes	A = assignment
– Has not demonstrated proficiency of Learner Outcomes at this time	O = observation
	% = percentage correct/test

Science					
The Learner will					
Compare and contrast related living things that reproduce in similar ways.					
• identify examples of plant reproduction (spores, seeds, cuttings, buds, shoots)	+O	+O	*O		
• identify examples of related living things that reproduce in similar ways	*O	+A	+O		
Analyze the reasons for changes observed in plant growth (or lack of growth)					
• observe the changes in plant growth (or lack of growth)	*O	*O	53%		
• record plant growth	+A	+A			
Identify plant parts					
• know plant parts (for example, roots, stems, leaves, flowers)	+O	*O	77%		
• know the effect of gravity on roots and stems	+O	*O	88%		

Source: Susan A. Colby. "Grading in a Standards-Based System." *Educational Leadership* (March 1999): 55.

Step 2: Create codes for assessing and documenting the type of student performance. Colby suggests, "P for performance assessment, A for assignment, O for direct observation, and % for percentage of correct answers [on test or quiz].[36] Another set of codes defines levels of performance: "+ for 'Has demonstrated proficiency of learner outcomes' ✓ for 'In progress on learner outcomes,' and – for 'Has not demonstrated proficiency of learner outcomes at this time.'"[37] A third code defines when the assessment occurred (e.g., red for the first quarter and green for the second quarter).

Step 3: Create a grade book (e.g., three-ring binder) that permits easy access for logging assessment information. Table 11.6 shows an example from a standards-based grading book.

Step 4: Monitor the assessment process and make certain that all the data are being collected efficiently and effectively.

Notice that in *standards-based grading* systems there is clear alignment among standards, assessment, and instruction. Such alignment should occur in traditional forms of grading, but it is often absent. That is, far too many teachers assign and grade individual assignments without really connecting the particular assignments to broader standards and learner expectations.

Colby reports that several real advantages occur with standards-based grading. First, it is easier to quickly assess learner strengths and weaknesses. Second, it is easier to communicate to parents and students the specific nature of their learning progress. Third, the conferences between parents and teachers are more focused and less subjective.[38]

There may be one other advantage, and that relates to the fact that students' performance is assessed in relation to a specific standard, not in relationship to how peers are performing. As we noted earlier, most grading systems are based on comparisons and not on an individual student's performance relative to a standard. Consider the grading systems used to assess you in school. Were you assessed based on a standard or based on how others performed?

Form of Grades

The most popular form in which grades are presented is the *letter grade.* The letter grade represents a translation from a number base, resulting from a combination of test scores, ratings, and the like.

Good teachers use grades to show how well students have learned material in relationship to an established absolute criterion level—what the teacher intended them to learn. That's an appropriate form of grading. A much weaker (but frequently used) form is to compare students' performances and then to give grades based on those relative performances.

The conversion from numbers to letters (*A, B, C*) to some extent distorts meaning and masks individual student differences. Because a letter represents a range of numbers, different students might receive the same letter grade from the same teacher for different levels of performance. Although the number system is more precise, often the difference between two or three points for a final grade is not that meaningful.

Most schools convert letters to an even more general statement of evaluation as follows:

A = superior, excellent, outstanding, and firm command and mastery of content

B = good, above average, and mastery is evident in most but not all areas

C = fair, competent, average, and mastery is evident at basic but not at advanced levels

D = minimum passing, weakness or problems, and limited understanding of content

F = failure, serious weakness or problems, and little if any mastery of content

The standards upon which grades are based vary considerably among school districts, so that a *C* student in one school may be an *A* student in another school. Schools and school districts eventually get reputations about how low or high standards are or about how rigorous their programs are.

One way in which states are beginning to deal with this "unevenness" in school districts is by creating "exit exams" or "end of course exams" that are administered on a statewide basis. A student taking Algebra I, for example, must take an exit exam, and his or her performance can be assessed against certain criterion levels of content mastery. In this way, the grade reflects what a student truly knows relative to a broader performance expectation as opposed to representing an assessment of a small group of students in a single class. It is helpful when you look at student grades to know whether absolute or relative standards have been used to make judgments about the level of student performance.

Exit exams are being used by more than one-third of the states in areas such as science and social studies, and by 2008 over half of the states will be using such exams. State exit exams incorporate both traditional and open-ended types of questions. For example, fifteen states now use some sort of essay writing in exit exams, and within the next six years at least fifteen states will use short answer question in their exit exams. All this effort is intended to ensure that a high school diploma means something to students and to employers. State legislators are trying to show the public that students are receiving a quality education, and one way they can do this is by requiring such exams.

Many critics argue that the exams will exacerbate problems for those in high poverty areas. Specifically, the tests will likely lead to higher dropout rates and will do little to ensure that high need students receive the kind of educational experiences they need in order to be successful as learners. At this point, the critics are losing the battle, and the No Child Left Behind legislation is resulting in even more testing requirements for students.[39] As a new teacher you will be confronting the reality of making certain that all your students learn. One of the ways in which that learning will be assessed is through mechanisms like exit exams. In 2002 some of the states with exit exams in place were Alabama, Florida, Georgia, Indiana, South Carolina, Tennessee and Virginia. Other states are in the process of phasing them in but still do not withhold diplomas. Those states include Arizona, California, Massachusetts, Utah, and Washington.

The research to either support or refute the power of exit exams is still quite mixed. The Center for Education Policy (Washington, D.C.) is documenting the impact on student achievement, dropout rates, and opportunities after high school. No clear and concise evidence on any of these variables is available, though it does appear that a relationship *may* exist between exams and higher dropout rates.[40]

Absolute Grade Standards

Grades may be given according to fixed or ***absolute standards,*** as illustrated in Table 11.7. One disadvantage of this approach is that the standards may be subject to the *error of leniency;* that is, if students have an easy grader, many *As* and *Bs* will be assigned, or if they have a tough grader, many *Cs* and *Ds* will be assigned. Also, student scores depend on the difficulty of the tests given. In some tests a score of 75 percent may be above average, but with an absolute or fixed standard, as indicated in the table, this score would be a *D.* Many students who would be given a minimum passing grade under an absolute grading approach may benefit with a relative standard.

Despite these limitations, most teachers use this method of grading. It makes a great deal of sense as long as teachers have a firm idea of what students should be able to do and as long as standards are realistic and fair. One of the most difficult aspects of being a new teacher is understanding the difficulties in developing tests. As you gain more experience it becomes easier to understand how to assess student learning fairly.

An absolute grading standard usually is imposed by teachers, school administrators, and boards of education in more traditional contexts. The process assumes that the teacher can predict the difficulty level of his or her testing, thus predetermining the dis-

table 11.7   **Examples of Absolute and Relative Standards of Grading**

Absolute Standard	*Relative Standard Percent of Students**
A = 95% or above	A = 7%
B = 86–94%	B = 24%
C = 78–85%	C = 38%
D = 70–77%	D = 24%
F = Below 70%	F = 7%

*Based on a normal curve.

Source: Adapted from Robert E. Slavin. *Educational Psychology: Theory into Practice,* 4th ed. Needham Heights, Mass.: Allyn and Bacon, 1994.

tribution of scores, so that a specified number of students will get *As, Bs, Cs,* and so on. Not only is this task nearly impossible, but it also requires the teacher to play catch-up at the end of the semester, purposely administering an easy or difficult test to get a more even distribution of grades, or to ignore an uneven distribution of grades, skewed as too high or too low.[41]

Relative Grade Standards

Grades may be given according to how a student performs in relation to others. If a student scores 80 on an examination, but most others score above 90, the student has done less than average work. Instead of receiving a *B* under the relative, or norm-reference, method of grading, the student might receive a *C.* If a student scores 65, but most others score below 60, he or she has done well and might receive a *B* instead of a *D* or *F.*

   Relative grading can be based on a curve, either a normal bell-shaped curve or a curve derived from a simple ranking system. In a normal curve few students receive *As* or *Fs,* the majority receive *Cs* (midpoint of the curve), and many receive *Bs* and *Ds.* This is also shown in Table 11.7, which uses a 7-24-38-24-7 percent grade distribution. In a ranking system, which is more common, the teacher determines in advance percentage equivalents for each letter grade: for example, the top 25 percent will receive *A,* the next 30 percent *B,* the next 25 percent *C,* and the next 20 percent *D* or *F.* The grading on this curve is not always as precise as with the normal curve, and it tends to be a little easier for students to score higher grades.

   Grading on a curve and other relative grading practices assure that grades will be distributed on the basis of scores in relation to one another, regardless of the difficulty of the test. It takes into consideration that the ability levels of students vary, and that tests vary in difficulty; thus, the distribution of scores or grades cannot be predicted. However, researchers contend this process can create competition among students and inhibit them from helping each other in class.[42] It can also have a negative effect on the students' desire to learn—highly competitive environments cause unnecessary comparisons that cause lower-ability students to lose interest in a task and perhaps in school.

Indeed, some educators argue that unnecessary comparisons could be the reason so many students decide to drop out of school, physically or psychologically.

Combining and Weighting Data

Although researchers generally agree that grading should be based on several indicators that are directly related to the instructional program, there is less agreement on what should be included, how the indicators should be weighted, and whether indicators not directly related to instruction, such as participation, effort, neatness, and conduct, are appropriate at all.[43]

Grades based on little information, such as only one or two tests, are unfair to students and probably invalid. Assigning too much importance to term papers or homework is also invalid and unwise because these indicators say little about whether the students have really learned the material. Relying more heavily on test data is preferred, especially at the secondary school level, as long as there are several quizzes or examinations and the tests are weighted properly. One of the reasons for using multiple measures (and different forms of assessment) is that it helps students clearly demonstrate what they know and helps protect teachers against various forms of bias to which no human being is immune. Teachers can take measures to mitigate such biases (e.g., mask the identity of students or, with essays, grade all of the first-question responses at one time).

There are a number of problems related to combining several test scores into a single measure (or grade) for each student, including the fact that test scores may have different significance. For example, a teacher who wishes to combine scores on two separate tests might determine that each contributes 50 percent to the composite score. However, this rarely is the case, especially if one test was more difficult than the other; the composite score is a function not only of the mean but also of the standard deviation.

A question arises whether scores from different sources, representing different learning outcomes and levels of difficulty, can be combined into a composite score. Although there are arguments for and against this procedure, it is acceptable as long as the composite score is based on several sources that are independent of each other—see Tips for Teachers 11.3.

Contracting for Grades

A few schools permit teachers and students considerable flexibility in formulating grades. Teacher and students come to an agreement early in the term concerning grades for specific levels of performance or achievement on various tasks. Maximum, average, and minimum standards or performance levels are usually established. The teacher promises to award a specific grade for specified performance; in effect, teacher and student establish a contract. With this *contract grading* approach students know exactly what they have to do to receive a certain grade.

The plan seems suited to criterion-reference learning and to teaching and learning by a set of objectives. The approach is not recommended for elementary school students because of their lack of maturity, their inability to engage in independent work for a sustained period of time, and their inability to follow through on individual activities. The contract can be implemented at the upper elementary level (grade 5 or higher) if great care is taken to match student maturity and abilities with performance requirements. Different standards will be needed for different students.

tips for teachers 11.3

Advantages and Disadvantages of the Point System of Grading

 Most teachers, especially from the middle grades onward, rely on a point system of grading that assigns points or percentages for various tests and class activities. Some teachers even post summaries at regular intervals so students can see their point totals as the term progresses. The point system has advantages and disadvantages. Special caution is recommended for its use.

Advantages

1. It is fair and objective. The teacher is not apt to be swayed by subjective factors, and the need for interpretation is minimized.
2. It is quantifiable, explicit, and precise. Students and teachers know exactly what the numbers are and what they represent.
3. It facilitates the weighting of tests and class activities (e.g., ten points for each quiz, twenty-five points for a special project, twenty-five points each for the midterm and final).
4. It is cumulative. The final grade can be determined by a single computation at the end of the grading period.
5. It facilitates grading by establishing clear distinctions. Once categories are weighted and points totaled, assigning the grade for each student is a straightforward task.

Disadvantages

1. It emphasizes the objectivity of scoring, not learning. It conveys the message that learning is equivalent to the accumulation of points, not the acquisition of skills and knowledge.
2. It presents an illusion of objectivity. Every test and assignment result from a series of subjective decisions by the teacher (e.g. about what areas to cover and how to weight particular answers or aspects of performance).
3. It reduces a teacher's judgment. Point systems tend to be inflexible and minimize the teachers' professional input.
4. It leads to cumulative errors. A particular score or activity may not truly reflect the student's abilities or learning. The final total represents the sum of all such errors.
5. It is subject to misinterpretation. Without norms it is false to assume that a certain range (90 to 100) or number (93) represents a valid indicator (e.g., an A) of performance or that categories (breakpoints) can be decided in advance.

Source: Adapted from Robert F. Madgic. "The Point System of Grading: A Critical Appraisal." *NASSP Bulletin* (April 1988): 29-34.

Revised contracts can be designed for students whose work is not satisfactory or who expected a higher grade than they received. This grading system provides more latitude for teachers in responding to unsatisfactory work and gives students a chance to improve their work and their grade. Good grade contracts take into account both the quality and quantity of student work.

You will find this contract approach used with some frequency in classrooms where there are specific performance measures for students so that they know what *products* they must produce and, if they produce those products, the grades they will receive.

Mastery and Continuous Progress Grading

Many elementary schools and a few middle grade and junior high schools now stress *mastery grading* and *continuous progress grading,* an outgrowth of the mastery learning approach. Both approaches require that teachers maintain specific records for each student and report on the student's progress. Schools using these approaches usually do not use grades but evaluate the student in terms of expected and mastered skills and behaviors.[44] Reports for the student and parents describe how the student is performing and progressing without any indication of how the student is doing in relation to others. Although a judgment is made about the student, the absence of a standard for comparison reduces some pressure related to grades. In mastery learning situations and continuous progress reporting, grades are usually based on criterion-reference measurements. Richard Arends describes how this approach might be used in spelling:

> For example, in spelling, the teacher might decide that the correct spelling of 100 specified words constitutes mastery. Student grades would then be determined and performance reported in terms of the percentage of the 100 words a student can spell correctly. A teacher using this approach might specify the following grading scale: A = 100 to 93 words spelled correctly; B = 92 to 85 words spelled correctly; C = 84 to 75 words spelled correctly; D = 74 to 65 words spelled correctly; and F = 64 or fewer words spelled correctly.[45]

Grading for Effort or Improvement

To what extent should teachers consider effort or improvement as part of the grade? This question surfaces for most teachers when they grade their students' work. Problems with considering effort are that bright students may show the least improvement and effort and that, by raising the grade or average of low-achieving students to reflect effort rather than achievement, you are to some extent lowering the value of the grade given to high-achieving students.[46] Also, low-achieving students have more opportunity to improve by simple regression toward the mean; that is, statistically they have a better chance to improve their scores than do other students whose scores are already above the mean.

Most teachers, especially in the elementary and middle grade schools, leave some room for judgment in grading. The more effort and improvement are considered in deciding on final grades, the more subjective the grades will be and the more biased they are likely to be. The teacher must examine his or her perceptions for accuracy. If the teacher feels strongly about a judgment, then the movement in a grade from a B to a B+ or an A– to an A is acceptable. A major change in a grade, say from a C to an A, cannot be justified on the basis of the student's effort or teacher's hunches about the student.

Where effort does become important is in the teacher's efforts to communicate to parents and students the way in which students are approaching their learning tasks. Are they working hard? Are they putting forth good effort and trying to do strong work? Such information sheds light on what a student is like as an individual and what interests and intrinsic motivation characterize the child. Such information is important for parents to know and for teachers to use as they work with students.

Regardless of whether you decide to "reward" effort by modifying a student's grade, you should place an emphasis on effort as you interact with your students. Why? Students can change their effort levels; they cannot change their innate abilities. In this regard, educators might learn something from the Japanese, who do place an emphasis on effort:

> In Asia, the emphasis on effort and the relative disregard for innate abilities are derived from Confucian philosophy. Confucius was interested above all in the moral perfectibility of mankind. He rejected categorization of human beings as good or bad, and stressed the

potential for improving moral conduct through the creation of favorable environmental conditions. His view was gradually extended to all aspects of human behavior. Human beings were considered to be malleable, and like clay, subject to molding by the events of everyday life. Differences among individuals in innate abilities were recognized, for no one can claim that all people are born with the same endowments. But more important was the degree to which a person was willing to maximize these abilities through hard work.

A typical example of Confucian position is found in the writings of the Chinese philosopher Hsun Tzu, who wrote, "Achievement consists of never giving up. . . . If there is no dark and doffed will, there will be no shining accomplishment; if there is no dull and determined effort, there will be no brilliant achievement." Lack of achievement, therefore, is attributed to insufficient effort rather than to a lack of ability or to personal or environmental obstacles.[47]

Records and Reports of Performance

There is usually a difference in the way student performance is recorded and reported between elementary and secondary school. Elementary teachers are usually more sensitive about the student's feelings, attitudes, and effort and are willing to consider these factors in reporting performance. Elementary school report cards often contain a narrative or a combination of grades and narrative about the child's progress. The parents may be asked to write a reply instead of merely signing the report card, or to attend a conference perhaps two or three times a year at which they can discuss with the teacher the child's work.

Fewer middle grade and junior high schools have such elaborate reporting systems, and at the high school level this human (or social) dimension of reporting is almost nonexistent, partly because teachers have more students (perhaps 150 or more) and thus cannot easily write narratives and hold conferences with the parents of each student.

Report Cards

The teacher's judgments and scores on tests are communicated to students and parents by means of a report card. The reports should not come as a surprise to students. Both students and parents should know how marks or grades are computed and to what extent tests, class participation, homework, and other activities contribute to their overall grade. It is reasonable for students and parents to become anxious if they do not know the basis for the marks or grades on the report card.

At the lower elementary grade level (below grade 4) and to a lesser extent at the upper elementary and junior high school levels, the school may use a ***mastery*** or ***progress report card*** that gives a list of descriptors or categories for which the teacher checks off "very good" (VG), "good" (G), and "needs improvement" (NI), or "outstanding" (O), "satisfactory" (S), and "unsatisfactory" (U). Following is a list of common reading descriptors and the accompanying progress options.

	O	S	U
1. Reads orally at appropriate level	—	—	—
2. Reads with comprehension	—	—	—

	O	S	U
3. Identifies main ideas in stories	—	—	—
4. Recognizes main characters in stories	—	—	—
5. Finds details in stories	—	—	—
6. Draws conclusions from reading stories	—	—	—
7. Demonstrates appropriate vocabulary	—	—	—
8. Reads with appropriate speed	—	—	—
9. Finishes reading assignments on time	—	—	—
10. Persists even if understanding does not come immediately	—	—	—

Teachers can make up their own lists for any basic skill or subject. A mastery report might also involve individualized rather than standardized descriptions of progress or problems. At some levels and for some types of course content the list of descriptors or categories can be precise, with a date for achievement or mastery to be shown relative to some defined learning standard—refer again to Table 11.6.

The approach fits with a criterion-reference system of evaluation and is useful for schools that wish to eliminate grades and put more emphasis on progress or mastery. The same approach can be used for various subjects and grade levels. For example, eighth-grade math might consist of the following mastery items: 1) fractions and decimals, 2) solving equations, 3) geometric figures, 4) percentages and probability, 5) powers and roots, 6) areas and volumes, and 7) graphs and predictions. Space can also be provided for the teachers' comments—permitting in-depth analysis of the students' strengths and areas for improvement. See Tips for Teachers 11.4 for more ideas about mastery report cards and other reporting tools.

A traditional report card uses letter or numerical grades. At the elementary grade level, the emphasis is on reading and language skills, but there are also grades for citizenship or conduct, work habits or social habits, and absenteeism and lateness. At the secondary level, the emphasis is on academic subjects (such as English, mathematics, and science), but there is some place for reporting on minor or elective subjects (such as music, art, or physical education). Most schools, regardless of grade level, should have a space on report cards for a parent's signature, teacher comments, and parent or teacher requests for a conference to discuss the report.

Electronic Recordkeeping

Careful recordkeeping is an important part of the teacher's evaluation of students and has financial and legal implications for the school. Research shows that the average teacher, with the assistance of a calculator, takes eighty-seven minutes to average and record grades for thirty students in a traditional record book. The same teacher with a computerized recordkeeper takes fifteen minutes to do the same work—a savings of sixty-two minutes for one class during a single grading period.[48]

The ***computerized recordkeeper*** can generate school reports and parental reports, as well as customized letters and printout lists concerning student grades by numerous categories, in ten to twenty seconds per report, compared to an average of twenty minutes per report required by traditional methods. Figuring on a minimum of one school

Innovative Practices for Reporting Student Performance

 In lieu of traditional report cards, teachers might experiment with new procedures for reporting on student performance and progress. A number of innovative ideas are listed here. Some are in practice in a few schools. Just how innovative you can be will depend, to a large extent, on your school's policy and philosophy about grading.

1. Consider more than a single grade or mark. Develop a progress report for each activity detailing specific instructional tasks and student performance.
2. List more than cognitive development and specific subjects. Include social, psychological, and psychomotor behaviors and creative, aesthetic, and artistic learning as well as scientific and technical abilities.
3. Develop forms of report cards specifically suited to particular grade levels rather than using one form for the entire school. The absolute standards should be clearly defined so that the students understand what they need to know.
4. Grade students on the basis of both an absolute standard and a relative standard (especially in lower grades).

5. Report each student's progress. Feedback to students is critical to their academic growth.
6. Replace or use in addition to standard letter grades or categories (such as "excellent," "good," and "fair") new categories or written individual statements that clearly define what students know and need to learn.
7. Stress strengths of the student. Include ways to share some of the student's best work with others in the class.
8. Point out only two or three weaknesses or problem areas, and specify ways for improving weak or problem areas.
9. Organize committees of students, teachers, and parents to meet periodically (every three or four years) to improve the school district's standard report card.
10. Supplement report cards with frequent informal letters to parents, parent-teacher conferences, and student-teacher conferences.

Source: Adapted from Allan C. Ornstein. "The Nature of Grading." *ClearingHouse* (April 1989): 65–69; David A. Payne. *Measuring and Evaluating Educational Outcomes.* New York: Macmillan, 1992.

report per week for forty weeks and two customized letters or progress reports per year for thirty parents, the savings is another thirty-three hours.

Two researchers have listed twenty-two tasks that computerized recordkeeping can accomplish more effectively than a traditional recordkeeping book. Selected ones are listed here.

1. Making easy and quick modifications of recorded scores, correcting clerical errors, or accommodating retest scores or new test scores
2. Computing grade averages and applying weighted formulas to grade students on various categories (e.g., 40 percent for exams, 30 percent for weekly quizzes, 15 percent for homework, and 15 percent for class participation)
3. Converting numerical grades to letter grades according to specific standards
4. Providing records of student performance by ranking, percentages, frequency distributions, and so on for subgroups or the entire class

5. Making comparisons of one student or subgroup on any recorded category for purpose of placement, diagnostic, formative, or summative evaluation

6. Providing printouts of student performance on specific tests or subtests for purposes of instruction

7. Designating or flagging students according to specific levels of performance on specific tests (e.g., students who failed or who received 80 percent or higher)

8. Generating reports that include standardized comments for one student or groups of students

9. Generating personal letters for individual students, including specific comments about grades

10. Reusing names for different reports, labels, printouts, or another grading period; creating class lists for attendance, lateness, extra credit, phone numbers, addresses, and so on.[49]

We are in the technology age, and the pen-and-pencil method of recording data is quickly becoming dated. It behooves teachers to manage information efficiently and use various databases and spreadsheets for grading, evaluating, and reporting student performance. These methods provide many alternatives for busy teachers in the twenty-first century. Whether technology really makes a difference will depend on a couple of critical factors—such as your technology skills and the availability of a computer in your room. It may also depend on the availability of colleague "expert" teachers who know how to use the systems.

Cumulative Record

Each student has a permanent record in which important data are filed during his or her entire school career. It contains information about subject grades, standardized test scores, family background, personal history, health, school service, parent and pupil interviews, special aptitudes, special problems (learning, behavioral, or physical), number of absences, and tardiness.

The *cumulative record* is usually stored in the main office or guidance office. Teachers are permitted access to the cumulative records of the students in their classes to obtain information about them. They are also required to add to the information at the end of the term to keep the records complete and up-to-date.

Although the information found in the cumulative records is extremely helpful, a major criticism of these records is that they may prompt a teacher to make prejudgments about students before even meeting them in class. For this reason, some educators argue that a teacher should not look at cumulative records until a month or more after the school year begins. When you read Case Study 11.2 later consider whether you think the potential problems of teacher "prior knowledge" warrant not looking at cumulative folders.

Since federal legislation permits the records of a child to be open to inspection and review by the child's parents, most educators are reluctant to write statements or reports that may be considered controversial or negative, unless supported with specific data. Sometimes important information is omitted. When parents review information in cumulative records (they also have the right to challenge the information), a qualified employee of the school (principal's secretary or guidance counselor) should be present to give assistance.

Salvia and Ysseldyke assert that there are three principles that should govern what is placed in a cumulative folder:

Principle 1: Include information in a folder only for the length of time that it is absolutely required.

Principle 2: Parents have the right to review, inspect, challenge, and even supplement information that is in a folder.

Principle 3: The cumulative records of students are classified information and should only be accessible to those school personnel who have a "need to know."[50]

Student Portfolios

Student portfolios (see also Chapter 10) can be used to demonstrate students' work—to show a range of performance or the "best" pieces of work. Through most portfolios, students are expected to show a variety of skills and the ability to improve performance. Portfolios tell an in-depth story, especially if they are maintained for the entire year and cut across domains or subjects. They may consist of a written autobiography; a statement about work (including a résumé); an essay on a particular subject or a series of essays; a special project, paper, or experiment; a series of photographs, drawings, or plans; or even a video, computer printout, or software developed by the student.[51] See Case Study 11.1 for an example of how a mathematics teacher uses portfolios. The teacher is experimenting with how to use portfolios and you can see her thinking through how and when to use them correctly and efficiently.

Portfolios are becoming increasingly popular because they are considered an excellent way for the teacher to get to know the student. They are particularly useful in inclusion classrooms in which students exhibit a wide range of needs and abilities. They help students (and teachers and parents) see the "big" picture, heightening the students' awareness of their own learning. Allowing students to select the contents of the portfolio also enables them to take an active role in their own instruction and assessment. The portfolio makes it possible to document instruction and learning over time and is an excellent resource for teacher, parent, and student when discussing overall school performance and progress. Portfolios portray a wide and rich array of what students know or can do. In effect, they capture multiple dimensions of learning, not only right answers or cognitive dimensions. They illuminate the process by which students solve problems, produce work, or perform in real-life contexts—what some educators call "authentic" assessment. Portfolios also help students integrate instruction and reflect on personal efforts.[52] As a tool for developing habits of reflection, they can lead to greater student confidence in their own learning, especially when they acquire information about their learning in ways that help them manage their learning.[53]

case study 11.1   How to Use Portfolios in Mathematics

Teachers may use portfolios for assessment in all subject areas. What follows is a math teacher's story about how she incorporates portfolios in her algebra class.

. . . My county department of education had established a portfolio network for math teachers who each month shared ideas. The first meeting was wonderful! There must have been 60 people there. By the third meeting the number had dwindled to 20; the last meeting had just enough people to sit comfortably around one table.

I was disturbed by the narrow scope of what my colleagues were suggesting should go into the portfolios. They wanted to include only their students' efforts at problem solving. While problem solving is a portion of the mathematics I teach, there is a lot more to algebra than problems of the week. As the semester came to a close, I was surprised at the absolute quantity of work my students had done. Examples of this work included long-term projects, daily notes, and journal entries about troublesome test problems. . . .

One day I handed the folders to the students, then went to the board and wrote the word portfolio. *I asked the class what should be included in a portfolio. What would show their effort and learning in algebra? What activities had been the most meaningful? I noted their suggestions: daily notes, the Personal Budget long-term projects, Lottery Project, scale drawing, their best tests, their worst tests, problems of the week, daily class notes, and homework. Next, I had them search through their folders and collect five items that they believed represented their math knowledge and effort. At this time I was really glad I had all their work for the semester because the students attached significant value to assignments that I would not have.*

The class then discussed the format of a good portfolio. We decided it should be neat, typed or in ink, in a cover, and include a table of contents. In addition, each entry was to contain a personal statement as to why this piece was important to the learner. I gave the class a week to organize portfolios.

After I collected the portfolios, I immediately handed them out again to a different person in the class. I wanted my students to see their classmates' work. Almost instantly those who had put little time into this project became uncomfortable when they saw the effort of others. I asked my students whether they would like four extra days to revisit their portfolios. There was obvious relief. . . .

I eventually decided to have the portfolios peer graded. Students were to write comments and suggestions for improvement on grading sheets, not on the actual portfolio. I devised a grading matrix and weighted the portfolio grade to be equivalent to about one-fifth of a test grade. After the students wrote comments, I added my own.

Having students grade one another's portfolios served two purposes. First, they received immediate, constructive feedback from a peer. Second, graders had an opportunity to read another student's work carefully. Some student graders felt that the introductions they read were so insightful that they asked me to read the comments aloud to the whole class. This is [one] excerpt from an 8th grader's portfolio:

"I chose these papers for my portfolio because they show my best work and my worst work. They portray both sides of my academic performance in math this last semester."

> *My students are now collecting work for their next try, which they are calling "Son of Portfolio."*
>
> *As a result of trying to implement portfolio assessment, my classroom has definitely changed. It became apparent early on that if I wanted variety in my children's portfolios, I had to provide variety in assignments. I have changed my curriculum to include more problem-solving opportunities with written explanations. I have also had my students do two long-term situational problems. In the past, although I knew my algebra classes found such projects entertaining, I had questioned their lasting value. Now I see that these problems are the ones the kids remember most. . . .*

Questions for reflection:

1.   Notice that this teacher purchased some of the supplies to make the portfolios possible. It is a small amount of money but a big issue for some teachers. Teachers use a lot of personal resources to support their students. Should they?

2.   The notion of a portfolio network is interesting. One advantage is that it helps teachers see different ways to handle student assessment. What factors make it difficult for such networks to become established in many schools?

3.   Should portfolios be the only way to assess student learning? Why or why not?

Source: Excerpted from Pam Knight. "How I Use Portfolios in Mathematics" *Education Leadership* (May 1992): 71–72.

Despite the compelling reasons for using portfolios, certain potential problems accompany their use. Unless the portfolio system is designed carefully, accurate conclusions about what learning outcomes have been achieved cannot be made. The work in the portfolio may not be representative of what the student knows or can do, the criteria used to evaluate the product may not reflect relevant dimensions of the course content or skill, and the work that a student puts into the portfolio may not really be "authentic" or reflect the curriculum.[54]

Defining selection and assessment criteria becomes crucial. The work assigned to students for the portfolio should match the behavior and content the teacher is trying to assess. For example, teachers cannot conclude the writing sample or research project in the portfolio is "typical" work for the student, if the student has selected only his or her "best" sample. The significance or value of the portfolio product also changes with the teacher analyzing it. Teacher bias and subjectivity in grading are much harder to control with this assessment system than with a short-answer test or when grading is based on right answers or a prescribed answer key.

Portfolios represent an assessment and grading strategy that can reveal much about a variety of learning outcomes; however, while most educators seem to favor their use, there is no single agreed-upon way to design a portfolio system. Effective use really depends on your intended purpose and audience, as well as your definition of a "good" portfolio. As a teacher, if you do not fully understand how portfolios can be developed and to what end, what content or skills should be assessed, and what criteria or standards should be used, then you are likely to become confused as you implement them as part of your assessment plan. Since many schools are using them in one form or another, it is advisable to ask experienced teachers for help. Listen, for example, for advice in the words of two experienced teachers who use portfolios:

> When it came time to measure cumulatively students' progress for the report cards, student portfolios were our main tool for assessment along with our observations. We knew that all of our children entered the school year on different levels with a variety of gifts. The portfolio would document growth from September through June and include teacher-suggested, student-elected work. . . . [O]ur students gained ownership of their portfolios early on. These portfolios comprised the children's work across the curriculum, with an emphasis on their reflective writing pieces. By looking at samples of their writing month after month, we could tangibly assess their growth in grammar, spelling, and sentence structure, along with their developing thought processes.
>
> We wanted our students to become self-reflective learners. At the end of each marking period, we asked them to review their work to examine the growth they had made. Each wrote a reflection for the different curriculum areas, reviewing the strides they had made and how they wanted to improve in the upcoming months. These pieces went into their portfolios along with the reflections that they had been writing throughout the year; students became engaged in their own learning as they engaged in self-assessment. . . . [55]

QUESTIONS FOR REFLECTION

Grading is one of the most difficult aspects of the teaching-learning process. As you get to know students, you will develop natural biases based on their responsiveness in class or their behavior during your lessons. Some students will work hard and still not learn the material well. Others will hardly study, and yet their performance will be exceptional. As you observe all these different students, it is very human to want to reward students who are trying but may not be learning. To what degree do you think effort should be considered as grades are awarded? Should you give a student a higher grade because that student has really worked hard? If not, how will you deal with these types of students who begin to "lose heart" because they are trying but still not succeeding?

Guidelines for Grading Students and Reporting Student Progress

Here are some suggestions for deriving grades:

1. *Become familiar with the grading policy of your school and with your colleagues' standards:* Each school has its own standards for grading and procedures for reporting grades. Your standards and practices should not conflict with those of the school and should not differ greatly from those of your colleagues.

2. *Explain your grading system to the students:* To young students, explain your grading system orally and with concrete examples. Older students can read handouts that describe assignments, tests, test schedules, and grading criteria, although this information can also be explained orally.

3. *If possible, base grades on a predetermined set of standards:* For example, a student who is able to perform at a significantly higher performance standard than another student should receive a higher grade. Limit the degree to which student comparisons are used to determine grades.

4. *Don't count everything when calculating grades:* Teachers may decide to drop the weakest assignment or grade of each student. This is especially true if a lot of new and complex material is being taught.

5. *Base grades on a variety of data sources:* The more sources of information used and weighted properly, the more valid is the grade. Although most of the grade should be based on objective sources, some subjective sources should also be considered. For example, a student who frequently participates in class may be given a slightly higher grade than her test average.

6. *As a rule, do not change grades:* Grades should be arrived at after serious consideration, and only in rare circumstances should they be changed. Of course, an obvious mistake or error should be corrected, but if students think you will change grades, they will start negotiating or pleading with you for changes.

7. *When failing a student, closely follow school procedures:* Each school has its own procedures to follow for failing a student. You may be required to have a warning conference, to send a pending failure notice to parents, and so forth.

8. *Record grades on report cards and cumulative records.* Report cards usually are mailed to parents or given to students to give to parents every six to eight weeks. Cumulative records are usually completed at the end of the school year.[56]

Remember to use the evaluation procedure as a teaching and learning device, to be fair in your evaluation of students, to interpret evaluative data properly, and to give students the benefit of the doubt.

Communication with Parents

The importance of parent involvement is well documented. How the teacher can help the parents improve the child's academic work and behavior is often the major concern among parents and teachers alike. According to Joyce Epstein, more than eighty-five percent of parents spend fifteen minutes or more helping their child at home when asked to do so by the teacher. Parents claim they can spend more time, forty minutes on the average, if they are told specifically how to help, but fewer than twenty-five percent receive systematic requests and directions from teachers to assist their children with specific skills and subjects.[57] Epstein further notes that parents become involved most often with reading activities at the lower grades: reading to the child or listening to the child read, taking the child to the library, and helping with teaching materials brought home from school for practice at home.[58] Parents of older students (grade 4 and above) become more involved with specific homework and subject-related activities.

Including the student in parent-teacher conferences encourages open communication.

Parent involvement in school matters and children's learning decreases with the level of schooling. Involvement and concern are considerable at the elementary school level, less at the middle school or junior high school level, and least at the high school level. Research also shows that children have an advantage in school when their parents support, participate, and communicate on a regular basis with school officials.[59] Figure 11.1 shows the levels of parental involvement for different types of families. Schools typically communicate with parents in three ways: through reports cards (already discussed), conferences, and letters. Parents expect feedback from the teachers and school, and they usually welcome the opportunity to meet with the teacher and to stay in touch through phone calls and letters.

Parent Conferences

Scheduling parent-teacher conferences is becoming increasingly difficult because an increasing number of children have only one adult living at home, have two parents in the workforce, or have parents with more than one job. Few parents are able to attend school activities or conferences during normal school hours, and many have trouble scheduling meetings at all. Today's teacher must adjust to these new circumstances with greater efforts through letters and telephone calls to set up meetings and greater flexibility to accommodate the needs of the parents.

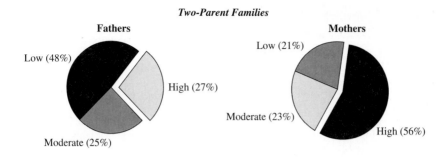

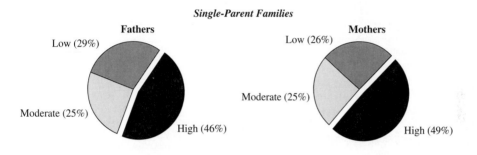

figure 11.1   Level of Fathers' and Mothers' Involvement in School, by Family Type: Students in Grades K–12, 1996

Low involvement is participation in none or only one activity; moderate involvement is participation in two activities; and high involvement is participation in three or four activities.

Source: U.S. Department of Education, National Center for Education Statistics.

Usually both teacher and parents are a little apprehensive before a conference, want to impress each other favorably, and don't know exactly what to expect. Teachers can reduce their anxiety by preparing for the conference, assembling in advance all the information pertinent to the student and the subject to be discussed with parents. This might include information regarding the student's academic achievement, other testing results, general health, attendance and lateness, social and emotional relations, work habits, special aptitudes, or other noteworthy characteristics or activities. If the conference is about subject grades, the teacher should assemble the student's tests, reports, and homework assignments. If it is about discipline, the teacher might have on hand written and detailed accounts of behavior.

The conference should not be a time for lecturing parents. If the teacher asked for the conference, the teacher will set the agenda but should remain sensitive to the needs of the parents. The atmosphere should be unrushed and quiet. The information presented should be based on as many sources as possible, and it should be objective in content. See Tips for Teachers 11.5 for suggestions on making communication objective for classroom management problems. It is advisable to begin and end on a positive

tips for teachers 11.5

Directing a Parent Conference

1. *Call a parent by the correct name:* If unsure, ask: "Is this Latoya's mother?"
2. *Identify yourself and provide a neutral focus for contact:* "I'm Mrs. Dawson and I'm calling to talk about John's behavior in math class."
3. *State the purpose for contact:* State the specific behavior(s) in *objective,* not *subjective* terms. In objective (what actually occurred) you'd say, "Today Rana grabbed a classmate's book and hid it." In subjective (your interpretation of what occurred) terms, you'd say, "Rana is very immature."
4. *Enlist parent support by stating the desired student behavior:* "I'm sure *you* want Clark to leave his classmates' property alone and concentrate on math."
5. *Identify parent's responsibility:* "I believe it will help if you tell Mohammad to leave his classmates' property alone and concentrate on math."
6. *Ask the parent for additional ideas:* "What ideas do you have that might help me as I work with Paquita?"
7. *Reinforce parent and teacher responsibility:* "I believe it will help if you tell Angel to keep his hands, feet, and objects to himself and concentrate on math. Please remind him that failure to do so is the reason he must serve detention tomorrow. In addition, I will attempt to involve him in more group activities."
8. *State if and when a follow-up contact will occur:* "I will contact you next week to share how Emma is doing. With your help Emma can correct her behavior."
9. *Finish contact on a cooperative note:* "Thank you for your time. Please don't hesitate to call me if you have questions or concerns."

Source: Adapted from a form developed by Charlene Sinclair. The form appeared in Thomas J. Lasley. "Teacher Technicians: A 'New' Metaphor for New Teachers." *Action in Teacher Education,* 16 (no. 1): 11–19.

note, even if a problem has to be discussed. The idea is to encourage parents. The teacher should not monopolize the discussion, should be truthful yet tactful and constructive, and should remain poised. The teacher should be cautious about giving too much advice, especially with regard to the child's home life. The average conference, unless there is an important problem, lasts twenty to thirty minutes.

The parent-teacher conference is helpful for both parties. The conference helps teachers 1) understand and clarify parents' impressions and expectations of the school program or particular classes, 2) obtain additional information about the child, 3) report on the child's developmental progress and suggest things the parents can do to stimulate development, 4) develop a working relationship with parents, and 5) encourage parents' support of the school. According to some educators, the conference, in turn, helps parents 1) gain a better understanding of the child's school program, 2) learn about school activities that can enhance the child's growth and development, 3) learn about the child's performance and progress, 4) learn about the school's faculty and support staff, 5) communicate concerns and ask questions about the child, and 6) both provide and receive information that can benefit the child's development in school and at home.[60] Clark, Starr, and others also point out that the conference should examine 1) how the student behaves in class (or school), 2) how the student gets along with classmates, 3) whether the student is working up to potential, 4) the strengths of the student, 5) the special abilities or interests of the student, 6) ways for the student to improve, 7) how the parent can help the student, and 8) how the parent can help the teacher.[61]

Letters to Parents

Letters to parents fall into three categories. First, letters are sent to make parents aware of or invite them to participate in certain classroom or school activities or functions. Second, letters may be sent out regularly, perhaps weekly or bimonthly, to keep parents up-to-date about their children's academic work and behavior. Parents are entitled to and appreciate this communication. Informing parents and seeking their input and support may help stop minor problems before they become serious. Third, letters may address specific problems. Such letters describe problems, ask parents for their cooperation in one or more ways, and request a conference.

Guidelines for Communicating with Parents

Over the years many suggestions have been offered for teachers communicating with parents. The following guidelines emphasize the need for 1) establishing a friendly atmosphere, 2) discussing the child's potential and limitations in an objective manner, 3) avoiding arguments and remaining calm, and 4) observing professional ethics.

Mechanics of the Parent Conference

1. Make an appointment for the conference well in advance.
2. Provide two or more options for the parent's visit.
3. Greet the parent courteously using his or her proper name. Stand up to greet the person.
4. Take the parent's coat and show him or her to a comfortable chair.
5. If parents are upset or emotional, let them express their feelings without interruptions. Do not become defensive; remain calm.
6. Be objective in analyzing the child's progress; also, show interest in the child's development, growth, and welfare.
7. Never get trapped into criticizing another teacher or the principal.
8. Explain how you and the parent can work together to help the student.
9. Set up a date for a follow-up conference, if needed.
10. Walk the parent to the door. If possible, end on a positive note.

Discussion About the Child

1. Begin on a positive note.
2. Be truthful and honest.
3. Accept the parent's feelings.
4. Emphasize the child's strengths.
5. Be specific about the student's learning difficulties—use objective, not subjective language (e.g., "Trent has not turned in homework for five straight days" rather than "Trent is irresponsible").

6. Have ready samples of the student's class work and homework as well as a record of his or her test scores, attendance, and so on.

7. Be receptive to the parent's suggestions.

8. Let the parent have the opportunity to talk about his or her concerns.

9. Avoid arguments; avoid pedantic language.

10. Provide constructive suggestions.

11. Be willing to explain activities or changes in the school curriculum that meet the needs of the child.

12. Close on a positive note, with a plan of action.[62]

As you consider all the material presented thus far on evaluating students, study carefully Case Study 11.2. In this Case Study, Mrs. Jones confronts the problem of student failure. As you read the case you will see how she solved the problem. Do you think her approach made the most sense? What other approaches might you use if you were confronted with such a situation? How might she have prevented the failures from ever occurring? You will also notice that once again highlighted in parentheses the relevant Pathwise criteria. Using the Pathwise concepts does not ensure teaching success, but it does help teachers better understand why some lessons may succeed or fail.

Accountability

Throughout Chapter 10 and this chapter, we have been focusing on how to set standards for student learning and then assess the degree to which students are learning the material taught. We have also discussed high-stakes (large-scale) testing (i.e., the type of tests students must pass in order to move to another grade level or to graduate). Until the late 1990s, such information would have been sufficient to capture the "state" of the assessment process. For good or bad, and the issue is highly debatable, your students' performance is now being used to hold you and your professional colleagues accountable, just as it is being used to hold students accountable. That accountability is evidenced at a number of different levels and has been punctuated in importance by the No Child Left Behind (NCLB) legislation of 2002.

Summarized here are two of the ways in which you will experience accountability in the next decade. The first is as a means to reward and sanction high- and low-performing schools. The second is as a way to benefit students.

All states must now establish clear guidelines for adequate yearly progress (AYP) for all students. Such guidelines, which have never existed before, will influence the climate within which you find yourself functioning as a professional. Specifically, here are some AYP components:

- A timeline to ensure all students reach proficiency by 2013–2014

- A baseline percentage of students meeting or exceeding the state's proficiency guidelines in each subject tested from which adequate yearly progress can be measured

- Intermediate goals that establish regular increases in the percentage of students meeting or exceeding proficiency guidelines

- Annual measurable assessment objectives

case study 11.2   **Assessing Student Progress: Seeking Help from Colleagues**

Mrs. Jones is an entry-year mathematics teacher in an urban high school that serves 1,500 students. She has been assigned a trained mentor, Mr. Bass, who is also the chair of the twelve member math department. The high school is on a block schedule system in which each math class meets for eighty minutes per day for one semester. Mrs. Jones teaches two sections of Math I to freshmen and one section of Algebra I containing 60 percent freshmen and 40 percent sophomores. She just computed her first six weeks' grades for report cards and is dismayed to find out that 10 percent to 15 percent of the students in each class failed and about the same percent earned a letter grade of D. *She finds this most disturbing since she knows that the rest of the year will build on the review skills that made up over half of the content that she covered the first six weeks (A). Math I is the most basic of all the math offerings in the high school and is the only math option for freshmen who are at the lowest levels. She realizes that she must determine why so many students are not successful and what she can do differently (D).*

As soon as her students' six-week grades are entered into the computer, she e-mails Mr. Bass and requests a meeting after school (D). She takes her grade book, a printout of the distribution of six weeks' grades, a list of students earning a D *or an* F, *and her lesson plan book to the meeting. Her opening comment to Mr. Bass is, "I feel like a failure. In each of my classes 20 percent to 30 percent of my students were unsuccessful. What am I doing wrong (D)?"*

Mr. Bass acknowledges how difficult it is to feel "like a failure" and then encourages her to think of the methods that produced success for the 70 percent to 80 percent who were successful in her class. After some discussion about what approaches seemed to be effective, he tells her how much he appreciates her wanting all of her students to be successful (B). They then begin to focus on her concerns about her students' performance and to analyze what might have happened (D).

They retrace her steps from the time she began to plan for the school year. Mr. Bass finds out that Mrs. Jones had chosen not to look at her students' cumulative records because she was afraid she would develop preconceived notions about who was likely to be successful and who was not (B). Thus, she had neither analyzed the students' standardized math achievement test scores nor reviewed their cumulative math performance indicator checklists, both of which were in their cumulative records. She had decided to base her lessons on the math academic content standards and had sequenced coverage of the topics in the Math I and Algebra texts in an order consistent with the sequence of performance indicators (A). For the same reasons, she had chosen not to contact the eighth-grade math teachers to determine who had done well and who had not.

Mr. Bass questions her about what pretesting or informal diagnostic evaluation measures she had used the first week of classes to determine students' present levels of performance. Mrs. Jones indicates that she had not used any, because it would delay for several days the students beginning the course content while she gave the pretests and analyzed the results. However, as they talk, she realizes the value of gathering information on students' current skill levels and decides to begin her new six weeks with a teacher-made diagnostic math assessment that will enable her to determine which students have deficits in specific math skills (A). She also decides to review cumulative folders to gain additional information about her students' past performance in math (A). What she finds out from the pretests and folder review is that approximately 50 percent had at least two significant skill deficits in either basic math computations, math reasoning, or both. She also finds that in one class, she had four students with specific learning disabilities (SLD) who had even greater math skill deficits (A).

She then meets again with Mr. Bass (D) to determine her next steps. They discuss ways in which she could group and teach students to address their mathematics skill deficits (A). They also discuss how she could incorporate various forms of formative assessment into her ongoing instruction to monitor student progress on a systematic basis (A). She also meets with Mrs. Ricardo, the ninth-grade intervention specialist, to find out why students with such significant math deficits had been placed in her mathematics class (D). Mrs. Ricardo tells her that there was no more room in the ninth-grade special education mathematics class. The four students with SLD assigned to Mrs. Jones actually had the highest math performance of all the students in special education receiving services outside of the general education classroom.

Mrs. Jones then contacts the students in Algebra I whose pretesting showed that their skill levels were better matched with the content covered in Math I to see if they would be willing to transfer into Math I. She also contacts their parents to see if they would come in to discuss the progress of their children (D). All but one student agrees to switch to Math I. Mrs. Jones then redesigns her Math I lesson plans to include two sets of learning objectives: 1) those built on the grade-level academic content standards and 2) those built to address the skill deficits of the group of students who had not been successful the first six weeks (A). She then expands her "point system" for earning six weeks' grades to include the accumulation of points for completion of homework, accuracy of homework, participation in class, improvement across tests and quizzes, and performance on tests and quizzes (A). Individual learning contracts are established for the students with identified learning disabilities whose math skill deficits were so significant that they would be responsible for only certain components of specific skill lessons (A).

Mrs. Jones knows that explaining her new system will be a challenge since not all students will be expected to accomplish the same goals and do the same work. She realizes that if they do not understand why she is going to differentiate her instruction (C), they might view the system as "unfair" (B). She develops a lesson that will enable her to introduce the new system through a simulation (A). Her goals for the lesson are to enable her students to recognize the sequential nature of mathematics and the need to have prerequisite skills (A and A) to learn successfully more complex mathematics concepts and skills. She develops a small group activity using jigsaw puzzles (A) and makes plans for the students' daily "grade" to be based on their small groups' "success" in putting together their jigsaw puzzles (A).

Before class that morning, Mrs. Jones rearranges the desk-top chairs into groupings of four and assigns a color to each grouping using colored index cards taped to the chairs (B). She puts the puzzle pieces for each group in a plastic bag. Only one group will receive all the pieces needed to successfully complete their puzzle. All the other groups will have bags of puzzle pieces with one or more pieces missing. Furthermore, the puzzles are of varying degrees of difficulty.

As students enter, Mrs. Jones greets them at the door with a friendly smile (B) and hands each a colored card (B) that indicates to what group the student has randomly been assigned. She laughingly tells them that their "reward" for completing all the pretests the previous day is to begin the class with a game (B).

Once all students are seated, Mrs. Jones explains that today they are going to begin their lesson with an activity designed to build skills in working as teams (C). She tells the students that their grade for the first half of the class will be based on their successful completion of the puzzle they will be given and on how well they work together to accomplish their goal (C). She also reminds them of the small group rules that they used during the first six weeks and indicates that any violations of the rules will result in a thirty-second time-out for that group, during which time the group cannot manipulate the puzzle pieces (B).

Mrs. Jones then randomly distributes the bags of puzzle pieces (B) and tells students they have twenty minutes to accomplish their task. She sets a timer and tells them she will warn them when five minutes and then one minute remain (C). She tells them that these are challenging puzzles, but that she knows they are up to completing the task (B).

As students work together, Mrs. Jones monitors the groups' progress (C). Some groups receive positive feedback (C4) while others are told she does not know why they are having such difficulty since they have such easy puzzles (B). As Mrs. Jones begins to give the five-minute warning, one group becomes so boisterous that the other groups cannot hear the warning. The loud group has to stop working on the puzzle for thirty seconds before resuming their activities (B). As the time draws to a close, two groups tell her in frustration that they do not have all the puzzle pieces needed to complete their puzzles. She responds with a shrug of the shoulders and "There is nothing I can do about it. Just work a little harder please." (C). Another group complains that the puzzle the neighboring group is working on seems easier (B). The noise level increases with the frustration. This time, she does nothing to stop the noise (B).

When the timer buzzes, all work stops and she quickly snaps a picture of each group surrounding their puzzle as "evidence" of how much of each puzzle has been completed. She then puts three questions on the overhead projector and asks the students to spend the next five minutes writing an entry to the following questions: 1) What difficulties did you have putting your puzzle together? 2) Do you think this was a fair activity? Why or why not? and 3) What does this puzzle activity have to do with math instruction? (C) The small groups discuss these questions. Finally Mrs. Jones facilitates a discussion of student responses to these questions in a whole-group format (C).

Following this discussion, Mrs. Jones restates the goal of the puzzle activity and indicates that, for the purpose of the activity, all groups will receive "full credit" since some groups had been at a disadvantage by not having all the puzzle pieces

(B). She then says that to be "fair" to all her students she needs to make sure that they have all the "mathematics" puzzle pieces they need to learn mathematics. Mrs. Jones describes how she will be splitting the class into groups and that different groups will be working on the math skills they needs to be successful (A). She shares both the overall point system with the class and the fact that students may have different learning goals, different assignments, and different criteria for earning their course grade, depending on what she has learned from her pretests about the number of "puzzle pieces" they are missing.

Mrs. Jones spends the remainder of the period answering student questions and explaining in greater detail how the system will work (C). Initial assignments to "groups" will be tentative and students' progress and performance will determine future groupings. Before the bell rings, she distributes a letter to parents explaining the system and encouraging them to contact her if they have any questions (D). She thanks her students for their participation in the simulation (B) and says that they will begin the new system tomorrow.

Questions for reflection:

1.   The goal of all students being successful in the classroom is admirable. Is it realistic? Is it achieveable?
2.   Notice the references to pretesting Do you think most teachers do such pretesting? Why or why not?
3.   Mrs. Jones uses a simulation to teach her students her "new" system. Do you think the simulation is really necessary? Explain.

Source: This Case Study was developed by Linda Morrow, Muskingum College

A Focus on School Performance

Helping parents understand how effective the schools are that their children attend is a fundamental part of the NCLB legislation. That legislation requires that *all states* test the reading and mathematics skills of students in grades 3 through 8, though it does leave the types of tests used to make such assessments up to the individual states.

The NCLB legislation is proving to be extremely problematic for many states because schools (to be successful) must show that students from each racial and demographic group are succeeding and showing annual improvement. The fear is that with such an expectation, far too many of the nation's schools will be classified as failing.

The original hope of those who argued for the accountability movement and the NCLB legislation was that students and parents would end up with better school options; that is, through an analysis of the results of those tests, parents would have a better understanding of what students know and how much they have learned. Parents would also have a general sense of the overall effectiveness of a school. And those schools that are performing poorly would be singled out for either remedial action or suffer some other form of penalty.

On one level, the accountability movement is focusing on identifying those schools that may not be succeeding or that are "low-performing." On another level, the movement is labeling districts based on their overall performance against certain state-defined criteria. In Ohio, for example, annual report cards are issued for each school district. Table 11.8 is the state report card for Smithville, Ohio, that was mailed in 2003. You will notice that there are twenty-two criteria, and the State of Ohio identifies the minimum level of student performance for each. Depending on the number of criteria met, the district is labeled anything from "academic emergency" to "academic excellence." District "labels" influence how parents perceive the schools and even the property values within a school district. It matters how well teachers and schools are helping students learn requisite academic material and it matters in ways that influence whether teachers are retained or schools remain open.

A Focus on Student Performance

Though a lot of attention has been given to the labeling of school districts and individual schools through the use of statewide standardized tests, other educators are beginning to look at how that same data can be used to foster student growth. Another state that has received a lot of attention lately for its learning standards and assessment system is Massachusetts through its use of the Massachusetts Comprehensive Assessment System (MCAS). Some educators are carefully examining standardized data to try to see student learning patterns that suggest areas of instructional focus. For example, three researchers describe how MCAS data are part of a data-driven school culture that attempts to create better learning opportunities for students.[63] They describe one district, Sound Public Schools, where they analyzed MCAS data in mathematics, science, and language arts. They noticed that writing fluency correlated with overall proficiency. The same district examined other diagnostic data from Terra Nova (see the section on diagnostic tests in Chapter 10) and noted that a close association existed between student reading scores and overall MCAS performance.

As a result of these close relationships, the Sound Public Schools created performance assessments in reading and writing and developed additional opportunities for teachers to provide assistance to students in skill areas where they experience problems or have academic weaknesses.

In the Sound Public Schools situation, accountability requirements are viewed as an opportunity for the teachers and administrators to find ways to analyze data to create better instructional responses. Their approach has meaning for what you do as a teacher. You must be able to use data to improve teaching practices. Table 11.9 is a model to help teachers focus on questions and data that will foster enhanced instructional effectiveness.

Clearly, accountability is creating threats and opportunities. The threats are being stressed by people like Alfie Kohn who argue that excessive testing mitigates student intrinsic motivation.[64] Students are simply, critics suggest, being tested to death—in some school districts one-sixth of the school year is devoted to testing. Proponents of testing, on the other hand, assert that testing is essential to help monitor student progress. Tests help identify student weaknesses, and teachers can then intervene, remediate, and create ways to ensure student success.

What you need to know is that accountability is here for the foreseeable future. It will likely influence what and how you teach. You should try to find ways to create opportunities from what some would view as threats. Find ways to link teaching to assessment.

table 11.8   **Smithville's 2001–2002 Preliminary Proficiency Test Results (to be reported on the 2003 School District Report Card mailed to parents in February 2003)**

| | **Percentage of Students Passing the Test** | | |
Performance Standards	*2001–2002 Minimum State Performance*	*2001–2002 Results in Smithville*	*Did Your 2001–2002 Performance Meet the Standard?*
Grade 4 Performance Standards			
1. Citizenship	75%	85.9%	Yes
2. Mathematics	75%	79.0%	Yes
3. Reading	75%	83.8%	Yes
4. Writing	75%	92.1%	Yes
5. Science	75%	82.2%	Yes
Grade 6—Class of 2008—Spring 2002			
6. Citizenship	75%	89.7%	Yes
7. Mathematics	75%	83.1%	Yes
8. Reading	75%	78.1%	Yes
9. Writing	75%	95.6%	Yes
10. Science	75%	77.2%	Yes
Grade 9—Class of 2005—Spring 2002			
11. Citizenship	75%	95.6%	Yes
12. Mathematics	75%	92.9%	Yes
13. Reading	75%	97.7%	Yes
14. Writing	75%	97.9%	Yes
15. Science	75%	94.5%	Yes
Grade 9 (tenth-grade students)			
16. Citizenship	85%	98.5%	Yes
17. Mathematics	85%	96.7%	Yes
18. Reading	85%	99.5%	Yes
19. Writing	85%	99.8%	Yes
20. Science	85%	98.0%	Yes
21. Student Attendance Rate	93%	95.6%	Yes
22. Graduation Rate	90%	95.9%	Yes

Source: Ohio Department of Education. Columbus, Ohio. Smithville is a pseudonym for one of Ohio's 612 school districts.

table 11.9   How Teachers Can Be Data Savvy

1. *Identify questions related to student performance:* You are likely to be most interested in information related to your classroom, but schoolwide, districtwide, and statewide patterns can also be informative.

2. *Identify data and gather necessary information:* Take into account demographic information, such as gender, race, eligibility for free or reduced lunch, and language spoken at home. Student responses to individual test questions tell you things that you can't learn from a single test score.

3. *Examine and use data:* Look at student performance in focused areas to target particular groups for assistance. Examine data from previous years. Regardless of how convincing patterns look, do not jump to conclusions. Look beneath the surface and ask more questions.

4. *Ask useful questions:*

   • How does performance for individuals and groups relate to state standards?

   • Is there variation across content areas?

   • How does the performance compare with that of other like groups, such as among students, schools, districts, states, and across the nation?

   • Are there data trends over time?

   • Are there existing initiatives in the school, district, or classroom that might help improve student performance? On the basis of what evidence?

   • What are the implications for your instructional practices or for your curriculum?

   • Do your findings suggest that you need more professional development?

   • How might other stakeholders benefit from this information?

Source: Penny Noyce, David Preda, and Rob Traver. "Creating Data-Driven Schools." *Educational Leadership* (February 2000): 55.

The best way to do that is to know the academic standards (for your state) in your teaching area, then to structure instruction and assessments around those standards, and to do so in a way that helps students grow as learners. This prescription sounds easy, but it will take great pedagogical skill on your part.

QUESTIONS FOR REFLECTION

The accountability emphasis has put real pressure on teachers and school administrators. The large-scale testing and accountability mania of the past decade has produced heated debate about the efficacy of testing—are teachers gearing instruction to just raise test scores or are they really promoting student learning? That is, are teachers simply teaching to the test to make themselves look good? This question is drawing considerable discussion. What do you think? Is it wrong to teach to the test? Does such an emphasis limit or promote student learning?

Also being debated is whether the testing is causing some students to drop out of school altogether. Quite simply, many students who cannot cope with the high stakes may be coping by dropping out. Is this circumstance avoidable? How?

technology viewpoint

Technology Viewpoint from a Classroom Teacher

Jackie Marshall Arnold
K–12 Media Specialist

 Evaluating students can be a challenging and time-consuming process. Technology applications exist to make the process more meaningful to students and less time intensive for teachers. Two technology tools that support the evaluation process are electronic grade books and electronically created rubrics.

Highly flexible and robust grading programs are available for teachers to use in their evaluation process. Software programs such as Grade Machine (http://www.mistycity.com/), ThinkWave Educator(http://www.thinkwave.com/), and Gradebook (http://www.gradebook.com/) are high-quality programs for purchase for teachers to use in their evaluation and grading. When selecting a program to use, an effective teacher will want to look for some specific features in the software program. First, know the computer that you will be using and make sure it can meet the requirements of the software package. Second, think about your evaluation practices, what you currently do and what you would like to do. Make sure the package that you choose meets your needs. Third, preview the package to verify that it has the features that you want and that it is easy to use. Many now provide the option of Internet use, al-lowing for example progress reports to be sent through e-mail. Fourth, verify that the package comes with customer support should you need assistance at any point. Finally, check with your building or district technology coordinator to confirm that the software is compatible with and acceptable to district policy.

Effective teachers often use rubrics to evaluate student work. The creation of quality rubrics can be time intensive. A technology tool exists that will allow you easily to create a rubric or to use an already created rubric for any subject matter. Rubistar (http://rubistar.4teachers.org) is a high-quality site that provides teachers an easy step-by-step process to create his or her own personalized rubrics or use ones already designed. Categories of created rubrics are easily accessible for oral projects, multimedia projects, science, math, and more. Teachers can click on any subject area and view the previously created rubrics. Any of these can then be customized and saved for continued access. A teacher can also choose to create his or her own rubric following the step-by-step directions provided at the site. Any of the created rubrics can then be saved at the site and accessed with the rubric's identification number and a password.

Effective teachers value the importance of evaluation in the teaching and learning process. By using technology applications to support the evaluative process, effective teachers can build quality evaluative practices that benefit themselves and, most importantly, their students.

Theory into Practice

We live in groups, and regardless of how noncompetitive we want others to be, we will always be evaluating people and making comparisons. As teachers you are expected to assess your students and to give them a grade. You need to temper your judgments with balance and humanness. Give your students the benefit of the doubt and try to reduce the anxiety and stress that often accompany the testing and grading process.

Following are questions to consider for improving your own grading system.

1. Does your evaluation system coincide with your instructional objectives? And are those objectives clearly linked to the school district curriculum guide and state academic content standards?
2. Do you make use of previous evaluation information for purposes of beginning instruction?

3. Is your grading system understood by your students?
4. Does your grading system adequately represent the content and skills you expect students to attain?
5. Are your grades derived from multiple sources (tests, quizzes, homework, papers, projects, class participation, and so forth)? Are these sources weighted according to importance?
6. Do students know in advance how grades are to be determined?
7. Is your grading system fair and objective? Does it consider the students' abilities, previous achievement, and maturity level?
8. Does your grading system enable students to demonstrate their progress and capabilities?
9. Do you use both formative and summative evaluation techniques? Are you willing to modify or reteach content, based on evaluation results?
10. Does your grading system coincide with school policy or school guidelines?

Summary

1. The reasons for evaluating students include motivating students, providing feedback to students and teachers, informing parents, and making selection decisions.
2. Four types of evaluation are placement, diagnostic, formative, and summative.
3. Sources of information for evaluation in addition to tests and quizzes include classroom discussion and activity, homework, notebooks, reports, research papers, and peer evaluations.
4. Grades are based on absolute or relative scales. Alternative grading practices include contracts, mastery grading, and grades for effort and progress.
5. Portfolios provide another vehicle for showing what students have learned and how they are progressing.
6. The conventional report card emphasizes basic subject areas and uses letters to designate grades; more contemporary methods of reporting include mastery and progress reports, statements about progress, and performance assessments.
7. The cumulative record is a legal document that includes important data about the student's performance and behavior in school; it follows the student throughout his or her school career.
8. Communication with parents takes place in the form of report cards, conferences, and letters.
9. Accountability systems are now in place for teachers.

Questions to Consider

1. Can a teacher be objective in evaluating student performance? Explain.
2. How would you distinguish between placement, diagnostic, formative, and summative evaluation?
3. How might you improve your own grading practice compared to that of teachers you had in school?
4. What are the differences between absolute and relative standards in grading? Which do you prefer? Why?
5. Why is it desirable to use several sources of data when arriving at a grade for a student?
6. Are there instances when alignment between standards, assessment, and accountability are not possible?
7. What testing systems are mandated in the state in which you will teach? What accountability systems are in place?

Things to Do

1. From your past school experiences, list some examples of inappropriate evaluation techniques.
2. Outline a grading procedure you expect to follow as a teacher.
3. Visit local schools, obtain sample report cards, and discuss their major characteristics in class. Analyze how various report cards differ.
4. Pretend you are about to have a general conference with a parent for the first time. Discuss with your classmates what topics might be important to include in a conference.
5. Examine the test scores for area school districts near where you are located. What are the high-performing districts? The low-performing districts? Are some districts in categories that you would not expect?

Recommended Readings

Airasian, Peter. *Classroom Assessment: Concepts and Applications,* 4th ed. New York: McGraw-Hill, 2000. This practical text examines how assessment and grading procedures can be used to enhance instruction and learning.

Barr, John R. *Parents Assuring Student Success.* Bloomington, Ind.: National Evaluation Service, 2000. This is a wonderful resource that teachers can use to help parents understand how they can support a student's academic learning within the classroom.

Bloom, Benjamin S., J. Thomas Hastings, and George F. Madaus. *Handbook of Formative and Summative Evaluation of Student Learning.* New York: McGraw-Hill, 1971. This mammoth-size text can serve as an excellent source for technical questions about evaluation.

Gronlund, Norman E., and Robert L. Linn. *Measurement and Assessment in Teaching,* 8th ed. Upper Saddle River, N.J.: Prentice-Hall, 1999. This text offers an appreciation of the advantages and disadvantages of various tests and evaluation procedures.

Johnson, Dale D, and Bonnie Johnson. *High Stakes: Children, Testing, and Failure in American Schools,* Lanham, Maryland: Rowman and Littlefield, 2002. This is a thoughtful analysis of accountability and its impact on students in American schools.

Popham, W. James. *Educational Evaluation,* 3d ed. Needham Heights, Mass.: Allyn and Bacon, 1992. This work presents various models and strategies for evaluating student outcomes. Popham is one of the most prolific writers in the area of assessment and evaluation. His most recent book, *The Truth About Testing* (2001), which is published by the Association for Supervision and Curriculum Development, is also an excellent resource.

Tucker, Marc and Judy B. Codding. *Standards for Our Schools.* San Francisco: Jossey-Bass, 1998. A thoughtful analysis of standards, assessment and accountability that describes both the political and practical implications of standards-based reform.

Key Terms

absolute standards   514
computerized recordkeeper   520
continuous progress grading   517
contract grading   516
cumulative record   522
diagnostic evaluation   496
formal evaluation   498
formative evaluation   496
informal evaluation   498
mastery grading   517
mastery report card   519
placement evaluation   495
quizzes   499
relative grading   515
standards-based grading   512
summative evaluation   497

End Notes

1. Kay Burke. *Authentic Learning,* 3d ed. Arlington Heights, Ill.: Merrill Prentice Hall, 1999.
2. Philip W. Jackson. *Life in Classrooms,* 2d ed. New York: Teachers College Press, Columbia University, 1990, p. 19.
3. Bruce W. Tuckman. *Measuring Educational Outcomes,* 2d ed. San Diego: Harcourt Brace Jovanovich, 1985, p. 300. Also see Bruce W. Tuckman, "The Essay Test: A Look at the Advantages and Disadvantages." *NASSP Bulletin* (October 1993): 20–27.
4. Norman E. Gronlund and Robert L. Linn. *Measurement and Evaluation in Teaching.* 6th ed. New York: Macmillan, 1990.
5. Jeanne Ellis Ormrod. *Educational Psychology,* 4th ed., Upper Saddle River, N.J.: Prentice Hall, 2003.
6. Michael Scriven. "The Methodology of Evaluation." In R. W. Tyler, R. Gagné, and M. Scriven (eds.), *Perspectives on Curriculum Evaluation.* Chicago: Rand McNally, 1967, pp. 39–83.
7. Benjamin S. Bloom, J. Thomas Hastings, and George F. Madaus. *Handbook on Formative and Summative Evaluation of Student Learning.* New York: McGraw-Hill, 1971, p. 20.
8. Paul Black and Dylan Wiliam. "Inside the Black Box: Raising Standards Through Classroom Assessment." *Phi Delta Kappan* (October 1998): 140.
9. Norman E. Gronlund. *How to Make Achievements Tests and Assessments,* 5th ed. Needham Heights, Mass.: Allyn and Bacon, 1993. Robert M. Thorndike et al. *Measurement and Evaluation in Psychology and Education,* 5th ed. New York: Macmillan, 1991.
10. Jackson. *Life in Classrooms,* p. 19.
11. Ibid., p. 20.
12. Nancy S. Cole. "Conceptions of Educational Achievement." *Educational Researcher* (April 1990): 2–7. Penelope L. Peterson. "Toward an Understanding of What We Know About School Learning," *Review of Educational Research* (Fall 1993): 319–326. W. James Popham. "Why Standardized Tests Don't Measure Educational Quality." *Educational Leadership* (March 1999): 8–15.
13. Benjamin S. Bloom, George F. Madaus, and J. Thomas Hastings. *Evaluation to Improve Learning.* New York: McGraw-Hill, 1981. Tom Kubiszyn and Gary Borich. *Educational Testing and Measurement,* 4th ed. New York: HarperCollins, 1993. Merlin C. Wittrock and Eva L. Baker. *Testing and Cognition.* Needham Heights, Mass.: Allyn and Bacon, 1991.
14. Jan La Bonty and Kathy Everts-Danielson. "Alternative Assessment and Feedback in Methods Courses." *Clearing House* (January–February 1992): 186–190. Allan C. Ornstein, "Assessing Without Testing," *Elementary Principal* (January 1994): 16–18.
15. David Johnson and Frank P. Johnson. *Joining Together: Group Theory and Group Skills,* 5th ed. Needham Heights, Mass.: Allyn and Bacon, 1994.
16. Black and Wiliam. "Inside the Black Box," pp. 143–144.
17. Herbert J. Walberg. "Homework's Powerful Effects on Learning." *Educational Leadership* (April 1985): 75–79. Melanie F. Sikorski, Richard P. Niemiec, and Herbert J. Walberg. "Best Teaching Practices," *NASSP Bulletin* (April 1994): 50–54.
18. Thomas L. Good and Jere E. Brophy. *Looking in Classrooms,* 8th ed., Reading, Mass: Addison Wesley, 2000.
19. M. R. Moran, B. S. Myles, and M. S. Shank. "Variables in Eliciting Writing Samples." *Educational Measurement* (Fall 1991): 23–26. Carol Ann Tomlinson. "Invitations to Learn." *Educational Leadership* (September 2002): 6–11.
20. Kenneth A. Kiewra. "Providing the Instructor's Notes: An Effective Addition to Student Note-Taking." *Educational Psychologist* (Winter 1985): 33–39. Kenneth A. Kiewra. "Aids to Lecture Learning." *Educational Psychologist* (Winter 1991): 37–53.
21. Maureen McLaughlin and Mary Beth Allen. *Guided Comprehension: A Teaching Model for Grades 3–8.* Newark, Del.: International Reading Association, 2002.

22. Kieran Egan. "Start With What the Student Knows or With What the Student Can Imagine" *Phi Delta Kappan* (February 2003): 443–445. Allison Zmuda and Mary Tomaino. "A Contract for the High School Classroom." *Educational Leadership* (March 1999): 59–61.

23. Ibid., p. 60.

24. David W. Johnson and Roger J. Johnson, *Learning Together and Alone,* 5th ed. Boston, Mass.: Allyn and Bacon, 1998.

25. Elizabeth G. Cohen. *Designing Groupwork.* New York: Teachers College Press, Columbia University, 1994. Peter M. Martorella, *Elementary Social Studies.* Boston: Little Brown, 1985. Also see Alfie Kohn. *What to Look for in a Classroom.* San Francisco: Jossey Bass, 2000.

26. Robert L. Ebel and David A. Frisbie. *Essentials of Educational Measurement,* 5th ed. Needham Heights, Mass.: Allyn and Bacon, 1991. Gary Natriello and James McPartland. *Adjustments in High School Teachers' Grading Criteria.* Baltimore: Johns Hopkins University Press, 1988.

27. Ellis D. Evans and Ruth A. Engleberg. "Student Perceptions of School Grading," *Journal of Research and Development in Education* (Winter 1988): 45–54. Mary A. Lundeberg and Paul W. Fox. "Do Laboratory Findings on Test Expectancy Generalize to Classroom Outcomes?" *Review of Educational Research* (Spring 1991): 94–106.

28. William W. Cooley. "State-Wide Student Assessment," *Educational Measurement* (Winter 1991): 3–6. Deborah Meier. "Standardization Versus Standards." *Phi Delta Kappan* (November 2002): 190–198.

29. Robert E. Slavin. "Classroom Reward Structure: An Analytical and Practical Review." *Review of Educational Research* (Fall 1977): 633–650. Robert E. Slavin. "Synthesis of Research on Cooperative Learning." *Educational Leadership* (February 1991): 71–82.

30. Neville Bennett and Charles Desforges. "Matching Classroom Tasks to Students' Attainments." *Elementary School Journal* (January 1988): 221–234. W. James Popham. "Appropriateness of Teachers' Test-Preparation." *Educational Measurement* (Winter 1991): 12–15. Robert E. Stake. "The Teacher, Standardized Testing, and Prospects of Revolution." *Phi Delta Kappan* (November 1991): 243–247.

31. Robert L. Bangert-Drowns. "The Instructional Effect of Feedback in Test-Like Events." *Review of Educational Research* (Summer 1991): 213–238. Gary Natriello and Edward L. McDill. "Performance Standards, Student Effort on Homework and Academic Achievement." *Sociology of Education* (January 1986): 18–31. Alvin C. Rose. "Homework Preferences." *NASSP Bulletin* (March 1994): 65–75. Marge Scherer. "Do Students Care about Learning?" *Educational Leadership* (September 2002): 12–17.

32. Natriello. "The Impact of Evaluation Processes on Students." Marv Nottingham. "Grading Practices—Watching out for Land Mines." *NASSP Bulletin* (April 1988): 24–28.

33. Robert F. Madgic. "The Point System of Grading: A Critical Appraisal." *NASSP Bulletin* (April 1988): 29–34. Margot A. Olson. "The Distortion of the Grading System." *Clearing House* (November–December 1990): 77–79.

34. E. D. Hirsch. *The Schools We Need.* New York: Doubleday, 1996, pp. 181–182.

35. Susan A. Colby. "Grading in a Standards-Based System." *Educational Leadership* (March 1999): 52–55.

36. Ibid., p. 53.

37. Ibid.

38. Ibid.

39. Paul S. George. "A+ Accountability in Florida?" *Educational Leadership* (September 2001): 28–32.

40. *State High School Exams: A Baseline Report.* Washington, D.C.: Center on Education Policy, 2002.

41. William A. Mehrens and Irvin J. Lehmann. *Measurement and Evaluation in Education and Psychology,* 4th ed. Fort Worth, Tex.: Holt, Rinehart, and Winston, 1991. Payne, *Measuring and Evaluating Educational Outcomes.*

42. Carole Ames. "Motivation: What Teachers Need to Know." *Teachers College Record* (Spring 1991): 409–421. Pamela A. Moss. "Shifting Consequences of Validity in Educational Measurement," *Review of Educational Research* (Fall 1992): 229–258. Lynda A. Baloche. *The Cooperative Classroom.* Columbus, Ohio: Prentice Hall, 1998.

43. David A. Payne. *Measuring and Evaluating Educational Outcomes.* New York: Macmillan, 1992.

44. Benjamin S. Bloom. "The 2 Sigma Problem: The Search for Methods of Instruction as Effective as One-to-One Tutoring." *Educational Researcher* (June–July 1984): 4–16. Robert E. Slavin. "Grouping for Instruction in the Elementary School." *Educational Psychologist* (Spring 1987): 109–128. Robert E. Slavin. "On Mastery Learning and Mastery Teaching." *Educational Leadership* (April 1989): 77–79.

45. Richard Arends. *Learning to Teach,* 4th ed. Boston: McGraw-Hill, 1998, p. 228.

46. S. Alan Cohen and Joan S. Hyman. "Can Fantasies Become Facts?" *NASSP Bulletin* (Spring 1991): 20–23. George F. Madaus. "The Effect of Important Tests on Students." *Phi Delta Kappan* (November 1991): 226–231.

47. Harold Stevenson and James W. Stigler. *The Learning Gap.* New York: Summit Books, 1992: pp. 97–98.

48. Edward L. Vockell and Donald Kopenec. "Record Keeping Without Tears." *Clearing House* (April 1989): 355–359.

49. Ibid.

50. John Salvia and James Ysseldyke. *Assessment,* 8th ed. Boston: Houghton Mifflin, 2001.

51. F. Leon Paulson, Pearl R. Paulson, and Carol A. Meyer. "What Makes a Portfolio a Portfolio?" *Educational Leadership* (February 1991): 60–64. Richard J. Shavelson and Gail P. Baxter. "What We've Learned About Assessing Hands-On Science." *Educational Leadership* (May 1992): 20–25.

52. Judith A. Arter and Vicki Spandel. "Using Portfolios of Student Work in Instruction and Assessment." *Educational Measurement* (Spring 1992): 36–44. Doris Sperling. "What's Worth an 'A'?: Setting Standards Together." *Educational Leadership* (February 1993): 73–75. Baloche. *The Cooperative Classroom.*

53. Stephen Chappuis and Richard J. Stiggins. "Classroom Assessment for Learning." *Educational Leadership* (September 2002): 40–44. Darlene M. Frazier and F. Leon Paulson, "How Portfolios Motivate Reluctant Workers," *Educational Leadership* (May 1992): 62–65.

54. Arter and Spandel. "Using Portfolios of Student Work in Instruction and Assessment." Richard J. Stiggins. "Relevant Classroom Assessment Trainers for Teachers." *Educational Measurement* (Spring 1991): 7–12.

55. Julie Heiman Savitch and Leslie Ann Serling. "I Wouldn't Know I Was Smart If I Didn't Come to Class." In A. Lin Goodwin (ed.) *Assessment for Equity and Inclusion.* New York: Routledge, 1997, pp. 157–158.

56. Allan C. Ornstein. "The Nature of Grading." *Clearing House* (April 1989): 365–369.

57. Joyce L. Epstein. "Parents' Reactions to Teacher Practices of Parent Involvement." *Elementary School Journal* (January 1986): 277–294. Joyce L. Epstein. "School/Family/Community Partnerships: Caring for the Children We Share." *Phi Delta Kappan* (May 1995). 701–712.

58. Joyce L. Epstein. "How Do We Improve Programs for Parent Involvement?" *Educational Horizons* (Winter 1988): 58–59. Joyce L. Epstein. "Parent Involvement: What Research Says to Administrators." *Education and Urban Society* (February 1987): 119–36.

59. James P. Comer and Norris M. Haynes. "Parent Involvement in Schools." *Elementary School Journal* (January 1991): 271–277. Anne T. Henderson. "An Ecologically Balanced Approach to Academic Improvement." *Educational Horizons* (Winter 1988): 60–62. Judith A. Vandegrift and Andrea L. Greene. "Rethinking Parent Involvement." *Educational Leadership* (September 1992): 57–59.

60. Jeffrey L. Gelfer and Peggy B. Perkins. "Effective Communication with Parents." *Childhood Education* (October 1987): 19–22.

61. Leonard H. Clark and Irving S. Starr. *Secondary and Middle School Teaching Methods,* 5th ed. New York: Macmillan, 1986. Richard Kindsvatter, William Wilen, and Margaret Ishler. *Dynamics of Effective Teaching,* 2d ed. New York: Longman, 1992.

62. Allan C. Ornstein. "Parent Conferencing: Recommendations and Guidelines." *Kappa Delta Pi Record* (Winter 1990): 55–57.

63. Penny Noyce, David Perda, Rob Traver. "Creating Data Driven Schools." *Educational Leadership* (February 2000): 52–55.

64. Alfie Kohn. "Offering Challenges, Creating Cognitive Dissonance." In J. Cynthia McDermott (ed.), *Beyond the Silence.* Portsmouth, N.H.: Heinemann, 1999.

Professional Growth

In the first two sections of this text, we outlined the relationship of the art and science of teaching (Section I) and the skills of teachers (Section II) who seek to create best practice for students. In this section (Chapter 12), we look ahead for you and for the profession. Good teachers necessarily understand that teaching is complex. And to deal with that complexity, they must find ways to push themselves academically and pedagogically.

Professional growth requires that you understand what your professional education experiences (your teacher education program) did and did not do for you. You must then assess how you can grow so that your abilities are expanded, not encapsulated. We begin Chapter 12 with a discussion of the problems facing, and the supports that should be available to, the beginning teacher. Then we describe the variety of assessments that are now used. Finally, we close with a description of collegial associations. Most teachers think of these as the AFT or NEA, but other associations are just as important, in particular those that are related to the subject, grade level, (or in some cases the special-type student) you are teaching.

Your professional preparation program provided you with many ideas, but for those ideas to have power, they need to be used. Similarly, this book documents a lot of what is now known about teaching. And even as this book is being written, new data is emerging. For example, in the 1960s, James Coleman argued that family socioeconomic status was the strongest influence on student achievement. In the 1990s and early 2000s, researchers began to challenge that notion. William Sanders (University of Tennessee) asserted teachers are an equally important factor influencing student achievement. What you do in the classroom does make a difference for students. And, what you do to sustain your professional growth will ultimately influence how students view their own learning.

Professional Growth

Pathwise criteria relevant to the content of this chapter:

- Reflecting on the extent to which the learning goals were met (D1)
- Building professional relationships with colleagues to share teaching insights and to coordinate learning activities for students (D3)

INTASC principles relevant to the content of this chapter:

- The teacher is a reflective practitioner who continually evaluates the effects of his/her choices and actions on others (students, parents, and other professionals in the learning community) and who actively seeks out opportunities to grow professionally. (P 9)
- The teacher fosters relationships with school colleagues, parents, and agencies in the larger community to support students' learning and well-being. (P 10)

focusing questions

1. Is teacher education necessary for teacher professional status?

2. What are some methods for improving the support of and learning opportunities for teachers during the first few years of their teaching careers?

3. How does self-evaluation improve a person's capabilities as a teacher? What methods of self-evaluation might a teacher use?

4. How do peer evaluation and supervisory evaluation contribute to evaluating teachers?

5. What sources and products can supply information to be used for teacher evaluation and growth?

6. How do professional organizations serve teacher development?

You can always improve your teaching. The extent of improvement is related to how much improvement you need to meet the learning needs of students and how hard you work at it. Beginning or novice teachers, in particular, should expect to encounter problems and frustrations, but they will also learn from their experiences and improve their pedagogical skills over time.

If you hope to be an effective teacher who enjoys his or her work, not only will you need to be well prepared for each day's lessons, but you will also need to acquire a variety of skills in working with people—students, colleagues, supervisors, and parents. You will need to have a good general education, knowledge of the subject you teach, and training in teaching at a particular grade level with several different types of students. Though there is a lot of controversy about what qualities characterize effective teachers, there is reasonable consensus that the teachers who foster enhanced student achievement have high verbal ability, are well grounded in the discipline(s) they teach, and know how to translate that content into good learning opportunities for students. The preceding chapters in this book dealt with methods of teaching and the principles of practice that determine when those different methods should be used. This final chapter is intended to help you consider what it means to grow as a teacher and what sources of support are available as you begin your professional journey.

Reforming Teacher Education

Professions have a monopoly on certain knowledge that separates their members from the general public and allows them to exercise control over those who are professionals. Indeed, years ago, one social critic observed that professions were nothing more than a conspiracy against the laity. Members of a profession have mastered a body of abstract knowledge that establishes their expertise and protects the public from quacks, untrained amateurs, and special interest groups. Further, they can use that abstract knowledge to deal with particular problems or cases.[1]

There is, however, no agreed-upon body of abstract knowledge that clearly constitutes what might be described as good education or teaching. Whereas the behavioral sciences, physical sciences, and professions such as law and medicine are guided by extensive rules of procedure and established methodologies, education has no agreed-upon set of procedures to guide teachers in the classroom as they diagnose student learning problems, make inferences about what to do, and then make decisions about how to proceed.

As a result, many talk about education as if they were experts—resulting in a great deal of conflicting and sometimes negative conversation about teachers and the pedagogy of teaching. Another result of this ill-defined body of knowledge is that the content of teacher education courses varies from state to state, among teacher preparation institutions within states, and even within specific departments and schools of education. Thus, according to Kenneth Sirotnik, "two students in the same program [at the same college or university] could end up with very different experiences."[2] Given such variation, what does it mean to be professionally prepared for the classroom? Do teacher education students (do you?) know how to diagnose the learning problems of students and then make informed decisions on how to proceed?

Becoming a Teacher

Julian C. Stanley

Professor of Psychology and Director of the Study of
Mathematically Precocious Youth (SMPY)
Johns Hopkins University

 I entered teaching during the Great Depression, perhaps chiefly because of having graduated from a state teacher's college. The year was 1937, and I was barely nineteen years old. Teaching positions for high school chemistry teachers were not scarce, but the ones offered me paid little: $75 per month for seven months in a Georgia village, and the munificent sum of $120 per month for ten months in the county surrounding Atlanta. Of course, those dollars were worth far more than now. I began in the lowest socioeconomic level high school the Atlanta area had—only white students.

Imagine my surprise when, shortly before school started, the assistant principal told me I would be teaching commercial arithmetic to ninth graders and general business training to eighth graders, subjects of which I (who had graduated in the "classical" curriculum from another high school in the same Fulton County system) had never heard. Other teachers "owned" chemistry and physics. I was even more disconcerted to discover that about two-thirds of my arithmetic students had failed the subject the preceding year.

I somehow managed to survive the nine months (including five classes, management of large study halls, and many other duties). During my four-and-a-half-year high school teaching career, which ended when World War II called me into service, I taught ten different subjects, including spelling, remedial mathematics, and English.

Other aspects were strange. We had only six days of sick leave each school year at half pay, so my only absence in 810 days was for three consecutive days of influenza. Women could not teach in high school initially unless they were in home economics or library science; they had to start in elementary schools, no matter what their college major had been. One I knew served six years there, at far less pay than high school teachers received, before getting to teach mathematics in the same high schools that had hired me straight out of college.

Women could not even get married and continue to teach in this school system. Fortunately, these utterly sexist rules were changed after the war.

Maybe in the "good old days" discipline was considerably easier than it is in some schools nowadays, but in many respects teaching is more attractive now than then. Also, the type of college I attended, which prepared only for teaching, has virtually vanished. You have more choices. Consider them well!

In short, there seems to be no overriding philosophy or body of defined abstract knowledge in teacher education programs, no agreed-upon pedagogy that must be learned by all candidates, and no set of criteria for making professional decisions in classrooms. This situation is clearly starting to change, but the diversity of views is still more common than consensus about what abstract knowledge teachers should use and apply. Nearly everyone has his or her own values, philosophy, and views about pedagogy. Insight and intuition—what some call the "art of teaching"—tend to rule in far too many institutions instead of scientifically based procedures, as in the case of medicine, or professional procedures, as in the case of law.

Although most education departments and education schools continuously formulate committees to revise and improve teacher education and continuously debate the course content, far too many decisions are still made on the basis of personal ideologies and institutional politics. The result is often a hodgepodge of professional courses packaged together as a program, driven by state guidelines of faculty member interests, and varying from one teacher-training institution to another. Some might argue this is an unfair criticism of teacher education, but mandates to improve and better coordinate teacher education efforts still go largely unheeded, though there are clear signs of change. Evidence of the problem can be seen in the *Improving Teacher Quality* report issued by *Education Week* in early 2003. In that report, no state was given an *A* grade for its overall approach to teacher quality, and well over half the states received grades of *C* or *D*.[3] Though there are many reasons for the low grades, a primary one relates to the lack of common abstract knowledge that educators can use to ground professional program content.

The debate over teacher preparation goes back to the 1960s when James Conant pointed out that professors of arts and science and professors of education were at war with each other over several important questions: the proper mix of courses, who should teach these courses (professors in content areas or professors of education), and even whether courses in pedagogy were worthwhile at all.[4] James Koerner described the problem further in his highly critical book *The Miseducation of American Teachers*. Koerner argued that, by requiring too many education courses—as many as 60 hours at some teacher colleges—and by making these courses too "soft," colleges of education were producing teachers versed in pedagogy at the expense of academic content.[5] Both critics argued that the academic quality of teachers needed to be upgraded.

Quality of teacher education was apparently still a problem in the 1970s and 1980s, as a substantial percentage of prospective teachers were unable to demonstrate minimum competency on basic skills and writing tests. Critics argued that prospective teachers were weaker academically than their professional peers. Whether this "competency problem" is still manifest is now a matter of continued debate, but there are signs that teachers are just as academically able as others who attend college. For example, some reports during the 1990s suggested that the average SAT scores of prospective teachers were slightly above the national average for entering college students and that the performance of education and of noneducation students in general education coursework was quite similar.[6]

Critics suggest that certain factors are keeping good people out of teaching: pay, as compared to that of other "skilled" professions; rigid teacher education programs with many requirements; too little flexibility for employers to hire those persons they want to employ; and a compensation system that is based far too much on years of experience and advanced graduate work and far too little on the actual performance of teachers in terms of fostering student learning.

Even teacher education advocates such as John Goodlad and the authors of this book have pointed to a host of shortcomings in teacher education; namely, that departments and schools of education are fraught with instability, they lack institutional identity, their research base is limited, their programs often lack curricular cohesiveness, and professors of education too easily yield to personal ideology (rather than scientifically based research) to determine what constitutes good teaching.[7] In short, teacher education programs are not sufficiently in control of their own mission or policies. E. D. Hirsch writes,

> The very thing which Horace Mann called upon teacher-training schools to do and which the American public assumes that such schools *are* doing—the teaching of effective pedagogy—is a domain of training that, according to both sympathetic and unsympathetic ob-

servers, gets short shrift in our education schools. Instead, it is mainly theory, and highly questionable theory at that, which gets more attention in education-school courses. That point should be stated even more strongly: not only do our teacher-training schools decline to put a premium on nuts-and-bolts classroom effectiveness, but they promote ideas that actually run counter to consensus research into teacher effectiveness.[8]

Goodlad proffered in the 1980s and 1990s nineteen recommendations, or what he called "postulates," for improving teacher education. They centered around screening candidates on the basis of moral and ethical decency, establishing well-defined program procedures and measurable outcomes, enhancing research and reflective practices, expanding the education faculty to include the entire university and public schools, resisting curriculum regulation by external authorities, and taking responsibility for the induction year of teaching.[9] Bold, new suggestions? Although there are differences in emphasis, much of what Goodlad advocates has been argued for before—from the time the findings of Conant and Koerner were published up to present-day reform movements such as the Carnegie Task Force on Teachers, the Holmes Group, and the National Network for Educational Renewal.[10]

The problem of teacher education is an ongoing national concern that needs to be addressed by establishing national standards for teacher preparation. The National Council for Accreditation of Teacher Education (NCATE) has set standards for professional content that outline the qualifications of the faculty who teach at NCATE teacher education courses. However, by the early 2000s only half of the 1,200 colleges involved in preparing teachers were accredited by NCATE.

Although many states have collaborative agreements with NCATE, teacher-training institutions can still receive state approval even if they are not accredited by NCATE. Moreover, the graduates of non-NCATE accredited institutions find jobs just as readily as graduates of accredited institutions. The current director of NCATE, Arthur Wise, hopes to remedy this confusing situation by making all teacher-education institutions measure up to more rigorous national standards by a single accrediting organization—and both the American Federation of Teachers and National Education Association support this idea.[11] Nonetheless, the confusion will persist until educators reach greater agreement about the candidates most likely to succeed as teachers (what combination of variables predicts teacher success?), the basic body of professional knowledge that teachers need to learn (what foundations and pedagogical courses are needed in order to teach?), and the clinical and field experiences needed to prepare teachers for being thrust into the classroom on their own.

You should find out if the institution you attend is NCATE accredited. If it is not, it might hold Teacher Education Accreditation Council (TEAC) accreditation. Though the number of TEAC institutions is quite small, TEAC still represents an important alternative that, like NCATE, seeks to ensure that teachers prepared by institutions have the skills essential for teaching success. If your institution is not accredited, you might ask why not. Is it because of cost? Discuss with a faculty member the advantages and disadvantages of institutional accreditation.

The preparation of teachers tends to be very ideological. Everyone has an opinion on how to prepare teachers and on whether extensive teacher preparation is even necessary. During the late 1990s and early 2000s some new critics of teacher preparation programs emerged. None of those voices has been more prominent than that of

Chester E. Finn Jr., President of The Thomas B. Fordham Foundation.[12] Finn has attempted to cause policymakers to loosen, if not eliminate, extant requirements for those entering the field of education. To Finn, teaching has a weak knowledge base, and what teachers need is more content and less pedagogy, especially progressivist pedagogy. In essence, by opening up the field to all who want to teach, classrooms will be accessible to many intellectually capable people who now decide against teaching because of all the requirements. Further, some individuals will not be "force fed" progressivist ideology.

Progressivist pedagogy includes ideas like constructivism and inquiry learning—student-centered learning approaches, which tend to be emphasized in teacher education programs. Finn and others, such as Jeanne Chall, argue that teacher-centered instruction, which this book describes more specifically as *direct instruction,* is the best way to foster enhanced academic results for students. They claim that such direct instruction strategies are especially powerful for children who come from poor families or for "those [with] learning difficulties at all social and economic levels."[13]

Some of the people who critiqued this book argued for more constructivism (more student-centered strategies) because that is what they emphasize in their education classes. Critics like Finn would argue that young people don't need more progressivist ideas (because those show no real history of success), and instead they need more teacher-centered approaches and more content. We have tried to achieve a balance between progressivist and traditionalist ideas, but it is difficult to do. Where you teach, who you teach, and what you teach will dictate what approach makes sense. Good teachers know how and when to use constructivism and how and when to use direct instruction. They know how to be both traditional and progressivist. How you teach depends on your goals for instruction. One size does not fit all students in all situations.

This section concludes with an analysis provided by Linda Darling-Hammond, who is one of the staunchest and most articulate defenders of current teacher education programming. Her voice stands in stark contrast to the critics' calls of people like Koerner, Finn and other conservative reformers. Darling-Hammond writes,

> Other research confirms the effectiveness of teachers who comprehend their subject matter, understand student learning and development, know a wide range of teaching methods, and have developed their skills under expert guidance in clinical settings. Over two hundred studies illustrating the positive effects of teacher education contradict the long-standing myth that "teachers are born and not made." This research also makes it clear that teachers need to know much more than the subject matter they teach. Teachers who have had more opportunity to study the processes of learning and teaching are more highly rated and successful with students in fields from early childhood and elementary education to mathematics, science, and vocational education.[14]

The words of Linda Darling-Hammond suggest that good teachers are *born* and *made.* The more effective you are as a teacher, the more your students will learn in your classroom. You can make a difference. That is a scientifically based fact. And you make that difference by being well-read, knowing your subject, and using what you know about how students learn to foster enhanced achievement in what you are having them learn.

Helping the Beginning Teacher

What are the general needs of the beginning teacher? Most schools offer teacher orientation, but in spite of efforts to help teachers succeed, many teachers still encounter adjustment problems. A review of the research on the problems of beginning teachers shows that feelings of isolation; poor understanding of what is expected of them; heavy workloads and extra assignments that they are unprepared to handle; lack of supplies, materials, or equipment; poor physical facilities; and lack of support or help from experienced teachers or supervisors contribute to their feelings of frustration and failure.[15] The result is that many potentially talented and creative teachers find teaching unrewarding and difficult, especially in inner-city schools, with approximately 11 percent leaving after one year of classroom experience and nearly 40 percent of newly hired teachers leaving the profession within five years.[16] The actual percentages vary by state and region. For example, teacher attrition tends to be a bit higher in Southern states than in Northern ones, but the attrition facts suggest that without proper support and positive working conditions, many teachers in all regions will decide to leave teaching.[17]

Problems of Education Students and Beginning Teachers

Several years ago, Frances Fuller suggested a progression in the type of concerns teachers have about teaching. Education students (at the preservice level) are characterized by "nonconcern"; student teachers are characterized by "increased concern"; beginning teachers are preoccupied with "survival concerns"; and experienced teachers focus on the tasks and problems of teachers (they have moved past initial survival) and are more involved with a variety of "self" concerns.[18]

A number of factors may contribute to the increasing concerns and anxieties student and beginning teachers have about the difficulty of teaching, beyond the fact that most people have concerns about the unknown when they start new jobs (especially their first jobs). Clearly, one factor is the content of and experiences associated with introductory teacher education courses, which do not seem to prepare teachers for the realities of the job, even if the course experiences are positive. Another factor is that age and optimism may be inversely related. It takes a few years of seasoning to face reality, and college students at the pre-student teaching level tend to have confidence in their own abilities and to believe they are better equipped than others (older people) to be teachers. What young student cannot, after all, reasonably criticize many former teachers, thinking, "I can do a better job"? But once those same persons confront certain school and classroom realities, their optimism far too often evolves to pessimism—and a decision to leave teaching.

In a recent study, education students and beginning teachers were asked to rank problems they expected in the classroom. Although there was some agreement between the groups in the ranking of important problems, there was significant disagreement on the perceived difficulty of the problems. First-year teachers consistently ranked their perceived problems significantly more difficult than did preservice education students.[19] A logical deduction is that experience brought the "veterans" up against the challenges posed by day-to-day work in the classroom. The major problems they identified centered around workload, improving the academic performance of low-achieving students, dealing with misbehavior and maintaining control, and adapting materials to the needs and abilities of their students.

Numerous reports over the last several years document the shock for the new teacher that accompanies the realities of school and classrooms. Organized programs and internal support systems for beginning teachers are emerging, but they are still uneven in quality.[20] Mentor relations between experienced and beginning teachers and support from colleagues for continued learning and professional development are still exceptions, not the rule, even though they are being mandated by a large number of states and school districts. One of the more highly publicized new teacher support and assessments systems is in Connecticut (see Case Study 12.1). Connecticut's system is not an exception, though it is somewhat unique. As you read the case, look at all the different ways data are collected to help teachers think about and improve their teaching. Such programs, when implemented properly, seem not only to provide teachers with data for self-improvement, but also to be enhancing teacher satisfaction and retention.

Without question, the induction period, the first two or three years of teaching, is critical in developing teachers' capabilities. Beginning teachers should not be left alone to sink or swim. Over thirty states have recently developed induction programs for new teachers, while other states have increased staff development activities, and fifteen states have provided partial funding for such programs.[21] Most important for the professional development of new teachers are the internal support systems and strategies that many schools adopt—that is, the daily support activities and continual learning opportunities.

Common causes of failure of new teachers need to be identified and addressed. One school administrator has identified six general causes of failure that the schools should rectify:

1. *Assignment to difficult classes:* "Good" courses and "good" students are assigned to teachers on the basis of seniority; beginning teachers are given the "dregs" or "leftovers" to teach. A better balance is required (actually the opposite assignments) to permit beginning teachers to survive and learn from their mistakes in the classroom.

2. *Isolation of classrooms from colleagues and supervisors:* The classrooms farthest from the central office are usually assigned to beginning teachers. Isolating the new teacher from experienced teachers contributes to failure. Beginning teachers need to be assigned to rooms near the main office and near experienced teachers to encourage daily communication.

3. *Poor physical facilities:* Classrooms, room fixtures, and equipment are usually assigned on the basis of seniority. Providing the leftovers to new teachers is damaging to morale. A more equitable assignment of facilities is needed.

4. *Burdensome extra class assignments:* Extra class duties are cited as a source of ill feelings more than any other item. New teachers are often assigned burdensome or tough assignments that they were unprepared for and did not expect as teachers, such as yard patrol, hall patrol, cafeteria patrol, or study hall duties. Assignments given to beginning teachers should not be so burdensome that they affect the quality of their teaching.

case study 12.1   Connecticut's Approach to New-Teacher Assessment and Support

Despite growing diversity in the [Connecticut's] student population (increases in minority, poor, and language diverse students), student achievement increased continually and sharply throughout the 1990s. Connecticut students ranked at the top in performance on the National Assessment of Educational Progress in elementary reading and mathematics and in science and writing. The state increased teacher salaries significantly and ensured that low-wealth districts could compete for qualified teachers. State leaders also enforced a stepped-up system of teacher standards and pushed forward with reforms in teacher education. As a result, Connecticut has one of the best-prepared teaching cadres in the nation.

One hallmark of Connecticut's Beginning Educator Support and Training (BEST) system, which was launched in the mid-1980s and has been continually improved, is its beginning teacher mentoring and assessment program. In explaining Connecticut's reading achievement gains, a National Educational Goals Panel report cited the state's teacher policies, especially those associated with beginning teacher assessment and support system, a critical element in its success.

Connecticut replaced a traditional new-teacher "teaching observation" process with an ambitious subject-specific portfolio system based on a more sophisticated approach to teaching and learning. Each district provides ongoing support and portfolio assessment in English, mathematics, biology, chemistry, physics, earth science, general science, special education, elementary education, middle school (4–8) education, history/social studies, art, music, and physical education. Most recently, the state has piloted new-teacher assessments in world languages and bilingual education.

The highly structured teacher portfolio is developed over a two-year period. It comprises lesson logs, videotapes, teacher commentaries, and student work. The new teacher documents a unit of instruction on a significant concept, producing a series of subject-specific lessons, assessing students' learning, and reflecting on the impact of his or her teaching on student achievement. This system is framed by an elaborate support structure, which spans up to three years of a new teacher's career. Provisional certification is contingent on successful portfolio completion, and beginning teachers have learned to take the program seriously.

Mentors in Connecticut meet regularly with first-year teachers to plan instruction and assess their practices (although time available to mentors varies across districts). Mentors observe or videotape first-year teachers' classroom instruction and analyze their teaching and student learning with them. The state currently requires mentors to participate in three days of standardized BEST support-teacher training. During this training, mentors actually assess the work of novices, use specific skills to promote inquiry, relate instructional practice to teaching standards, and provide portfolio-related support.

Since the mid-1990s, the state has offered content-specific seminars for its novice teachers. These seminars are designed by the state Department of Education's teachers-in-residence and are facilitated by teachers, administrators, and teacher educators who are also trained to score beginning teacher portfolios. The year-long seminars (which average twenty-five to thirty hours) help new teachers align unit and lesson objectives, instructional strategies, and assessments. They emphasize the critical connection between student and teacher performance and show novices how to analyze results with that connection in mind. In 2002–2003, the state will pilot distance-learning seminars that will cover portions of this program. The first and last seminars will be regional, on-site sessions; those in between will be accessible online.

Connecticut's portfolio process is reminiscent of the system developed for National Board Certification. New teachers must include a description of their teaching context, a set of lesson plans, two videotapes of instruction during the unit(s), samples of student work, and written reflections on their planning instruction, and assessment of student progress. The portfolio requirements are highly structured and content specific, revealing much about how new teachers think and how they act on behalf of students. The portfolio assessors grade the novices on the logic and coherence of their curriculum, the suitability of instructional decisions, the scope of teaching strategies they use effectively, the quality of their assessments, their skill in assessing student learning, and their capability to shape new classroom practices based on evidence of student learning.

Each portfolio is scored by two trained assessors who teach in the same content area as the candidate they are judging. They use a content-specific instrument to rate the novice. On average, it takes about five hours for the assessors to score a portfolio. Based on recent data gathered from program administrators, somewhere between 85 and 92 percent (depending on content area) initially pass Connecticut's new-teacher assessment. Pass rates appear to vary according to the university that novices attended, suggesting that some university programs do a better job of preparing novices for the assessments and for teaching. The state predicts a 98 percent success rate when third-year candidates are re-examined.

The purpose of the Connecticut process is to develop new teachers, not simply to screen weaker candidates out of the profession. Still, program officials report that the process is sufficiently rigorous to convince some weaker candidates to leave teaching before they complete the portfolio accounting, at least in part, for the high initial passing rates.

Source: Adapted from Barnett Berry et al. *Assessing and Supporting New Teachers: Lessons from the Southeast.* Raleigh, N.C.: The Southeast Center for Teaching Quality, 2002, p. 8. see: www.teachingquality.org/ResearchMatters/current_issue.htm.

5. *Lack of understanding of the school's expectations:* School officials should clarify the school's goals and priorities and the responsibilities of teachers early in the first term. Orientation sessions and written guides are usually provided; the problem seems to be the dearth of *continuing* communication and reinforcement as the teacher progresses through various stages of role acquisition.

6. *Inadequate supervision:* Most problems of beginning teachers could be either prevented or curtailed with proper supervision. Supervision often consists of only two or three formal visits to the classroom a year and possibly a few informal contacts and one or two meetings. The need is for increased supervisory contact, both formal and informal, so that assistance is provided regularly in the early stages of the teacher's career.[22]

In another study conducted by The Sallie Mae Foundation Institute in 1999, researchers identified a variety of reasons for high ability teachers' decisions to leave the profession.[23] In the order identified by this select group of teachers, the reasons were family-motherhood, salary, career advancement, stress and demands of job, lack of support, student behavior, and lack of respect. In examining the causes of failure for new teachers and the reasons of more experienced teachers for leaving the profession it is quite clear that students and student behavior are not the only (perhaps even primary) reasons for most teachers to exit the classroom. The quality-of-life issues that bother the "exiting" teachers relate to the lack of student respect and administrative support.

Interestingly, the nature of the problems that teachers confront in classrooms has changed little over time. Even though slight changes have occurred in the types of problems, the frequency and magnitude of the specific problems remain relatively stable. For years the *Phi Delta Kappan* poll highlighted areas such as student discipline as significant. Interestingly, in the 2002 poll, parents expressed more concern with how schools are funded and with overcrowding than they did with issues such as discipline.[24] Even this fact, however, highlights the notion that the types of problems that teachers will face are *contextually* specific and will not be significantly different from those evidenced in classrooms in the past.

The degree to which issues like student misbehavior or respect are problematic for you will likely be more a factor of *where* you teach. In high poverty schools, student misbehavior is an issue that impacts teacher perceptions of working conditions. Poverty influences many different aspects of school life, and one of those is how the students act on their impulses and how responsive students are to the learning environment. There are great rewards to teaching in urban schools; there are also, quite candidly, real challenges. Knowing that those challenges are there is the first step toward identifying the theoretical and practical knowledge you need for success with high-need students.

Teaching Inner-City and Culturally Diverse Students

Teachers assigned to inner-city schools tend to feel significantly greater anxiety and even symptoms of exhaustion and battle fatigue. They may deal with classroom management and discipline problems, the inability of many of their students to grasp basic fundamentals, especially reading and writing, the nonresponsiveness or nonavailability of parents, and lack of meaningful assistance from supervisors and administrators.

Several years ago, Ornstein and Levine summarized forty years of research aimed at understanding and overcoming the problems of teaching low-achieving and inner-city students. The problems are categorized into ten classroom realities, illustrated in Table 12.1. The first five are teacher related and the remaining five are student or school

t a b l e   1 2 . 1   **Realities of Teaching Inner-City, Low-Achieving Students**

1. *Differences in teacher-student backgrounds:* Teachers with middle-class backgrounds may have difficulty understanding and motivating inner-city students; this may be particularly salient for white teachers working with minority students.

2. *Teacher perceptions of student inadequacy:* Many teachers working with inner-city students conclude from achievement test scores that large numbers are incapable of learning; hence the teachers may work less hard to improve student performance.

3. *Low standards of performance:* By the time many inner-city students reach middle or senior high school, low performance has become the norm, expected and accepted by both students and teachers.

4. *Ineffective instructional grouping:* Low achievers are frequently grouped into slow classes (or subgrouped in regular classes) where instruction proceeds at a slow rate.

5. *Poor teaching conditions:* As inner-city students fall further behind academically, and as both they and their teachers experience frustration and disappointment, classroom behavior problems increase and teachers find working conditions more difficult; the terms "battle fatigue," "battle pay," and "blackboard jungle" have been used in the literature to describe teaching conditions in inner-city schools.

6. *Differences between parental and school norms:* Differences between the way the inner-city home (physical punishment) and the school (internalization of norms) punish, shame, or control youngsters make it difficult for many students to follow school rules or for teachers to enforce them.

7. *Lack of previous success in school:* Lack of academic success in earlier grades hinders the learning of more difficult material and damages a student's perception of what he or she is capable of learning.

8. *Negative peer pressure:* High-achieving inner-city students are frequently ridiculed and rejected by peers for accepting the middle-class school norms.

9. *Inappropriate instruction:* As inner-city students proceed through school, academic tasks and concepts become increasingly more abstract, and many of these students fall further behind because their level of mastery is too rudimentary to allow for fluent learning.

10. *Delivery of services:* The tasks of delivering effective instruction and related services to students are increasingly more difficult in a classroom or school comprised mainly of lower-achieving, inner-city students (because their learning problems are more serious) than in a middle-class classroom or school that has a small percentage of lower-achieving, inner-city students.

Source: Adapted from Allan C. Ornstein and Daniel U. Levine. "Social Class, Race, and School Achievement: Problems and Prospects." *Journal of Teacher Education* (September–October 1989): 17–23.

related. The inference is that the finger of responsibility should not be pointed at any one group or one person. The researchers provide six teacher-education solutions for the teacher-related problems: 1) increase the number of minority teacher-education students, 2) improve instructional strategies for low achievers (e.g., know how to use direct instruction), 3) permit student teachers more opportunity to work with an effective cooperating teacher, 4) promote greater assistance to teachers during the first three years (intern period) of teaching, 5) put greater emphasis on classroom management techniques (see Chapter 9) during the preservice and intern periods, and 6) examine several different teacher effectiveness models in the preservice and intern stages of education.[25] These "solutions" continue to be evidenced in the reports of commissions and researchers who are working on teacher quality issues in the early 2000s.

The increasingly rich diversity of American classrooms has created a challenge for teacher education. Many beginning teachers prefer to teach white middle-class students because they are white and from middle-class communities, but the reality is that most of them will teach a very diverse group of students, even if they are in suburban teaching contexts. Even affluent suburban communities are more diverse than they were thirty to forty years ago. If preservice teachers are unprepared to deal with this diversity in the classroom, they will be unsuccessful. In California, almost 140 distinct cultural groups are represented in the classrooms. Nationally, of America's 53 million elementary and secondary students, 35 percent are from racial or ethnic minority groups, and 25 percent come from home environments characterized by poverty. Present evidence suggests that current approaches in far too many institutions do not adequately prepare teachers—in terms of attitudes, behaviors, and teaching strategies—for dealing with this diverse student population.[26]

Legal immigration now accounts for up to one-half of the annual growth in the U.S. population. From 1930 to 1950, 80 percent of the immigrants to the United States came from Western Europe and Canada. From 1970 through 1990, however, as many as 90 percent came from non-Western, or Third World, countries—chiefly and in rank order from Mexico, the Philippines, South Korea, Taiwan, Vietnam, Jamaica, India, Dominican Republic, and Guatemala. Moreover, estimates of the illegal population, mainly from Latin America and the Caribbean, total about one million people in a given year (with approximately half establishing permanent residence).[27] Partly as a result of these immigrant trends and the current birth rate trends of whites, blacks, Hispanics, and Asian Americans, in the year 2000 nearly one-third of the U.S. population and 40 percent of the student population (and in Arizona, California, Colorado, Texas, New Mexico, and New York, more than 50 percent) are minorities.[28]

A significant number of these culturally diverse and immigrant families are "structurally poor," meaning that the family conditions are unstable or disorganized and the children have few chances to escape from poverty. The majority of minority children are at risk in school and lack the requisite cognitive skills for learning because of poverty and lack of strong family structure. Such children are far too often labeled "learning disabled" or "slow" primarily because of cultural differences in learning styles and thinking patterns. This circumstance is regrettable.

Interestingly, the school performance of immigrant children suggests that, in almost all academic subjects, the immigrant students outperform native children who come from similar economic backgrounds.[29] Ironically, the longer immigrant students are in the United States, the more poorly they perform in school. Laurence Steinberg describes quite poignantly this phenomenon:

> We would hypothesize, therefore, that students born outside the United States would be doing worse in school than those who are native Americans, and that native Americans whose families have been in this country for several generations would be faring better than their counterparts who arrived more recently.
>
> Surprisingly, just the opposite is true: the longer a student's family has lived in this country, the worse the youngster's school performance and mental health. . . . Foreign-born students—who, incidentally, report significantly more discrimination than American-born youngsters and significantly more difficulty with the English language—nevertheless earn higher grades in school than their American-born counterparts. . . .

It is not simply that immigrants are outperforming nonimmigrants on measures of school achievement. On virtually every factor we know to be correlated with school success, students who were not born in this country outscore those who were born here.[30]

QUESTIONS FOR REFLECTION

The Steinberg quote is a sad commentary on American education. It also suggests something about the nature of American culture. Assuming that Steinberg's argument is correct, what, if anything, can you as a teacher do to counteract this "diminished return" reality that he describes? Can you as *one teacher* really make a difference in mitigating the progression of weak performance of non-mainstream–culture students? What can you do that would really help non-mainstream students succeed?

Beginning teachers often do not learn to make modifications in their pedagogical efforts or in subject matter to adjust to culturally diverse learners. If you ask teachers (novice or experienced) about culturally diverse learners, you usually get socially acceptable responses since teachers may not want to admit to ignorance or biases. But responding to scenarios or questions in education classes or on job interviews is obviously not the same as teaching. Teacher education programs and even internship programs in the first three years of teaching need to explore the attitudes that teachers have toward students who are culturally different from themselves, their attitude toward related learning and pedagogy issues, the teacher's role, and the effects of teacher expectations and behavior on the performance of minority students.[31]

At the same time, it is imperative to explore the problem behaviors of at-risk student populations regardless of the racial, ethnic, or socioeconomic implications. To ignore the impact on schooling of such factors as early sexual activity, truancy, delinquency, and early use of drugs can result in the creation of educational underclasses under the guise of tolerance or political correctness. You need to know how to deal with "problem" students in order to empower them as learners. Identify a successful teacher in an urban school—this is someone who is not just surviving but whose students are academically thriving. Observe the person in a classroom lesson. What makes him or her unique? Successful?

How Beginning Teachers (Novices) Teach

The personal styles and images of beginning teachers, commonly called *novices,* tend to remain inflexible throughout their preservice training. Candidates tend to use the information provided in coursework to confirm rather than to reconstruct their views about teaching. Further compounding the problem of adjusting to future classroom life, teacher candidates are often presented with contradictory and inconsistent views of teaching and learning in their coursework and while student teaching, with teacher education emphasizing one approach and a classroom teacher (in student teaching) encouraging another. As a result, novices come to their first job with an inadequate or conflicted notion of classroom practice and are unprepared to adjust their approach in response to varied problems of instruction, classroom management, and student learning. As beginning teachers acquire knowledge on the job, they must begin to use it to modify, adapt, and reconstruct their views and their teaching methods. Eventually, those who are successful move from focusing on their own behaviors to focusing on the performance of their students; they move from emphasizing classroom management to emphasizing instructional techniques and, finally, to the matter of how and whether students learn.

Many teacher educators oversimplify the reality of student teaching and ignore many complex teaching and learning variables that affect a teacher's classroom decisions. As a result, both student teachers and beginning teachers are expected to function at levels beyond their capacity; in fact, many possess only minimal survival skills. At issue is the failure of teacher educators to provide student teachers with sufficient procedural knowledge to deal with the unique needs of students with special needs. Lacking sufficient knowledge when thrust into the classroom as beginning teachers, novices tend to rely on their own recent experiences as students—an approach that is inappropriate or insufficient for teaching younger pupils.[32] Experience does not ensure future success. What you need is guided, purposeful experience, built on the best available knowledge about what practices foster enhanced student success and that also entails involvement with a mentor teacher who has demonstrated success using those practices. The lack of consistency between what you learn and what a mentor or cooperating teacher models has historically been problematic. It is also the reason, in part, for the increased popularity of PRAXIS and INTASC: they foster a common approach to what occurs in teacher education and classrooms.

Although mastering procedural routines or generic teaching methods is important, another group of teacher educators contend that beginning teachers, or novices, must be concerned with learning how to teach content and helping students learn it.[33] This position stresses the importance of subject matter *and* subject-matter pedagogy—if there are any methods to learn, they are methods related to subject matter delivery. This school of thought is rooted in the post-Sputnik era and in the old schism between professors of arts and science and professors of education over the centrality of disciplinary knowledge versus knowledge of pedagogy. Arts and science faculty today, as in the past, continue to advocate the necessity of subject matter and are likely to remain skeptical of pedagogy.

More recently, Lee Shulman introduced the phrase "pedagogical content knowledge" and sparked a whole new wave of scholarly articles on teachers' knowledge of their subject matter and the importance of this knowledge for successful teaching.[34] For the most part, content knowledge was ignored by researchers on teaching in the 1970s and 1980s when generic methods and principles of effective teaching were emphasized. In the 1990s and 2000s, the shift in interest is toward specialized or content-based methods and toward enhanced teacher reflection relative to selected scientifically based practices—that is, toward an emphasis on techniques that research supports as effective in helping students learn.[35] Researchers began to examine specific strategies for teaching mathematics, science, or reading and to look for evidence that knowing how to teach something effectively is an important complement to possessing the requisite and essential disciplinary knowledge.

In Shulman's theoretical framework, teachers need to master two types of knowledge: 1) content, or "deep" knowledge of the subject itself, and 2) knowledge of curricular development. Content knowledge encompasses what Jerome Bruner would call the "structure of knowledge"—the theories, principles, and concepts of a particular discipline. Especially important is content knowledge that deals with the teaching process, including the most useful forms of representing and communicating content and how students best learn the specific concepts and topics of a subject.

Teachers' orientation to their subject matter influences their method of planning, choice of content, the use of textbooks, the supplementary materials that teachers use, pedagogical strategies, and teacher perceptions of students' instructional needs. Likewise, it determines the way teachers formulate, demonstrate, and explain the subject so that it is comprehensible to learners. All this suggests that beginning teachers need to integrate subject-matter content and pedagogy.[36] Teachers must know process *and* content. Pam Grossman and others conducted research to determine the effects of teacher education coursework in subsequent professional practice. Grossman concluded that teachers who do and those who do not have teacher education backgrounds do teach differently.[37] More specifically, they make different assumptions about the students as learners. Grossman writes in describing six teachers (three with and three without formal teacher preparation):

> The six teachers in this study represent, in many ways, the best and the brightest of prospective teachers. All are well prepared in their subject matter; four of the six hold BAs in literature from prestigious colleges and universities, while one teacher was completing his doctorate in literature at the time of the study . . . All six of the teachers were technically first-year teachers, although three of them had had prior experience as teaching interns or aides. Of the six teachers, three taught in suburban public schools and three taught in independent schools. Two of the teachers, one with and one without teacher education, taught at the same independent school, which provided opportunity for at least one cross-case analysis in which teaching context was controlled.
>
> The results of this study suggest that, in this case, subject specific coursework did make a difference in these beginning teachers' pedagogical content knowledge of English. The two groups of teachers differed in their conceptions of the purposes of teaching English, their ideas about what to teach in secondary English, and their knowledge of student understanding.[38]

If beginning teachers are to be successful, they must wrestle simultaneously with issues of specialized pedagogical content as well as issues of general pedagogy (or generic teaching principles). The authors of this book stress generic teaching principles in this text, but specialized pedagogical approaches and generic teaching principles are not mutually exclusive. You will use some generic principles to learn to teach reading; you will also need more highly defined skills for phonetics instruction. Only by integrating both forms of pedagogy can a teacher personally define and understand the purpose of teaching, understand students' learning, and develop realistic curricular and instructional strategies.

In the ideal, you will have matriculated through a program that combines theory and practice (and general and specialized methods) in ways that help you see the connections between what is known and how that known knowledge can be applied. You should be able to negotiate the problems of teaching in ways that improve your practice and foster enhanced opportunities for your students and to mitigate some of the common problems that often plague novice teachers. You will develop, in essence, your artful twist on the known science of teaching. This vision of success is only possible if you have had long-term exposure to teacher education content through your own long-term professional development and growth. You will, in essence, always be on a professional journey, and though you may find accomplishment, you may never feel as though you have reached your goal. Teachers cannot and should not "short-course." Some evidence is emerging to suggest that although good intentions are necessary, they are not a sufficient condition for success. Such anecdotal evidence comes from an analysis of teachers who have been "short-coursed" into the classroom:

> Even very bright people who are enthusiastic about teaching find that they cannot easily succeed without preparation, especially if they are assigned to work with children who need skillful teaching. Perhaps the best example of the limitations of the "bright person" myth about teaching is Teach for America (TFA), a program created to recruit talented college graduates to disadvantaged urban and rural classrooms for two years en-route to careers in law, medicine, and other professions. If anyone could prove that teachers are born and not made, these bright, eager students, many of them from top schools, might have been the ones to do it. Yet four separate evaluations found that TFA's three-to-eight-week training program did not prepare candidates to succeed with students.
>
> Many recruits know that their success, and that of their students, had been compromised by their lack of access to the knowledge needed to teach. Yale University graduate Jonathan Schorr was one of the many to raise this concern. He wrote:
>
> I—perhaps like most TFAers—harbored dreams of liberating my students from public school mediocrity and offering them as good an education as I had received. But I was not ready . . . As bad as it was for me, it was worse for the students. Many of mine . . . took long steps on the path toward dropping out. . . . I was not a successful teacher and the loss to the students was real and large.[39]

Support from Colleagues for Beginning Teachers

In general, having to learn by trial and error without support and supervision has been the most common problem faced by new teachers. Expecting teachers to function without support is based on the false assumptions that 1) teachers are well prepared for their initial classroom and school experiences, 2) teachers can develop professional expertise on their own, and 3) teaching can be mastered in a relatively short period of time. Researchers find that there is little attempt to lighten the class load and limit extra class assignments to make the beginning teacher's job easier. In the few schools that do limit these activities, teachers have reported that they have had the opportunity to "learn to teach."[40]

Unquestionably, new teachers need the feedback and encouragement experienced teachers and professional peers can provide. The exchange of ideas can take place in school and out, such as while sharing a ride to a local meeting. Experienced teachers must be willing to open their classrooms to new teachers. Because of the desire for autonomy in the classrooms, there is seldom sufficient communication or visitation between classrooms. No matter how successful individuals are as student teachers and how good their preservice training is, they can benefit from the advice and assistance of experienced colleagues. Talking to other teachers gives novices the chance to sound out ideas and assimilate information. *Peer coaching* and *mentoring* are nothing more than purposeful faculty collaboration where you as a new teacher work with colleagues to share ideas about instruction and student learning.

Peer interaction and feedback are essential for the teacher's professional growth.

Teachers expect to learn from one another when the school provides opportunities for teachers 1) to talk routinely to one another about teaching, 2) to be observed regularly in the classroom, and 3) to jointly participate in planning and lesson preparation. Teachers who are given opportunities to 1) develop and implement curriculum ideas, 2) join study groups about implementing classroom practices, or 3) experiment in new skills and training feel more confident in their individual and collective ability to perform their work.[41]

During peer coaching or mentoring, classroom teachers observe one another, provide feedback concerning their teaching, and together develop (or reflect upon) instructional plans. The new teachers should look for techniques of teaching and lesson planning that are unfamiliar to them, that coincide with their teaching style, and that are an improvement over what they are doing. Mentor programs are in place in a number of states such as California. These programs were established to help new teachers be successful and to reduce high teacher attrition rates. In California, the goals of the program include the following:

- Providing an easy transition into teaching for new teachers
- Encouraging professional success and teacher retention
- Providing strong and individualized support for new teachers
- Ensuring that teachers are more effective working with culturally, linguistically, and academically diverse student populations.[42]

According to Joyce and Showers, an experienced teacher who acts as a peer coach or mentor teacher for an inexperienced teacher performs five functions: 1) companionship, or discussing ideas, problems, and successes; 2) technical feedback, especially related to lesson planning and classroom observations; 3) analysis of application, or integrating what happens or what works into the beginning teacher's repertoire; 4) adaptation, or helping the beginning teacher adapt to particular situations; and 5) personal facilitation, or helping the teacher feel good about himself or herself after trying new strategies.[43]

Similar data have been reported by Neubert and Bratton. They studied visiting mentor teachers in Maryland school districts who, rather than observe classroom teachers, teach alongside them. From this study they identified five characteristics of resource teachers that promote an effective coaching relationship: 1) knowledge—more knowledge about teaching methods than the classroom teacher; 2) credibility—demonstrated success in the classroom; 3) support—a mix of honest praise and constructive criticism; 4) facilitation—recommending and encouraging rather than dictating, assisting rather than dominating in the classroom, and 5) availability—accessibility to the classroom teacher for planning, team teaching, and conferences.[44]

In one Pennsylvania school district, a "buddy system" has been developed for beginning and experienced teachers who need additional assistance. Continuous peer support is provided, with teachers teamed together from the same subject or grade level. The teacher "coaches" who are selected work full-time (and often after school) helping their less-experienced colleagues become better teachers. Four characteristics help define this program: 1) collegiality and teamwork, such as in the case of coaches covering classes so that their colleagues can observe other teachers and gather ideas to adapt to their own teaching style or in the case of coaches engaging in direct peer coaching; 2) instructional support, such as in the case of coaches introducing new instructional strategies that enhance student learning; 3) professional growth, in which coaches take an active role in presenting in-service sessions so that new teachers are helped to better understand the school philosophy and policies; and 4) special services and programs provided by coaches that can be used by all teachers in the school (visiting authors, artists in residence, environmental projects, computer assistance, etc.).[45]

Data suggest, however, that beginning teachers are selective about whom they ask for help. They seek help from experienced teachers whom they perceive as "knowledgeable," "friendly," and "supportive," independent of whether the teachers are formally recognized as their "mentors" or "coaches." In a study of 128 teachers in 90 different schools, 75 percent sought help from teachers who were not their assigned mentors; only 53 percent were generally satisfied with the mentors they were assigned.[46]

Although mentors are usually comfortable offering help to their inexperienced colleagues, the success of any mentoring program hinges on whether the inexperienced teacher is comfortable seeking help from his or her experienced counterpart. The decision for adults to seek help and then to accept it is influenced by numerous variables. The tension that impacts the decision process about asking for help is the tension between the embarrassment of continued failure without help and the embarrassment of asking for help to solve a problem. Indeed, the staggering number of teachers who leave the profession after only a few years of service suggests the need to be sensitive to the concerns of beginning teachers and the need to improve mentoring programs, which is why so many states in the early 2000s are developing more formalized mentoring systems for their new teachers—see Case Study 12.1.

Perhaps the most important strategy for a coach, resource teacher, or mentor teacher is to allow new teachers to reflect, not react or defend. An integral part of any good program for helping beginning teachers is observation of experienced teachers on a regular basis and then observation by experienced teachers of the novice teachers. With both observational formats, there is a need to discuss what facilitated or hindered the teaching-learning process and to identify the steps or recommendations for improving instruction. The "coach" or mentor needs to serve as a friend and confidante and function in a nonevaluative role. The term "peer sharing and caring" best describes the new spirit of collegial openness and learning advocated here.

Some educators, such as James Stigler and James Hiebert, are outlining new ways for teachers to help teachers by relying on models used in Japan for professional development. The *jugyoukenkynu* (or Japanese study lesson) takes different forms but often includes a group of teachers collaborating to develop lesson plans—they essentially plan together.[47] One "appointed" teacher then teaches the lesson, and professional colleagues from the planning group watch and take notes on a variety of classroom dynamics, especially the students' reactions to the lesson. After the lesson, they hold a general discussion about what happened and how the students responded (what they learned). This model is quite unique but some American schools are trying it with the goal of making teachers less isolated and more focused on working with others to improve teaching performance. Even if the school where you eventually teach has no such program (and it likely will not), find someone to talk to about your teaching and find ways to have him or her watch you teach—whether in person or on tape.

Support from Other Beginning Teachers

The *induction period*—the first two or three years of teaching—is critical in developing teachers' capabilities. Beginning teachers should not be left alone to sink or swim. The internal support systems that schools adopt (both the daily support activities and continual opportunities for growth) are vital for the professional development of new teachers.

Unfortunately, some schools (and school districts) do not respond adequately to the needs of their new teachers and expect too much from them in terms of expertise. In such schools other support activities can fill the vacuum or, they can serve as a supplementary support mechanism at schools with strong support programs. One supplementary activity is for beginning in-service teachers to share classroom experiences, to tell their stories, and to reflect on ways of addressing problems within the structure of a college course or as part of a staff development program at the school district level. Beginning teachers from various schools can share, organize, and apply what they know about teaching in sort of a self-help process.[48] Preservice teachers, especially student teachers, have been doing this for years, returning from their field experiences to meet in groups with a supervisor. Such sharing of personal stories and experiences, with feedback and interpretation from peers, can have a nurturing effect and help change and improve the lives of teachers at many stages of their professional growth.

Still another method for supporting beginning teachers is the use of a computer network. Across the country in various schools and colleges, teachers, administrators, professors, and even students frequently communicate with each other using electronic mail (e-mail). One network is the Beginning Teacher Computer Network (BTCN) initiated at Harvard University to help its first-year teacher graduates, now based in schools across the country, stay in touch with each other.[49] Unlike larger computer conferencing systems such as Bitnet or Prodigy, the BTCN network is small and relies on personal computers and modems. It is an inexpensive way for teachers to work out small problems; to offer peer diagnosis, rather than expert or supervisor analysis; and to provide nonevaluative feedback. The network provides support, collegiality, and opportunity for professional growth; participants know that a friend and former classmate are close at hand to listen and offer ideas and advice. Beginning teachers who graduate from any teacher education program can form their own networks with or without the assistance of their professors or principals.

Guidelines for Improving Support for Beginning Teachers

Whatever the existing policies regarding the induction period for entry teachers, there is a need to improve provisions for continued professional development, to make the job easier, to make new teachers feel more confident in the classroom and school, to reduce the isolation of their work settings, and to enhance interaction with colleagues. Following are some recommendations for achieving these goals. They are written from the perspective of those providing assistance, but they also suggest what you as a new teacher might expect. Talk to a teacher in the field and find out which of these strategies is used at the school in which he or she teaches.

1. Appoint someone to help beginning teachers set up their rooms. Beginning teachers should actively seek a good mentor.

2. Pair beginning teachers with master teachers to meet regularly to identify general problems before they become serious. Beginning teachers should identify teachers with whom they can discuss content and instructional process.

3. Provide coaching groups, tutor groups, or collaborative problem-solving groups for all beginning teachers to attend. Beginning teachers can teach each other just as they can learn from master teachers.

4. Provide for joint planning, team teaching, committee assignments, and other cooperative arrangements between new and experienced teachers. Beginning teachers should find professional partners to support them.

6. Plan special and continuous in-service activities with topics directly related to the needs and interests of beginning teachers. Eventually, integrate beginning staff development activities with regular staff development activities. Beginning teachers should communicate common problem areas to those responsible for staff development.

7. Carry on regular evaluation of beginning teachers; evaluate strengths and weaknesses, present new information, demonstrate new skills, and provide opportunities for practice and feedback. Beginning teachers should expect administrator evaluation and should engage in personal self-evaluation.

Self-Evaluation

Teaching presents ample opportunities for self-evaluation. The teacher who does a good job and knows it has the satisfaction of seeing students grow, feeling their respect and affection, and obtaining the recognition of colleagues, parents, and the community.

Self-evaluation by the teacher can contribute to professional growth. This idea is a logical outgrowth of the modern belief in the value of teacher-supervisor cooperation. If teacher evaluations are accepted as an integral part of an effective supervisory situation for professional development, then teachers should be involved in the clarification and continual appraisal of their goals and effectiveness.

Part of that clarification process is the teacher's ability to identify areas of need in terms of his or her own teaching skills or to add information to data that might be collected by a mentor or administrator. Self-assessments have embedded problems (some self-evaluations are not especially accurate), but they are important for professional growth.[50]

According to Good and Brophy, one of the first steps to better teaching is to evaluate your current professional strengths and weaknesses. In order to improve your teaching, you need to decide what you want to do and how to determine whether your plans are working. In their words, "Resolutions [to improve teaching] are more likely to be fulfilled when . . . [teachers] specify the desired change: 'I want to increase the time I spend in small-group and project-based work by 25 percent.'"[51]

There are good and practical reasons for thoughtful self-evaluation and for seeking out mentor support. For example, several years ago a United States government survey of 10,000 secondary teachers and 400 schools revealed that about one-fourth (26 percent) of the respondents were "never" evaluated by their building principal or supervisor the previous year, and another 27 percent had received only one visit. When teachers were asked how many times they visited other teachers to observe or discuss teaching techniques, 70 percent said, "Never."[52] Some states are attempting to change this circumstance. For example, Ohio is instituting a PRAXIS III assessment process (that reflects the Pathwise criteria used in this book) to observe all first-year teachers in the state. Trained evaluators are using the criteria to assess how well new teachers are using the various skills in their delivery of instruction.

Many school districts have also established their own intern or new teacher evaluation process.[53] Of those systems, few have received more national publicity than the system of the Toledo Public Schools. All newly hired teachers in Toledo are in the program for two semesters. They are assigned a consulting (mentor) teacher who works with them to determine their progress and success in meeting the school district's teacher development performance standards.

The mentor teacher has the final responsibility for each semester's evaluation, which is based on mutually defined teacher goals. At the last evaluation date, the mentor teacher recommends to an Intern Board of Review the future employment status of the novice teacher.[54] The Toledo system has resulted in the termination of some teachers and the nonrenewal and resignation of others. Table 12.2 provides data on the Toledo system from 1991 to 2001.

Clearly, evaluation systems like Toledo's are making a difference in potentially improving teacher quality, but they still represent an exception rather than the rule. As

table 12.2   **Status Report of Intern Teachers**

School Year	Teachers Placed in Intern Program	Nonrenewed	Terminated	Resigned	% Failure
1991–1992	109	9		4	11.9
1992–1993	249	5	3	17	9.6
1993–1994	170	7	1	10	10.6
1994–1995	160	6	2	8	10.0
1995–1996	No Program				
1996–1997	175	7	2	8	9.7
1997–1998	196	1	5	15	11.0
1998–1999	400	3	9	20	8.0
1999–2000	285	13	2	16	10.9
2000–2001	140	3	1	8	8.6
TOTALS	3,025	88	31	139	8.5

Source: "Intern Intervention Evaluation: The Toledo Plan." Toledo, Ohio: Toledo Public Schools, 2001.

a consequence, you need to be able to self-assess your own teaching, and you will need to continue the self-evaluation process throughout your career. Few school districts have the type of evaluation and supervisory systems needed for ongoing professional growth.

Far too many teachers operate with virtual autonomy in the classroom and receive minimal assistance from supervisors or colleagues. It follows, therefore, that a thoughtful self-evaluation may be more useful and possibly less biased than an outside evaluation based on one or two visits from an adminstrator who is rushed or going through motions to satisfy some school policy.

What is thoughtful self-evaluation? Some self-evaluation involves *reflection in action.* The teacher is thinking about the teaching act as it occurs. New teachers may find this difficult to do because they are still trying, all too often, to survive the moment. As a result they may engage in more *reflection on action,* which is reflection after the teaching occurs. There are basically two forms of reflection on action.

First, teachers can assess themselves on their teaching methods at the classroom level by using some type of self-evaluation form. This type of evaluation form can be developed by the teacher, a group of teachers, the school district, or by researchers. Teachers should either have input in devising the instrument (to build acceptance of the process) or in selecting an instrument already developed and may be in use in another school district and then modifying it according to their own purposes. The point is that teachers should feel comfortable with (and understand) the evaluation instrument. Two types of instruments can be used for such self-evaluation of instructional practices. One type (shown in Table 12.3) is general in nature and focuses on general instructional effectiveness and just determines the presence of a teaching behavior; the second

table 12.3   **General Instructional Effectiveness**

....

This evaluation form is used to assess whether a teacher is presenting content in a clear, logical way to students. It evaluates the presence of certain salient teacher behaviors.

	Yes	No
Establishing the Purpose of a Lesson		
1. Teacher states purpose of lesson	_____	_____
2. Teacher lists objectives on board	_____	_____
3. Teacher ties objectives to defined content standards	_____	_____
4. Teacher provides students with some type of advanced organizer	_____	_____
Presenting the Lesson		
1. Teacher begins lesson promptly	_____	_____
2. Teacher has materials ready for student use	_____	_____
3. Teacher speaks clearly and fluently	_____	_____
4. Teacher is enthusiastic in presenting content	_____	_____
5. Teacher defines or clarifies abstract terms	_____	_____
6. Teacher presents material in step-by-step fashion	_____	_____
7. Teacher provides time for students to ask questions	_____	_____
8. Teacher requires students to demonstrate that they understand content	_____	_____
9. Teacher provides feedback to students during lesson as students demonstrate their knowledge	_____	_____
10. Teacher paces lesson to fit student learning needs	_____	_____
Closing the Lesson		
1. Teacher summarizes content covered	_____	_____
2. Teacher provides students with an opportunity to do their own summary	_____	_____
3. Teacher allows students an opportunity to ask questions	_____	_____
4. Teacher provides meaningful independent practice	_____	_____

type is specific in nature and focuses on particular instructional skills, such as those related to direct instruction (see Table 12.4) and looks for both the presence and degree to which a teaching behavior is evidenced.

Second, teachers can rate themselves on their professional responsibilities at the school and community levels. According to administrators, this form might include 1) classroom climate, 2) student learning, 3) contractual responsibilities, 4) service to school, and 5) professional development.[55] To this list might be added 6) relations with students, 7) relations with colleagues, 8) relations with parents, and 9) service to the community.

California is building these types of "environment" requirements into its formative evaluation systems. (Remember, formative systems are intended to provide feedback for improvement, not to summatively assess effectiveness or ineffectiveness.) For example, one "element" of the California Formative Assessment and Support System for Teachers (CFASST) is "Creating a physical environment that engages all stu-

table 12.4 **Direct-Instruction Assessment**

	Not Evident	Somewhat Evident	Clearly Evident
Phase I: Review			
1. The teacher reviews ideas from the previous day's lessons.	_____	_____	_____
2. The teacher reteaches content material that students had difficulty understanding.	_____	_____	_____
Phase II: Presenting New Material			
1. The teacher clearly states the objectives for the lesson.	_____	_____	_____
2. The teacher teaches the skill or action sequence in a step-by-step fashion.	_____	_____	_____
3. The teacher lets students see the standard connected to the objective.	_____	_____	_____
Phase III: Guided Practice			
1. The teacher frequently asks questions to assess student understanding.	_____	_____	_____
2. The teacher calls on both volunteers and nonvolunteers.	_____	_____	_____
3. All students have an opportunity to respond to the teacher's questions.	_____	_____	_____
4. Students successfully respond to the teacher's questions (at approximately an 80 percent rate of success).	_____	_____	_____
5. The teacher continues to practice the skill until student understanding appears firm.	_____	_____	_____
Phase IV: Feedback and Correctives			
1. The teacher provides specific feedback to students when their responses are hesitant.	_____	_____	_____
2. The teacher reteaches material when student responses are incorrect.	_____	_____	_____
Phase V: Independent Practice			
1. The teacher provides an appropriate number of problems for independent practice.	_____	_____	_____
2. Students are assigned homework that is meaningful and appropriate.	_____	_____	_____
3. Students appear to know how to do the homework successfully.	_____	_____	_____

Source: Adapted from Thomas J. Lasley II, Thomas J. Matczynski, and James Rowley. *Instructional Methods: Strategies for Teaching in a Diverse Society.* Belmont, Calif.: Wadsworth, 2002. pp. 288–289.

dents."[56] Beginning teachers need to be conscious of both what students are learning and the environment within which that learning is occurring.

    Quite obviously, how you self-evaluate will be dictated by how and what you teach. A teacher who uses step-by-step (teacher-centered) direct instruction (see Table 12.4) will look at a lesson on teaching fractions in a much different way than will a constructivist teacher who has students engaged in exploring the same concept. To complicate matters, that constructivist teacher might be a rational constructivist (Piagetian) or dialectical constructivist (Vygotskian): If the former, the teacher will be guiding students toward a more complete understanding of the concept, and if the latter, the teacher and student will be co-constructing the knowledge—that is, the students might develop personal representations of a concept that differ from but are equally valid to those identified by a teacher.[57] All the teachers do have a common goal: student understanding of fractions. The question for self-evaluation is whether that goal was achieved.

Reflection

The terms **reflection** and **reflective practice** are partially based on the works of Carl Rogers and Donald Schon, who studied the actions and thoughts of workers in a variety of fields in which reflection is needed for personal development and day-to-day practice. According to these authors, each person is capable of asking questions and analyzing the answers about their own professional performance for the purpose of improvement. Through open-mindedness and maturity and with the help of colleagues, individuals can discover new ideas and illuminate what they already understand and know how to do.[58]

Reflection is increasingly becoming a part of mandated evaluation systems such as the California FASST program. Carline Lucas describes this approach:

> Reflection is an important part of professional development. Teachers need to look at their intended objectives and to determine their effectiveness. New teachers must learn to observe outcomes and to determine the reasons for success or failure. The role of the support provider is to guide the novice in reflective experiences, such as examining delivery of instruction and student outcomes. BTSA/CFASST [Beginning Teacher Support and Assessment/California Formative Assessment and Support System for Teachers] support providers are trained to make and record objective observations of beginning teachers. New teachers in California become familiar with the California Standards for the Teaching Professions; . . . therefore, when provided with objective feedback after an observation, teachers center their reflective conversation on what and how they meet or fall below any given standard.[59]

Reflection can help beginning and experienced teachers alike, and it can be incorporated into preservice, internship, and in-service or staff development programs. Most participants are resistant at the beginning and usually express some ambivalence or confusion about what is required, especially as unsettling questions about their teaching are examined. But more often than not, for teachers, reflection results in more questions, clearer perceptions of themselves, and better plans for solving individual problems.[60]

One of the more sophisticated tools for analyzing teachers' reflective thoughts at the preservice level was developed by Dorene Ross, who contends that reflection becomes increasingly complex with greater maturity and perception of safety in expressing one's views. Ross identifies three levels of complexity in the reflection process: 1) describing a teacher's practice with little detailed analysis and little insight into the reasons behind teacher or student behaviors; 2) providing a cogent critique of a practice from one perspective but failing to consider multiple factors; and 3) analyzing teaching and learning from multiple perspectives and recognizing that teachers' actions have a pervasive impact beyond the moment of instruction.[61]

In the later stages, individuals come to realize that behaviors (and feelings) are contextually based. Rather than dealing in absolutes, they begin to deal in relative pedagogical truths and points of view. In the third stage, people are open to more change and willing to admit that they don't always know the answer. The third stage suggests the presence of considerable professional experience and maturity. It can be inferred that beginning teachers operate at the lower levels of reflection and, therefore, are more singular in their approaches and unwilling to accept other viewpoints about their teaching. This is only an educated inference, yet it does conform to research data that suggest that only one out of five preservice teachers function above level 2 and then only for particular topics.[62]

Through reflection, teachers focus on their concerns, come to better understand their own teacher behavior, and help themselves or colleagues improve as teachers. Through reflective practices in a group setting, or forums, teachers learn to listen carefully to each other, which also helps provide insight into their own work. In turn, as researchers hear teachers reflect on their practices in the classroom and the basis for those actions, they are in the position to translate the teachers' practical knowledge and particular points of view into theoretical knowledge and to integrate it with other viewpoints.

As you reflect on practice, don't just select exceptional events for guided reflections—the ordinary and the extraordinary offer equally useful opportunities to think in more depth about teaching. Hole and McEntree articulate a four-step process consisting of asking critically reflective questions:[63] Select a classroom event (e.g., students excitedly working on a project but then ignoring teacher calls for their attention or students playing a game such as "around the world" and then getting angry when a high performing student wins the game, again) and then focus on the following questions about it to foster your personal reflection on what occurred:

Step 1: What happened? Be specific and detailed in describing the "critical incident."

Step 2: Why did it happen? Look at both the surface and hidden contextual clues to explain the critical event.

Step 3: What might it mean? What is the potential or real meaning of the event?

Step 4: What are the implications for my practice? This guided reflection should suggest ways of rethinking or modifying practice.[64]

The Hole and McEntree Guided Reflection Protocol is a way to help you think through the classroom events you experience. At times, there is simply no colleague with whom you can discuss a classroom event. The key to this protocol is that it moves you from classroom instruction *as it is* to envisioning how it *might be.*

As teachers probe and further examine specific teaching situations, a language of practice can emerge that allows you to understand better how you cope and deal with the complexity of your work. The goal of such self-reflection is to make sense of what happens in a classroom, to clarify and elaborate particular scripts or situations, and to delineate the meaning these reflections have for you and for students.

Guidelines for Self-Evaluation and Reflection

Self-evaluation can serve as the initial step in an ongoing attempt to improve teaching and instructional procedures. A written self-evaluation instrument focuses your attention on specific aspects of your teaching and ensures that you not overlook anything important. Reflection, because it involves no instrumentation, keeps you open to probing deeper and deeper as you discover more about your teaching. Follow these guidelines when reflecting on and evaluating your own teaching:

1. The teacher's ability to assess his or her weaknesses and strengths is important for self-improvement. This ability can be enhanced through good relations and communication between the teacher and supervisor.

2. If professional growth contracts are used in a school, self-evaluations may be included as part of the contract or formal evaluation process.

3. Self-ratings should be compared with student ratings if the same items are included in the forms. Discrepancies between the ratings should be interpreted or analyzed.

4. Self-evaluations can be used as a starting point for the formal supervisor evaluation of the teacher.

5. Teachers wishing to focus on specific behaviors or instructional activities should videotape a particular lesson in conjunction with the self-evaluation of that lesson. The same videotape can be used for the purpose of reflection. You can use forms such as those in 12.3 and 12.4 to focus your analysis of a taped lesson you teach.

6. Reflection takes place when teachers volunteer to collaborate and exchange ideas with colleagues about shared pedagogical concerns.

7. Through reflection teachers can come to understand better their strengths and weaknesses.

8. The key to reflection is the ability to be honest with yourself and with colleagues or peers and to listen to and dialogue with them as they help you analyze your own teaching.

Supervision and Evaluation

Beginning teachers should welcome evaluation as a means to develop professionally. In general, the evaluation a beginning teacher receives takes two forms. Some evaluation is formative and summative, just as good student evaluations are. It is intended to reassure new teachers that they can succeed and can foster student growth. The other evaluation is intended to help teachers know how they are performing relative to the specific criteria of a school district's evaluation system.[65] Find out from your supervisor (your principal) how you will be evaluated and who will be doing the evaluation. Or, if you are currently involved in a field experience, ask your cooperating teacher to review with you the process that is followed to evaluate teacher performance of regular classroom teachers. Is that process different for new teachers than it is for experienced teachers?

Evaluation systems take on many different forms. As you review the evaluation procedures used in different school districts, several models will emerge. Some of those models will be relatively ineffective in helping you grow professionally or in identifying specific areas needed for professional growth. Peterson describes several evaluative models that are ineffective:

- *Testimonials,* or the use of third-party claims about a teacher's abilities or expertise
- *Student assessments,* in which students who have worked with a particular teacher assess his or her abilities
- *Competency-based approaches,* which use highly specific descriptions of teacher behavior that do not take into account the context within which you teach[66]

Peterson does argue that standard-based systems (like those with Pathwise and INTASC) can be problematic because they have not yet demonstrated a clear relationship to student achievement. Though true, such systems are based on a body of research that does relate teacher behaviors and student achievement. For that reason, we have used Pathwise and INTASC as a framework for this textbook.

These models are only problematic when they become selected methods for assessing teacher performance rather than parts of a broad system of teacher assessment. No one type of supervision is used by all school districts. The options are too numerous to discuss, but we will consider two relatively common options.

A relatively small number of school districts (and teacher education institutions) use a form of supervision known as clinical supervision, which is more collaborative. In **clinical supervision,** members of the supervisory and administrative staff create a partnership with the new teacher focused on inquiry into the instructional process. As the school year gets under way, a grade-level or subject-related supervisor works with the novice to plan lessons, discuss appropriate materials and media, and dialogue about curriculum suggestions. Ideally, he or she informally visits the class for short periods of time to learn about the new teacher's style, abilities, and needs. Later, at the teacher's invitation or by mutual agreement, the supervisor observes a complete lesson. Such a visit is often formally planned in conjunction with a preobservation conference to talk over the plans for the lesson and a postobservation conference to discuss the observation and evaluation of the lesson. Clinical supervision is a time demanding process for the supervisor and the novice teacher and it can be either directive or nondirective.

This three-step clinical process (preobservation conference, observation, and postobservation conference) has been enlarged to eight phases by Morris Cogan, a major theorist in the area of supervision of teachers: 1) establishing the teacher-supervisor relationship, 2) planning the lesson with the teacher, 3) planning the strategy of observation, 4) observing instruction, 5) analyzing the teaching-learning process, 6) planning the strategy of the conference, 7) holding the conference, and 8) renewed planning.[67]

Robert Goldhammer, a student of Cogan, developed a similar model consisting of five stages: 1) preobservation conference, 2) observation, 3) analysis and strategy, 4) supervision conference, and 5) postconference analysis. In both of these models the teacher's behavior and techniques are observed, analyzed, and interpreted, and decisions are made in order to improve the teacher's effectiveness.[68]

According to Ben Harris, the teacher can learn to assume increasing responsibilities for each step in the process. As the teacher learns to analyze and interpret observational data and confronts his or her own concerns and needs, he or she should become less dependent on the supervisor and more capable of reflection and self-analysis.[69]

Obviously, several observations and conferences are needed before any formal judgment is made about a teacher's performance. However, even one or two observations by a skilled supervisor can be helpful to the teacher, especially for the new teacher who lacks practical experience in the classroom. There is also evidence that beginning (and experienced) teachers value supervisory feedback and appreciate supervisors' and principals' input in diagnosing, prescribing, and recommending teaching strategies and skills. The input helps teachers learn to teach and to understand the expectations of the school district.[70] This type of support is considered important in view of the fact that the turnover among new teachers (those with fewer than three years of experience) may be as high as 40-50 percent.

Another form of supervision is ***technical coaching,*** which is more structured and directive. That is, the coach or mentor is more specific about the teaching behaviors that the novice needs to use. Technical coaching assists teachers in developing new teaching strategies and skills over longer time periods. Technical coaching, however, tends to inhibit professional dialogue and peer exchange because the focus is on teacher acquisition of a particular teaching skill such as how to teach fractions using inquiry or how to teach the same concept using direct instruction. Discussions often focus on the presence or absence of a particular behavior or teaching skill not on its development.

Technical coaching assumes that objective feedback, given in a nonthreatening and constructive climate, can improve teaching, especially if a novice teacher understands the theory behind a particular approach that is used and then has opportunities to view its use by an expert and subsequently to practice the teaching skill on his or her own.

Whether a clinical or technical approach is best for you may depend on how you think about teaching. Carl Glickman distinguishes between teachers who think in concrete terms and those who think in abstract terms. Both teacher types are willing to accept feedback and evaluation. However, concrete types (to whom Glickman attributes low conceptual professional thought patterns) are confused about their instructional problems, lack ideas about what to do, and need assistance in clarifying such issues— i.e., they profit from specific and highly structured recommendations. They want answers, and technical approaches may be good ways to start. Highly conceptual, abstract supervisor or mentor recommendations will only confuse them. The second teacher types (who function at a high conceptual level) can identify instructional problems and seek and generate multiple sources of ideas about what can be done; they can visualize and verbalize the consequences of various choices or actions and easily make modifications to their teaching. A subtle, more generalized clinical approach to supervision is more likely to succeed with them. In practice, a good number of teachers are moderately abstract and fall between the two groups.[71]

Teachers are at different stages of development, in part due to experience and age and in part because of different thresholds or levels of willingness to accept recommendations for change. Different supervisory approaches—from directive (technical) to collaborative or nondirective (clinical)—should be considered in the context of the developmental stage and thinking pattern of the teacher to enhance positive changes in teaching. Certainly, an experienced and/or older teacher needs different types of coaching than does an inexperienced and/or younger teacher. As a new teacher, you may prefer a more directive style, but your professional goal should be to collaborate with mentors and colleagues for your own personal development and that will mean developing comfort with a more nondirective approach.

New Forms of Evaluation

Some school districts and states are experimenting with new forms of evaluation. These were limited in use until the early 1990s, but since that time many schools and institutions have been exploring how to use them effectively.

Authentic Evaluation

Authentic evaluation relies on a variety of different artifacts of the teaching process. *Artifacts of teaching* are sources of data for teacher reflection and growth. These products offer teachers prime examples of their teaching performance and of student learning:

1. *Lesson plans and unit plans:* Examination of lesson plans and unit plans should reveal whether the curriculum or course syllabus is being taught, whether the teacher's pace and focus are appropriate, how individual student differences are provided for, whether the instructional objectives are clear, whether the activities are appropriate, and whether study and homework exercises are adequate. (Also, it should be possible to determine the connection between academic standards and material required for students to learn.)

2. *Assessments:* Do quizzes and examinations reflect the important objectives and learning outcomes? Are the test questions appropriately written? Are there different types of assessments being used?

3. *Laboratory and special projects:* Handouts for these projects should be examined for clarity, spelling, punctuation, and appropriateness. They should coincide with the important objectives and content of the course and serve to motivate students and enrich their learning experiences.

4. *Materials and media:* The quality and appropriateness of materials and media and the way they are incorporated into the instructional process can reveal the teacher's knowledge, skills, and effort to facilitate student learning.

5. *Reading lists and bibliographies:* These current lists should accommodate varied student abilities, needs, and interests.

6. *Student outcomes:* Samples of student work and test results indicate students' mastery of skills and subject matter. They provide feedback for teachers and provide a basis on which to judge whether the teacher has achieved his or her own objectives as well as the standards set by the school.[72]

7. *Teacher portfolios:* Portfolios, although difficult to construct and vulnerable to misrepresentation, provide a rich portrayal of the teacher's performance. Such materials as videotapes, lesson plans, teacher logs or personal commentaries, student work (writing samples, laboratory exercises, etc.), and records of teacher observations can be used for purposes of documentation, assessment, and/or reflective analysis. Ideally, a teacher portfolio needs to be based on extant teaching standards and defined school goals. And, it should contain examples of both student and teacher work.[73]

You may be fortunate enough to work in a school district or be in a teacher education program that has a more comprehensive perspective on evaluation and uses authentic evaluation. Certain principles of practice will be evidenced in such authentic systems.

> *Principle 1:* Authentic teacher evaluation enables teachers to collect and show real artifacts of student learning. The focus is on whether students (all students) are learning the requisite content. What examples can you provide that suggest specifically what your different students are learning and that document the extent of their learning? And, can you connect that learning to defined state and national standards?
>
> *Principle 2:* The authentic representations of student learning can be illustrated through teacher-developed portfolios of student work. These portfolios should include examples of student work (e.g., assignments, tests, homework, projects) and of the teacher's work (e.g., lesson plans, videotapes of lessons).

Clearly, these authentic representations are not perfect. They only work if teachers make good decisions about what to include in the portfolios and if supervisors comment on and discuss them.

By the time you begin to teach, you will likely be assessed in multiple ways. You may be observed to see if you evidence particular teaching skills or dispositions (e.g., the Pathwise criteria or INTASC standards) and you may be expected to collect a wide variety of artifacts to use to demonstrate what students have learned and how you have taught the content. Use all of the information to help you reflect on your teaching and use it as a means of fostering personal and professional growth.

One of the newest forms of teacher assessment, especially for new teachers, is the PRAXIS series. The Education Testing Service initiated the series in 1987. The first two PRAXIS phases focus on skills in basic performance areas (PRAXIS I) and in content and professional areas (PRAXIS II). In the third phase (called *Pathwise* for preservice teachers), PRAXIS III Classroom Performance Assessments, beginning teachers are expected to exhibit a certain level of performance in each of four domains: 1) planning and preparation, 2) the classroom environment, 3) instruction and 4) professional responsibility.

If you are not in a PRAXIS state, you are likely in a state that embraces the Interstate New Teacher Assessment and Support Consortium (INTASC). Those standards correlate well with the PRAXIS III domains because both are based on essentially the same body of research—they just represent different ways of organizing the "effective teaching" concepts.

Some school districts are creating standards-based evaluation systems that are complex and relatively comprehensive. One, in particular, that has received national attention is the Cincinnati Public School District in Cincinnati, Ohio. The standards from the National Board for Professional Teaching Standards, the PRAXIS III Framework, INTASC, and especially Charlotte Danielson's *Enhancing Professional Practice: A Framework for Teaching* were all used to ground the system.

The Cincinnati system is based on four domains:

- Planning and Preparing for Student Learning
- Getting an Environment Ready for Learning

- Teaching for Learning
- Professionalism

You can see that they are similar to the PRAXIS domains. PRAXIS III is used for entry-year assessments and PATHWISE is used at the preservice level. Within each domain there are standards of performance. The district has created a clear description of who is evaluated and when that evaluation is to occur. New teachers are involved in the assessment process. Each teacher creates a portfolio that includes artifacts of high-quality student work. The portfolios are organized by standards within the four domains. Artifacts included are

- Evidence of acquiring knowledge of students as learners
- A long-range plan
- Two samples of work from two students
- Tracking of student progress
- Evidence of family communication
- District/School/Team participation log
- Record of professional development activities completed[74]

In Connecticut, the INTASC framework has been used to develop a performance-based assessment system (see Case Study 12.1). The Connecticut Beginning Educator Support and Training Program provides for both the support and mentoring of new teachers.[75] Throughout the first three years of teaching, new teachers receive a variety of sources of support. "During their second year [of teaching, new] teachers must compile and submit a discipline-based teaching portfolio. In the portfolio, teachers document their methods of planning, teaching, assessment of student learning, and self-reflection in a 7- to 10-day unit of instruction."[76] This should sound familiar. A lot of these models (PRAXIS III, INTASC, etc.) draw from parallel research but represent slightly different ways of thinking about effective teaching. The Connecticut model focuses on both content and pedagogy.

As you look at supervision and evaluation practices across the country you will see a wide variety of practices in place. Some schools will want you to set goals and then evaluate you relative to those goals—a clinical approach. Some schools will have specific methodologies that they want you to use, such as, Direct Instruction or Success for All—and they will *train you,* evaluate you accordingly, and then provide (usually) some form of technical coaching. Finally, some schools will use a variation on the model used in Cincinnati. They will use established standards for what constitutes good teaching and they will then evaluate you relative to those criteria.

With all the variations and alternative structures, some common characteristics among the targets of these new assessments are evidenced. Specifically, as a teacher you must:

- Know your content.
- Know how to teach that content.
- Know how to provide appropriate feedback to students.
- Know how to assess student learning in a variety of ways.
- Know how to document that learning.
- Know how to reflect on what students are learning in order to modify instruction for students with special needs.

If you know how to do these things, you will almost assuredly be successful. Even with such knowledge, however, there is room for growth. One of the most acknowledged approaches to continued professional growth is National Board Certification.

National Board Certification

Founded in 1987, the *National Board for Professional Teaching Standards* (NBPTS) launched a massive research and development program to improve teacher certification and teacher assessment. Its mission is to develop a voluntary (advanced) certification system that establishes high standards of what teachers should know and be able to do and identifies a governing board (comprised mainly of teachers) to enforce these standards. The specific mission of the NBPTS can be reviewed by visiting its website (www.nbpts.org). In general its goals are

- Maintaining high and vigorous standards for what accomplished teachers should know and be able to do.
- Providing a voluntary certification system for those who meet those standards.
- Advocating related education reforms to integrate National Board Certification into American education.

The National Board Certification process emphasizes the APPLE criteria. The criteria require that assessments be *A*dministratively feasible, *P*rofessionally acceptable, *P*ublicly credible, *L*egally defensible, and *E*conomically affordable.

The NBPTS process is not inexpensive. It costs $2300 to secure a certificate valid for ten years. It is available for any person who holds a baccalaureate degree and has three years of teaching experience in a public or private school.

The process is also not without controversy. A very high percentage of teachers who pursue NBPTS are not successful, and critics argue that there is simply no good evidence to show that teachers who hold NBPTS certificates create greater learning gains in the students they teach. Current research is being undertaken to determine whether NBPTS certification does make a "value-added" learning difference for students, but that research will likely not resolve the controversy completely. NBPTS has conducted research to suggest that those who hold NBPTS certificates do perform better on a variety of performance indicators, but critics often argue that the key variable is student learning. Do NBPTS teachers create enhanced student learning? The answer is not known. What is known is that the NBPTS teachers believe that the process does benefit them the most but also benefits their students with their enhanced pedagogical skill. Even though NBPTS teachers receive salary incentives in most states, most do not cite that as a motivation for pursuing advanced certification. They argue that the personal challenge coupled with the enhanced professional development provides the incentive for pursuing the NBPTS certificate.[77]

The new NBPTS "advanced" certification system consists of over thirty different teaching certificates (developed or underdeveloped) that consider two dimensions: 1) developmental level of students (*how* they should be taught) and 2) subject matter (*what* should be taught). In the developmental-level dimension there are four categories: early childhood (ages 3–8), middle childhood (ages 7–12), early adolescence (ages 11–15), and adolescence/young adulthood (ages 14–18+). This structure differs from traditional practices of state licensing by school grade level. In the subject matter dimension there are teaching certificates for generalists (e.g., early and middle childhood generalists) and subject specialists (e.g., early adolescence English/language arts, adolescence and young adult math). The National Board has also developed certificates for exceptional needs, English as a new language, and world languages other than English.

The National Board issues guidelines for the assessment of teachers. These guidelines emphasize that assessment tasks should be

- Authenticated and therefore complex
- Open-ended so that teachers can show their own practice
- Structured to provide teachers with opportunities for analysis and reflection
- Opportunistic, to exemplify good practices

The number of National Board Certified teachers is still quite limited. In early 2003, North Carolina and Florida had the highest number of Board Certified teachers in the country, 5,111 and 3,489, respectively. Closely behind were South Carolina (2,358), California (1,960), and Ohio (1,771). All states have some Board Certified teachers, though in some states the actual numbers are quite small (e.g., North Dakota, 13, and Pennsylvania, 225).

Professional Associations and Activities

Membership in professional organizations and participation in meetings, research, and advanced study can contribute to professional growth and help improve conditions for teachers.

Teacher Associations

There are two major teacher associations, the American Federation of Teachers (AFT) and the National Education Association (NEA). In most school districts teachers vote on which of the two associations all the teachers will join. In some school districts, the choice of joining or not joining a local chapter of the AFT or a state affiliate of the NEA is left to the individual. If you have a choice, you should not be rushed into making a decision. Keep in mind, however, that both organizations have helped improve salaries, benefits, and working conditions for teachers and that you should probably join one of them. At present over three-quarters of all public school teachers belong to either the AFT or the NEA.[78]

The AFT has approximately one million members (in 2003) and is organized in locals, mainly in cities. The AFT advocates a wide variety of reforms including

- High academic standards and vigorous curricula
- Solid school discipline policies
- Higher standards for teacher certification
- Peer review to ensure a high-quality teacher corps
- Well-crafted charter schools
- Voluntary advanced teacher certification

The AFT is affiliated with the AFL-CIO and bills itself (see www.AFT.org) as one of the country's oldest advocates of "free public education."

Disproportionately suburban and rural, the National Education Association (NEA) membership is served by a large network of affiliates in every state, Puerto Rico, and the District of Columbia. There are 13,000 local affiliate groups, but unlike the AFT (in which local affiliates are powerful), most of the NEA's power is derived from the state affiliates. In terms of actual numbers, the NEA represents the second largest lobby force in the country, trailing only behind the Teamsters. There are nearly 2.7 million current NEA members. Founded in 1857, it is also committed to advancing public education.

Although the two organizations occasionally take different positions on educational matters and battle over membership, "no raid" efforts have been discussed at the state level. Most important, both organizations seek to improve the status of the teaching profession, agree on many issues concerning teachers and schools, and sometimes join forces on policy matters.

You might find it useful to visit the organizations' websites to see where each stands on salient educational issues. On the day when this chapter was written, the www.nea.org site offered positions on the following "hot topics": accountability and testing, charter schools, class size, school safety, and teacher quality. The NEA position, for example, on accountability and testing (as posted on its website) is that "Schools, teachers, and students should all be held to high standards, and NEA believes that accountability should be shared by schools, educational employees, and parents—with the ultimate goal of helping every student succeed."

Professional Organizations

At the working level of the classroom, the professional organization of greatest academic benefit to a teacher (and preservice teacher) is usually one that focuses on his or her major field. Each professional association provides a meeting ground for teachers of similar interests. The activities of these professional organizations usually consist of regional and national meetings and publication of a monthly or quarterly journal that describes accepted curriculum and teaching practices.

Some organizations are subject centered such as the National Council for the Social Studies, the National Council of Teachers of English, the Modern Language Association, the National Science Teachers Association, and the National Council of Teachers of Mathematics. Others such as the Council for Exceptional Children, the National Association for Bilingual Children, the National Association for the Education of Young Children, and the National Scholarship Service and Fund for Negro Students, focus on the needs of specific students. Such associations are organized to ensure that specific children and youth are served by well-prepared school personnel and to improve specialized teaching techniques.

Still another type of professional organization cuts across subjects and student types. These organizations tend to highlight innovative teaching and instructional practices in general. They describe, in their journals, new trends and policies that affect the entire field of education; have a wide range of membership including teachers, administrators, and professors; and work for the advancement of the teaching profession in general.

Keeping up with the professional literature and enrolling in professional coursework are important for developing and maintaining teacher effectiveness.

Perhaps the best known organization of this type is Phi Delta Kappa (www.pd-kintl.org), which includes 649 local chapters in the United States, Canada, and abroad. Its membership is available to graduate students, administrators, and grade school and college-level teachers. Even undergraduates may join if they are pursuing teacher certification. The membership in 2003 stood at approximately 120,000. Originally open only to men, it opened its membership to women in 1974. The purpose of the organization is to promote quality and equality in education, with particular emphasis on public education. Members receive *Phi Delta Kappan,* a highly respected journal that is published ten times a year, and the fraternity newsletter. Paperback (Fastback) publications of interest are available at reduced rates for members and are published on a variety of topics, including *Portfolio Development for Preservice Teachers* and *Student Literacy: Myths and Realities.*

Professional Activities

If you are to continue to do a good job teaching, you must keep up with your subject and the latest teaching and instructional trends in your specialization. Without continued updating, your teaching will become dated and dry. To keep abreast of developments in your field you will need to do three things: 1) read professional books and journals, 2) attend professional conferences, at least one or two a year, and 3) enroll in advanced courses in conjunction with a university-sponsored program or a school district in-service program. All three activities will help you keep up on changes in methods and materials, teaching and learning theories, and current experimentation.

Readings

Almost any professional organization you join should have a monthly or quarterly journal. The journal that will have the most immediate value for you is the one that focuses on your subject and grade level. For example, reading teachers might subscribe to the *Journal of Reading, Reading Teacher,* or *Reading Today.* Math teachers might want to subscribe to *Teaching Children Mathematics* or *Mathematics,* and social studies teachers would do well to read *Social Education and The Social Studies.* Elementary teachers who are more tuned to their grade level, might subscribe to *Childhood Education* or *Young Education* and high school teachers might want *Middle Ground* or *High School Journal.*

There are many professional journals in education. Pick and choose wisely because of time and the cost of subscriptions. The answers to two questions can help determine your reading and subscription focus: "Do I want practical advice and easy-to-read articles or theoretical and in-depth reading?" and "Do I want to focus on subject or grade-level issues, or do I want a broad discussion of education issues?" Practitioner journals such as *Instructor* will have easy to read, practical articles, while journals such as *Educational Researcher* will have more complex, research-based articles.

In addition to reading books and journals, you might also want to subscribe to virtual services that provide daily updates on significant issues relevant to classroom practices. One of the very best is ASCDBrief, which can be contacted through 1.6200.Fa-TAmb_TNFYqsR.1@smbl.cc. The ASCDBrief offers daily information on a wide variety of topics, with links to specific stories of interest. On any given day, you will find information on topics ranging from special education to high-stakes testing.

Meetings

The two major teacher organizations—the American Federation of Teachers and the National Education Association—meet annually in different cities. If you become a member of one of these organizations, it would be beneficial to be an active participant and attend the annual meeting. The various subject-related associations and specialized student associations also have local and regional conferences. Keep an eye on your local colleges and universities; their departments or schools of education often sponsor professional meetings and short seminars that are excellent for updating your knowledge about teaching and for meeting other professionals in the local area. State departments of education and local school districts frequently organize in-service workshops and one- or two-day conferences on timely educational topics and teaching techniques.

Choose wisely which meetings and conferences best serve your professional needs and interests and organize your schedule so you can attend them. Become acquainted with the scheduling and travel policy of your school district. If the meetings take place during the school calendar, you will need special permission to attend. Some school districts give travel reimbursement for certain meetings. Local meetings sponsored by colleges or universities, state departments, regional education agencies, or local school districts often happen after school hours or on weekends. These sessions are easier to attend in terms of scheduling, time, and cost.

Coursework

You should take advantage of university coursework and programs that lead to graduate degrees and state certification in a field of study. You may also attend summer sessions, workshops, special institutes, and in-service courses conducted by a local university or the school district.

Check to see whether special stipends, scholarships, or grants are available through the school district or state in which you teach. Several states offer monetary incentives for enrolling in programs in special fields, especially science education, math education, and special education. Many school districts offer partial or full reimbursement for graduate work.

Although many of the recent reports on excellence in education recommend reducing the role of teacher-training institutions in the preparation and certification of teachers by limiting the number of professional educational courses, others, such as the Carnegie Report *A Nation Prepared* and the National Commission on Excellence in Education, call for increased professional education and field experiences.

As you consider your future professional growth, you might find it useful to consider how you want to focus your future professional growth experiences. Here are some prescriptions that are logical extensions of research reported in *Teaching Quality Research Matters*. These ideas have real relevance to whatever pedagogical experiences you participate in as a prospective teacher.

1. Professional development experiences that are very focused on acquisition of a particular pedagogical practice are predictive of a teacher's use of that practice. Learning a lot about everything will likely limit what you use correctly. To develop skill in *direct instruction* or *constructivist* teaching requires focus and practice. Watch others who use an approach and then engage in that practice and try to receive feedback on your practice.

2. Technology related to professional development that involves teachers with similar backgrounds and teaching interests (even grade-level focus) results in better outcomes instructionally.

3. Find a mentor or a study group to work with as you develop your professional skills. Good teachers do not isolate themselves; they collaborate.[79]

Researcher-Teacher Collaboration

In what is often called the ***collaborative research model,*** university researchers are increasingly joining with schools in an effort to deal with a range of educational problems by involving teachers in the solutions to these problems. The model has spread because of the belief that, through cooperative problem solving, researchers can get a better grasp of practitioners' problems and develop strategies that improve teaching and benefit teachers and schools. In fact, a large portion of the new research on teacher effectiveness is derived from such cooperative efforts. The new collaborative centers (sometimes called *R&D education centers* or *laboratory research centers*) tend to focus less on theory and what researchers want to study and more on practical and enduring problems of teachers.

Decisions regarding research questions, data collection, and reporting are jointly determined by the university and the school. Collaboration between teachers and researchers is stressed, with both groups working together to improve the theory and practice of education. Researchers are learning to respect teachers and to conduct research of practical value, and teachers are learning to appreciate the work of researchers and to do research.[80]

A most interesting development in collaborative relationships is that many teachers no longer want anonymity in the studies conducted by researchers. In the old relationship, the desire was to protect the rights and anonymity of "informants" or "respondents." Now teachers often seek full partnership in the research, so they can share in the recognition when it is published. This is an ethical issue that has not been pressed in the past and may very well become an issue as experienced teachers develop relationships with researchers—and perceive only the researchers' benefit when the materials are published. This issue involves teachers' sense of ownership and empowerment as well as teacher-researcher relations. To better blend theory and practice in the future these relations need to be improved.[81]

As we conclude this chapter, it is important to note that teaching can be difficult and rewarding. True, there are problems, but few roles are more exciting and important than teaching. When competent teachers work with young children, there is rarely a dull moment. Through their students, teachers can contribute to the shaping and growth of the community and the nation; the teachers' impact is long-term—and we are unable to determine when the influence ceases. Teaching is a proud profession, and professional growth and development are an important part of the life of a teacher. Unfortunately, it is likely that you will not receive all the professional development that you need to be successful. Most American teachers do not. Interestingly, Japanese teachers receive almost twenty days of in-service training during their first year of teaching. You will be lucky to receive more than a couple, which leads us to the final point of this chapter.

As you begin your professional practice, be aware of two negative realities that are in a large part are not your fault, but rather by-products of the structure of American education. One is burnout; the other is a lack of personal and professional self-esteem. Both are caused, directly or indirectly, by a lack of personal and professional growth. That is, you will be placed in classrooms and expected to do too much, too soon, with too little. The best way for you to counter the potential negative realities is to identify ways to continue to extend your own skills (through computer networks) and to understand the complexity of teaching. Jennifer Bradford, an experienced teacher, also offers some "fun" lessons for you to consider when you need renewal:

- Get a massage. Find a way to relax.
- Exercise.
- Get a dog or at least some perspective.
- Don't expect "outsiders" to understand.
- Realize that schools have many faculty members for a reason.
- Vacation means vacate. Find ways to "recharge."[82]

Technology ViewPoint from a Classroom Teacher

Jackie Marshall Arnold
K–12 Media Specialist

 Professional development is critical for an effective teacher to stay effective. It is important that teachers continue their professional growth in all content-appropriate areas and instructional methods. This final viewpoint will detail how technology can be the tool to provide the professional development that effective teachers need and desire.

The Internet provides a wealth of online resources to support professional growth. Teachers can use the Internet to research content, read current journal articles, and stay involved with professional organizations like the National Council of Teachers of English. Websites are also available to support growth in a specific area. For example, Teacher Tap (http://eduscapes.com/tap/) is a free resource that supports teachers with technology-integration questions. It provides online resources, activities, and tools that support technology integration.

Teachers can find discussion rooms and threaded discussions to share thoughts, ideas, and challenges with one another. These synchronous and asynchronous ways of collaborating allow busy teachers to "talk" with other teachers and support each other's growth. For example, Tapped In (http://www.tappedin.sri.com/) allows teachers to collaborate with other educators around the world. It hosts after-school discussion sessions on most disciplines and provides a wealth of resources. Teachers can participate in a variety of discussions by responding to a person's question or thought and then coming back at a later time to read other responses.

Online courses are now readily available for teachers to continue their coursework and professional practice without ever having to "go" anywhere. By taking a course online teachers can gain college credit and develop their area of interest and/or need. Online courses respect the intensely busy life of the teacher and allow for flexibility in when and where the teacher completes the coursework.

Finally, effective teachers will always be looking to enhance their technology skills and ideas to support technology integration. They seek out the media specialist and/or technology coordinators to provide ideas and resources to continue growth in this area. Attending technology conferences, reading technology journals, and belonging to area technology organizations will also allow effective teachers to keep their technology understanding current.

Technology is a tool that can support an effective teacher's professional development in a multitude of ways. It can provide teachers the resources and information they need and allow for the flexibility that busy teachers require.

A book such as this one necessarily examines teaching practices. As a teacher who grows professionally, you must be able to see how the different practices can be commingled to address the inherent complexity of the teaching-learning process. But for now, or very soon, you will need to consider how to make sense of all the "parts" of teaching to prepare for interviews. We hope that this book helps you as you prepare for those interviews. You will be asked questions about:

- Your philosophy of teaching to bring together the science and art of professional practice.
- Your ability to create meaningful instruction around the academic content standards in your state and school district.
- Your approach to adapting instruction to address the multiple learning needs of students.

- Your approach to classroom management and discipline.
- Your own professional short and long-term goals.

Our goal in this text was not to give you answers to these areas of concern but to give you information to use to shape your answers!

We hope your professional journey for the next 20 to 30 years is rewarding. To become an effective teacher is to make a difference in children's lives. It will also make a difference in how you feel about yourself as a professional educator.

Theory into Practice

We have discussed in this chapter a lot about how teachers are prepared and then subsequently develop as professionals. We'll conclude with one of the most troubling issues of the early 2000s: How do schools keep good teachers? This question is at the nexus of theory and practice. There are theories about how to prepare teachers, but in practice many of those "prepared" teachers decide to leave the profession.

Research is mixed about why teachers drop out of teaching. Clearly, some drop out for very common reasons (e.g., to start families) while others drop out because they simply feel unsupported and unfulfilled. William Sanders believes that teachers reach their peak effectiveness between their seventh and twenty-fifth years of practice.[83] Teachers develop skills (years one to seven), attain proficiency (years seven to twenty-five) and then begin to diminish in effectiveness. That pattern is not always the norm. For some, the decline never occurs; for others, the "decline" in performance may occur early in a career or may be evident only during a particular year. In order to prevent this decline, teachers need challenging and practical programs. Each school has to concentrate on a few of its most serious problems and then develop in-service programs to meet these problems. In-service programs can be vastly improved if the staffs of teacher education institutions and school districts work together to identify and focus on serious problems.

If you expect to be an effective teacher, you will need to be able to cope with the frustrations and problems that arise on the job. Regardless of the amount of satisfaction you obtain from teaching, there will be dissatisfying aspects of the job. What follows is a list of *mental health strategies*—keys to professional well-being in the form of questions that are a mix of common sense and psychology for self-understanding. They are intended to help you deal with problems or dissatisfactions that may arise on the job.

Key 1. *Are you aware of your strengths and weaknesses?* The ability to make realistic self-estimates is crucial, given the fact that your students and colleagues will observe and make judgments about your behavior, attitude, and abilities. Learn to see yourself as others see you and to compensate for or modify areas that need to be improved.

Key 2. *Are you aware of your social and personal skills?* You will need to understand the attitudes and feelings of your students, colleagues, and supervisors; how to adapt to and interact with different persons; how to learn from them; and how to work cooperatively with them.

Key 3. *Can you function in a bureaucratic setting?* Schools are bureaucracies, and you must learn the rules and regulations, as well as the norms and behaviors of the school. As a teacher, you are an employee of an organization that has certain expectations of you and all its employees.

Key 4. *Can you cope with school forms and records?* Schools expect teachers to complete a host of forms, reports, and records accurately and on time. The more quickly you become familiar with this work, the smoother it will be for you. At first the various forms, reports, and records may seem burdensome, yet neither you, your supervisors, nor the school can function without them.

Key 5. *Can you study and learn from someone else with similar problems?* It helps to assess people with similar problems to see what they are doing wrong to avoid making the same mistakes.

Key 6. *Do you look for help on specific questions?* Often teacher dissatisfaction pertains to a specific problem, such as, the inability to maintain discipline. Consulting with an experienced colleague or supervisor sometimes helps.

Key 7. *Do you take out your frustrations in class?* Don't vent your dissatisfactions on your students. It solves nothing and adds to your teaching problems.

Key 8. *Do you understand your roles as a teacher?* The teacher's role goes far beyond teaching a group of students in class. Teaching occurs in a particular social context, and much of what you do and are expected to do is influenced by this context. Different students, supervisors, administrators, parents, and community members expect different things from you. You must expect to perform varied roles depending on the realities, demands, and expectations of a school's culture.

Key 9. *Are you able to organize your time?* There are only so many hours in a day, and many demands and expectations are imposed on you as a person and professional. You will need to make good use of time, set priorities, plan, and get your work done.

Key 10. *Can you separate your job from your personal life?* Never let the teaching job (or any job) overwhelm you to the point that it interferes with your personal life. There are times when you may have to spend a few extra hours in school helping students or working with colleagues, and there are times when you will have to spend extra after-school hours grading papers and tests, preparing lessons, and performing clerical tasks, but for your own mental health be sure you have time left for your private, family, and social life.

The professional mental health of many teachers is being influenced by things like the No Child Left Behind legislation. Tye and O'Brien discuss a number of the reasons teachers have left the profession during the past several years. The reasons they list include accountability, increased paperwork, student attitudes, no parent support, unresponsive administration, low status of the profession, and salary considerations.[84] Of particular interest is the concern of teachers relative to accountability and increased paperwork. Teachers are now required to do more testing and more curriculum development work that relates to that testing (see Chapters 10 and 11). What appears to be especially problematic is that teachers are not given the time to really think through many of the curriculum instruction issues that they will confront. American teachers have less time to plan and are in front of students more than teachers in many other countries. Without adequate planning time teachers are at a disadvantage in terms of their overall effectiveness. Although the increased accountability focus may have positive aspects it will be limited in its effectiveness unless teachers are given the professional time to plan and think about their teaching.

Summary

1. There is little agreement on a national basis regarding the number and mix of educational courses for teacher preparation.
2. Beginning teachers need support and assistance to ease into their position and improve their instructional skills.
3. To become a master teacher, you will need continually to improve your teaching abilities and focus your professional development. People closely associated with your teaching and instruction, including peers and supervisors, are best able to provide feedback and evaluation.
4. Several different types of formative and summative evaluations will help you assess your progress as a teacher.
5. There are a variety of associations for teachers to join; the two largest ones and the ones that have probably done the most to improve teacher salaries and working conditions are the American Federation of Teachers and the National Education Association.
6. Several opportunities exist to help teachers grow as professionals, including reading the professional literature, attending conferences, taking courses, and collaborating with researchers.

Questions to Consider

1. Why should you begin now as a preservice teacher to consider ways for improving your skills as a regular classroom teacher?
2. What are some ways for coping with problems or concerns related to the job of teaching?
3. Which of your experiences as a preservice teacher do you think will help you as a beginning teacher? In what ways has your teacher education program *focused* your acquisition of important teaching skills and dispositions?
4. Of the following evaluation alternatives—student, peer, self, and supervisory—which would you prefer as a beginning teacher? Why? As an experienced teacher? Why?
5. Name two or three professional organizations you expect to join as a teacher. Go to their websites and review the qualifications for membership. Are preservice teachers permitted to join? How do you expect to benefit from membership in these organizations? What is the explicitly stated mission of each association?

Things to Do

1. Survey the class members (in the course you are taking) on the anticipated problems of new teachers. Rank order them. Discuss in class how problems considered important (top five) can be addressed through preparation experiences. For example, if classroom management is an anticipated problem, what specific steps can you take to deal with that problem?
2. Evaluate a class member's teaching of a sample lesson in his or her subject geared for students at a particular grade level. Evaluate the lesson in terms of instructional methods, use of media, and organization of subject matter.
3. Invite a representative of the AFT and NEA to your class to discuss each organization's purposes and mission. What are their views on specific topics: class size, high stakes testing? Do you think their views are consistent with the best interests of students.
4. This text lists several professional organizations and several professional journals. Identify the ones that offer potential for your professional development. Explain the reasons to the class.
5. Obtain the evaluation instrument for your student teaching experience. On what standards is it based?

Recommended Readings

Beerens, Daniel. *Evaluating Teachers for Professional Growth.* Thousand Oaks, Calif.: Corwin Press, 2000. This is a thoughtful analysis of all the different ways to evaluate teaching practice.

Darling-Hammond, Linda. *Professional Development Schools.* New York: Teachers College Press, Columbia University, 1994. This is a discussion concerning how to improve teacher education and schools of education.

Ladson-Billings, Gloria. *Crossing Over to Canaan.* San Francisco: Jossey Bass, 2001. This wonderful book outlines the experiences of eight novice teachers learning how to teach for diversity.

Marzano, Robert J. *What Works in Check Schools: Translating Research into Action.* Alexandria, Va.: Association for Supervision and Curriculum Development, 2003. A description of packages that teachers and schools can use to enhance student success.

Meeting the Highly Qualified Teachers Challenge. Washington D.C.: U.S. Department of Education, 2002. This short monograph released by the government highlights information about how states need to address the issue of having highly qualified teachers in every classroom, which is a requirement of the No Child Left Behind legislation of 2002.

No Dream Denied: A Pledge to America's Children. Washington, D.C.: National Commission on Teaching and America's Future, 2003. An analysis of the state of the teaching profession and a description of promising practices to ensure a highly qualified teacher in each classroom.

Testing Teacher Candidates. Washington, D.C.: National Academy Press, 2001. A thorough analysis of practices and policies related to teacher licensure in the United States.

Key Terms

artifacts of teaching 579	induction period 568	peer coaching/mentoring 565
authentic evaluation 579	mental health strategies 590	reflection/reflective
clinical supervision 577	National Board for Professional	practice 574
collaborative research	Teaching Standards	technical coaching 578
model 587	(NBPTS) 582	

End Notes

1. Robert J. Yinder and Amanda L. Nolen. "Surviving the Legitimacy Challenge." *Phi Delta Kappan* (January 2003): 386–390.
2. Kenneth A. Sirotnik. "On the Eroding Foundations of Teacher Education." *Phi Delta Kappan* (May 1990): 714.
3. "Improving Teacher Quality: The State of the States." *Education Week* (January 9, 2003): 90.
4. James B. Conant. *The Education of American Teachers.* New York: McGraw-Hill, 1964.
5. James D. Koerner. *The Mideducation of American Teachers.* Boston: Houghton Mifflin, 1963.
6. Susan Chira. "In the Drive to Revive Schools: Better Teachers but Too Few." *The New York Times.* (2 August 1990): A1, A12. "School Administrators Report New Teachers Are Better Prepared Than Predecessors." *AACTE Briefs.* (13 May 1991): 1, 8.
7. John I. Goodlad, Roger Soder, and Kenneth Sirotnik. *Places Where Teachers Are Taught.* San Francisco: Jossey-Bass, 1990.
8. E. D. Hirsch Jr. *The Schools We Need and Why We Don't Have Them.* New York: Doubleday, 1995.
9. John I. Goodlad. *Teachers for Our Nation's Schools.* San Francisco, Jossey-Bass, 1990. John I. Goodlad. *Educational Renewal.* San Francisco: Jossey-Bass, 1998.
10. James W. Fraser. "Preparing Teachers for Democratic Schools: The Holmes and Carnegie Reports Five Years Later." *Teachers' College Record* (Fall 1992): 7–39.
11. "Meeting Teaching's Toughest Critic." *NEA Today* (April 1991): 8–9. Telephone conversation with Arthur E. Wise, Director of NCATE, March 1, 1993.
12. Thomas J. Lasley II, William L. Bainbridge, and Barnett Berry. "Improving Teacher Quality: Ideological Perspectives and Policy Prescriptions." *Educational Forum* (Fall 2002): 14–25.
13. Jeanne S. Chall. *The Academic Achievement Challenge.* New York: The Guilford Press, 2000: p. 182.
14. Linda Darling-Hammond. "Educating Teachers." *Academe.* (January–February 1999): 29.
15. Hilda Borko. "Research on Learning to Teach." In A. Woolfolk (ed.), *Research Perspectives on the Graduate Preparation of Teachers,* 3. Englewood Cliffs, N.J.: Allyn and Bacon, 1989, pp. 69–87. Simon Veenman. "Perceived Problems of Beginning Teachers." *Review of Educational Research* (Summer 1984): 143–178. Sylvia M. Yee. *Careers in the Classroom: When Teaching Is More Than a Job.* New York: Teachers College Press, Columbia University, 1990.
16. The research of Richard M. Ingersoll effectively documents the teacher attrition problem. See, for example, Richard M. Ingersoll. "Teacher Turnover and Teacher Shortages." *American Educational Research Journal* (Fall 2001): 449–534.
17. Bridget Curran and Liam Goldrich. *Mentoring and Supporting New Teachers.* Education Policy Studies Division, National Governor's Association Center for Best Practices, 2002.
18. Frances F. Fuller. "Concerns for Teachers." *American Educational Research Journal* (March 1969): 207–226.
19. Carol S. Weinstein. "Preservice Teachers' Expectations About the First Year of Teaching." *Teaching and Teacher Education* no. 1 (1988): 31–40. Weinstein. "Prospective Elementary Teachers' Beliefs About Teaching." *Teaching and Teacher Education* no. 6 (1990): 279–290.
20. Marilyn Cochran-Smith and Susan Lytle. "Research on Teaching and Teacher Research." *Educational Researcher* (March 1990): 2–11.
21. Scott Joftus. *New Teacher Excellence: Retaining Our Best.* Washington D.C.: Alliance for Excellent Education, 2002.
22. William H. Kurtz. "How the Principal Can Help Beginning Teachers." *NASSP Bulletin* (January 1983): 42–45. Also see Thomas J. Sergiovanni. *Building Communities in Schools.* San Francisco: Jossey-Bass, 1994.
23. Diane Davis and Marjorie Leppo. *A First Class Look at Teaching.* Washington D.C.: Sallie Mae Education Institute, 1999.
24. Lowell C. Rice and Alec M. Gallup. "The 34th Annual Phi Delta Kappa/Gallup Poll of the Public's Attitudes toward the Public Schools." *Phi Delta Kappan* (September 2002): 41–56.

25. Allan C. Ornstein and Daniel U. Levine. "Social Class, Race, and School Achievement Problems and Prospects." *Journal of Teacher Education* (September–October 1989): 27–33.

26. Mary H. Futrell, Joel Gomez, and Dana Belden. "Teaching the Children of a New America: The Challenge of Diversity." *Phi Delta Kappan* (January 2003): 381–385. Maria Enchautequi. *Immigration and County Employment Growth.* Washington, D.C.: Urban Institute, 1992. Jason Juffus, *The Impact of the Immigration Reform and Control Act of Immigration* Washington, D.C.: Urban Institute, 1992.

27. Michael Fix and Wendy Zimmermann. *Educating Immigrant Children.* Washington, D.C.: Urban Institute, 1993.

28. Allan C. Ornstein. "Enrollment Trends in Big City Schools." *Peabody Journal of Education* (Summer 1988): 64–71. Roger Passel and Edward Edmonston. *Immigration and Race in the United States: The 20th and 21st Centuries* (Washington, D.C.: Urban Institute, 1992).

29. Laurence Steinberg. *Beyond the Classroom.* New York: Simon and Schuster, 1996.

30. Ibid., p. 97.

31. James A. Banks. "Multicultural Education: For Freedom's Sake." *Educational Leadership.* (December–January 1992): 32–36. Carl A. Grant. "Desegregation, Racial Attitudes, and Intergroup Contact: A Discussion of Change," *Phi Delta Kappan.* (September 1990): 125–132.

32. F. Michael Connelly and Jean Clandinin. *Shaping a Professional Identity.* New York: Teachers College Press, 1999. Margaret Eisenhart, Linda Behm, and Linda Romagnano. "Learning to Teach: Developing Expertise or Rite of Passage?" *Journal of Education for Teaching* (January 1991): 51–71. Anne Reynolds. "What Is Competent Beginning Teaching?" *Review of Educational Research* (Springs 1992): 1–36.

33. Pamela Grossman. "Why Models Matter: An Alternative View on Professional Growth in Teaching." *Review of Educational Research* (Summer 1992): 171–179.

34. Lee Shulman. "Those Who Understand: Knowledge Growth in Teaching." *Educational Researcher* (March–April, 1986): 4–14. Lee Shulman. "Knowledge and Teaching: Foundations of the New Reform." *Harvard Educational Review* (February 1987): 1–22. Lee Shulman. "Ways of Seeing, Ways of Knowing, Ways of Teaching, Ways of Learning About Teaching." *Journal of Curriculum Studies* (September–October 1992): 393–96.

35. Susan E. Wade. *Preparing Teachers for Inclusive Education.* Mahwah, N.J.: Erlbaum, 1999.

36. Sigrun Gudmundsdottir. "Values in Pedagogical Content Knowledge." *Journal of Teacher Education* (May–June 1991): 44–52. Rick Marks. "Pedagogical Content Knowledge: From a Mathematical Case to a Modified Conception." *Journal of Teacher Education* (May–June 1990): 3–11. Barbara Scott Nelson. "Teachers' Special Knowledge." *Educational Researcher* (December 1992): 32–33.

37. Pamela L. Grossman. "A Study in Contrast: Sources of Pedagogical Content Knowledge in Secondary English." *Journal of Teacher Education* (September–October 1989): 24–32.

38. Ibid., pp. 25–26.

39. Linda Darling-Hammond. "Educating Teachers": 30.

40. Karen Carter. "Teachers' Knowledge and Learning to Teach." In W.R. Houston (ed.), *Handbook of Research on Teacher Education.* New York: Macmillan, 1990, pp. 291–310. Daniel L. Duke. "How a Staff Development Program Can Rescue At-Risk Students." *Educational Leadership* (December–January 1993): 28–30.

41. Thomas D. Bird. "Early Implementation of the California Mentor Teacher Program." Paper presented at the annual meeting of the American Educational Research Association, San Francisco, April 1986. Auroro Chase and Pat Wolfe. "Off to a Good Start in Peer Coaching." *Educational Leadership* (May 1989): 37–38. Donna Gordon and Margaret Moles. "Mentoring Becomes Staff Development." *NASSP Bulletin* (February 1994): 62–65.

42. Bridget Curran and Liam Goldrich. *Mentoring and Supporting New Teachers.* Education Policy Studies Division, National Governor's Association Center for Best Practices, 2002. For copies of the report contact bcurran@nga.org.

43. Bruce Joyce and Beverly Showers. *Power in Staff Development Through Research in Training.* Alexandria, Va.: Association for Supervision and Curriculum Development, 1983. Bruce Joyce and Beverly Showers. *Student Achievement Through Staff Development,* 3d ed. Alexandria, Va.: Association for Supervision and Curriculum Development, 2002.

44. Gloria A. Neubert and Elizabeth C. Bratton. "Team Coaching: Staff Development Side by Side." *Educational Leadership* (February 1987): 29–32.

45. Judith T. Witmer. "Mentoring One District's Success Story." *NASSP Bulletin* (February 1993): 71–78.

46. Kip Tellez. "Mentors by Choice, Not Design." *Journal of Teacher Education* (May–June 1992): 214–21.

47. Tad Watanabe. "Learning from Japanese Lesson Study." *Educational Leadership* (March 2002): 36–39.

48. Mary R. Jalongo. "Teachers' Stories: Our Ways of Knowing." *Educational Leadership* (April 1992): 68–73.

49. Katherine K. Merseth. "First Aid for First-Year Teachers." *Phi Delta Kappan* (May 1992): 678–83.

50. Kenneth D. Peterson. *Teacher Education,* 2d ed. (Thousand Oaks, Calif.: Corwin Press, 2000).

51. Thomas L. Good and Jere E. Brophy. *Looking in Classrooms,* 6th ed. New York: Harper & Collins, 1994, p. 463.

52. *High School and Beyond: Teacher and Administrator Survey.* Washington, D.C.: National Institute for Education, 1985.

53. Many school districts around the country are using variations of INTASC or PATHWISE-PRAXIS criteria to develop district evaluation systems for new teachers.

54. "Intern Intervention Evaluation: The Toledo Plan." Toledo, Ohio: Toledo Public Schools, 2001.

55. Carol A. Dwyer. "Teaching and Diversity: Meeting the Challenges for Innovative Teacher Assessment." *Journal of Teacher Education* (March–April 1993): 119–129. Carolyn J. Wood. "Toward More Effective Teacher Evaluation." *NASSP Bulletin* (March 1992): 52–59.

56. Margaret Olebe, Amy Jackson, and Charlotte Danielson. "Investing in Beginning Teachers—The California Model." *Educational Leadership* (May 1999): 41–44.

57. Wayne K. Hoy and Cecil G. Miskel. *Educational Administration,* 6th ed. Boston, Mass.: McGraw Hill, 2001.

58. Carl Rogers. *A Way of Being.* Boston: Houghton Mifflin, 1980. Donald A. Schon. *The Reflective Practitioner: How Professionals Think in Action.* New York: Basic Books, 1983. Donald A. Schon, ed. *The Reflective Turn.* New York: Teachers College Press, Columbia University, 1991.

59. Caroline Allyson Lucas. "Developing Competent Practitioners." *Educational Leadership* (May 1999): 46–47.

60. Linda Darling-Hammond and Gary Sykes (eds.). *Teaching as the Learning Profession.* San Francisco: Jossey-Bass, 1999.

61. Dorene D. Ross. "First Steps in Developing a Reflective Approach." *Journal of Teacher Education* (March–April 1989): 22–30.

62. Ibid.

63. Simon Hole and Grace Hall McEntree. "Reflections in the Heat of Practice." *Educational Leadership* (May 1999): 34–37.

64. Ibid.

65. Kenneth D. Peterson. *Teacher Education,* 2d ed. Thousand Oaks, Calif.: Corwin Press, 2000.

66. Ibid.

67. Morris Cogan. *Clinical Supervision.* Boston: Houghton Mifflin, 1973.

68. Robert Goldhammer et al. *Clinical Supervision: Special Methods for the Supervision of Teachers,* 2d ed. New York: Holt, Rinehart, 1980.

69. Ben M. Harris. *In-Service Education for Staff Development.* Needham Heights, Mass.: Allyn and Bacon, 1989. Ben M. Harris. *Personnel Administration in Education.* Needham Heights, Mass.: Allyn and Bacon, 1992.

70. Allan A. Glatthorn. *Supervisory Leadership.* New York: Harper Collins, 1990. Arthur E. Wise et al. *Effective Teacher Selection: From Recruitment to Retention.* Santa Monica, Calif.: Rand Corporation, 1987.

71. Carl D. Glickman. *Supervision of Instruction: A Developmental Approach,* 2d ed. Needham Heights, Mass.: Allyn and Bacon, 1990. Mary D. Phillips and Carl D. Glickman. "Peer Coaching: Developmental Approach to Enhance Teacher Thinking." *Journal of Staff Development* (Spring 1991): 20–25.

72. John G. Savage. "Teacher Evaluation Without Classroom Evaluation." *NASSP Bulletin* (December 1982): 41–45. Lee Shulman. "A Union of Insufficiencies: Strategies for Teacher Assessment in a Period of Educational Reform." *Educational Leadership* (November 1988): 36–41.

73. Elizabeth A. Hebert. "Portfolios Invite Reflection." *Educational Leadership.* (May 1992): 58–61. Thomas J. Sergiovanni and Thomas J. Starratt. *Supervision: A Redefinition.* Boston, Mass.: McGraw-Hill, 2002.

74. *Teacher Evaluation System.* Cincinnati, OH: Cincinnati Public Schools, 2001.
75. *Testing Teacher Candidates.* Washington, D.C.: National Academy Press, 2001.
76. Ibid., p. 153.
77. *Teaching Quality Research Matters.* Chapel Hill, N.C.: The Southwest Center for Teaching Quality, Issue 2 (November 2002).
78. Allan Ornstein and Daniel Levine. *Introduction to the Foundations of Education,* 7th ed. Boston: Houghton Mifflin, 2000.
79. *Teaching Quality Research Matters.*
80. Christopher Clark. "Teacher Preparation: Contributions of Research on Teacher Thinking." *Educational Researcher* (March 1988): 5–12. Michael O'Loughlin. "Engaging Teachers in Emancipatory Knowledge Construction."*Journal of Teacher Education* (November–December 1992): 42–48.
81. Judith H. Shulman. "Now You See Them, Now You Don't." *Educational Researcher* (August–September 1990): 11–15.
82. Jennifer J. Bradford. "How to Stay in Teaching (When You Really Feel Like Crying)." *Educational Leadership* (May 1999): 67–68.
83. William Sanders. Presentation to the Governor's Commission on Teaching Success. Columbus, Ohio, July 2002.
84. Barbara Benham Tye and Lisa O'Brien. "Why Are Experienced Teachers Leaving the Profession?" *Phi Delta Kappan* (September 2002): 24–32.

Photo credits:

Name Index

Note: Page numbers in *italics* indicate illustrations; those followed by *d* indicate display text; and those followed by *t* indicate tables.

Subject Index

Note: Page numbers in *italics* indicate illustrations; those followed by *d* indicate display text; and those followed by *t* indicate tables.